LIGHT-SIGNAL CODES

	Meaning of the signal	
Type and color of signal	Aircraft on the ground	Aircraft in flight
Steady green	Cleared for takeoff	Cleared to land
Flashing green	Cleared to taxi	Return for landing (followed by steady green at proper time)
Steady red	Stop	Yield to other aircraft and continue circling
Flashing red	Taxi clear of runway in use	Airport unsafe—do not land
Flashing white	Return to starting point on airport	
Alternating red and green	General warning signal—exercise extreme caution	

HOURLY SEQUENCE REPORT LEGEND

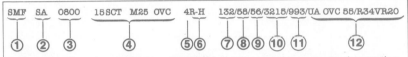

Translation: Sacramento Metropolitan Field: hourly sequence report; observation taken at 0800 UTC; 1500 feet scattered clouds; measured ceiling, 2500 feet overcast; visibility 4 statute miles because of light rain and haze; sea level pressure is 1013.2 millibars; temperature 58 degrees Fahrenheit; dew point 56 degrees Fahrenheit; wind from 320° at 15 knots; altimeter setting 29.93 inches of mercury; pilot reports top of overcast at 5500 feet MSL; runway 34 visual range 2000 feet.

VFR WEATHER MINIMUMS

Uncontrolled airspace

1. **Below 1200 feet AGL,** you need only **one mile visibility** to fly VFR, and you must remain **clear of the clouds.**

2. In the altitude range between **1200 feet AGL and 10,000 feet MSL,** you still only need **one mile visibility,** but you must remain at least **500 feet below, 1000 feet above, or 2000 feet horizontally from clouds.**

3. **At or above 10,000 feet MSL, and above 1200 feet AGL,** the requirements change significantly. You now need **five miles visibility,** and you must remain at least **1000 feet below, 1000 feet above, or one mile horizontally from clouds.**

Controlled airspace

1. **Below 10,000 feet** you need **three miles visibility** to fly, and you must remain at least **500 feet below, 1000 feet above, or 2000 feet horizontally from clouds.**

2. **At or above 10,000 feet MSL** the requirements are the same as in uncontrolled airspace: **five miles visibility** and at least **1000 feet below, 1000 feet above, or one mile horizontally from clouds.**

GENERAL TRANSPONDER CODES

1200: For VFR flight
7500: For aerial hijacking in progress

7600: For loss of two-way radio communications
7700: For an airborne emergency

The time will come when gentlemen,
when they are to go on a journey,
will call for their wings as regularly
as they call for their boots.
BISHOP WILKENS

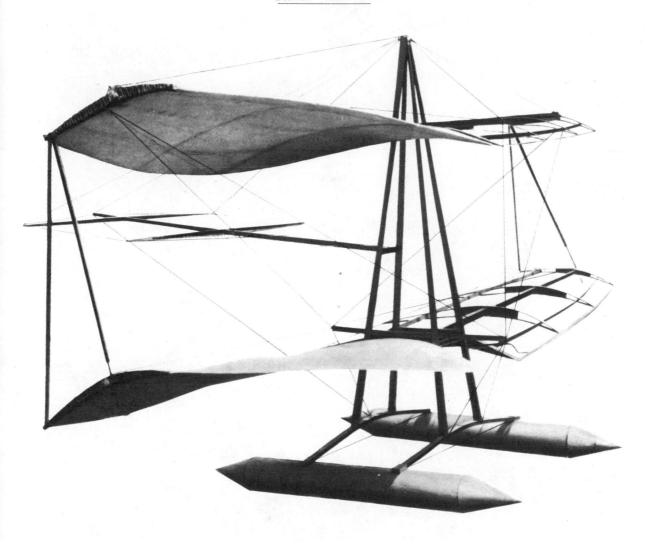

The first powered flight took place at 10:35
on the morning of December 17, 1903.
Orville guided the *Flyer* down a long wooden track,
lifted into the air, and remained aloft for
twelve seconds and flew 120 feet.

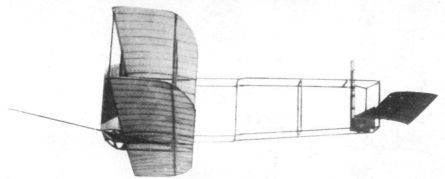

The Literary Digest

(Title Reg. U.S. Pat. Off.)

CAPRONI PLANE SUPPLYING FOOD TO ITALIAN TROOPS ON OUTPOST GUARD DUTY

New York FUNK & WAGNALLS COMPANY London

PUBLIC OPINION New York combined with The LITERARY DIGEST

Vol. 58, No. 3. Whole No. 1474   JULY 20, 1918   Price 10 Cents

Lindbergh Lands Safely in Paris at 5:21 P.M.;
3,800-Mile Flight in 33½ Hours Thrills World.
NEW YORK HERALD TRIBUNE, MAY 22, 1927

I do not believe (the airplane) will supplant
surface transportation. I believe it will always be limited to
special purposes. It will be a factor in war. It
may have a future as a carrier of mail.
WILBUR WRIGHT

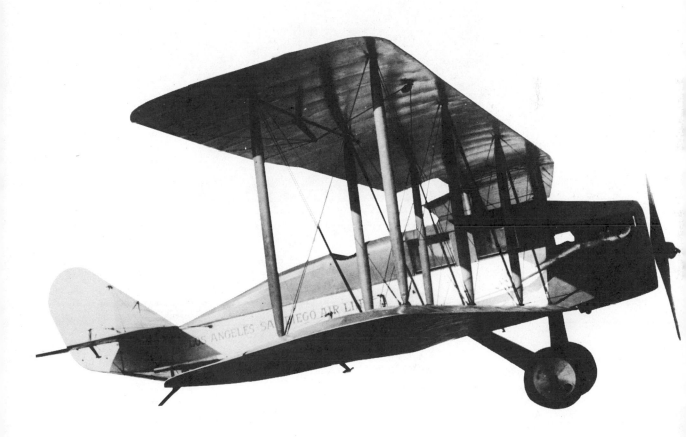

WADSWORTH PUBLISHING COMPANY
BELMONT, CALIFORNIA
A DIVISION OF WADSWORTH, INC.

AN INVITATION TO FLY

Basics for the Private Pilot

THIRD EDITION

DENNIS GLAESER
PARKS COLLEGE

SANFORD GUM
COLLEGE OF SAN MATEO (EMERITUS)

BRUCE WALTERS

Aviation Editor: Anne Scanlan-Rohrer

Editorial Assistant: Sally Uchizono

Production Editor: Sandra Craig

Managing Designer: James Chadwick

Print Buyer: Karen Hunt

Art Editor: Marta Kongsle

Copy Editor: Thomas L. Briggs

Design: McQuiston & Daughter

Technical Illustrations: Joan Carol; Scientific Illustrators, Champaign, Illinois; Sirius Productions, Ltd.

Cover Design: James Chadwick

Cover Photograph: Tom Brouwer/Artistic Photography

Printed in the United States of America   85

  2 3 4 5 6 7 8 9 10—93 92 91 90 89

Library of Congress Cataloging-in-Publication Data

Glaeser, Dennis.
    An invitation to fly : basics for the private pilot / Dennis Glaeser, Sanford Gum, Bruce Walters.—3rd ed.
        p.   cm.
    Includes indexes.
    Updated ed. of: An invitation to fly / Sanford Gum & Bruce Walters.
    ISBN 0-534-09390-6
    1. Private flying. I. Gum, Sanford. II. Walters, Bruce (Bruce E.) III. Gum, Sanford. Invitation to fly. IV. Title.
    TL721.4.G53 1989
    629.132′5217—dc19
                                                          88-17348
                                                          CIP

Special note: One of our objectives is to acquaint you with the various publications available from the Federal Aviation Administration and other sources that will be useful to you as a pilot. This book is not a substitute for such publications, although it reflects the most accurate and recent information available when we went to press. Since some information changes each year, we encourage you to take the responsibility of keeping current by referring to up-to-date manuals, regulations, and directories.

Photo and Illustration Credits

Beech Aircraft Corporation: 39, 40, 41, 48, 62, 69, 70, 73, 74, 75, 80, 81, 88, 98, 102, 104, 105, 110, 118, 119, 123, 125, 485, 506, 508

Bell Helicopter Textron: 6

Benson Aircraft Corporation: 7

Paul Bowen Photography, Inc. (Paul Bowen, Mike Fizer, Dan Moore): viii, 2, 25, 63, 96, 129, 152, 153, 176–177, 178, 226, 276, 327, 430–431, 432, 433, 457, 478, 513, 554–555, 556, 557, 586, 587

Cessna Aircraft Corporation: xx–1, 6, 22–23, 277, 512

Marguerite Comstock Photography: 3, 601

Eipper Aircraft, Inc.: 6

Fairchild National, Inc. 14437 North 73rd Street, Scottsdale, Arizona 85260: 540, 544, 550, 551

Historical Collection—Title Insurance and Trust: vi, vii

Iowa State University Press: 34, 41, 51

King Radio Corporation: 479, 498, 500, 504

Lewis Engineering Company: 115

Library of Congress: iv

Napa Valley Aviation: 6

National Oceanic and Atmospheric Administration: 269

Photophile/Gordon Menzie: 224–225, 256, 257, 258, 259, 261, 318–319, 320, 321

Piper Aircraft: 6, 24, 128, 227, 344

San Diego Aerospace Museum: i, ii, iii, v, 6, 514

CONTENTS

Preface

Welcome to *An Invitation to Fly: Basics for the Private Pilot*. The excellent reception of this text by the aviation training community is a tribute to the efforts of Sanford Gum, Bruce Walters, and the entire team who contributed to the original text.

Preparing this Third Edition of *An Invitation to Fly* has largely been an exercise in tracking changes to Regulations and Airspace as they were implemented by the FAA. The good news is the entire National Airspace System is currently undergoing a sweeping modernization program. The bad news is that the changes are not yet complete. Therefore, it is of utmost importance for pilots to stay informed about these changes through aviation magazines, pilot organizations, and FAA publications.

Of course, we have also incorporated quite a few suggestions and corrections submitted by instructors and students who use this text. User feedback is an integral part of our revision process, and we encourage your participation.

Some of the many changes made in this edition include:

▶ All changes in Federal Air Regulations and FCC regulations are reflected in the text overall, as well as in Chapter 11, Federal Aviation Regulations.
▶ Proficiency Check questions now cover material in the same order as the text.
▶ A number of specific discussions have been expanded or reorganized or both to improve clarity and flow.
▶ In Chapter 1, the discussion of FCC license requirements was revised, and a brief discussion of insurance was added.
▶ In Chapter 2, the explanations of parts of an airplane, turns, and creation of lift were expanded and revised, and a discussion of angle of incidence was added.
▶ In Chapter 4, the attitude indicator figure was revised, and the definition of true altitude was expanded.
▶ In Chapter 6, the discussion of best angle of climb and best rate of climb were expanded, and "carpet plot" performance charts and an explanation of how to use them were added.
▶ In Chapter 7, coverage of airport lighting was moved to follow the discussion of runways to improve continuity, and discussions of ARSAs, common traffic advisory frequency, and ADIZ and DEWIZ were added.
▶ In Chapter 9, the area forecast explanation was updated and expanded.
▶ In Chapter 10, the *Airport/Facility Directory* legend was updated.
▶ In Chapter 12, the discussion of LORAN was revised and expanded.
▶ Chapter 15 was reorganized for better continuity, and the discussion of the inner ear was expanded.

Acknowledgments

I want to thank Anne Scanlan-Rohrer, Wadsworth's aviation editor, for leading the effort on this edition. I also had the pleasure of working with Sandra Craig, the production editor; Marta Kongsle, the art editor; and James Chadwick, the designer. Their efforts and the work of the entire production team are heartily appreciated.

My gratitude is extended to the following individuals for their contribution as reviewers of the Third Edition: Herbert B. Armstrong, Hampton University; Len Kastner, Hanover Park Regional Adult School; Vern Knock, Indiana State University; Hugh M. Miller, Embry-Riddle Aeronautical University, Daytona Beach; Robert H. Pearson, University of Alaska, Anchorage; Michael Peloquin, Foothill College; Don Taylor, San Diego Mesa College; Jacqueline Waide, Ohlone College. I would also like to thank Vern Knock for checking the galleys.

In addition, I would like to acknowledge the reviewers of the Second Edition: Marvin Bay, Aims Community College; Lee Cash, Auburn University; Jerry Houser, Palomar College; David P. Hunter, University of New Haven; Dr. Lamon Marcom, Middle Tennessee State University; Robert Pearson, Anchorage Community College; Jeff Richmond, Embry-Riddle Aeronautical University; Gerald Schreve, San Jose State University.

It was also my good fortune to work with Sandy Gum. I want to thank him for his encouragement and support as well as his contributions to this revision as coauthor.

Finally, I thank my wife, Anne, for her support.

DENNIS GLAESER

Ancillaries

A complete teaching and learning package is provided for students and instructors.

Study Guide. Written by George Semb, University of Kansas, and Don Taylor, San Diego Mesa College, the Study Guide provides the 1988 FAA examination questions and answers matched to the corresponding sections in the text, a review of main points in the text, key terms and concepts, and discussion questions. The Study Guide will be revised every year new FAA questions are released.

Instructor's Manual. This manual provides support materials for the instructor, including sample syllabi, sample reading assignments, answers to text proficiency checks, and **transparency masters.** The number of transparency masters has been increased in the Third Edition.

Flight Maneuvers Manual. The Flight Maneuvers Manual offers students additional instruction for the flight portion of basic training.

NEW Computerized Testing System. This testing system for IBM-PCs and compatibles is available to instructors upon adoption of the text. The system includes 1988 FAA test questions and all objective questions from the Study Guide.

NEW Electronic Study Guide. Students can test themselves on the FAA questions and receive immediate feedback with the Electronic Study Guide, available for IBM-PCs and compatibles.

Videotapes. A set of 30 half-hour videotapes is available from KCSM-TV (at College of San Mateo) for the classroom, learning laboratory, or telecourse. These tapes are being revised for the Third Edition of *Invitation to Fly.* A **Viewer's Guide** is available to accompany the tapes.

Update Newsletter. Information on FAA regulation changes is provided to adopters twice a year in a newsletter format.

Preface to the First Edition

An Invitation to Fly: Basics for the Private Pilot is designed to help you, the potential private pilot, to become a safe and competent pilot and to successfully complete the ground portion of your training. It is designed to be used in ground schools that are approved under part 141 of the Federal Aviation Regulations. It is, of course, also suitable for those individuals who seek a Private Pilot Certificate under FAR part 61 and who are not affiliated with an approved school.

This is perhaps your first opportunity to learn about the principles of flight, weather, and the operation of airplanes *and* perhaps your introduction to some of the basic skills of flying. Thus we have tried to avoid technical language and aeronautical jargon as much as possible in favor of plain English. Points that are appropriate to a beginning level are thoroughly discussed without the introduction of detail that might be appropriate at a more sophisticated level of training. And because looking at a diagram is frequently as helpful as reading about a point, the book is amply illustrated, with color highlighting important features of photographs and schematic drawings.

To help you get the most from each chapter, Checkpoints appear at the beginning of the chapter to indicate the essential ideas to watch for as you read. Checks at the end of the chapter pose questions to help you review and check your knowledge. The *Workbook* that accompanies *An Invitation to Fly* provides aids for further review, for checking your understanding, and for preparing for the Federal Aviation Administration written examination. It contains a concise summary of each chapter, a review of key terms, questions that require short answers, and a bank of questions that are similar to those asked by the FAA.

Thirty half-hour videotapes have been developed in conjunction with *An Invitation to Fly*. All chapters of the book are illustrated through scenes taken in flight and at airports and through computer graphics. Further information is available from KCSM, College of San Mateo, San Mateo, California 94402. A *Viewer's Guide* that integrates text, the workbook, and the videotape programs is available from Wadsworth Publishing Company.

This book and the materials that accompany it are truly the result of a team effort. Special thanks go to our reviewers from FAA-approved (FAR part 141) ground schools: George Sachen, College of San Mateo; Betty Hicks, Foothill College; Jacqueline Waide, Ohlone College; Roy Grumback, Miami Dade Community College; and Tom Emanuel, Jr., University of Illinois. We are especially grateful to Anne Gallagher, director of flight training for Beech Aircraft Corporation, who reviewed the complete manuscript of this text and who helped arrange for photographs and charts. Particular chapters owe a debt to industry specialists: Wallace Jorgenson, power plant instructor, College of San Mateo; Joel Bartlett, pilot and meteorologist, KPIX-TV, San Francisco; Dr. Michael Cowan, FAA Medical Examiner; and the Beechcraft flight engineers.

Other individuals who were instrumental in the development of the book include: Betty Steele and Leanne Ferranti, who coordinated the flow of paper and people: Nancy Taylor, our editor at Wadsworth; and Jay Wurts, whose writing skills and background in flying and aeronautical engineering contributed enormously to the readability and teachability of this text. The production team—Sandra Craig, Douglas Pundick, and Li Greiner—deserves a special tribute for performing the unusually difficult job of coordinating the editorial functions, design, and illustration program. Ultimately we must thank Stewart Chiefet and his staff at KCSM for initiating the telecourse and making this whole project possible. And thanks to the Aircraft Owners and Pilots Association for the information they provided, and to Kathryn Gum for her support.

Finally, all who worked on this book owe a special tribute to Bruce Walters. For sixteen years he encouraged scores of beginning pilots and guided their interests in aviation. Many people around the world owe their start to his dedication and enthusiasm. His own aviation background was extensive. He held both fixed wing and helicopter ratings, served in World War II and with a MASH unit in Korea, was pilot to the Emperor of Ethiopia, and was a very active bush pilot in Alaska. He started his second career as the "Pied Piper" of aviation at the College of San Mateo, dedicating long hours to his students, his church, and his family. This book owes its own start to Bruce Walters. In some small measure, it conveys his love of teaching and of aviation.

SANFORD GUM, ED. D.

AN
INVITATION
TO
FLY

PART I
HOW TO GET STARTED

Until the present century, people lived very much as did those who founded our country. These early pioneers and all others before them to the dawn of civilization lived in the age of the wheel. Today we live in the age of the wing. . . .

Robert M. Kane and Allan D. Vose
Air Transportation

C H E C K P O I N T S

Why do people learn to fly?  What is general aviation? What is the difference between air*craft* and air*planes?* What does a private pilot ground and flight course consist of? How do I become a student pilot? What are the private pilot examinations like? What does becoming a pilot *really* mean?

ON BECOMING A PILOT

Congratulations on your decision to become a pilot. Although flying takes hard work and concentration, it also offers exhilaration, great beauty, and the satisfaction of accomplishing an important goal.

Nearly everyone today takes airplanes for granted. It is easy for us to forget that less than a hundred years ago, transportation was almost completely confined to the earth's surface—on the ground or across the water. Horse-drawn wagons or carriages competed with a fledgling system of railroads, and intercontinental travel was the province of wind- or steam-driven sailing ships. Flight, for all but a few brave balloonists, was confined to the imagination.

Today, of course, you can accomplish in hours journeys that took your grandparents months to complete. Modern airliners and private airplanes are marvels of speed, comfort, and safety. Because of aviation's rapid growth and technical development, even people with little or no interest in flying can avail themselves of all its conveniences. This book was not written for them; it was written for those people who are ready to accept the joys and responsibilities of piloting an airplane.

Flying itself—the manipulation of aircraft controls and the exercise of aeronautical judgment and skill—is still very much for dreamers. By reading this book, you have begun the process of realizing that dream. Private or commercial piloting has never been more popular or accessible to the average citizen.

This chapter will orient you to the world of the **private pilot**. It will explain how you may gain admittance to that world through the process of ground and flight training.

THE AVIATION COMMUNITY

The aviation community has three sectors. The scheduled public air transportation to about 500 locations throughout the country and to every part of the globe is known as **commercial aviation**. The aircraft flown by the armed forces constitute **military aviation**. Any aeronautical activity that does not fall into one of these two sectors is called **general aviation**.

Although most people think of the private pilot who flies for pleasure on weekends or of student pilots and their instructors as representing general aviation, these activities are really a very small part of the total picture. Business jets, charter air taxis, crop dusters, and even NASA's Space Shuttle are all general-aviation aircraft. And this list is just a tiny sample. The Aircraft Owners and Pilots Association estimates that there are over 200,000 general-aviation aircraft operating from about 15,000 airports in the United States. General aviation is the backbone of the American aviation community, since most military and commercial pilots got their start in general aviation.

The governing agency of the commercial- and general-aviation sectors of the aviation community is the **Federal Aviation Administration (FAA)**. The FAA is the government agency responsible for regulating and promoting the growth of aviation in the United States. It issues and enforces the **Federal Aviation Regulations (FARs)**, which govern all aspects of aviation. There are FARs for the design and construction of aircraft, for flight operations, for the certification of pilots, and for a multitude of other aviation-related matters. Chapter 11 presents a number of FARs that student pilots should be familiar with. The FAA also operates **Flight Service Stations**, which provide vital weather and operational information to pilots. At busy airports the FAA operates **air traffic control towers**, which coordinate the flow of aircraft, both commercial and general. The underlying purpose behind all the FAA rules and procedures is to make flying as safe as possible.

THE CLASSIFICATION OF AIRCRAFT

Although all airplanes are aircraft, not all aircraft are airplanes. An **aircraft** is any structure that is intended for navigation through the air and that is supported either by its own buoyancy or by the dynamic action of the air against its surfaces. A brief look at the various kinds of aircraft is in order, since you may fly a number of them during your aviation career and since FAA rules for pilot or airman certification are based on aircraft classification. The classification begins with categories; within a category, specific classes are identified; and within a class, types are identified.

Category.   Aircraft that use the same method of staying aloft and use similar means of propulsion are grouped into the same **category**. This is the broadest classification of aircraft. The FAA currently recognizes the four categories of aircraft shown in Figure 1.1: lighter-than-air, rotorcraft, glider, and airplane.

Class.   Within each category, aircraft with similar operating characteristics are grouped into a **class**. For instance, within the *airplane* category there are four classes: single-engine land, single-engine sea, multiengine land, and multiengine sea.

Type.   When you refer to a specific make and model of aircraft, you are defining its **type**. Here are some aircraft types you may be familiar with: Cessna 152, Piper Tomahawk, Beech Bonanza, Boeing 727, McDonnell Douglas DC-10.

The Different Categories and Classes of Aircraft
Lighter-than-air (LTA) aircraft ascend by displacing a free mass of heavier air with an enclosed mass of lighter gas. There are two classes of lighter-than-air aircraft: **balloons** and **airships**. Balloons are unpowered aircraft that ride air currents. Hot-air balloons were common in the nineteenth century and are used today for sport. Airships are powered and have controls to direct their movement. Inflatable/deflatable airships are called **blimps.** **Dirigibles** are airships built on rigid frames; the famous German Zeppelins were dirigibles.

A **rotorcraft** is easily recognized by its large overhead propeller, called a *rotor*. There are two classes of rotorcraft: **helicopters** and **gyroplanes**.

Lighter-than-air

Balloon

Airship

Glider

Sailplane

Rotorcraft

Helicopter

Gyroplane

Airplane

Single-engine land

Multiengine water

Multiengine land

Helicopters have powered rotors that provide both vertical and horizontal motion through the air. On a gyroplane the rotor is freewheeling; propulsion is provided by an engine and propeller mounted in either a tractor (pulling) or pusher configuration.

A **glider** is an unpowered aircraft with wings and a tail. A **sailplane** is a high-performance glider capable of remaining aloft on rising air currents. These aircraft can be towed aloft by an airplane or a winch, or they can be launched over the edge of a cliff. Once aloft, a glider or sailplane is always coasting down through the air immediately around it. A sailplane pilot stays aloft by finding rising air currents produced by the local terrain or weather conditions.

An **airplane** is a powered aircraft with wings and a tail. The airplane category has four classes: **single-engine land, single-engine water, multiengine land,** and **multiengine water**. Chapter 2 is devoted to describing airplanes and how they fly.

These descriptions of category, class, and type are used by the FAA in defining *pilot limitations*. Your pilot certificate will always specify each category and class of aircraft you may legally operate. When you move up to jet-powered aircraft or any aircraft that has a maximum takeoff weight of over 12,500 pounds (about the size of a Lear jet or bigger), you will need a *type rating* in each make and model you fly. The term *category* is also used in another context: In the *certification of aircraft*, category refers to the operating limitations or intended use of the aircraft. The aircraft's Operating Handbook will discuss each category for which it is certified and the limitations to be observed.

There is one type of airborne vehicle that is treated differently by the FAA. An *ultralight* is a lightweight, single-person, recreational aircraft like that shown in Figure 1.2. The FAA defines these as "vehicles" and does not regulate their design or construction. You do not need a pilot's certificate to fly one.

You will need a pilot's certificate to fly any kind of airplane, and you will need training before you can obtain that certificate. The following section provides a brief overview of what that training entails.

Figure 1.1 *(opposite)* The various categories and classes of aircraft.

Figure 1.2 An ultralight.

THE PILOT TRAINING PROCESS

When did you really decide to become a pilot? You, like many people, may have been inspired by a lifelong fascination with airplanes and the glamour of flying as depicted in books and films. Perhaps you have a friend or relative who is a pilot, or perhaps you are simply curious and answered an advertisement for a low-cost demonstration flight at your local flying school. Or you may have been attracted to aviation because you are interested in precision machines and modern technology. Whatever your initial motivation, you have one thing in common with other student pilots: a desire to learn more not only about flying—an important element of the world around you—but also about yourself and the range of your abilities.

The focus of the rest of this chapter, and in fact the entire text, is learning to fly airplanes. To avoid confusion, the training requirements for other aircraft categories, where different from airplanes, are not discussed.

Flight Instruction

You may take flying lessons at any age, but you cannot **solo** (fly the aircraft by yourself, without an instructor) until you are sixteen (FAR 61.87), and you will not be able to receive a Private Pilot Certificate before your seventeenth birthday (FAR 61.103). Assuming that you face no age restriction, you will probably want to begin your search for a flight instruction program right away, if you have not done so already.

How do you go about finding a good flight instruction program? A good place to start, of course, is a company at a local airport that offers flight training. Such businesses are called **fixed-base operators (FBOs)**. Besides instruction, FBOs generally offer aircraft rental and sales, charter services (air taxi), maintenance, tie downs (aircraft parking), fuel, and many other goods and services required by the flying community. An FBO is not your only option, however. Anyone who is a **Certified Flight Instructor (CFI)** can give you inflight training called **dual instruction**. You may want to investigate flying clubs in your area or talk to freelance instructors (instructors who are not on staff at an FBO). Some colleges offer flight training as part of their aviation academic program; in fact, there are a number of colleges that specialize in aviation programs. Most instructors and flight schools offer a short introductory flight lesson to prospective students (who get to operate the controls of the airplane for most of this flight). You may want to take an introductory flight with more than one school or instructor before you decide who your instructor will be.

Many FBOs meet the criteria set out by the FAA to be an **FAA-approved flight school**. To earn this status they must have training facilities, personnel, and course syllabuses that comply with the regulations established for flight schools (FAR Part 141). A list of approved schools can be obtained at no cost from the Publications Section, U.S. Department of Transportation, Washington, D.C. 20590.

Ground Instruction

Your training program must include **ground instruction** as well as flight instruction (FAR 61.35). Again, there are several means of acquiring the knowledge you will need to pass certification tests and to be assured of having all information necessary to your skill and safety as a pilot.

Formal ground school classes are offered by most FBOs as part of their training program. An FAA-approved syllabus always calls for a mandatory number of ground instruction hours. Many colleges offer formal ground schools for academic credit.

A number of private-pilot home-study courses that use programmed learning methods are available. You may also use appropriate materials (such as this book and the associated workbook) to study on your own. Self-study courses are most effective when you consult regularly with a CFI, who can check your progress and explain ambiguous material.

"Weekend ground school" courses provide intense preparation for the FAA written exam. These courses are not designed to provide in-depth coverage of the material. But for a person who has studied the course matter and who wants a quick, well-organized preparation for the written exam, these reviews are remarkably successful.

The Cost of Learning to Fly

In essence, you will be paying for two things during flight training: the *airplane rental charge* and the *instructor's fee*. Most aircraft used for instruction have a recording digital clock, called the *Hobbs meter*. This device records either the total time the engine was running or the time the electrical system was turned on, depending on the airplane. You note the reading before you start and after you stop the airplane, and the charge is based on the number of hours recorded. Your instructor's fee is usually based on the total time of your lesson, which includes some preflight and postflight discussion in addition to the flight time.

Most flight schools have package deals for flight training. It is extremely important for you to understand exactly what each package covers. Some cover all training up to your solo flight. Others cover a fixed amount of instruction and of solo time. There are even fixed-price programs for you to earn your pilot's certificate, with no maximum limit on the number of hours. And there are undoubtedly other variations on packaging and pricing. The following data will give you some means of estimating and comparing costs: an average student will solo after 12 to 15 hours of dual instruction and will earn a pilot's certificate after about 65 total hours (40 dual, 25 solo). The number of hours you require will probably differ from this total, but these averages provide the basis for realistic planning. The FAA requires a *minimum* of 40 hours—20 dual, 20 solo. (These minimums are discussed later in this chapter.)

Ground school is usually a separate cost item. Your choice of home study, formal classes, and/or a weekend course will determine the exact amount. Select the method that best suits your learning habits and schedule.

Your training will also entail a few miscellaneous costs, briefly described here. You will need:

1. A **logbook**, used to record your flight experience.

2. A copy of the **Pilot's Operating Handbook** for the airplane you will be flying.

3. *Aeronautical charts* for your local area.

4. An *aeronautical computer* and *plotter*, used to plan cross-country flights. (They are described more completely in Chapter 12.)

5. The *books* required for your ground school course.

6. A *medical examination*, required for your Student Pilot Certificate (described below).

7. Fees for the *FAA-designated examiners*, who will administer your written and flight tests.

Insurance is another cost item to consider. The extent to which renter pilots are covered by the FBO's insurance varies considerably. It is only prudent to know what you may or may not be held financially responsible for. Should you desire additional coverage, numerous insurance companies offer "Renters Policies" to supplement the coverage provided by the FBO. It is entirely your decision whether or not to purchase additional insurance.

The FAA Medical Examination and Student Pilot Certificate
It is probably wise to obtain your **Student Pilot Certificate** as soon as you decide to invest in flying lessons. You do not need it as long as you are flying dual, but it is required before you may fly solo. This document will be issued if the following conditions are met:

1. You are at least 16 years of age.

2. You are able to read, speak, and understand the English language.

3. You obtain at least a **Third Class Medical Certificate**.

The third class is the least demanding **FAA Medical Certificate**. Anyone with good general health should qualify easily. Wearing eyeglasses or contacts is usually no problem, and even certain physical limitations or handicaps can be accommodated (possibly with operating restrictions something like those issued with automobile licenses).

If your long-range plans include flying for hire (as a flight instructor, charter pilot, or corporate pilot, for instance), you should consider obtaining a **Second Class Medical Certificate**. If flying for an airline is your objective, then look into a **First Class Medical Certificate**. These certificates are more restrictive than the third class (and the examinations are more expensive, of course), but it makes sense to verify early that no roadblocks stand between you and your goals.

No matter which examination you take, your Student Pilot Certificate is good for 24 calendar months. It will expire in two years at the end of the month in which it was issued. If you have not earned your **Private Pilot Certificate** by that time, you will have to repeat the process.

The actual Student Pilot Certificate, shown in Figure 1.3, is on the same form as your medical certificate. On the back are spaces for your instructor's

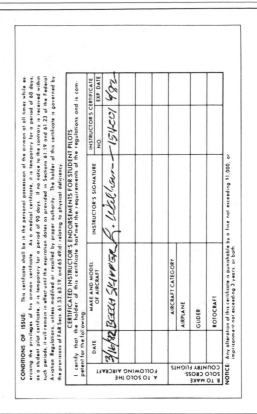

Figure 1.3 An example of an FAA medical certificate, which also serves as a Student Pilot Certificate.

signature, to verify that you qualify to solo an airplane, and, later, that you are ready to go cross-country alone.

Where do you go for an FAA medical examination? Your local FAA office can provide you with a list of physicians who are **Aviation Medical Examiners (AME)**. It may be just as easy to ask other pilots you know, including your instructor, for the names of the doctors they use.

After you become a certified pilot, FAR 61.23 requires you to pass a third-class medical exam (or better) every two years. If you start flying for hire, you will need to renew your second-class medical every year (12 calendar months). Airline captains must take a physical every 6 months.

A TYPICAL TRAINING PROGRAM

Now let us examine all the steps you will take, both in flight and ground training, in the process of becoming a pilot. Figure 1.4 outlines the process described in the next few paragraphs.

Presolo Instruction

Your program of dual instruction will begin with such basics as preflight inspection of the airplane, taxiing, flying straight and level, turns, climbs,

Figure 1.4 The pilot training process.

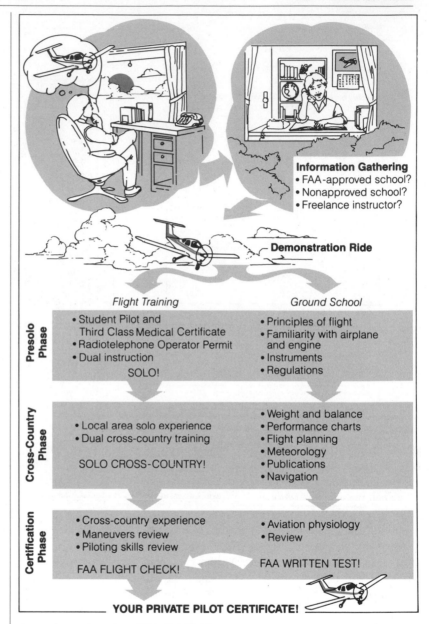

Information Gathering
- FAA-approved school?
- Nonapproved school?
- Freelance instructor?

Demonstration Ride

	Flight Training	*Ground School*
Presolo Phase	• Student Pilot and Third Class Medical Certificate • Radiotelephone Operator Permit • Dual instruction **SOLO!**	• Principles of flight • Familiarity with airplane and engine • Instruments • Regulations
Cross-Country Phase	• Local area solo experience • Dual cross-country training **SOLO CROSS-COUNTRY!**	• Weight and balance • Performance charts • Flight planning • Meteorology • Publications • Navigation
Certification Phase	• Cross-country experience • Maneuvers review • Piloting skills review **FAA FLIGHT CHECK!**	• Aviation physiology • Review **FAA WRITTEN TEST!**

YOUR PRIVATE PILOT CERTIFICATE!

and descents. Within a short period of time your skills will expand to takeoffs and landings, maneuvering the airplane around objects on the ground, and exploring the limits of the airplane's flight envelope. You will also become familiar with aircraft emergency procedures, local airport procedures, the use of the radio, and the boundaries of the *practice area*, the geographical area specified by your instructor for practicing flight maneuvers. (It is usually near the airport but away from local air traffic and populated, noise-sensitive areas.)

Your ground school will support this activity with courses on the principles of flight; a general description of the airplane and its systems, including its power plant and engine instruments; familiarization with the basic flight instruments; and a study of pertinent regulations, such as FAR Part 61 (pilot certificates), FAR Part 91 (general flight rules), and National Transportation Safety Board (NTSB) Part 830 (accident reporting).

Flying Solo

When you are competent to fly solo (alone in the aircraft), your instructor will make sure you are familiar with the regulations and flight procedures that apply to solo flight (FAR 61.87). Your Student Pilot Certificate and logbook will be endorsed (see Figures 1.3 and 1.5), and you will be released for a *supervised solo flight*. This first solo excursion usually consists of flying around the airport for a number of takeoffs and landings while your instructor observes from the ground. Upon the completion of your first solo, your instructor will host a small ceremony to initiate you as the world's newest pilot. After this momentous occasion, there will be a few more dual flights to review procedures and to assure your familiarity with the practice area. These flights are usually followed by a repeat of your first solo performance. Then you will spend a few solo hours in the practice area as directed by your instructor.

Going Cross-Country

The next training phase is aimed at qualifying you to fly cross-country. At least three hours of dual cross-country flight instruction is required (FAR 61.109).

Your flight instructor will make sure that you know all the pertinent pilot operations (FAR 61.93). These include various methods of aerial navigation, reading aeronautical charts, flight planning, and the gathering and use of weather information. You will practice controlling the airplane while referring only to the flight instruments and will learn procedures to follow if you become unsure of your position.

All these subjects will also be discussed in ground school. In fact, some instructors think it best to teach navigation methods, flight planning, regulations, and the like before starting the cross-country phase of flight training. Ground school also teaches airplane weight and balance computations, how to calculate airplane performance, and basic meteorology, as well as how to use available weather data. A valuable part of the curriculum is to have you become familiar with publications containing airport information and safety-related data.

After you demonstrate the necessary skills on dual cross-country flights, your instructor will endorse your student certificate for solo cross-country. Before *each* solo jaunt, your preflight planning will be examined, and *your logbook must be endorsed*. This logbook entry is required by FAR 61.93, so don't leave home without it!

In order to qualify for a Private Pilot Certificate, you must log at least 10 hours of solo cross-country flight. Each flight must have a landing at an

DATE 1982	AIRCRAFT MAKE & MODEL	AIRCRAFT IDENT.	POINTS OF DEPARTURE & ARRIVAL		REMARKS, PROCEDURES, MANEUVERS	NO. INSTR. APP.	NO. LDG.
			FROM	TO			
3/5	Beech Skipper	177 BA	SQL	LCL	Normal LDG's, coordination exercises attitude control L. Walker 154000 CFI		6
3/7	Beech Skipper	177 BA	SQL	LCL	Review short FLD LDG's — stalls, emerg. LDG's and go-arounds L. Walker 154000 CFI		6
3/9	Beech Skipper	177 BA	SQL	LCL	Review slow FLT, T.O's & LDG's L. Walker 154000 CFI		6
3/12	Beech Skipper	177 BA	SQL	LCL	X-wind T.O's & LDG's and pattern work L. Walker 154000 CFI		6
3/14	Beech Skipper	177 BA	SQL	LCL	Full and no flap LDG's, SLR's to LDG's L. Walker 154000 CFI		5
3/16	Beech Skipper	177 BA	SQL	LCL	FIRST SOLO L. Walker 154000 CFI		5
3/18	Beech Skipper	177 BA	SQL	LCL	Stalls, slow FLT, traffic pattern PWR control L. Walker 154000 CFI		6

3/16/81 Pat Llewellyn is competent to make SOLO FLIGHTS in a Beechcraft SKIPPER. Max. cross wind component 5 Kts. Max. wind 15 Kts. Min weather – ceiling 3000 ft. Vis. 5 st. miles.

I certify that the statements made by me on this form are true.

PILOT'S SIGNATURE _Pat W. Llewellyn_

PAGE TOTAL

AMT. FORWARD

TOTAL TO DATE

AIRCRAFT CATEGORY			CONDITIONS OF FLIGHT					TYPE OF PILOTING TIME			TOTAL DURATION OF FLIGHT	
AIRPLANE SEL	AIRPLANE MEL	CROSS COUNTRY	DAY	NIGHT	ACTUAL INSTR.	SIMULATED INSTR.	SYNTHETIC TRAINER	DUAL RECEIVED	PILOT IN COMMAND			
1 0			1 0					1 0			1 0	
1 2			1 2					1 2			1 2	
1 1			1 1					1 1			1 1	
1 2			1 2					1 2			1 2	
1 0			1 0					1 0			1 0	
1 3			1 3					3	1 0		1 3	
1 0			1 0					1 0			1 0	
7 8			7 8					6 8	1 0		7 8	
6 1			6 1					6 1			6 1	
13 9			13 9					12 9	1 0		13 9	

Figure 1.5 An example of a student pilot's logbook.

airport more than 50 nautical miles from your home base. One *long cross-country* flight is required. This trip must be at least 300 nautical miles long, with landings at three (or more) airports. One of the airports must be at least 100 nautical miles from the departure airport (FAR 61.109).

Flying at Night

It is possible to earn a pilot's certificate without flying at night; however, your certificate will restrict you to daytime flying. Because no pilot can be sure of *never* getting caught by the setting sun, virtually all training programs call for at least three dual hours of night flight, including ten night takeoffs and landings (the minimum required by FAR 61.109). Your ground school program will cover the physiological aspects of night flight.

QUALIFYING FOR YOUR PILOT'S CERTIFICATE
The Written Exam
It is best to complete your ground school training before the flight training ends. In fact, you should finish ground school before your first solo cross-country, because you will need the information the ground school offers to assure a safe and error-free flight. Besides teaching you the skills necessary to be a good pilot, ground school will prepare you to take the *Private Pilot Written Exam*. One of the books used in your ground school program, the *FAA Private Pilot Question Book* (or a commercially available equivalent), is invaluable both in learning the material and in preparing you for the exam. It is actually a compilation of all the questions that could be asked. Your actual exam will consist of 60 questions from the question book.

The exam will be administered by an instructor who is also an FAA-designated examiner. Your local FAA office or FBO can provide a list of these individuals. Before taking the test, you will be required to present some form of personal identification and evidence that you have prepared for the written exam. An entry in your logbook or simply a note from your ground school or flight instructor is acceptable. Some home study courses provide a certificate of completion, which serves as evidence. If your home study course provides no certificate, you must show the course materials to the examiner to qualify for the test.

Your completed test will be sent to the FAA for grading. The results will be mailed to you—usually within two weeks—informing you of your score and listing the questions (from the FAA Question Book) you answered incorrectly (see Figure 1.6). A satisfactory written test (a score of 70 percent or better) is good for 24 calendar months. If your practical (flight) test has not been completed within that period, you must retake the exam.

Dual and Solo Flight Time
Your flight training program will prepare you for two things: a lifetime of safe flying and your private pilot practical test. Before recommending you for the test, your instructor will verify that you meet the aeronautical experience (flight time) requirements of FAR 61.109: you will have had *at least* 40 hours of total time, 20 dual and 20 solo. FAR Part 141–approved schools can recommend students with a minimum of 35 hours (20 dual, 15 solo).

Although regulations specify the dual cross-country and night times discussed previously, the majority of your dual flying will be structured by your instructor rather than by regulations. Regulations do specify that you must spend at least 3 hours preparing for your practical test, within the preceding 60 days.

Your instructor will also spell out what you should do during solo flight, recommending the procedures and maneuvers you need to practice. Reg-

Figure 1.6 A sample report from
the FAA written test. Shown with
the score are questions missed from
the FAA Private Pilot Question
Book.

DO NOT DESTROY THIS TEST REPORT
This Test Report must be presented
for retesting or certification

DEPARTMENT OF TRANSPORTATION   FEDERAL AVIATION ADMINISTRATION

AIRMAN WRITTEN TEST REPORT (RIS: AC 8080-2)

3829
SSN 019-36-2819

TEST		GRADES BY SECTION							FAA OFFICE NO.	TEST DATE	EXPIRATION DATE
TAKE NO.	TITLE *	1	2	3	4	5	6	7			
01	PA	83							CE 62C	11-07-84	11-30-86

EXPIRATION DATE *Last day of month*							

See codes on reverse side.

MECHANICS ONLY - EXPIRATION DATE CODES
The first character designates the month; the second
and third characters, the year. January through September
as shown by numbers 1 through 9; October as
"O"; November as "N"; December as "D".

LAST NAME, FIRST MIDDLE

LLEWELLYN PAT W.
COUNTRY CLUB HEIGHTS
MUNSON MA   01057

EXAMPLES:
Month (June)_____ 6 75   D 75
Year (1975)_____
Month (December)_____
Year (1975)_____

NOTE: MACHINE SCORING OF TEST PA 102 INDICATES AN INCORRECT ANSWER
WAS SELECTED FOR THE FOLLOWING QUESTIONS.

SECTION   QUESTION NUMBERS - SEE QUESTION BOOK FAA-T-8080-1 .

1   1056 1105 1254 1269 1343 1420 1464 1789 1796 1878

When applicable, an authorized instructor may complete and sign this statement:

I HAVE GIVEN THIS APPLICANT ADDITIONAL INSTRUCTION IN EACH OF THE SUBJECT AREAS FAILED AND CONSIDER THE APPLICANT COMPETENT TO PASS THE
TEST.

LAST_____INITIAL_____CERTIFICATE NO._____TYPE_____INSTRUCTOR'S SIGNATURE_____
     INSTRUCTOR'S NAME (Print)

FRAUDULENT ALTERATION OF THIS FORM BY ANY PERSON IS A BASIS FOR SUSPENSION OR REVOCATION OF ANY CERTIFICATES OR RATINGS
HELD BY THAT PERSON.
AC Form 8080-2 (10-83)

ISSUED BY   ADMINISTRATOR
             FEDERAL AVIATION ADMINISTRATION

ulations require the cross-country flights mentioned above. At least three
of your solo landings and takeoffs must be at an airport with an operating
control tower.

The flying time requirements set out in the FARs represent an absolute
minimum, not an average. Very few pilots earn a certificate after only 35
or 40 hours unless they have previous flying experience (in gliders or helicopters, for instance). In fact, the requirements are designed to minimize
the burden on those with previous experience, not to establish guidelines
for the novice. An average student pilot requires about 65 hours of flight
time to achieve the proficiency necessary for passing the flight test. Developing your flying skills is a continuous learning process. Earning your
pilot's certificate is simply a checkpoint along the way.

Taking the Practical Test

Like your written test, your practical test will be administered by an FAA
Designated Flight Examiner. The job of the examiner is to assess your
skills relative to established standards. He or she does not alter those standards for individuals or enforce personal flying techniques.

The examiner will quiz you informally on your knowledge of airplane
documents, certificates, performance, weight and balance, preflight inspections, and radio communications, usually while you are engaged in these
activities in the course of your practical test. The examiner will probably
emphasize any areas noted on your written exam report as requiring further
study.

Since this is a practical test, you will prepare a typical cross-country flight (the examiner will specify the destination). This exercise will include a weather briefing, navigation calculations, and preparation of a complete flight plan. You will also compute the actual weight and balance of the airplane as loaded for the flight.

The flight usually begins with your demonstrating navigation skills as you proceed toward your destination. At any time you may be tested on your reactions to such unusual flight conditions as flying only by reference to the flight instruments, engine failure (simulated), or equipment malfunctions. The examiner may want to see the procedures you use when you are unsure of your position. Since you have practiced these situations during your training, you should have no trouble taking the proper actions.

Next, you will be asked to demonstrate ground reference maneuvers and such basic flight maneuvers as climbs, descents, steep turns, and slow flight. Finally, you will execute maximum performance takeoffs and landings. This scenario for a practical test is, of course, only an example. The content of each practical test is determined by the examiner.

When your practical test is complete, the examiner will debrief you on your performance and provide constructive hints on improving your techniques where appropriate. Since few instructors will recommend a marginal student for a practical test, you can reasonably expect to pass the test on your first try. But if you do not, the examiner will explain the reasons for your not passing and will discuss in detail what will be required to pass. Normally you will not have to repeat the entire practical test, simply those skills you failed to demonstrate acceptably on the first try. The applicant for initial practical tests and retests always provides the aircraft used in the examination.

When you have passed the test, the examiner will issue you a temporary Private Pilot Certificate, good for 120 days. From that moment on you may enjoy the privileges of a private pilot. You will receive your permanent certificate by mail some time after your practical test. A sample Private Pilot Certificate is shown in Figure 1.7. There are no charges for any certificates issued by the FAA, although a civilian Designated Flight Examiner, like the civilian Medical Examiner, will charge you a fee for services rendered.

Private Pilot Responsibilities

Even after you have earned a Private Pilot Certificate, there will be limits to your flying privileges. Although you will now be able to take your family, friends, and associates on local or cross-country flights, you may not conduct such flights for compensation. Sharing traveling expenses, however, such as the cost of fuel, is not considered flying for hire. Only pilots holding a commercial or airline transport certificate may fly for hire. Your certificate will be limited to the category and class of aircraft in which you took your practical test, usually a single-engine land airplane. You may not, nor would you want to, operate an unfamiliar class of aircraft without receiving dual instruction. Private pilots are eligible to earn additional certificates and

Figure 1.7 A Private Pilot
Certificate.

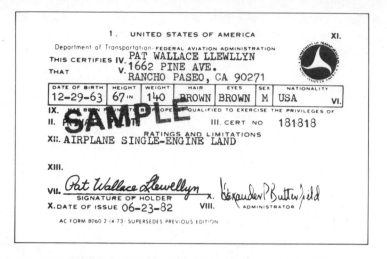

ratings in many different classes and categories of aircraft, from multiengine airplanes to helicopters. Appropriate training from a qualified CFI and
an FAA practical test are always prerequisites, however.

Similarly, you would not be allowed, nor would you normally wish to
continue, flights into regions where **Visual Flight Rules (VFR)** are not in
effect and the aircraft would have to be operated in accordance with **Instrument Flight Rules (IFR)**. Visual Flight Rules are those rules established
by the FAA pertaining to safe flight clear of clouds and in areas of adequate
visibility. Instrument Flight Rules are those rules that apply to aircraft
operating in weather conditions below VFR minimums or in other special
circumstances as specified by the FAA. Although you will have received
some preliminary instrument flight training as part of your private pilot
program, this training is precautionary in nature only. A separate rating
must be obtained to operate an aircraft in low visibility or poor weather
conditions, or even to file an Instrument Flight Rules flight plan.

Finally, though all pilots enjoy sharing their experiences, no aviators
other than CFIs are permitted to give flight instruction.

THE PSYCHOLOGY OF PILOTING

Flying is literally a process that takes a lifetime to learn. Nothing in flying
encourages success like a little humility; nothing leads to disaster more
quickly than overconfidence.

Pilots as Individualists

The stereotype of the white-scarfed, goggled Red Baron dies hard. This
image of pilots as confident individualists frequently attracts people to
flying. Yet while self-confidence is important and necessary to all pilots
(an aircraft must be operated *properly*, not timidly), the best pilots are far
more than confident individuals. They are strong team players as well.

Pilots as Team Players

The best pilots have learned that they are important components in the aviation system. As pilots who must share with others a finite amount of airspace, they accept the responsibilities of safe flying as easily as they accept the many freedoms flying offers. The best pilots are:

1. **Knowledgeable.** They know the appropriate regulations and the valid reasoning behind them. They know the performance characteristics and limitations of their aircraft and observe them carefully. They also know their own limits of ability as pilots and do not try to overstep those limits.

2. **Prepared.** They review and practice their flying skills regularly. They plan each flight and fly their plan.

To say that safe flying demands careful, deliberate action and self-discipline is not to rob it of its excitement or adventure. Far from it. These are the precise qualities that will allow you to turn your dreams of flight into reality.

The best way to start is with a quality ground school experience. That is the purpose of the rest of this book.

KEY TERMS

category
Certified Flight Instructor (CFI)
class
cross-country flight
Designated Flight Examiner
dual instruction
Federal Aviation Administration
  (FAA)
Federal Aviation Regulations
  (FARs)
fixed-base operator (FBO)

general aviation
logbook
pilot-in-command
private pilot
Private Pilot Certificate
solo
student pilot
Student Pilot Certificate
Third Class Medical Certificate
type

PROFICIENCY CHECK

1. What branch of the Department of Transportation is responsible for regulating and promoting the growth of civil aviation? Name at least three ways in which this organization accomplishes these goals.

2. Name the four categories of aircraft and give an example of each.

3. What requirements must an applicant meet to obtain a Student Pilot Certificate?

4. A student pilot decides on a career as a CFI. What class of FAA medical certificate should this person obtain?

5. What is the minimum number of flying hours a student pilot must log before applying for a private pilot practical test?

6. If the FAA approves a CFI to administer aviator practical tests on its behalf, what will the instructor's new title be?

7. Aviator certificates carry with them certain limitations as well as privileges. What are three major limitations the FAA places on the student pilot? What are three major limitations placed on the private pilot?

8. Assuming you take your private pilot flight test in a single-engine land airplane, will you be eligible to pilot any other category, class, or type of aircraft?

9. Good pilots should be team players as well as self-confident individualists. Name the two characteristics mentioned in the text that are commonly found in the best pilots.

PART II
HOW
AN AIRPLANE
WORKS

> Get rid at the outset of the idea that the airplane is only an air-going sort of automobile. It isn't. It may sound like one and smell like one, and it may have been interior-decorated to look like one; but the difference is—it goes on wings.
>
> Wolfgang Langewiesche
> *Stick and Rudder*

C H E C K P O I N T S

What are the parts of an airplane? ✈ What forces cause an airplane to leave the ground and stay aloft? ✈ How do airplanes go up and down and turn? ✈ What does it mean to "fly the wing"? ✈ What is the cause of an airplane stall? ✈ How do pilots recover from it? ✈ What is a spin and how is it caused? ✈ How do pilots recover from it?

THE PRACTICAL SCIENCE OF FLIGHT

66"It will never get off the ground," they said of the first simple airplanes. But some did get off the ground, and some actually flew. How and why do airplanes fly? Although every component on an airplane has an important function, the wing is what allows an airplane to fly. In a very real sense, everything else on airplanes is put there primarily to control or otherwise use the wings. As a pilot, you should know how the parts of your craft operate and how physical forces act on the plane as it moves through the air.

THE PARTS OF AN AIRPLANE

Figure 2.1 shows the basic components of an airplane. Although each manufacturer and each model have their own design features, these general components are found on every airplane and are called by the same names. The entire structure of an airplane is called the **airframe**. The components of the airframe are: the wing, the fuselage, and the tail assembly, or empennage.

Wings are the major characteristic of an airplane. Wings can be mounted above the cabin (high wing), below the cabin (low wing), or anywhere between (mid wing). Each manufacturer has its own preference. Most modern airplanes are **monoplanes**; that is, they have one wing. Airplanes with two wings are called **biplanes**. There have even been *triplanes*, the most famous of which was the Fokker triplane flown by the Red Baron in World War I.

The most commonly used wing construction consists of airfoil-shaped *ribs* attached to *spars*. Those components are then covered by a thin *skin*, which forms the wing's outer surface.

Figure 2.1 The parts of an airplane.

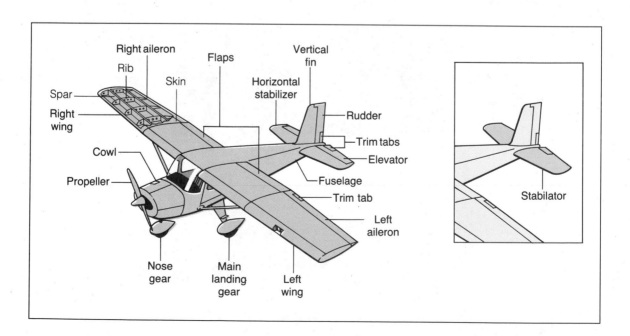

On the *trailing* (rearmost) edge of the wing are two sets of movable surfaces. Those farthest from the center of the airplane (outboard) are called **ailerons**. The ailerons move when you turn the control wheel or move the control stick side to side. They move in opposite directions, one going up while the other goes down. **Flaps** are the movable surfaces closest to the center (inboard). They are controlled by a lever or switch in the cockpit. Flaps only move downward (sometimes backward as well as downward), and both flaps always move simultaneously.

On most airplanes, the wings contain the fuel tanks. This is both structurally efficient and practical. The weight of the fuel is distributed along the structure that is doing the lifting, and it leaves the rest of the airframe available for other things, like people and cargo.

When you observe an airplane from the front or rear, you will notice that the wings are not parallel to the ground but form a slight V (see Figure 2.2a). This angle is called **dihedral**. The purpose of dihedral will be discussed later in this chapter.

The **fuselage** is the body of the airplane. It holds the pilot, passengers, and cargo. The fuselage is designed to be as small as possible for performance reasons yet spacious enough for comfort. When viewed from the side, the wings may appear to be attached at a slight angle with respect to the fuselage (see Figure 2.2b). This is called the **angle of incidence,** and its purpose is to keep the fuselage level in cruising flight.

The **tail assembly** or **empennage** consists of two sets of surfaces, usually one horizontal and one vertical. (There are airplanes that use a V configuration, but these are not discussed here, to reduce confusion.) The vertical element has a fixed part called the **vertical stabilizer** and a movable part called the **rudder**. The rudder is controlled by pedals on the cockpit floor. The horizontal surface usually has a fixed **horizontal stabilizer** and a movable **elevator**. On some airplanes the entire horizontal surface moves, in which case it is called a **stabilator**. The elevator or stabilator is controlled by the fore and aft movement of the control wheel or stick.

The **engine** and **propeller** on most single-engine airplanes are mounted on the front of the fuselage. This is called the *tractor (pulling) configura-*

Figure 2.2 **(a)** Wing dihedral. **(b)** Angle of incidence.

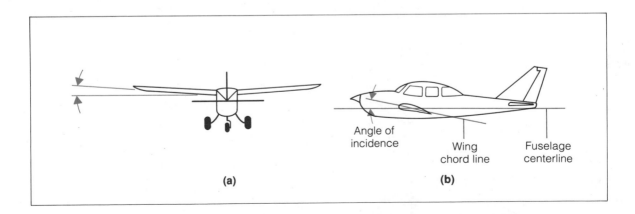

Angle of
incidence

Wing
chord line

Fuselage
centerline

(a)   **(b)**

tion. The protective skin around the engine is called the **cowl**. It provides a smooth exterior surface and channels cooling air around the engine.

The **undercarriage** of an airplane is its landing gear. Early airplanes had two main wheels under the fuselage or wings and a smaller wheel under the tail. Since this was the original method of designing landing gear, it is called **conventional landing gear** (see Figure 2.3). Today most airplanes are designed with the main wheels farther aft on the fuselage or wing and with a nose wheel rather than a tail wheel. This is the *tricycle configuration*. Tricycle gear airplanes are easier to control on the ground, especially during landing.

The landing gear on an airplane is either fixed or retractable. Fixed gear is cheaper, easier to maintain, and foolproof (you don't have to remember to put it down before landing). Aerodynamically, a retractable gear is preferable because with the wheels and struts placed inside the wing or fuselage, there is less interference with the flow of air.

WHY AIRPLANES FLY
The Forces of Flight

An airplane in flight is at the center of a continuous tug-of-war between two pairs of opposing forces (see Figure 2.4). *Lift opposes weight* and *thrust opposes drag*.

Gravity constantly pulls the airplane toward earth. We measure the effects of gravity by the **weight** of the aircraft and its cargo.

Thrust is any force acting in the same direction as the airplane flight path (the motion of the airplane through the air). Typically the power plant system (the engine and propeller) provide this force.

Lift and **drag** are the forces produced by the motion of the airplane through the air. As a pilot, you must understand how these forces are generated in order to use them properly. Lift acts *perpendicular* (at a 90-degree angle) to both the flight path and the wing's *span* (the wing tip to wing tip direction) (see Figure 2.5). Drag is any force acting *parallel* to the flight path but in the opposite direction.

Whenever the airplane is flying at a constant airspeed along a steady **flight path** (a steady climb, a steady descent, or straight and level), it is in *static* flight conditions. In static flight the opposing forces on the airplane

Figure 2.3 Conventional and tricycle landing gear.

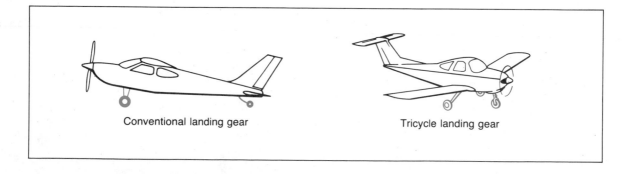

Conventional landing gear

Tricycle landing gear

are balanced; that is, lift equals weight and thrust equals drag. Whenever an airplane is turning, changing speed, or changing rate of climb or descent, the opposing forces are not balanced. However, under any changing conditions the airplane is always attempting to equalize the opposing forces and return to static flight.

The Creation of Lift

The actions of the physical forces that support an aircraft in flight are not visible. But rest assured that these forces keep an airplane aloft while it moves. Two basic laws of physics, Newton's Third Law of Motion and Bernoulli's Principle, help explain the phenomenon of flight. These principles are not difficult to understand when they are explained in practical, flight-related terms.

Newton's Third Law of Motion.   This law states that *for every action there is an equal and opposite reaction*. If you could observe the airflow in front of and behind an airplane in flight, you would see that the air behind the airplane is redirected downward (see Figure 2.6). The downward force caused by the wing is called **downwash**. The *action* of redirecting the air down causes the *reaction* of lifting the airplane. In other words, *an airplane stays up because it makes the air go down.*

Newton's Third Law of Motion describes the *effect* the wing has on the air it passes through: the wing redirects air downward. It does not, however, explain *how* the wing makes this happen. Later in this section Bernoulli's Principle will explain what the wing does to the air to cause it to be redirected downward.

Airfoils.   Any structure that moves through the air for the purpose of obtaining a useful reaction is called an **airfoil**. Although airfoils are found

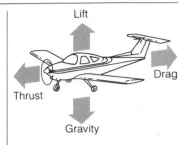

Figure 2.4 The forces on an airplane in flight.

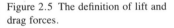

Figure 2.5 The definition of lift and drag forces.

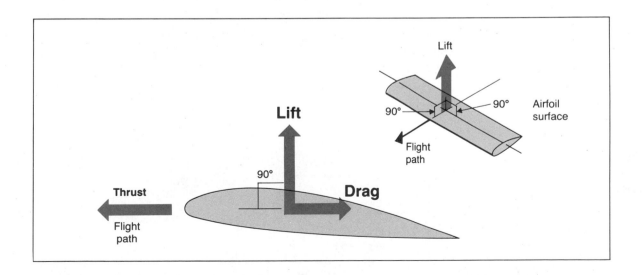

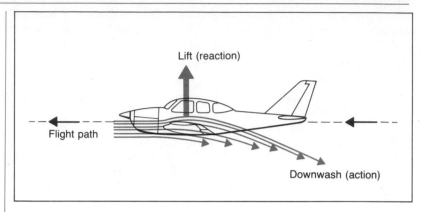

in a number of places on an airplane—the wing, tail surfaces, and propeller—the wing is the most important. The special shape of the wing is
the secret to its success. Figure 2.7 shows a cross-section of a typical airfoil
in motion through the air. The airfoil has a rounded *leading edge* and a
sharp *trailing edge*. The curved shape of the upper and lower surfaces is
called **camber**. The **chord line** (or chord) is a hypothetical straight line
that passes through the leading and trailing edges of the airfoil.

Relative wind and angle of attack.   The stream of air approaching the
airfoil is called **relative wind** since it is a moving mass of air and has a
direction relative to the airfoil. The direction of the relative wind is exactly
opposite that of the flight path of the airfoil. In fact, relative wind is the
result of the flight path. The angle that the relative wind makes with the
chord line is called the **angle of attack**. When describing the magnitude
of this angle, the term *low angle of attack* means a small angle between
the relative wind and the chord line. As the angle between the relative wind
and the chord line increases, the angle of attack gets *higher*.

Figure 2.7 A cross-section of an
airfoil in flight.

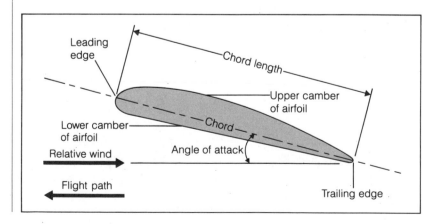

Although these effects hold for every airfoil on the airplane, the wing is the primary airfoil of interest to you as a pilot. The wing's relative wind is a result of the flight path of the entire airplane. Realizing this is an important step toward gaining a pilot's understanding of flight mechanics.

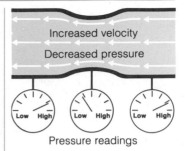

Figure 2.8 The venturi tube.

Bernoulli's Principle. The eighteenth-century Swiss physicist Daniel Bernoulli discovered that if air were forced through a tube with a constriction in it (a **venturi tube**), the pressure of the air was the same at both ends but *less* at the constriction. The reason for this, he theorized, was that the mass of air had to speed up in order to pass the constriction. The total energy of the air at any point in the tube must be constant, because of the conservation of energy (a law of physics that holds at all times). Bernoulli then deduced that at the constriction, more energy was used to accelerate the air molecules, leaving less energy to exert pressure on the walls of the tube. He determined that *any time the velocity of air is increased, its pressure is decreased.* He observed that the reverse is also true: *when the velocity of air is reduced, its pressure increases.* Figure 2.8 shows a venturi tube and these pressure-velocity relationships.

How does this principle apply to airfoils? The special shape of an airfoil causes the air passing over it to speed up while the air below the airfoil is slowed. The change that occurs along the upper surface is the most significant of the two. The higher-velocity air over the top of the airfoil results in a large low-pressure area above the wing. The decreased air velocity below the airfoil creates a smaller high-pressure area below the wing (Figure 2.9a).

The large low-pressure area (which could also be called a partial vacuum) pulls the wing up into it. The action of pulling up on the wing causes a reaction of pulling down on the passing airflow (Figure 2.9b). A similar activity is taking place below the wing, but on a much smaller scale. High pressure below the wing acts by pushing it up, causing the reaction of pushing the air down.

The net result is an upward force on the wing called the *resultant force.* The portion of this resultant force that acts perpendicular to the flight path (or relative wind) is called *lift.* The downward force transmitted to the passing airflow is *downwash.* The most important point to remember is that the upper surface of the wing produces most of the force we call lift.

The Creation of Drag
Induced drag. Drag, you recall, is any force acting parallel to the flight path but in the opposite direction. The resultant force created by an airfoil is basically in the correct direction for lift, but not exactly. Note that the resultant force arrow in Figure 2.9 is not perpendicular to the relative wind; the slant is in the same direction that the relative wind is moving. Figure 2.10 breaks this force down into two components and shows that while lift is created (perpendicular to the relative wind), some drag is also induced by the creation of lift. This component of the wing's resultant force is called **induced drag.**

Figure 2.9 **(a)** How Bernoulli's
Principle causes downwash.

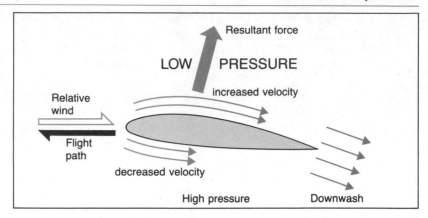

Figure 2.9 **(b)** The effect of
Bernoulli's Principle on an airfoil.

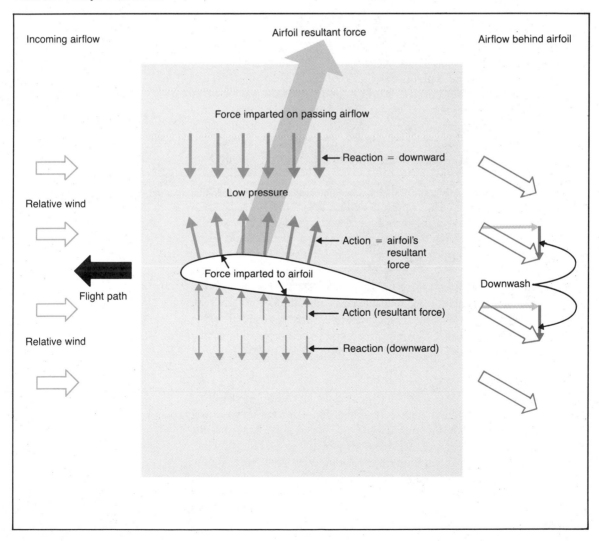

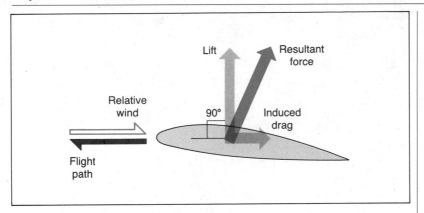

Figure 2.10 Lift and induced drag
are components of the wing's
resultant force.

Parasite drag.   Any solid object (an airplane, for instance) that moves
through the air must disturb and displace the air molecules along its path.
The air molecules resist this disturbance, and the resistance is manifested
as a drag force called **parasite drag**. The amount of parasite drag depends
on a number of interacting factors, such as the size of the object, its shape,
and the roughness of its surface.

The effective size of an object as it moves through the air is called its
frontal area (see Figure 2.11a). You can visualize frontal area as the shadow
an object would cast if a light source came from the same direction as the
relative wind. A given object's frontal area can vary depending on its
orientation with respect to the relative wind—just as the shape of its shadow
depends on how it is presented to the light. A thin board placed edge first
into the wind has a small frontal area compared to the same board placed
broadside into the wind.

In general, the larger the frontal area, the higher the drag force. However,
the shape of the object also has a powerful effect on drag. A flat plate
facing the wind broadside creates a very large drag force, but if that same
frontal area is enclosed in a teardrop shape, the drag is reduced enormously
(see Figure 2.11b). This aspect of parasite drag, which depends on both
frontal area and shape of the object, is called **form drag**. Most aircraft
have protrusions that add unwanted but necessary frontal area, such as
radio antennas, wing struts, or fixed landing gear. Aircraft designers often
enclose these items in a metal or plastic shroud called a **fairing**, which is
shaped and oriented to reduce drag as much as possible.

The slowing of air molecules due to **skin friction drag** is another component of parasite drag (see Figure 2.11c). Smooth surfaces are obviously
better than rough ones. The amount of skin friction drag is proportional to
the total amount of surface area of the object.

When two different shapes are joined together, such as a wing and a
fuselage, air may not flow smoothly near the intersection, creating **interference drag**. Designers often add a specially shaped piece of metal or
plastic, called a *fillet*, to blend the surfaces and reduce the interference drag
(see Figure 2.11d).

Total drag.   The total drag on an airplane in flight is the combination of its induced drag and parasite drag.

Factors That Influence Lift and Drag
The aerodynamic forces on a airplane are influenced by four variables:

1. Its size and shape.
2. The density of the air through which it is flying.
3. The angle of attack of its wing.
4. The speed at which it is moving through the air.

Figure 2.11 The various forms of parasite drag.

Size and shape.   Although the manufacturer determines the basic size and shape of an airplane, the pilot does have some ability to modify shape by

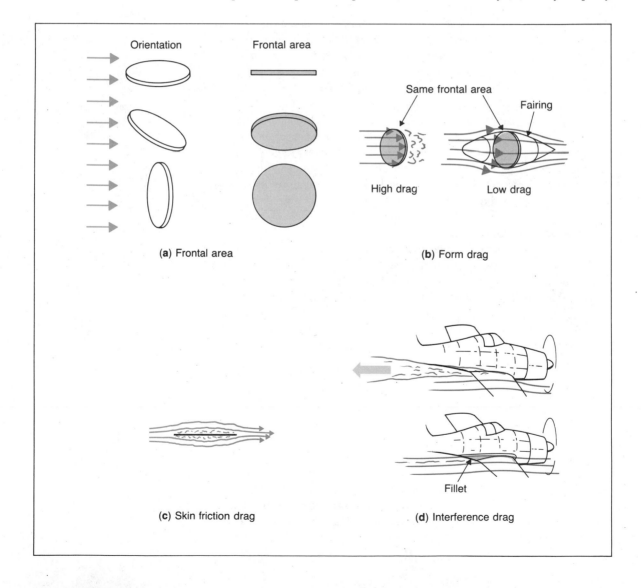

using the control surfaces. A later section of this chapter discusses these controls in detail, so for now we will assume that size and shape remain constant.

Air density.   An airplane creates forces by moving air molecules around, so naturally those forces are influenced by the density of the air. Density is the number of molecules in a given volume of air. Lift and drag increase with air density because more molecules are being affected (all other factors being constant). The relationship between air density and the way an airplane performs is the subject of *performance*, covered in Chapter 6. The discussions in this chapter assume that air density is not changing.

Lift and drag versus angle of attack: stalls.   The most direct way a pilot can control lift is through the angle of attack of the wing. Increasing the angle of attack increases lift and induced drag (all other things being equal).

There is, however, an upper limit to what the wing can do. Figure 2.12 shows a cross-section of a wing flying at increasing angles of attack. At low angles of attack, the airflow follows the airfoil surface closely and is efficiently redirected downward. As the angle of attack increases, the airflow begins to *separate* from the upper surface of the airfoil at its trailing edge, and this separation produces an area of disturbed air. The separated airflow hinders the creation of downwash and increases drag significantly. This separation continues to increase as the angle of attack increases. When enough lift-producing downwash is replaced by swirling eddies of disturbed air, lift begins to decrease. At this point the airfoil is stalled. By definition, a **stall** occurs when lift decreases as a result of an increase in angle of attack. The angle of attack at which the stall begins is called the **critical angle of attack.**

It must be emphasized that only angle of attack is responsible for the stall process; neither speed nor the attitude of the aircraft controls it. An airfoil stalls any time the critical angle of attack is exceeded. *A stall can occur at any airspeed and in any aircraft attitude.* The only way to recover from a stall is to *reduce the angle of attack*.

The wing of most airplanes is designed so that stalling occurs *progressively* rather than all at once. The designer's goal is to make the inboard

Figure 2.12 The airflow over an airfoil at various angles of attack. (Note: Angles shown are for illustrative purposes only.)

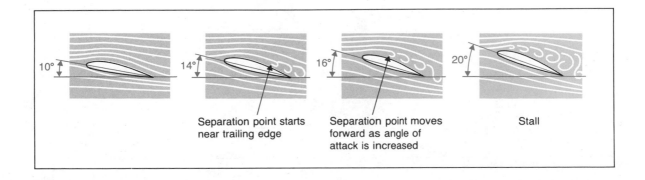

10°   14°   Separation point starts near trailing edge   16°   Separation point moves forward as angle of attack is increased   20°   Stall

part of the wing stall first and the tips last (see Figure 2.13). There are two benefits to this scheme. First, the disturbed air from the stalled inboard wing strikes the fuselage and tail, creating a **buffet** (noise and/or shaking) on the airframe. Because it comes early in the stall process, this important warning signal should not be ignored. Second, the control surfaces on the outboard part of the wing (the ailerons) remain effective even while most of the wing is stalled, so the pilot has control of the airplane as long as aerodynamically possible. One way to achieve progressive stall characteristics is to place different airfoil shapes along the span of the wing. Another is to use wing *twist,* which means building the wing with its tips at an angle of attack lower than the inboard part. Most airplanes have a combination of the two.

Lift and drag versus speed.   The most powerful factor in the creation of lift and drag is the speed at which the airplane moves through the air. If all other variables are held constant, lift and drag vary with the *square of the speed*. This means that if speed is doubled, the lift and drag forces increase four times. Conversely, if speed is halved, the aerodynamic forces become one-fourth their initial value.

In the real world of flying, of course, other variables are not constant. In fact, in steady flight (constant speed, no change in altitude), *lift* is held constant (equal to weight). So let us examine the effect of speed on an airplane in level flight.

Figure 2.13 A partially stalled wing. Wing twist and different airfoils along the span cause the wing to stall progressively.

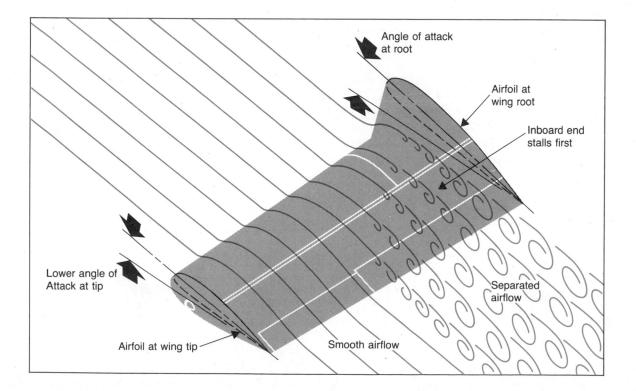

Lift and drag in level flight. As an airplane changes speed, it must simultaneously change its angle of attack in order to keep lift constant. For instance, an increase in speed must be counteracted by a decrease in angle of attack. But changes in speed and angle of attack also affect the various types of drag.

We know that induced drag changes with angle of attack. Therefore, in level flight, as speed increases, induced drag decreases (see Figure 2.14).

Since parasite drag is a function of the number of air molecules being disturbed, it follows that parasite drag increases with speed, whether the airplane is in level flight or not.

Total drag in level flight is more complicated because induced drag and parasite drag behave differently. Figure 2.14 shows how each drag force varies with speed. Thrust from the engine is the force that opposes drag. That is why the curve labeled "total drag" in Figure 2.14 has the alternate label of "thrust required for level flight."

Normally, airplanes in flight move at speeds high enough to make parasite drag the predominant drag force. Any increase in speed requires more thrust, and you slow down by reducing thrust. Notice that the total drag curve has a characteristic U shape. This indicates that slowing down reduces drag only to a certain point. The bottom of the U is the point of minimum drag. If you slow down beyond the point of minimum drag, induced drag predominates. Total drag now *increases* as speed *decreases*. This means that below a certain speed power must be increased to fly slower! The speed at which minimum drag occurs is typically a few mph faster than normal takeoff speed.

Learning to control an airplane at slow flight speeds is an essential part of flight training. Understanding the drag characteristics of an airplane will simplify the learning process.

Flying the Wing: A Pilot's-Eye View of Flight

To successfully apply the forces of flight in your flying, you must have a frame of reference different from that used to drive an automobile or ride

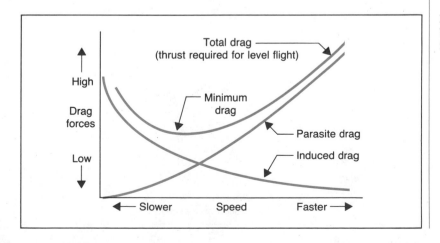

Figure 2.14 The relationship between airspeed and drag in level flight.

a bicycle. As a pilot, you must constantly imagine that you are "flying the wing." That is, you should imagine that the plane is nothing but a wing, except for a place to carry the pilot.

In time, your body's senses will provide subtle clues about the way the airplane is flying. This use of the senses is called "flying by the seat of your pants" because the location of the primary sensory input about the plane's motion and attitude is there. The sensory clues and your responses are similar to the sense of balance you develop to ride a bicycle or your knowing how fast you can drive around a sharp corner and still be in control. Your sensory organs may be fooled on occasion by the motion of the airplane, but good training can assure that your brain never is.

CONTROLLING THE AIRPLANE IN FLIGHT
Using the Flight Controls

The axes of rotation.   The flight controls are used by the pilot to position the wing and to move the airplane along the desired flight path. The motion of any object can be described by its movement about the three *axes of rotation*. The point at which the axes meet is called the **center of gravity (CG)** (see Figure 2.15).

The lateral axis and pitch.   The **lateral axis** of rotation can be imagined as a line running from wing tip to wing tip through the center of gravity. Movement about this axis is called **pitch** and is controlled by the elevator or stabilator on the tail (see Figure 2.1). When you pull back on the control wheel or stick, the trailing edge of the elevator moves up. This deflects air upward, forcing the tail down and the nose up. Pushing the controls forward lowers the elevator and consequently the nose. ("Deflecting the air" is a descriptive term, not a literal one. Control surfaces such as the elevator change the shape of the airfoil they are part of. The deflected air is actually the change in the downwash due to the control movement.) (See Figure 2.16). The terms "raising the nose" and "lowering the nose" are conventions adopted from cockpit references.

Figure 2.15 An airplane's axes of rotation, the motions around each axis, and the controlling mechanisms.

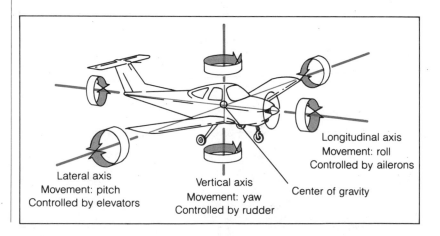

Longitudinal axis
Movement: roll
Controlled by ailerons

Lateral axis
Movement: pitch
Controlled by elevators

Vertical axis
Movement: yaw
Controlled by rudder

Center of gravity

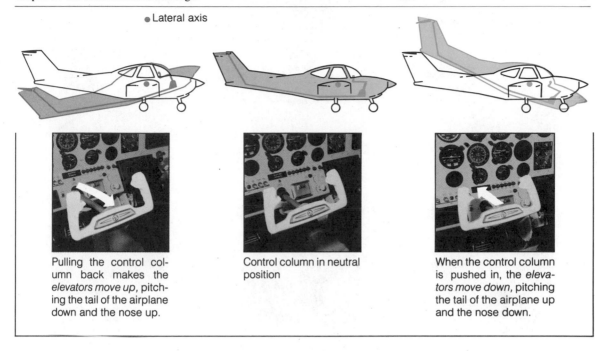

● Lateral axis

Pulling the control col-
umn back makes the
elevators move up, pitching the tail of the airplane
down and the nose up.

Control column in neutral
position

When the control column
is pushed in, the *eleva-
tors move down*, pitching
the tail of the airplane up
and the nose down.

The vertical axis and yaw.   The **vertical axis** is an imaginary line running
through the ceiling and floor of the fuselage, through the center of gravity
(see Figure 2.15). Rotation about the vertical axis is called **yaw** and is
controlled by the rudder on the tail. Figure 2.17 shows that pressing on the
right rudder pedal deflects the trailing edge of the rudder to the right. This
redirects the airflow, causing the tail to move to the left and the nose to the
right. Pressing the left rudder pedal produces the opposite result.

The longitudinal axis and roll.   The **longitudinal axis** is an imaginary
line running from the nose to the tail through the center of gravity (see
Figure 2.15). Rotation around this axis is called **roll** and is controlled by
the ailerons on the wings (see Figure 2.18). When the control wheel is
turned (or the stick is moved from side to side), the ailerons move simultaneously but in opposite directions. To roll right, for example, the control
wheel is turned to the right, which causes the right aileron to move up and
the left aileron down. The aileron that moves down increases lift on that
wing, causing it to rise. The aileron that moves up reduces lift on that wing,
causing it to descend.

There is a simple way to check that the ailerons are moving correctly.
Grasp the control wheel, or stick, with your thumb pointing up. When the
control is moved left or right, your thumb will point to the up aileron. The
other aileron will be down, of course. Study Figure 2.18 until it is obvious
that this simple check always works.

The airplane will continue to roll as long as the ailerons are deflected.
The more they are deflected, the faster the rate of roll. When the wings

Figure 2.16 Operation and effect of
the elevators.

● Vertical axis

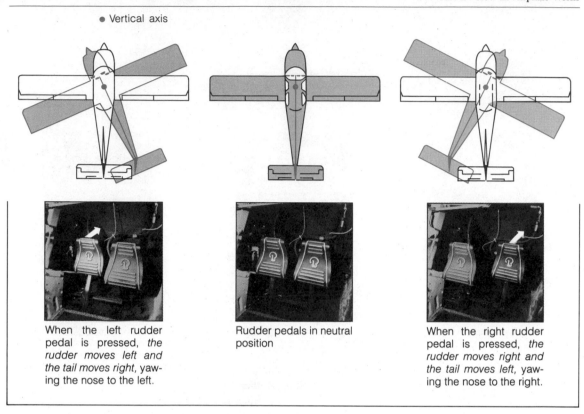

When the left rudder pedal is pressed, *the rudder moves left and the tail moves right,* yawing the nose to the left.

Rudder pedals in neutral position

When the right rudder pedal is pressed, *the rudder moves right and the tail moves left,* yawing the nose to the right.

Figure 2.17 Operation and effect of the rudder.

reach the angle with the horizon that the pilot wants for the particular maneuver he or she is executing, the aileron control must be neutralized to stop the rolling motion. Rolling the airplane is called **banking,** and the angle with the horizon is called the **bank angle**. To roll out of an existing bank, the control must be turned opposite the direction of bank. For example, to roll level from a right bank, turn the control wheel to the left. The ailerons are then neutralized when the wings return to level.

Coordinated Flight

The ailerons operate by changing the amount of lift on the outboard portion of the wings. Of course, lift alone cannot change because induced drag is part of the same force. (Recall that lift and induced drag are two components of the total resultant force created by the wing.) The aileron that increases lift also increases drag on that wing tip. At the same time lift and drag are reduced on the other wing tip. Figure 2.19 shows an airplane beginning to bank to the left. The left aileron is up, which reduces the lift and drag on the left wing tip. The right aileron is down, creating more lift and drag on that wing tip. The changes in lift cause the airplane to bank left as desired; however, the changes in drag at the wing tips create a yaw to the right. This unwanted reaction is called **adverse yaw** because it always opposes the action of the ailerons. You must add rudder input, in the same direction

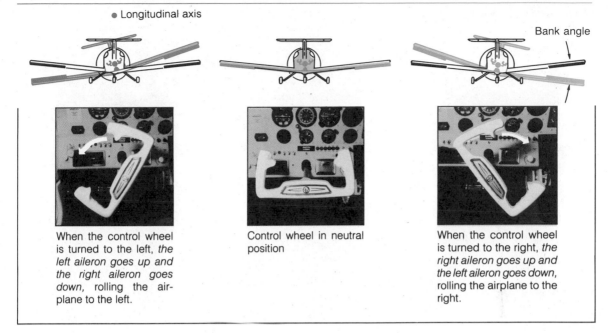

When the control wheel is turned to the left, *the left aileron goes up and the right aileron goes down*, rolling the airplane to the left.

Control wheel in neutral position

When the control wheel is turned to the right, *the right aileron goes up and the left aileron goes down*, rolling the airplane to the right.

as the turn, to counteract adverse yaw. Entering a right bank, for instance, you will use right aileron and right rudder until the desired bank is achieved. Then both controls are neutralized. Rudder input is always required when the ailerons are deflected, both rolling into and out of turns. Rolling level from a right bank requires left aileron and left rudder until the wings are level. Proper use of the ailerons and rudder results in **coordinated flight**. When pilots refer to flight as "uncoordinated," they are not maligning the

Figure 2.18 Operation and effect of the ailerons.

Figure 2.19 The creation of adverse yaw.

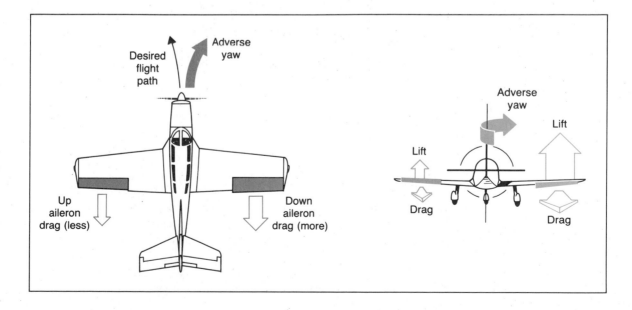

Figure 2.20 Forces acting on an airplane in a turn.

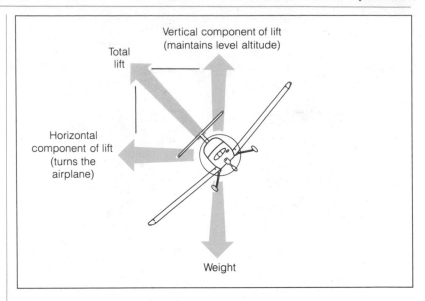

pilot's physical abilities but referring to improper use of the ailerons and rudder.

Turns and Load Factor

In order for an object in motion to change directions, it must create a force in the direction it wishes to go. An automobile turns because its tires create a sideways force to push it around the corner. An airplane creates this sideways force by banking its wings and *redirecting the lift force* (see Figure 2.20).

The total lift force in a turn can be broken down into two components: one in the direction of the turn, the other, opposing weight. If the airplane is to remain in *level* (constant altitude) flight (which is assumed throughout this discussion), the portion of lift opposing weight must remain constant. Therefore, whenever the wings are banked, the total lift created by the wings must increase because the lift vector is now doing two jobs—lifting and turning. Figure 2.21 shows pictorially the relationship between total lift and its two components for various bank angles. Notice that the vertical component remains constant. The horizontal component grows with increasing bank angles, as does total lift. Notice also that the forces on a turning airplane *do not balance,* and in this case the result is a flight path that is not in a straight line. Therefore, turning is one condition where an airplane is in *accelerated* flight.

The ratio of total lift produced to the weight of the airplane is called the **load factor**. When the wings are level (zero degrees of bank), the load factor is one because lift and weight are equal. Since total lift increases with bank angle, the load factor also increases. Figure 2.22a shows the relationship between load factor and bank angle. Load factor is expressed in **G units,** where one G is the normal force of gravity.

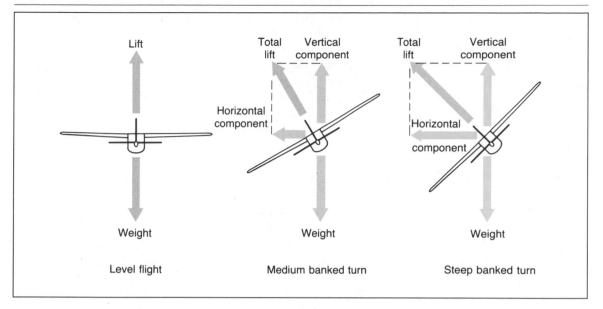

While turning, the airplane transmits forces to things inside (people and cargo) through contact with structure, seats, and belts. These forces cause the things inside to remain inside during the turn. Of course the things inside respond with an equal and opposite reaction, which occupants feel as a G force pushing them down into their seats. Figure 2.22b illustrates this reaction as a function of bank angle. In a 60-degree banked level turn, the occupants feel 2 Gs because the airplane is producing twice the lift required when the wings are level (load factor is 2).

Figure 2.21 Turn forces versus bank angle.

Figure 2.22 Load Factor **(a)** and Gs **(b)** as a function of bank angle in a level turn.

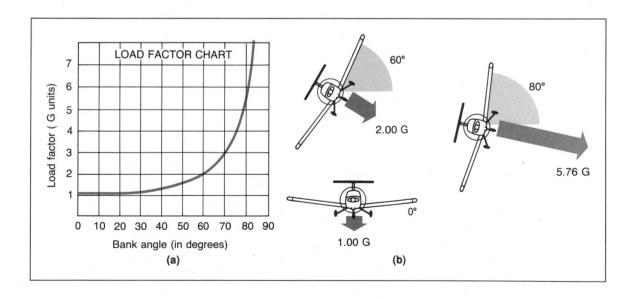

Turns and stall speed.   In a turn you will increase lift by pulling back on the control wheel or stick, which increases the wing's angle of attack. When the plane is flying at cruise airspeeds while doing moderately banked turns, the demand for extra lift is well within the capabilities of the wing. But performing steep turns, even at what appears to be sufficient airspeed, can suddenly demand more lift than the wing has to offer.

Recall that every wing has a critical angle of attack, above which the airfoil stalls. At cruise speeds, the wing is operating at a low angle of attack. The difference between the current operating angle of attack and the stall angle is effectively a "reserve angle of attack" to draw on for extra lift. The magnitude of extra lift available is thus a function of both speed and the reserve angle of attack.

As you fly slower, the operating angle of attack increases, which reduces the reserve. (The stall angle does not change.) If you fly slow enough, the operating angle of attack becomes identical with the stall angle, and there is no reserve. The speed at which you run out of reserve angle of attack in level flight is called the **stall speed**, for obvious reasons. Stall speed is also defined as the minimum speed required for level flight.

The extra lift required in a turn is generated by increasing the operating angle of attack. If the airplane is banked far enough, the entire reserve angle of attack will be used and the wing will stall, at whatever speed the plane is flying. At high speeds there is lots of reserve, allowing large bank angles. The slower you go, the smaller the bank angle you can afford before you use up the reserve angle of attack. Figure 2.23 shows how the stall speed varies with bank angle. *The steeper the bank, the higher the stall speed in level, turning flight.*

Maneuvering Speed

Every airframe has a maximum load it can handle without damage. These loads are the aerodynamic forces created by the wing and tail. At high airspeeds any sudden increase in angle of attack can impose loads capable

Figure 2.23 The relationship between stall speed and bank angle.

Stall speeds–mph IAS (indicated airspeed)				
Gross weight 1600 lbs. _____ Condition	Angle of bank			
	0°	20°	40°	60°
Flaps up	55	57	63	78
Flaps 20°	49	51	56	70
Flaps 40°	48	49	54	67
Power off — AFT CG				

of damaging the structure. Flying through turbulent air and moving controls abruptly are the two most common ways of inducing these damaging loads.

At high speeds, the wing is capable of creating loads that far exceed the airframe's capability. The maximum increase in load that the wing *can* produce is a function of airspeed and the wing's reserve angle of attack (the difference between the current operating angle of attack and the stall angle of attack). Therefore, the increase can be limited by reducing airspeed.

Knowing this, airframe designers can designate the speed that will limit the load increase the wing can produce to just within the airframe's structural limit. This speed, called the **maneuvering speed,** is the *maximum* speed to use during maneuvers or in turbulent air or any time you anticipate the need to use abrupt control inputs. Flying at slower speeds during these times provides even more protection, since it limits the wing's ability to increase the load. As long as you are flying at or below maneuvering speed, the wing will stall before the airframe can be damaged by aerodynamic loads.

As the airplane weight decreases (fewer people or less cargo or fuel), so does the angle of attack required to maintain level flight. This means that the reserve angle of attack is greater, and the maneuvering speed must be lowered to compensate (the airframe has not changed). In other words, *when an airplane is operated at light weights, the maneuvering speed decreases.*

The Pilot's Operating Handbook, and sometimes placards in the cockpit, contain this speed information. When only one speed is listed, it is for the airplane's maximum legal weight. If no other information is available, reduce the given airspeed 2 knots for each 100 pounds your weight is below the maximum legal weight.

Wing Flaps

Pilots want an airplane that cruises at very high speeds yet slows down to a fast walk for takeoffs and landings. An airplane equipped with wing flaps has the capability of altering the shape and sometimes the size of the wing to accommodate both speed requirements. Figure 2.24 shows the various kinds of flaps found on general aviation airplanes. Flaps effectively increase the critical (or stall) angle of attack of the airfoil. This reduces the stall speed of the wing, as shown in Figure 2.23. Flaps also add to both induced and parasite drag, because of the changed camber and profile of the airfoil. One type of flap, the Fowler flap, also increases the surface area of the wing when extended, adding to its effectiveness.

Flaps provide three benefits during landings. First, they allow the fuselage to assume a more nose-down attitude during low-speed flight, thereby improving visibility. Second, flaps allow a steeper glide path. Figure 2.25 shows how this steeper path helps shorten the landing distance required. This capability is especially useful when you must land over an obstacle. Finally, using flaps allows both lower approach speeds and lower touchdown speeds. These reduced speeds translate into shorter stopping distances as well as reduced tire and brake wear.

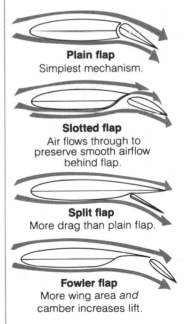

Plain flap
Simplest mechanism.

Slotted flap
Air flows through to preserve smooth airflow behind flap.

Split flap
More drag than plain flap.

Fowler flap
More wing area *and* camber increases lift.

Figure 2.24 Types of wing flaps found on general aviation airplanes.

Figure 2.25 The benefits of wing flaps for landings.

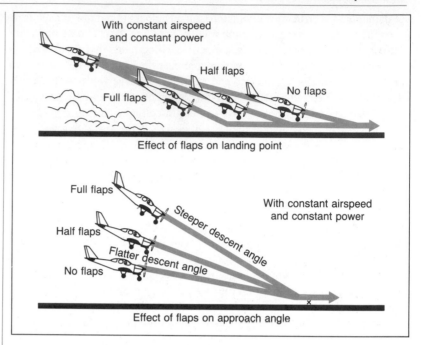

Figure 2.25 The benefits of wing flaps for landings.

There are times when partially extended flaps are used on takeoff. Some aircraft do this as a normal procedure; others do it only when maximum takeoff performance is desired. Partially extended flaps often provide a significant increase in low-speed lift with little drag penalty. The airplane can thus become airborne at a lower speed and in a correspondingly shorter distance. The Pilot's Operating Handbook outlines recommended procedures for each type of airplane.

Trim Tabs

On the trailing edge of most primary control surfaces there is a small adjustable cutout or an extended tab (see Figure 2.26). These minicontrols are called **trim tabs**. An example best describes their use: suppose you found it necessary to keep maintaining pressure on the elevator control to hold a desired pitch attitude. This constant exercise would soon become very tedious. *The purpose of a trim tab is to hold the primary control surface in the deflected position aerodynamically instead of through control pressure*. In this example you would adjust the elevator trim tab until no more pressure was necessary to maintain the required attitude (see Figure 2.27). In other words, trim tabs allow you to maintain the position of a primary control surface without keeping your hands on the control wheel or stick.

The trim tab deflection creates a small force on the trailing edge of the control surface, and this force holds the surface in the desired position. Notice in Figure 2.27 that the trim tab is deflected *down* to hold the elevator *up*; the downward angle of the trim tab creates a small upward force at the

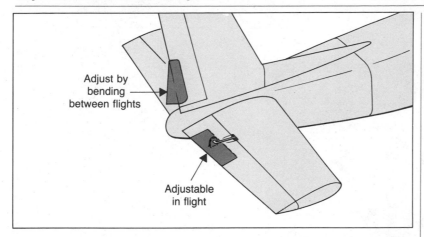

Figure 2.26 Location of trim tabs on a primary control surface.

trailing edge of the elevator. *Trim tabs always move opposite the direction of the primary control surface deflection.*

All airplanes have a pitch trim control (elevator control) in the cockpit, usually a small wheel (see Figure 2.28). Since any change in airspeed or power or the extension of flaps may affect pitch trim, it must be adjustable in flight (see Figure 2.28). In contrast, the trim tabs on the ailerons and rudder of many single-engine airplanes are metal tabs permanently attached to the primary control surfaces. Adjustments to these tabs can be made only by bending them between flights. Such adjustments should be made only by a trained pilot or mechanic.

It is important to develop proper habits in your use of trim. Use the primary controls to position the airplane in the desired attitude. Then use trim to relieve control pressures and allow the airplane to fly "hands off." Any time the airplane is changing speed, the control pressures will be constantly changing, so hold a constant attitude long enough for the speed to stabilize before adjusting the trim. It should take you only a few seconds

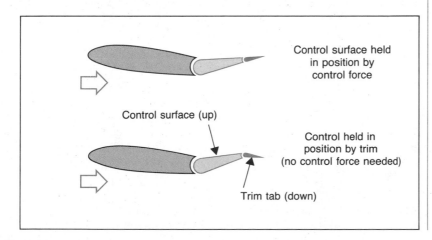

Figure 2.27 Effects of trim on a primary control surface.

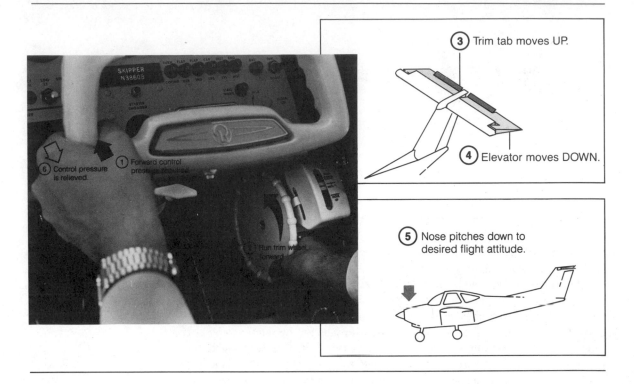

3 Trim tab moves UP.

4 Elevator moves DOWN.

5 Nose pitches down to desired flight attitude.

6 Control pressure is relieved.

1 Forward control pressure required.

2 Run trim wheel forward.

Figure 2.28 Operation and effect of elevator trim.

to properly trim the airplane. Good pilots do not constantly play with the trim. A well-trimmed airplane is a joy to fly because it needs very little help from you.

STABILITY: THE AIRPLANE'S BUILT-IN CHARACTERISTICS

The attitude and airspeed that an airplane will maintain "hands off" is called the *trimmed condition*. The tendency of the airplane to return to these conditions after a change in attitude or speed caused by turbulence or by movement of the controls is called **stability**.

Kinds of Stability

Positive stability means there is a tendency to *return* to the original trim condition. Most general aviation airplanes have positive stability about all three axes. *Neutral stability* is the tendency to *remain* in the condition produced by the disturbance; that is, there is no tendency to return to the original condition or diverge away from it. *Negative stability* is the tendency to constantly move away from the original condition (to go from bad to worse).

Static stability. When an aircraft is flying in trimmed condition and that condition is disturbed, our first concern is the aircraft's *initial* tendency

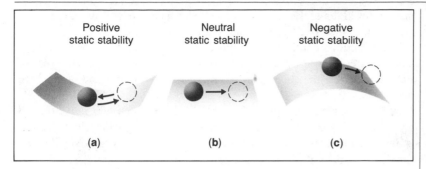

Figure 2.29 Types of static stability.

when the disturbance is removed. This tendency constitutes the airplane's **static stability** characteristics. Static stability can be positive, neutral, or negative. Figure 2.29 presents a simple illustration, using a marble. If you move the marble on the surface, then release it, it may act in one of three ways. If the initial response is back toward the original position, then static stability is positive (Figure 2.29a). If there is no immediate response either toward or away from the original position, static stability is neutral (Figure 2.29b). When the initial movement is away from the original position, stability is negative (Figure 2.29c).

Dynamic stability.   Even when the initial tendency (static stability) is positive, the object may still overshoot its starting position and have to come back again from the other direction. For example, an airplane trimmed for level flight finds itself nose-high due to a gust. If the nose pitches back down on its own, the initial reaction is correct, and the airplane has positive static stability. However, as the nose pitches down, it will probably overshoot level flight and enter a shallow dive. The recovery from the dive will probably also overshoot level flight. The trend of an object's motion with time describes its **dynamic stability** characteristics. Figure 2.30 illustrates

Figure 2.30 Types of dynamic stability. (**a**) Positive. (**b**) Neutral. (**c**) Negative.

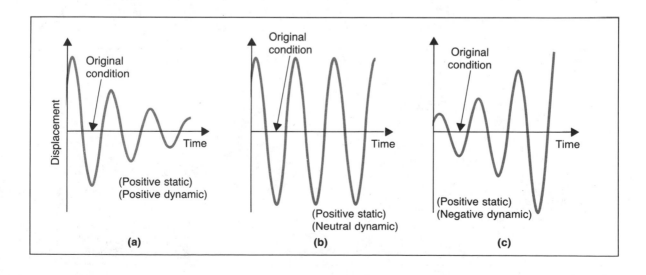

the various kinds of dynamic stability. If all successive motions get smaller and smaller, then positive dynamic stability exists (Figure 2.30a).

If the motions continue back and forth without growing or subsiding, this indicates neutral dynamic stability (Figure 2.30b). Negative dynamic stability is when the oscillations continue to grow larger and larger each time (Figure 2.30c).

In the example cited above, the nose of the airplane will move up and down according to one of the three graphs in Figure 2.30. If the airplane is dynamically stable, the nose will oscillate up and down by smaller and smaller amounts until it returns to level flight.

Longitudinal stability.   The tendency of an airplane to resist pitch displacement is called **longitudinal stability**. The airplane's longitudinal axis, you recall, lies along the fuselage, so longitudinal stability essentially describes the motion of the fuselage. Longitudinal stability is probably the most important characteristic to you as a pilot, since it affects angle of attack, airspeed, and altitude. All airplanes certified by the FAA must have positive static and dynamic longitudinal stability.

Longitudinal stability is strongly influenced by the location of the center of gravity of the airplane. *As the CG moves forward, the aircraft becomes more stable. Any airplane can become unstable if the CG is too far aft.* Chapter 5 covers the subject of weight and balance and discusses in detail the effects of CG on longitudinal stability.

Directional stability.   The tendency of an airplane to assume a straight flight path after a yaw displacement is called **directional stability**, or **yaw stability**. Feathers on an arrow and the rudder on an airplane both serve the same function: they provide added surface area behind the CG so that if the arrow or aircraft is yawed, the airflow pushes against the fuselage and tail, or feathers, and tends to straighten it out. The position of the CG affects yaw stability in the same way it affects longitudinal stability: forward CG makes it more positive; aft CG, more negative (see Figure 2.31).

Figure 2.31 Contribution of the vertical stabilizer on directional stability.

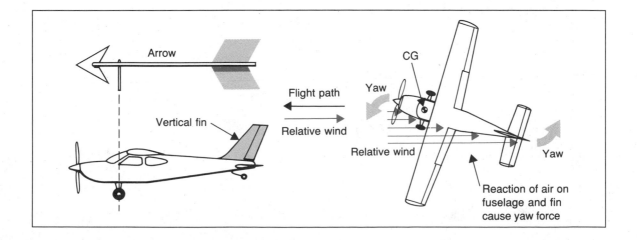

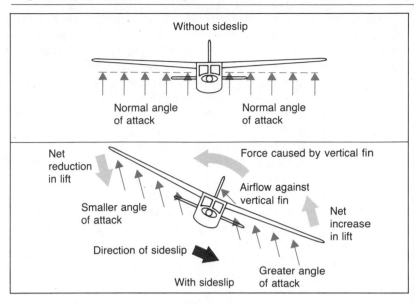

Lateral stability. The tendency of an airplane to roll its wings back to level when it is banking is called **lateral stability**. The movement of the lateral axis when the airplane rolls gives it this name. The dihedral of the wings (see Figure 2.2) is primarily responsible for the lateral stability characteristics of an airplane. When the pilot's control or an air gust creates a banked attitude, the airplane begins to slip sideways. The sideslip motion combined with the forward motion produces a change in the angle of attack on the wings. Dihedral causes the downward wing to receive an increase in angle of attack and the upward wing to receive a reduction in lift (see Figure 2.32). The vertical fin also helps roll the airplane level in a sideslip. The fin extends well above the center of gravity, and therefore any sideways forces on it cause a rotation about the longitudinal axis.

The next time you are at the airport, observe that, in general, low-wing airplanes have more dihedral than those with high wings. Figure 2.33 shows that in a sideslip the fuselage of the high-wing airplane magnifies the desired rolling forces and reduces the amount of dihedral required.

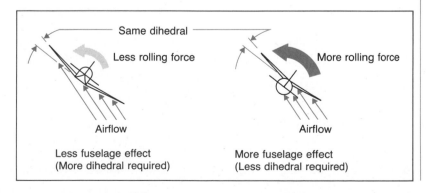

Figure 2.33 Effect of wing position on the amount of dihedral required for lateral stability.

Airplanes are designed to have only limited lateral stability, because they must have acceptable handling qualities while turning. An airplane with strong positive roll stability would be difficult to put into a banked attitude and would immediately roll level when the control pressures were relaxed. Most pilots prefer an airplane to roll easily and stay banked without much effort. Therefore, most airplanes exhibit positive roll stability only when banked less than 15 or 20 degrees. As bank angle increases, roll stability becomes more negative. An airplane in a steep spiraling turn will usually not recover by itself. Nevertheless, the airplane remains totally controllable. As long as a pilot maintains reference to the horizon, recovering from even the most unusual attitudes is no problem. However, when visibility is low, the position of the horizon may not be obvious. If you are not proficient in using the flight instruments in place of the real horizon, recovery is not assured. Always remember that only shallow bank angles can assure positive roll stability.

SPECIAL FLIGHT SITUATIONS
Ground Effect

When an airplane is operated very near the ground, there are special changes to the airflow around the wing. This effect, called **ground effect,** reduces induced drag and increases lift for any given angle of attack. The effect is of significant magnitude only when the wing is less than half the wing span from the ground—that is, when taking off and just before touchdown.

When taking off from a **soft field**—a runway surface that hinders the airplane's forward motion (mud, long grass, slush, or snow)—you may have to perform a *soft field takeoff* (a procedure you will learn during your flight training). To do this, you will attempt to get airborne at the slowest possible speed since acceleration to normal takeoff speed may be difficult or impossible. Ground effect will allow the airplane to start flying at a lower-than-normal airspeed. However, once off the ground, if the airplane is allowed to continue climbing at this low airspeed, it will fly out of ground effect and probably sink back to the soggy runway. The correct procedure is to level off immediately after leaving the ground. Allow the airspeed to build while flying only a few feet off the runway until normal climb speed is attained, then climb.

Ground effect also plays an important role during the landing phase of flight. As the airplane gets closer to the runway, it loses a little drag and picks up a little lift. This usually causes the plane to travel a little farther than you expected (pilots call this *floating*). Every extra bit of speed carried into the **flare** (the level-off just before touchdown) translates into a longer landing distance. For this reason, the secret to a successful short field landing is precise airspeed control.

Wake Turbulence

The disturbed air behind any aircraft producing lift contains a special flight hazard called **wake turbulence.** At the tip of a wing in flight, the high pressure below the wing has the opportunity to spill into the low-pressure

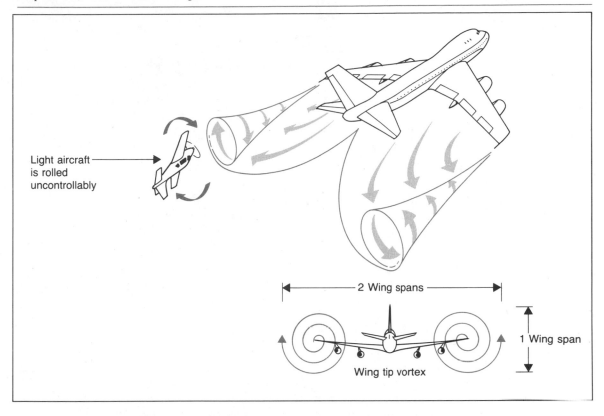

Light aircraft is rolled uncontrollably

2 Wing spans

1 Wing span

Wing tip vortex

area above it. This flow, combined with the forward motion of the aircraft, produces a horizontal, tornado-like swirl at each wing tip, called a **wing tip vortex** (see Figure 2.34). Large aircraft produce vortices powerful enough to roll light aircraft uncontrollably.

These vortices begin when the airplane's nose wheel leaves the ground and continue throughout the flight until the nose wheel touches down again after landing. In flight the vortices descend below the aircraft's flight path. They cover an area about a wing span in height and two wing spans wide. Wake turbulence is strongest behind aircraft that are heavy, slow, and have landing gear and flaps retracted. However, *the wake of any aircraft significantly larger than the one you are flying, regardless of its configuration, should always be avoided*.

The simplest way to avoid wake turbulence is to stay at or above the flight path of the aircraft creating it, or at least 1000 feet below. Figure 2.35 illustrates the recommended techniques. On takeoff, be sure to lift off from a point well behind the one from which the aircraft before you took off. Stay upwind of its flight path during climbout. When landing behind a large aircraft, stay above its glide path and touch down farther down the runway.

Vortices generated during takeoffs and landings sink to the ground and then move away from each other at a speed of 5 to 7 knots (see Figure

Figure 2.34 Wake turbulence.

Figure 2.35 The ways to avoid wake turbulence.

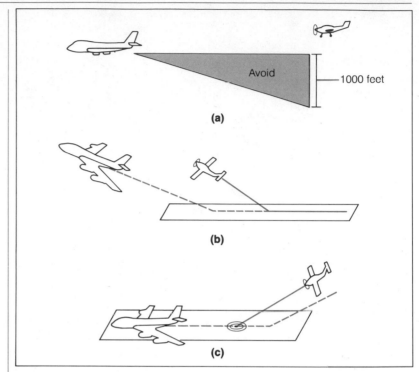

Figure 2.36 Motion of wing tip vortices near the ground.

2.36). However, *if the wind has a slight component blowing across the runway (a light crosswind), the upwind vortex remains stationary over the runway while the downward swirl departs quickly.* That stationary vortex is an invisible but deadly hazard, at least for a short period of time. If you are departing behind a large aircraft, wait at least 2 minutes before starting

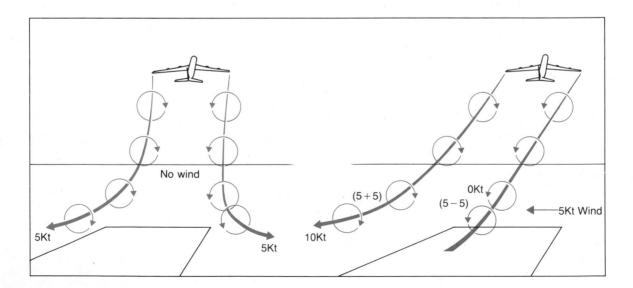

your takeoff roll (2 minutes is the minimum value recommended by the FAA). Crosswinds in excess of 10 knots will move both vortices away from the runway almost immediately, but be sure to stay upwind of the large aircraft's flight path.

Propeller Effects (Left-Turning Tendency)

P-factor.   A rotating propeller produces a uniform thrust force only when the plane of rotation is exactly perpendicular to the flight path. During flight with a nose-high attitude, the propeller disk meets the relative wind at an angle, as shown in Figure 2.37. (The propeller on all single-engine airplanes built in the United States rotates clockwise when viewed from the cockpit.) This attitude gives the *descending* blade (on the right side) a greater pitch angle, and the *ascending* blade a smaller pitch angle. The right side of the prop disk therefore produces more thrust than the left. The unbalanced thrust induces a yaw force to the left, called **P-factor**. You counteract P-factor with right rudder, to keep the airplane flying straight. P-factor is most pronounced at high-power settings and slow airspeeds, such as during takeoffs, climbs, and slow flight (any situation in which the angle of attack is high).

Torque.   The action of turning the propeller creates the reaction of **torque** on the airplane. The torque on an airplane built in the United States will

Figure 2.37 P-factor.

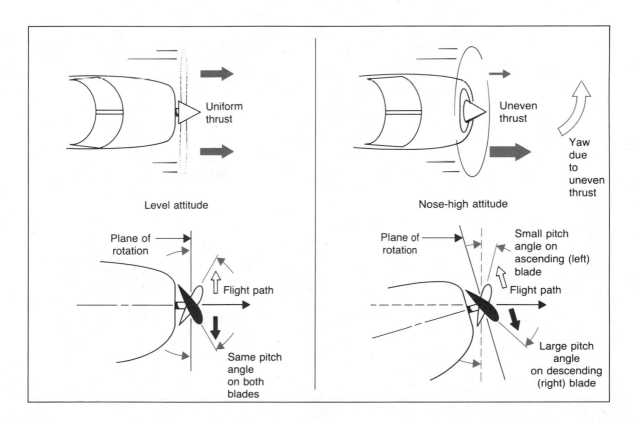

Figure 2.38 Torque.

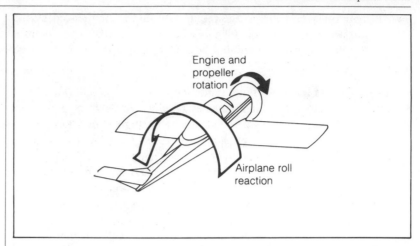

Engine and
propeller
rotation

Airplane roll
reaction

always induce a left-rolling force, as shown in Figure 2.38. At high-power settings the effects of torque add to P-factor in making the airplane tend to turn left.

Gyroscopic effects.   The spinning mass of a propeller takes on the characteristics of a gyroscope. Whenever a force attempts to tilt the plane of rotation of a gyroscope, the force causes a reaction 90 degrees ahead of, and in the direction of, rotation (see Figure 2.39). This reaction is called **precession**. What these effects mean for flying is that raising the tail (or lowering the nose) of an airplane applies an effective forward force at the top of the propeller disk. The precession reaction results in force being applied on the right side of the propeller, which, in turn, produces yawing to the left (as shown in Figure 2.39). This situation exists when a conventional gear airplane raises its tail as it rolls down the runway preparing to take off. A tricycle gear airplane, which moves the tail down for takeoff, would experience a yaw to the right. These yawing forces are counteracted with rudder, of course. Similarly, when the aircraft is yawed, precession causes a pitch reaction (left yaw—pitch up; right yaw—pitch down).

Slipstream effects.   The high-speed rotation of the propeller causes a corkscrew or spiraling motion to the airflow behind it. The spiral of air is called the **slipstream.** When the slipstream strikes the vertical fin, it causes both a left yawing tendency and a right rolling tendency (see Figure 2.40). The spiral is most compact, and therefore strongest, at high revolutions per minute (rpm) and low forward speeds (for instance, takeoffs or approaches to power-on stalls). At higher speeds the spiral becomes elongated and less effective.

Stalls
An important focus of all pilot training is stalls. First, and most important, pilots must recognize the *situations* that can cause a stall. Second, they

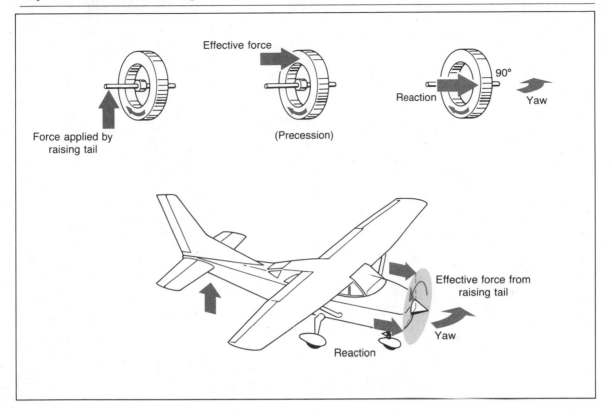

must recognize the *indications* of a stall. Finally, of course, they must become proficient in *recovery* procedures.

Figure 2.39 Gyroscopic effects of the propeller.

The FAA requires most certified airplanes to be equipped with a **stall warning device**. This device usually consists of a sensor on the wing's leading edge and either a warning light or audible horn (or both) inside the cockpit. As the angle of attack increases on a wing, the point where the airflow splits to go over and under the wing moves down on the leading edge. The sensor is placed to detect when the airflow is near, but not quite at, the stall point, thus providing a *warning* that the stall is near.

Most airplanes experience an aerodynamic buffet when the stall is near, an effect of the separated flow from the wing passing over the fuselage and tail. As the stall approaches, the controls will also lose effectiveness (become *mushy*, in pilot jargon). Flight training always includes situations that produce these indications of an *incipient* or imminent stall.

Stalls are practiced at altitude for obvious safety reasons. The procedures used to practice stalls are admittedly artificial because it is impossible to practice an unintentional maneuver. However, the goal of training is to teach *avoidance* of or immediate recognition of a stall. Stalls are practiced in the following flight conditions: takeoff and departure, approaches to landing, and turning or accelerated flight. They are practiced with the flaps (and landing gear, if applicable) both extended and retracted—in short,

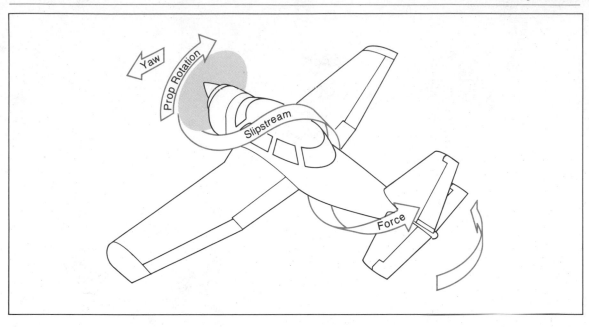

Figure 2.40 Propeller slipstream effects.

under every possible airplane configuration and flight condition. Each airplane reacts differently in a stall, so this procedure is repeated each time you fly a new type of airplane.

Stall recovery. The recovery from any stall situation has three main goals: (1) to maintain control of the airplane at all times; (2) to unstall the wing; and (3) to minimize the loss of altitude. Any time there are indications of a stall, positive action is required to effect recovery immediately. Unless the Pilot's Operating Handbook for your airplane states otherwise, the correct actions are:

1. Move the control wheel forward to break the stall (reduce the angle of attack).
2. Simultaneously add full engine power.
3. Level the wings.
4. Return to level flight as soon as possible, minimizing altitude loss.

Rudder control is vitally important during a stall. Any time a wing drops during a stall, immediate rudder input is required to keep the nose from yawing toward the low wing. If the airplane is stalled in a banked attitude, the high wing will usually stall first and drop, immediately becoming the low wing. By maintaining directional control, the wing will not drop farther before the stall is broken, and a *spin* will be averted. Continued practice of stalls will help you develop a more instinctive and prompt reaction in dealing with an *incipient spin*.

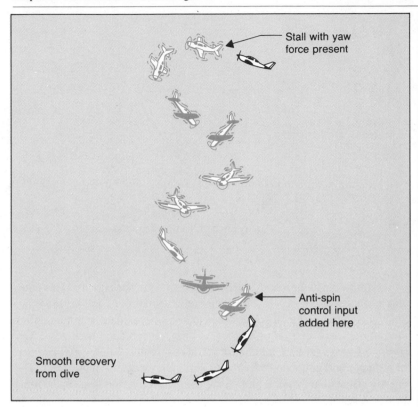

Figure 2.41 A spin.

Stall with yaw force present

Anti-spin control input added here

Smooth recovery from dive

Spins

If a yawing force is present when an airplane stalls, the craft will begin to descend with a steep corkscrew path, called a **spin** (see Figure 2.41). By themselves, spins are no more dangerous than any other aerobatic maneuver, provided the pilot is competent and the aircraft has been certified for them. **If the airplane's handbook or cockpit placards (signs) prohibit spins, you should assume that the airplane will become uncontrollable in a spin.** Most modern training airplanes must be blatantly mishandled to produce a spin. However, a spin is *always possible* whenever these two conditions exist together:

1. The wing is stalled.
2. A yawing force is present.

The yawing force can come from a number of sources:

1. Uncoordinated flight (improper use of the rudder).
2. Adverse yaw from the ailerons.
3. P-factor.
4. Torque.
5. Turbulence.

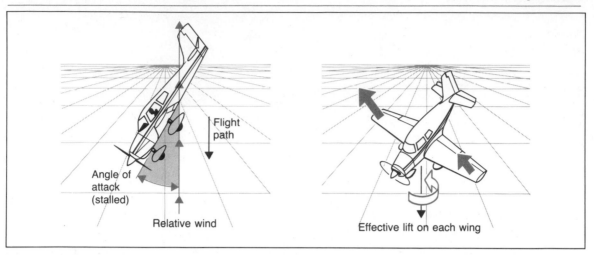

Figure 2.42 The flight path, angle of attack, and effective lift on the wings during a spin.

In a spin both wings are stalled, of course, but not equally. The outer wing produces *more effective* lift than the inner wing, as shown in Figure 2.42. This combination of forces tends to keep the airplane spinning. After one to three turns (depending on the airplane), the situation becomes a *fully developed spin*. This means the forces in the spin become stabilized and the airplane will continue to spin until anti-spin forces are introduced. The objective of stall and spin training is to recover before the spin can become fully developed.

Spin recovery.   Take the following actions to recover from a spin in a light single-engine airplane (unless the Pilot's Operating Handbook indicates otherwise):

1. Close the throttle completely and neutralize the ailerons.
2. Add full rudder input opposite the direction of the spin (for example, a left spin requires right rudder). A brisk input is the most effective.
3. Move the control wheel (or stick) forward to reduce angle of attack and break the stall. Again, a brisk input is most effective.
4. Level the wings, with the ailerons if necessary.
5. Neutralize the rudder as the spinning stops.
6. Smoothly recover from the resulting dive. This is where pilot skill is demanded most. Pulling up too quickly can result in another (*secondary*) stall. Pulling up too slowly can result in exceeding the maximum allowable airspeed.
7. Return to level flight.

Inadvertent spins occur most commonly during approach and landing, where little altitude is available for a correct recovery. Avoidance is the only acceptable solution in these situations. Plan ahead to use shallow bank angles and recommended airspeeds when maneuvering near the ground.

Be aware of the airplane's flight path, attitude, and airspeed at all times. Don't be afraid to add power and go around. You can use the experience gained from one poor approach to improve your next attempt.

KEY TERMS

ailerons	maneuvering speed
airfoil	P-factor
airframe	pitch
angle of attack	propeller
attitude	relative wind
bank	roll
center of gravity (CG)	rudder
critical angle of attack	slipstream
dihedral	spin
drag	stability
elevator	stall
flaps	torque
fuselage	trim tabs
ground effect	undercarriage
horizontal stabilizer	vertical axis
lateral axis	vertical stabilizer
lift	wing tip vortex
load factor	yaw
longitudinal axis	

PROFICIENCY CHECK

1. Describe the two *pairs* of forces that act on an airplane in flight.

2. How are angle of attack and relative wind connected? How does this relationship account for lift?

3. Explain the significance of Bernoulli's Principle and Newton's Third Law of Motion to airplane flight.

4. What is the *single* reason an airfoil (wing) stalls? What advance warning does your airplane give you before a stall? What is the stall-recovery technique?

5. What do we mean by "flying the wing"?

6. What are the airplane's primary flight controls? What are the three airplane axes about which each of them works? What are the names given to the movements about each axis?

7. If you were flying a modern light airplane in an out-of-trim condition and suddenly released the controls, what would happen?

8. What are wing tip vortices? When are they most dangerous? How might you avoid them in flight? On takeoff? On landing?

9. On takeoff you notice a strong pull to the left, correctable only by moderate pressure on the right rudder. Is this condition normal? What could explain this yawing tendency?

10. List three uses of an airplane's rudder.

Despite the great deal of attention and fanfare which has been attached to the design of turbojet . . . aircraft since World War II . . . one has only to look at the number and dollar value of light aircraft produced annually to realize that the propeller is alive and well in Wichita.

Leland M. Nicolai
Fundamentals of Aircraft Design

C H E C K P O I N T S

What is a reciprocating engine and how does it work? ✈ What are the parts of a power plant system and what do they do? ✈ What controls do pilots use to operate the power plant? ✈ What instruments do pilots use to monitor the power plant? ✈ How do propellers make an airplane move? ✈ How do pilots operate the power plant during the course of a typical flight?

THE POWER PLANT AND ITS SYSTEMS

We remember the Wright brothers' flight in 1903 not because it was the first time a winged craft had flown with a human being aboard but because it was the first time any such manned craft had flown with an engine—under its own power. Since that time, the growth of aviation has been, in a very real sense, the story of the growth of engine efficiency and reliability. Early aircraft engines were big and heavy and produced barely enough power to justify their weight on the airplane. Since they were industrial rather than aeronautical designs, they sometimes tore themselves from their mountings or imparted such strain on the airplane that the airframe literally shook itself to pieces. All pilots were mechanics because repairs were often made not in hangars but in cow pastures or other remote places after a forced landing. It was a colorful and romantic time, but only for those who survived it. Pilots and designers thought there had to be a better way. There was, and the modern reciprocating aircraft engine is the result.

Today's pilots need to understand power plant principles and systems in order to operate those systems safely and efficiently. Repairs, fortunately, are the province of **airframe and power plant (A&P) mechanics**, FAA-certified specialists who meet specific legal and professional standards. A good pilot is one who not only can fly safely but can converse with these specialists and relay accurate information about power plant system operations.

PRINCIPLES OF RECIPROCATING ENGINES

All engines operate because they provide a means for releasing the chemical energy stored in fuel. An *internal combustion* engine (the type of reciprocating engine that powers cars and airplanes) does this by combining a small quantity of fuel with a larger quantity of air (all materials need the oxygen in air in order to burn) and compressing them in a chamber. When a source for **ignition** is supplied—that is, when a way is provided for combustion to begin—the fuel and air mixture burns and expands rapidly. This expansion begins a series of mechanical actions that result in the rotation of a shaft, which is then harnessed to accomplish useful work. The goal of all internal combustion engines is to produce this useful rotary motion, or **torque**.

When this torque is harnessed, we can measure the work it is capable of doing in units of **horsepower**. The amount of horsepower an engine produces relative to the energy contained in the fuel is the measure of its efficiency.

The Anatomy of a Reciprocating Engine

Let us begin where engine power originates, with fuel and air. Like your automobile, your airplane carries a supply of fuel. Air is free, fortunately, and is drawn into the engine compartment from the atmosphere. The fuel and air are mixed to form a combustible mixture by either a *carburetor* or through *fuel injection*. (Both methods are described later in this chapter.)

The fuel and air mixture then flows through the *intake manifold* into the engine's **cylinders** (see Figure 3.1). Cylinders are juglike vessels where the energy in the fuel is released and translated into mechanical work. The combustible mixture enters the cylinder through the **intake valve** at the top, or *head*, of the cylinder.

Inside each cylinder is a **piston**, which is a rugged metal plunger. Precision **rings** fit in grooves in the pistons and form a tight seal against the cylinder walls. The chamber formed by the top of the piston and the cylinder head must be virtually airtight for efficient engine operation.

The four-stroke operating cycle.   The intake valve opens as the piston begins to move down (away from the cylinder head). This motion, called the *intake stroke*, creates a suction that draws the fuel/air mixture into the cylinder (see Figure 3.2). When the maximum amount of fuel and air that a cylinder can hold has been drawn in, the intake valve shuts. Now the piston moves up, compressing the gases in the *compression stroke*. Just before the piston reaches the end of its upward movement, the **ignition**

Figure 3.1 Basic components of a reciprocating engine.

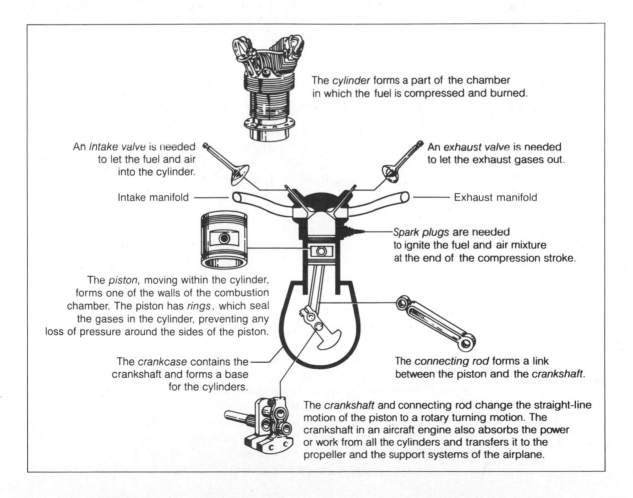

The *cylinder* forms a part of the chamber in which the fuel is compressed and burned.

An *Intake valve* is needed to let the fuel and air into the cylinder.

An *exhaust valve* is needed to let the exhaust gases out.

Intake manifold

Exhaust manifold

Spark plugs are needed to ignite the fuel and air mixture at the end of the compression stroke.

The *piston,* moving within the cylinder, forms one of the walls of the combustion chamber. The piston has *rings*, which seal the gases in the cylinder, preventing any loss of pressure around the sides of the piston.

The *crankcase* contains the crankshaft and forms a base for the cylinders.

The *connecting rod* forms a link between the piston and the *crankshaft*.

The *crankshaft* and connecting rod change the straight-line motion of the piston to a rotary turning motion. The crankshaft in an aircraft engine also absorbs the power or work from all the cylinders and transfers it to the propeller and the support systems of the airplane.

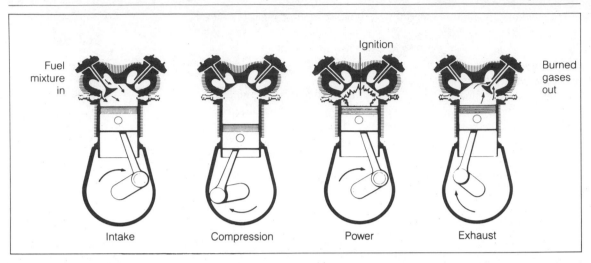

Figure 3.2 The four-stroke
operating cycle.

system generates a spark at the electrodes of the **spark plug**. The fuel/air
mixture burns instantaneously, expanding with tremendous pressure. This
release of energy forces the piston back down in the *power stroke*. Finally,
the **exhaust valve** opens in the cylinder head and the *exhaust stroke* of the
piston pushes the spent gases out through the *exhaust manifold*. The piston
is once again at the top of the cylinder, ready to start the cycle over again.
The four strokes of the piston (intake, compression, power, exhaust) give
the operating cycle its name: **four-stroke cycle.** The alternating up-and-
down movements of the pistons are the reason this type of engine is called
a **reciprocating engine.**

How does a piston moving up and down in a cylinder produce useful
torque? A **connecting rod** is attached to each piston with a *wrist pin*. This
rod connects the piston to the **crankshaft**, which translates the linear motion
of the piston into rotary motion. Figure 3.3a shows the unusual shape of the
crankshaft, which makes this transformation possible. Each connecting rod
is attached to a pin offset from the centerline of the crankshaft. The amount
of offset is called the **throw**. The **crankcase** is the protective case around
the crankshaft and also the structure on which the cylinders are mounted.
Notice that the crankshaft makes *two* revolutions for *one* complete power
cycle. If an engine has four or more cylinders, power is applied continuously to the crankshaft.

Engine arrangement.   Engines are described and classified by their cylinder arrangement. *Inline* engines have their cylinders aligned in a straight
line. Other engines have the cylinders arranged in the form of a V. When
the cylinders form a circle around the crankshaft, the engine has a *radial*
cylinder arrangement. Most aircraft engines use the *horizontally opposed*
cylinder arrangement. The major advantages of this design are its light
weight and low frontal area for the power produced. Figure 3.4 illustrates
some of these engine arrangements.

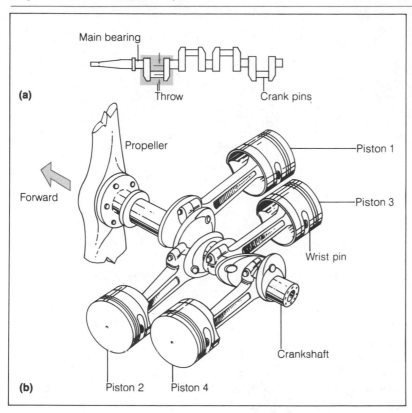

(a)

Main bearing

Throw Crank pins

Propeller

Forward

Piston 1

Piston 3

Wrist pin

Crankshaft

(b) Piston 2 Piston 4

Figure 3.3 The crankshaft converts the piston's linear motion to rotary motion. **(a)** Crankshaft. **(b)** Piston arrangement.

Converting Torque into Thrust

However the engine is arranged, it is useless unless the torque it generates can be transformed into thrust. Power from the engine is harnessed by attaching the device to be driven to the crankshaft. In an airplane, the crankshaft drives the propeller, and, in fact, the propeller is usually bolted directly to the crankshaft (see Figure 3.3).

A propeller is an airfoil that rotates in a plane roughly 90 degrees to the flight path. The *drag* from the propeller's airfoils is the force that is overcome by the engine's *torque*. The *lift* produced by the rotating airfoil is in the direction we have defined as *thrust* for the airplane.

The propeller is actually made up of a continually changing series of airfoils along the length of the blade. A cross-section of the propeller at any point is called a **blade element** (see Figure 3.5). Blade elements are set at continually *decreasing* angles of attack from hub to tip. The propeller is designed this way because the elements near the tip are traveling *faster* than those near the hub, and they will generate an amount of "lift" (actually thrust) at this lower angle of attack equivalent to the thrust produced by the thicker, highly cambered, and slower-moving elements near the center. This design, necessary if the propeller is to produce a uniform amount of thrust across its disk, gives the propeller blade its characteristic twisted

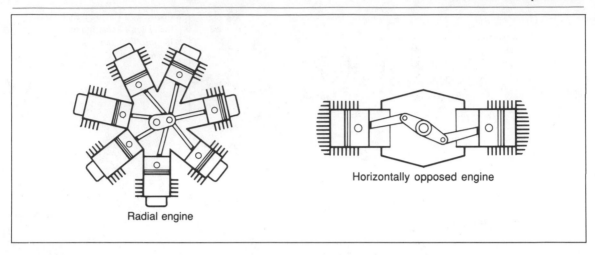

Radial engine

Horizontally opposed engine

Figure 3.4 Various engine
arrangements.

appearance. The term used to describe the propeller blade angle of attack
is its **pitch** (not to be confused with "pitch" meaning motion about the
lateral axis).

Types of Propellers

A propeller is tied to a "best" altitude and airspeed for producing thrust
unless it can change the angle of its blade elements for different flight
conditions. A propeller designed for high-altitude cruising speeds, for
example, would not be efficient for takeoffs and landings, and vice versa.
Pilots and designers both wanted to be able to "redesign" the propeller in
flight in much the same way they found they could redesign the airplane's
wing in flight by lowering the flaps. Invention of the *controllable pitch
propeller,* also called the **constant-speed propeller,** gave planes the desired
flexibility. On this type of prop, the blades are capable of rotating in the
hub to change their angle of attack. Figure 3.6 shows both fixed-pitch and
constant-speed propellers.

The position of the blades is controlled by a device called the **governor**.
(Most governors use engine oil to hydraulically move the blades; however,
there are various other designs.) The governor is, in turn, controlled by

Figure 3.5 Propeller blade elements
and the change in pitch angle of the
elements along length of the blade.

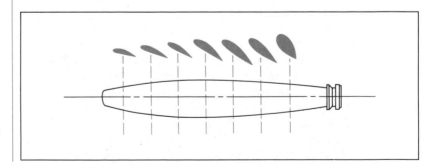

the **propeller control** in the cockpit. The purpose of the governor is to keep the prop spinning at a constant speed (hence the name). High rpm requires the blades to be set to low pitch (low drag). To slow the rpm, the governor commands a higher pitch, which increases the drag on the prop airfoils and slows engine speed. Figure 3.7 illustrates the relationship between blade pitch and rpm. Low-speed flight requires a setting at high rpm, low pitch. As the forward speed of the airplane increases, so does the optimum blade-pitch angle. Therefore, a setting at a lower rpm (higher pitch) is best for cruising flight.

Nearly all training airplanes use **fixed-pitch propellers** because of their operating simplicity and low cost. You will undoubtedly encounter constant-speed propellers as you fly a wider variety of airplanes and add ratings to your license.

Power Plant Controls

The amount of power an engine produces is a function of two things: the pressure of the air/fuel mixture entering the cylinders—called **manifold pressure**—and the crankshaft's rotational speed (rpm). The faster an engine turns and the higher the manifold pressure, the greater the engine's power.

The pilot can control the fuel/air pressure available to the cylinders, and therefore change power, by using the **throttle control**. It controls a valve

(a)

(b)

Figure 3.6 **(a)** Fixed-pitch propeller. **(b)** Constant-speed (controllable pitch) propeller.

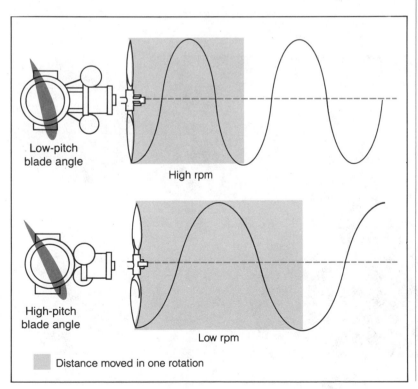

Figure 3.7 Propeller pitch setting versus rpm.

in the intake manifold, on both carburetor and fuel injection systems. On engines like those we are discussing, the maximum pressure of the fuel/air mixture is limited by atmospheric pressure. This type of engine is called *normally aspirated*. (Turbocharged engines mechanically boost the air pressure going into the engine, but those engines are not discussed in this text.)

The rpm of the engine is controlled by the drag of the propeller blades. A **tachometer** (Figure 3.8b) indicates engine rpm in the cockpit. On a fixed-pitch propeller airplane, the only way to change propeller drag is to change rpm. Therefore, rpm is a direct indication of engine power on fixed-pitch airplanes.

Power plant control for a fixed-pitch airplane is relatively simple. Power is controlled with the throttle, and the amount of power being generated is indicated on the tachometer.

As altitude increases, the drag on the prop *decreases* as a result of lower air density. Therefore it takes less power to maintain a given rpm at a higher altitude. In other words, *if engine power is held constant, rpm will increase with altitude* (for a fixed-pitch prop). (The discussion of performance in Chapter 6 illustrates this relationship.)

An airplane with a constant-speed prop is a bit more complex. Since you can control the engine rpm and manifold pressure independently, you must have instrumentation for both. Therefore, airplanes with constant-speed props have both a tachometer and a **manifold pressure (MP) gauge** (Figure 3.8c and Figure 3.9), which shows pressure in inches of mercury.

Figure 3.8 Engine power controls and instruments. (a) Power controls. (b) Tachometer. (c) Manifold pressure gauge.

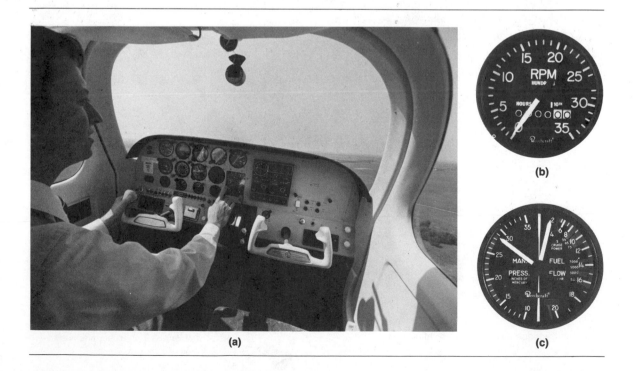

(a)   (c)

(b)

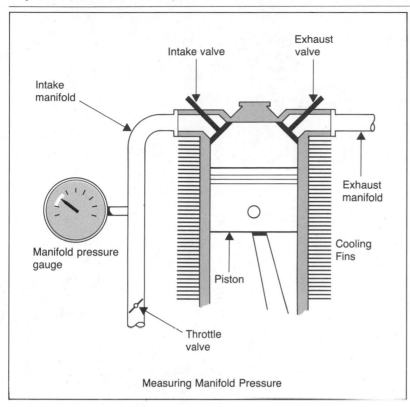

Intake valve

Exhaust valve

Intake manifold

Exhaust manifold

Manifold pressure gauge

Cooling Fins

Piston

Throttle valve

Measuring Manifold Pressure

Figure 3.9 A manifold pressure gauge installation.

Controlling engine power of a plane with a constant-speed prop involves using the throttle to set manifold pressure and the propeller control to set rpm. (Actually the propeller control sets the governor, which sets rpm, but the result is the same.) Figure 3.8 shows the controls and instrumentation necessary for a constant-speed propeller airplane.

Changing power on a constant-speed prop airplane requires you to use the prop and throttle controls in the proper order.

To increase power: 1. Increase rpm (the prop control), then
                               2. Increase MP (the throttle)

To decrease power: 1. Decrease MP (the throttle), then
                               2. Decrease rpm (the prop control)

These procedures are necessary to avoid having the engine operate at a low rpm and high manifold pressure. To do so could be compared to driving your car up a steep hill in fourth gear. Such improper use of the controls puts undesirable loads on the engine and invites engine problems.

Engine Cooling

The engine's power cycle is repeated with amazing speed. A four-cylinder engine running at 2400 rpm produces 80 "fuel fires" every *second*. All this heat must be dissipated by an effective cooling system. There are two basic

Figure 3.10 **(a)** Airflow through an air-cooled engine. **(b)** Cooling fins and baffles.

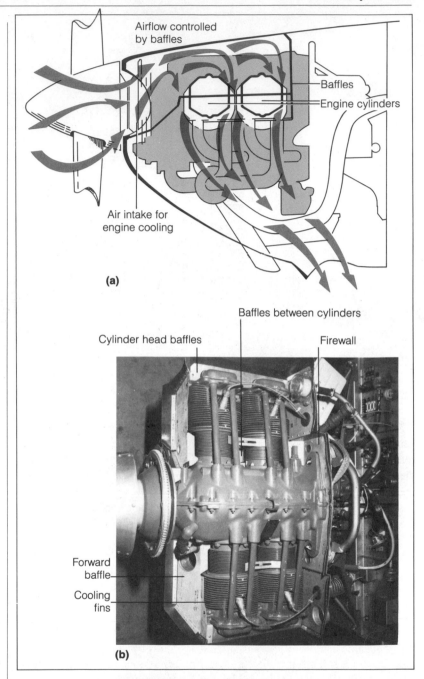

ways to transfer an engine's excess heat to the passing airflow: by means of a liquid or by direct air contact.

In a liquid cooling system, the cylinders have an elaborate system of passages called a *jacket* through which cooling fluid is circulated by a pump. After passing the cylinders, the fluid is hot. It is then routed through a *radiator*, where outside air reduces its temperature before the fluid is returned to the engine. This type of cooling allows the cylinders to be closely spaced

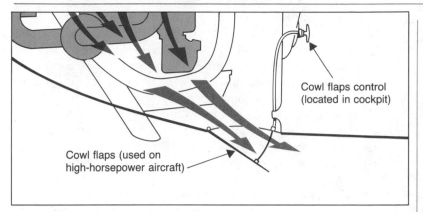

Figure 3.11 Cowl flaps allow the pilot to control the volume of cooling air.

Cowl flaps control (located in cockpit)

Cowl flaps (used on high-horsepower aircraft)

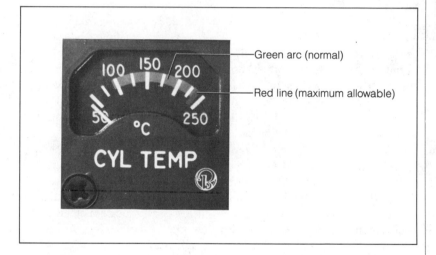

Figure 3.12 Cylinder head temperature gauge.

Green arc (normal)

Red line (maximum allowable)

and tightly cowled. Properly designed radiator air ducts add very little drag. (In fact, under the right conditions thrust can be produced.)

Most of the technology for current air-cooled aircraft engines was developed during World Wars I and II. Because liquid cooling systems were extremely vulnerable to damage, major emphasis was placed on the design of air-cooled engines, which have no fluid to lose and no pumps to break down.

An air-cooled engine is constructed with a large number of thin *cooling fins* around each cylinder (see Figure 3.10). These fins increase the surface area of the hot cylinder and allow more heat to be carried away with any given volume of air. Close-fitting **baffles**, inside the engine cowl, channel the airflow around the engine to provide uniform cooling.

High-horsepower engines often need more cooling air during low-speed, high-power flight—climbs, for example—or at high altitudes, where the air is very thin. For these situations, movable **cowl flaps** are designed into the cowling (see Figure 3.11). A **cylinder head temperature (CHT) gauge** (Figure 3.12) allows the pilot to monitor engine temperature and adjust the cowl flaps accordingly.

THE OIL SYSTEM

An engine's oil system serves two main purposes. It removes internal engine heat, complementing the external cooling systems described above. Oil also coats the moving parts of an engine, reducing friction enormously. Without adequate lubrication, an engine will fail within minutes. Figure 3.13 shows a typical reciprocating engine oil system. A mechanic or pilot adds oil to the system by putting it into a sump, or reservoir, attached to the lower side of the engine. The oil level is read directly from a **dipstick**, as it is in an automobile.

Various types of oil are available for your airplane. **Mineral oil** (also called *nondetergent* oil) is typically used only during the break-in period of a new engine. From that point on, **ashless dispersant (AD) oil** (detergent oil) is used. Oils are further categorized by their viscosity, or grade. The Society of Automotive Engineers (SAE) has established the standards for these grades. The higher the grade, the thicker the oil, so SAE 50 oil is thicker than SAE 20. Aviation oils are identified by *aviation grades*, which are exactly double the SAE value. For instance, aviation grade 100 is equivalent to SAE 50 weight oil. There are even multiviscosity oils for aircraft; these change their thickness in response to changes in temperature. Automotive oils should never be used in aircraft engines, since the two oils are formulated differently. Refer to your Pilot's Operating Handbook for the type and grade of oil to use. If single-viscosity oil is used, you will need to change it when the outside climate changes.

Aircraft engines use up oil at a regular rate, unlike automobiles, which generally use little oil. It is very important to check the oil level before every flight. Keep in mind that there are no service stations in the sky.

An oil pump draws the oil out of the **sump** through an intake that is screened to trap contaminants. The oil then passes through another, much finer screen, or a replaceable **oil filter** (similar to the one in your car) on its way to the rest of the engine. Some engines have an oil cooler, which is a small radiator exposed to the airflow. In most engines, the oil is cooled sufficiently in the sump, which is exposed to the airflow in the cowling.

Oil System Gauges

Oil pressure and temperature sensors exist at strategic locations in the oil system and register their findings on gauges in the cockpit. The **oil pressure gauge** (Figure 3.14b) indicates the pressure, in pounds per square inch (psi), of the oil being sent to lubricate the engine. Since different engines tend to hold different pressures, it is less important to read particular values from the gauge than it is to notice general needle position and trends. The needle should show movement within 30 seconds after a normal start and should stay within the green arc for the duration of the flight, with no radical changes of position. If the needle fails to move during this 30-second period, shut down the engine and report the problem to a power plant mechanic. The oil pressure gauge will help you remember this by

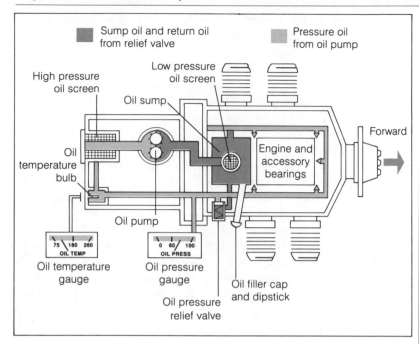

Figure 3.13 An engine oil system.

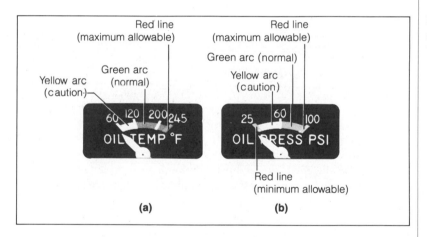

Figure 3.14 (a) Oil temperature gauge. (b) Oil pressure gauge.

showing two red lines on its face instead of only one. The lower line is for minimum allowable pressure, while the upper depicts the maximum allowable value.

The **oil temperature gauge** (Figure 3.14a) is located next to the oil pressure gauge in the cluster of engine instruments. Like the oil pressure gauge, it should be read for a steady value within the green arc.

You can expect higher oil and cylinder head temperatures during hot weather and during prolonged climbs. Monitor the gauges closely and take appropriate action (level off or reduce power) *before* temperature limits are reached. You must take note of any *unexpected* high temperatures and have the engine investigated by a mechanic.

AIRPLANE FUELS AND FUEL SYSTEMS

Just as automobile engines use unleaded, regular, or premium gasoline, aircraft engines must be provided with the appropriate **aviation fuel: aviation gasoline (avgas)** for aircraft with reciprocating engines and jet fuel for aircraft with jet engines.

Aviation gasoline is identified by its **octane number**. The octane rating of a fuel is a measure of how fast it burns. Higher-octane gasoline burns slower and in a more controlled manner. Figure 3.15 illustrates the difference between a normal, controlled combustion and a rapid, uncontrolled explosion, which is called **detonation**. The higher the octane of a fuel, the better it can resist detonation.

The various grades of aviation fuel are color coded for positive identification. Table 3.1 lists the colors for each grade of fuel. The dyes used to create these colors are designed to cancel each other if different grades of fuel are mixed. An unequal blend will have the color of the predominant grade but will be weaker than normal. An equal mixture of two different fuels will be clear.

Table 3.1 Color Identification for Aviation Fuel

Fuel octane	Color
80	Red
100 regular	Green
100 low lead	Blue
Jet fuel (kerosene)	Clear or straw colored

If the proper grade of fuel for your type of airplane is not available, you can use a *higher* grade of fuel but *never a lower grade*. Using a lower grade than the one specified can (and usually does) result in detonation, which in turn brings loss of power and catastrophic engine damage. Using jet fuel in a piston engine is another sure way to cause catastrophic detonation. *Never* put jet fuel in a piston engine aircraft.

Another form of abnormal combustion is **preignition**. This problem is caused by excessively hot exhaust valves, carbon particles, or spark plug electrodes heated to an incandescent, or glowing, state. These conditions can cause fuel to ignite before the ignition normally coming from the spark plugs and thus create abnormally high pressure in the cylinder. Preignition effects are so harmful that the engine will continue to operate normally for only a short period. If detonation occurs simultaneously with preignition, engine life is especially short.

Preignition can be difficult to detect because it may occur in only one or two cylinders. Detonation is usually easier to detect because the conditions that cause it usually exist in all cylinders.

The corrective actions for preignition include anything that will reduce engine temperature: enriching the fuel mixture (with the mixture control—discussed later), retarding the throttle (reducing power), opening cowl flaps (if available), and leveling off if climbing (thereby increasing the amount of cooling air).

Fueling Operations

When adding fuel to the airplane, you should always take steps to prevent fire due to sparks produced by static electricity and contamination of the fuel system.

Fire precautions.   Fuel moving through the fueling equipment creates static electricity in a way similar to shuffling across a thick carpet on a winter day in stocking feet. Since fuel is highly volatile, a spark in the vicinity of the fueling nozzle can be dangerous. To prevent this, be sure to clip a **grounding wire** on the airplane before starting any fueling operations—even before removing the cap from the tank with the intention to refuel. The fueling nozzle and the fuel truck should also be grounded before fuel is allowed to flow into the airplane tanks.

Contamination precautions.   Although strainers and filters appear at many points in fueling systems and equipment, some contamination by either sediment or water is always possible. Fuel obtained at remote locations or drawn from drums should always be strained through a chamois cloth before being put into the tanks. The *pilot* is responsible for seeing that the proper grade of fuel is used. Remember the appropriate fuel color for your airplane.

Finally, you must also be certain that all **fuel vents** are clear while the tank is being filled. Failure to do this can lead to inadequate fueling and fuel system malfunctions in flight, such as the failure of one tank to feed the engine.

It is good practice to keep the fuel tanks full when the airplane is not in use, especially overnight, in order to minimize the chances of getting water in the fuel. The empty space in a partially filled tank traps outside air, which always contains some moisture. Overnight, when the outside temperature drops, the water vapor in the air condenses into liquid on the walls of the tank. The effect is similar to the water drops that form on the outside of a cold glass of tea or beer in the summertime. A poorly sealed or improperly installed filler cap can also allow rainwater, or water from a wash job, to enter the fuel. Engines that are fed water instead of fuel do not run very well. To eliminate any water that may have collected, a small drain, called a **sump**, exists at the lowest point on each tank. There is also a sump in the **fuel strainer**, which is located at the lowest point in the entire fuel system. Because water is heavier than fuel, it will collect at these points and can be easily disposed of by manual draining. Your preflight check should always include draining the sumps into a transparent

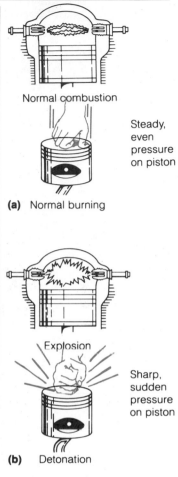

Normal combustion

Steady, even pressure on piston

(a)   Normal burning

Explosion

Sharp, sudden pressure on piston

(b)   Detonation

Figure 3.15 Normal combustion versus detonation. **(a)** Normal burning. **(b)** Detonation.

container. Any water present will stand out as a clear bubble at the bottom of the colored fuel. Continue to drain fuel samples until no water is present. If a large quantity of water is found, or if water is found on a regular basis in a particular airplane, the cause should be investigated by a mechanic.

Fuel Systems

The sole function of any fuel system is to provide the engine with an uninterrupted flow of clean fuel. It is your responsibility, as pilot-in-command, to assure that the airplane is supplied with the right type of fuel, in sufficient quantity, for your intended flight (see FAR 91.22).

Two general kinds of fuel systems are used in light airplanes: gravity systems and pump systems. Gravity systems are common in high-wing airplanes, where the tanks are mounted above the engine. A constant pressure flow is provided as long as the airplane maintains an upright attitude or positive load factor. Figure 3.16 shows a typical gravity fuel system.

For low-wing airplanes or airplanes with auxiliary tanks mounted in the fuselage, some kind of **fuel pump** is required to make the fuel go uphill to the engine. Figure 3.17 illustrates a pump-fed arrangement. Notice that

Figure 3.16 A gravity fuel system.

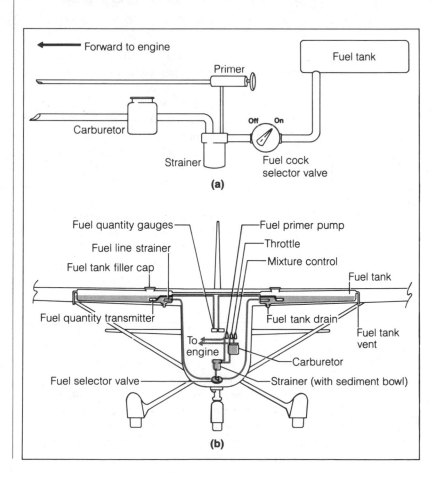

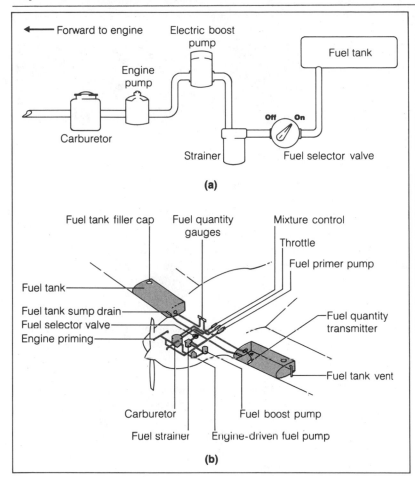

Figure 3.17 A pump-fed fuel system.

there are *two pumps* in this system. Since the engine will not run unless at least one pump is operating, it makes sense to have a backup. The system usually includes the primary fuel pump and at least one **boost pump**. The primary pump is usually driven by the engine, and the boost pump by the electrical system. The boost pump provides fuel pressure to help start the engine, and for emergency operations, when the primary pump fails.

Fuel gauges and controls.   All airplanes are required to have **fuel quantity gauges** indicating the fuel level in each tank (see Figure 3.18), but it is unwise to depend on these gauges to judge your fuel load. You should look into the tanks and see for yourself the quantity of fuel on board before every flight.

A **fuel pressure gauge** (Figure 3.19) allows the pilot to monitor operation of the fuel pumps. A sudden drop in fuel pressure indicates the need to turn on the boost pump. The Pilot's Operating Handbook gives the specific procedures to follow in this event.

Figure 3.18 Fuel gauges.

Left tank

Right tank

As the fuel proceeds toward the engine, it passes through a **fuel selector valve**. This valve allows the pilot to select fuel from one wing tank or the other or both or an auxiliary tank. Some pilots run one fuel tank dry before switching to another tank, but this practice is considered unwise because a pump may draw air from the dry tank into the fuel lines, causing vapor lock and subsequent engine malfunction. The fuel selector valve can also be used as an emergency shutoff valve to prevent fuel from feeding a fire in or near the engine compartment.

The engine primer.   The engine primer is a device used by the pilot to inject fuel directly into the cylinders before starting. The extra fuel is helpful during cold weather or if the engine has not been started recently.

The carburetor.   Once the fuel reaches the engine, it must be vaporized and mixed with the proper amount of air for combustion. This is the job of the carburetor. A **carburetor** is basically an air passage with a venturi in it (see Chapter 2). A fuel discharge nozzle is placed near the throat of the venturi. The pressure drop, which occurs as a result of Bernoulli's Principle, draws fuel into the passing airflow.

When you open or close the throttle, you are really adjusting the **butterfly valve**, or **throttle valve**, in the carburetor. This valve is an oval disk that moves to open or constrict the flow of the fuel and air mixture out of the carburetor into the engine (see Figure 3.20).

Most training aircraft use a **float-type carburetor** (see Figure 3.21). The essential parts of the carburetor are:

Figure 3.19 A fuel pressure gauge.

1. *Float mechanism*. Fuel entering the carburetor passes through a valve into a float chamber. When the fuel level in the chamber is high enough, the float closes the valve. This feeds fuel to the venturi at a constant pressure, and also keeps fuel from leaking out when the engine is not in use.

2. *Fuel strainer*. This filters small particles that might clog the flow of fuel in the narrow carburetor channels.

3. *Main metering system*. The **main metering system** controls the amount of fuel used in the higher-power settings, such as those required for takeoff and cruising flight.

4. *Idling system*. When the engine idles, the airflow through the venturi is too low to draw a sufficient amount of fuel to keep the engine running.

Figure 3.20 Butterfly valve.

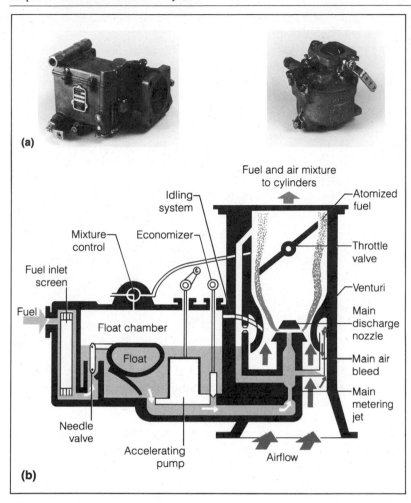

Figure 3.21 **(a)** Two examples of a float-type carburetor. **(b)** Schematic of a float-type carburetor.

The **idling system** automatically provides more fuel than would normally be commanded with the throttle nearly closed.

5. *Economizer system.* The **economizer system** provides a leaner mixture for cruising speeds and a richer mixture for full-throttle operations.

6. *Accelerating system.* The accelerating system compensates for sudden throttle movements. Since fuel may lag momentarily behind changes in throttle position, this system automatically enriches the mixture to prevent engine missing due to lack of fuel.

7. *Mixture control system.* At reduced power settings and high-altitude flight, the carburetor provides more fuel than the engine needs. The **mixture control system** allows you to manually adjust the fuel flow to match the engine's requirements.

Carburetor ice.   Whenever a liquid is vaporized into a gas, as fuel is in a carburetor, it draws heat out of its surroundings. You have experienced

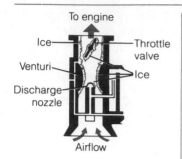

Figure 3.22 Carburetor ice.

this phenomenon if you ever spilled some fuel on your hand. As the liquid evaporated, your hand got quite cold.

If moist air enters the carburetor, the temperature drop causes the moisture to condense into liquid form. If the temperature drops below the freezing point (32 degrees Fahrenheit), the liquid will freeze as ice on the walls and throttle valve of the carburetor. This **carburetor ice** tends to choke off the flow of air as shown in Figure 3.22, reducing power output. Uncorrected, it will eventually cause total loss of power.

Under what conditions can you expect carburetor ice? The answer may surprise you. Any time the outside air temperature is between 20 and 80 degrees Fahrenheit and there is high humidity, carburetor ice is possible. In fact, the warm, moist days of summer offer the greatest danger. Also, carburetor ice is most likely to accumulate at reduced power settings because the position of the throttle valve already nearly blocks the carburetor throat.

How can you detect carburetor ice? With a fixed-pitch propeller, your first indication of carburetor ice will be a gradual loss of engine rpm on the tachometer. With a constant-speed propeller, the engine manifold pressure will start to decrease. Your airspeed indicator is another effective tool in detecting carburetor ice. Since carburetor ice reduces engine power, your airspeed will decrease, as long as you hold a constant altitude. This signal will warn an alert pilot before the engine instruments do.

Removing carburetor ice is the job of the **carburetor heat system** (see Figure 3.23). Pulling the carburetor heat control out (toward the pilot) directs heated air into the carburetor, melting any ice that has formed. If ice is present, the engine will run rough as the ice melts and the water goes through the engine. The warming of the fuel and air mixture reduces its density, which has two effects: *the mixture is made richer*, since there are fewer air molecules, and *engine power will be less than normal*, even when the ice is gone.

Some airplane manufacturers recommend the use of carburetor heat during the landing approach. If this is the case in a plane you are flying, do not forget to turn off carburetor heat if full engine power is needed for an aborted landing or a touch-and-go landing. Notice in Figure 3.23 that the heat source for carburetor heat is the exhaust manifold. In order for it to be effective, the engine must be producing power. Turn on carburetor heat *before* reducing the throttle. Obviously, you need to correct carburetor ice as early as possible. If ice is allowed to reduce the power of the engine significantly, there may not be enough heat available to remove it.

Outside air entering the exhaust shroud does not pass through an air filter (unheated air normally *is* filtered, as shown in Figure 3.23). Unfiltered air can draw abrasive contaminants into the engine. Therefore, the use of carburetor heat on the ground, especially in dusty conditions, should be kept to a minimum.

Carburetors have the advantages of simplicity and low cost; however, they have some operational drawbacks. Carburetor ice is obviously one. Another is that the distribution of the fuel/air mixture can vary significantly between cylinders. The engine components must be built strong enough to

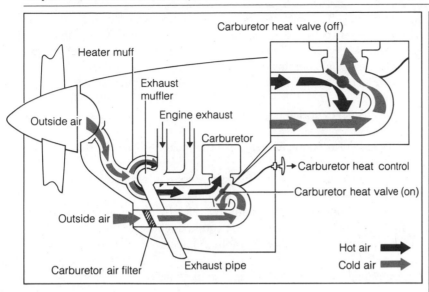

Figure 3.23 Carburetor heat system.

withstand such imbalances in power among the cylinders. On lower-performance engines the penalty is minimal, but as horsepower increases, the added weight becomes prohibitive.

A way to mix fuel and air without using a carburetor is with *fuel injection*. As the name implies, this method injects the fuel into the air as it enters the cylinder (see Figure 3.24). **Fuel injectors** are precisely drilled nozzles placed in the intake manifold near the intake valve of each cylinder. Fuel

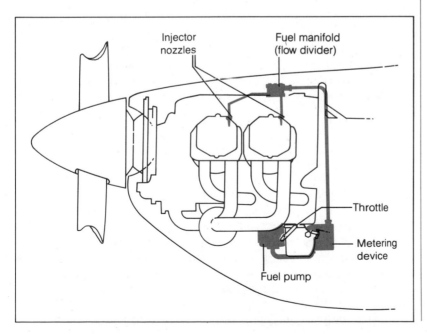

Figure 3.24 Fuel injection.

injection always requires a fuel pump to provide sufficient fuel pressure. The throttle on fuel-injected engines controls a butterfly valve similar to the one in the carburetor, but it also is connected to a metering device that controls the rate of fuel flow to the cylinders.

Fuel injection has numerous advantages over a carburetor:

1. No tendency to ice up, since the fuel is mixed with the air right at the cylinder.

2. Precise distribution of fuel to each cylinder, provided by the precision injectors.

3. Faster throttle response. The throttle control is connected to both the butterfly valve and the fuel control system.

4. Precise control of the mixture, provided by the metering device.

5. Easier cold-weather starts. The boost pump can be used like a primer to place a charge of fuel directly in the cylinders.

There are also some disadvantages to fuel injection:

1. Higher cost. The complexity of a fuel injection system means higher manufacturing and maintenance costs.

2. There is a greater likelihood of vapor lock. **Vapor lock** is trapped fuel vapor bubbles in the fuel lines leading to the cylinders; the bubbles block the normal flow of fuel. This situation often occurs immediately after shutting down the engine because residual heat boils the fuel in these lines. Running a fuel tank dry and thus allowing air to be drawn into the fuel lines can also cause vapor lock and make restarting the engine difficult.

The mixture control.   The amount of fuel drawn into the carburetor is a function of *air velocity* through the venturi. As altitude increases, the density of the air decreases (fewer molecules for a given volume), but the velocity of the air through the carburetor does not change. As a result, the mixture becomes more fuel-rich as altitude increases. A similar situation exists in a fuel injection system, since the metering device must send enough fuel for the engine to operate in the highest-density air anticipated. Consequently, in both systems, the mixture will be undesirably fuel-rich at high altitudes, reducing engine performance and wasting fuel, without pilot use of the mixture control.

The mixture control allows you to manually reduce the fuel flow as required. This process is called **leaning**, because it makes the fuel/air mixture more fuel-lean. Most manufacturers recommend leaning any time the engine power is below a certain level, typically 75 to 80 percent of rated power.

You should consult your Pilot's Operating Handbook for specific leaning procedures for the airplane you are flying. For a fixed-pitch propeller airplane the procedure is usually as follows:

1. Establish the airplane in level flight and set the power.

2. Slowly pull the mixture control out (aft) until the rpm peaks and then begins to drop off or until the engine begins to run a bit rough.

3. Slowly enrich the mixture (push the control forward) until the peak rpm is reached or until the engine runs smoothly.

This procedure must be repeated any time you change altitude or power settings. Of course, the mixture should be enriched (probably full rich) before increasing power. It should also be set (again, probably full rich) as part of your pre-landing checklist, in case power is needed. If you are operating at high altitudes or out of high-altitude airports, a full-rich mixture may not be appropriate, even for full power. The Pilot's Operating Handbook will specify the procedures to be used in these situations.

THE IGNITION SYSTEM

The function of an **ignition system** is to supply a properly timed spark, which ignites the fuel and air mixture in each cylinder. The heart of an aircraft ignition system is a **magneto**. This single device performs a number of functions:

1. It *generates the electricity* that will eventually become the spark igniting the fuel/air mixture. Current is generated by mechanically rotating a magnet inside a coil of wire.

2. It *steps up the voltage* by sending the current through a set of breaker points and a secondary coil. The voltage is increased to approximately 20,000 volts.

3. It *distributes the high voltage* by connecting to the proper spark plug at the right time. The action of the distributor and the breaker points is *timed* to send the high-voltage pulse to the cylinder when the piston is in the proper position.

Dual Ignition

Dual ignition systems have *two* magnetos, and each cylinder has two spark plugs. Figure 3.25 shows that each magneto powers one spark plug in each cylinder. The engine, then, can operate with only one system working, but it will be less efficient.

The entire engine ignition system is independent of any other airplane system and its operation is self-sustaining. Once the engine is running, the rotary motion of the crankshaft will continue to turn the magnetos and provide the sparks necessary to sustain ignition. Turning the electrical system's master switch off has no effect on the engine's operation (try it!). You can stop ignition only by turning off the magnetos from the cockpit or by stopping engine rotation.

Ignition Controls

Ignition and starter operations are controlled by a single rotary switch, called the **ignition control switch,** labeled (from left to right) Off, R (right magneto), L (left magneto), Both, and Start. The Start position must be

Figure 3.25 Dual ignition system.

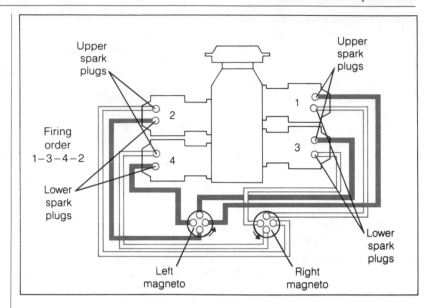

held manually against a spring so that it will automatically return to the Both position when it is released after the start cycle. The Pilot's Operating Handbook will provide details on starting procedures for your airplane.

An important procedure before any flight is the **magneto check**, or *mag check*, the verification that both magnetos are operating as part of the dual ignition system. Before takeoff, set the engine rpm to the recommended mag check setting, then move the magneto switch from Both to Right (grounding out the left magneto) and observe whether the drop in rpm is within the manufacturer's tolerances. The rpm will drop a certain amount if both magnetos are functional, since combustion is less efficient when the engine is running on only half its set of spark plugs. Return the switch to the Both position and repeat the check for the left magneto, setting the switch to the Left position. If the engine begins to die or loses more than the allowable rpm when switched to either magneto, you know that one magneto is malfunctioning or that there is some other problem with the ignition system. The aircraft should not be flown until the trouble is investigated and corrected by a power plant mechanic.

The absence of any drop in rpm during the mag check is also significant, because it may indicate a faulty magneto switch. An unsafe and potentially dangerous situation exists if the switch does not properly ground the magneto. If a magneto cannot be grounded, that means it cannot be disabled in flight if it should malfunction. It also means that *any movement of the propeller could start the engine*, even if only momentarily. (In pilot jargon, the prop is *hot*.) Obviously, this situation is dangerous because any unsuspecting person who moves the propeller by hand could be hurt. For your own safety never move the propeller by hand, and **always assume the engine will start if the propeller is moved**. If you suspect a faulty mag switch, you can check it as follows: with the engine idling at the slowest possible rpm, *momentarily flip the switch to Off*. If the engine dies, the switch is operating correctly. If the engine continues to run, do not fly the airplane until the problem is corrected.

The proper way of shutting down any aircraft engine is by pulling the mixture control to full lean, not by turning off the ignition. Although turning off the ignition will, in fact, shut down the engine, it will leave unburned fuel in the cylinders.

STANDARDIZATION OF CONTROLS

You may be reassured to know, as you sit for the first time in a cockpit full of unfamiliar dials and levers, that there is a great deal of standardization on controls and displays among the airplanes you may fly as a private pilot. It makes sense that since modern pilots tend to fly many types of airplanes during their careers, there should be a built-in margin of familiarity whenever a new cockpit is encountered. The FAA has determined that it is a good idea if all flap handles, for example, are shaped the same: little flaps aligned horizontally in the cockpit. Similarly, all landing gear handles (for aircraft with retractable gear) have knobs shaped like little wheels aligned vertically to the cockpit, like the tires themselves. The list continues: all carburetor heat controls are capped with a square handle; mixture controls have a handle with knurled (rough) edges; and throttle grips are round and smooth. Each control must be distinguishable from another, by touch alone if necessary. (This standardization, while increasingly widespread, is still not universal. Some older aircraft still have unique controls, and you will have to exercise great care when operating them.) Almost all airplane controls and displays you will encounter are very similar and are grouped in standard areas on the panel. If you become familiar with one cockpit, you will have learned your way around a good many others. Figure 3.26 shows a typical control panel with a standard arrangement.

Figure 3.26 Typical control panel.

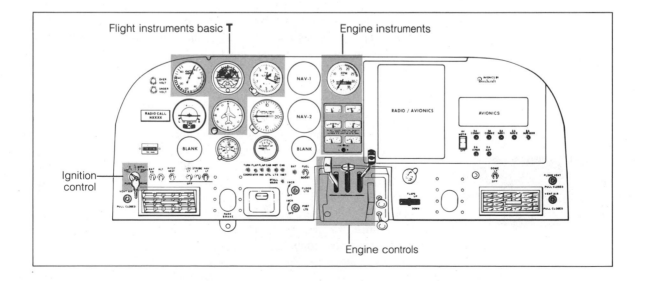

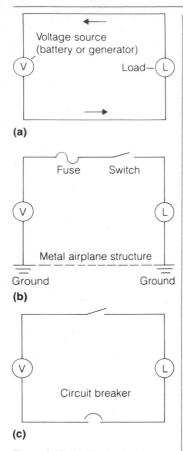

(a)

(b)

(c)

Figure 3.27 **(a)** Simple electric circuit. **(b)** Fuse-protected circuit. **(c)** Circuit breaker protection.

THE ELECTRICAL SYSTEM
The Principles of Electricity
Electricity comes from matter—from materials composed of atoms and electrons—and from nowhere else. When one kind of matter has a surplus of electrons, which have a negative charge, and another kind of matter associated with it has a shortage of electrons and therefore has a positive charge, the electrons from the negatively charged material will flow into the positively charged material. This flow of electrons is called **electric current** and is measured in *amperes (A)*, or *amps*. The amount of electrical potential stored in a material (that is, the potential for an electric current of some size) is called its **voltage** and is measured in *volts (V)*. When a material of higher voltage is connected to a material with lower voltage, a **circuit** is formed. Like a continuously circulating fountain, the conducting material (usually a copper wire) must go *from* the voltage source to the **load** (receiver of current) and *back to* it as well. It is necessary to *complete the circuit* for electrons (current) to flow. Figure 3.27a shows a simple electrical circuit.

Airplane Electrical Systems
A battery provides the electricity required to start the engine. It powers the **starter motor**, by means of the ignition switch. The starter motor rotates the engine to get it going, then disengages. Once the engine is running, it drives a **generator** or **alternator**, which provides electrical energy. Even though the battery is not used after the generator or alternator is operating, it is continuously charged to maintain its energy. It is then ready to power the starter for the next flight or to serve as a source of emergency electrical power if the generator/alternator were to fail.

Ammeter. The **ammeter** (see Figure 3.28) displays the electrical current flowing into the airplane battery when the alternator or generator is on line. A deflection of the needle toward the right-hand side of the case shows proper battery charging. A left deflection shows a battery discharge. Your Pilot's Operating Handbook will tell you the minimum rpm at which the engine-driven generator or alternator must operate to power the electrical system.

Load meter. Some airplanes are equipped with a gauge that indicates the electrical load, in amperes, being placed on the alternator or generator. With all electrical equipment off except the master switch, the **load meter** will indicate the amount of charging current being demanded by the battery. As each item of electrical equipment is turned on, the additional load will be registered on this gauge. If the alternator or generator fails, the load meter will indicate no load (0 amperes).

In some aircraft, there is a warning light either in place of or in addition to the ammeter or load meter. The light goes on whenever the alternator or generator is not producing enough power to handle the entire electrical

Figure 3.28 The ammeter.

load (when the battery is being discharged). Warning lights are useful because they usually catch your attention immediately, alerting you to the problem. If your airplane does not have a warning light, you will only be able to spot a problem by noticing a discharge indication on the ammeter or a no-load indication on the load meter. Too often, a pilot fails to pay attention to these signals and only realizes there is a problem when the radios or lights begin to malfunction because the battery has become too weak to support their function. Good instrument scanning habits are necessary to catch the problem early in planes that have no warning light.

What is the difference between a generator and an alternator? Both create electricity by rotating a magnet inside a wire coil. The generator produces **direct current (DC)** electricity, which is required by the airplane's electrical system. The alternator produces **alternating current (AC)**, which is immediately transformed into direct current by **rectifiers** attached to the alternator case. Generators were required before efficient rectifiers were available to transform AC to DC. Alternators are simpler to make, lighter in weight, and provide more electrical power at low engine speeds, which is why they have replaced generators on most airplanes (and cars).

Electrical controls and protection devices.   The airplane's entire electrical system is activated (or deactivated) by a **master switch**. Once it is on, each electrical component can be individually controlled by its own On/Off switch.

If a piece of equipment malfunctions, it can cause a **short circuit**—that is, creation of an undesired electrical path somewhere in the circuit. The component with the short circuit then draws more current than it can safely handle, creating a fire hazard. To guard against this, circuits are protected by **fuses** or **circuit breakers**, which open the circuit when the current flow exceeds a predetermined value (see Figure 3.27b and c). The fuses or circuit breakers (a plane will have one or the other) are usually found together on the instrument panel and are labeled to identify the component they protect.

A fuse is made of a special material that melts to stop the current flow. A blown fuse may be replaced with a fuse of the same or lower amperage rating but *never by a fuse of a higher rating*. FAR 91.33 requires spare fuses to be carried during flights conducted at night. Common sense dictates carrying spares all the time.

Circuit breakers operate like automatic push-button switches. When one trips, the button pops out and is noticeable when touched. Also, its popping out usually exposes a white band, so it can be easily seen. A circuit breaker should never be used as a switch, since it is not designed for repeated use. However, if one trips in flight it can be reset once, to see if the problem was a temporary condition. If it continues to pop, leave it alone until the problem can be solved by the proper technician. *Never hold a circuit breaker in place manually*. Holding it down will aggravate the malfunction and perhaps start an electrical fire.

Figure 3.29 Typical electrical system schematic for a light airplane.

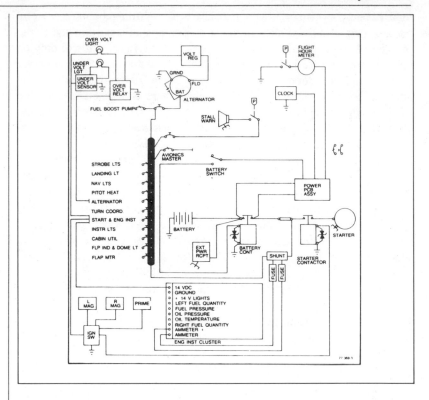

Figure 3.29 is a schematic drawing of a typical electrical system for a light airplane. It shows how all the components of the electrical system are connected.

POWER PLANT OPERATIONS

Although each engine model and installation is unique, certain general procedures are useful in the safe operation of all airplane reciprocating engines. While *your Pilot's Operating Handbook is still the primary source of operating information*, the following section will help you interpret that information and use it efficiently. Remember, this section deals with *engine* operation only. Other airplane components and instruments must be checked as part of normal flight operations as well.

Preflight Operations

1. Visually check the fuel level in the tanks.

2. Drain all the fuel sumps. Verify the grade of fuel by its color. If any water or other contaminant is found, continue draining until none can be seen.

3. Visually check the engine oil level. If oil is needed, refer to the Pilot's Operating Handbook for the correct grade to use. Make sure the dipstick and filler cap are properly secured. Visually check the engine and cowling for evidence of an oil leak.

4. Ensure that all plugs and covers are removed from cooling air inlets. Be sure that no foreign objects are under the engine cowling (bird nests, rags, tools, or the like). Be sure to secure the cowl properly if it was opened for this inspection.

5. Check the propeller and spinner for nicks or damage.

6. If the weather is cold, say, 20 degrees Fahrenheit or below, the engine should be preheated. A heated hangar is the best solution. A portable hot-air blower, to heat the engine compartment, will also do the job.

Starting the Engine and Warm-up Operations

Even though you have prepared the airplane for flight and have entered the cockpit and closed the door, ground personnel or airport visitors may not be aware that you are about to start the engine. Always make sure that the area around the airplane (especially near the nose) is clear and always shout "Clear!" outside the pilot's window or door before engaging the starter.

The following procedures should be observed when starting the engine in normal or hot weather:

1. If the engine has been standing idle for some time or if it is the first start of the day, use the engine primer, following the manufacturer's recommendations.

2. After the engine has started, check the oil pressure gauge for immediate reaction. If the needle has not moved within 30 seconds, shut down the engine at once.

3. Check the ammeter for positive indication.

4. Running the engine at high rpm for magneto and carburetor heat checks should be as brief as possible and should always be conducted while the aircraft is headed into the wind to aid engine cooling. Be sure to use the manufacturer's recommended power settings.

5. Keep all ground operations to a minimum to avoid engine overheating. Avoid lengthy taxiing or long periods of time parked on the ramp with the engine at idle to prevent spark plug fouling.

6. Cowl flaps, if installed, should be full open for all ground operations. If the flight is aborted (canceled) for any reason, be sure to leave the cowl flaps open after shutdown to help the engine cool down.

When you start the engine in cold weather:

1. Enter the cockpit and make sure that the ignition switch and electrical master switch are off. Then (and *only then*) turn the propeller by hand for at least six revolutions in the direction of rotation.

2. Prime the engine as recommended by the Pilot's Operating Handbook.

3. Once the engine has started, check the oil pressure gauge. If the needle has not moved within 1 minute or the recommended time after starting, shut down the engine at once and report the problem to a power plant mechanic.

4. Set the throttle to 1000 rpm until the oil pressure needle rests steadily in the green zone. Fluctuating oil pressure usually means that air is in the gauge lines. The engine should be shut down at once and checked by a power plant mechanic. If the weather is very cold, additional preheating of the engine may be required.

5. If the engine is equipped with a constant-speed propeller, activate the propeller control three or four times ("exercise" the propeller) to cycle the propeller governor and allow the mechanism to fill with warm engine oil. Refer to your Pilot's Operating Handbook for specifics.

Takeoff and Climb

Your Pilot's Operating Handbook will list specific procedures to use during the takeoff and initial climb phase of flight. Check your engine instruments frequently to ensure that they are operating steadily in the green zones of normal operation. If the airplane is equipped with a cylinder head temperature gauge, be certain CHT is within limits and cowl flaps are set.

1. Use full throttle on takeoff unless otherwise instructed by the Pilot's Operating Handbook.

2. Set the fuel mixture at full rich, except at airports with high-density altitudes, where the engine will operate more efficiently with a leaner mixture. Consult your Pilot's Operating Handbook for the proper procedure.

3. Use full power for initial and other climbs unless otherwise instructed by the Pilot's Operating Handbook.

4. On hot days use a climb airspeed that is slightly higher than normal to force more air over the cylinders and assist engine cooling.

5. Check the CHT, if your airplane is so equipped, and adjust the cowl flaps to maintain the operating temperature required by the handbook.

Cruise

When you reach your desired cruise altitude, level off and let the airplane accelerate to cruise speed before reducing power. This will greatly simplify trimming the airplane for level flight. Set cruise power in accordance with your Pilot's Operating Handbook. Use the recommended procedure to lean the mixture at this time. Do not forget to monitor the engine gauges regularly throughout the flight.

Descent and Landing

1. Maintain sufficient engine power to keep engine temperature within the normal (green) operating zone and keep the alternator or generator on line. Plan all your descents so that partial power can be maintained. Avoid overcooling the engine.

2. Gradually enrich the fuel mixture to ensure smooth engine operation as you descend.

3. Keep the cowl flaps closed to avoid overcooling.

4. Set mixture full rich before landing, unless you are landing at an airport with high-density altitude. Consult your Pilot's Operating Handbook for operations into these airports.

The Role of Good Judgment in Power Plant Operations

Read your Pilot's Operating Handbook and know how to put its information to use in your airplane. A good pilot couples a sound understanding of general power plant principles with knowledge of specific procedures—normal and emergency—required by the manufacturer and the FAA. A skilled, well-informed pilot can minimize the potential dangers of most equipment malfunctions, should they occur, and can cope readily with changes in the flying environment. A little effort and forethought, after all, is a small price to pay for the many joys and freedoms of powered flight.

KEY TERMS

airframe and power plant (A&P) mechanic
alternating current (AC)
alternator
ammeter
aviation gasoline (avgas)
baffles
blade element
boost pump
carburetor
carburetor heat system
carburetor ice
circuit breaker
connecting rod
constant-speed propeller
cowl flaps
crankcase
crankshaft
cylinder
cylinder head temperature gauge
detonation
direct current (DC)
dual ignition system
engine primer
fixed-pitch propeller
fuel injectors
fuel pressure gauge
fuel pump

fuel quantity gauge
fuel selector valve
fuel strainer
fuses
generator
grounding wire
horsepower
leaning
load meter
magneto
magneto check
manifold pressure gauge
master switch
mixture control
oil pressure gauge
oil temperature gauge
piston
pitch
preignition
propeller
reciprocating engine
rings
starter motor
sump
tachometer
throttle control
torque
vapor lock

PROFICIENCY CHECK

1. What is meant by a four-stroke engine? What is its ultimate purpose, regardless of how it is used?

2. What is the function of the propeller? Is it reasonable to compare a propeller to a wing? Why or why not?

3. Name two advantages of a fixed-pitch propeller. Name two advantages of a constant-speed propeller.

4. Name two ways airplane engines are cooled. What are the advantages and disadvantages of each?

5. You are on a cross-country flight in a low-horsepower trainer airplane and have just landed at a small airport in a remote area. The airport operator informs you that he has only 100-grade aviation fuel available and that it is stored in 50-gallon steel drums. Is it safe to fuel your airplane for the return flight with the gasoline available? If you decide to refuel at this airport, list three precautions you should take.

6. What are the two main purposes of the carburetor? What is carburetor ice and how can you detect it? Remove it?

7. What are the components of a dual ignition system and how does the system work? Describe the mag check preflight procedure. What are the indications of a malfunctioning magneto?

8. What is an ammeter? How does a pilot use the information it provides?

9. What are the similarities and differences between a circuit breaker and a fuse?

It is only by putting ourselves in harmony with Nature
that we get sound instruments. . . .

Admiral W. H. Henderson
The [London] *Times*, 1925

C H E C K P O I N T S

How do cockpit instruments work? 🛩 How do pilots use cockpit instruments? 🛩
What are the limitations of each flight instrument? 🛩 How are flight instruments used
to coordinate airplane attitude with respect to outside references?

FLIGHT INSTRUMENTS

As you saw in Chapter 2, the actions of an airplane in flight, while logical and predictable, can be complex. Early aircraft designers were absorbed in discovering the principles of stability and control we now take for granted. The development of aeronautical technology was the early designers' priority, not the convenience of pilots.

Early fliers had to rely on the force of the wind on their faces and the sound of the wind in the airplane's rigging to gauge the speed and direction of the airflow. The only measure of airplane attitude was the surrounding world, so all flight information came from scanning the horizon and comparing it to the position of the airplane's nose and wing tips. Not surprisingly, flights at night or in areas of low visibility often ended abruptly.

As aeronautical technology progressed, it became important to provide better cockpit instrumentation. These devices add safety to the operation of an aircraft. Your flight training will integrate the use of visual references and instrument indications for control of the airplane, in the interest of making you a safer pilot. It also lays the groundwork for an advanced pilot rating, when you will be able to fly *solely* by instrument reference.

In this chapter you will become familiar with the basic **flight instruments** found in general aviation aircraft. These instruments give the pilot information about the attitude, flight path, and performance of the airplane. The operation and use of each one is explained in detail. Your flight instructor will teach you how to use them safely and effectively as a private pilot.

THE PITOT-STATIC INSTRUMENTS

Ram air, or **pitot air**, (moving air that hits the airplane head-on) is captured in a device known as the **pitot tube**. This hollow tube projects from the aircraft in such a way that it can capture this impact air with minimum disturbance from other airframe features, such as struts or airfoils. A frequent location for the pitot tube on light airplanes is on the outboard part of the wing, where it is mounted on a short pedestal below the lower surface, clear of the wing's pressure zones (see Figure 4.1a). Pitot pressure registers both the impact pressure resulting from the motion of the airplane and the static pressure of the atmosphere.

The **static ports** (Figure 4.1b) measure the local atmospheric pressure,

Figure 4.1 **(a)** Pitot tube. **(b)** Static port.

(a)

(b)

or **static air**. This pressure is called static because its value would be the same even if the airplane were standing still. The static ports are typically one or more holes oriented normal (90 degrees) to the surface they occupy. Some aircraft have one static port; others have two, mounted on opposite sides of the fuselage. Aircraft designers select the locations to provide accurate readings across as wide a range of airspeeds as possible and regardless of aircraft attitude.

Figure 4.2 is a diagram of the instruments connected to the pitot and static ports—the **pitot-static instruments** that make up the **pitot-static system**. The **altimeter** and **vertical speed indicator (VSI)** are connected only to the static ports. The **airspeed indicator** is the only instrument connected to both.

The Airspeed Indicator

Function.   The airspeed indicator registers the total pressure from the pitot head and subtracts from it the static pressure supplied from the static ports. This remainder is called **dynamic pressure**, and it is the measure of the airplane's forward speed. This speed is displayed on the instrument's face on a graduated scale called the **indicated airspeed (IAS)**. Remember that this value represents the airplane's speed through the air, not necessarily its speed across the ground. Why? Once it is airborne, the airplane becomes part of the local mass of air. If the mass of air is moving (that is, if the wind is blowing), the airplane will move with the air. While this is an important consideration during takeoffs and landings (when the airplane is making the transition between flight and ground operations) and for navigation (the moving air mass can carry the plane off course, like a ship on ocean currents), it means very little to the pilot in terms of normal flight

Figure 4.2 The pitot-static system.

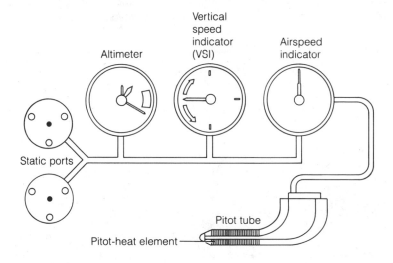

dynamics. The airplane flies because of the speed of the relative wind, and this is what the airspeed indicator measures, not ground speed.

Most airspeed indicators have scales for both statute miles per hour (mph) and nautical miles per hour, called **knots (kts)**. Older airplanes have mph on the outer ring of numbers (the most prominent scale on the instrument). This was done, supposedly, to ease the transition from driving a car to flying an airplane. All aircraft (old and new), however, use nautical distances and speeds, especially when communicating with Air Traffic Control facilities (control towers and radar services). Consequently, newer airplanes have knots on the outer scale and mph on the inner ring.

Mechanism. The heart of your airspeed indicator is an airtight chamber containing a flexible metallic diaphragm (a thin elastic partition). Pitot pressure is supplied to the diaphragm while static pressure is supplied to the chamber. The diaphragm then expands or contracts, depending on the amount of pitot pressure (speed at which the outside air is entering the pitot head) and the prevailing atmospheric (static) pressure. The diaphragm is linked to a pointer with levers and gears. Figure 4.3 shows a cutaway view of the mechanism of the airspeed indicator.

Types of Airspeed

Indicated airspeed (IAS). Indicated airspeed, the direct reading from the face of the instrument, is a valid indication of airplane performance, since it depends on the number of air molecules encountered with time. Pilots rely most heavily on indicated airspeed during takeoffs and landings. *The proper indicated airspeeds for takeoffs and landings are always the same, regardless of altitude.*

Calibrated airspeed (CAS). An airplane affects the air through which it is flying; in turn, the pressures sensed by the pitot-static system (primarily

Figure 4.3 Mechanism of the air-speed indicator.

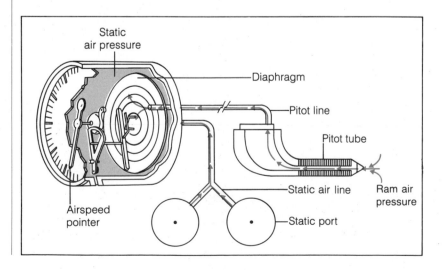

the static ports) are affected. The amount of disturbance depends on the design of each type of airplane—in particular, on where the ports are placed on the airframe. Manufacturers can measure the effects due to this *position* or *installation error* for various airspeeds. The airspeed indicator itself has known inherent *instrument errors*. **Calibrated airspeed (CAS)** is indicated airspeed corrected for position and instrument errors. There is no direct reading of CAS in the cockpit. Instead, every airplane's Pilot's Operating Handbook has a table listing calibrated versus indicated airspeed across the entire speed regions of the airplane.

True airspeed (TAS).   An airspeed indicator is calibrated for standard sea level air. Therefore, when the airplane is flying at altitudes other than standard sea level, the airspeed indicator does not reflect the actual speed through the air. The amount of error is a function of temperature and altitude. **True airspeed (TAS)** *can be approximated by increasing indicated airspeed 2 percent per thousand feet of altitude*. For example, if you are flying at 6000 feet and your indicated airspeed is 110 knots, your true airspeed is approximately:

$$\text{correction} = 2\% \times 6\,(\text{thousands of feet}) \times \text{IAS}$$
$$= 12\% \times 110\,\text{knots}$$
$$= 13.2\,\text{knots}$$
$$\text{TAS} = 110 + 13.2$$
$$= 123.2\,\text{knots}$$

Remember, this is an approximation. An exact solution will be given when the flight computer is explained in a later chapter.

Markings and use.   Figure 4.4 shows the face of a typical airspeed indicator. The instrument is marked with color-coded arcs to help you associate needle position with the operating limits of your particular airplane. Although the numerical values of operating limits will change from one airplane design to another, the color codes are standardized.

Important airspeeds you should know about will often be presented as subscripted **V** (velocity) **speeds**. The following V speeds and speed ranges are color coded on the airspeed indicator:

1. The *white arc* is the flap operating range. The low-speed end of the white arc is the *stall speed in the landing configuration*, $\mathbf{V_{S0}}$. The high-speed end of this arc is the *maximum flap extension speed*, $\mathbf{V_{FE}}$.

2. The *green arc* is the range of airspeeds for normal operation. The *stall speed with the gear and flaps up*, $\mathbf{V_{S1}}$, is found at the low-speed end of the green arc. The green arc's high-speed end is called the *maximum structural cruising speed*, $\mathbf{V_{NO}}$.

3. The *yellow arc* is the caution range, or the smooth-air operating range. Operations are permitted in this region only if there is *absolutely no turbulence*. The yellow arc ends at the *red line* speed. The designation $\mathbf{V_{NE}}$ indicates that this is the *never-exceed airspeed*.

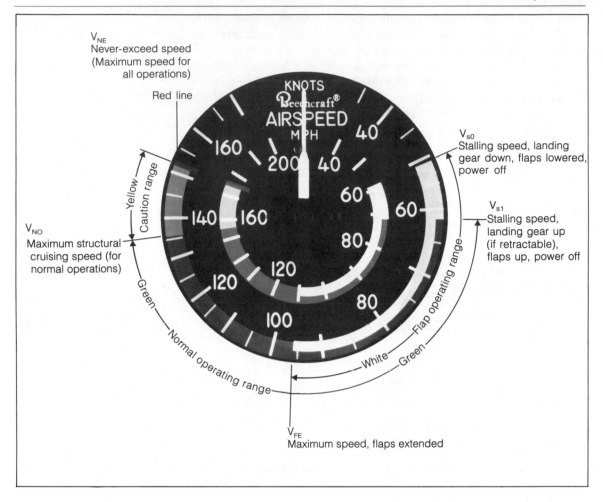

Figure 4.4 Color-coded markings on the airspeed indicator.

The airspeed values of the color arcs give *indicated airspeed* on newly certified airplanes (since 1977). The color markings have been positioned to account for any position error that may apply at that airspeed.

Aircraft certified before that time have color markings that are *calibrated airspeed* values. The colored arcs *do not account for position error* on these airplanes. This means that you must know (or look up in the book) the correction that converts CAS to IAS. For example, let us assume you are flying an older airplane, and the low-speed end of the green arc is at 60 mph (CAS). You look in the airplane handbook and determine that 60 mph CAS will indicate 51 mph. This means the airplane will stall in the clean configuration at 51 mph IAS, even though the green arc ends at 60. It is obvious why this change was made on newer airplanes. If yours were a new airplane, the green arc would end at 51 mph.

A number of important airspeeds are *not* color coded on the instrument. These include maximum landing gear extension speed (for aircraft with

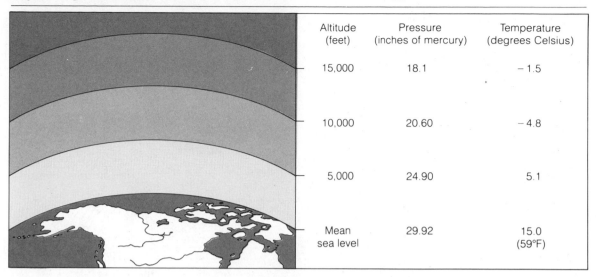

Altitude (feet)	Pressure (inches of mercury)	Temperature (degrees Celsius)
15,000	18.1	-1.5
10,000	20.60	-4.8
5,000	24.90	5.1
Mean sea level	29.92	15.0 (59°F)

retractable gear); maneuvering speed; and some maximum-performance climb speeds, which will be discussed in Chapter 6.

Figure 4.5 Properties of the standard atmosphere.

Limitations.   Like all mechanical devices, airspeed indicators can sometimes fail. The most common cause of failure is blockage of the pitot tube, sometimes because the pilot forgot to remove the protective cover from the pitot head before takeoff. Other causes of blockage are ice accumulation or obstruction by foreign objects such as insects or dirt. Obviously, the first problem can be prevented by a careful preflight inspection, and the last can be easily averted by re-covering the pitot tube after each flight. Since many pitot heads are electrically heated, obstruction by ice is also easily preventable.

The Altimeter
Function.   The altimeter translates barometric pressure into a display of elevation in feet.

Mechanism.   The altimeter works on the principle that atmospheric pressure decreases with altitude. Figure 4.5 shows the relationship between altitude and pressure in the **standard atmosphere** (an internationally standardized set of atmospheric properties versus altitude). Inside an altimeter are *aneroid wafers*, thin metal canisters sealed with a known reference pressure inside (see Figure 4.6). Levers and gears connect the aneroids to the pointers on the face of the instrument. The static air source is connected to the altimeter case, exposing the aneroids to static atmospheric pressure. As the airplane climbs or descends, the aneroids expand or contract, and these processes are reflected by the altimeter reading.

Unfortunately, atmospheric pressure changes not only with altitude but with every fluctuation in the weather. The altimeter must account for these changes in order for it to provide useful information. The **altimeter setting**

Figure 4.6 Mechanism of the
altimeter.

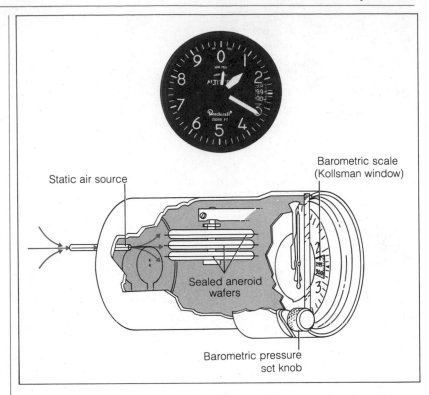

Figure 4.6 Mechanism of the
altimeter.

is the current sea level barometric pressure, expressed in inches of mercury.
An adjustment knob is provided to set this reading in the **Kollsman window**
on the face of the instrument. *A change of 1 inch of mercury on the Kollsman window results in approximately a 1000-foot change in altitude on the
needles*. This is a useful conversion value to remember. Increasing the
value in the window increases the altitude reading, and vice versa.

You will obtain the altimeter setting from the airport control tower or a
Flight Service Station (an FAA facility that provides weather information
to pilots) before you take off. If neither source of information is available
to you, then set the field elevation on the altimeter. After you are under
way, you must use an altimeter setting from a reporting station within 100
miles of your location (see FAR 91.81).

Markings and use.   Figure 4.7a shows the face of a typical three-hand
barometric altimeter. The shortest hand, or the triangle on the outer perimeter, is the 10,000-foot pointer. The next largest hand is the 1000-foot
pointer, and the longest pointer is the 100-foot pointer. These names describe
the amount of altitude change when the needle moves one numbered increment on the face.

To read the 10,000- and 1000-foot hands, look at the closest number that
has been *passed* (as you do when you read the hour hand on a clock). In
Figure 4.7a, the 10,000-foot pointer is between the 0 and 1 (much closer

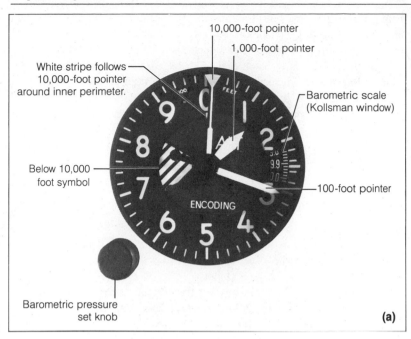

10,000-foot pointer

1,000-foot pointer

White stripe follows 10,000-foot pointer around inner perimeter.

Barometric scale (Kollsman window)

Below 10,000 foot symbol

100-foot pointer

ENCODING

Barometric pressure set knob

(a)

Figure 4.7 (a) Three-pointer altimeter. (b) Number drum altimeter.

(b)

to the 0); this means the altitude is between 0 and 10,000 feet. The 1000-foot hand is between the 1 and 2, which translates into 1000 feet. The 100-foot pointer is read directly, in increments of 20 feet. In Figure 4.7a, the hundreds hand points to 3, and the indicated altitude is therefore 1300 feet.

If reading an altimeter seems complicated, you are right. It is very easy to misread, especially when the altitude is above 10,000 feet. Practice will help minimize errors, but awareness of the difficulty is the real key. Take an extra second to think, before registering the reading in your mind. All pilots, from airline captains to students, will misread the altimeter from time to time, especially when rushed. New altimeter designs use number drums (like the odometer on your car) rather than pointers, to simplify things (see Figure 4.7b). However, most light airplanes are equipped with the less expensive pointer altimeters.

Limitations.   Even though altimeters are precise instruments, they have some inherent characteristics that result in operational errors of varying degrees:

1. *Scale error*. Sometimes the aneroids do not assume the exact size required to reflect the appropriate change in pressure. Such **scale error** is irregular, although the tolerance for error is larger as altitude increases. An error of plus or minus 50 feet at lower altitudes may become an error of plus or minus 200 feet at 40,000 feet.

2. *Friction error*. You may observe the altimeter needles moving in fits and starts through certain altitude ranges. This **friction error** is due to friction between the mechanical parts. Usually, the vibration of the engine is enough to overcome any tendency of the instrument to stick. If you notice this error, tap the glass on the case lightly with your finger. This will usually get the instrument moving again.

3. *Hysteresis*. The material used to make the aneroids is not perfectly elastic. After a long flight at altitude, the wafers may become "set" in their new shape. This condition is called **hysteresis**. If a rapid descent is initiated, the altitude shown on the altimeter may be a bit higher than your actual altitude. The error should be less than 100 feet for a modern altimeter. A few minutes at a new altitude is enough for the aneroids to "remember" their correct shape.

Types of altitude.   Several values can be assigned to an altitude, depending on the reference plane used. The following altitude definitions are important to all pilots (see Figure 4.8):

1. Pressure-altitude is defined as the reading on an altimeter when the Kollsman window is set to 29.92 inches of mercury (standard sea level pressure). This altitude will be used in performance calculations (discussed in the next chapter) and for flights above 18,000 feet (where pressure altitudes are called **flight levels**).

2. True altitude is the true height above **mean sea level (MSL)**. Sea level is a fixed position on earth; therefore, MSL altitudes do not change with atmospheric conditions. A properly functioning and correctly set altimeter will indicate true altitude only if it is in a standard atmosphere. Since this is rarely (if ever) the case, true altitude must be computed based on actual conditions.

3. Indicated altitude is what your altimeter reads at any point in time.

4. Absolute altitude is your altitude above ground level (**AGL**). It is computed by subtracting the true elevation of the surface from your indicated (true) altitude.

The local altimeter setting is used to adjust your altimeter for local pressure conditions, but this setting does not compensate for nonstandard pressure or for temperature gradients aloft. Therefore, even a correctly set altimeter does not indicate MSL altitude. However, all flying is done with respect to indicated altitudes, and all altimeters in the local area are affected similarly by nonstandard conditions. Therefore, in actual practice, we treat a properly set altimeter as if indicated altitude is the same as MSL altitude. In fact, virtually all references to "MSL" altitude you will encounter as a pilot are really indicated altitude on a properly set altimeter.

Figure 4.8 Types of altitude.

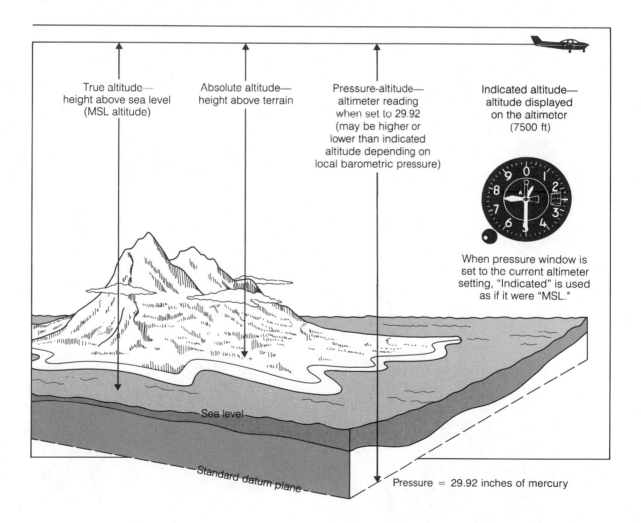

True altitude—
height above sea level
(MSL altitude)

Absolute altitude—
height above terrain

Pressure-altitude—
altimeter reading
when set to 29.92
(may be higher or
lower than indicated
altitude depending on
local barometric pressure)

Indicated altitude—
altitude displayed
on the altimeter
(7500 ft)

When pressure window is
set to the current altimeter
setting, "Indicated" is used
as if it were "MSL."

Sea level

Standard datum plane

Pressure = 29.92 inches of mercury

Weather and the altimeter. What is the danger if you *do not reset* the Kollsman window during a cross-country flight? When you fly a constant indicated altitude with the same Kollsman setting, you are flying a line of constant pressure. If you fly from high-pressure weather to low-pressure weather, your true altitude will reveal a descending flight path. This phenomenon is illustrated in Figure 4.9. A good way to remember how weather affects altitude is with the pilot rhyme: "From a high to a low, look out

Figure 4.9 The effects of changes in barometric pressure and temperature on altimeter readings.

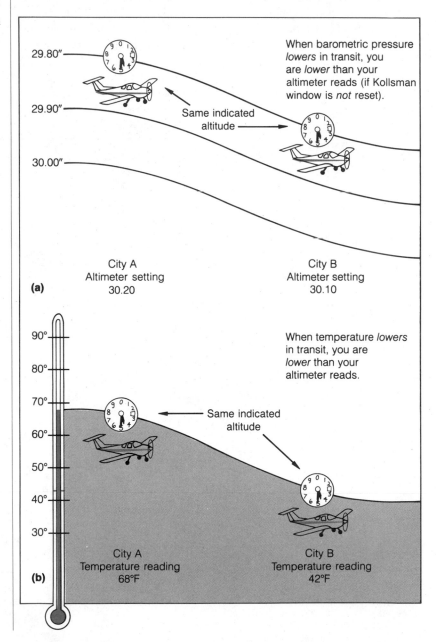

below; from a low to a high, you're high in the sky." Obviously, such problems are avoided by resetting the Kollsman window to local conditions.

The same rhyme applies when you encounter a change in temperature; that is, cooler-than-standard temperatures cause your true altitude to be lower than indicated. You cannot compensate for this effect, except by increasing your awareness of the terrain below. All altimeters in the same area will be affected similarly, so traffic separation is not compromised. Figure 4.9 also shows the temperature effect graphically.

Let us take a short flight from Sacramento, California, to Reno, Nevada, to illustrate the use of the altimeter. You climb into your airplane at Sacramento Executive Airport and receive from the tower the current altimeter setting: 29.85 inches of mercury.

You dial this number into the Kollsman window of your altimeter. Since the sign by the runway tells you the field elevation is 21 feet, you check your altimeter reading to see if it is in agreement. (As a general rule, the altimeter is considered safe for use if the indicated altitude is within plus or minus 75 feet of this value.) The needles read 30 feet, a difference of 9 feet. Since your altimeter reading is well within the acceptable tolerance, you proceed with the flight. If the reading you get is outside this tolerance, the instrument should be checked by a repair technician before proceeding.

As you fly past Lake Tahoe, you decide to check the current weather with the nearest FAA Flight Service Station. You are informed that the Lake Tahoe altimeter is 29.94. You dial this new number into the Kollsman window of your altimeter and adjust your altitude (FAR 91.81). As you descend into the traffic pattern at Reno, you receive landing instructions, including a new altimeter setting of 29.69. You know that the Reno traffic pattern is 800 feet AGL and that the field elevation at Reno is 4411 feet. You level off at 5200 feet indicated altitude. After landing, you notice that the field elevation is 4420 feet on your altimeter—again a difference of 9 feet, well within the acceptable tolerance.

Now let us assume that you failed to adjust your altimeter to the Reno setting. How far off would your altitude have been? Would you have been higher or lower than indicated? First, since you went from a high to a low (29.94 at Lake Tahoe to 29.69 at Reno), you have to look out below. In other words, you would have been *lower* than indicated. You can calculate how much lower as follows:

$$
\begin{aligned}
\text{Proper setting} &= 29.69 \\
-\ \text{Actual setting} &= \underline{-29.94} \\[4pt]
\text{Error} &= -0.25 \text{ inches of mercury}
\end{aligned}
$$

$$-0.25 \text{ in Hg} \times 1000 \text{ feet of altitude per inch} = -250 \text{ feet (or 250 feet low)}$$

Note that subtracting the *actual setting* from the *proper setting* will always yield an answer with the proper sign ($-$ = low, $+$ = high).

By flying 250 feet too low, you would not only have risked your own safety because of inadequate terrain clearance, you would probably have baffled the other pilots in the airport traffic pattern and possibly risked a midair collision with those who could not see you. Maintaining the current altimeter setting is a team effort requiring the cooperation of every pilot.

Vertical Speed Indicator (VSI)

Function.   The vertical speed indicator registers the rate of change of static pressure and converts this to an indication in feet per minute. This information is valuable because it is difficult to judge rate of climb or descent using only our human senses.

Mechanism.   The VSI is housed in an airtight case. Static pressure is routed to one side of a thin metal diaphragm (see Figure 4.10). The other side of the diaphragm senses static air that must pass through a small calibrated hole. Levers and gears connect the diaphragm to a needle on the face of the instrument.

When the airplane is in level flight, both pressures are equal, and the needle reflects this fact. As the airplane changes altitude, the metering hole limits the change in pressure to one side of the diaphragm, while the other side senses actual static air immediately. The faster the change in altitude, the greater the difference in these two pressures, and the greater the resulting needle deflection.

Figure 4.10 Mechanism of the vertical speed indicator.

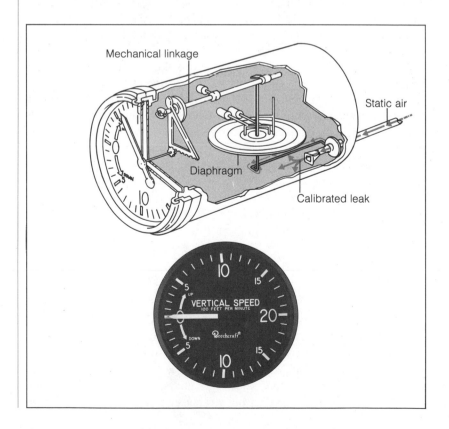

Limitations.   Whenever a change in altitude is made, the diaphragm reacts immediately, and the needle indicates this *trend*. However, the flow of air through the calibrated "leak" does not stabilize for several seconds, and therefore the value the needle registers is not valid during this time. Once the climb or descent is stable for 5 to 7 seconds, the needle accurately reports the rate. Because of this lagging tendency, you must be careful not to overreact to momentary fluctuations of the needle.

During flight maneuvers or during flights in turbulence, the VSI may give a brief indication of movement *opposite* to the actual direction of movement. This indication is only momentary and is caused by the sudden pressure changes at the static ports. Again, the best procedure is to remain patient and allow the instrument to stabilize before taking action.

THE MAGNETIC COMPASS

A magnet is a piece of metal that attracts another piece of metal. The two ends, or *poles*, of a magnet are labeled north and south. Similar poles (north-north) repel each other, and opposite poles (north-south) attract. Lines of magnetic force flow between the poles. A free-floating magnet will align itself with these force lines.

The earth has the properties of a giant magnet, but unfortunately its magnetic pole does not coincide with its rotational axis (called its geographical pole). This difference is called **variation**, and its use will be explained in Chapter 12, when navigation is discussed. For now, examine Figure 4.11 to see how the magnetic pole and geographical pole differ.

Function.   The **magnetic compass** indicates the direction your airplane is heading with respect to magnetic north. This simple instrument is vital when navigating over unfamiliar terrain, or any time ground contact cannot be maintained (flying over or through clouds, for instance).

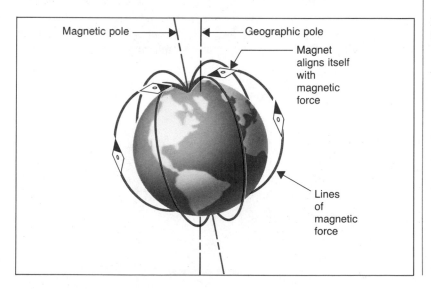

Figure 4.11 The earth's magnetic field.

Mechanism.   The magnetic compass operates because the earth is a giant magnet, not because of any airplane power system or other phenomenon of flight. It contains two bar magnets fixed to a compass card (see Figure 4.12b). Although the card is free to turn and tilt up to 18 degrees, liquid within the instrument case tends to stabilize the card. This liquid dampens but does not prevent motions of the card resulting from flight maneuvers. A line (called the *lubber line*) mounted behind the glass of the instrument is used for a reference line to read headings on the compass card.

Markings and use.   Figure 4.12a shows the face of a magnetic compass. The compass display is graduated into 5° increments, with 30° increments labeled numerically and the **cardinal headings** (north, south, east, and west) labeled with the appropriate initial.

Limitations.   The magnetic compass provides reliable readings as long as the airplane is in level, unaccelerated flight or is parked on the ground. However, during turns, speed changes, or any sort of turbulence, the compass experiences significant fluctuations. The problem is that the magnets in the instrument attempt to remain aligned with the earth's magnetic force lines. As Figure 4.11 illustrates, near the equator, the force lines are parallel with the earth's surface. As you get closer to the poles, the force lines bend toward the surface, causing the magnets to have a ground-seeking tendency. At the poles these force lines are nearly vertical. The free-floating suspension of the magnets, combined with their attempt to stay aligned with the earth's force lines, cause the following types of errors in the reading:

   1. Acceleration-deceleration error. When an airplane accelerates or decelerates, the compass dips, as shown in Figure 4.13. This effect is most apparent on easterly or westerly headings (when the magnet is aligned with the wing tips). In the Northern Hemisphere, an *acceleration* causes the compass to dip and indicate a turn to the *north*. When the airplane *decelerates*, a turn to the *south* is indicated. The mnemonic **ANDS** (*A*ccelerate *N*orth, *D*ecelerate *S*outh) will aid you in remembering this.

Figure 4.12 Mechanism of the magnetic compass: **(a)** Face. **(b)** Mechanism.

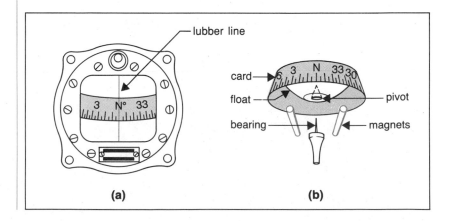

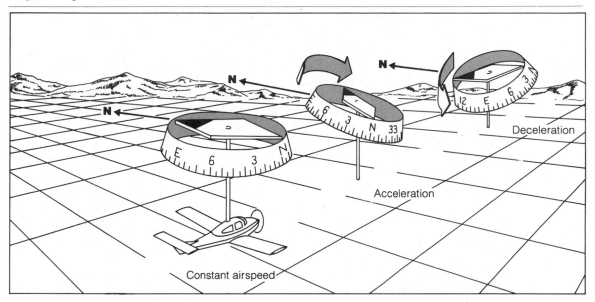

2. Turn error. When the airplane rolls into a bank, the magnetic compass card banks too. However, the magnetic force lines also influence the motion of the card and cause errors while the turn is in progress (see Figure 4.14). Turn errors are most pronounced when the airplane is headed north or south. When the airplane is turned from a heading of north, the compass

Figure 4.13 Acceleration and deceleration errors.

Figure 4.14 Turn errors.

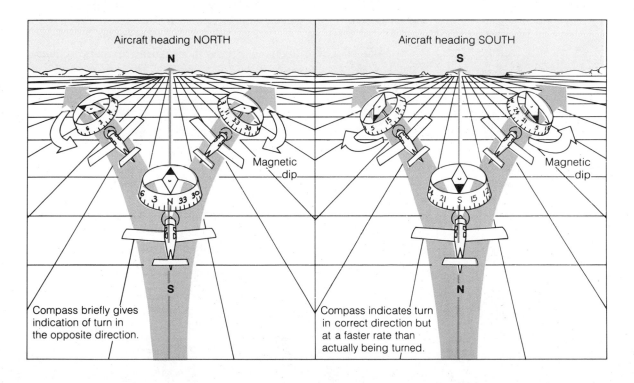

will initially indicate a turn in the *opposite direction*, and it will always *lag behind* the actual heading. When the turn begins from a heading of south, the compass will *jump ahead* of the actual heading, and it will remain ahead of the actual heading for a while. The amount of error is approximately the same as your latitude on headings of north or south; it becomes negligible on east-west headings. To illustrate these errors, let us do a 360-degree turn to the right, starting on a heading of due north. As we roll into the turn, the compass initially indicates 330°, opposite the direction we are actually turning. As our heading progresses toward 90°, the compass indication lags; however, the lag becomes smaller and smaller as an easterly heading is approached. As we pass 90°, the magnetic compass has caught up and indicates this passage correctly. Now the compass begins to lead our actual heading, and the lead grows as our heading approaches south. As our actual heading passes south, the compass has built up a 30-degree lead (indicating 210). As we continue the turn, the lead begins to decline as a west heading nears. By the time our actual heading is 270°, the compass is again correct, for the moment. Once again the compass indication begins to fall behind the actual heading of the airplane. As the compass slowly reaches an indication of 330, we begin to roll out on a heading of north.

3. Variation. As mentioned earlier, you may need to compensate for the difference between true north and magnetic north. The method for doing this is discussed in Chapter 12.

4. Deviation. Metallic or electrical components in the cockpit may affect the magnetic compass. When the instrument is first installed in the airplane, it is checked for accuracy. Any errors are published on a **compass correction card**, which is mounted on the compass case (see Figure 4.15).

During turbulence or flight maneuvers, the magnetic compass oscillates so much that it is impossible to read it accurately. These movements are the result of all the dip errors operating simultaneously. Do not try to use the magnetic compass for precise heading information unless the airplane is in straight, level, unaccelerated flight.

THE OUTSIDE AIR TEMPERATURE GAUGE

Since the **outside air temperature (OAT) gauge** works like a home thermometer, we need not say much about it here. Its external probe (the temperature-sensing bulb mounted outside the cockpit) is protected by a metal guard against direct sunlight or physical damage. The face of the instrument (see Figure 4.16) displays both Celsius and Fahrenheit degrees and is useful in planning cross-country flights and determining airplane

Figure 4.15 Compass correction card. (MH = magnetic heading; CH = compass heading.)

FOR (MH)	0°	30°	60°	90°	120°	150°	180°	210°	240°	270°	300°	330°
STEER (CH)	359°	30°	60°	88°	120°	152°	183°	212°	240°	268°	300°	329°
RADIO ON [X]						RADIO OFF [ ]						

performance. Obviously, a major use of the OAT gauge is as an indicator of subfreezing conditions, when ice may be a hazard. The OAT is discussed in Chapter 12, Basics of Air Navigation, as OAT is an important variable in calculating true airspeed in flight.

Figure 4.16 The outside air temperature (OAT) gauge.

THE GYROSCOPIC INSTRUMENTS

A **gyroscope** is a mass spinning rapidly about an axis (see Figure 4.17). The rotor (the part that spins) is typically suspended within a set of inter-connected frames, or *gimbals*. A spinning gyroscope exhibits two fundamental properties that make it useful for use in airplane flight instruments. These properties are:

1. *Rigidity in space.* A spinning gyroscope will tend to maintain its orientation in space and resist any forces that tend to displace it. A gyroscope with **universal mounting** (one mounted in three or more gimbals) will, in fact, maintain spatial orientation regardless of the motion of the item attached to the outermost gimbal (an airplane in this case).

2. *Precession.* When a gyroscope is displaced by a force, such as friction in the bearings of the gimbals or a restricted mounting (less than three gimbals), the reaction generated by the gyroscope is called **precession**. This reaction force acts 90 degrees from the applied force, in the direction of the rotation of the rotor (see Figure 4.17).

The following flight instruments contain gyroscopes for their operation: the *attitude indicator*, the *turn coordinator*, the *turn and slip indicator*, and the *heading indicator*. Let us look at each **gyroscopic instrument** in detail.

The Attitude Indicator

Function.   The **attitude indicator**, also called the *artificial horizon* or *gyro horizon*, provides the pilot with a visual representation of the airplane's flight attitude with respect to the horizon. Any change in airplane pitch or roll is displayed immediately on the face of the instrument exactly as it occurs, with no delay or time lag.

Mechanism.   Figure 4.18 shows a cutaway view of a typical attitude indi-cator. Since the gyroscope's rotor must be spinning to attain the desired gyroscopic properties, the attitude indicator (like the other gyro instru-ments) is a powered instrument. This means that, unlike the pitot-static instruments, it must have a source of energy if it is to operate. This power source is usually electricity, air pressure, or vacuum. Most attitude indi-cators used on lower-performance aircraft (not jet fighters or airliners, for example) have *suction- (vacuum) driven* or *air pressure–driven* rotors. A description of these systems will follow our discussion of the instruments themselves.

The gyro is universally mounted with a vertical spin axis. It is linked to the *attitude sphere* (the rotating ball or curved card on the instrument face),

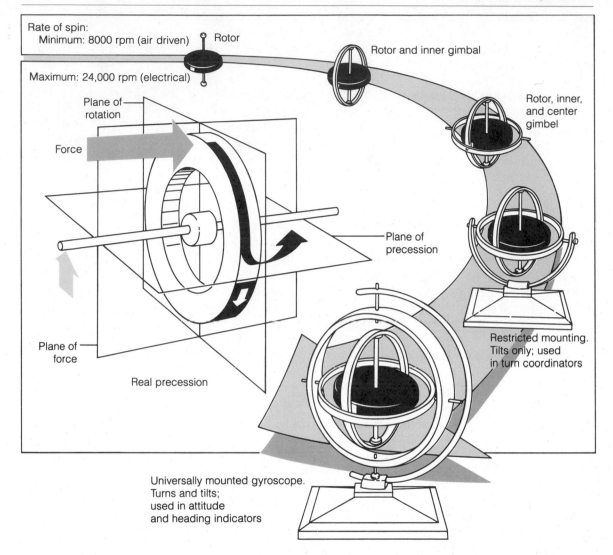

Rate of spin:
Minimum: 8000 rpm (air driven)   Rotor
Maximum: 24,000 rpm (electrical)

Rotor and inner gimbal

Rotor, inner, and center gimbel

Plane of rotation

Force

Plane of precession

Plane of force

Real precession

Restricted mounting. Tilts only; used in turn coordinators

Universally mounted gyroscope. Turns and tilts; used in attitude and heading indicators

Figure 4.17 The components and mounting of gyroscopes.

which is marked with a precise horizon line. A miniature airplane is fixed (we say "*fixed*" even though it is adjustable by the pilot within a narrow range) to the instrument case. When the airplane maneuvers in three-dimensional space, the attitude sphere remains rigid with the gyroscope, in line with the earth's horizon, while the miniature airplane rotates about it with the rest of the aircraft.

Markings and use.   The attitude indicator is a graphic display of the sky and earth with respect to the airplane. Modern instruments have a gray or blue "sky" and a black or brown "earth" on the horizon sphere. On older instruments, both are painted black and so are, understandably, harder to interpret.

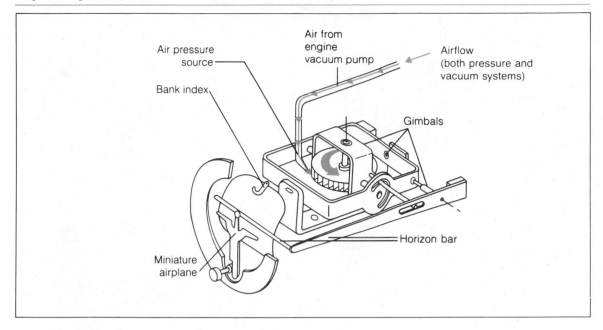

The attitude sphere and horizon line stay aligned with the earth's surface when you bank the airplane, showing the miniature airplane in a bank identical to the one held by the real airplane. A pointer at the top of the case moves along a series of index marks corresponding to 10, 20, 30, and 60 degrees of bank on either side of center. A change of pitch of the airplane is also reflected instantaneously on the instrument by the movement of the miniature airplane above or below the horizon bar. Figure 4.19 illustrates the attitude indicator display for various flight situations.

Since the gyroscope winds down without power, it must be *erected* (forced by precession into proper orientation) at the beginning of each flight. This is accomplished automatically in most airplanes. In some airplanes certified for aerobatics, the gyroscope can be *caged* (erected manually), but these instruments are expensive and not common. The pitch adjustment knob is used to move the miniature airplane upward or downward as needed to match the horizon line for any given trimmed flight condition. Never attempt to adjust the miniature airplane while maneuvering because an inaccurate setting will probably result.

Limitations.   For most suction-driven or pressure-driven instruments, there are limits of motion beyond which the gyros will "tumble," or lose their alignment. Your instructor will inform you if any such limits apply to your airplane. You should also find this information in the Pilot's Operating Handbook, since each instrument design has certain unique capabilities and limitations. But when the instrument is properly maintained and operated, it is very reliable.

Figure 4.18 Mechanism of the attitude indicator.

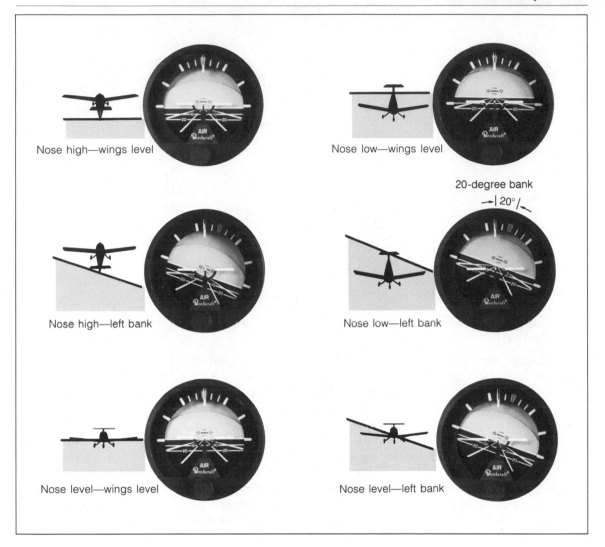

Figure 4.19 Attitude indicator
displays for various flight situations.

The Turn Coordinator

Function.   The **turn coordinator** is actually two instruments in one. The
airplane symbol, shown in Figure 4.20, indicates the airplane's rate of turn
once a constant bank angle is established. The ball in the tube, called the
inclinometer, provides information about the *quality* of the turn.

Mechanism.   The gyroscope in the turn coordinator is installed with the
fore and aft axis of the mounting canted slightly with respect to the airplane's longitudinal axis (see Figure 4.21). This makes the gyroscope sense
motions about both the airplane's yaw and roll axes, but primarily about
the yaw axis. The mounting is restricted to eliminate any reaction to pitching
motion.

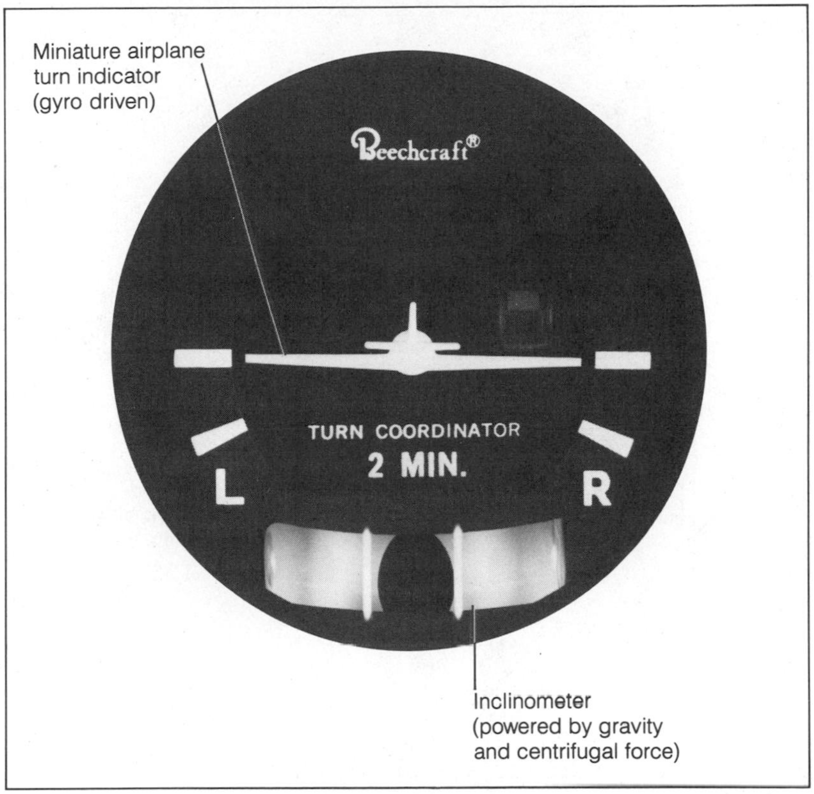

Figure 4.20 The turn coordinator.

The airplane symbol reacts to any roll input by rotating in the correct direction. When the bank angle is constant, the airplane symbol deflects proportional to the rate of turn.

The inclinometer is simply a black ball in a curved liquid-filled tube. The position of the ball is determined by the centrifugal and gravity forces present in the turn.

Markings and use.   The turn coordinator depicts a miniature airplane viewed from the rear (see Figure 4.20). Below the airplane are two reference marks and the printed legend 2 Min, or 2 Min Turn. This abbreviation means that if the airplane is banked so that the miniature airplane's wing tip is on the reference line, the real airplane will fly a 360-degree turn (go around in a circle) in 2 minutes. To beginning pilots, this time reference may seem of little value. But for instrument-rated pilots, who must on occasion fly precisely timed turns, it is of considerable assistance. This rate of turn (called **standard rate of turn**—3 degrees per second) may be a convenient and comfortable rate to use for normal en route movements and approaches to landing maneuvers.

Factors controlling turn rate.   An airplane's rate of turn depends on both airspeed and angle of bank. For any given airspeed, the greater the bank

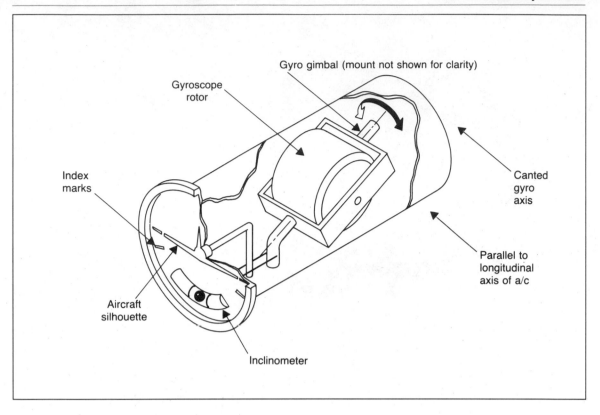

Figure 4.21 Mechanism of the turn
coordinator.

angle, the greater the turn rate. Conversely, for any given bank angle, the
greater the airspeed, the slower the turn rate.

The bank angle required to produce a standard rate turn can be approximated by the formula:

$$\text{Bank angle for standard rate turn} = \frac{\text{Airspeed}}{10} + 7 \text{ knots or } 5 \text{ mph}$$

This equation shows that as airspeed increases, so does the bank angle
needed to maintain a standard rate turn. For instance, if you were flying at
100 mph, you would need:

$$\frac{100 \text{ mph}}{10} + 5 \text{ mph} = 15 \text{ degrees bank angle}$$

Increasing the speed to 200 mph means you would need 25 degrees of bank
to make a standard rate turn.

Factors controlling turn radius.   Turn radius is the size of the circle you
scribe in the sky while turning. The higher the airspeed, the larger the
circle, for any given bank angle. If you hold airspeed constant, then steep

bank angles yield a smaller turn radius than do shallow ones. The tightest turning radius is obtained using a steep bank angle while flying at the slowest possible airspeed (not the safest combination of conditions).

Slips and Skids

The inclinometer registers the quality, or coordination, of the turn. (Review coordination in Chapter 2 if necessary.) If the ball is inside the turn (i.e., you are turning left and the ball is to the left), the airplane is in a **slip**. This condition results when the rate of turn is too slow for the angle of bank. The lack of centrifugal force moves the ball to the inside of the turn. To achieve coordinated flight from a slip requires that the bank be decreased or that more rudder pressure be applied in the direction of the turn (step on the ball), or a combination of both.

When the ball moves to the outside of the turn (i.e., you are turning left and the ball is to the right), the airplane is in a **skid**. Skid means that the rate of turn is too fast for the angle of bank. Excessive centrifugal force causes the ball to move to the outside of the turn. Correcting this situation requires an increase in bank angle or an increase in rudder pressure opposite the direction of the turn (again, step on the ball), or a combination of both.

The Turn and Slip Indicator

Function.   Some airplanes are equipped with a turn and slip indicator (Figure 4.22) instead of a turn coordinator, since it performs a *similar* function. In fact, the turn and slip is the predecessor of the turn coordinator.

Mechanism.   The fore and aft axis of the mounting in the turn and slip indicator mechanism is parallel to the airplane's longitudinal axis. This

Figure 4.22 Turn and slip indicator.

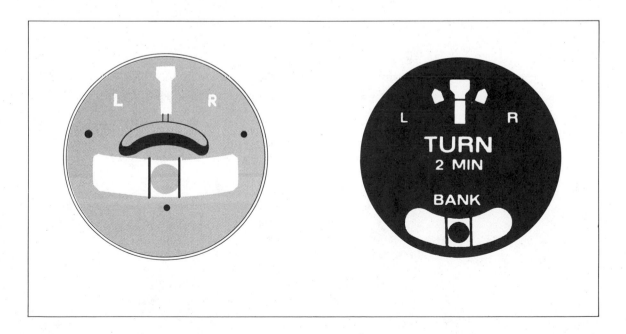

means that it reacts only to yaw motion. Neither roll nor pitch motions are sensed by this instrument.

Markings and use.   The display on the turn and slip is a vertical needle that deflects proportional to the rate of turn. When the needle is deflected one width, the airplane is making a standard rate turn. Some instruments have a special mark called the **doghouse**; on these, a standard rate turn is when the needle is aligned with the doghouse.

The inclinometer is exactly the same on both the turn and slip and the turn coordinator.

The turn coordinator versus the turn and slip.   The difference between the turn and slip and the turn coordinator (aside from the display) is the feedback provided during the recovery from steep turns. It is not difficult to turn sharply enough to make either instrument *peg* (the needle or the airplane symbol hits its stop on the instrument). Since the turn and slip reacts only to yaw, it will stay pegged as long as the turn rate is greater than the value that pegs the needle. If you were to begin to level out, you would not see any reaction on the turn and slip until your turn rate had slowed considerably. The turn coordinator, on the other hand, senses both yaw and roll. The moment you begin to recover from a steep turn, the turn coordinator reacts, indicating that you have responded correctly. If your flight visibility is good, this difference is immaterial since you can easily see what is happening. However, if you inadvertently (or carelessly) fly into poor visibility, the situation changes. The lack of meaningful feedback from the turn and slip is a drawback; in fact, it is the reason the turn coordinator was developed. Even in the steepest turns, the turn coordinator will immediately react when you start to roll out, showing that you responded correctly.

The Heading Indicator
Function.   The **heading indicator**, also called the **directional gyro (DG)**, displays the airplane's heading from a gyroscopically rigid platform. The DG's heading must be set initially to agree with the magnetic compass (before takeoff or during straight and level, unaccelerated flight). The DG will maintain an accurate heading reference throughout a wide range of attitudes and maneuvers. It has none of the errors associated with the magnetic compass.

Mechanism.   The axis of the rotor in a heading indicator is aligned horizontally, as shown in Figure 4.23. The universal mounting allows the gyroscope to remain in a fixed position as the airplane turns. Gears connect the mount to the circular compass card on the face of the instrument.

Markings and use.   The display on a DG is a **planform** airplane symbol (planform means viewed from above) superimposed over circular compass cards. The airplane symbol is fixed to the case while the compass card

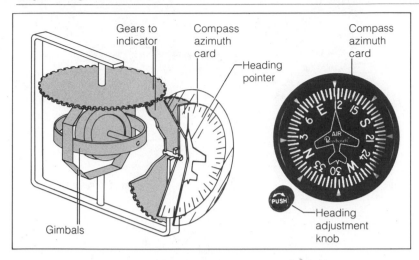

Figure 4.23 Mechanism of the heading indicator.

rotates. The current heading is read under the lubber line at the top of the case.

Limitations.   The heading indicator must be checked regularly against the magnetic compass and reset if necessary. Precession, caused by friction in the bearings, can cause the gyro to drift. These checks should be made about every 15 minutes, while the airplane is in straight and level, unaccelerated flight.

Power Systems for Instruments That Have Gyroscopes

The wonderful properties of the gyroscope are available only as long as the rotor is kept spinning. Each instrument uses either air pressure or electricity to power its rotor.

Vacuum or air-pressure systems.   Because of their low cost and relative simplicity, vacuum or air-pressure systems power the attitude and heading indicators on most general-aviation airplanes. **Vacuum systems** begin with an engine-driven vacuum pump that converts the engine's rotary motion directly into a source for low-pressure air. The suction produced by the pump, transmitted through tubes connected to the gyroscopes, draws air over the rotors and keeps them moving (see Figure 4.24).

Positive pressure systems are similar in design, but they place the pump at the opposite end of the system. A vacuum or pressure gauge in the cockpit allows you to monitor the operation of the system.

Electrical systems.   An electrically driven gyroscope is actually an electric motor, where the motor's rotating member doubles as the gyroscope rotor. An indicator on the face of the instrument is usually provided to warn you when the power supply has been interrupted.

Figure 4.24 Vacuum system.

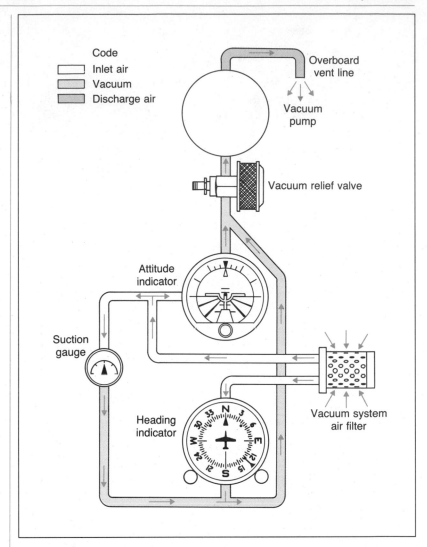

Code
☐ Inlet air
▨ Vacuum
▨ Discharge air

Overboard vent line

Vacuum pump

Vacuum relief valve

Attitude indicator

Suction gauge

Heading indicator

Vacuum system air filter

Redundancy.   As part of your flight training, you will learn how to maintain control of the airplane solely by reference to the flight instruments. In order to do this, either the attitude indicator or the turn coordinator must be operational (you will normally have both). The attitude indicator and directional gyro are usually air powered. The turn coordinator is normally electric. The use of different power sources for the attitude indicator and turn coordinator is designed to reduce the chance of having both instruments inoperative simultaneously. This **redundancy** is vital on any airplane equipped for instrument flight.

USING THE FLIGHT INSTRUMENTS TOGETHER
No single instrument in the panel presents enough information to control the airplane and its flight path. Your limited instrument training will intro-

duce you to the concept of *scanning* the instruments. The instrument panel of most airplanes has been standardized to facilitate this process.

Figure 4.25 shows a panel with all the flight instruments in a standard layout. The most important instruments are arranged in a T configuration. The instruments across the top provide pitch information. The vertical group presents directional data. Notice that the attitude indicator is the only one that provides both. For that reason, it is in the most prominent position, the center of the panel.

The turn coordinator (or turn and slip indicator) and the VSI fit into the corners not occupied by the **basic T** instruments. The turn coordinator (or turn and slip) acts as a backup for the attitude indicator, as mentioned previously. The VSI provides valuable trend information.

Learning to use the flight instruments skillfully is one of the greatest rewards—and challenges—in flying. The instrument training you receive as part of your private pilot curriculum is for emergency use only. With additional training, you can develop those skills into an instrument rating.

COMPOSITE FLYING

Although you will see that the airplane can be controlled by reference to the flight instruments only, just as it can be flown without reference to any instruments at all, neither method is used exclusively by pilots all the time. Even in bad weather, instrument pilots occasionally glance out of the cockpit to check for visual references. Pilots flying VFR sometimes consult the instruments to confirm a flight condition assumed from the position of the real horizon, wing tips, and nose.

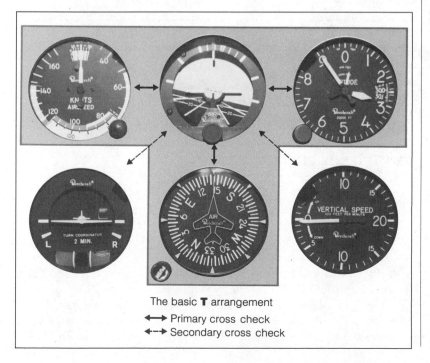

The basic **T** arrangement
⟷ Primary cross check
⟵⇢ Secondary cross check

Figure 4.25 Standard instrument panel layout.

This process of cross-referencing visual data from the world outside the cockpit to instrument readings within the cockpit is called **composite flying**. Just as one instrument is used to confirm the readings of another, so the cues given to the pilot from both external and internal sources are used to form an accurate picture of how the airplane is really flying.

Modern flight instruments and the quality of aeronautical design make piloting easier today than it was even a decade ago. But the true capabilities of your airplane will only be realized after you have learned to use these instruments correctly. The best flight instruments are no substitute for sound judgment and respect for one's limitations.

KEY TERMS

above ground level (AGL)
absolute altitude
acceleration-deceleration error
airspeed indicator
altimeter
attitude indicator
basic T
calibrated airspeed (CAS)
compass correction card
composite flying
deviation
flight instruments
friction error
gyroscope
heading indicator
inclinometer
indicated airspeed (IAS)
indicated altitude
knots
Kollsman window
magnetic compass
mean sea level (MSL)

outside air temperature (OAT)
    gauge
pitot-static instruments
pitot tube
precession
pressure-altitude
skid
slip
static ports
true airspeed (TAS)
true altitude
turn and slip indicator
turn coordinator
turn error
variation
vertical speed indicator (VSI)
V_{FE}
V_{NE}
V_{NO}
V_{S0}
V_{S1}

PROFICIENCY CHECK

1. Name the flight instrument(s) that require(s) static pressure in order to operate. Name the instrument(s) requiring pitot pressure.

2. Airspeed is not the same as ground speed. True or false? Why or why not? How is calibrated airspeed different from indicated airspeed?

3. Name the four kinds of altitudes important to pilots and the reference datum (basis for measurement) assigned to each.

4. Two airplanes are sitting on the ramp preparing to taxi. The tower informs the two pilots that the current altimeter setting is 29.90. They set this value into their Kollsman windows as required. Airplane A's altimeter is shown on page 127, as is airplane B's. Which altimeter is within recommended tolerances? Airplane A? Airplane B? Both? Neither? Explain your answer.

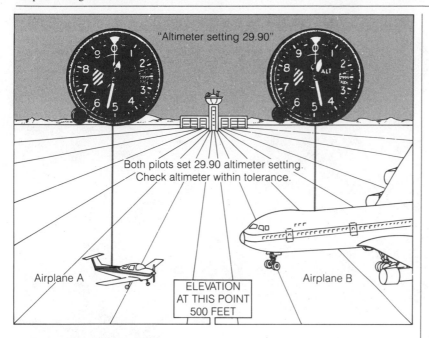

"Altimeter setting 29.90"

Both pilots set 29.90 altimeter setting.
Check altimeter within tolerance.

Airplane A

Airplane B

ELEVATION
AT THIS POINT
500 FEET

5. Name the function of the magnetic compass. Name the operating limitations mentioned in the text that apply to the magnetic compass and describe the recommended procedure for overcoming each limitation.

6. What are the two properties of the gyroscope that make it useful in airplane instrumentation? Name three gyroscopic instruments and their functions.

7. Give two reasons why most general-aviation airplanes have both a vacuum power system and an electric power system.

8. What is the basic T of airplane instrumentation? What is composite flying and why is it important?

A false balance is abomination to the Lord:
but a just weight is His delight.

Proverbs 11:1

C H E C K P O I N T S

How does the weight of an airplane affect the way it flies? ✈ How does the location of an airplane's cargo affect the way it flies? ✈ How do pilots calculate an airplane's weight and balance? ✈ What are the effects on flight if an airplane is loaded near or beyond its balance limits? ✈ How does the Pilot's Operating Handbook present weight and balance data?

AIRPLANE WEIGHT AND BALANCE

Barnstormers used to entice customers into their airplanes with a promise that they would "defy gravity." Since gravity holds us firmly to the earth's surface and the airplane allowed them to "float" up in the air, this sales pitch was very effective.

The physical property of weight is an important element in nearly all aspects of human activity and technology. It is an especially vital consideration in the design of aircraft because the technology of aviation is specifically aimed at overcoming the effects of gravity and weight.

If the weight that we carry increases by more than a few pounds, we find that it is more difficult for us to perform certain tasks. An otherwise pleasant hike in the woods can become an ordeal when carrying a 50-pound backpack. Similarly, since *lift* opposes *weight* in flight, anything that changes airplane weight necessarily changes the lift required for level flight.

The *distribution* of weight is critical on an airplane. Since the tail surfaces control movement about the center of gravity (CG), any change in the airplane's center of gravity affects its stability and control. Changing the position of the CG also affects the total lift the wing must produce, even when the aircraft's weight remains constant. It is clear that the airplane's *weight* and *balance* are of fundamental concern to pilots. An appreciation of these concerns, plus forethought and care when you load your airplane with passengers and cargo, will assure you of a safe and efficient flight. As you progress in your flying career, you will probably operate larger, more powerful airplanes. Because of these airplanes' greater flexibility in carrying passengers and cargo, you will have to pay even closer attention to their weight and balance limits than you do to those of your training airplane. More capability brings with it more responsibility. High-performance jet transports have elaborate procedures for controlling their weight and balance. The Anglo-French Concorde, a supersonic airliner, has a complicated system of fuel pumps and storage tanks just to maintain its balance during flight.

As a private pilot, your knowledge of weight and balance will not need to be so sophisticated, but the principles involved are the same and the need for safety is just as great. The time you spend now learning the fundamentals of this important area will be repaid later in many hours of safe and efficient flying.

PRINCIPLES OF WEIGHT AND BALANCE

As a child you might have spent a number of happy hours traveling up and down on the end of a teeter-totter. All you needed to make it work was a friend about the same size. In fact, one of the first things you learned about a teeter-totter was that it took two people to make it work. Sitting on it by yourself simply gave you a very low and uncomfortable seat, since there was nobody on the other end to *balance* your weight. Similarly, when your friends ganged up on you and piled onto the opposite seat, you were left up in the air, unable to overcome the force of their collective weight. When they climbed off, leaving you and your original partner in place, the teeter-totter resumed its normal action.

A more precise way to describe the actions of a teeter-totter is to say that you and your friend represented weights in balance on an **arm** (extension of a lever) on either side of a *fulcrum,* or the support point of a lever (see Figure 5.1). The force of your body (its weight) acting at the end of this lever arm is called a **moment**. Since you and your friend were roughly the same weight and the positions of the teeter-totter seats were equidistant from the fulcrum, the moments that your weights produced were *balanced,* and each of you "floated" easily up and down. Your *equilibrium* was disturbed only when you kicked your feet against the ground.

This relationship can be expressed by the mathematical formula:

$$\text{Moment} = \text{Weight} \times \text{Arm}$$

Naturally, this relationship can be rearranged to solve for any value that happens to be missing, such as:

$$\text{Weight} = \frac{\text{Moment}}{\text{Arm}} \quad \text{or} \quad \text{Arm} = \frac{\text{Moment}}{\text{Weight}}$$

Let us say that you and your friend weighed 60 pounds each and that you were on a teeter-totter 200 inches long. The support point (fulcrum) is in the middle, 100 inches from both of you. Each of you produced a moment about the fulcrum of 100 inches × 60 pounds, or 6000 inch-pounds.

Recall from Chapter 2 that the center of gravity (CG) is the point where the entire weight of an object appears to be concentrated for balance purposes. When the teeter-totter balances, it means that the CG is aligned with the fulcrum (see Figure 5.1).

What happened if two more friends climbed on the other end of the teeter-totter? The balance was upset, and the heavy end sank to the ground,

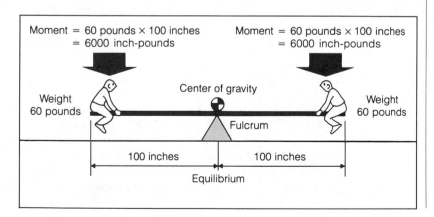

Figure 5.1 A balanced teeter-totter.

Figure 5.2 An unbalanced teeter-totter.

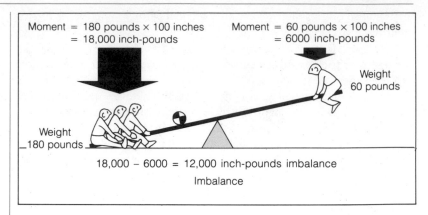

Moment = 180 pounds × 100 inches = 18,000 inch-pounds

Moment = 60 pounds × 100 inches = 6000 inch-pounds

Weight 60 pounds

Weight 180 pounds

18,000 − 6000 = 12,000 inch-pounds imbalance

Imbalance

leaving you suspended in midair. More precisely, when your friends climbed aboard, they shifted the CG of the teeter-totter toward them, away from the support point. Figure 5.2 shows that three children (60 pounds each) create a moment of 180 pounds × 100 inches, or 18,000 inch-pounds. This easily overpowers the 6000 inch-pounds you are producing.

There are two ways to make the teeter-totter balance again. The first method is to shift the children until the CG once again falls over the support. The other possibility is to calculate the location of the new CG and move the support to that point.

Shifting Weight to Move the CG

If we are going to move the group of three children so that the teeter-totter will balance, where, exactly, should they be placed? Since we are looking for a distance, or arm, the following form of the moment equation applies:

$$\text{Arm} = \frac{\text{Moment}}{\text{Weight}}$$

We are trying to balance your 6000 inch-pounds with their weight of 180 pounds, so the calculation becomes:

$$\frac{6000 \text{ inch-pounds}}{180 \text{ pounds}} = 33.33 \text{ inches}$$

The three children should therefore move to a point 33.33 inches from the support (see Figure 5.3). Checking the moments for this new configuration:

$$180 \text{ pounds} \times 33.33 \text{ inches} = 6000 \text{ inch-pounds}$$

$$60 \text{ pounds} \times 100 \text{ inches} = 6000 \text{ inch-pounds}$$

Since the moments are equal, the CG is once again aligned with the support.

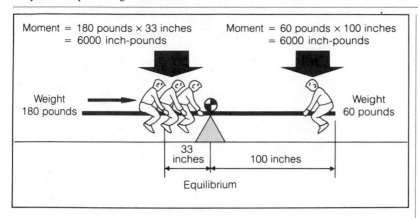

Moment = 180 pounds × 33 inches = 6000 inch-pounds

Moment = 60 pounds × 100 inches = 6000 inch-pounds

Weight 180 pounds

Weight 60 pounds

33 inches | 100 inches

Equilibrium

Calculating the Position of the CG

Now assume that all four children are left in their original positions on the teeter-totter. We will have to apply the second method and figure out where to move the support to make the teeter-totter balance again.

As before, we will measure all distances from the fulcrum's existing location. But now we will need to identify direction as well as distance so that we can know which way to move the fulcrum. (In many situations, common sense will identify the direction, but not always, so we must also be able to express directions mathematically.) Therefore, we will identify all distances (arms) on the *left* side of the fulcrum as "minus" and those on the *right* as "plus" (see Figure 5.4). The assignment of "plus" and "minus" is arbitrary. We could reverse the convention (make left "plus" and right "minus") without changing the results. Once a convention is selected, however, it must be used consistently throughout the problem. The procedure to calculate the new CG begins as follows:

1. Add up all the weights to get total weight.

2. Calculate all the moments and add them up to get total moment.

3. Divide the total moment by total weight, using the following mathematical formula:

$$CG\ inches = \frac{Total\ moment\ inch\text{-}pounds}{Total\ weight\ pounds}$$

This answer is the location of the CG from the fulcrum's existing location, with the children as shown in Figure 5.4.

Additional data are needed to calculate the new CG. Since we will be moving the support point, the *empty* teeter-totter will no longer be balanced. We must account for this in our calculations. Assume that the teeter-totter board weighs 60 pounds. Its arm is zero because its CG is exactly at the fulcrum when it is empty.

Figure 5.4 Assigning directions to the arms of each side of the fulcrum.

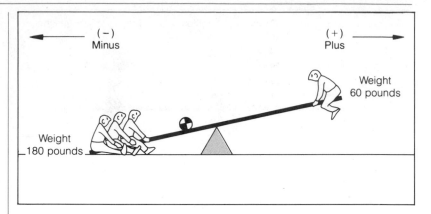

The easiest way to calculate the new CG is to make a four-column table as follows:

Item	Weight (pounds)	Arm (inches)	Moment (in-lb)
1 Child	60	+100	+6,000
3 Children	180	−100	−18,000
Teeter-totter	60	0	0
Total	300	~	−12,000

Then apply the formula to these figures:

$$\text{CG location} = \frac{-12{,}000 \text{ inch-pounds}}{300 \text{ pounds}} = -40 \text{ inches}$$

That is, moving the support 40 inches in the minus direction (left) should balance the teeter-totter (see Figure 5.5).

In checking the moments about the new fulcrum, remember that the teeter-totter board contributes:

(3 children)   180 pounds × 60 inches   = 108,000 inch-pounds

(1 child)   60 pounds × 140 inches
+(Teeter-totter)   60 pounds × 40 inches   = 108,000 inch-pounds

Weight and Balance Terms

In the teeter-totter example, all the distances were measured from the original fulcrum because it was the most convenient location. The teeter-totter worked correctly only when the CG fell right on the fulcrum. In contrast, an airplane has an allowable *range* of CG locations rather than one fixed

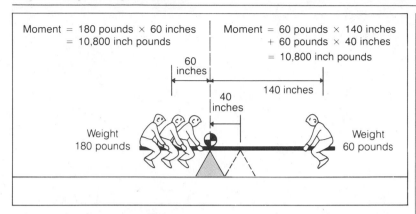

Figure 5.5 Moving the fulcrum to the new center of gravity location.

position. Therefore, we will calculate where the airplane's CG is located and verify that it lies within the allowable range.

The datum.   On an airplane, the manufacturer chooses an imaginary location from which to measure all distances. This fixed reference is called a **datum.** The actual location of the datum is immaterial, but, once established, *all locations must be measured from the same datum*. The location of the CG is described with respect to the datum. This concept is illustrated in Figure 5.6. Note that, by convention, all distances aft of the datum are positive, and those forward of the datum are negative.

Terms for the empty airplane.   The term **licensed empty weight** or **empty weight** is used to describe an airplane with all installed equipment, hydraulic fluid, and all *unusable* fuel and oil. Every airplane has some fuel and oil that cannot be completely drained or used by the engine. For weight and balance purposes, this small amount of fluid is considered part of the empty airframe.

   Since you will never fly without engine oil, the empty weight described here is not a particularly convenient value to use. A more practical weight is that of the empty airplane (as described here) plus the normal supply of engine oil. The term **basic empty weight** is used to describe this condition.

   The licensed empty weight or basic empty weight is obtained by *actually weighing the airplane*. The empty airplane moment and CG are computed from these actual readings. This information is entered on the aircraft's **weight and balance record,** which is required, by FAR 91.31, to be on the airplane at all times.

Terms for the loaded airplane.   Useful load includes all **usable fuel,** passengers, and cargo (and *usable oil* if licensed empty weight is used instead of basic empty weight). The weight and balance data in the Pilot's Operating Handbook will have the information you need to determine the amount each item will contribute to the loaded airplane.

Figure 5.6 Datum versus center of gravity location.

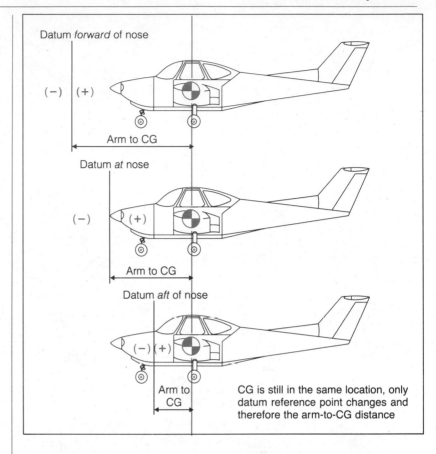

Gross weight is the actual total weight of the airplane and everything it is carrying. It is the combination of empty weight and useful load. Some manufacturers specify maximum weights for various operating conditions. **Maximum ramp weight** is the highest weight approved for ground maneuvering. It includes a fuel allowance for starting, taxiing, and engine run-up. **Maximum takeoff weight** applies to the start of the takeoff roll. The airplane must be at or below **maximum landing weight** before the landing touchdown. If none of these special weights is mentioned in the Pilot's Operating Handbook, then one *maximum gross weight* applies to all ground and flight operations.

The weight of fuel and oil.   The following values will be used in the calculations you make later in the chapter to determine balance: gasoline weighs 6 pounds per gallon; oil weighs 7.5 pounds per gallon (4 quarts).

DETERMINING GROSS WEIGHT AND CENTER OF GRAVITY

In the teeter-totter example, we used the *computation method*. It demonstrates the principles of weight and balance most completely. However, its use for airplanes requires multiplying and adding large numbers. Even if you were to use your trusty pocket calculator, there are plenty of chances for error before you are through. For this reason, most manufacturers provide tables or graphs (or both) to simplify the process. We will work through examples of each method.

The Computation Method

Assume that your four-place airplane has a maximum ramp weight of 2650 pounds. Your first step is to compile a list of all people and items you intend to load onto the airplane and note the actual weight of each. You also need the weight and balance data for the airplane when it is empty. Your list might look like that shown in Table 5.1.

Table 5.1 Sample List of Items for a Flight

Item	Weight (pounds)
Basic empty weight	1600
Pilot and front-seat passenger	340[a]
Rear-seat passengers	340[a]
Baggage	35
Fuel (55 gallons at 6 lb per gallon)	330
Total	2645

[a]Assumes a standard value of 170 pounds for each occupant. You should always use actual weights whenever possible.

Add up the weights first, just to verify that you can take everything and everyone on your list. If you find that this load is within the legal limit, you still must determine whether everything is safely balanced. To do so, first consult the Pilot's Operating Handbook to find the arms for each item listed. Figure 5.7 shows one way this data may be presented. The CG of the empty airplane is, of course, obtained from the papers on board that airplane. In this example, the CG of the basic empty airplane is 82.0 inches aft of the datum.

Now expand your list to a four-column table with the same headings used in the teeter-totter example (item, weight, arm, and moment). Opposite each item list the appropriate arm. Multiply each weight by its respective arm to fill in the moment column. Find the total moment. Table 5.2 presents the computations for the items in Table 5.1.

Table 5.2 The Computation of Takeoff Weight and Moment

Item	Weight (pounds)	Arm (inches)	Moment (inch-pounds)
Basic empty weight	1600	82.0	131,200
Pilot and front-seat passenger	340	85.5	29,070
Rear-seat passengers	340	118.0	40,120
Baggage	35	140.0	4,900
Fuel	330	95.0	31,350
Total	2645		236,640

Figure 5.7 Sample loading diagram.

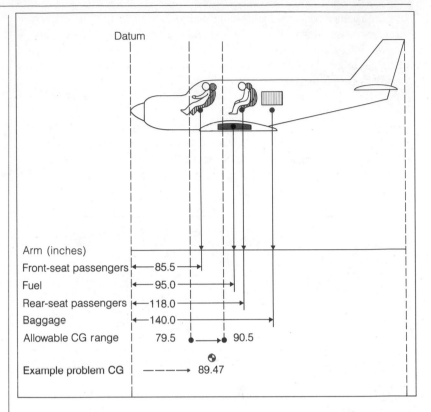

Arm (inches)

Front-seat passengers	85.5
Fuel	95.0
Rear-seat passengers	118.0
Baggage	140.0
Allowable CG range	79.5 ● ━━➤ ● 90.5
Example problem CG	━ ━ ━ ➤ 89.47

Finally, divide the total moment by the total weight to find the location of the CG:

$$\text{Takeoff CG} = \frac{236{,}640 \text{ inch-pounds}}{2645 \text{ pounds}} - 89.47 \text{ inches}$$

When you refer to Figure 5.7, you see that the CG location for the takeoff condition falls within the allowable range.

You must also check the airplane's balance at the anticipated landing weight before you take off. Assume that you will burn 45 gallons of fuel during this flight. Subtract the weight and moment of this amount of fuel from the takeoff totals, and compute the new CG, as in Table 5.3 and the accompanying equation.

Table 5.3 The Computation of Landing Weight and Moment

Item	Weight (pounds)	Arm (inches)	Moment (in-lb)
Takeoff	2645		236,640
Fuel burned	− 270	95.0	− 25,650
Landing	2375		210,990

$$\text{Landing CG} = \frac{210{,}990 \text{ inch-pounds}}{2375 \text{ pounds}} = 88.84 \text{ inches}$$

The center of gravity has shifted slightly but is still within the allowable range. You can conclude that this flight is safe from a weight and balance standpoint.

The Tabular Method

With the appropriate forms from the Pilot's Operating Handbook, you are ready to figure a sample weight and balance problem using *tabular* data. Figure 5.8 shows the worksheet we will be using. Notice that the "arm" column is missing from this worksheet. Moment information is simply looked up in a table rather than calculated, relieving you of some messy math (see Figure 5.9). Here are the steps to take:

1. Find the basic empty weight and moment from the data on board the airplane and enter them on the worksheet. In this particular handbook, the moment is divided by 100 to correspond to the useful load weights and moment tables. The data are presented this way to make the numbers more manageable.

2. Record the weight and moment of each useful load item (except fuel) to be carried on the airplane for this flight (see Figure 5.9b and c). Since our sample aircraft is a two-passenger model, let us assume that both seats

Figure 5.8 Weight and balance form used for the tabular method.

WEIGHT AND BALANCE LOADING FORM

MODEL _____ DATE _____
SERIAL NO. _____ REG. NO. _____

ITEM	WEIGHT	MOM/100
BASIC EMPTY CONDITION		
OCCUPANT - LEFT	170	151
OCCUPANT - RIGHT	170	151
BAGGAGE	—	—
SUB TOTAL ZERO FUEL CONDITION	1530	1325
FUEL LOADING (gal.)	150	122
SUB TOTAL RAMP CONDITION	1680	1447
*LESS FUEL FOR START, TAXI AND RUNUP	-5	-4
SUB TOTAL TAKEOFF CONDITION	1675	1443
LESS FUEL TO DESTINATION	-120	-98
LANDING CONDITION	1555	1345

*Fuel for start, taxi, and runup is normally 5 pounds at an average moment/100 of 4.

USEFUL LOAD WEIGHTS AND MOMENTS

USABLE FUEL (6.0 LB/GAL)
ARM = 81.5

GALLONS	WEIGHT (LBS)	MOMENT/100 (LB-IN)
5	30	24
10	60	49
15	90	73
20	120	98
25	150	122
29	174	142

(a)

USEFUL LOAD WEIGHTS AND MOMENTS

BAGGAGE*
ARM = 119

WEIGHT (LBS)	MOMENT/100 (LB-IN)
10	12
20	24
30	36
40	48
50	60
60	71
70	83
80	95
90	107
100	119
110	131
120	143

*Baggage shall be prevented from shifting by using the baggage net.

(b)

USEFUL LOAD WEIGHTS AND MOMENTS

OCCUPANTS

WEIGHT (LBS)	FWD POSITION ARM = 89	AFT POSITION ARM = 97
	MOMENT/100 (LB-IN)	
100	89	97
110	98	107
120	107	116
130	116	126
140	125	136
150	134	146
160	142	155
170	151	165
180	160	175
190	169	184
200	178	194
210	187	204
220	196	213
230	205	223
240	214	233
250	223	243

(c)

Figure 5.9 Tabular weight versus moment data.

will be occupied for a local training flight and that no baggage will be carried. (Note: The value used in the example assumes the seats are in the forward position.)

3. Get a subtotal for the weight and moment columns. This gives you the weight and moment of the airplane with no fuel load, or its *zero fuel condition.*

4. Now assume that you are going to fill the tanks for flight: 25 gallons × 6 pounds per gallon = 150 pounds. Figure 5.9a gives you this information and its moment on the airplane. Enter this value in the space marked Fuel Loading and add it to the zero fuel condition value. This gives you another subtotal, **ramp condition,** the weight of the airplane ready to taxi.

5. Subtract the moment and weight of fuel allowed for start, taxi, and runup. This information is provided at the bottom of the worksheet. This new subtotal gives you the **takeoff condition.**

6. A later chapter will show you how to compute fuel consumption for a cross-country flight. For now, let us assume that you will burn 20 gallons. Consulting Figure 5.9a again, you see that this amount of fuel weighs 120 pounds and has a moment value of 98 inch-pounds/100. Since this is fuel burned, *subtract* it from the takeoff condition to determine the airplane's *landing condition.*

7. Now consult Figures 5.10 and 5.11. You want to make sure that the zero fuel condition, takeoff condition, and landing condition moments all fall within the allowable tolerances of CG travel for each weight. The table and the chart show the same information, so use the one that is easiest for you. We will demonstrate both. Remember that all moment values are divided by 100.

In the table shown in Figure 5.10, the moment of 1325 inch-pounds for a zero fuel condition of 1530 pounds falls well within the limits of 1304

MOMENT LIMITS VS WEIGHT

WEIGHT (LBS)	MOMENT/100 (LB-IN)		WEIGHT (LBS)	MOMENT/100 (LB-IN)	
	MIN MOMENT	MAX MOMENT		MIN MOMENT	MAX MOMENT
1100	935	978	1400	1190	1245
1110	944	987	1410	1198	1253
1120	952	996	1420	1207	1262
1130	960	1005	1430	1216	1271
1140	969	1013	1440	1224	1280
1150	978	1022	1450	1232	1289
1160	986	1031	1460	1241	1298
1170	994	1040	1470	1250	1307
1180	1003	1049	1480	1259	1316
1190	1012	1058	1490	1268	1325
1200	1020	1067	1500	1277	1334
1210	1028	1076	1510	1286	1342
1220	1037	1085	1520	1295	1351
1230	1046	1093	1530	1304	1360
1240	1054	1102	1540	1313	1369
1250	1062	1111	1550	1322	1378
1260	1071	1120	1560	1331	1387
1270	1080	1129	1570	1341	1396
1280	1088	1138	1580	1350	1405
1290	1096	1147	1590	1359	1414
1300	1105	1156	1600	1368	1422
1310	1114	1165	1610	1377	1431
1320	1122	1173	1620	1387	1440
1330	1130	1182	1630	1396	1449
1340	1139	1191	1640	1405	1458
1350	1148	1200	1650	1414	1467
1360	1156	1209	1660	1423	1476
1370	1164	1218	1670	1433	1485
1380	1173	1227	1675	1437	1489
1390	1182	1236			

Figure 5.10 Weight versus moment in tabular form.

inch-pounds (minimum) and 1360 inch-pounds (maximum). The takeoff condition moment of 1443 inch-pounds (corresponding to a takeoff weight of 1675 pounds) likewise falls within the minimum and maximum values for that weight. The landing weight of 1555 pounds, however, does not fall evenly on the table. You can *interpolate* between values on the table by subtracting the minimum moment for 1550 pounds from the minimum moment for 1560 pounds and making that difference *proportional* to the number of pounds your actual landing weight is above 1550. Since 1555 is exactly halfway between 1550 and 1560, you should take half the difference between the two moment values as the correct moment value for the actual landing weight. This results in a minimum moment of 1326.5 inch-pounds. Follow the same procedure for the maximum moment values; this results in a maximum moment of 1382.5 inch-pounds for your actual landing weight. Since your calculated moment is 1345 inch-pounds, you see at once that you fit well within this range.

Alternatively, you may prefer to use the chart shown in Figure 5.11. The weights lines run horizontally with the weight values listed on the right-hand side of the chart. Moment values run up the left side of the chart and refer to the diagonal lines that increase in value as you go up the chart. To solve our landing condition problem, find 1555 pounds on the right-hand margin (it lies about one-tenth of the distance between 1550 and 1600 pounds). Now follow this point across the chart, parallel to the horizontal

Figure 5.11 Center of gravity versus moment and distance from datum.

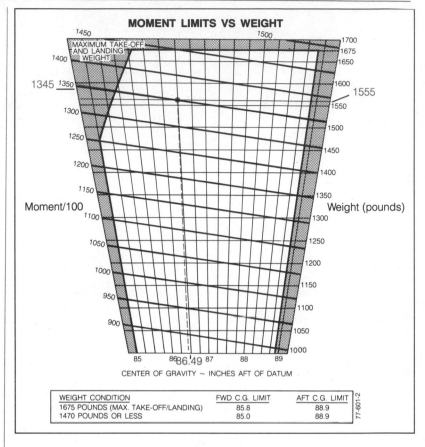

weight reference lines. Stop when you hit the line that would correspond to the 1345 inch-pound moment. The 1345 inch-pound line would be about one-tenth of the distance down from the 1350 inch-pound line to the 1300 inch-pound line. From this point of intersection drop down, paralleling the vertical CG lines, and read the CG location for that particular flight condition from the scale across the bottom of the chart. This scale and the table below the chart show that this CG is within the margins of safe flight.

The Graphical Method

Some operating handbooks present weight and balance data in *graphical* form. Figure 5.12 shows the **loading graph** that relates the weight of any useful load item to its moment. Figure 5.13 is called the **weight-moment envelope** because it shows the minimum and maximum moments for any given weight. These charts abbreviate moments by dividing them by 1000.

Let us assume that your airplane is a four-seater this time, with a licensed empty weight of 1424 pounds. You are taking along three friends and 100 pounds of baggage. You plan to have 38 gallons of usable fuel on board. Figure 5.14 shows your worksheet for this problem. This time, since your airplane data showed *licensed* empty weight, add engine oil to your list.

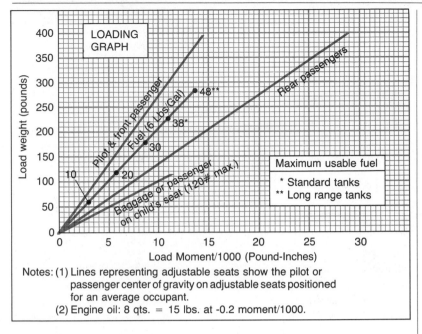

Figure 5.12 Sample loading graph.

1. Your airplane's weight and balance record lists the empty weight moment as 60,800 inch-pounds. You enter 60.8 on the worksheet (60,800/1000).

2. The loading chart (at the bottom) gives the weight and moment of a full complement of engine oil. The moment is negative, indicating that it is located forward of the datum. This information is added to the worksheet.

3. Enter the loading graph on the vertical scale with the combined weights of the two front-seat passengers. The two of you weigh 380 pounds in this example. Follow the line for this weight horizontally until you come to the

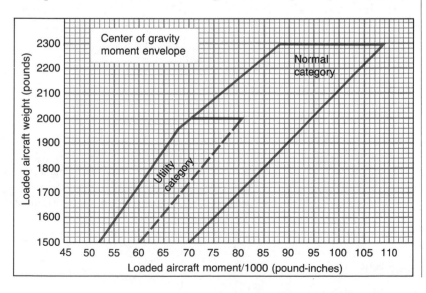

Figure 5.13 Sample weight versus moment envelope.

Figure 5.14 Worksheet for the
graphical method.

ITEM	WEIGHT (POUNDS)	MOMENT (IN-LB./1000)
EMPTY WEIGHT	1,424	60.8
OIL	15	− 0.2
FRONT SEATS	380	14.0
REAR SEATS	195	14.3
FUEL 38 GAL	228	11.0
BAGGAGE	100	9.5
TAKEOFF	2,342	109.4 (Unsafe)
Less 7 gal fuel	− 42	− 2.0
TAKEOFF	2,300	107.4 (Safe)
Fuel used	− 150	− 7.5
LANDING	2,150	99.9 (Safe)

reference line for the *pilot* and *front passenger,* then drop down vertically
to the moment/1000 value of 14.0. Enter this on the worksheet.

4. Your rear-seat passenger weighs 195 pounds. Use the same method
to find the moments for the rear-seat passenger, baggage, and fuel. Read
the moment values carefully. Figure 5.14 shows the correct values.

5. Now total the weights and moments.

6. Enter the CG-moment envelope graph with the total weight (2342
pounds) on the vertical scale. Trace this weight horizontally until you intersect the vertical line that has the value of the total moment (109.4 inch-
pounds/1000).

This point falls *outside* the envelope, so the CG location is *not* safe for
flight. In order to understand how to correct this situation, let us examine
the boundaries of the **center of gravity envelope** and what they represent.

The *top* of the envelope (the horizontal line) represents *gross weight*.
Any value above this line means that useful load must be reduced. You
may reduce your fuel load or leave some baggage behind, or even a passenger, depending on the amount of weight involved.

The *left-hand border* represents the *forward CG limit*. If your point falls
to the left of this border, then your actual CG is forward of the forward
limit. Assuming that you are within gross weight, you can solve this problem by shifting the load aft. This transfer creates more moment for the
same total weight and moves the CG aft.

The *right-hand border* represents the *aft CG limit*. When your actual
CG falls to the right of this line, then you have the dangerous situation of
your CG being aft of the aft limit. Again, assuming that gross weight is
not a problem, shift weight forward. This transfer reduces total moment
for a given weight, and the CG moves forward.

Once you have determined what the problem is, make the appropriate
changes on your loading chart and calculate another CG. Repeat the process
until your CG is within limits.

In the example we have been working with, the point is above the top of the envelope. Notice that the gross weight line is at 2300 pounds, which means that you are 42 pounds too heavy. You decide to reduce your fuel load by that amount to get your weight within limits. (Of course, you have verified that adequate fuel reserves will still be maintained.) By removing 7 gallons of fuel, you reduce your weight the exact amount needed. You subtract the weight and moment of the fuel removed from the previous totals. The new values (2300 pounds gross weight, and 107.4 inch-pounds/ 1000 of moment) are now within limits.

You can complete the problem by computing the landing condition. Suppose you plan to burn 150 pounds of fuel during this flight. This would reduce your weight to 2150 pounds, and the moment to 99.9 inch-pounds/ 1000 (see Figure 5.14). Referring to Figure 5.13, you verify that this point is also within the envelope.

Operations at High Gross Weights

The problems we have used to demonstrate methods of calculating weight and balance have necessarily been simple ones. In the real world, things are rarely so straightforward. Airplanes are designed with spacious cabins able to hold generous supplies and large fuel tanks, because manufacturers want their airplanes to have flexibility. If you want to go great distances, you can, but with a limited cabin load. You can load the cabin with everything in sight, including the proverbial kitchen sink, by limiting the fuel load. Rarely can you fill both the cabin and the fuel tanks without exceeding the gross weight limit. The temptation to do so is always there, but you must not give in. An overweight airplane is an unknown commodity. An extra fuel stop (or two) may be inconvenient, but not as inconvenient as an unsuccessful takeoff would be.

Exactly what are the problems associated with an overweight airplane? As weight increases, so does the lift being generated by the wing. This is done by increasing the operating angle of attack of the wing. Consequently, you have less reserve angle of attack separating you from the stall and therefore higher stalling speeds. *An overweight airplane will stall at higher speeds than those shown in your Pilot's Operating Handbook.* Higher lift also means higher drag forces (since both are part of the same force; see Figure 2.10), so the overall performance of the airplane suffers too. You will experience longer takeoff rolls, lower climb rates, and slower cruise speeds as well. Flying overweight also compromises the safety factors built into the aircraft structure. Gusts and maneuvers that are safe in a properly loaded airplane may cause structural damage in one that is overloaded.

Flight at Various CG Positions

We have stated that as long as the CG falls within the limits specified by the manufacturer, the airplane will behave in a normal manner. But is there a difference in how the airplane flies as the CG is moved *within* the allowable range? And what happens when the CG limits are not observed?

Figure 5.15 shows the relationship between CG and the lift forces on the wing and tail for a stable airplane. Notice that the wing's lift acts through a point *behind* the CG. (The point through which an airfoil's aerodynamic forces appear to act is called the *center of pressure*.) If lift and weight were the only two forces present, the airplane's nose would pitch down uncontrollably because only the lift force would be causing a moment about the CG. The tail, therefore, must create a *downward* force to keep things in balance. The total lift the wing must create is the combination of the airplane's weight and the negative lift created by the tail.

It may appear paradoxical that the tail acts opposite the wing, but this configuration is required for positive longitudinal stability. Imagine the airplane shown in Figure 5.15 in level flight. If the airplane pitches up for any reason, the wing and tail will react to the change in angle of attack. The wing's angle of attack will be increased, which will create a moment about the CG that will lower the nose. Although the tail's change in angle of attack is similar, the fact that it is "lifting" in the opposite direction from the wing means that it actually undergoes a decrease in angle of attack. The decrease reduces the load on the tail, which helps to lower the nose. As the nose is lowered, the angles of attack return to their previous values, removing the pitch-down moment. The airplane eventually stabilizes in its original attitude. If the airplane had pitched down initially, a similar but opposite reaction would take place.

As the CG moves forward, stability increases, but performance decreases. Let us examine why this is so. If the CG were even farther forward than shown in Figure 5.15, the stabilizing effect would become more pronounced. Larger tail forces would be required to make pitch changes, which means that the pilot would have to exert heavier pressure on the controls. Also, a forward CG produces a greater nose-down moment, which requires more counteracting down-load on the tail. The total lift created by the wing must increase to counteract this extra down-load. The wing must fly at a higher angle of attack for any given airspeed. As a result, induced drag increases, causing reduced speed or requiring more power to keep the same speed. Remember that all we did was move the CG forward; the total weight of the airplane did not change.

In summary, *moving the CG forward increases stability but decreases performance*. If you fly with the CG forward of the forward limit, you can expect the following difficulties:

Figure 5.15 Center of gravity location on a stable airplane.

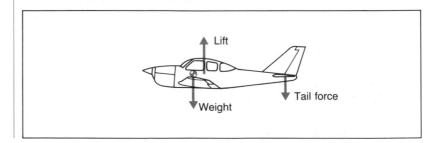

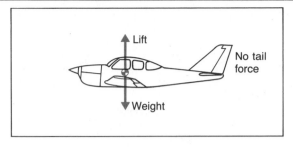

Figure 5.16 Center of gravity
aligned with lift.

1. The elevator control forces increase (the control wheel becomes harder to move) because the airplane is too stable and resists any pitch changes.

2. The horizontal tail is less effective in holding the nose up during low-speed operations like takeoff and landing. Higher speeds are required for adequate elevator control, which results in longer takeoff and landing distances.

3. The tail is operating at high angles of attack to create the required down-load. The wing is operating at a higher angle of attack than normal to overcome the excessive down-load from the tail. Therefore, both the wing and tail are also generating abnormally high amounts of induced drag, reducing overall airplane performance. The airplane will not climb as well, and it will not go as fast for a given power setting.

4. Stall speeds increase because the wing and tail are operating at higher angles of attack than normal. As you slow down (or bank the wings), the critical angle of attack will be reached at a higher speed than normal.

5. Conventional gear airplanes have more of a tendency to nose over. The nose wheel of a tricycle gear airplane is subjected to higher loads, increasing the chances for damage or failure.

As you would expect, moving the CG aft reverses all of these trends. When the CG is closer to the wing's center of pressure, the nose-down moment is reduced, as is the balancing tail down-load. The wing now operates at a lower angle of attack, resulting in better airplane performance.

Figure 5.16 shows the CG moved far enough aft that it is aligned with the wing's lift force. Notice that since no nose-down (or nose-up) moment is produced, no load is required from the tail. The lift force needed from the wing is now equal to the airplane weight, a reduction from the situation discussed above.

Continuing to move the CG aft produces the condition shown in Figure 5.17. Now the weight and lift forces create a nose-up moment, which must be balanced by an *upward* tail force. This upward force further reduces the wing's lift force because the tail now joins the wing in opposing gravity.

That is the good news. Unfortunately, moving the CG aft also creates a problem: decreased stability. When the airplane in Figure 5.17 is flying straight and level, everything is balanced. But suppose you want to start to descend. You would push the control wheel forward, increasing lift on

Figure 5.17 Center of gravity aft of the lift force.

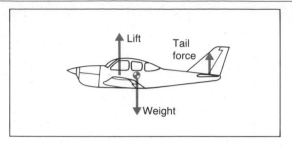

the tail, and the airplane would pitch down. This action reduces the angle of attack of the wing, which also causes more of a nose-down moment. Two nose-down reactions for the price of one! The situation is destined to get worse because as the nose pitches down, it creates more of a nose-down moment. In other words, the airplane is *unstable*. (Prove to yourself that a similar but opposite reaction would take place if the nose were raised from level flight.) Obviously, this situation is extremely dangerous. You can see why all airplanes have an aft CG limit.

So, *moving the CG aft increases performance but decreases stability.* Flying an airplanc with a CG aft of the aft limit produces the following undesirable reactions:

1. Unstable flying characteristics. Any pitch disturbances will require active pilot input to maintain control of the airplane, because the craft may not return to the original condition by itself. The airplane will be difficult, if not impossible, to trim for hands-off flight.

2. Very light control forces. Because the control wheel is *very* easy to move, the airplane is easier to overcontrol. It is thus easier for the pilot to impose high load factors unintentionally.

3. Violent stall characteristics. The airplane may have no tendency of its own to recover from a stall. If the airplane spins, recovery may be impossible.

Figure 5.18 summarizes the undesirable characteristics caused by a center of gravity that is outside the allowable range.

WEIGHT, BALANCE, AND THE ART OF PILOTING
Someone once said that piloting an airplane is a balancing act between caution and persistence. When the act becomes literal, it means you must have the caution to recognize the airplane's limits and the persistence to observe them—even though it may take a few extra minutes before each flight for weight and balance planning. Here are some practical tips that make the process easier.

Use All Relevant Publications
Become familiar with the weight and balance data in your Pilot's Operating Handbook and the airplane's weight and balance records. Be certain that

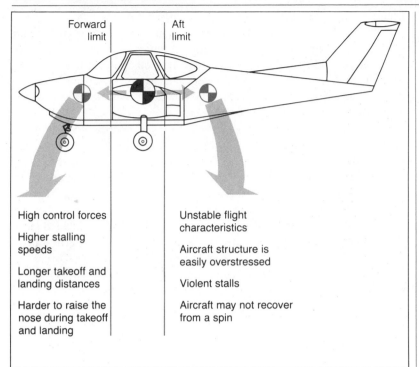

Figure 5.18 The problems expected when the center of gravity is outside the prescribed limits.

all equipment changes have been noted in the weight and balance record and then *use* the current basic empty weight to begin your calculations. Most people like to take the course of least resistance, and after you are familiar with your airplane, it is easier to *assume* that a particular loading is safe simply because it is similar to other loadings you have flown safely with in the past. Sometimes it is. But as we will see in the next chapter, operating conditions can change drastically from location to location. The departure end of the runway is no place to find out that your airplane has been loaded incorrectly for the prevailing conditions. If it is any extra incentive, FAR 91.31 expressly requires a pilot to ensure that the aircraft is within the prescribed weight and balance limits prior to flight. Good pilots make weight and balance planning a *habit,* not a stratagem reserved for check flights.

We have shown that the most efficient way to load your airplane is close to, but not beyond, the aft CG limit. If your gross weight looks good but the CG is too far forward or too far aft, then just rearrange the load. Work the problem on paper until you have a valid solution. Then be sure to load the airplane according to your plan.

As we saw in the sample problem, the CG often changes as fuel is burned. Be certain ahead of time by calculating a landing weight and moment that this change will not put you beyond the CG envelope. Planning becomes even more important in airplanes with auxiliary fuel tanks, stretched (extra long) fuselages, and/or swept wings.

Monitor Your Progress

The elevator trim tabs are a useful tool in monitoring the rate and amount of CG change in flight. If the trim setting becomes extreme or shifts in a direction you did not anticipate, you may have computed a false balance, traceable to inaccurate documentation or calculation errors. Your awareness of how the airplane is flying can help you catch these tendencies early, before they have a chance to become serious.

Watch also for CG changes whenever you alter the basic load en route. An airplane that is well balanced on its initial departure can become seriously imbalanced after one or two stops en route, where passengers and cargo are loaded, unloaded, or shifted. Add to this new airport and atmospheric conditions—and the usual pilot's inclination to press on with the flight—and trouble could well be brewing in your flight plan. "Defying gravity" can be fun, and modern airplanes, with a little planning and attention from their pilots, are designed to do just that, safely and efficiently.

KEY TERMS

arm	loading graph
basic empty weight	maximum landing weight
center of gravity envelope	maximum ramp weight
datum	maximum takeoff weight
gross weight	moment
licensed empty weight	useful load

PROFICIENCY CHECK

1. What are the two major factors a pilot needs to know about the airplane's weight and balance before it flies?

2. Name three effects of high gross weight on an airplane's flying characteristics.

3. What are three characteristics of flight at the *forward* CG limit? What are three characteristics of flight at the *aft* limit?

4. What is the airplane's datum and how is it determined?

5. What is the difference between basic empty weight and licensed empty weight?

6. Refer to the sample *tabular* weight and balance problem in the text (Figures 5.8 and 5.9). Assuming one occupant (pilot only) and a fuel load of 10 gallons, compute a new landing condition for the airplane. Is the airplane's CG at landing within its operating envelope? What is the new center of gravity (in inches aft of the datum)?

7. Refer to the sample *graphical* weight and balance data and to the tabular data on the facing page.

Allow 8 pounds of fuel—0.4 inch-pounds/1000 for engine start, taxi, and runup. Is this airplane safe for flight from a weight and balance standpoint? (If not, what must be done to bring it within the CG envelope?)

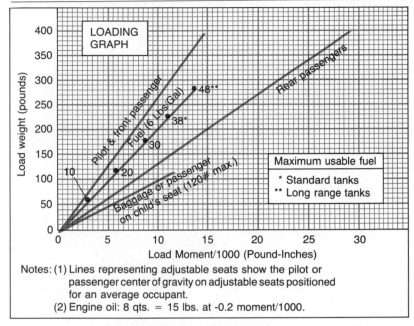

Notes: (1) Lines representing adjustable seats show the pilot or
passenger center of gravity on adjustable seats positioned
for an average occupant.
(2) Engine oil: 8 qts. = 15 lbs. at -0.2 moment/1000.

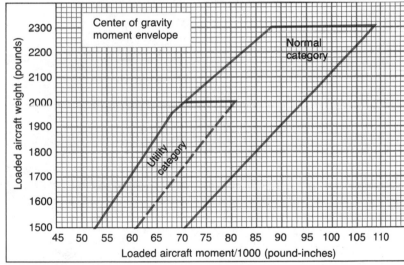

A/C empty weight	1364 pounds
A/C empty moment	60.8 inch-pounds/1000
Pilot	185 pounds
Front-seat passenger	115 pounds
Rear-seat passengers	350 pounds
Fuel	40 gallons

What you theoretically know, vividly realize.

Francis Thompson
"Shelley," *Works,* Volume III

C H E C K P O I N T S

How do atmospheric conditions affect airplane performance? How is an airplane's performance determined? How do wind and runway characteristics affect takeoffs and landings? How do pilots use data from the Pilot's Operating Handbook to calculate airplane performance?

PERFORMANCE: MEASURING AN AIRPLANE'S CAPABILITIES

I t is vital that a pilot be able to accurately determine whether an airplane can safely complete a flight under existing weather, wind, and runway conditions. The takeoff, climb, cruise, and landing capabilities of an airplane are collectively called **performance**, and performance varies, depending on existing conditions. Be familiar with the performance limitations of any airplane you fly, and always stay within them. Your safety depends on it.

THE SOURCE OF PERFORMANCE DATA

The *demonstrated* capability of an airplane design is published in the Performance Section of the Pilot's Operating Handbook. "Demonstrated" means that the data come not from plugging numbers into theoretical formulas but from actual flights of an airplane of that design. Recording of flight-test data is done to give you confidence in the performance information (and because the FAA requires it).

Keep in mind, however, that manufacturers want to present their products in the most favorable manner possible. The performance flight tests are done with a brand-new airplane and engine. The pilot performing the tests is an experienced test pilot. The performance data printed in the handbook are achievable if your skill and equipment are in similar shape. The data are presented in chart or graph form in a way that allows you to determine performance for any weather conditions. This chapter will teach you how to use the performance data in your airplane's handbook.

THE INFLUENCE OF AIR DENSITY ON PERFORMANCE

We learned in Chapter 2 that all aerodynamic forces are created by the moving airfoil reacting with air molecules. The actions of an airplane are directly related to the *number* of air molecules encountered as the airplane moves through the air. That is, *airplane performance is a function of the density of the air through which it is flying*. Three factors determine air density: atmospheric pressure, temperature, and humidity.

Atmospheric pressure, or air pressure, is the result of gravity acting on air molecules. In other words, atmospheric pressure is caused by the weight of the air above you. As air pressure increases, so does the number of molecules in a given volume of air; that is, air density is increased. The reverse is true also: lowering air pressure reduces air density. Figure 6.1 shows that on an average day, a 1-inch square column of air weighs about 14.7 pounds on the earth's surface. As you go up in the atmosphere, the weight of the air above you decreases. Notice that the same 1-inch column of air 18,000 feet above the earth weighs only 7.35 pounds. *Atmospheric pressure (and therefore air density) decreases as altitude increases*.

Temperature affects air density because when gases are heated, they expand. Warm temperatures, then, make any given volume of air less dense. *Air density decreases as air temperature increases*.

Humidity is the presence of water vapor molecules in the air. We usually think of water in its liquid form, which is quite dense and therefore heavy.

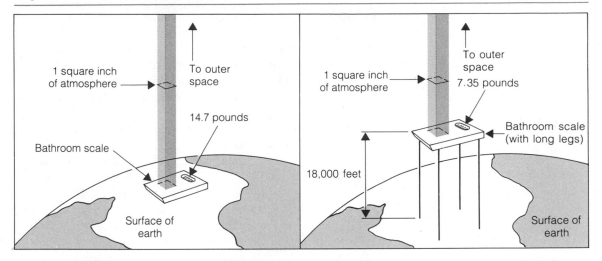

However, in its gaseous form, water vapor is less dense than dry air. You can see the difference in density by comparing the molecular weight of water vapor to that of oxygen and nitrogen, the primary gases in the atmosphere:

H_2O: molecular weight = 18 (water vapor)

O_2:   molecular weight = 32 (oxygen)

N_2:   molecular weight = 28 (nitrogen)

Clearly, *air density decreases as humidity increases*. However, the number of water vapor molecules in the air compared to the number of other molecules (primarily N_2 and O_2) is only a tiny fraction, even in the highest humidities. Therefore, the effect of humidity on the density of air is small compared to the effect of temperature and pressure.

When all three factors are considered together, it should be evident that the highest air densities are found at low altitudes on cold, dry days. A hot, humid day in the mountains (high elevations) produces the lowest air density.

Figure 6.1 The pressure of the atmosphere is the result of the weight of the entire column of atmosphere above.

The Standard Atmosphere

Describing airplane performance would be impossible without some sort of a standard to use for atmospheric conditions. The **International Standard Atmosphere (ISA)** was created to fulfill this need. In the ISA, at sea level, the temperature is 59 degrees Fahrenheit (15 degrees Celsius), and the barometric pressure is 29.92 inches of mercury, with low humidity. The density of the air is also defined (the exact value is only relevant to an engineer). Temperature, pressure, and density of the air are computed for any altitude, under these standard conditions. Manufacturers are required to report the performance of their aircraft relative to the ISA. However, since the real atmosphere rarely, if ever, matches this theoretical standard, pilots must use techniques to convert actual conditions to standard conditions for the purpose of computing aircraft performance.

Pressure-altitude.   **Pressure-altitude** is the altitude in the standard atmosphere where the current outside air pressure will be found. If you were to obtain the current outside air pressure, then find the altitude where that *pressure* exists in the standard atmosphere, you would get *pressure-altitude*. Pilots have a very simple way to do this. *If you set your altimeter to 29.92, the resulting indication is pressure-altitude*.

When you do not have an altimeter handy—for example, when you are at home doing some preflight planning—you can nevertheless obtain pressure-altitude by using a table like the one shown in Figure 6.2b. The technique requires a current altimeter setting and a sea level elevation (usually an airport elevation). You can get the altimeter setting by calling the nearest Flight Service Station. Airport elevations are shown on aeronautical maps. To use the table, simply look up the altimeter setting in the left column, then note the corresponding *altitude correction* in the right column. This altitude number is added to (or subtracted from) the airport elevation to obtain pressure-altitude. For example, if the current altimeter setting were 29.70, you would add 205 feet to the airport elevation to get pressure-altitude. If you were to run out to the airport and set any altimeter there to 29.92, you should get the same result.

Density-altitude.   **Density-altitude** is the altitude in the standard atmosphere where the current outside air *density* will be found. Since your airplane's performance is a direct function of air density, density-altitude is very important. It cannot be measured directly by an instrument; instead, it must be calculated, using pressure-altitude and outside air temperature.

Figure 6.2a is a chart for converting pressure-altitude and temperature into density-altitude. Pressure-altitudes are depicted by the slanted lines. The vertical lines represent air temperature, and the horizontal lines indicate density-altitude. To use the chart, you must know both pressure-altitude and temperature. Let us use 86 degrees Fahrenheit and pressure-altitude of 6000 feet as an example. First, find the location of 86 degrees along the bottom scale. Next, move vertically until you intercept the slanted line representing 6000 feet pressure-altitude. Finally, from that point, move horizontally to the left and read the density-altitude (8800 feet) on the vertical scale.

The solid diagonal line marked "standard temperature" depicts the ISA temperature versus altitude. Notice that pressure-altitude equals density-altitude at any point along this line. If the outside air temperature is higher than standard, density-altitude is *greater* than pressure-altitude. Density-altitude is *lower* than pressure-altitude at below-normal temperatures.

Since air density decreases with altitude, the term *high density-altitude* refers to low-density air, whereas *low density-altitude* means higher-density air. (Be careful not to mistake high *density-altitude*—for *high-density* air—the two are opposite in meaning.)

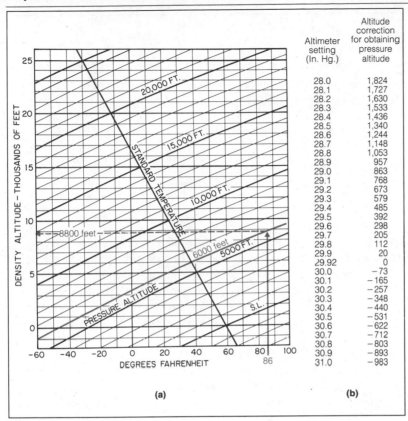

Altimeter setting (In. Hg.)	Altitude correction for obtaining pressure altitude
28.0	1,824
28.1	1,727
28.2	1,630
28.3	1,533
28.4	1,436
28.5	1,340
28.6	1,244
28.7	1,148
28.8	1,053
28.9	957
29.0	863
29.1	768
29.2	673
29.3	579
29.4	485
29.5	392
29.6	298
29.7	205
29.8	112
29.9	20
29.92	0
30.0	−73
30.1	−165
30.2	−257
30.3	−348
30.4	−440
30.5	−531
30.6	−622
30.7	−712
30.8	−803
30.9	−893
31.0	−983

(a)   (b)

Figure 6.2 **(a)** Density-altitude chart. **(b)** Pressure-altitude correction versus altimeter setting.

TAKEOFF PERFORMANCE

The distance an airplane will travel on takeoff, from a standing start until it leaves the ground, is appropriately called the *ground roll*. The FAA requires manufacturers to determine required ground roll distance and also the total distance required for the airplane to clear a 50-foot obstacle. Takeoff performance depends on the following factors:

Density-altitude. The engine, propeller, and wing produce their highest output in high-density air. Therefore, low density-altitudes provide the best takeoff performance. The combined lowered performance of these parts at high density-altitudes causes dismal takeoff performance, as illustrated in Figure 6.3.

Aircraft weight and balance. The airplane cannot fly until it generates enough lift to support its weight. As weight increases, more lift must be generated. Recall that loading an airplane so that its CG is forward also increases the lift required from the wing. Extra lift is generated by increasing the takeoff speed, which translates into a longer takeoff roll.

Headwinds. Any wind that approaches the aircraft from a frontal direction and acts opposite to its course is a **headwind.** Headwinds assist the airplane by giving the wing an effective "running start." A 10-knot headwind means that the wing is creating 10 knots of lift before the airplane

Figure 6.3 The combined effects of temperature, altitude, and humidity on takeoff.

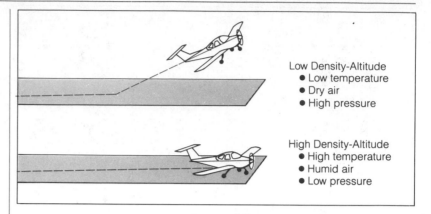

even starts moving. Headwinds reduce the takeoff roll considerably. In contrast, any wind that approaches the aircraft from a rearward direction and acts in conjunction with its course is a **tailwind.** Tailwinds lengthen the takeoff run even more dramatically and must be avoided.

Runway gradient and surface. Ideally, you would always take off from level, dry, hard-surfaced runways. Any deviation from these conditions will worsen takeoff performance. The runway **gradient** is its slope. Naturally, a downhill slope assists the airplane in reaching its takeoff speed, because gravity helps propel it forward. Taking off uphill is only recommended when strong headwinds are present or when dictated by the surrounding terrain. A *soft* runway surface, such as rain-soaked turf, prevents normal acceleration to takeoff speed. A hard-surfaced runway with water, slush, snow, or ice causes similar problems. The *soft field takeoff* is a technique designed to get the airplane off the ground at the slowest possible speed under such conditions (see Chapter 2).

Flaps. Generally, the extra lift from partial flaps will shorten the ground roll, but the extra drag they produce harms climb performance. (These effects are different for each type of airplane.) The Pilot's Operating Handbook specifies the procedures to follow to obtain the published takeoff performance.

Computing Takeoff Performance

Every manufacturer has its own method of presenting performance data; some use tables, some use graphs. You must take the time to learn how to use the data for the airplane you are flying. The Performance chapter of your operating handbook will probably have a tutorial section containing sample problems. We will work through some examples using various types of data.

Figure 6.4 is a sample graph for computing takeoff distance under various conditions of density-altitude. Assume that we know the density-altitude to be 4000 feet. What ground roll distance is necessary for takeoff? And what distance is needed to clear a 50-foot obstacle? Simply find 4000 on the left-hand border and move horizontally to the appropriate reference

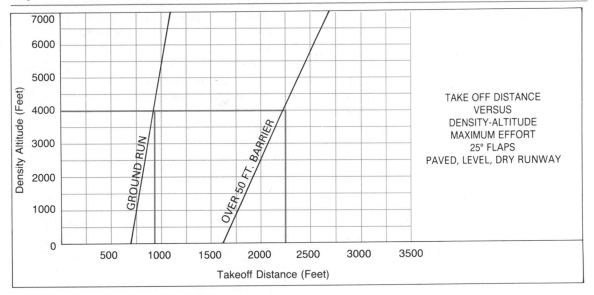

line, then drop vertically to find the distance in feet. In this example the ground roll is approximately 950 feet, and you will travel a total of 2250 feet to clear a 50-foot obstacle. Notice that this manufacturer has specified that to obtain this performance, the flaps must be set to 25 degrees and the runway conditions must be ideal.

A sample of a manufacturer's tabular data is shown in Figure 6.5. This chart lists information for various gross weights and headwinds for figuring takeoff distance. Notice that each takeoff altitude specifies a standard tem-

Figure 6.4 Takeoff distance versus density-altitude.

Figure 6.5 Example of tabular take-off data.

Take-Off Data										
Take-Off Distance From Hard Surface Runway With Flaps Up										
			At Sea Level & 59°F		At 2500 Ft. & 50°F		At 5000 Ft. & 41°F		At 7500 Ft. & 32°F	
Gross Weight Pounds	IAS At 50° MPH	Head Wind Knots	Ground Run	Total To Clear 50 Ft OBS	Ground Run	Total To Clear 50 Ft OBS	Ground Run	Total To Clear 50 Ft OBS	Ground Run	Total To Clear 50 Ft OBS
2300	68	0	865	1525	1040	1910	1255	2480	1565	3855
		10	615	1170	750	1485	920	1955	1160	3110
		20	405	850	505	1100	630	1480	810	2425
2000	63	0	630	1095	755	1325	905	1625	1120	2155
		10	435	820	530	1005	645	1250	810	1685
		20	275	580	340	720	425	910	595	1255
1700	58	0	435	780	520	920	625	1095	765	1370
		10	290	570	355	680	430	820	535	1040
		20	175	385	215	470	270	575	345	745

Notes: 1. Increase distance 10% for each 25°F above standard temperature for particular altitude.
2. For operation on a dry, grass runway, increase distances (both "ground run" and "total to clear 50 ft. obstacle") by 7% of the "total to clear 50 ft. obstacle" figure.

perature and that the first note explains how to correct for nonstandard temperatures. This means that the altitudes listed are pressure-altitudes, and since temperature variations are accounted for, you do not have to compute a density-altitude to use this chart.

Let us assume that you are about to take off from Denver, Colorado, for a flight to Wichita, Kansas, under the following conditions:

Pressure-altitude: 5000 feet
Gross weight: 2300 pounds
Temperature: 91 degrees Fahrenheit
Wind from: 140° at 20 knots
Runway in use: 20

Using the tabular data, we will find the total distance required to clear a 50-foot obstacle. In order to do this, however, we first need to know how to compute the amount of headwind present.

Computing Headwinds and Crosswinds

When the wind is not blowing straight down the runway (it never does, it seems), only a portion of the total wind speed acts as a headwind. Therefore, some part of the wind also blows directly across the runway, a **crosswind.** Figure 6.6 is a chart for determining the various components of any wind. To use this chart, you need to know the angle between the runway heading and the wind direction.

Runways are numbered according to their magnetic direction. To convert a runway number to a magnetic direction, add a zero to the end. For example, runway 3 has a magnetic direction of 030° magnetic. For the purposes of takeoff and landing, surface winds are reported with respect to the magnetic direction they are coming *from*. The angle we are interested in is simply the difference between the runway direction and the wind direction. If the wind is from 310 degrees and you are planning to use runway 27, the angle is 310 − 270 = 40 degrees. You should be able to visualize whether the wind is from the left or right. In the airplane, a glance at the directional gyro (DG) will help the visualization; on the ground, a look at the wind sock or a quick sketch will do the same. In this example the wind is from the right.

Now let us figure the winds in Denver today. The wind is from 140 degrees at 20 knots. You plan to use runway 20. The angle between the wind and the runway is 200 − 140 = 60 degrees, and the wind is from the left. Refer to Figure 6.6. The circular arcs represent wind speed, and the radial lines are the angle between the runway and wind. Find the intersection of the 20-knot arc and the 60-degree radial line. From this point move horizontally to the left and read the headwind component: 10 knots. Drop down vertically from the intersection point to get the crosswind component of 17 knots (from the left).

We now have enough information to use the table in Figure 6.5 for determining your takeoff distance. First, find the 2300-pound gross weight

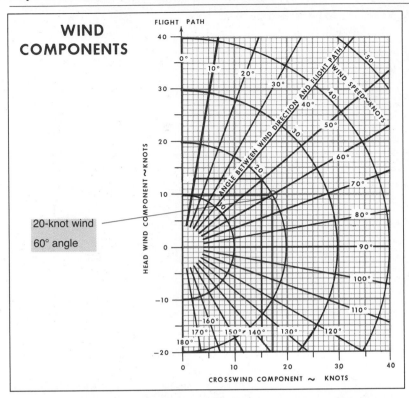

Figure 6.6 Crosswind component chart.

block on the left-most column of the table. Next, find the 10-knot headwind line two columns over. This 10-knot figure identifies the horizontal row you should use (the second from the top in this example). Now find the "At 5000 ft and 41° F" column heading and the "Total to Clear 50 ft Obs" column below it. The second number in this column is 1955 feet. Now we have to correct for the nonstandard temperature. Referring to Note 1, we see that 1955 feet must be increased by 10 percent for each 25 degrees above the standard shown for an altitude of 5000 feet. The temperature in Denver is 50 degrees higher than standard (91 − 41), so we will increase our number by 20 percent. The answer is:

$$1.20 \times 1955 = 2346 \text{ feet}$$

(for a hard-surface runway and flaps up). This chart also has a factor for operations from a dry grass runway.

Figure 6.7 is yet another type of chart for computing takeoff distance. To demonstrate the use of this chart, the following conditions apply:

Pressure-altitude: 5650 feet
Gross weight: 2950 pounds
Temperature: 59 degrees Fahrenheit
Headwind: 9.5 knots

TAKE-OFF DISTANCE

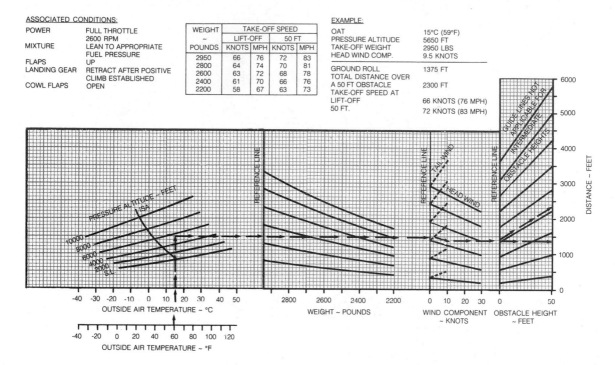

Figure 6.7 Takeoff distance chart.

The first step is to find 59 degrees Fahrenheit (15° C) on the temperature scale (lower left-hand portion of the chart). From this point, move vertically upward to a pressure-altitude of 5650 feet. There is no line drawn for this exact altitude, so you must estimate this location based on the altitudes shown on the chart.

From that point, move horizontally until you intersect the first reference line. From there, move parallel to the sloped lines to the vertical line representing Gross Weight. (In this example, the reference line itself represents the given gross weight, so no horizontal movement is necessary.)

Now move horizontally again and intersect the next reference line. This section adjusts for headwinds. This time, horizontal movement is needed, and we parallel the slanted lines until we reach the 10-knot vertical line. Once again, move horizontally to the last reference line. This panel figures the effect of obstacle height. Ground roll is determined by continuing horizontally to a value of 1375 feet. The distance required to clear a 50-foot obstacle—2300 feet—is found by paralleling the slanted lines to the distance line.

The box in the top-center section of the chart lists the takeoff speeds required to achieve best performance.

CLIMB PERFORMANCE

Whenever an airplane gains altitude against the force of gravity, *work* is performed. An airplane is capable of climbing whenever the thrust or power available from the power plant exceeds the thrust or power required for level flight. The terms *thrust* and *power* are mentioned separately here because, while they are related, they are not the same. An in-depth discussion of work, thrust, and power is beyond the scope of this text. However, we need to distinguish between thrust and power to discuss climb performance.

Thrust determines how much work is done *per distance traveled*. Power relates the amount of work done *per unit of time*. This means if we wish to discuss the ability of an airplane to gain altitude versus distance traveled, we must determine excess thrust. If altitude gain versus time is of interest, the amount of excess power is the key.

Figure 6.8 shows characteristic plots of thrust and power versus airspeed for a propeller-driven airplane at a single altitude. On each graph, the distance between the "available" curve and the "required" curve at any given airspeed is called *reserve*. The airspeed that has the maximum reserve will give the best climb performance. Note that maximum reserve thrust occurs at a different airspeed than does maximum reserve power. This means that there is no one "best" airspeed for climbing. There are, in fact, two: best angle of climb and best rate of climb.

Best Angle of Climb

The airspeed that has maximum reserve thrust will let the airplane gain the most altitude for any *distance traveled* and is called the **best angle of climb**

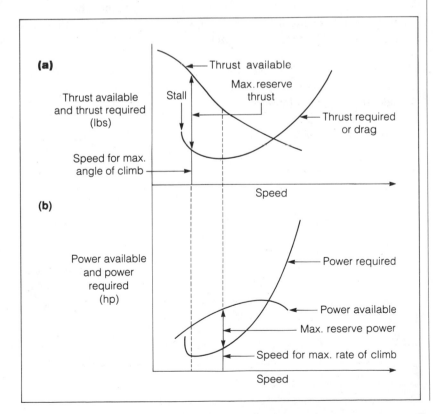

Figure 6.8 **(a)** Thrust available and thrust required versus airspeed. **(b)** Power available and power required versus airspeed.

speed (V_x). You will use this speed on takeoffs when there are obstacles to clear at the end of the runway.

Best Rate of Climb

The airspeed that has the maximum reserve power will allow the airplane to gain the most altitude for any *unit of time* and is called the **best rate of climb** speed (V_y). You will use this speed when you want to gain altitude as quickly as possible.

Figure 6.9 compares these two ways to climb. Both airplanes started the takeoff roll simultaneously, and this picture represents their relative positions one minute later. The airplane on the left used the best angle of climb speed (V_x). This climb allowed it to clear the obstacle, but it gained less altitude than the other airplane (for the same time period). The aircraft on the right used the best rate of climb speed (V_y), which allowed it to gain more altitude in the given time period, but notice that its flight path is shallower. It would not have cleared the obstacle. The best technique generally is to start your climb at the best angle of climb speed, then, once clear of any obstacles, change to the best rate of climb speed.

The Effect of Altitude on Climb Performance

Not surprisingly, climb performance decreases with altitude. Best angle of climb data are the basis for the "total to clear a 50-foot obstacle" data on a Takeoff Performance chart, and the effects of altitude there have already been discussed. Figure 6.10a shows how best rate of climb varies with altitude. These data may also be presented in tabular form, as in Figure 6.11.

Figure 6.10b shows how the airspeeds for V_x and V_y vary with altitude. Best angle of climb speed is the lower of the two speeds and *increases* with altitude; best angle of climb speed *decreases* with altitude. These airspeeds vary noticeably with the correct airspeeds for the altitude at which you are operating. The altitude where two climb speeds meet is called the airplane's

Figure 6.9 Best angle of climb (V_x) compared with best rate of climb (v_y).

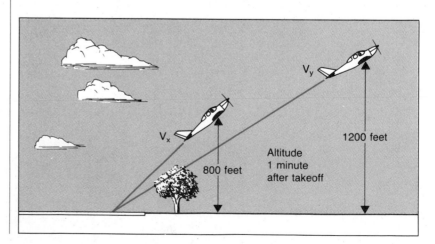

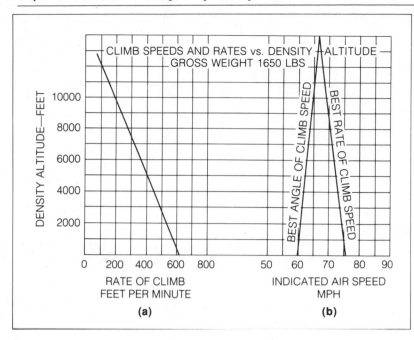

Figure 6.10 **(a)** Climb rate versus altitude. **(b)** Best climb performance speeds versus altitude.

absolute altitude. This is the maximum altitude the airplane is capable of achieving.

Computing Climb Performance

We will use the Denver conditions given for the takeoff problem to compute climb performance in conjunction with Figure 6.11. Read the 2300-pound gross weight row and the 5000-foot altitude column to get a standard rate of climb of 435 feet per minute and a climb speed of 81 mph. Note 3 gives the correction for nonstandard temperatures. Since the given temperature is 50 degrees above normal, we need to reduce the rate of climb by 100

Figure 6.11 Climb performance chart.

Maximum Rate-Of-Climb Data												
	At Sea Level & 59°F			At 5000 Ft. & 41°F			At 10,000 Ft. & 23°F			At 15,000 Ft. & 5°F		
Gross Weight Pounds	IAS MPH	Rate Of Climb Ft/Min	Gal. Of Fuel Used	IAS MPH	Rate Of Climb Ft/Min	From S.L. Fuel Used	IAS MPH	Rate Of Climb Ft/Min	From S.L. Fuel Used	IAS MPH	Rate Of Climb Ft/Min	From S.L. Fuel Used
2300	82	645	1.0	81	435	2.6	79	230	4.8	78	22	11.5
2000	79	840	1.0	79	610	2.2	76	380	3.6	75	155	6.3
1700	77	1085	1.0	76	825	1.9	73	570	2.9	72	315	4.4

Notes: 1. Flaps up, full throttle, mixture leaned for smooth operation above 3000 ft.
2. Fuel used includes warm up and take-off allowance.
3. For hot weather, decrease rate of climb 20 ft./min. for each 10°F above standard day temperature for particular altitude.

feet per minute (5 × 20 feet per minute). This means that *initially* your rate of climb will be 335 feet per minute. Note 1 indicates that you will need to lean the mixture for smooth engine operation since you are indeed above 3000 feet.

As you continue your climb into lower-density air, your climb rate will deteriorate. Your minimum rate of climb will be at your cruising altitude, just before leveling off. An average of your initial and final climb rates can be used to compute the approximate time it will take to climb to your cruising altitude.

You plan to cruise to Wichita at an altitude of 9500 feet, so let us check the climb rate at this altitude. We will use the 10,000-foot column on the chart, which yields a standard rate of climb of 230 feet per minute. (To be totally accurate, we should interpolate the values to 9500 feet, but the difference would be so small that the computation is probably not worth the effort. Also, since we assumed a higher cruising altitude than actual, 10,000 versus 9500, the error will be on the safe side.) No other data are given on this problem, so we will assume the same 50 degrees above standard temperature. (Information on air temperatures aloft will be discussed in Chapter 9.) The chart indicates that you will be climbing at 130 feet per minute just before you level off at your cruising altitude.

We have now determined the initial and final climb rates to be expected. Of course, your average climb rate will be about halfway between the two values:

$$\text{Average climb rate} = (335 + 130)/2 = 232 \text{ feet per minute}$$

Average climb rate is needed to calculate an approximate time to climb to your cruise altitude:

$$\text{Approximate time to climb} = \frac{(9500 - 5000)\,\text{feet}}{232\,\text{feet per minute}} = 19\,\text{minutes}$$

Note that the chart in Figure 6.11 also has a column for climb speed (IAS). During this ascent, your climb speed must gradually change from 81 mph to 79 mph IAS.

This chart also allows you to estimate the amount of fuel burned during the climb. First, note that a "climb" to sea level takes 1.0 gallons of gas. This value represents the fuel allowance for engine start, taxi, and runup. The data entries for each of the higher altitudes include this allowance. The entry under the 10,000-foot column indicates that a takeoff and climb from sea level would consume 4.8 gallons of gas. However, you are not climbing from sea level but from 5000 feet. So we will first subtract the fuel the chart says you would have burned taking off and climbing to 5000 feet (2.6 gallons). The *difference* between these two values, 2.2 gallons, represents *only the climb* from 5000 to 10,000 feet. It does not include the ground allowance fuel. When ground allowance fuel is added to the fuel required for the climb, we see that we use a total of 3.2 gallons for a takeoff and climb from Denver to your cruise altitude. In practice, this value can vary greatly, depending on your leaning technique. It is prudent to assume that you will burn about 50 percent more fuel than the chart indicates.

Climb Airspeed Considerations

Some other factors can affect the airspeeds you use after ground obstacles have been cleared. Since your engine is likely to be air cooled, you will want to avoid the lower airspeed ranges, particularly in warm weather. The best rate of climb airspeed may also put the nose in an attitude too high to safely look for other traffic. Adding a few knots to your climb speed will solve both of these problems. This alternative is not a departure from recommended procedures. Most manufacturers recommend *cruise climb* speeds that are higher than the best performance speeds, for the reasons mentioned.

Of course, using a higher climb speed changes both the amount of time and amount of fuel to climb (because V_y was assumed). The difference will not be extreme, but it must not be ignored. Assuring an adequate fuel supply is the primary concern. The safety factor of assuming you will burn 50 percent more than the chart indicates should still provide a reasonable estimate.

CRUISE PERFORMANCE

Power and Speed Effects

Pilots use a variety of airspeeds in climb to suit different needs, as you have seen. Similarly, the cruising speed you choose depends on your objective for the flight. Cruise speed is directly controlled by the engine power setting. If you choose to fly a certain distance in the shortest amount of time, you will select the *maximum allowable* power setting. The price you will pay for the added speed is a higher fuel consumption. If you want to fly the longest distance on a given amount of fuel, you will use the **maximum range** power setting. If you wish to stay aloft as long as possible and the number of miles you travel is of secondary importance, then select **maximum endurance** power.

Regardless of the power setting you use, it is important to correctly lean the mixture. Lean the mixture any time you are in cruise flight, at any altitude. An engine runs best on a properly leaned mixture, so if you ignore this important process, you will reduce engine performance. The fuel consumption, range, and endurance data in the Pilot's Operating Handbook always assume a lean mixture.

Altitude Effects

In Chapter 2 you learned that in cruise flight parasite drag is the predominant drag on the airplane. Increasing altitude reduces parasite drag because there are fewer air molecules to resist. In general, then, performance improves at higher altitudes.

Engine power is also a function of altitude. Recall from Chapter 3 that the air pressure entering the cylinders (manifold pressure) is one of the determinants of engine power. The maximum manifold pressure an engine can obtain decreases with altitude. Performance begins to drop off with altitude when the engine can no longer produce enough power to maintain the desired speed. The fuel penalties of the climb to altitude must also be weighed against the benefits of efficiency once at that altitude. Short flights rarely benefit from a long climb to an efficient cruising altitude, since you will spend so little time there.

In order to plan a flight properly, you must also consider the weather and winds en route. These factors are beyond the scope of this chapter but will be covered completely in Chapter 12. For the moment, we will assume that there is no wind.

Computing Cruise Performance

Figure 6.12 shows cruise performance data in tabular form. To use the chart, select the altitude and power setting you desire. For the example flight from Denver to Wichita, you have chosen to cruise at 9500 feet. If you run the engine at 2500 rpm, your true airspeed will be 95 knots and

Figure 6.12. Cruise performance chart.

CRUISE PERFORMANCE*
STANDARD DAY
AVERAGE CRUISE WEIGHT = 1600 POUNDS

ALTITUDE FEET	THROTTLE SETTING RPM	FUEL FLOW GPH	IAS KNOTS	TAS KNOTS
2500	2700	8.0	101	105
	2500	6.4	94	97
	2400	5.7	90	93
	2300	5.2	85	88
3500	2700	7.8	100	105
	2500	6.3	92	97
	2400	5.7	88	93
	2300	5.2	84	88
4500	2700	7.7	99	105
	2500	6.3	91	97
	2400	5.6	87	93
	2300	5.1	82	88
5500	2700	7.6	97	105
	2500	6.2	89	97
	2400	5.5	85	92
	2300	5.0	81	87
6500	2700	7.4	96	105
	2500	6.1	88	97
	2400	5.4	84	92
	2300	5.0	79	87
7500	2500	6.0	86	96
	2400	5.3	82	91
	2300	4.9	77	86
8500	2500	5.8	85	96
	2400	5.3	80	91
	2300	4.9	76	85
9500	2500	5.7	83	95
	2400	5.2	79	90
	2300	4.8	74	85
10500	2500	5.6	81	95
	2400	5.1	77	90
	2300	4.7	72	84
11500	2500	5.5	80	94
	2400	5.0	75	89
	2300	4.7	70	82

*Cruise performance is based on best power mixture. Lean to maximum rpm for best performance.

the engine will be burning 5.7 gallons of fuel per hour (with the engine leaned, of course).

The maximum range and endurance you can expect at this speed and altitude can be determined with the graphical data shown in Figures 6.13 and 6.14. These charts are very useful because they include a fuel allowance for start-up, taxi, takeoff, climb, and a 45-minute reserve. (You must make such allowances if the handbook data do not.) To use the charts, find your cruising altitude on the left-hand margin, then move horizontally until you encounter the desired cruising rpm guideline. Now drop down vertically from that point to read the range or endurance. These values assume no wind. With full fuel tanks and the example flight conditions, the range would be 392 nautical miles, and the endurance would be 4.2 hours.

Let us compare these values to those obtained with another power setting. What if you were to use 2300 rpm instead of 2500 at the same altitude? Figure 6.12 lists the new true airspeed as 85 knots, or 10 knots less. Obviously, the flight would take longer. Now refer to Figure 6.13. The range at the lower power setting goes up to 412 nautical miles, and endurance (Figure 6.14) increases to 4.95 hours. Overall, the lower power setting trades speed for efficiency.

Suppose you needed to circumnavigate some bad weather during your flight. You may be able to safely go the extra distance by reducing speed

Figure 6.13 Range performance chart.

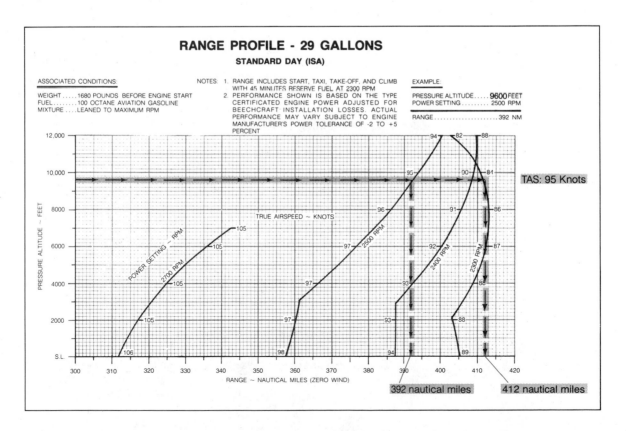

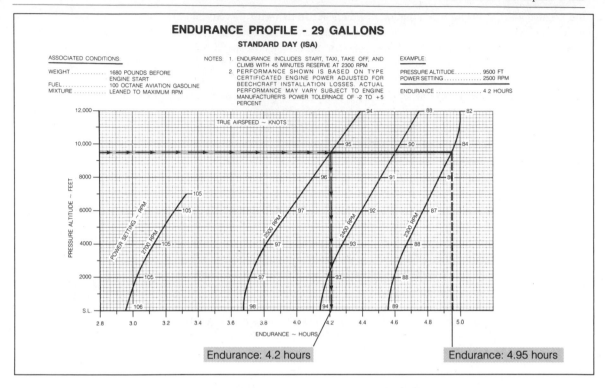

Figure 6.14 Endurance performance chart.

to increase range (the effects of wind must be considered also). If you fly into a very busy air terminal, you may have to **hold** (fly around in circles over a fixed position) while awaiting your turn to land. Again, a speed reduction is in order, to increase your endurance. You would have to recalculate your remaining range and/or endurance, on the basis of the fuel remaining when the power change is made. You will learn to do this quickly and accurately with your flight computer in a later chapter.

TIPS ON FUEL ECONOMY

Conserving fuel has always been a tradition in aviation. Plenty of fuel on board can overcome most of the problems that might come between a pilot and a safe, expeditious landing—variables such as weather, wind, and navigational error. High fuel costs and shortages mean that pilots must now watch fuel usage on even the most routine flights. Here are some hints on how to keep your bills for avgas as low as possible:

1. A dirty airplane uses more fuel than does a clean one. Dirt, mud, and bird droppings all add drag.

2. Do not take unnecessary weight aboard the airplane. Every 1 percent increase in gross weight reduces your range by approximately the same amount. Load the airplane near (but *never beyond*) the aft CG limit.

3. Turn directly on course as soon as possible after takeoff. Consider using a climb speed that provides adequate visibility over the nose. This will reduce (but not eliminate) the need for turns to check for traffic, which slow your climb.

4. Lean the engine properly during all phases of flight.

5. Plan shallow descents (300 to 500 feet per minute) from cruise flight to the landing pattern. Keep normal power on the engine and take advantage of the speed increase (unless turbulence does not allow it). Steep, power-off descents are hard on the ears and on the engine.

LANDING PERFORMANCE

There are two indisputable facts about landings that every pilot must learn. First, any landing that you can walk away from is a "good" landing. (However, some good landings are better than others.) Second, no matter how carefully you plan a flight, or how skillfully you execute it, your passengers will judge the entire flight by the landing. Now that the important points are out of the way, we can move on to the details of landing performance.

Perhaps no other factor contributes more to a safe and efficient landing than the early establishment of the proper final-approach attitude and airspeed. Make corrections as early as possible in the landing process, to establish the proper crosswind correction, airspeed, trim, and glide path. Catch any discrepancies early, so that only small corrections are necessary in your final approach. Large corrections close to the runway are an invitation to disaster and reflect poor planning. A final approach that is stabilized early, on the desired glide path, at the proper attitude and airspeed, is hard to spoil.

There are various maximum-performance landing techniques, just as with various takeoff procedures. A **short field landing** is designed to touch down near the end of the runway and get the airplane stopped in the shortest possible distance. Proper airspeed control is essential for two reasons. First, your approach will be made at the slowest safe airspeed. Understandably, the slower you are going, the easier it is to stop in a short distance. Second, any excess airspeed will cause unwanted floating due to ground effect. A short field landing requires little or no floating to be successful. A *soft field landing* strives to delay touchdown until the airplane is at the minimum possible forward speed. The danger here is that the airplane will sink into the soft surface and flip over if the forward speed is too high. As with the soft field takeoff, ground effect and power are used to hold the airplane off the ground as long as possible. You will practice both these special landings as part of your flight training program.

Computing Landing Performance

Figure 6.15 shows a typical landing distance chart. As you arrive in Wichita to conclude the example flight, we will assume the following conditions:

NORMAL LANDING DISTANCES

ASSOCIATED CONDITIONS

POWER	OFF
FLAPS	35
GEAR	DOWN
RUNWAY	PAVED, LEVEL, DRY SURFACE
WEIGHT	2750 POUNDS
APPROACH SPEED	85 MPH/74 KTS IAS

NOTES:

1. GROUND ROLL IS APPROXIMATELY 45% OF TOTAL DISTANCE OVER 50 FT. OBSTACLE
2. FOR EACH 100 LBS. BELOW 2750 LBS. REDUCE TABULATED DISTANCE BY 3% AND APPROACH SPEED BY 1 MPH.

WIND COMPONENT DOWN RUNWAY KNOTS	SEA LEVEL		2000 FT		4000 FT		6000 FT		8000 FT	
	OAT °F	TOTAL OVER 50 FT OBSTACLE FEET	OAT °F	TOTAL OVER 50 FT OBSTACLE FEET	OAT °F	TOTAL OVER 50 FT OBSTACLE FEET	OAT °F	TOTAL OVER 50 FT OBSTACLE FEET	OAT °F	TOTAL OVER 50 FT OBSTACLE FEET
0	23	1578	16	1651	9	1732	2	1820	-6	1916
	41	1624	34	1701	27	1787	20	1880	13	1983
	59	1670	52	1752	45	1842	38	1942	31	2050
	77	1717	70	1804	63	1899	56	2004	49	2118
	95	1764	88	1856	81	1956	74	2066	66	2187
15	23	1329	16	1397	9	1472	2	1555	-6	1644
	41	1372	34	1444	27	1524	20	1611	13	1707
	59	1414	52	1491	45	1575	38	1668	31	1770
	77	1458	70	1540	63	1626	56	1727	49	1833
	95	1502	88	1588	81	1682	74	1784	66	1898
30	23	1079	16	1142	9	1212	2	1289	-6	1372
	41	1119	34	1186	27	1260	20	1341	13	1430
	59	1158	52	1230	45	1308	38	1395	31	1489
	77	1199	70	1275	63	1357	56	1449	49	1548
	95	1240	88	1320	81	1407	74	1502	66	1608

Figure 6.15 Landing performance chart.

Landing weight: 2050 pounds
Pressure-altitude: 2000 feet
Temperature: 70 degrees Fahrenheit
Headwind: 15 knots

The runway in Wichita is hard surfaced and is 5000 feet long. Determine the landing distance over a 50-foot obstacle, as well as the ground roll.

This chart is very similar to those used previously for other performance calculations, so we will not repeat how to use the chart. For the given conditions, an airplane weighing 2750 pounds would require 1540 feet to clear the obstacle. Since your landing weight is 700 pounds less than that, Note 2 applies as follows:

$$7 \times 3\% = 21\% \text{ reduction of table value}$$

$$1540 - (0.21 \times 1540) = 1217 \text{ feet to land over an obstacle}$$

Next, Note 1 applies to compute the ground roll:

$$\text{Ground roll} = 1217 \times 0.45 = 548 \text{ feet}$$

A runway length of 5000 feet is more than adequate. You end the example flight with a precise approach and a very smooth touchdown. We are suitably impressed.

FLYING BY THE BOOK

In the midst of all these tables and charts you may come to think that a pilot is some sort of robot that functions best by thinking least. This is far from the case. Charts and tables do not fly the airplane.

As stated before, the charts and tables in the Pilot's Operating Handbook are based on data determined by a skilled test pilot using a new, clean airplane with a new, finely tuned engine. In actual fact, the typical pilot using an airplane with dents and dirt and a used engine cannot duplicate this performance. Additionally, the manufacturer used exact runway temperature; on a sunny day this can be 10 to 30 degrees Fahrenheit more than the reported temperature. The prudent pilot assumes the actual performance will be less than that calculated using existing conditions and the charts and tables. Conditions change constantly in the flying environment, and no two situations are ever precisely alike. The flexibility to meet ever-changing conditions makes the pilot the most valuable "device" in the cockpit.

KEY TERMS

atmospheric pressure	performance
best angle of climb	pressure-altitude
best rate of climb	runway gradient
crosswind	short field landing
density-altitude	soft field landing
headwind	standard atmosphere
maximum endurance	tailwind
maximum range	

PROFICIENCY CHECK

1. Test pilots are highly skilled, disciplined fliers. Since performance data in the Pilot's Operating Handbook is derived from FAA flight test experience in the airplane, can the average pilot hope to match this performance? Explain.

2. How are density-altitude and pressure-altitude related? How are they different? How does each affect airplane performance?

3. Refer to the *density-altitude conversion chart* in Figure 6.2 (repeated on page 174) and the takeoff performance problem presented on page 160. Using the chart, find the corresponding density-altitude for the takeoff conditions at Denver. Is this altitude higher or lower than the ISA altitude?

4. Using the charts supplied in the text and the data below, compute: takeoff distance; distance to clear a 50-foot obstacle; fuel, time, and distance to climb to cruise altitude; maximum range and maximum endurance, giving the TAS, pressure-altitude, and rpm setting required for each; and landing ground run.

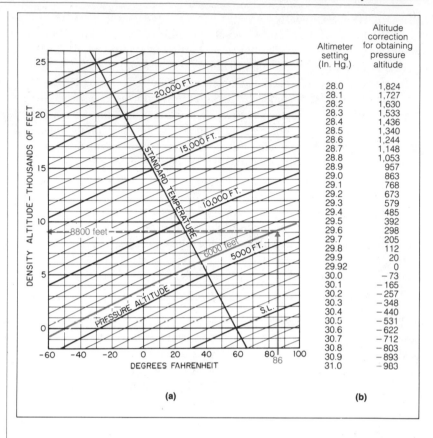

Altimeter setting (In. Hg.)	Altitude correction for obtaining pressure altitude
28.0	1,824
28.1	1,727
28.2	1,630
28.3	1,533
28.4	1,436
28.5	1,340
28.6	1,244
28.7	1,148
28.8	1,053
28.9	957
29.0	863
29.1	768
29.2	673
29.3	579
29.4	485
29.5	392
29.6	298
29.7	205
29.8	112
29.9	20
29.92	0
30.0	−73
30.1	−165
30.2	−257
30.3	−348
30.4	−440
30.5	−531
30.6	−622
30.7	−712
30.8	−803
30.9	−893
31.0	−903

(a)   (b)

Airplane takeoff weight: 2000 pounds
Departing airport conditions:
    OAT: 75 degrees Fahrenheit
    Field elevation: 2388 feet
    Altimeter setting: 29.82
    Runway: 18R, 5000 feet long, concrete surface
    Winds: 110° at 15 knots
Cruise conditions:
    Desired altitude: 7500 feet pressure-altitude
    OAT: 32 degrees Fahrenheit
    Winds aloft: zero
Landing conditions:
    OAT: 45 degrees Fahrenheit
    Field elevation: 4275 feet
    Altimeter setting: 28.76
    Runway: 9, hard surface
    Winds: calm
    Landing weight: 2000 pounds

5. An airplane takes off into a direct 20-knot headwind. The stalling speed of the airplane is 50 knots, and its indicated airspeed in a climb is 65 knots. If the pilot turns the airplane downwind and the 20-knot headwind becomes a 20-knot tailwind, will the airplane stall? Explain why or why not.

6. True or false? When landing at an airport with a high density-altitude, a pilot should add extra speed to the final-approach indicated airspeed to compensate for the thinner air. Explain your answer.

PART III
THE FLYING ENVIRONMENT

Those who praise the FAA do so because of the careful way in which so many of its faceless employees all around the country go about their jobs. There are people who check airport equipment, check out pilots, check out flying schools, airplanes—you name it. In almost all cases they know the vital importance of their jobs, and they take them seriously, without pulling rank.

F. Lee Bailey
Cleared for the Approach

C H E C K P O I N T S

How do airports relate to the national airspace system? ✈ How does a pilot plan and conduct a typical local flight? ✈ What kinds of airports are there and how do pilots use their facilities? ✈ How do pilots use aeronautical radios?

AIRPORTS, AIRSPACE, AND LOCAL FLYING

One of the benefits you will enjoy as a private pilot is the choice of a wide range of airfields to visit on cross-country flights or to claim as your home airport. Airports are owned and operated by either private interests or public agencies. Commercial air carriers require facilities with elaborate servicing equipment and passenger terminals, in addition to air traffic control assistance and hard-surface runways—a combination available at fewer than 500 airports. As a general-aviation pilot, however, you have at your disposal many remote or local privately owned airfields in addition to all public airports—a total of nearly 15,000 facilities. Private airports outnumber public airports by nearly two to one, though most of them have unimproved (grass- or dirt-surface) runways. Most public airports are owned and operated by municipalities, though a lesser number are operated by counties or special airport districts. Whatever their source of funding, *all* airports are under the jurisdiction of federal regulations governing runway and approach-zone identification, lighting, condition, operating procedures, traffic control, and communications. Airports with operating towers to supervise and coordinate the flow of ground and air traffic are called **controlled airports**, though the tower may be operated by a private or municipal agency as well as the FAA. Airports without operating control towers are called **uncontrolled airports**, but, as you will see, that does not imply disorderly flight operations. Uncontrolled airports have definite procedures prescribed by the FAA and supervised by the pilots themselves. You will learn about both types of airports in this chapter.

AIRPORT AND RUNWAY MARKINGS AND IDENTIFICATION

Airports must provide the means to launch and retrieve many high-speed vehicles (runways), to guide them safely to their destinations (taxiways), and to park them in an appropriate area (the airport ramp). Although the ground traffic systems may seem complex at first, especially at large terminals, airport and runway markings are a logical and concise system for traffic coordination developed over many years of use.

Taxiways

Taxiway markings.   A single 6-inch-wide yellow line is used to mark the centerline of taxiways. The edge of the taxiway may also be marked by two thinner, parallel lines 6 inches apart. Where a taxiway meets a runway, **holding lines** are painted across the taxiway (see Figure 7.1). You must always stop short of the holding line until you are cleared by the tower to cross it. On a landing roll, however, you should clear the active runway (cross the line onto a taxiway) without the tower's permission. At uncontrolled airports, you must hold short until you have determined that you are clear of all traffic, both before takeoff and on approach for landing.

At some airports you may find an additional set of holding lines, called *category II holding lines,* which consist of two solid lines joined by bars crossing the taxiway. Category II refers to marginal weather conditions, during which sensitive precision-approach aids are used at the airport. Since your airplane and its equipment might interfere with these systems, you

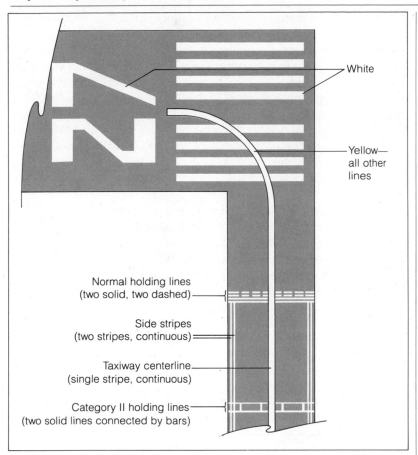

White

Yellow—
all other
lines

Normal holding lines
(two solid, two dashed)

Side stripes
(two stripes, continuous)

Taxiway centerline
(single stripe, continuous)

Category II holding lines
(two solid lines connected by bars)

Figure 7.1 Taxiway markings. All
taxiways are marked in yellow paint.

must hold a farther distance from the runway threshold than under normal circumstances. The tower will inform you if category II equipment is being used.

Taxi signs.   Many airports have a system of taxi signs that assist pilots in moving airplanes from place to place on the ground with minimal instructions from the tower. There are two types of taxi signs: destination and intersection. Destination signs indicate the route to certain facilities, such as Ramp (parking area), Fuel, and HGR (hangar). Intersection signs are marked with the identification numbers of the runway they intersect, such as 9-27. At some airports the taxiways are identified by a letter, such as taxiway A (spoken as "taxiway alpha"), and you may be directed by the tower to use that particular route.

Runways
Runway markings.   The **runway identification number** is always presented as one or two numerals representing the "hundreds" and "tens" digits

of the runway's magnetic heading. For headings of less than 100° magnetic, the first zero is deleted for easier reading. Thus, the first zero in a heading of east, 090, is deleted along with the last, giving a runway with a due-east heading an identification number of 9. Since a runway can usually be used in both directions, the identification number at the other end of the runway is the **reciprocal heading** of the first. A reciprocal heading is the opposite of any given heading, obtained by adding (or subtracting) 180° to (or from) the original number. For example, the reciprocal of 090 is 270, or west. Therefore, runway 9 would have a reciprocal identification number of 27 at its opposite end. Parallel runways are identified by L for left, C for center, or R for right. You will always be told which runway of a series of runways you should use for takeoff or landing.

The other types of runway markings depend on whether or not the runway can be used for instrument approaches. A **basic runway** (see Figure 7.2a), or one *without* a published instrument approach procedure, is marked with a white runway number and dashed centerline. A runway *with* a published (but nonprecision) instrument approach has both of these features plus threshold identification markings (see Figure 7.2b). The **threshold** is the boundary that marks the usable part of the runway. The pilot should land beyond this portion of the runway. Runways with more sophisticated precision approach landing aids have all of the above markings plus side stripes and a touchdown zone or fixed-distance markers. **Side stripes** delimit the boundary of the runway. The **touchdown zone** or **fixed-distance markers** are a series of parallel stripes in line with the runway heading placed in diminishing numbers (four, three, two, and finally one) every 500 feet from the threshold (see Figure 7.2c). Typically, you will see these latter markings only at larger airports.

Displaced threshold.   Sometimes an entire runway is not suitable for landing because of obstructions or the like. The need to keep off a particular runway section is indicated by marking the runway with a **displaced threshold**, as shown in Figure 7.3. This threshold marking is a solid line across the runway with chevrons along one side of it. If arrows point to the displaced threshold, then the nonlanding portion may nevertheless be used for taxi and takeoff.

Unusable areas.   Any surfaces marked with yellow chevrons, or parallel yellow stripes, as shown in Figure 7.4, are for emergency use only. **Stabilized areas**, **overrun areas**, and **stopways** are marked in this manner. These areas should not be used for takeoffs, landings, or taxiing.

Closed runways.   A runway closed for repairs or one that has been deactivated permanently is marked with a broad X at both ends (see Figure 7.5). This mark must always be respected, since the landing surface may be obstructed by workers or equipment.

Closed taxiways may also be marked in this manner.

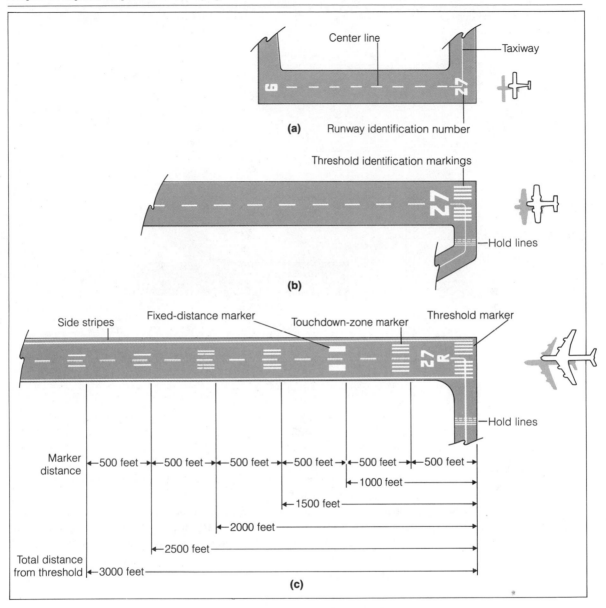

Figure 7.2 Runway markings.
(a) Basic runway. (b) Runway served by a nonprecision approach. (c) Runway served by a precision approach.

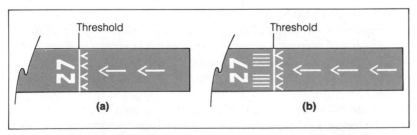

Figure 7.3 Displaced thresholds.
(a) Basic runway. (b) Runway served by an instrument approach.

Figure 7.4 Overrun and stopway areas.

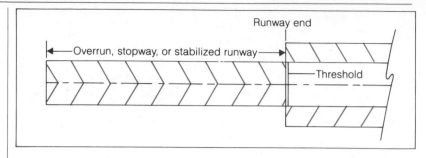

Figure 7.5 Closed runway or taxiway markings.

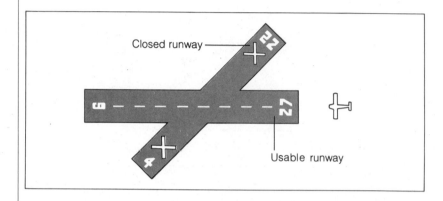

Airport Lighting

Standard runway lighting includes white lights along the sides of the runway, green lights along the threshold, and red lights at the runway's departure end. Blue lights mark the taxiway turnoff points and frequently the taxiways themselves. Extra caution must be used whenever you land at night, especially when the airport is unfamiliar or poorly equipped. Civilian airports can be recognized at night by a rotating beacon featuring an alternating white and green light. Military airports feature a double-flashing white light alternating with the green. Obstructions are marked with red lights, such as those commonly seen on radio towers, tall buildings, and bridges (see Figure 7.6). If you see an airport's rotating beacon illuminated during the day, it means that current weather conditions are *below* VFR minimums.

TRAFFIC PATTERNS

A preestablished **traffic pattern** allows a large volume of aircraft to use the airport with maximum safety and efficiency. A **standard traffic pattern** (Figure 7.7a) is flown using left turns only (except at entry, as shown in the figure). **Nonstandard traffic patterns** are flown to the right (Figure 7.7b).

The **takeoff** or **upwind leg** of any pattern consists of a climb straight ahead (position 1 in Figure 7.7) to within 300 feet of pattern altitude, unless

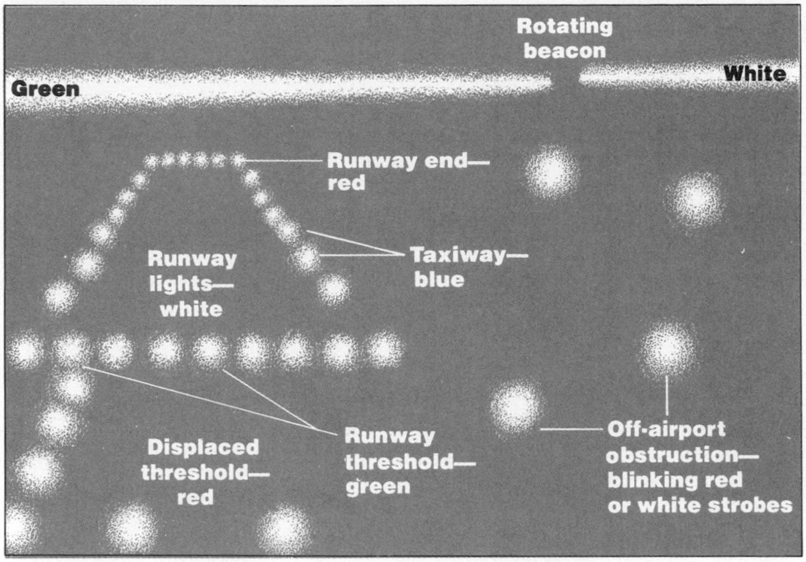

Figure 7.6 Airport lighting.

local procedures differ. The **crosswind leg** (2) is flown at 90 degrees to the takeoff leg. The timing of this turn is based on your clearance from other airplanes in the pattern, but it should never be commenced before crossing the departure end of the runway. The **downwind leg** (3) parallels the runway but is flown in the opposite direction from the takeoff leg. The downwind leg is usually flown at 1000 feet AGL, although this altitude may be different at some airports. This altitude is known as the **pattern altitude** and is determined by adding the pattern altitude to the airport's field elevation. For example, a 1000-foot pattern altitude flown above an airport at a 1700-foot elevation would read 2700 feet MSL on the altimeter.

When your airplane is opposite the intended touchdown point (as traffic spacing permits), use your before-landing checklist, reduce power, and start your descent. At an appropriate distance from the touchdown point, turn 90 degrees onto the **base leg** (4), at which time you should perform the procedures on your pre-landing checklist. **Final approach** (5) is flown into the wind, in line with the runway, in the direction of landing. The term *long final* refers to the portion of the final approach just after the turn from base leg. The term *short final* refers to that segment of the final approach just prior to the threshold. You may have to extend your base turn sometimes because of traffic congestion on base or final approach. In such cases, your long final may be considerably longer than usual, and you will have to delay your descent from pattern altitude somewhat to avoid a *dragged-in* (too low) final approach.

Procedures for entry into the traffic pattern (6) can vary, but generally an angle of 45 degrees to the downwind leg is preferred. As you can infer from the diagram, this point in the traffic pattern has potential for conflict. As a new arrival to the pattern, you must yield right of way when necessary to other aircraft established on the downwind leg. While waiting your turn,

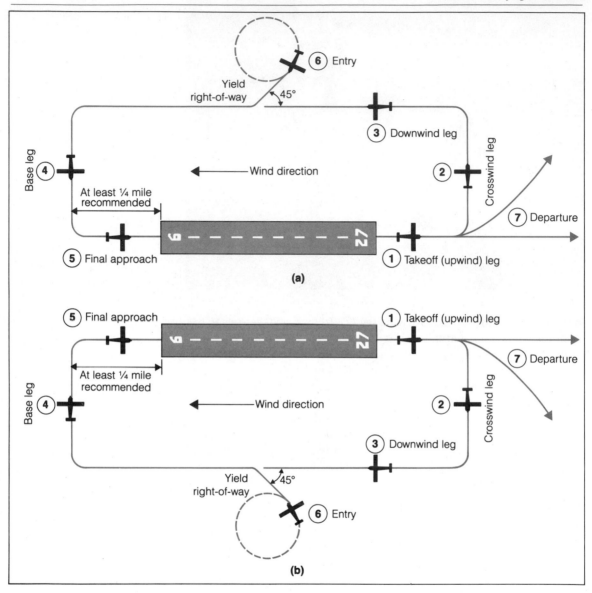

Figure 7.7 Traffic patterns.
(a) Standard (left turning).
(b) Nonstandard (right turning).

you continue in a circle in the direction of the entry turn until space on the downwind leg is available.

Traffic pattern departures (7) usually involve a 45-degree turn away from the crosswind or downwind leg, or in some cases they can be flown by climbing straight ahead. At controlled airports you may ask for or the tower will specify the method of entry and departure you must use. At uncontrolled airports, you should look up the local procedures in your flight information publications and abide by them. Your instructor will show you how to fly these patterns, how to judge distances and where to turn, and the techniques used to compensate for winds.

The Segmented Circle

There are a number of ways to determine which type of traffic pattern (left or right) to use for a particular runway. In a later chapter you will see that this information can be found in flight publications you will use during preflight planning. This discussion will deal with the methods available in flight.

At controlled airports, the tower will give you takeoff and landing information and instructions over the radio. At uncontrolled airports, traffic information may be available by radio on the Common Traffic Advisory Frequency (CTAF), discussed later in this chapter. In cases where radio information is unavailable, the pilot should fly over the airport well above pattern altitude and inspect the **segmented circle** installed near the runway (see Figure 7.8a). This circle may contain a number of components that vary from airport to airport.

Usually, a wind direction indicator is placed in the center of the segmented circle, as shown in Figure 7.8a. The wind indicator may be a **wind sock**, a **tetrahedron**, or a **wind T**. All three are pictured in Figure 7.8b.

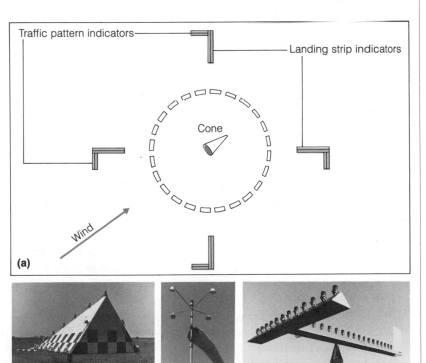

Traffic pattern indicators——

Landing strip indicators

Cone

Wind

(a)

(b)

Figure 7.8 **(a)** Segmented circle with landing strip and traffic pattern indicators. **(b)** Wind direction indicators (from left): a tetrahedron, a wind sock, a wind T.

The wind T is sometimes confusing to interpret. Notice that the body of the T has a rudder mounted on it, which acts like the rudder on an airplane. The crossbar resembles the airplane's wings. *The crossbar of the wind T always points into the wind.*

At airports with more than one runway, you may find two wind indicators in the circle. One is usually a wind sock, the second either a tetrahedron or wind T. The tetrahedron or wind T will be tied into a fixed position to indicate the preferred runway. In this role it is called a **landing direction indicator**. The wind sock is always free to show the actual wind conditions.

Around the segmented circle you may find **traffic pattern indicators**. There is an L-shaped marker representing the *approach end* of each runway. One leg of the L points toward the circle, showing the direction of the runway. This is the *landing strip indicator.* The other leg is called the *traffic pattern indicator* because it specifies the direction of the traffic pattern for that runway. The L represents the *base to final turn* for that runway. The direction of that turn (left or right) is the direction of the traffic pattern.

Look at Figure 7.8a. The landing strip indicators tell us that there are two runways, one oriented north-south, the other east-west. To land to the north, we would approach the south end of the north-south runway. The base to final turn indicated (at the bottom of the picture) is to the left. Now let us land to the east (left to right in Figure 7.8a). The appropriate indicator is the one on the left (the approach end of the runway). This time right turns are indicated.

A flashing **amber light** in the segmented circle, on top of the control tower, or on an adjoining building is another way to indicate that a right-hand traffic pattern is in effect. If no L markers are found outside the segmented circle and if no amber light is flashing, then all runways have left-hand traffic patterns.

Visual Landing Aids

On a normal final approach path of 3 degrees to the horizon, even the largest runway can become a pretty small target (see Figure 7.9a). It is very easy to establish a **glide path** (the angle of descent on final approach) that is too low or too high. Low or dragged-in approaches are dangerous because the airplane may not have adequate terrain clearance in case of turbulence or engine malfunction. High approaches are also undesirable because they may lead a pilot to "dive" for the runway, creating a very high rate of descent and creating the possibility of a hard landing or of overflying the touchdown zone.

To assist pilots in maintaining a safe glide path, many airports have installed a **visual approach slope indicator (VASI)**. This system (see Figure 7.10) uses two groups of high-intensity lights, mounted on one, or both, sides of the runway. The first group, called the *downwind bars,* is approximately 600 feet from the threshold. The second group, the *upwind bars,* is approximately 700 feet beyond the first group. Viewed from the perspective of the cockpit, the downwind bars appear lower on the wind-

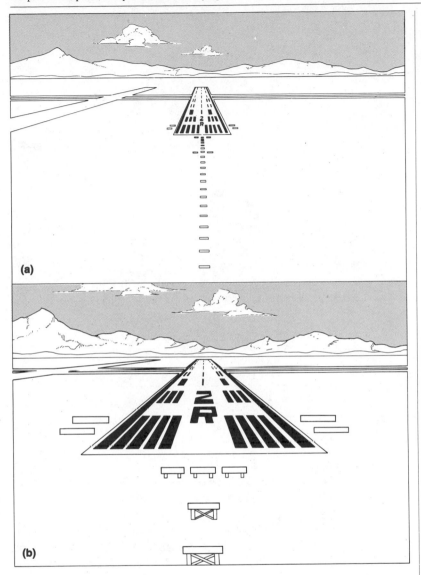

Figure 7.9 Landing perspectives for a 3-degree approach. **(a)** One-half mile from threshold, 200 feet high. **(b)** One-eighth mile from threshold, 80 feet high.

screen while the upwind bars appear above the downwind bars. A color filter assembly splits the light emitted into red and white components. When the pilot flies a normal **glide slope** (the glide path defined by the VASI), the downwind or lowest group of lights shows white, and the upwind or upper group shows red. If the airplane begins to descend below the glide slope, the upper group stays red, and the lower group turns pink and finally red, indicating that the airplane is well below the glide slope. If the airplane begins to climb above the glide slope, the upper group becomes pink, and the lower group remains white. When the airplane is well above the glide slope, both groups are white. The lights are calibrated to guide the airplane

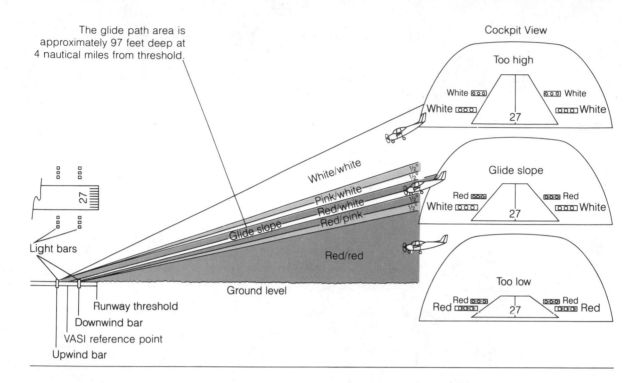

The glide path area is approximately 97 feet deep at 4 nautical miles from threshold.

Cockpit View

Too high

White ▭▭▭   ▭▭▭ White
White ▭▭▭   ▭▭▭ White
                27

White/white

Glide slope

Red ▭▭▭   ▭▭▭ Red
White ▭▭▭   ▭▭▭ White
                27

Pink/white
Red/white
Red/pink
Red/red

Too low

Red ▭▭▭   ▭▭▭ Red
Red ▭▭▭   ▭▭▭ Red
Red   27   Red

Ground level

27

Light bars

Runway threshold
Downwind bar
VASI reference point
Upwind bar

Figure 7.10 Visual approach slope indicator (VASI).

to a runway touchdown point approximately 1000 feet from the threshold. The correct approach is one in which *red* is maintained *over white*.

Uncontrolled Airports

As we mentioned earlier, the term *uncontrolled airport* is a bit of a misnomer. Although there may be no tower to clear aircraft to taxi, take off, and land, those functions are accomplished quite smoothly by pilot reference to airport markings and adherence to established procedures. Quite often, airport advisory information is available over the radio, even at uncontrolled airports. All airports have a radio frequency designated for this purpose called the Common Traffic Advisory Frequency (CTAF). The CTAF may be a UNICOM, MULTICOM, FSS, or tower frequency and is identified in appropriate aeronautical publications.

UNICOM.   To aid pilots at an uncontrolled airport, a local facility (flying school, FBO, or airport manager) may be designated an **Aeronautical Advisory Station (AAS)** and be allowed to operate a private radio service, called **UNICOM**. Figure 7.11 illustrates a portion of an aeronautical chart showing how to identify uncontrolled airports and their UNICOM frequencies. The information this service provides includes the active runway, winds, and any other notices pertinent to safe operations. UNICOM does *not,* however, provide any sort of traffic control service. Pilots using uncon-

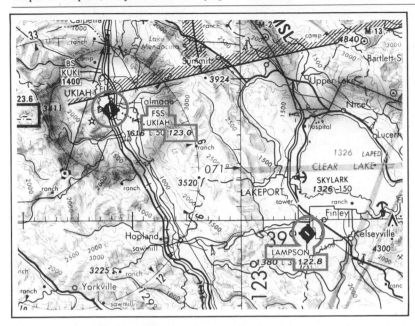

Figure 7.11 Uncontrolled airports. The data are printed in magenta on aeronautical charts.

trolled airports are responsible for adequate spacing between aircraft for takeoff, in the traffic pattern, for landing, and during ground operations.

UNICOM may also be used for general information, such as inquiries about the availability of fuel, food, lodging, or ground transportation at the airport. It can often be of assistance in arranging for these services when necessary. More important, it can be of significant aid in an emergency, since flight instructors or mechanics are often nearby.

Keep in mind that UNICOM is a voluntary service provided by the airport. Many UNICOMs are unattended, or the airport personnel may be busy with other duties, so you cannot depend on a UNICOM to provide information or services. Perhaps the greatest value of UNICOM is its use as a common frequency by all airplanes in the airport area. By monitoring UNICOM and by reporting their own positions (such as taxiing to the active runway, entering the pattern, or turning onto final approach), pilots can assist each other in keeping track of airport traffic. Obviously, then, using the frequency to hold extended chats with friends or the ground operator is not only inconsiderate but potentially dangerous, since it prevents use of the frequency for its intended purpose. Think of UNICOM as a telephone party line in a crowded building, and use it only for essential communications.

Once again, be aware of the limitations of UNICOM. Using UNICOM in the traffic pattern is not mandatory. There may be airplanes in the area that do not even have radios. Always assume that there are pilots in the area who are *not* using UNICOM, and plan your actions accordingly.

FAA Flight Service Stations.   A very important service to pilots at controlled or uncontrolled airports or en route is the **FAA Flight Service Sta-**

tion. This facility provides you with detailed information about terminal and en route weather and operating conditions, assists you in opening and closing your flight plan, and follows your progress. During flight, the station is addressed over the radio by the name of its location and the word *radio;* thus the FSS in Phoenix, Arizona, is addressed Phoenix Radio. You can also contact the FSS before your flight in person, by telephone, or on the ramp if it is within range of your airplane radio. If the FSS is located on an uncontrolled field, airport advisory services are also available on its frequency, 123.6 MHz. Frequencies for other FSS services are provided in a later chapter.

MULTICOM and other frequencies.   When you fly into public airports that have no control tower, FSS, or UNICOM, the frequency 122.9 MHz (called **MULTICOM**) should be used for communications at and around the airport. If you fly into a private airport, you should use either 122.725 or 122.75. (Since these airports are not open to the public, you need to make prior arrangements with the owner/operator, who can tell you the proper frequency.) Frequency 122.75 is also to be used for air-to-air communications. Certain general-aviation operations (such as crop dusting, skydiving, and fire fighting) often use the air-to-air frequency, so it is a good one to monitor when flying in an area where these activities are taking place.

Controlled Airports and Supporting Services
Airports with a high volume of traffic or traffic with a regular mix of high-performance and low-performance airplanes generally have control towers. To be a *controlled airport*, however, the tower must be operational. Many airports have towers that operate only during certain hours. When the tower is not operating, the field is uncontrolled, and procedures for uncontrolled airports are in effect. The tower frequency becomes the CTAF under these circumstances (*not* the UNICOM frequency, if one is listed). If there is an FSS located on the field, it will provide airport advisory service, also over the tower frequency (*not* 123.6).

Airport traffic area.   Flights into and out of controlled airports bring with them increased pilot duties and responsibilities. This means abiding by the rules of the **airport traffic area (ATA)** (Figure 7.12b), an area extending from the ground up to, but not including, 3000 feet above the airport elevation, with a radius of 5 statute miles around the airport—but *only* when the tower is operating. (Note: There are a few specially designated airports that have nonstandard ATAs.) No aircraft movement is allowed on the ground or in the air inside the ATA without two-way radio communications with and authorization from the tower. The one exception to this rule is when you are operating at an uncontrolled field within the tower's area of responsibility. The boundaries of the ATA are not depicted on aeronautical charts; however, all airports that have a control tower are given a *blue* airport symbol on the chart (uncontrolled airports have magenta

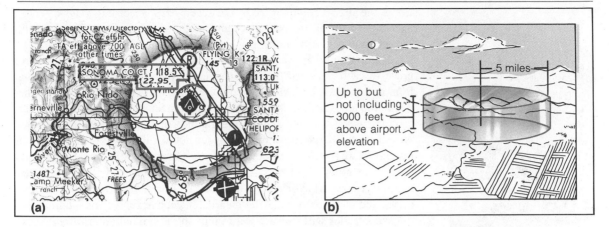

symbols). Controlled airports also have a "CT" designation, followed by the tower frequency in the airport data key (see Figure 7.12a).

When you first contact the tower for either taxi or landing instructions, you will be given the active runway and winds and any other relevant information about the airport's operational status, as well as the correct altimeter setting.

Automatic Terminal Information Service.   At many busy airports, an **Automatic Terminal Information Service (ATIS)** broadcast is available. This is a prerecorded message containing noncontrol information relevant to the airport and its operations, including weather conditions, surface winds, altimeter setting, active runway information, tower frequencies, and any special advisories concerning airport hazards or equipment, such as runways or taxiways under repair. When ATIS is available, the radio frequency at which it can be received is listed on aeronautical charts. Each ATIS message is identified by a letter assigned in alphabetical order as each message is updated. For example, the first ATIS broadcast of a sequence would be labeled *information alpha*. This message would be broadcast continuously until the information was updated. The second broadcast would then be labeled *information bravo*, the next *charlie*, the next *delta*, and so forth. The information designator is given at the beginning and end of each broadcast cycle.

When ATIS is available, you should receive its information before contacting the tower (in flight) or ground control (prior to taxi) to avoid unnecessary radio traffic. On initial contact with the tower or ground controller (or approach control if you are arriving cross-country), state that you have received the current ATIS broadcast by repeating the current letter designator. For example, a pretaxi radio call might be: "Los Angeles Ground, Beechcraft two zero eight eight foxtrot, ready to taxi, information bravo."

As you would expect, all aircraft flying in the ATA are monitored by the tower. This means that you may be asked to give a position report when you reach a certain location within the area, even if you do not intend to

Figure 7.12 **(a)** Controlled airport data are printed in blue on aeronautical charts. **(b)** An airport traffic area (ATA).

Figure 7.13 Using a light-signal gun.

land at the airport being served by the tower. Also, according to FAR 91.70, the airspeed for all reciprocating engine aircraft within the ATA must not exceed 156 knots (180 miles per hour) for safety.

It is important that you maintain awareness of the radio frequency appropriate to each phase of flight, particularly when arriving at or departing from a controlled airport. On departure, you will generally tune into the ATIS frequency if one is available, then contact ground control for your taxi clearance. You will stay on the ground control frequency until in the vicinity of the active runway. After your initial call to the tower, you will maintain tower contact until released by the tower controller to the departure control (or other) frequency. On arrival, the sequence is reversed. After listening to the ATIS message, you will call up approach control, if one exists, and then the tower. After clearing the active runway on landing, the tower controller will instruct you to tune in the ground control frequency, which you will use until the airplane is parked on the ramp.

The two important things to remember about communications in controlled airspace are: maintain awareness of which controlling agency *should* have jurisdiction over your current phase of flight, and do not leave an assigned frequency until you are cleared to do so by the controller involved.

Procedures in case of an inoperative radio. Since operations in the ATA are heavily dependent upon radio communications, what happens if your radio fails in flight? Fortunately, this is a comparatively rare occurrence, and it is even rarer that a tower is unable to initiate or receive communications. But when two-way radio communications are not possible, a system of light signals is used to clear airplanes for taxi, takeoffs, and landings, and to transmit a variety of other messages. Figure 7.13 shows a light gun in use, and Table 7.1 gives the meanings of various light signals. It is even possible to fly an airplane without a radio (uninstalled or inoperative before takeoff) into a controlled field if prior arrangements are made with the tower by telephone.

Table 7.1 Light-Signal Codes

	Meaning of the signal	
Type and color of signal	*Aircraft on the ground*	*Aircraft in flight*
Steady green	Cleared for takeoff	Cleared to land
Flashing green	Cleared to taxi	Return for landing (followed by steady green at proper time)
Steady red	Stop	Yield to other aircraft and continue circling
Flashing red	Taxi clear of runway in use	Airport unsafe—do not land
Flashing white	Return to starting point on airport	
Alternating red and green	General warning signal—exercise extreme caution	

If your radio fails in flight, remain outside or above the airport traffic area until you have determined the traffic pattern in use. Then you should join the traffic pattern using the standard downwind entry discussed previously. If there is the slightest possibility that *only the receiver* has failed, transmit your intentions to the tower. Even if you cannot receive a reply, this may allow the tower controller to plan for your stated actions. (*Your* actions will be the same, whether your transmissions are being received or not.) Watch the tower for light signals, and act accordingly.

It is also possible for your receiver to be operative but not the transmitter. Again, enter the traffic pattern in the normal manner. When the tower controller spots the added traffic, he/she will normally ask "the red Cessna (or whatever) entering downwind, please rock your wings (or flash your lights) if you receive this transmission." If you respond to this request, you will continue to acknowledge instructions in this manner and forgo the light-gun signals.

CONTROLLED AND UNCONTROLLED AIRSPACE

In good weather, *all* aircraft operate under the principle of *visual separation*. This principle means that pilots are responsible for seeing and avoiding other aircraft. The FARs specify the minimum weather that must prevail for **Visual Flight Rules (VFR)** to apply. (These regulations are discussed in the following paragraphs.) Most airplanes, and many pilots, are capable of flying in poor weather, called **instrument meteorological conditions (IMC),** where visual separation is impossible. Under these conditions the pilots are flying solely by reference to their instruments, so **Instrument Flight Rules (IFR)** apply. Air Traffic Control (ATC) is responsible for keeping aircraft separated in IMC. In order to give ATC the authority it needs to do its job, **controlled airspace** was created. As air travel progressed and matured, various types of controlled airspace evolved to fulfill special needs. This evolution continues even today.

There are areas, however, where ATC has no authority or responsibility for controlling aircraft, regardless of the weather. Appropriately enough these areas are called **uncontrolled airspace**.

In VFR weather, also called **visual meteorological conditions (VMC),** *most* controlled airspace below 18,000 feet is treated as uncontrolled: no contact with ATC is necessary to fly. In VMC, even aircraft using ATC IFR services must maintain their vigilance for VFR traffic.

In IFR weather, the reverse is true. All aircraft *must* have clearance from ATC to fly in controlled airspace. Of course, the aircraft and pilot must be qualified for IFR flight. VFR flight is prohibited in IFR weather, in *any* controlled airspace.

VFR Weather Minimums

FAR 91.105 specifies the weather requirements to fly VFR. Figure 7.14 is a pictorial summary of this regulation for airplanes in both controlled and uncontrolled airspace. Notice that the requirements depend on your altitude as well as on the type of airspace.

Figure 7.14 VFR weather
minimums.

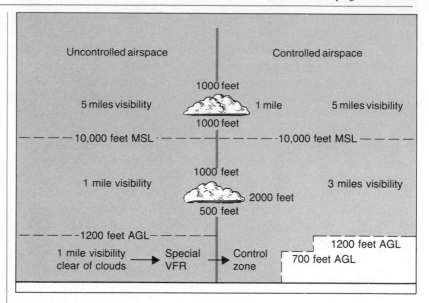

Uncontrolled airspace is basically broken into three altitude sectors:

1. *Below 1200 feet AGL*, you need only *1 mile visibility* to fly VFR, and you must remain *clear of the clouds*.

2. In the altitude range between *1200 feet AGL and 10,000 feet MSL*, you still only need *1 mile visibility*, but you must remain at least *500 feet below, 1000 feet above, or 2000 feet horizontally from clouds*.

3. *At or above 10,000 feet MSL, and above 1200 feet AGL*, the requirements change significantly. You now need *5 miles visibility*, and you must remain at least *1000 feet below, 1000 feet above, or 1 mile horizontally from clouds*.

Controlled airspace has only two divisions:

1. *Below 10,000 feet* you need *3 miles visibility* to fly, and you must remain at least *500 feet below, 1000 feet above, or 2000 feet horizontally from clouds*.

2. *At or above 10,000 feet MSL* the requirements are the same as in uncontrolled airspace: *5 miles visibility* and at least *1000 feet below, 1000 feet above, or 1 mile horizontally from clouds*.

Types of Controlled Airspace
Starting from the ground up, the following material describes the characteristics of the various types of controlled airspace.

Control zones. **Control zones** were established to buffer IFR pilots from VFR traffic. They are found around airports with an instrument approach capability and thus work to separate IFR from VFR traffic when weather at the airport is below VFR minimums. By definition, they extend upward from the surface of the earth to the base of the continental control area (CCA), described later in this section. (Actually, *any* overlying controlled airspace effectively forms the top of a control zone.)

If the control zone does not underlie the CCA, or any other controlled airspace, it has no upper limit. Normally, the zone extends outward from its airport for a 5-mile radius; several airports can be included in the same zone. Extensions to the zone, required for instrument approach and departure corridors, give the control zone its distinctive keyhole appearance on aeronautical charts. The control zone is depicted on charts by a dashed line (see Figure 7.15a).

A control zone is often confused with the **airport traffic area (ATA)**, discussed earlier. It is important to understand the differences between the two:

1. Size and shape. An ATA is always 5 miles in radius and 3000 feet tall (with a few rare exceptions). The shape of a control zone varies from airport to airport. Its upper limit may vary, depending on the airspace above it (see Figure 7.16).

2. An ATA is a communications area, *not* a controlled airspace. The type of airspace (controlled or uncontrolled) where the ATA exists determines the weather minimums that apply. There are no weather minimums for an ATA itself. The control zone, on the other hand, *is* controlled airspace. In other words, an *ATA places a communication requirement on the pilot; a control zone has a weather requirement.*

3. An ATA exists any time there is an operating control tower. If the tower ceases operation, the ATA disappears. A control zone does not depend

Figure 7.15 **(a)** Control zones are indicated on aeronautical charts with a dashed blue line. **(b)** The boundaries of a control zone.

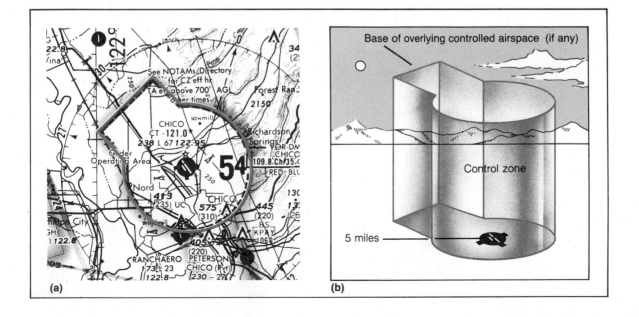

(a)

(b)

Figure 7.16 Comparison of an airport traffic area and a control zone.

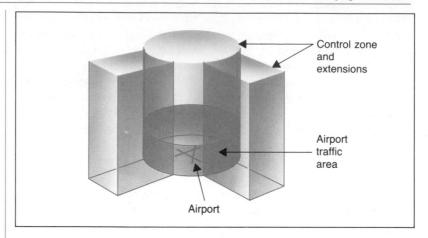

on the existence of a control tower. An airport without a control tower can have a control zone.

4. Depiction on a chart. An ATA is indicated by the existence of a control tower frequency in the airport data block. All such airports are colored blue; airports without a control tower are colored magenta. A control zone is shown directly on a chart by dashed blue lines.

In VFR weather there are no restrictions to flight within a control zone (it is still there but has no operational meaning). Normally, the visibility must be at least 3 miles and the cloud ceiling must be at least 1000 feet AGL. It is possible to get a **special VFR clearance** to fly in a control zone in weather as low as 1 mile visibility and clear of clouds (uncontrolled airspace below 1200 feet minimums). When operating on a special VFR clearance, you are separated from other traffic by ATC. There are four limitations you need to know about special VFR clearances:

1. IFR traffic is given priority into a control zone, so there may be delays in obtaining a special VFR clearance.
2. Special VFR clearances *at night* will be issued only if the pilot and airplane are qualified for IFR flight.
3. Some larger airports do not allow special VFR operations at all, because of their heavy volume of IFR traffic. Such a restriction is indicated on the chart when the control zone is bounded with "T"s rather than dashed lines.
4. Special VFR only applies within a control zone. Outside a control zone it has no meaning.

Transition areas.   Extending outward from our typical control zone is the **transition area**. These additional areas are established to buffer IFR airplanes from VFR airplanes. Airplanes departing federal airways and descending to land under IFR require an area of controlled airspace to accommodate their transition from airway to runway (and vice versa, of course, on departure). Transition areas extend from 700 feet AGL (when used in conjunction with airports) or 1200 feet AGL (when used in conjunction with airways) to the base of overlying controlled airspace. They are marked on aeronautical charts with magenta for transition areas around airports and blue for transition areas around airways (see Figure 7.17). Therefore, controlled airspace begins at 700 feet AGL in areas designated with magenta bands, and at 1200 feet in areas that are marked with blue bands.

Control areas.   We now find ourselves in **control areas**—the airspace designated for airways, other control areas with extensions, and transition areas. The federal airway system links most major airports and terminal areas together, and you will make considerable use of them on cross-country flights as a student or private pilot. We will have much more to say about airways and navigation in a later chapter. The control areas around federal airways (indicated on aeronautical charts by a blue line) extend 4 miles on either side of the airway's centerline and from 1200 feet AGL up to 18,000 feet MSL (see Figure 7.18).

Between control areas and transition areas, controlled airspace effectively begins at 1200 feet AGL over most of the continental United States. There are pockets of airspace where this is not true, but they are located in remote or mountainous areas.

Continental control area.   The **continental control area (CCA)** is all airspace at and above 14,500 feet MSL that lies over the 48 contiguous states, the District of Columbia, and Alaska east of the 160° meridian. In

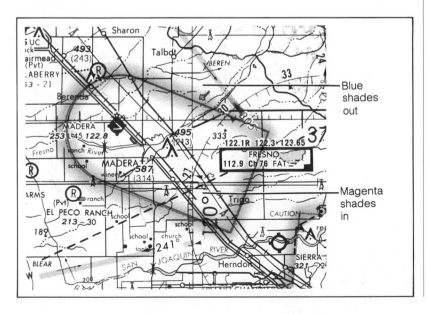

Figure 7.17 The transition area. Transition areas are marked on aeronautical charts as feathered blue and magenta lines.

Figure 7.18 Control areas surround
federal airways, which are indicated
by a blue line on aeronautical
charts.

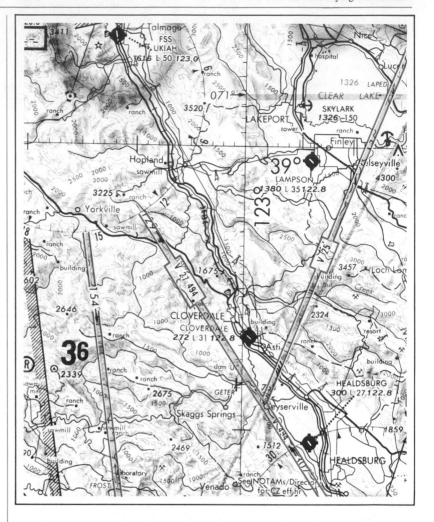

mountainous areas, there is a 1500-foot AGL buffer zone of uncontrolled
airspace. This airspace caps any pockets where controlled airspace does
not begin at 700 or 1200 feet AGL.

Positive control area.   Over the continental United States and Alaska all
VFR airspace ends at 18,000 feet MSL, at which point **positive control
area (PCA)** is in effect. At and above this altitude all pilots and airplanes
must be qualified for IFR flight and must have an IFR clearance from ATC.
Beginning at 18,000 feet, all pilots set their altimeters to 29.92 rather than
to the local altimeter setting. Altitudes beginning at 18,000 feet are actually
pressure-altitudes, not MSL. To make this distinction, pressure-altitudes
are referred to as **flight levels**, and they are identified by their first three
digits only. For example, 21,000 pressure-altitude is called flight level 210
(FL 210).

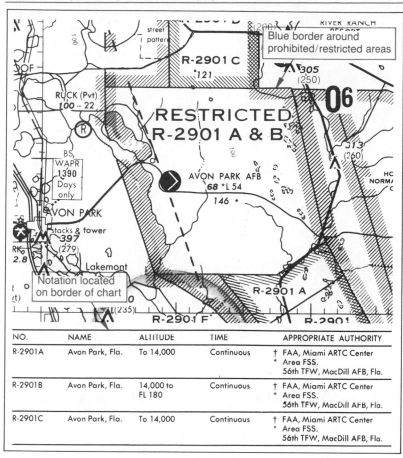

Figure 7.19 Prohibited and restricted areas. Each has an entry in a table on the border of the chart.

NO.	NAME	ALTITUDE	TIME	APPROPRIATE AUTHORITY
R-2901A	Avon Park, Fla.	To 14,000	Continuous	† FAA, Miami ARTC Center * Area FSS. 56th TFW, MacDill AFB, Fla.
R-2901B	Avon Park, Fla.	14,000 to FL 180	Continuous	† FAA, Miami ARTC Center * Area FSS. 56th TFW, MacDill AFB, Fla.
R-2901C	Avon Park, Fla.	To 14,000	Continuous	† FAA, Miami ARTC Center * Area FSS. 56th TFW, MacDill AFB, Fla.

Special-use airspace.   You would not want to fly over a parcel of ground while the Army or Navy bombarded it with artillery shells, and you would not want to fly over the White House, where security forces suspect the birds themselves of malicious intent. Such areas must be protected—in the former case from doing harm to the intruder, and in the latter case from intrusion. The FAA's system of **special-use airspace** satisfies both these needs. **Prohibited areas** are flatly forbidden to all aircraft, usually for reasons of national security. **Restricted areas**, usually military-training corridors or weapons testing ranges, may be flown over at certain times and at certain altitudes, as shown on aeronautical charts (see Figure 7.19), or with prior permission from the controlling authority. Failure to obtain this permission is not only a violation of FARs but frequently very hazardous.

Airspace over international territory that may or may not contain similar hazards is called a **warning area**. The FAA can only warn you about such hazards; it cannot restrict your movement into such areas because international territories are outside its jurisdiction. The careful pilot, however, treats all warning areas with caution. Figure 7.20 shows how warning areas are depicted on an aeronautical chart.

Figure 7.20 Warning areas.

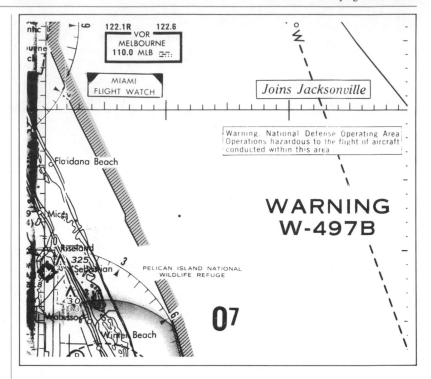

Military Operations Areas (MOA). Areas used by the military services for high-volume or high-speed flights or for unusual aircrew training missions are called **Military Operations Areas (MOA)**. These areas may be particularly hazardous to transient aircraft. MOAs are shown on sectional charts by a magenta hatched border, as shown in Figure 7.21. An **alert area** may contain extensive pilot-training activity or other unusual (but regularly conducted) aerial operations. Alert areas are bordered by a blue crosshatch (similar to a restricted or prohibited area), as shown in Figure 7.22. While permission is not required to enter these areas, extra vigilance is. The nearest FSS can advise you on the current status of military or alert area activities.

Military Training Routes (MTR). As a joint venture by the FAA and the Department of Defense, military aircraft conduct low-altitude, high-speed training in **Miltary Training Routes (MTR)**, generally at speeds in excess of 250 knots below 10,000 feet MSL. Route segments may be defined at higher altitudes for purposes of route continuity, such as descents, climbouts, and in mountainous terrain. When only VFR operations will be conducted, the route is denoted as a **visual route (VR).** Routes that will be used regardless of weather conditions are called **instrument routes (IR)**. VRs and IRs that are entirely at or below 1500 feet AGL are identified by four-digit numbers (for example, IR1006, VR1007). Routes that may have segments both above and below 1500 feet AGL are identified by three-digit

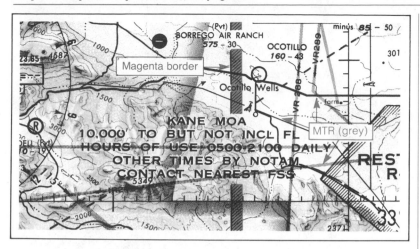

Figure 7.21 Military Operations Areas (MOA) and Military Training Routes (MTR).

numbers (such as VR008, IR009). On aeronautical charts, these routes are depicted as grey lines (see Figure 7.21).

Air Defense Identification Zone (ADIZ) and
Distant Early Warning Identification Zone (DEWIZ)

All aircraft approaching domestic U.S. airspace must be properly identified prior to entry. The **Air Defense Identification Zone (ADIZ)** and (in Alaska) the **Distant Early Warning Identification Zone (DEWIZ)** represent established areas along the boundaries of U.S. and international airspace for this purpose (see Figure 7.23).

The regulations regarding national security, as it relates to the control of air traffic, are found in FAR Part 99. A complete discussion of these rules

Figure 7.22 Alert area depiction on a chart.

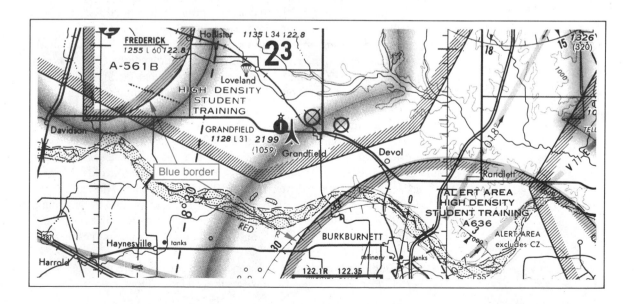

Figure 7.23 Air Defense
Identification Zone (ADIZ) chart
depiction.

is beyond the scope of this text. However, all pilots should know that there
are specific requirements regarding flight plans, two-way radio communications, and position reporting while flying in these areas. Aircraft operating in an ADIZ or DEWIZ that are not properly identified are subject to
being intercepted, usually by military aircraft.

Prior to departing on a flight into an ADIZ or DEWIZ, you must familiarize yourself with the relevant regulations and procedures. The *Airman's
Information Manual* and an appropriate aeronautical facility (FSS, ATC
center, or FAA office) should be consulted in preparation for such a flight.

Airport Radar Services

The advent of ground-based air traffic control radar has greatly reduced the
need for two-way radio communications and has greatly enhanced flight
safety. However, the primary responsibility for collision avoidance, both
with other aircraft and the terrain, remains with the pilot. Airplanes under
radar guidance are *vectored* (given a heading to fly, or **vector**) by the ground
controller. Even though you may be given vectors by the controller, you,
as a conscientious pilot, should constantly monitor your position using radio
aids or ground references.

Although we will discuss radar and traffic control more thoroughly in a
later chapter, you ought to know a little bit now about radar's uses and

limitations. **Radar** works on the following principle: a radio wave is transmitted in a certain direction, bounces off a target, and is received and analyzed by the radar unit. From this procedure, both *azimuth* (direction) and distance data are available for use by the ground controller. Naturally, big, dense, metallic targets provide the best radar return, or *echo*. Unfortunately, most general-aviation airplanes are neither big nor dense, and sometimes they are not even made out of metal! Thus, an airborne **transponder**—a radio device that transmits a coded signal to ATC radar equipment—is a valuable piece of equipment for modern airplanes. Transponders are used universally on airplanes at high altitudes—airspace above 12,500 feet MSL, excluding the airspace at or below 2500 feet AGL. When your airplane is not equipped with a transponder, it may not present a clear return on the ground-based radarscope, even in the terminal area. In this case, more frequent communications are required to ensure that your position is properly monitored by the controller.

Terminal Radar Programs.   Certain airport areas are provided with radar-assisted **Terminal Radar Service Programs**. There are several levels of service and assistance for the general-aviation pilot, depending on the airport. *Basic radar service* (formerly called Stage I) is provided to the VFR general-aviation pilot on a workload-permitting basis. This service provides traffic advisories and limited vectoring. *Stage II service* provides sequencing for arriving VFR and IFR traffic and traffic advisories for departing VFR aircraft. *Stage III service*, available in a **terminal radar service area (TRSA)**, provides *positive separation* (vectors for spacing as well as navigation) for all *participating* VFR and IFR airplanes operating in the TRSA. Only *Stage III* TRSAs are shown on sectional aeronautical charts, identified by a magenta-colored boundary (see Figure 7.24).

While use of these services is not mandatory, it is strongly recommended for all pilots. Not using radar capability is like flying with one eye closed. When you operate from a Stage III facility, in fact, the tower will assume you want the service unless you decline it on your initial contact with the controllers. Even with this service, however, you must be vigilant of non-participating aircraft. To depart an airport using Stage III service, you will be given a *departure clearance*—that is, instructions on what heading to fly after takeoff, what altitude to climb to (consistent with your flight plan), what frequency to use on your radio to talk to the radar controllers after you have been cleared off tower frequency, and what code to set on your transponder. Your VFR radar service will be terminated at your request or on the decision of the controller.

Terminal control area (TCA).   At very busy airports, an area extending beyond the ATA has been established to separate arriving and departing traffic. The **terminal control area (TCA)** extends a number of miles around the airport with altitude floors and ceilings unique to each location's needs. These dimensions are marked plainly on aeronautical charts (see Figure 7.25). Generally, these control areas are shaped like an upside down wed-

Figure 7.24 Terminal radar service area (TRSA). TRSA boundaries are shown as magenta lines on aeronautical charts.

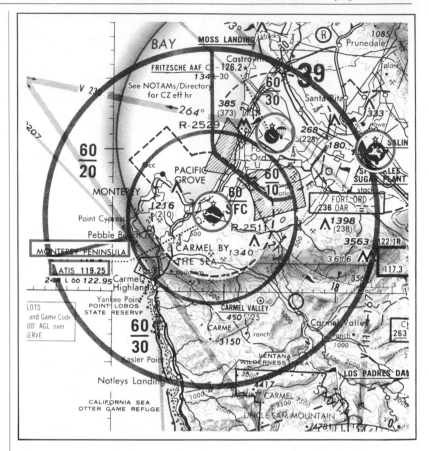

ding cake, each layer having a greater diameter than the one below. FAR 91.90 gives the specific rules to be used and equipment required for TCA operations. There are two types of TCAs (group I and group II); all pilots flying into or out of them must have authorization from TCA controllers and must follow the vector and altitude directions given. These radar services cannot be declined. As a VFR pilot, you must provide your own safety clearance from clouds. You must have a functioning two-way radio, VHF omnirange (VOR) navigation equipment, and a 4096 code transponder that encodes its altitude with the transponder signal for operation in a group II TCA. A group I TCA is identical to a group II TCA except that no student pilots flying solo are permitted to take off or land at the primary airport. ATC may authorize deviations as outlined in FAR 91.24(d). (Note: Prior to December 1987, group II TCAs did not require altitude encoding equipment.)

Airport radar service area (ARSA). The most recent addition to the controlled airspace arena is the **airport radar service area (ARSA).** This airspace is shaped like a simple one-tier TCA, as shown in Figure 7.26a. The inner cylinder of airspace has a 5-nautical-mile radius and extends from

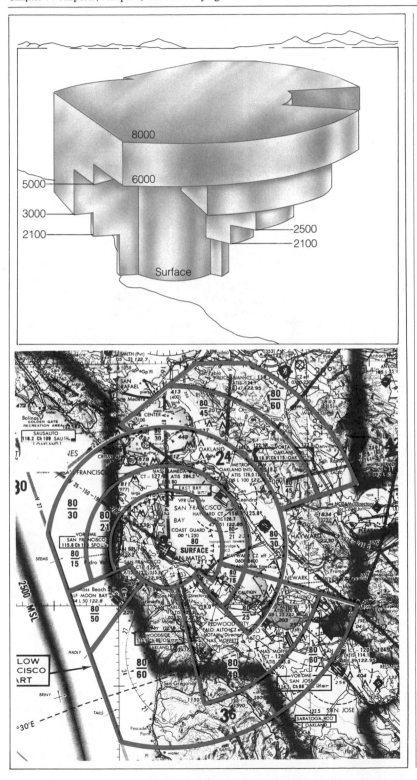

Figure 7.25 Terminal control area (TCA). TCA boundaries are shown as blue lines on aeronautical charts. Altitude limits are shown by two numbers separated by a line, with the numbers representing hundreds of feet. For example, if the number is 80, it represents 8000 MSL; if the number is 30, it represents 3000 MSL.

Figure 7.26 (a) Airport radar service area (ARSA) diagram. (b) ARSA chart depiction.

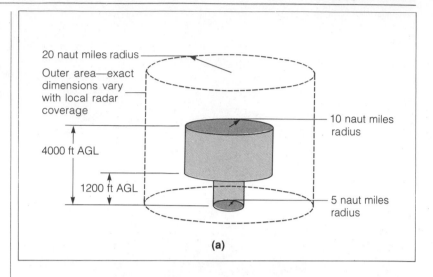

(a)

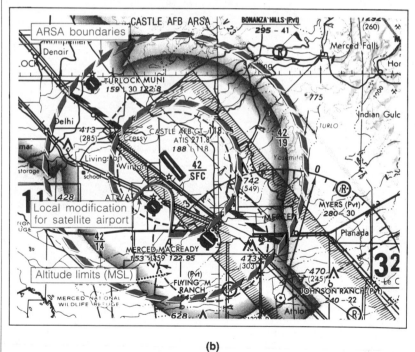

(b)

the surface to approximately 4000 feet above the airport. The outer ring has a 10-nautical-mile radius and extends vertically from about 1200 feet AGL to 4000 feet above the airport. Figure 7.26b shows how ARSAs are depicted on aeronautical charts. The definition of an ARSA includes an outer area (not depicted on the charts), which is normally 20 nautical miles in radius; the exact dimensions may vary due to site-specific requirements. The floor of the outer area is defined by the limits of radar and radio coverage and extends upward to the ceiling of the approach control's delegated airspace.

Pilots are required to establish two-way radio communication with ATC prior to entering or departing an ARSA, and to maintain radio contact with ATC while in the ARSA. Pilots departing airports nearby the primary airport (satellite airports) must establish radio communication with ATC as soon as possible. ARSAs that overlap nearby airport traffic areas have procedures established to allow an orderly transition to and from those areas. While you are in an ARSA, ATC provides the following services:

1. Sequencing of all arriving aircraft to the primary ARSA airport.

2. Standard IFR separation between IFR aircraft.

3. Traffic advisories and conflict resolution between VFR and IFR aircraft. This means ATC will assure a minimum horizontal and/or vertical separation between IFR and VFR aircraft.

4. Traffic advisories and, as appropriate, safety alerts between VFR aircraft. This means ATC keeps VFR pilots aware of other VFR traffic in the immediate area to help them establish visual contact and maintain visual separation.

Within the outer area ATC will provide these same services, as long as two-way communication and radar contact are maintained. Pilot participation, however, is voluntary, and service can be discontinued at the pilot's request (only in the outer area; participation is mandatory in the ARSA). Service *outside* the outer area is provided on a workload-permitting basis. This means the controller can discontinue service if he or she becomes too busy.

RADIO COMMUNICATION TECHNIQUES
Up to this point we have discussed the "whys and whens" of using aeronautical radios but have said nothing about the "hows." Few other aspects of aviation seem to carry as much mystique to novices as "talking on the radio"; when it comes to saying our first few words over the airplane's transmitter, we can become strangely tongue-tied. Whatever the cause, any apprehension you may feel about using the radio is unwarranted. Sounding like a "pro" on the airplane radio is no problem once you have mastered a few conventions. It is less like learning a new language than like developing a slang for the one you already speak.

How Aeronautical Radios Work
Like ground-based radios, airplane radios transform sonic vibrations (your voice into the microphone) into electrical impulses that are broadcast from your airplane's antenna and received by any other antenna within range of your transmission. Radios tuned to transmit and receive on the same frequency (118.000 to 135.975 **megahertz**, or **MHz**—the frequency range reserved for aeronautical voice communications) can therefore communicate with each other. This communication can be blocked, however, by

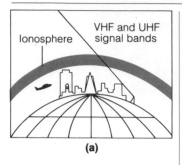

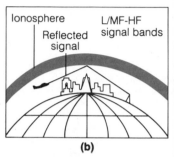

Figure 7.27 Radio signal characteristics. **(a)** VHF and UHF signals. **(b)** HF signals.

line-of-sight obstructions, such as a mountain or the curvature of the earth (see Figure 7.27a). Also, only one transmission at a time can be received, so when one airplane or ground station in the area is transmitting on your frequency, you must wait until that transmission is finished before speaking or you will block the other transmission. The frequencies we have discussed so far fall in the range of **very high frequencies (VHF)**. These frequencies are used by the transmitters and receivers you will find in most general-aviation airplanes. **Ultrahigh-frequency (UHF)** radios are used mostly by the military and for certain ground-based navigation and landing aids. **High-frequency (HF)** radios can broadcast and receive over very long distances—halfway around the world, in fact—since their signal bounces off a screen of electrically charged particles called the **ionosphere**, which blankets the earth at high altitudes. Unfortunately, these radios lack the clarity and dependability of shorter-range equipment, and so they are used mainly for long-distance communications on airplanes flying over water (see Figure 7.27b).

Your airplane's radio will probably have its transmitter and receiver combined into one unit called a **transceiver**, which is mounted behind the instrument panel or away from the cockpit in an equipment rack. You select the desired frequency and control the volume and the **squelch** (balance between volume and static) from a control mechanism mounted on the instrument panel. Messages coming in on the receiver are heard through a cabin speaker. The microphone is usually hand held, though most airplanes have provisions for earphones and a small boom microphone attached to the headset. With this arrangement, the pilot's hands are free to fly the airplane, since the microphone is activated by a button on the control wheel.

How to Use the Microphone

Positioning the microphone so that your voice is both clear and readable (understandable) and the background noise of the cabin is minimized is basic to good radio technique. You should always speak directly into the microphone, usually with your lips gently touching its surface. This allows you to speak in a conversational tone without straining, while shielding the mike from cockpit interference. Depress the mike button (or slide the mike switch, depending on its action) when you wish to talk, and leave it alone the rest of the time. "Keying" the mike while you are thinking or for any other reason blanks out other transmissions and may preempt important communications. If you are in a busy area but have not heard any radio traffic (conversations) for more than a few minutes, after simply checking the volume control, you might suspect that you have a failed receiver, or, more likely, that your mike button is stuck in the transmit position. First, check to see if you are on the correct frequency and ask for a *radio check*. If there is no reply on this or likely alternate frequencies, disconnect the microphone immediately and monitor your original frequency. Even with the mike disconnected, you will continue to receive normally. When you wish to speak, use a second microphone, or plug in your mike just long enough to transmit.

The Radiotelephone Accent: Phraseology and Pronunciation

Since every frequency has a number of simultaneous users at any given instant, a "shorthand" English has been developed for certain key phrases and concepts, thus ensuring standard, unambiguous, and—above all—*brief* communications.

Phonetic alphabet.   Have you ever tried to give information to a switchboard operator and spent many valuable minutes spelling and respelling your name? It is a common experience, and you probably resolved it by reverting to some kind of phonetic code, substituting common words for single letters, such as "J as in John," "D as in dog," and so forth. Airplane radios are similar to telephones, and, due to atmospheric conditions and range, they are sometimes less clear. To complicate matters further, regional accents often lead to different pronunciations of the same word. Even though English is the internationally agreed-upon language of aviation, you may also hear those same terms pronounced with a foreign accent as well. The solution to this problem is the standard **phonetic alphabet** that is used to relay aircraft call signs, clarify information, and facilitate many other types of communications required for navigation and traffic control. Table 7.2 presents this alphabet.

Table 7.2 The Phonetic Alphabet and Numbers

Letter	Phonetic equivalent	Pronounced	Letter	Phonetic equivalent	Pronounced	Number	Phonetic equivalent	Pronounced
A	Alpha	*Al*-fah	N	November	No-*vem*-ber	1	One	(WUN)
B	Bravo	*Brah-voh*	O	Oscar	*Oss*-cah	2	Two	(TOO)
C	Charlie	*Char*-lee	P	Papa	Pah-*pah*	3	Three	(TREE)
D	Delta	*Dell*-tah	Q	Quebec	Keh-*beck*	4	Four	(FOW-ER)
E	Echo	*Eck*-oh	R	Romeo	*Row*-me-oh	5	Five	(FIFE)
F	Foxtrot	*Foks*-trot	S	Sierra	See-*air*-rah	6	Six	(SIX)
G	Golf	Golf	T	Tango	*Tang*-go	7	Seven	(SEV-EN)
H	Hotel	Hoh-*tell*	U	Uniform	*You*-nee-form	8	Eight	(AIT)
I	India	*In*-dee-ah	V	Victor	*Vic*-tah	9	Nine	(NIN-ER)
J	Juliet	*Jew*-lee-*ett*	W	Whiskey	*Wiss*-key	0	Zero	(ZEE-RO)
K	Kilo	*Key*-loh	X	X-ray	*Ecks*-ray			
L	Lima	*Lee*-mah	Y	Yankee	*Yang*-key			
M	Mike	Mike	Z	Zulu	*Zoo*-loo			

Numbers.   Certain numbers, like certain letters, sound like other words when they are spoken. Because of this, and since numbers are so critical to flying safety, they are spoken over the radio using a definite technique. Numerals are usually spoken separately, as you would normally pronounce them, with the exception of the number nine, which is pronounced "niner." (This is to preclude confusion with the German word *nein,* pronounced the same as the English *nine*.) Multidigit numbers are given by saying each number individually, in sequence, such as "heading one eight zero" for a course of 180°. Radio frequencies are read saying "point" or "decimal" at the appropriate place. Thus, a UNICOM frequency for an uncontrolled airport would be read "one two two point eight." Barometric pressure, however, is read without the decimal point, and standard sea level pressure would be given as "two niner niner two." Below 10,000 feet, altitudes are read in *thousands* and *hundreds,* such as "seven hundred" for 700 feet, "six thousand five hundred" for 6500 feet, and so forth. At and above 10,000 feet, the thousands digits are stated separately, followed by the hundred as required, as in "one zero thousand" for 10,000 and "one six thousand five hundred" for 16,500. At 18,000 feet and above, altitudes are referred to as flight levels, as in "flight level two three zero" for FL 230, or 23,000 feet.

Time.   Aeronautical, maritime, and military agencies tell time by reference to a 24-hour clock. By international convention, "world time" begins the day at the **prime meridian**, which runs though the observatory at Greenwich (pronounced "*Gren*-itch"), England, at 0000, or midnight. An hour later, the time is 0100, spoken as "zero one zero zero hours," or the equivalent of 1:00 A.M. As the day continues, the hours progress normally, until 12 noon is passed. From this point on, the hours are counted consecutively toward 24. One o'clock in the afternoon is 1300, spoken as "one three zero zero hours." Six-thirty P.M. is 1830, or "one eight three zero hours," and so on. Time given with reference to the Greenwich meridian is called **coordinated universal time (UTC)** (it is also called **Z time** or—using the phonetic alphabet—**zulu time**). Since you will usually be flying in the United States instead of England, your local time will be several hours different from Greenwich time, just as the time in Los Angeles is three hours earlier than the time in New York. The chapter on navigation will explain the time zones and how to convert from UTC to local time.

Clock position reference system.   Another sort of "clock" system is used by controllers and pilots to identify the position of airborne traffic relative to a given airplane. Under this system, a conventional 12-hour clock is mentally superimposed over the airplane, with the nose of the airplane pointing to twelve o'clock, the tail pointing to six o'clock, and the left and right wing tips to nine and three o'clock, respectively. Aircraft flying in your vicinity can then be positioned relative to your airplane by referring to their clock position. For example, an airplane flying off your right wing tip would be said to be at your "three o'clock position." An aircraft directly ahead of you would be at your twelve o'clock position, and so on.

When a radar controller issues traffic reports, the clock reference will be with respect to your aircraft's **track** (path along the ground), not its **heading** (the direction in which the nose is pointed). Unless you are fighting a significant crosswind, the difference is minor. However, on those not so rare occasions when the wind is significant, you must account for this difference while scanning for the other traffic.

Traffic callouts from ATC. In addition to the relative direction, you are also given distance and altitude information when ATC reports traffic to you. When the controller knows the altitude of the other aircraft, it is stated: "You have traffic at one o'clock, three miles, at four thousand feet." When the controller is not talking directly to the other aircraft but has an altitude readout from the plane's transponder, the altitude will be given as *unverified*: "The traffic is at eleven o'clock, two miles, two thousand five hundred, unverified." If the controller has no altitude information on the traffic, he or she says so directly: "Your traffic is at ten o'clock, five miles, altitude unknown." Always tell the controller whether you see the traffic (say "contact") or not (say "looking, no contact"). If you report the traffic in sight, you may be told to "maintain visual separation." As this implies, you are now responsible for seeing and avoiding the other aircraft—the controller will not issue further advisories. If you subsequently lose sight of the traffic, *tell the controller immediately.*

Call signs. Like automobiles, all aircraft in the world are registered with their respective governments. In the United States, all civil aircraft registration numbers begin with the prefix *N,* or *november.* This **N prefix** is deleted from all radio transmissions, and the remaining numerals and letters are used as a **call sign** to identify the aircraft. Thus Beechcraft N2088F would be addressed "Beechcraft two zero eight eight foxtrot" over the radio. Note that the make (manufacturer) of the aircraft is part of the call sign.

Pilots initiating a radio contact should always use the full call sign on initial contact. Usually, ATC will respond by calling the aircraft by its make and the last three elements (numbers and/or letters), to expedite communications. Once the controller has used the abbreviated call sign, the pilot should do likewise in future communications. If the controller continues to use the full call sign, so should the pilot, because the controller may be talking with another airplane whose last three elements are similar, and the full call sign is necessary to eliminate confusion.

Ground facilities are addressed by their name, as we described earlier. The UNICOM at Falcon Field, Arizona, for example, would be addressed "Falcon UNICOM"; Los Angeles Air Route Traffic Control Center would be addressed "Los Angeles Center." The ground controller at Los Angeles International Airport would be addressed "Los Angeles Ground Control" or "Los Angeles Ground," and the tower controller, "Los Angeles Tower." Approach and departure controllers in the same area would be addressed "Los Angeles Approach Control" or just "Los Angeles Approach," and "Los Angeles Departure Control" or "Los Angeles Departure," respectively.

Standard phraseology. Because most air-to-ground and ground-to-air communication is routine in nature, pilots and controllers have found it convenient to adopt a standard way of exchanging information and standard phrases for concepts that are repeated often. Whenever you initiate a radio communication from the air, for example, it is customary to follow the sequence below:

1. State by name the ground facility you are calling, then identify your airplane by its full call sign.

2. Wait for an acknowledgment of your call.

3. Give your approximate location and altitude. Geographic landmarks are permissible if they are well known in the local area; otherwise, give your location with respect to the number of miles and compass direction from the airport or navigational fix concerned.

4. State your intentions or your request for service—*briefly.*

5. Finish your transmission with any other information that may be relevant to communications, navigation, or the status of your flight, such as the receipt of ATIS information or an unusually low fuel condition.

A typical contact initiated by a pilot might go as follows: "Los Angeles Approach, Beech two zero eight eight foxtrot." You would wait until the controller responds: "Beech eight eight foxtrot, Los Angeles Approach, go ahead." You then continue: "Beech eight eight foxtrot is three-zero miles south, at six thousand five hundred, inbound for landing at Los Angeles, with information bravo, over."

The reply might be: "Roger, Beechcraft eight eight foxtrot, this is Los Angeles Approach. Turn right heading zero four five, descend to and maintain four thousand, vectors to Los Angeles final approach course runway two six right, squawk four zero one six."

And the pilot would respond: "Beechcraft eight eight foxtrot turning right, zero four five, out of six thousand five hundred for four thousand, squawking four zero one six."

To translate, Beechcraft N2088F contacted Los Angeles Approach Control thirty miles south of the airport at an altitude of 6500 feet MSL and informed the controller that the pilot desired to land at Los Angeles International Airport. The airplane's current VFR transponder setting was mentioned to assist the controller in recognizing the airplane on the radar screen. The pilot also confirmed that Los Angeles Airport ATIS information bravo had been received. The radio shorthand term *over* was used (this is optional) to denote that the transmission was finished, that there was no further relevant information, and that a reply was expected.

The controller responded using radio shorthand for "I have received all of your transmission" ("roger") and directed the airplane (you will notice that the controller repeated the call sign in its abbreviated form) to make a heading change to 045° magnetic (from that moment on the pilot is flying vectors and is no longer following the preplanned route of flight) and to descend from the airplane's current altitude to a new altitude of 4000 feet MSL. The controller also identified the active runway at Los Angeles International, to which the airplane was being routed. The pilot was also asked to set a new transponder code ("squawk") to further aid in identifying that particular aircraft in a decidedly busy terminal area.

The pilot read back the heading and altitude assignment, notifying the controller that the airplane was vacating the old altitude for the new one. The transponder code was repeated so that the controller could look for the new display on the radar scope and confirm the location of this latest "customer."

As you can see, it took a good deal more space to repeat in "plain English" what was said with great efficiency using radio shorthand. Table 7.3 lists a number of other standard terms and phrases you should remember

Table 7.3 Standard Radio Phraseology

Radio phrase	Meaning
Acknowledge	The message has been received and understood.
Affirmative	Yes.
Confirm	Tell me if this correct. For example, "Confirm clear to land on 28R."
Correction	An error was made in the previous information. Here is the correct information.
Go ahead	Proceed with the transmission.
How do you hear me? or How do you read me?	How did you receive the transmission (quality of radio signal)?
I say again	I repeat (usually added for emphasis).
Negative	That is incorrect; no.
Out	The message is completed, and no response is expected. The word *out* is seldom used since modern radios are so reliable that there is usually no question that the transmission was ended intentionally.
Over	The transmission is ended, and a response is expected. The word *over* is usually omitted unless a reply ordinarily would not be made.
Progressive taxi instructions	Please tell me when, and which way, to turn as I taxi. (Don't be shy about asking for this type of assistance when moving around an unfamiliar airport. It's safer for you and easier on the controller if you ask for help.)
Read back	Repeat all of the transmission that has just been received.
Roger	All of your last transmission has been received and understood.
Say again	Would you repeat (a request usually to clarify a garbled message).
Stand by	Please wait for further information to be transmitted momentarily.
Verify	Double-check the accuracy of the transmission; usually followed by a repetition of the message in question.
Wilco	I understand and will comply.
Words twice	Please repeat each phrase or key word twice (usually required because of radio interference).

as you use the radio. Continuing to practice proper phraseology will help you become a more professional pilot. The main thing to bear in mind, however, is that communication—not style—is the object. If the correct phraseology slips your mind, make your request or statement in plain English, and *never* "roger" a controller's instructions when you did not fully understand what was said. Ask the controller to "say again" the message. Ground-based controllers are interested in the same thing you are—the safe, expeditious completion of the flight.

FLYING AT NIGHT
Airplanes fly just as well at night as they do during the day; during the warmest months, they fly even better, due to the effects of nocturnal cooling and smoother air. FAR 61.109 requires all student pilots to receive at least 3 hours of dual night instruction and to perform ten night landings. This is wise even if the new private pilot decides to avoid flying at night. Long cross-country flights can be delayed en route, and you might find yourself still aloft as the sun is setting.

Illumination Systems
Airplane lighting.   Most airplanes flying at night have three basic lighting features (see Figure 7.28). An **anticollision light** (or lights), usually in the form of a red rotating beacon or flashing white strobes, is (are) installed above and/or below the fuselage. Strobes may also be installed in the wing tips. **Position lights**, sometimes called navigation lights, such as those on a boat, are installed to form a directional triangle—a red light on the left wing tip, a green light on the right wing tip, and a white light on the tail. The orientation of these lights will always tell you an airplane's relative direction of movement. **Landing lights**, functionally similar to the headlights on a car, are installed under the wing near the leading edge, in the leading edge, or on or near the landing gear. If the landing lights are retractable, you will have to lower them (as well as turn them on) by activating a switch in the cockpit. Be sure to observe the limiting airspeed for their deployment, just as you would for the flaps or landing gear. The landing lights are used only in the vicinity of the airport, and then only for

Figure 7.28 Airplane lighting.

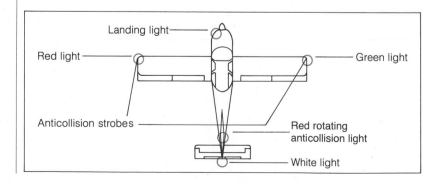

takeoffs and landings. (Some pilots turn them on miles away for identification and collision avoidance.) Landing lights can momentarily blind other pilots if they are left on while taxiing near other aircraft. For ground operations, use taxi lights if your airplane has them; if your airplane does not have taxi lights, use the *taxi* position of your landing lights. Should your radio fail during a night flight, respond to the tower controller by blinking your landing lights or position lights in acknowledgment of the light-gun signals.

Personal equipment.   Although you will inspect your airplane's internal and external lighting systems before flying at night, there is always a possibility, however remote, that cockpit lighting might fail in flight. To prevent a serious situation from becoming a real emergency, you should always carry a flashlight and a spare complement of batteries on each night flight.

Advantages and Disadvantages of Night Flying

Flying at night opens a whole new world to the private pilot. It allows more flexibility to scheduled cross-country flights and presents a rewarding and aesthetically pleasing side to flying that many pilots enjoy. But airplanes have a special vulnerability after dark that should not be ignored. A forced landing, should one be necessary, can be exceptionally difficult, and weather conditions—always a reasonable concern to VFR pilots—can be deceiving. The anticipated route of flight should be analyzed ahead of time for possible emergency landing sites, and the forecast weather, even for local flights, should be carefully considered.

In the last analysis, all pilots become more dependent upon their flight instruments after dark. In this comparatively unfamiliar world of night flying, you should be aware of two general rules that can prevent or minimize the effects of spatial disorientation:

1. Rely primarily on your airplane's flight instruments for indications of airplane attitude, airspeed, altitude, heading, and vertical speed.

2. When and if your sense of sight disagrees with your body's sensations of motion, disregard your motion senses and give full attention to the airplane's instruments.

NOISE ABATEMENT: MAINTAINING THE FRIENDLY SKIES

It is hard for some residents of communities around airports to share your enthusiasm for flight. To many people, airplanes are devices built to convert expensive fuel into noise. You should remember that every pilot is aviation's ambassador to the nonflying public. Frequently, your behavior is the standard by which all the rest of us are judged.

You will find that some airports have formal noise abatement traffic patterns. Even though these patterns may differ from standard procedures, you should observe them at all times. Usually they involve mandatory turns on departure to avoid certain areas or a minimum altitude at particular places in the pattern. The only excuse for noncompliance is the safety of the aircraft.

Besides at airports, special procedures to minimize noise are required at certain parks and wildlife preserves. Many open-air areas are centers of recreation and conservation. Low-flying aircraft can be most annoying to people and sometimes actually harmful to wildlife. Give these areas a comfortable altitude margin—2000 feet is a good minimum—even though FARs may give you latitude to fly a little lower. (Some state laws or the Fish and Wildlife Service may prescribe a 2000-foot minimum.)

PLANNING AND CONDUCTING A LOCAL FLIGHT

The **local flying area** is a zone up to 25 miles from a given airport. Flights of a greater distance are defined by FAR 61.109 as cross-country flights. Within the local area are parcels of airspace informally set aside for training by the local FBOs, even though anyone can fly through them for any other purpose, such as cross-country flights or sightseeing. Training areas are situated over sparsely populated locations, where practice maneuvers will not disturb residents. Your CFI will familiarize you thoroughly with your local area, and you will not be allowed to leave it during solo flight until your logbook has been properly endorsed.

General Flight Planning

Common sense and the FARs require you to familiarize yourself with all information pertinent to your flight: the weather, the airplane, and the airport.

The weather.   A call or visit to the nearest Flight Service Station will tell you what the current weather is and what is forecast. The briefer will want to know your aircraft number and where you intend to fly. If your flight is going to be local, this kind of a weather briefing is not required, but it is recommended practice. Before leaving on a cross-country flight you *must* obtain a weather briefing.

The airplane.   Know the airplane's operating limitations, limiting airspeeds, G-loads, cockpit controls and displays, performance charts, and emergency procedures before you attempt any flight as pilot-in-command. Be sure the airplane is loaded appropriately and within its CG and weight limits. Check its maintenance status prior to all operations. If your airplane is equipped with an auxiliary fuel system, plan ahead of time *when* to switch tanks.

The runway.   FAR 91.5 also requires you to have all available information about the runway—including its length and elevation—the wind and temperature, and your airplane's gross weight and performance. The purpose of this exercise, of course, is to determine that your airplane is capable of operating in and out of the airports you intend to use.

Checklists

Human memory is a biological marvel, unduplicated by even the most sophisticated computer. It is not perfect, however. The safe operation of an aircraft requires the pilot to perform a number of important, albeit simple, tasks. Normally, forgetting to do some of these tasks (e.g., setting the altimeter, setting the DG, checking to make sure the door is locked) is only inconvenient or embarrassing. Neglecting other tasks, such as checking the fuel or oil supply, can be outright dangerous.

A **checklist** is a simple but powerful backup to your memory. It is simply a complete list of tasks you must perform. Every airplane has one supplied by the manufacturer. (If yours does not, *get one*.) The operation of the airplane is usually broken down into phases, with a checklist for each phase. The proper way to use a checklist is to:

1. Do the tasks from memory first.
2. Use the checklist to verify that each task is complete.

Some pilots use a checklist as a *do*list; that is, they simply read the checklist and perform the tasks as they read them. This is better than not using the checklist at all, but the two-step process provides a real check mechanism. After all, that is why it's called a *check*list!

Preflight inspection. By **preflight inspection**, we mean that you must examine the item named on the checklist and compare it to your mental picture of a properly installed, functional component. Your flight instructor will show you how each component you inspect should look and operate. The airframe should be free of dents, skin wrinkles, or popped rivets. Transparent surfaces such as position lights, strobe lights, and windows should be free of cracks. The pitot tube and static ports should be clear of obstructions. Tires should be properly inflated and free of cuts, blisters, or bald spots. There should be no evidence of hydraulic leaks (red-orange fluid) around the brakes. Control surfaces should move freely. If you have any questions as to the item's airworthiness or its proper configuration, now is the time to ask about it or have it checked—not after the flight. Be sure to take your time and give proper attention to each item, including those that may be awkward or hard to reach.

Ground operations. Never start the engine without first making sure the area around the propeller is clear and shouting outside the pilot's door or window, "Clear!" Wait a moment or two before engaging the starter to allow any outside observers to move away from the airplane.

Taxiing an airplane seems hard at first, because you steer with your feet, not your hands. After a few tries, it will become second nature. The control wheel cannot be ignored however, especially if the wind is blowing. When high surface winds are blowing, position the ailerons *into* the wind when taxiing into a quartering headwind and *away* from the wind when the wind is coming from a rear quarter. This will help keep the airplane's weight

Figure 7.29 Correct position of the
controls for various wind directions
relative to a tricycle gear airplane
during taxiing.

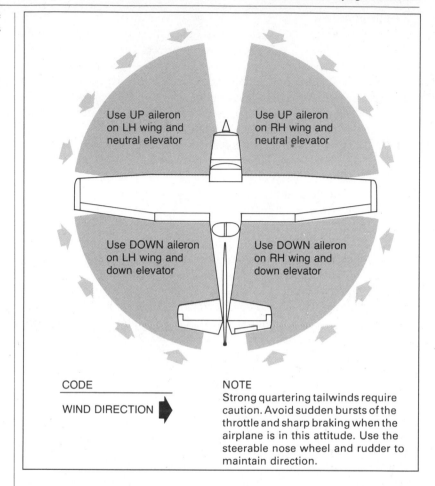

Figure 7.29 Correct position of the controls for various wind directions relative to a tricycle gear airplane during taxiing.

Use UP aileron on LH wing and neutral elevator

Use UP aileron on RH wing and neutral elevator

Use DOWN aileron on LH wing and down elevator

Use DOWN aileron on RH wing and down elevator

CODE

WIND DIRECTION ▶

NOTE
Strong quartering tailwinds require caution. Avoid sudden bursts of the throttle and sharp braking when the airplane is in this attitude. Use the steerable nose wheel and rudder to maintain direction.

evenly distributed on the landing gear and prevent control problems or upset due to gusty air moving over the wing's upper surface. Figure 7.29 shows the proper positioning of the controls versus wind direction.

At large airports or those with elaborate services for transient airplanes, you may be guided into or out of your parking spot by a ground crew employee called a **signaler**. The signaler will use a set of standard hand and arm signals to direct you in various phases of pretaxi or parking operations (see Figure 7.30). You should always keep the signaler in sight and follow the instructions given, since the signaler usually has a full view of your aircraft and can assist you in negotiating a crowded ramp safely and efficiently. At night, the signaler will hold lighted batons (flashlights with cones fitted over the ends) to help you see the signals. You can communicate visually with the signaler from the cockpit using similar signals or by simply shaking or nodding your head.

Local area procedures.   As we mentioned earlier, most of your flights as a student pilot will be in your local training area. The boundaries of this

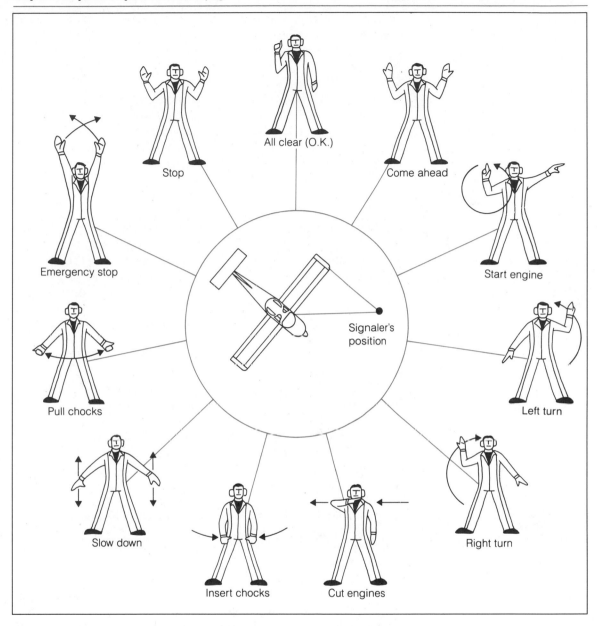

All clear (O.K.)

Stop

Come ahead

Emergency stop

Start engine

Signaler's position

Pull chocks

Left turn

Slow down

Insert chocks

Cut engines

Right turn

Figure 7.30 Standard arm and hand signals used by aircraft signalers.

area will usually be apparent during flight by reference to landmarks (towers, mountains, rivers, and so forth) and occasionally by radio navigational aids. We will discuss those later. Your CFI will show you how to identify and use these references. Since most of your local flights will be for the purpose of practicing maneuvers for your FAA check flight, you will find your attention primarily focused on flight attitudes, cockpit indications, and ground references for those maneuvers. This is proper and necessary, but it must not prevent you from scanning the surrounding airspace for other airplanes. Remember, airplanes move in a vertical as well as a horizontal plane. Make certain that the sky above and below you, as well as the horizon, is clear before beginning any maneuver.

KEY TERMS

Air Defense Identification Zone (ADIZ)
airport radar service area (ARSA)
airport traffic area (ATA)
anticollision light
Automatic Terminal Information Service (ATIS)
base leg
continental control area
control area
controlled airport
controlled airspace
control zone
crosswind leg
Distant Early Warning Identification Zone (DEWIZ)
displaced threshold
downwind leg
FAA Flight Service Station
final approach
glide slope
IFR
landing direction indicator
landing lights
local flying area
N prefix
pattern altitude
phonetic alphabet
position lights

positive control area (PCA)
preflight inspection
prime meridian
runway identification number
segmented circle
signaler
special-use airspace
special VFR
standard traffic pattern
takeoff (upwind) leg
terminal control area (TCA)
terminal radar service area (TRSA)
Terminal Radar Service Programs
threshold
traffic pattern indicators
transceiver
transition area
transponder
uncontrolled airport
uncontrolled airspace
UNICOM
vector
very high frequencies (VHF)
VFR
visual approach slope indicator (VASI)
wind sock
wind T

PROFICIENCY CHECK

1. Can you land on the surface immediately in front of a displaced threshold? How is a displaced threshold identified?

2. What is a VASI system? What does a *white over white* indication mean? What does a *red over red* indication mean? How should a pilot respond to each?

3. Give a brief description of the following FAA-controlled airspace areas and state the altitude and geographic limits of each:

    a. terminal radar service area (TRSA)

    b. terminal control area (TCA)

    c. positive control area (PCA)

    d. continental control area

    e. control zone

    f. transition area

    g. control area

    h. airport radar service area (ARSA)

4. List the phonetic alphabet and write out each term.

5. Name some precautions you should take when preparing for a night flight.

6. During a night flight you find yourself continually lining up the airplane with a pattern of ground lights and stars that seems to resemble a natural horizon. This gives the airplane a slight wing-low attitude, and you find that you must constantly correct it. As you bank the airplane to a wing-level attitude for the fourth or fifth time, you notice that you have a strong sensation that you are banking in the opposite direction. In a few seconds, these two conflicting sensations—the lights outside the cockpit and the sensation of a turn—begin to disorient you. What should you do? Explain your answer.

PART IV
WEATHER

It is the weather . . . that reminds me now and then
that, although I can span continents in a single leap,
I am not always so godlike as I feel. . . . Clouds are
watchkeepers over [the] arrogant. . . .
Richard Bach
Stranger to the Ground

C H E C K P O I N T S

What is the composition of the atmosphere and what is its structure? ✈ Why is the atmosphere called a giant "heat engine"? ✈ What causes circulation of the air in the atmosphere? ✈ How does global air motion affect local winds and weather? ✈ What aspects of meteorology are of most concern to pilots? ✈ How are clouds used as the "signposts" of weather? ✈ How do air masses and fronts affect flying?

METEOROLOGY: A PILOT'S VIEW OF WEATHER

In Chapter 1 we made a comparison between the ocean of water and the ocean of air as media for transportation systems. The analogy continues to be very apt, especially when our discussion turns toward weather. Navigating the sea—a footless (seemingly bottomless), fluid medium—out of sight of familiar landmarks, risking storms, currents, and deadly fog has always been the sailor's lot. When modern mariners traded their sails for wings, the technology of the voyage changed, but not the dangers. The sky is neither evil nor benign, but absolutely neutral. Like the sea, it is extremely unforgiving of mistakes. The thought is both a comfort and a caution and should be taken to heart by every pilot.

Meteorology, the science of the atmosphere, has made enormous gains over the last few years, both in understanding the basic phenomena of the atmosphere and in applying that understanding to more effective weather surveillance and forecasting. Laborious land-based observations and manual record keeping are being supplemented by orbiting weather satellites, automated data acquisition and processing systems, and computer-controlled analyses. More information is available now in a matter of minutes than was generated in months by the entire corps of meteorologists when the science was begun in earnest at the turn of the century. It is one of the chief responsibilities of the pilot to use this knowledge wisely and effectively.

While most meteorologists are not pilots, all pilots are in some part meteorologists. Your forecaster can provide you with data and assist you in interpreting it, but it is the pilot, not the meteorologist, who captains the airplane. Once aloft, a helping voice may be available at the other end of the radio, but the hand on the wheel is yours. It is your responsibility to complete the flight safely. Although you need not be a scientist to fly an airplane, you can never know too much about the weather. This chapter will help you begin that career-long process of learning.

THE ATMOSPHERE DEFINED
The Composition of the Atmosphere

Sometimes we use the words *air* and *atmosphere* synonymously, but this is imprecise. **Air** is a mixture of gases, specifically nitrogen (78 percent), oxygen (21 percent), and argon (0.9 percent), with a variety of trace elements rounding out the last percentage point. Air also contains water vapor, but in percentages that vary according to air pressure and temperature. The **atmosphere** contains not only air and water vapor but a large number of particles and impurities called condensation nuclei. These include dust, unburned hydrocarbons emitted by vehicles and industrial power plants, salt spray, and plant pollen, to name a few. Air is necessary to most living things. It causes airfoils to fly and allows engines to "breathe." Water vapor, as we will see shortly, is a major force behind weather of all kinds—both good and bad. Particulate matter is of concern to pilots both because it is a catalyst for precipitation and because it can restrict vision. We will look at both later. For the moment, let us get a better feeling for what elements make up the atmosphere as a whole and how these basic elements interrelate.

The Structure of the Atmosphere

The atmosphere literally begins at our feet and continues until it fades away into space above the earth. Gravity keeps the energetic air molecules trapped at comparatively high pressures near the surface of the earth.

Near outer space, the energy of the molecules exceeds the pull of gravity, and they escape into space. Due to the relationship of pressure, temperature, and the nature of the air's constituent gases and vapors, we can divide the atmosphere into three basic spheres, or blankets, that surround the earth. From the lowest to the highest, these are: the *troposphere,* the *stratosphere,* and the *ionosphere* (see Figure 8.1).

Troposphere.   If you like weather, here is where you will find the action. The **troposphere** extends from the surface of the earth to an altitude of 5

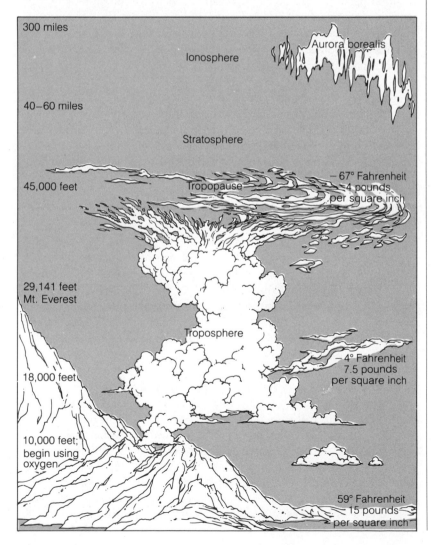

Figure 8.1 The structure of the atmosphere.

to 10 miles. It slopes from about 20,000 feet over the poles to about 65,000 feet over the equator. The troposphere is higher in the summer than in the winter. The bulge at the equator is due to equatorial heat and centrifugal force from the rotating earth. Many of the factors determining weather are a result of the earth's planetary motions, as well as atmospheric water content. These motions, and certain other factors, make the troposphere a boiling cauldron of changing temperatures, shifting pressures, windstorms, bubbling cloud formations, and precipitation of every description. Since these relatively low altitudes are where you will be flying as a private pilot, we will deal extensively with the phenomena and events of the troposphere.

Stratosphere.   Compared to the relative chaos of the troposphere, the **stratosphere** is a great, placid lake in the sky. Extending from the edge of the troposphere (called the **tropopause**) to about 40 to 60 miles above the earth, it is characterized by little vertical motion of the air, constant temperatures, and very low pressures. Only high-performance aircraft or gas balloons can operate in the stratosphere; you will see little of it except as a pilot or passenger of a jet airplane.

Ionosphere.   The remotest layer of the atmosphere is also one of the strangest. The most notable characteristics of the **ionosphere** are its electrical properties, which cause, among other things, the *aurora borealis* (the so-called northern lights) and modification of certain radio transmissions, some of which help and some of which hinder air-to-ground or ground-to-ground communications.

Atmospheric Pressure

Previously, we indicated that atmospheric pressure is measured in inches of mercury as displayed in a barometer. This is only one system of measurement. Pressure is defined as a force per unit of surface area, such as *pounds per square inch (psi)*. Meteorologists use a metric pressure measurement called **millibars (mb)**. One inch of mercury is equal to approximately 33.86 millibars. Thus, we will encounter the same variable (atmospheric pressure) under many guises: inches of mercury, pounds per square inch, and millibars. They all mean the same thing, and as a pilot, you will have to be familiar with each.

Pressure and altitude.   You already know that pressure decreases as altitude increases, and that, at sea level, ISA (International Standard Atmosphere) conditions call for a pressure of 29.92 inches of mercury. We can expand upon that now and say that this sea level pressure is also 14.7 pounds per square inch or 1013.2 millibars. The range of millibar pressures you will see on a weather map for sea level can run from 950 millibars (very low pressure) to about 1050 millibars (very high pressure). When meteorologists report the atmospheric pressure at an airport or other geographic location, they call it **station pressure**. This pressure, corrected to a sea level value, is the one to which your altimeter is set before taking off or landing at that location.

Although atmospheric pressure decreases continuously as altitude increases, the rate of decrease is not uniform. Lower altitudes show a greater decrease in pressure than do higher altitudes. Nearly half of the earth's atmosphere, in fact, is beneath you when you are flying as low as 18,000 feet MSL. At 40,000 feet MSL, the outside pressure is a sparse 2.27 pounds per square inch, or 5.54 inches of mercury (or 187.6 millibars). At these altitudes, an airplane's cabin is usually pressurized. We will learn more about the physiological aspects of high-altitude flight in a later chapter.

Atmospheric Moisture

In our examination of humidity and airplane performance, we saw how water vapor can affect the air around us. When the percentage of water vapor in the air becomes very high, the potential exists for **condensation**—the formation of clouds—and/or **precipitation**—the discharge of moisture from the atmosphere in the form of rain, snow, or hail. Besides the amount of water vapor itself, two things control precipitation: temperature and the presence of particles in the air onto which the water vapor can condense. Let us look at each of these factors.

Relative humidity.   Warm air has the capacity to hold more water vapor than does cold air. That is why summer days are frequently humid as well as warm, and winter days are usually dry. **Relative humidity** is the ratio (expressed as a percentage) of water vapor present in the air to the maximum amount of water vapor that same amount of air could hold under current conditions (see Figure 8.2). Thus, it is both a measure of water vapor content and an indicator of how close conditions might be to condensation or precipitation. When this value nears 100 percent, the air is almost saturated with water vapor. Since warm air can hold more moisture than cold air can, the relative humidity can be increased simply by lowering the temperature. If the temperature gets too low and there is particulate matter in the air, the water contained in the air can change abruptly from its gaseous to its liquid state. Clouds and precipitation are simply visible moisture. If the air is cold enough, the precipitation may become snow, hail, or freezing rain.

Dew point.   Relative humidity is important from the pilot's viewpoint because it reflects how close the water vapor is to condensation or precipitation. **Dew point** is the temperature to which air must be cooled to become saturated by the water vapor already present in the air. At the dew point or a lower temperature, the moisture in the air will condense, forming clouds at higher altitudes and fog on the ground. If conditions are otherwise suitable for it (moisture droplets attract and collide, growing large enough to respond to gravity), precipitation could occur as well. When the OAT (outside air temperature) and dew point are within 4 degrees Fahrenheit and

Figure 8.2 The relationship between temperature and relative humidity.

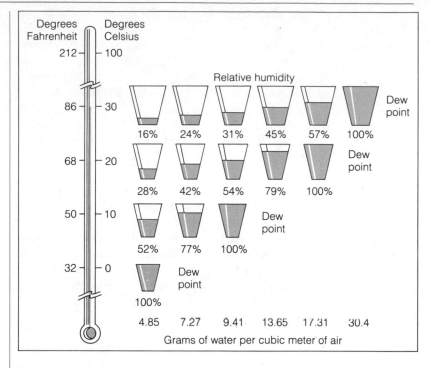

the difference between current temperature and dew point is narrowing, fog or low clouds should always be anticipated.

Condensation nuclei.   We mentioned earlier that the atmosphere contains not only air and water vapor but particles of matter as well. These particles range in size from barely visible grains of dust to molecule-size products of combustion (such as smog) and other impurities. As these particles float through the air, carried aloft by winds and vertical air currents, they come in contact with the molecules of water vapor. The vapor molecules adhere to the particle, and when enough of them are collected (a function of temperature and saturation), the particle becomes visible as a droplet of moisture, with the particle as the droplet's nucleus. Thus, these particles in a mass of air are called **condensation nuclei**.

Evaporation and sublimation.   If you have ever watched a rain puddle dry up, you are familiar with the process of *evaporation*, or the change of water from its liquid to its gaseous state. When a water puddle hardens overnight in the winter, you are witnessing the process of *freezing*, during which water changes from its liquid to its solid form (see Figure 8.3). What is less obvious is the process of **sublimation**, or the changing of a solid *directly* to its gaseous state, and vice versa. This occurs only at very low temperatures (below freezing, obviously) and can be somewhat surprising—a block of ice shrinks without leaving a pool of water, or frost forms on the airplane while flying under a clear blue sky.

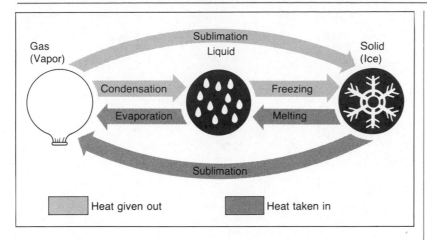

Figure 8.3 Changes in state.

Atmospheric Temperature

Temperature is a by-product of heat. We gauge the presence or absence of heat by readings on a thermometer, in much the same way a physician determines the presence or absence of life by the strength of the patient's pulse. But heat itself implies much more. Heat is energy and thus has the capacity to do work. While solar energy, if collected, might be able to light an entire city, we cannot evaluate the capacity of sunlight to generate electricity merely by the temperature of a summer day.

Sunlight is the place where we must begin our discussion of atmospheric temperature and heat. Some heat escapes the great compression in the rocks beneath the earth's surface in the form of *geothermal energy*. But this energy is trivial compared to the amount of energy that reaches the earth every day in the form of *solar radiation*. As we will soon see, the earth's atmosphere is a giant heat engine, powered by the furnace of the sun.

Because of the composition of the earth's atmosphere, less than half the sun's rays that strike it reach the surface of the earth. How intense this radiation is depends on several factors. If you have ever spent any time near a beach, you will be familiar with all of them (see Figure 8.4).

The earth's daily rotation.   Have you ever gone to the beach at night or in the early evening? You cannot have solar heat without the sun, and the air cools rapidly when the sun sets, though some residual heat remains trapped in the sand and water. This is true everywhere on earth during the night and day cycle, and much local weather depends on it. The coolest nighttime temperatures occur just before dawn, and this is significant too.

Unequal land and water heating.   As noted previously, the sand and water at the beach not only have different temperatures, but they tend to lose or gain temperature at different rates. The sand warms much more rapidly during the day than the water does—it can be hot under your feet while the water is cool. At night, the land gives up its heat quickly, but the water retains its heat for a longer period. Thus, a body of water that feels

Figure 8.4 The mechanism of atmospheric heating.

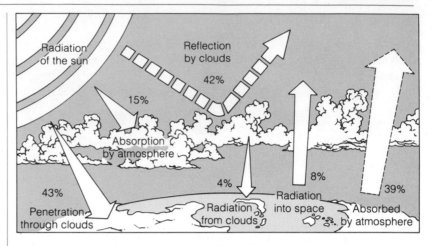

cold by day becomes more comfortable at night. This differential heating of land and water controls a number of local weather phenomena in coastal areas.

The earth's revolution around the sun.   Have you ever been to the beach in the winter? If you have, it was probably to dig for clams and light a bonfire—since the air was probably too cold for sunbathing and the water too cold for swimming. As the earth revolves around the sun, it presents its hemispheres alternately to direct sunlight in summer and less direct sunlight in winter. Thus, winters are cooler than summers, since air, land, and sea have less opportunity (owing to the shorter days) to receive the less intense radiation. Summer days are warm because the sun stays above the horizon longer and the rays fall on the earth and sea at a steeper angle (see Figure 8.5).

This angle at which the sun's rays strike the earth is called the sunlight's **angle of incidence.** Rays striking the surface from directly overhead tend to impart more energy to the earth than those falling at an acute angle. Hence, even in winter, afternoons are warmer than mornings or evenings.

Temperature and altitude.   Atmospheric temperature decreases as altitude increases. The reason for the difference in temperature is that air is not heated directly by the sun; instead, the surface of the earth absorbs the solar radiation, and the air passing closer to it gains temperature. The rate at which the atmosphere loses its temperature with altitude is called the **lapse rate,** and it averages about 2 degrees Celsius per thousand feet in the troposphere. However, as we will see shortly, a number of things can happen to increase, decrease, or even reverse this rate entirely.

The Transfer of Atmospheric Heat
Radiation.   *Radiation* is the fundamental process that starts all the other processes. Energetic rays of light arrive at the earth, striking both air and surface molecules, imparting a portion of their energy as heat.

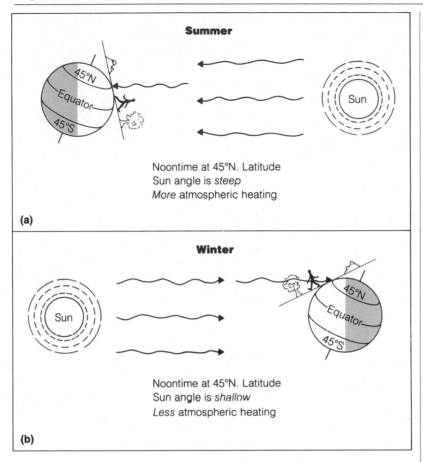

Summer

Noontime at 45°N. Latitude
Sun angle is *steep*
More atmospheric heating

(a)

Winter

Noontime at 45°N. Latitude
Sun angle is *shallow*
Less atmospheric heating

(b)

Figure 8.5 Effect of the earth's seasons on atmospheric heating. **(a)** Summer. **(b)** Winter.

Conduction.   When one molecule, energized through the heating process, comes in contact with another molecule, the second molecule absorbs some of this heat. This is why the air above a layer of hot concrete, for example, becomes warmer than other surrounding air. Heating by direct contact is called *conduction*.

Convection.   Any heat transfer by vertical motion is called *convection*. An example is the rippling effect of air above a hot runway or highway in the summer. The air over these hot surfaces rises; thus vertical currents are established in the atmosphere. Some parcels of air are heated and rise, and other parcels of air cool and descend.

Advection.   As we said earlier, when the wind blows, it is simply movement by or within the local air mass. Since that air mass has a certain temperature (as well as other properties), that temperature will be transferred horizontally over the surface of the earth by blowing winds or moving air masses. This process of horizontal heat transfer is called *advection*.

THE ATMOSPHERE IN MOTION

Heat is the power that drives the great machinery of the atmosphere. Solar radiation heats the surface of the earth and begins convective currents in the atmosphere. As the warm air rises, its place is taken by surrounding cooler air. As the heated parcel of air rises into cooler regions away from the surface, it loses its heat and falls away, replaced from below by a continually rising stream of air from the surface. In this manner the heat engine of the air operates over a patch of blistering desert sand just as it does on a global basis.

Global Circulation of the Atmosphere

Figure 8.6 shows a simplified model of a stationary earth and its atmosphere. The intense sunlight at the equator causes a convective upwelling of air in the tropopause, which flows north and south toward the poles. As it nears the polar regions, it cools and sinks, taking the place of the masses of air sucked into the "furnace" at the equator. The zones of rising air at the equator form regions of low pressure, while the zones farther north, filled with falling, cooler air, become high-pressure regions. The high-pressure air tends to fill the void behind the low-pressure air, and a pattern of global circulation is established.

Now let us take into account the rotation of the earth. What happens to the flow of air? Air is held close to the earth's horizontal movements only by the tenuous forces of surface friction. It tends to assume a course *dependent* upon the initial force that set it in motion but *independent* of any particular point on the ground beneath it. This apparent motion is called the **Coriolis force,** so named for the nineteenth-century French scientist who first described it.

Figure 8.6 The atmospheric heat power system.

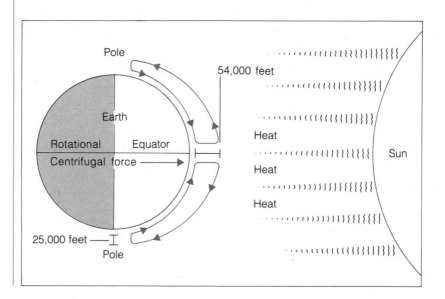

The Coriolis force.   Suppose you are riding in a balloon and are part of a mass of air rising at the equator. Since you (and the other air molecules) started at the surface, your horizontal speed is the same as the rotational speed of every other point on the equator, about 1000 miles per hour. As you reach the tropopause and begin your journey north toward the pole, you begin surveying the ground beneath you. At first, the earth's surface features rotate with you, neither gaining position on you to the east nor losing ground to the west. Gradually, though, after several hundred miles, you notice that the ground reference points are slowly drifting to the west. Are they? Or are *you* drifting to the east?

The answer is both viewpoints are correct, since the force you are experiencing, the Coriolis force, is *apparent*—a question of viewpoints—though its effect relative to air mass motion over the ground is very real. The reason for it is that 2000 miles north of the equator—say about 30° north latitude—the surface below you is rotating several hundred miles per hour *slower* than the surface at the equator. Why? Because a point on the equator simply has a *longer* distance to go before the end of its 24 hours. And the day on earth ends after the same number of hours have elapsed for everybody!

Thus, as you make your way north, following what seems to be a true course for the pole, the ground reference points beneath you gradually slip farther and farther west. Your path through the sky, to someone on the earth's surface, seems to bend increasingly toward the east (see Figure 8.7). Similarly, if you rode with the southward-flowing current from the pole to the equator, your slower "surface" speed would stay with you, and ground reference points would quickly pass you right to left, west to east, as you neared the rapidly rotating equator.

This relative motion imparts a lateral component to the north-south flow of winds (see Figure 8.8). The winds flowing south from the North Polar region come generally from the east as well as the north and hence are

Figure 8.7 The Coriolis force. **(a)** Effect of the earth's rotation. **(b)** The Coriolis force as seen from the North Pole.

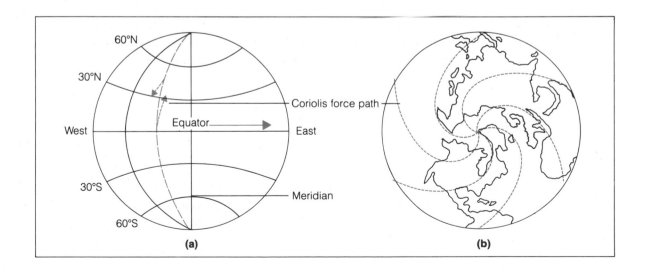

(a)   (b)

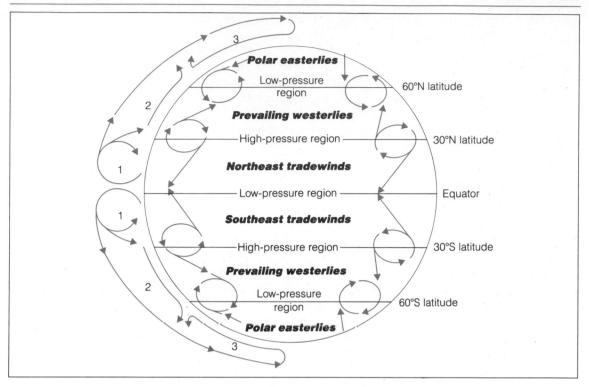

Figure 8.8 Zones of prevailing winds.

called the **polar easterlies**. A third of the way down toward the equator from the pole (at about 60° north latitude), they meet winds generally deflected west to east, called the **prevailing westerlies**. From 30° north latitude to the equator, the winds flow generally from the northeast and are called the **northeast trades**.

You should remember that in the Northern Hemisphere all winds circulate about a high-pressure area in a clockwise direction and in a counterclockwise direction about a low-pressure area. In the Southern Hemisphere, the atmospheric physics works the same way, but in the opposite direction. This is because the main polar-equator airflow itself is in the opposite direction. Spend a little time with Figure 8.8 until you have proved this to yourself.

The Effect of Pressure Gradients

We need to take a closer look at some of the details of pressure systems. We have seen that pressure in a given area can be measured in a number of ways, such as inches of mercury, pounds per square inch, or millibars. However they are measured, identical pressures can be plotted on a map and connected with lines. The lines representing these points of continuous equal pressure are called **isobars**. When all the equal pressure points are connected, the beginnings of a weather map have been constructed (see Figure 8.9).

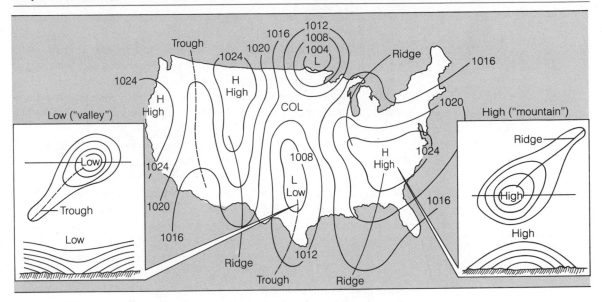

Figure 8.9 Isobaric pressure mapping.

Any map of isobars has a familiar appearance. It resembles very much a topographical map of the earth's surface and may be read in much the same way. The high-pressure areas on the map (areas where the isobars represent continually increasing pressures as they near the center) may be thought of as hills or mountains of pressure. The low-pressure areas of the map, conversely, may be thought of as valleys. When a high-pressure area takes an elongated form, it is called a **ridge,** after the geographic feature it resembles. An elongated low-pressure area is called a **trough.** The neutral area between the two highs and two lows is called a **col.** It also is the intersection of a trough and a ridge.

As we have seen, the high-pressure mountains have a constant tendency to fill in the low-pressure valleys. Because of the Coriolis force, the winds in a pressure area rotate around the high- or low-pressure centers *parallel* to their isobars (see Figure 8.10). Thus, if you see a high-pressure area on

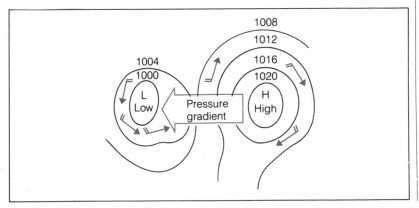

Figure 8.10 High- and low-pressure circulation.

a weather map, you know at a glance the general direction of the winds will be clockwise about the center (marked with a capital *H*) and parallel to the isobars. The same will be true for a low-pressure area (marked with a capital *L*), but the direction of circulation will be counterclockwise. Pressure patterns therefore have both circular and horizontal movement components. In the Northern Hemisphere, low-pressure areas and their associated rotational winds are called **cyclones**; high-pressure areas are called **anticyclones.**

On a topographical map, elevation lines that are close together represent steeply sloping terrain. Similarly, on a weather map, isobars that are close together represent a steep **pressure gradient**, or rapid change of pressure over a given distance—a steep slope from a high-pressure mountain to a low-pressure valley (see Figure 8.11). Pressure gradients always refer to the pressure changes *perpendicular* to the isobars. Flat or weak pressure gradients, like gently sloping terrain, show a gradual change in pressure and tend to have light winds. Strong (steep) pressure gradients, however, are like sharp mountain cliffs and tend to have higher winds.

Now that we know a little more about high- and low-pressure patterns, we can describe the mechanics of the earth's permanent and semipermanent pressure systems.

Three-Cell Circulation: The Zones of Weather

A fairly well defined pattern has been established in the global circulation of air. This pattern is most conveniently visualized as occurring in the three cells or zones mentioned earlier in the chapter (refer back to Figure 8.8) and bears the name **three-cell circulation**.

Equator to 30° latitude.   Warm air rises in great masses from the equator, forming a permanent low-pressure area. By the time air moving toward the poles reaches the vicinity of 30° latitude, however, the Coriolis force has diverted most of its apparent motion eastward, and the mass of air "piles up," sending much of it toward the earth again. This descending column of air forms a belt of high pressure straddling the 30° line in both hemispheres. Thus, the area from the equator to this latitude becomes a nearly self-contained cell of circulation.

30° latitude to 60° latitude.   The belt of prevailing westerlies is a very complex cell. Air from the northern and southern regions mixes in this region, causing large temperature variations. Storms appear frequently and

Figure 8.11 Pressure gradients. Steep gradients mean a rapid change in pressure and often higher-velocity winds.

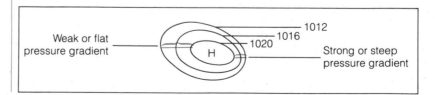

move through the region, varying in intensity with the season. The general motion of the wind is west to east (hence the name).

60° latitude to the pole.   Air coming north from the prevailing westerlies meets air moving south from the pole and begins to build a vertical column, forming a permanent area of low pressure all along the 60° line. When the vertical sheet of air joins the general northward stream again, it continues until it is cooled by the polar region and meets air from other parts of the globe. These masses of air descend and form a permanent area of high pressure above the polar caps, from which a southerly flow recommences. Some of the air continues on to the equator, while the rest of it meets the prevailing westerlies and combines to form the third cell of circulation in each hemisphere.

Other Forces Acting on Winds

Complications to the three-cell circulation pattern are virtually endless, particularly when dealing with winds near the surface. However, three major factors exert the most influence on final wind speed and direction. These are the forces of gravity and friction and centrifugal force.

Gravity.   Since gravity exerts a pull on all molecules all of the time, the result is denser air near the surface of the earth than aloft. The greater *inertia* of this lower air (its resistance to all forces that would try to move it) can affect all weather patterns.

Friction.   Just as airflow is disturbed on an airplane by struts, antennas, and other protrusions, the surface features of the earth—the **friction level**— work to retard, or otherwise deflect, the smooth flow of wind in the atmosphere. In areas without high mountains, the effect of surface features usually becomes negligible by 2000 or 3000 feet AGL. Above this altitude the winds generally follow the contours of the isobars. Below this altitude, friction causes the winds to flow *across* the isobars at an angle of about 30° *toward* the low-pressure area.

Centrifugal force.   Air moving along a curved path has a centrifugal force component. The speed of the wind along the isobars decreases as the center of a low-pressure area is approached and increases toward the center of a high-pressure area.

The altitude above which all these forces come into balance and at which the wind flows parallel to the isobars is called the **wind level.** Fortunately, there are enough predictable aspects of atmospheric winds so that pilots can use them to plan their flights. Isobaric lines can be compared to the desired route of flight and anticipated headwinds, tailwinds, or crosswinds located. The flight can be replanned if necessary to avoid heavy headwind areas or the turbulence expected when crossing steep pressure gradients. In fact, we are now ready to look at a whole range of meteorological phenomena that directly affect the pilot.

AVIATION WEATHER

To pilots the most important weather phenomenon is the one that currently confronts their airplane. Favorable winds aloft make little difference if your destination airport is closed by fog when you arrive. Clear, balmy weather at home base is of small comfort when thunderstorms cross your path. The sum total of any pilot's knowledge of meteorology is useful only to the extent that it helps solve the problems of a particular flight.

The primary concerns of any pilot, generally, are restrictions to visibility, icing, and turbulence. Although you will rely on meteorological information such as en route winds to plan your flight efficiently, you must also rely on your knowledge of these particular factors to keep your airplane flying safely.

Sky Cover and Ceiling

Sky cover is the term used to describe the extent of the clouds in a particular location. If less than one-tenth of the sky is covered, the sky condition is *clear. Scattered clouds* cover one-tenth to one-half of the sky. Clouds are reported as *broken* when they cover from six-tenths to nine-tenths of the sky. *Overcast* clouds cover more than nine-tenths of the sky. A *thin layer* of clouds is one that you can easily see through.

The lowest layer of clouds reported as broken or overcast, and not classified as thin or partial, constitutes a **ceiling.** For example, scattered, thin broken, and thin overcast clouds are *not* cloud ceilings. Broken or overcast conditions *do* constitute a ceiling.

Restrictions to Visibility

Visibility at an airport is based on a ground observer's ability to see and identify a prominent unlighted object, such as a mountain or broadcast tower, by day and a prominent lighted object at night. This **prevailing visibility** is reported in terms of statute miles for longer distances and in hundreds of feet when visibility is poor. Metric measurements are used in Europe.

There are a number of weather conditions that contribute to limited visibility. The most important of them are fog, precipitation, and natural and artificial obscurations.

Fog.   Technically, **fog** is any cloud that happens to lie on or near the ground. Like any cloud, the visibility inside fog is not good—ranging anywhere from a few hundred feet to zero. Although fog may seem gentle as you walk through it, it is among the most serious hazards you can encounter while flying.

The conditions necessary for fog are well known, though forecasting it has yet to be perfected for any given area at any specific time. Thus, as a pilot, you should know about the general conditions causing the formation of fog and be ready to supplement the meteorologist's estimate with precautions of your own. The following conditions are necessary for fog formation:

1. *High relative humidity.* This means that there is a small spread between the temperature and dew point.

2. *Presence of condensation nuclei.* The same requirement is true for any cloud.

3. *A cooling tendency.* Warmer air can hold more moisture, so a decrease in temperature is usually necessary.

These conditions are frequently achieved due to some relative motion of the air over the ground.

There are four basic types of fog that concern pilots:

1. *Radiation fog.* Also called **ground fog** or **tule fog, radiation fog** is caused by the radiational cooling of the ground at night and is most common under clear skies with calm winds in the hours just before and after sunrise. In warm weather it should quickly burn off with the rising sun, but if the fog occurs in valleys shaded from the morning sun, it may persist well into the morning or afternoon.

2. *Advection fog.* **Advection fog** forms when moist air moves over a cool surface, either land or water. For this movement to take place, some wind is necessary, usually 5 to 15 knots. It is commonly encountered in coastal areas, where moist sea air blows in over the cooler land. Advection fog is usually more extensive and much more persistent than radiation fog. It can move in rapidly regardless of the time of day or night.

3. *Upslope fog.* **Upslope fog** forms as a result of moist, stable air being cooled as it moves up rising terrain. The cooling is caused by the decreases in temperature and pressure associated with moving up in altitude. Upslope fog is common along the eastern slopes of the Rocky Mountains. It is also found less frequently along the eastern portion of the Appalachians.

4. *Frontal fog, or precipitation-induced fog.* **Frontal fog** can occur whenever warm rain falls through cooler, lower-level air. The rainwater evaporates into the cooler air, causing it to become saturated and form fog. The weather front that produces this combination usually causes widespread areas of rain and low visibilities.

Precipitation.   Precipitation is an all-inclusive term denoting drizzle, rain, snow, ice pellets, hail, and ice crystals (see Figure 8.12). Precipitation occurs when these particles grow in size and weight until the atmosphere can no longer support them and they fall. Visibility problems are most often encountered in rain, drizzle, and snow; in fact, drizzle or snow restricts visibility more than rain. Drizzle falls in stable air and therefore often accompanies fog, haze, or smoke. These combinations result in extremely poor visibility. Snow can reduce visibility to zero because it tends to descend slowly and has high reflectivity.

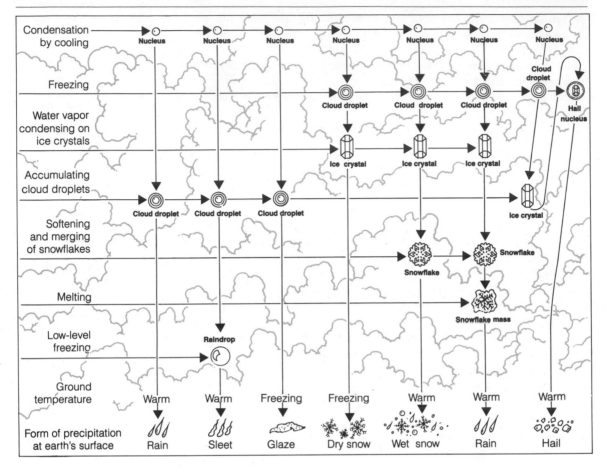

Figure 8.12 Formation and types of precipitation.

Obscurations. To be classified as an **obscuration,** the phenomenon restricting visibility must begin at the surface. When the sky is totally hidden by the surface-based phenomenon, an **indefinite ceiling** is reported. The distance value given is the vertical visibility from the surface upward into the obscuration. If clouds or part of the sky can be seen above the obscuration, only a **partial obscuration** exists. A partial obscuration does not necessarily constitute a ceiling. It may, if there is a cloud layer above it. Because an obscuration goes all the way to the ground, visibility becomes deceptive.

Pilot's visibility. Finally, there are a few visibility-related terms all pilots should learn to use precisely, especially when dealing with meteorologists or air traffic controllers. **Visual meteorological conditions (VMC)** means that the weather conditions are such that flight can be maintained by use of outside references. It is not the same thing as Visual Flight Rules, or VFR, which are the regulations under which visual flight is to be conducted. **Instrument meteorological conditions (IMC)** means that visual flight is not possible on account of restrictions to visibility, and the aircraft must be flown by reference to flight instruments only. Instrument Flight Rules, or IFR, on the other hand, are a specific set of rules governing any pilot who has filed an instrument flight plan (and who is certificated for instrument flight and whose aircraft is suitably equipped). All VFR flights are conducted under VMC. IFR flights, however, can be conducted under VMC and/or IMC. These terms are not interchangeable, and you may hear many student and private pilots—and even some controllers—using these terms improperly.

The most significant measure of visibility aloft, perhaps, is **slant range visibility** (see Figure 8.13). This is the "over-the-nose" visibility the pilot needs for maneuvering and landing. Under hazy conditions, pilots frequently see the ground beneath them before they see the runway. Even though the vertical visibility or a ground observer's reported prevailing visibility may seem satisfactory, it is slant range visibility that allows maneuvers by means of ground references.

Icing

Frost.   During clear nights with little or no wind, the surface of an object (like an airplane) often cools, by radiation, to a temperature below the dew point of the adjacent air. If the air temperature is below freezing, the water vapor clings to the surface as **frost.** The rough surface the frost produces can seriously degrade the performance of an airfoil; it increases drag and causes premature separation of the air passing over the airfoil. *Always remove all frost from the airplane before flight.*

Structural icing.   Two conditions are necessary for structural icing to form in flight:

1. You must be flying through visible water, such as rain or cloud droplets.
2. The surface temperature of the airframe, at the point where the moisture strikes the aircraft, must be below freezing.

Aerodynamic cooling can lower the temperature of an airfoil a few degrees below the ambient air temperature. *Most* icing occurs when the OAT is in

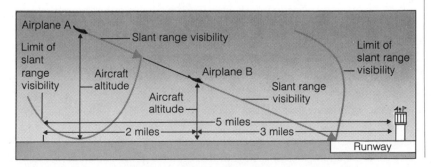

Figure 8.13 Slant range visibility. The tower reports 5 miles surface (horizontal) visibility; airplane A's slant range visibility equals 2 miles horizon; airplane B's slant range visibility equals 3 miles horizon.

the range from -5 degrees to $+3$ degrees Celsius (23 to 37 degrees Fahrenheit); however, airframe icing has been experienced at temperatures as low as -40 degrees.

The best defense against inflight icing as a VFR pilot is to *stay within legal limits* and stay out of clouds and away from freezing rain. All pilots, however, should be aware of how inflight icing occurs and what it looks like on the airframe. Structural ice comes in two forms: *clear* and *rime,* depending upon the size of the water droplets that strike the airplane's surface.

Clear ice.   Large water droplets that strike the airframe and freeze slowly form a smooth, conformal blanket of **clear ice.** This type of icing occurs in clouds with vertical development, which also produce turbulent flying conditions.

Rime ice.   Clouds that have little or no vertical development can produce very small water droplets. Small motionless water droplets often remain liquid even when the air temperature is many degrees *below* freezing. These *supercooled* droplets freeze instantly if anything, like an airplane, disturbs them. They form an opaque, irregular, granular deposit known as **rime ice** on the surface where they freeze. The freezing happens so rapidly that the ice can even form protrusions *into* the oncoming airflow.

Mixed icing forms when the water drops vary in size or when liquid drops are intermingled with snow or ice particles. This combination creates a very rough buildup, which can, like rime ice, extend into the airstream as a product of instantaneous freezing.

The detrimental effects of structural ice are cumulative:

1. *Lift is reduced* because the airfoil shape of the wing is deformed.

2. *Weight increases.* The ice becomes an unwanted addition to your airplane's total weight.

3. *Thrust decreases* because the propeller airfoil is also deformed.

4. *Drag increases* drastically because of increased frontal area, deformation of all airfoil surfaces, and surface roughness created by the ice.

5. *Stalling speed increases* as a result of all of the items mentioned above. Unfortunately, there is no way to predict the value of the new stall speed.

Flight into icing conditions usually involves IFR weather. Obviously, you have no business flying in such weather until you earn your instrument rating.

Turbulence

Any time air is in vertical motion, the air is *unstable. Atmospheric stability,* like the stability of the airplane itself, is the tendency of a parcel of air to return to its original condition after being displaced. Very stable air resists such changes and settles down again to a smooth horizontal motion. Very unstable air reacts positively to displacing forces and may reinforce them as well. When an airplane flies through such unstable air, it experiences **turbulence**. Turbulence can result from wind shear (discussed later) and from other sources too, but the most destructive usually involves air in vertical motion.

Instability and lapse rate.   We have already noted that the atmosphere normally loses 2 degrees Celsius per thousand feet of altitude. This **standard lapse rate** is an average value between the temperature lapse rates of dry and moist air. Dry air is relatively stable, while moist air is relatively unstable. Heat is only one ingredient in unstable and potentially turbulent air. The term **adiabatic lapse rate** is applied to the temperature change of mechanically lifted air, such as air being forced over a mountain ridge, without the injection or removal of heat to or from an outside source. The adiabatic lapse rate for dry air is about 3 degrees Celsius per thousand feet, while the rate for moist (or saturated) air is considerably less, ranging from 1.1 to 2.8 degrees Celsius (see Figure 8.14). As we will see later in this chapter, mechanically lifted moist air can become extremely unstable and turbulent.

Convective currents.   **Convective currents** develop over any warm surface and can be as localized as the size of a small plowed field. These parcels of warm air rise like bubbles in a saucepan until their temperature is reduced to that of the surrounding air. Amid these columns of rising air are columns of descending air, rushing down to fill in the low-pressure areas beneath them. The currents are strongest when the surface heat is the greatest, usually in the summertime and over dark surfaces. Barren sur-

Figure 8.14 Adiabatic lapse rates.

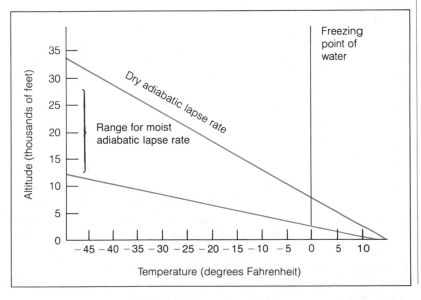

Figure 8.15. Effect of convective
currents on final approach.
Predominantly upward currents tend
to cause the aircraft to overshoot;
predominantly downward currents
tend to cause the craft to
undershoot. (Note that smooth flight
can be maintained above the
clouds.)

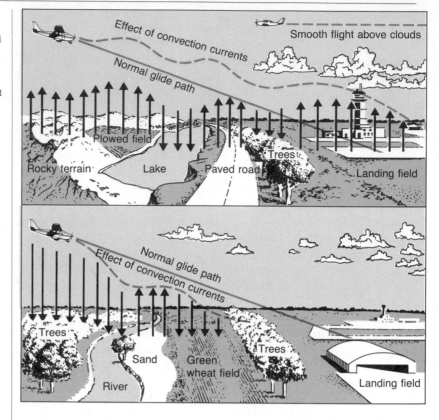

faces, such as sandy or rocky wastelands, and plowed fields heat more
readily than fields covered with grass or vegetation. Thus, the frequency
and strength of these **thermals,** as pilots call them, vary from place to
place. When an airplane flies through them, it experiences a sudden updraft,
followed by a sudden downdraft as it exits the thermal into the descending
air. While this sort of turbulence is seldom dangerous, it can be uncomfortable. Many pilots, when anticipating thermals, prefer to fly in the early
morning or evening during the warmer months of the year.

As air moves upward, it cools by expansion. The convective action stops
when the rising air's temperature is the same as that of the surrounding air.
If the air is moist and it cools to saturation, then a cloud forms. The cloud
top usually marks the upper limit of the convective current. If the clouds
are scattered enough that you can get above them, you will find smooth air
(see Figure 8.15).

We have already described the temperature variations between bodies of
land and bodies of water. During the day, the earth warms more quickly,
sending convective currents from its surface and drawing in cooler air from
the sea. This results in an **onshore wind,** or sea breeze (see Figure 8.16).
At night, the water retains its warmth while the land cools rapidly, and the
situation is reversed, creating an **offshore wind,** or land breeze. You can
therefore expect to encounter thermal turbulence when crossing or paralleling the shoreline or when flying in the vicinity of large lakes.

Figure 8.16 *(opposite)* Shoreline
convective current. **(a)** Generation
of onshore wind during the day.
(b) Generation of an offshore wind
during the night.

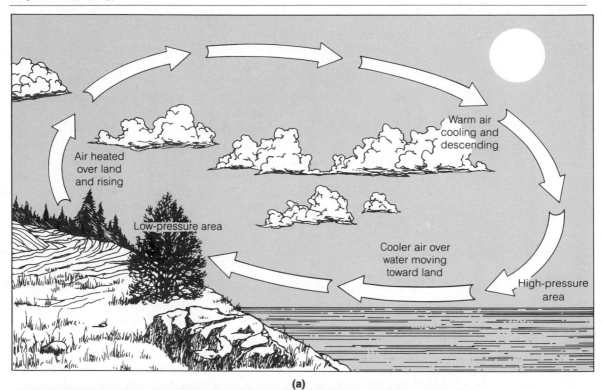

(a)

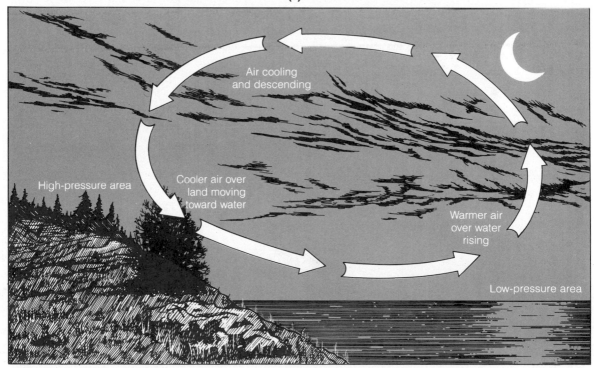

(b)

Surface obstructions. Surface features can affect the direction of the wind. The effect the particular feature has on breaking up or diverting the otherwise smooth flow of air is directly proportional to its size. We will look quickly at both the smallest features and the largest.

Land flow. At the lowest level, wind must flow around such things as houses, hangars, towers, trees, and hills (see Figure 8.17). But even if this action is not on the magnificent scale of global circulation, you should not take it lightly. Air is densest at the surface of the earth, which is where potentially hazardous takeoff and landing operations take place. Like rocks and branches in a fast-moving stream, these surface features snarl the wind in a complicated series of whirlpools and eddies, causing **land flow turbulence.** When the wind itself is gusty, these surface vortices can become vicious. If the wind exceeds 20 knots, these eddies will be detached from the object, carrying turbulence some distance away to areas where it may be unexpected. Pilots landing at airports with large natural or artificial obstacles in the vicinity of the runway should be alert for this type of turbulence.

Mountain wave. When stable air moves across a mountain barrier, the air flowing up the windward side is relatively smooth, and the air moving across the barrier also tends to flow in layers; however, the action of the barrier may set up waves on the downstream side. The waves remain nearly stationary while the wind blows rapidly through them. This wave pattern is called a **standing** or **mountain wave** because of these characteristic traits (see Figure 8.18). The wave pattern may extend 100 miles or more downwind from the barrier.

Wave crests extend well above the tops of the mountain, sometimes into the lower stratosphere. The updrafts and downdrafts in the waves are extremely powerful. If you are flying within the wave in a light aircraft, you will

Figure 8.17 Land flow turbulence.

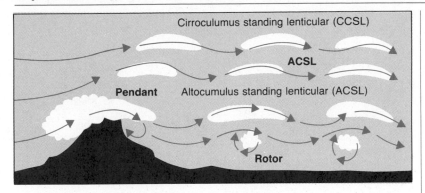

Figure 8.18 Schematic cross-section of a mountain wave. Note the standing wave pattern downwind from the mountain and the rotary circulation below the wave crests. When air contains sufficient moisture, characteristic clouds form.

follow the up and down motion of the wave whether you want to or not. Your airplane will not have enough performance to counteract the effects of the wave flow. Turbulence within the wave can range from none to extremely violent.

Under each wave crest, below the elevation of the mountain peaks, is an area of turbulent rotary motion. This rotor area is an area of violent turbulence.

Figure 8.18 shows the clouds often associated with a mountain wave. The mountain top may be covered by a *cap cloud*. The crests of the standing waves may be marked by standing **lenticular** (stationary lens-shaped) **clouds.** Although these clouds appear to be stationary, that appearance is misleading because the wind is continually moving through their area. The clouds form in the updraft portion of the wave and dissipate in the downdraft. The rotor area may be marked by a **rotor cloud.**

The existence of any of these clouds depends on sufficient moisture in the air, and dry mountain wave air is not uncommon. Always anticipate mountain wave conditions whenever stable air blows across mountains at speeds of 25 knots or greater.

Wind shear.   A **wind shear** is any sudden change in wind speed or direction. It can occur in a horizontal as well as vertical plane—and sometimes in both together. Wind shear can be encountered at any altitude, from just above the ground to high cruising altitudes (see Figure 8.19). Occasionally, there may be eddies of turbulence announcing it ahead of time, but this cannot be counted on. A wind shear may be anticipated whenever there is a **temperature inversion** (a reversal of the standard lapse rate) aloft (see Figure 8.20). During takeoff and landing phases, transition to a new, moving air mass can instantaneously change the relative wind, causing airspeed fluctuations and, in severe cases, stalling the airplane when it is especially vulnerable. A large difference between low-altitude winds and airport surface winds may indicate the presence of a wind shear as well.

Clear air turbulence.   Because temperature and moisture are so closely related to instability, there is a tendency among many pilots to feel secure

Figure 8.19 Wind shear. (a) High-altitude wind shear is caused by air moving in different directions.
(b) Wind shears in any direction are found in proximity to thunderstorms.
(c) Horizontal wind shear occurs at low altitudes due to temperature inversion when warmer air is above cooler air.

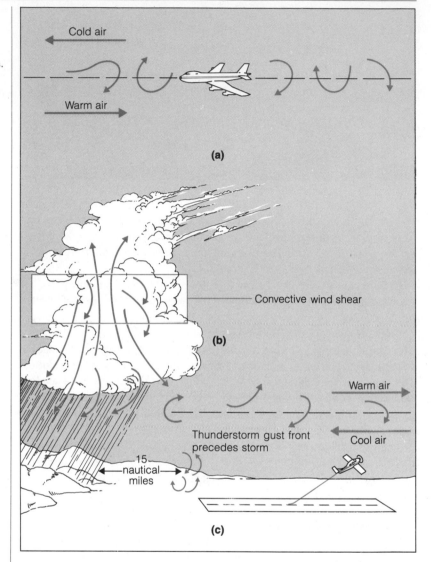

from turbulence when flying out of the sight of clouds or storm systems. This sense of security, unfortunately, can be misleading. **Clear air turbulence (CAT),** a phenomenon different from convection or surface turbulence, is comparatively rare but can strike anywhere, anytime—seemingly from "out of the blue." It is usually very mild, similar to what you experience when driving a car over a rough dirt road or cobblestone street at moderate speeds. Occasionally, at higher altitudes, clear air turbulence can be extreme and catastrophic. Although all significant weather information should be reported over the radio as soon as it is encountered, CAT reports are especially valuable, since the means for predicting it en route are, as yet, imperfect.

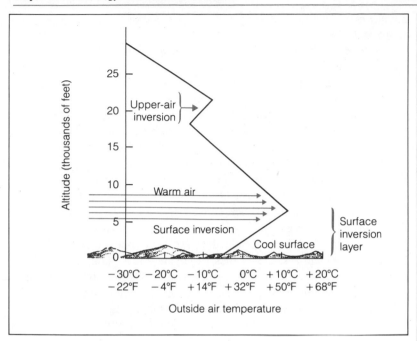

Figure 8.20 Temperature inversion.

CLOUDS: SIGNPOSTS IN THE SKY

You already know that **clouds** are nothing more than visible moisture. Moisture becomes visible through a process called condensation, and it is worth a quick review. When saturated air is cooled to its dew point and condensation nuclei are present in the air, liquid water forms from water vapor in the shape of millions of microscopic droplets. These droplets may freeze if the temperature is low enough, and the cloud will be composed of ice crystals.

Clouds are classified in two basic ways: by how they are formed and by their altitude. Other ways of describing them are added to these two dimensions to produce the classification of clouds. Two of these descriptors are cumulus and stratus. **Cumulus clouds** have a puffy, billowy appearance. The word cumulus means *accumulation* or *heap*. These clouds are formed by vertical currents of unstable air. **Stratus clouds** are those having a uniform sheet-like appearance. Stratus means *stratified* or *layered*. This type of cloud is formed by the cooling of a stable layer of air.

Cumulus and stratus clouds are divided into four *altitude families*: low, middle, high, and those with extensive vertical development:

1. *Low clouds* have bases that range from near the surface to about 6500 feet. These clouds are called simply stratus or cumulus (no prefix).

2. *Middle clouds* extend from about 6500 to 23,000 feet. The prefix *alto* is usually added to the cloud type (**altostratus,** *altocumulus*).

3. *High clouds* begin at approximately 16,500 to 45,000 feet. The high-cloud family is **cirriform clouds** and includes **cirrus,** *cirrocumulus,* and *cirrostratus*. They are composed almost entirely of ice crystals, and are wispy and fibrous in appearance.

4. *Clouds with extensive vertical development* have bases that range from 1000 to 4500 feet and tops that often extend into the lower stratosphere. These **cumuliform clouds** are discussed later in this chapter.

In addition to the foregoing, the prefix *nimbo* or suffix *nimbus* means rain cloud. Stratified clouds from which rain is falling are *nimbostratus*. A cumulus cloud that produces precipitation is called a **cumulonimbus cloud.**

Clouds broken into fragments are often identified by adding the suffix *fractus*. For example, fragmentary cumulus is called *cumulus fractus*.

Table 8.1 describes a number of the more significant cloud forms and details some of their characteristics. (See also the photos on pages 256–259.) Although these characteristics reveal much about the short-term weather picture, they perform a more immediate service to pilots by indicating the flying conditions in and around them. Here are a few examples.

Stratus. This form features long layers of uniform clouds, sometimes accompanied by intermittent drizzle. This type of cloud generally will not burn off and, if it is a low overcast, may limit flying for several days. Flying below it, the air is smooth and stable. Above the clouds, features of the terrain underneath may be revealed by means of lumps and depressions in the sheet of clouds.

Cumulus. Cumulus clouds indicate vertical development and instability, usually with bases that range from 4000 to 6000 feet. Flight below and in between the buildups is rough and bumpy due to the ascending and descending columns of air. Above the cloud tops, the air will be smoother, since the cumulus cloud quits its vertical development when it reaches a layer of stable air. If the instability is significant and there is a large amount of moisture in the air, certain cumulus clouds can continue their development into cumulonimbus, or thunderheads. These cloud forms are among the most awesome and powerful phenomena in nature, and they merit special attention from all pilots who hope to share the sky with them.

Stratocumulus. This form features layers of cumulus clouds, usually at a low altitude, frequently below 1000 feet AGL. If it is a thin layer, it may well burn off or dissipate with the heat of the day.

The Cumulonimbus

Variously called Cbs or *TRWs* (from their meteorological abbreviations), or **thunderstorms,** *thunderheads, thunderbumpers,* and other names less complimentary than respectful, cumulonimbus clouds can be encountered in a wide variety of circumstances: in isolated splendor over a desert mountain range, or by the dozen in fast-moving **squall lines,** strewn in ranks for hundreds of miles. They can even lurk embedded in great stratocumulus cloud masses, visible only on airborne or ground-based radars.

By any standard, cumulonimbus clouds are dangerous. Because of the great amounts of energy released in the course of their towering vertical development, they can spawn heavy rain, damaging hail, lightning, extreme

Type	Approximate height of bases (feet)	Description	Associated weather	
			Precipitation types	*General*
Cumulus	1500–10,000	Detached domes or towers, flat bases; brilliant white in sun, dark blue or gray in shadows	If building, rain or snow showers	Good surface visibility and fair weather if not building; if building, high winds, turbulence
Altocumulus	6500–16,500	White or gray layers, rolls or patches of wavy solid clouds	Intermittent rain or snow, usually light	Turbulence likely; generally good surface visibility
Stratocumulus	A few feet above surface to 6500	Gray or blue; individual rolls or globular masses	Light rain or snow showers	Strong, gusty surface winds, particularly if ahead of a cold front; turbulence
Cumulonimbus	1500–10,000	Large, heavy, towering clouds; black bases; cauliflowerlike or anvil-shaped tops	Heavy showers; possibility of hail	Associated with severe weather, turbulence, high surface winds; surface visibility usually fair to good outside of precipitation
Stratus	A few feet above surface to 3000	Low, gray, uniform, sheet-like cloud	Light drizzle, snow grains	Poor surface visibility; air smooth
Altostratus	6500–16,500	Gray or blue veil or layer of clouds; appears fibrous; sun may show as through frosted glass	Light, continuous precipitation	Usually poor surface visibility; air smooth; moderate surface winds
Nimbostratus	1500–10,000	Dark gray, thick, shapeless cloud layer (really a low altostratus with precipitation)	Continuous precipitation	Visibility restricted by precipitation; air smooth; calm to light surface winds
Cirrus	16,500–45,000	White, thin, feathery clouds in patches or bands	None	If arranged in bands or associated with other clouds, usually a sign of approaching bad weather
Cirrostratus	16,500–45,000	White, thin cloud layers; looks like sheet or veil; halo around moon or sun	None	Often a sign of approaching bad weather; surface winds bring overcast skies
Cirrocumulus	16,500–45,000	Thin clouds in sheets; individual elements look like tufts of cotton	None	Indicate high-level instability

Table 8.1 Cloud Forms and Characteristics

Cumulus.

Cu

"Woolpack"

Altocumulus.

Ac

"Sheep
backs"

Stratocumulus.

Sc

Flat, long
layers

Cumulonimbus.

Cb

Thunderhead

Stratus.

St ___

Layers or
sheets

Altostratus.

As

Ns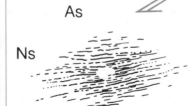

Thick, gray
curtain

Nimbostratus.

Ns

Illuminated
layers

Cirrus.

Ci

Feathery

Cirrostratus.

Cs

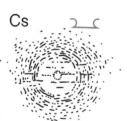

Halo-
producing

Mackerel
scales

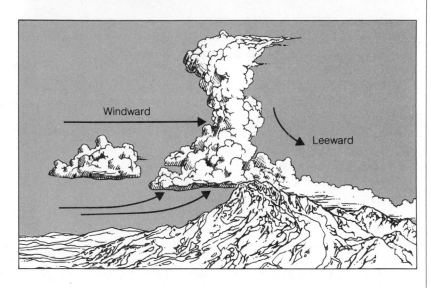

Figure 8.21 An orographic
thunderstorm.

turbulence, tornados, and the severest forms of airframe icing—frequently all at the same time! They are avoided scrupulously by all pilots everywhere—from private pilots to airline captains—regardless of the performance of the airplane. A towering thunderhead can be one of nature's most beautiful sights, but only from a distance.

Cb types.   Like all cumulus clouds, Cbs are a product of vertical motion and instability, but on an exaggerated scale. **Air mass thunderstorms** are caused by the heating of the air at the earth's surface according to the convection mechanisms previously discussed. **Orographic thunderstorms** are the product of the upslope lifting of moist, moving air approaching a mountain range (see Figure 8.21). **Frontal thunderstorms** are formed by the same vertical motion, though the impetus for development comes from the mechanical lifting of one air mass by another. We will define this process more precisely later in the chapter.

Thunderstorm Mechanics

For a thunderstorm to form, the air must have: (1) sufficient water vapor, (2) an unstable lapse rate, and (3) an initial lifting to start the process in motion. The initial lifting can come from any one of the mechanisms mentioned previously. Within the cumulus cloud itself there is another source of energy that contributes greatly to its development: the process of water vapor condensing into water droplets releases energy, called the *latent heat of condensation* (refer to Figure 8.3). The rate of energy released is proportional to the amount of water vapor being condensed within the cloud. The latent heat energy adds vertical momentum to the cloud, and that momentum helps draw in more moisture-laden air. The cloud becomes a self-sustaining heat engine, fueled by water vapor.

Thunderstorm life cycle.   Fortunately, the same mechanism that builds a thunderstorm eventually brings about its demise. A typical thunderstorm goes through three stages of development (see Figure 8.22):

1. The *cumulus stage*. The initial building stage is the cumulus stage. It is characterized by rapid vertical development and updrafts in and around the cloud. Air is drawn into the cloud from all sides, a process called *entrainment*.

2. The *mature stage*. The water droplets within the cloud begin to collide and form larger, more numerous drops. Eventually, they become large and heavy enough to fall against the updraft that formed them. This marks the beginning of the mature stage of the thunderstorm. The prevailing updrafts are now accompanied by downdrafts generated by the falling precipitation. Static electricity, produced by the friction between the updrafts and downdrafts, is discharged at irregular intervals as *lightning*. The mature stage is the most violent and dangerous phase of a thunderstorm. Duration of the mature stage usually determines a storm's severity.

3. The *dissipating stage*. Once the storm reaches the mature stage, it begins to die. The downdrafts dissipate the updrafts that earlier supported the development of the storm. A thunderstorm is considered over when it no longer produces rain.

Air mass thunderstorms are most often the result of surface heating in a warm, moist air mass. (An air mass is a body of air that has uniform temperature and moisture properties; its characteristics and actions are described in a later section.) These storms occur at random, last for only an hour or two, and produce moderate gusts and rainfall. When the storm reaches the mature stage, rain falls through or immediately beside the updraft. The friction of the falling precipitation retards the updraft and eventually reverses it to a downdraft. This action is self-destructive and

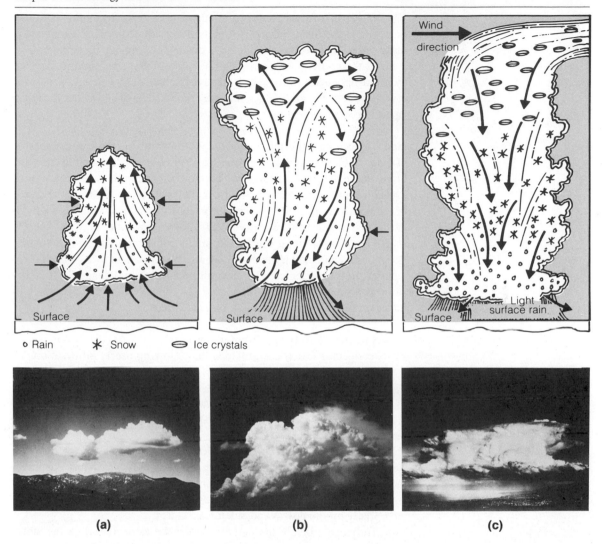

○ Rain   ✳ Snow   ⬯ Ice crystals

(a)   (b)   (c)

limits the severity of the storm. (They are nevertheless too dangerous to fly through.) The downdraft and precipitation cool the lower portion of the air mass and the surface, which further degrades the lifting action, resulting in less inflow of water vapor. All of this causes the storm to run out of energy and die. The life cycle of an air mass thunderstorm usually ranges from 20 minutes to an hour and a half. Since surface heating is the primary triggering mechanism, these storms occur most frequently over land during the middle and late afternoon. Offshore, they usually occur during late hours of darkness, when the water temperature is the warmest relative to the land temperature.

Steady state thunderstorms are usually associated with weather systems. Frontal activity, converging winds, and upper air disturbances create the lifting action that spawns these storms. Afternoon heating intensifies them.

Figure 8.22 The life cycle of a thunderstorm. (a) Cumulus stage. (b) Mature stage. (c) Dissipating stage.

The activity that forms them is often conducive to the formation of squall lines. Since the lifting action is usually the result of horizontal movement of the wind, the precipitation in these storms falls outside the updraft area. Without the cooling action of precipitation on them, the updrafts develop more strongly and last longer. A steady state thunderstorm may persist for several hours and can produce more severe weather over a wider area than an air mass thunderstorm.

Hail.   Precipitation often travels up and down inside the cloud a number of times before becoming large enough to fall out. Updrafts often carry the drops above the freezing level, where they become hail. Every time hail is cycled up and down through the freezing level, it can receive a new coat of water, which increases its size. Large hailstones occur with severe thunderstorms, which have extensive vertical development.

Hail may fall through warmer air and become rain. Rain at the surface does not preclude hail aloft. Hail may also be thrown up to 10 miles downwind of the storm center. The clear air under the anvil head of a thunderstorm is a very likely place to find hail. *Any* encounter with hailstones will inflict serious damage on the aircraft structure.

Flying in the Vicinity of Thunderstorms
Thunderstorm research has provided the following useful information:

1. There appears to be no correlation between the external appearance of a thunderstorm and the turbulence and hail within it.

2. In most well-developed thunderstorms, there is little variation in the intensity of turbulence with altitude.

3. The severity of turbulence decreases slowly with distance from the storm center. Remember that the storm cloud is only the visible portion of the turbulence area. Moderate to severe turbulence may be encountered at any altitude in the clear air surrounding the storm cloud. Turbulence is more likely on the downwind side of the storm.

4. Turbulence below the cloud base can be as severe as in the storm itself. Strong downdrafts can be encountered down to the earth's surface.

5. Avoidance, rather than penetration, of thunderstorms is always the best procedure. *Remain at least 20 miles from any thunderstorm cell.*

6. Beware of apparent holes between thunderstorm cells. Holes always seem to close up once you are in them, adding IMC to your list of problems. Holes are often the turbulence zone between two or more storm cells.

7. If you encounter strong turbulence despite your best efforts, you must accept the fact that (for the moment at least) you are part of the storm system. Your airspeed at this time must be below maneuvering speed. The most expeditious way out of most storms is straight ahead (perpendicular to the line of storms if there is a line). The time to turn back was *before* entering the storm area. Rule number one in such a situation is to *control yourself and your airplane's attitude*. Do not attempt to maintain altitude or any particular airspeed. Concentrate on holding a *level attitude,* because this will reduce the risk of losing control of the airplane or of overstressing it.

In the final analysis, the only explanation for flying near enough to a thunderstorm to be endangered by it is *poor judgment.* Proper flight planning and sensible decision making en route should prevent being exposed to a thunderstorm penetration.

AIR MASSES AND FRONTS

An **air mass** is a body of air that has uniform temperature and moisture properties. These characteristics are acquired by the air moving slowly over a geographical *source region* that itself has those temperature and moisture properties.

Source regions are many and varied, but air masses are most likely to form over large snow- or ice-covered polar regions, cold northern oceans, tropical oceans, and large desert areas. Figure 8.23 shows the source regions that influence the air masses that move across the United States. These air masses are classified as: (1) *polar* or *tropical,* describing the temperature of the source region; (2) *maritime* or *continental,* indicating whether the source region is land or water.

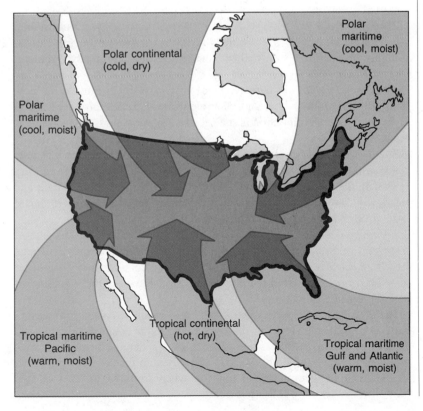

Figure 8.23 Air mass source regions for the United States.

Mid-latitudes are poor source regions because these areas are constantly disturbed. The disturbances give little opportunity for an air mass to stagnate and take on the properties of the underlying region.

Air Mass Characteristics

We already know enough about how the atmosphere works to make a few generalizations about air masses, regardless of their origin. When a cold air mass moves over a relatively warmer surface, convection currents are produced. Vertical-development cloud forms may be present, and obscurations near the surface will be carried aloft, improving low-altitude visibility. At the leading edge of such a mass, the warmer air previously at the surface will be propelled aloft. Therefore, cold air moving over a warmer surface is decidedly *unstable*.

When a warm air mass moves over a cooler surface, the situation is considerably different. The cooler air tends to stay where it is as the warm air approaches, so the warmer air initially moves over the back of the original air mass. Convection currents have no reason to form, so the air is relatively smooth. Obscurations are confined to the lower altitudes with the cooler air, so visibility can be poor. Therefore, warm air moving over a cooler surface is generally *stable*.

Now let us add a few more variables, like the source characteristics of particular warm and cold air masses. The results are interesting and important to all pilots.

Maritime Polar air masses. Since these are moist as well as unstable, precipitation and cumuliform clouds are typical. Away from the clouds, visibility and ceilings are excellent, though the air is generally turbulent. Cbs are likely.

Continental Polar air masses. Since this mass by definition has low moisture, humidity is low, and what clouds exist are usually confined to higher altitudes. Precipitation is sparse, and visibility and flying conditions are good.

Maritime Tropical air masses. Conditions within this air mass are usually stable with high humidity. Clouds tend to be stratiform and can be very low or on the ground as fog. When precipitation is present, it is light and steady. Skies tend to be overcast, with visibility beneath them poor due to haze or other trapped obscurations.

Continental Tropical air masses. This is a dry, relatively unstable air mass, and precipitation may be present but sparse. Cloud forms will depend largely on surface conditions but will usually be cumuliform. Visibility is good above or away from the clouds but variable below them because of possible trapped obscurations.

In the United States, the general pattern of weather moves from west to east, with polar and arctic air masses moving to the southeast and tropical air masses moving northeast. Cold air masses generally move faster than warm air masses, and both vary considerably with the seasons. However, a typical migrating air mass can cover anywhere from 240 to 700 miles per day (a rate of 10 to 30 miles per hour).

Fronts

As you would suspect, when one type of air mass meets another, "fireworks" can result. This mismatch of characteristics at the zone of transition between air masses has been compared to a battlefield in the sky, where the constituents of one system try to install themselves in place of a dissimilar air mass. Frequently, these fireworks are real, and the resulting thunder and lightning make the battlefield analogy appropriate. So well does this description fit, in fact, that the term *weather front* comes from the similar expression for the battle zone between two armies. The characteristics of these various battlefields can be as important to you as a pilot as the air masses behind them.

Frontal boundaries between air masses are comparatively narrow, the zone of mixing varying from 3 to 50 miles in depth before a homogeneous air mass is encountered again. A front is named for the *advancing* air mass. Thus, a **warm front** is an advancing mass of warm air superseding a mass of cold air. A **cold front** is the reverse. An **occluded front** is a combination of both of these, occurring when a very rapidly moving cold front outraces a slower front and forces it aloft. A **stationary front** is one in which the relative forces of both the warm and cold air masses are so well balanced that neither one of them prevails, and the *zone of discontinuity* (the boundary line between the two air masses) stays in virtually the same place for a period of time.

Remember too that the reason fronts move is the pressure gradient between air masses, and that within these systems of circulating winds are centers of high and low pressure. Thus, the movement of air masses and the generation and dissipation of fronts are very much related to the location and dynamics of high and low pressure areas.

The birth and death of fronts.   The ammunition that arms a front for battle is the temperature difference between the two air masses. When this temperature difference is pronounced, either by one air mass overtaking another or by the formation of a steep temperature gradient *within* an air mass, a front is born. This process is called **frontogenesis** (see Figure 8.24). When the two air masses normalize their temperatures after expending their energy, or when the formerly steep pressure gradient within the air mass flattens out, the front dissipates. This process is called **frontolysis** (see Figure 8.25). Since the air masses are characterized by temperature differences and are propelled by pressure gradients, and since wind circulates around highs and lows in a predictable way, these are the signs used to tell when frontal passage has occurred. Even when the fireworks are absent, all pilots should be able to recognize the passage of fronts from the following signs:

1. The temperature will change.
2. The wind will change direction.
3. The barometer will change.

Figure 8.24 Frontogenesis.

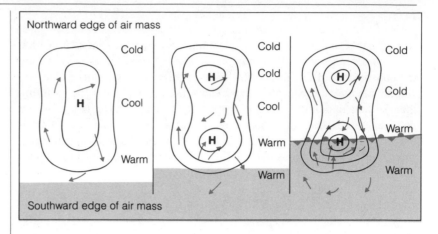

Figure 8.25 Frontolysis.

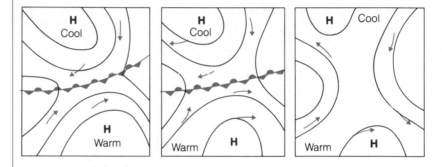

While all of these can happen at various times independently within the air mass, the only time they happen *simultaneously* is during a frontal passage.

Warm fronts.   When a warm front approaches, the less dense warm air lies on top of the retreating colder air (see Figure 8.26). When the warm, moist air climbs this wedge of cooler air, it loses temperature adiabatically and condensation begins.

Because of its long, sloping line of advance, a warm front announces itself first with high cirriform clouds that increase in density and decrease in altitude to become altostratus and finally nimbostratus layers. These clouds are normally seen between 500 and 1000 miles in advance of the front itself, losing about 1000 feet in altitude for every 20 miles of frontal advancement. Low-altitude nimbostratus and other stratiform clouds appear. Precipitation begins too, usually in the form of a steady drizzle. This moisture increases the water content of the cooler air below, and if further cooling occurs (such as radiation cooling after sunset), ground fog can form over a wide area.

If surface temperatures are cold enough, the steady precipitation usually associated with warm fronts can take the form of snow or freezing rain. Since there is no convection to speak of in a warm front, the water droplets

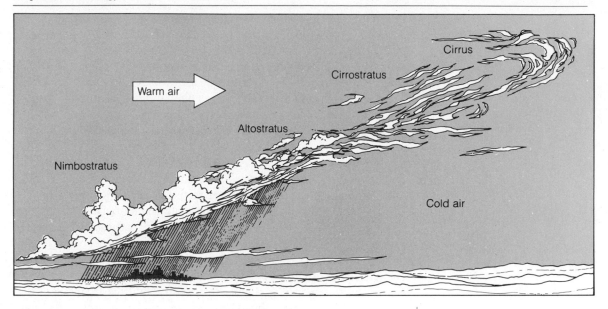

Figure 8.26 A warm front.

are small, and ice encountered in clouds or precipitation will usually be of the rime type.

Because of the stable, layered air, there is little turbulence in the frontal zone, but visibility is often restricted by precipitation or reduced to zero by clouds or fog. Low-altitude airways and the airports underneath a warm front are frequently IMC. If the air in the warm-air portion of the front is unstable, thunderstorms could develop amid the stratiform clouds and be undetectable without radar (*embedded thunderstorms*).

Passage of a warm front is marked by a gradual rise in temperature, a change in the wind direction, a steady or slowly falling barometer, and a moving away of the frontal weather, though stratus clouds or fog may persist if the warm air mass is exceptionally moist.

Flying the warm front.   VFR pilots usually encounter difficulties with warm fronts because of the extensive cloud cover. Because of the long, gradual slope of the approaching front and the likelihood of clouds at every altitude, it is difficult for most light airplanes to climb over them. Similarly, since cloud cover and precipitation can extend to the surface, flying under the disturbance can be risky. Even instrument-rated pilots are well advised to steer clear of clouds around the front due to the possibility of embedded Cbs. Perhaps the best way to handle warm fronts is to plan your flight to arrive at your destination well in advance of a frontal passage. If the front has already passed your destination, you may have to plan an intermediate stop and allow the weather to pass before continuing on, or delay the flight until the front has passed your home airport. We will show you a typical flight in the vicinity of a warm front in the next chapter.

Cold fronts. Cold fronts move faster than warm fronts, forcing the less dense air up "onto the back" of the cold air mass as it wedges between the mass of warmer air and the ground. This lifting of moist air gives rise to great cumuliform clouds and often thunderstorms (see Figure 8.27). Precipitation, though showery, can be intense—often featuring both rain and hail—and the surface winds gusty. Flight through the frontal zone is uncomfortable due to turbulence, and thunderstorms pose a continual hazard to all airplanes. The temperature and pressure gradients along the front are steep; hence, the frontal zone of the cold front is more compact than that of the warm front. A tightly knit zone of discontinuity and very violent weather that sometimes precedes the cold front is referred to as a **squall line** (see Figure 8.28). This storm line features a number of fully developed Cbs all along its length. Because the onset of a cold front can be very fast, stable warm-air conditions can persist until very near the arrival of the front or squall line. The faster the cold front is moving, the farther out in advance of it the squall line can be found. Sometimes these storms form more than one line and pass a given point in a number of ranks or chains of thunderstorms, each diminishing slightly in intensity until the front has passed. Spring and early summer squall line Cbs are among the most vicious thunderstorms in nature, frequently spawning tornados that can do considerable surface damage (see Figure 8.29).

Despite the ever-present dangers of thunderstorms and turbulent air, cold fronts do have a few redeeming qualities not found with warm fronts. Visibility can be excellent everywhere, except, of course, in the storm area

Figure 8.27 A cold front.

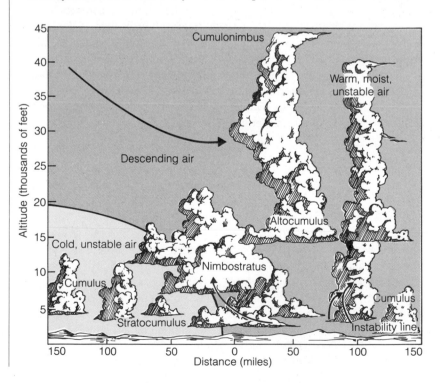

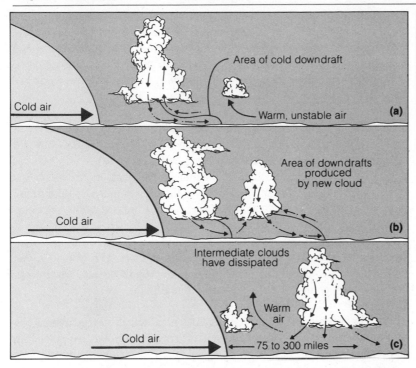

Figure 8.28 The formation of a squall line.

Figure 8.29 Thunderstorm tornado activity.

itself. Precipitation and cloud cover will be relatively brief, unless the front is very slow moving. In that case nimbostratus clouds may develop, and the system takes on more warm-front characteristics.

Passage of the cold front is marked by a drop in temperature, a change in wind direction, a rising barometer, and quick passage of the thunderstorms, usually followed by clear skies with unlimited ceilings and visibility.

Flying the cold front. All the advice we have offered concerning thunderstorms applies to operations around cold fronts. No matter how fast the cold front is moving, however, your airplane will still fly faster. Reversing course in the face of an oncoming storm and landing at the nearest suitable field is still the VFR pilot's best and surest way to avoid the front.

Occluded fronts. An occluded front is a front that has been overtaken from behind by a faster-moving cold front and forced aloft. Occlusions can be warm or cold, depending upon the nature of the overtaking front and the temperature of the air mass before it (see Figure 8.30).

When a cold front is occluded by another cold front, the frontal zones remain so close together that they are virtually indistinguishable and so are represented as one line on a weather map. Cold front occlusions are common in the eastern United States.

When a warm front is occluded by a cold front, the resulting frontal zones spread out over a wide distance, featuring warm front clouds and precipitation before and after a central core of thunderstorms. Warm front occlusions are common in the western United States.

Flying the occluded front. Occluded fronts are almost guaranteed to have thunderstorm activity embedded in the stratiform clouds. Approaching an occlusion from the east, a pilot may be misled into thinking the airplane is approaching a warm front. Approaching one from the west, the same pilot would think that a cold front lay ahead. Even an otherwise correct decision made at those points about penetrating the frontal zone under VFR stands a good chance of becoming the wrong decision a few miles later. Also, since the severest weather and turbulence is found near the crest of the occlusion, along its northernmost 50 to 100 miles, this area should be avoided at all costs. If the terrain is flat beneath the front, plan on flying beneath the clouds, even in a high-performance airplane, since the Cb cells

Figure 8.30 An occluded front.

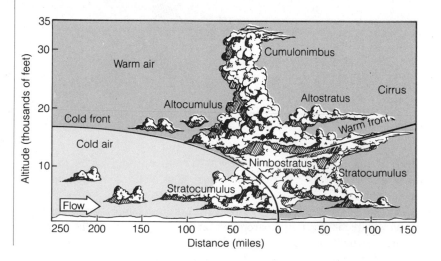

are most likely at intermediate altitudes. Only high-flying jet aircraft can hope to avoid frontal activity of any kind by flying over it.

Stationary fronts.   Any front moving slower than 5 miles per hour is considered a stationary front. Even though the front is not moving or is moving very slowly, winds may still be circulating behind or within the frontal zone, usually parallel to the zone of discontinuity. Weather encountered in a stationary front can include Cbs, though the storm activity will not be as violent or widespread as it is in a fast-moving front. It is more likely that warm front conditions will prevail, featuring days of drizzle and low cloud cover.

Flying the stationary front.   Stationary fronts are similar to occluded fronts in that there is a reasonable chance of finding Cbs embedded in the stratiform clouds. Generally, though, you will find warm front conditions throughout, with smooth air, poor visibility beneath the clouds, low ceilings, and persistent, widespread, and multilayered overcasts.

Frontal waves.   On slow-moving or stationary fronts, a phenomenon called **cyclogenesis,** or **frontal wave** formation, may occur (see Figure 8.31). This happens when the front begins to bow due to small disturbances in the winds and temperatures in the frontal zone (Figure 8.31b). The bow gradually becomes a wave, and counterclockwise rotation begins behind it (Figure 8.31c). The first arm of the wave acts as a new warm front, because it is drawing warmer air into the cold air mass. The one behind it acts as a cold front, because it is pulling cooler air into the mass of warmer air (Figure 8.31d). As the circulation develops, a low-pressure point forms at the crest of the wave, increasing the wave's cyclonic action (Figure 8.31e). Eventually, the cold front overtakes the warm front and occludes it (Figure 8.31f). At this point the cyclonic action is at its peak. Gradually, the occlusion absorbs the energy of the circulating air, and the low-pressure region weakens. While the disturbance diminishes in the area of the occlusion, the original stationary front is reestablished, and the zone stabilizes or begins a new wave cycle (Figure 8.31g).

The net effect of a frontal wave is to spawn a miniature low-pressure cell that takes off cyclonically into the air mass, widening the area of frontal disturbance and complicating the pilot's job of negotiating it safely and efficiently.

WEATHER AND THE VFR PILOT

While we may choose our climate by changing our residence, weather is thrust upon us at all locations. No matter where you live on the earth, the most pleasant weather conditions will eventually turn "sour." As human beings, dwelling on the floor of our ocean of air, we must accept whatever the currents bring us. As private pilots, however, we can and must pick the weather in which we choose to fly. Once aloft, our ability to discriminate between the hazardous and the safely challenging must continue undiminished.

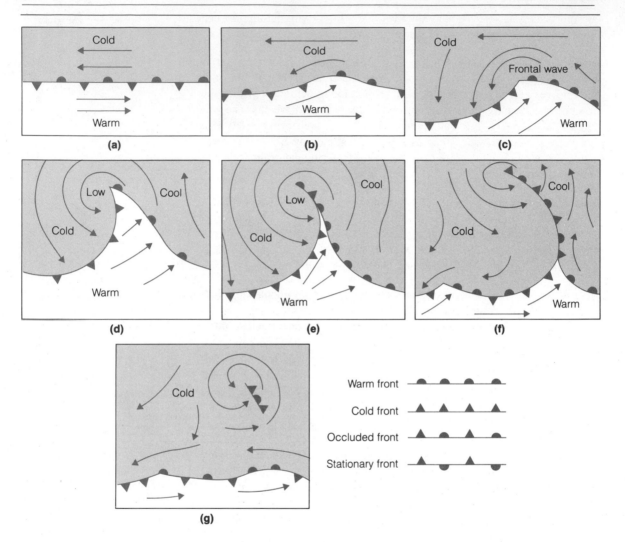

Figure 8.31 The life cycle of a frontal wave.

General Rules for Avoiding Weather Problems

1. As required by FAR 91.5, familiarize yourself with every relevant aspect of each flight. Even an hour's ride in the local area can be hazardous if marginal weather conditions develop at the airport behind you.

2. Decide ahead of time exactly at what point in the flight you will make your weather-related decision to continue the flight or not. Delaying a decision to abort the flight may put you irretrievably into a dangerous weather situation.

3. When you replan your course in-flight to fly around a weather disturbance, remember what you have learned about navigating the airplane. Weather diversions over unfamiliar territory can be disorienting. Avoid getting lost in an attempt to continue a flight into marginal conditions.

4. If you appear to be getting boxed in by hazardous weather, reduce your airspeed at once to low cruise or maximum endurance. This lower ground speed may give you valuable minutes to reverse course or analyze your options and avoid flight into an area of low (or zero) visibility.

5. Remember, a 180-degree turn is the quickest and best route out of danger. Just be sure you roll out of your turn on the opposite (reciprocal) compass heading and do not disorient yourself by inadvertently flying in circles. Although flight in turbulence and narrowing visibility can be anxiety producing, keep cool and maintain control of the aircraft.

Finally, you should realize that the truly dangerous flying situations usually involve *marginal* VFR weather rather than weather that is obviously dangerous. No rational private pilot is going to fly consciously into a hurricane or attempt a landing in zero-zero (zero visibility and zero ceiling) fog. But far too many pilots at one time or another attempt to press a marginal weather situation that "just might" open up enough to let them through under VFR. A safe, knowledgeable pilot has the self-control to resist these temptations and avoid the urge to challenge the unknown. A good rule is: when in doubt, wait it out.

The Beauty of Our Ocean of Air

No sailor who has ever captained a ship can look out over the ocean without experiencing special feelings for the ship, the sea, and the sheer physical joy of sailing. After you have flown awhile you will probably discover that you will be unable to look up at a sky in motion without recalling the many rare and wonderful sights you have enjoyed that remain hidden from earthbound observers: the glory of a circular rainbow, the delight of a zigzagging descent through a checkerboard of fair-weather "cu," or the grace of the sun setting below your wing tip in a crystal sky or frothy layer of stratus.

KEY TERMS

adiabatic lapse rate

advection fog

air mass

cirrus clouds

clear air turbulence (CAT)

clear ice

cold front

condensation

convective currents

Coriolis force

cumulonimbus clouds (Cbs)

cumulus clouds

dew point

frontal fog

indefinite ceiling

instrument meteorological
   conditions (IMC)

isobars

lenticular clouds

meteorology

millibar

mountain wave

obscuration

occluded front

partial obscuration

precipitation

pressure gradient

prevailing visibility

radiation fog

relative humidity

rime ice
sky cover
slant range visibility
squall line
standard lapse rate
stationary front
station pressure
stratus clouds

temperature inversion
troposphere
upslope fog
visual meteorological
    conditions (VMC)
warm front
wind shear

PROFICIENCY CHECK

1. Name the three basic layers of atmosphere and describe at least two characteristics of each layer.

2. What is *lapse rate?* What does the term *adiabatic* mean? What is the temperature value for the *standard, dry,* and *moist* adiabatic lapse rates? How does temperature inversion affect lapse rate?

3. Explain why meteorologists call the earth's atmosphere a giant "heat engine." How are these heating transfer principles related to global air circulation?

4. Because of the *Coriolis force,* high- and low-pressure areas rotate about their centers of pressure. In the Northern Hemisphere, what is the direction of rotation for each pressure area? Why do *highs* and *lows* begin to move?

5. How are *ceiling* and *sky cover* related?

6. What are the three conditions necessary for fog formation?

7. What are the conditions necessary for inflight icing? Describe the characteristics of the two main kinds of structural ice.

8. What are the characteristic cloud "signposts" for a *mountain wave?* Are they always present during mountain wave conditions?

9. What is a *wind shear?* What are two indicators of a possible wind shear?

10. Name and describe the basic cloud types. What are the flying characteristics associated with each?

11. What is a *cumulonimbus* cloud or *Cb?* What are the three stages of its life cycle and what are the characteristics of each?

12. How do *warm fronts* pose a flying hazard for pilots? How do *cold fronts* pose a flying hazard? What is the VFR pilot's best maneuver in case the weather begins to close in on the airplane in flight?

. . . Many [accidents] are caused by ignorance of weather phenomena, overconfidence in the face of uncertain conditions, or failure to use the weather information that is available. . . . Aviation accident statistics clearly show the wisdom of the old saying, "There are old pilots and there are bold pilots; but there are no old, bold pilots."

Malcolm W. Cagle and C. G. Halpine
A Pilot's Meteorology

C H E C K P O I N T S

What agency provides weather information and how is it collected? ⟶ What specific weather information do pilots need to plan their flights? ⟶ How do pilots read and interpret weather charts? ⟶ What weather reports and forecasts are available to assist flight planning? ⟶ What special warnings are there for adverse flying weather? How do pilots use aviation inflight weather services?

USING AVIATION WEATHER SERVICES

Few groups of people need timely and reliable weather information more than do pilots. Farmers may face crop losses without it; mariners may lose days from their schedule if it is delayed; public events may lose revenue if it is wrong; but pilots depend on it for their very survival.

Spurred by the rapid growth of aviation, weather services have, for the most part, kept pace with user needs. Meteorological information is gathered continuously, 24 hours a day, from a variety of sources—including pilots—and analyzed and reported at frequent intervals. A steady stream of accurate observations also provides the time histories for reliable forecasts. Contrary to folk wisdom, the weather forecaster is more often right than wrong, particularly in forecasts involving good weather, moderate to low ceilings, frontal passage, the onset of precipitation, and thunderstorms. Less accurate forecasts involve the prediction of severe weather (such as icing, turbulence, and squall lines) that subsequently does not materialize. But even these errors work in the careful pilot's favor. Zones of dangerous weather that you avoid will not be hazardous to you, and even if those dangerous conditions never appear, you are wise to minimize your risks. Changes to reported conditions or forecasts are made available immediately to pilots, and long-range forecasts are updated continually from short-term experience. There is simply no excuse for beginning a flight with inadequate weather information.

This chapter will explain how weather information is gathered, prepared, and disseminated to pilots. We will finish our discussion by taking simulated flights through two different weather systems.

THE SOURCES OF WEATHER INFORMATION
The National Weather Service
The National Weather Service (NWS) gathers information about the weather and provides that information to the Federal Aviation Administration (FAA), which makes it available to the flying public. The NWS is a branch of the National Oceanic and Atmospheric Administration (NOAA), reporting to the U.S. Department of Commerce. In addition to its public weather reporting and forecasting duties, the NWS also issues warnings about severe weather—such as hurricanes, tornados, and floods—and information to users with special needs, such as pilots and sailors. The far-flung NWS facilities are located throughout the continental United States, Alaska, and Puerto Rico, and on several islands in the Pacific. The military provides its own weather services, though there is considerable cooperation between the agencies, particularly concerning severe weather.

Observations.   All forecasts and reports begin with observations of current meteorological conditions. Data are gathered from a wide variety of sources, including surface observations taken at military and civilian airports and over 12,000 volunteer substations, balloon-mounted and rocket-mounted atmospheric probes called **radiosondes, pilot** (uninstrumented) **balloons** that are tracked by instruments as they rise, ground-based radar systems, weather reconnaissance flights, satellite observations, surface

automatic weather observation stations (AWOS) operating in remote areas, and reports from aircraft in flight and ships at sea.

Of these sources, surface, radar, satellite, and pilot reports are probably the most important. Surface observations are usually the most complete and relevant to pilots, since they are made directly at the airport or terminal. Radar observations are made using special units adjusted to produce a radar wave that is sensitive to rain drops (unlike ATC radars, which specifically minimize the effects of precipitation). Thus, these weather radars can track and very accurately diagnose areas of precipitation, including thunderstorms and their associated severe weather. Satellite observations allow a global (or at least hemispheric) picture of the weather and allow accurate tracking and prediction of large air mass movements and storm systems.

Inflight reports from general-aviation and commercial and military pilots complete the picture of the current weather. No one knows the flight conditions aloft better than a pilot who has just flown through them. **Pilot reports (PIREPs)** are especially useful in conditions of low visibility, icing, and turbulence; in making visual meteorological conditions (VMC) determinations; and in verifying nonstandard meteorological conditions, such as temperature inversions. As a member of the flying community, you will be asked on occasion to submit these inflight reports, or you may want to volunteer them on your own. They are another reason you will want to continually refine your weather diagnosing skills. You, too, are part of the national weather reporting system.

Distribution of weather information.   All weather data are transmitted electronically between observers, NWS data processing centers, and service outlets (such as Flight Service Stations, the military, ATC; see Figure 9.1). Some reports use words or codes based on words—textual reports— and some use drawings or graphs. Textual data are sent across teletype circuits, though these are being supplemented and replaced by higher-speed computer data lines. Graphical data are distributed using facsimile machines.

The network is designed to automatically give each outlet complete data within its immediate area (a few hundred miles). The automatic supply of data for remote locations is sparse, but complete data for any location are available upon request.

INTERPRETING WEATHER CHARTS

Given the massive amount of data that are produced every hour about the atmosphere and its phenomena, the resulting tables of numbers would be hopelessly inadequate to communicate even a fraction of their meaning. Thus, a series of charts is prepared to help the users of weather information to assimilate these data and make judgments about their meaning. The charts of greatest interest to aviators are the *surface analysis, weather depiction, prognostic,* and *radar summary* charts.

Surface Analysis Charts

The **surface analysis chart** is what most people visualize when you say "weather map." This chart depicts weather at the earth's surface, including

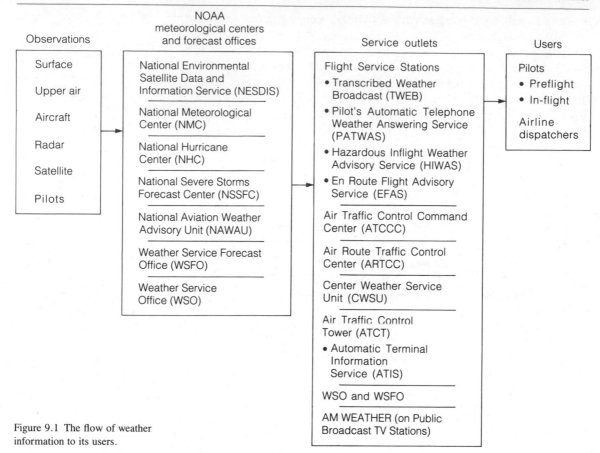

Observations

| Surface |
| Upper air |
| Aircraft |
| Radar |
| Satellite |
| Pilots |

NOAA
meteorological centers
and forecast offices

National Environmental
Satellite Data and
Information Service (NESDIS)

National Meteorological
Center (NMC)

National Hurricane
Center (NHC)

National Severe Storms
Forecast Center (NSSFC)

National Aviation Weather
Advisory Unit (NAWAU)

Weather Service Forecast
Office (WSFO)

Weather Service
Office (WSO)

Service outlets

Flight Service Stations
• Transcribed Weather
  Broadcast (TWEB)
• Pilot's Automatic Telephone
  Weather Answering Service
  (PATWAS)
• Hazardous Inflight Weather
  Advisory Service (HIWAS)
• En Route Flight Advisory
  Service (EFAS)

Air Traffic Control Command
Center (ATCCC)

Air Route Traffic Control
Center (ARTCC)

Center Weather Service
Unit (CWSU)

Air Traffic Control
Tower (ATCT)
• Automatic Terminal
  Information
  Service (ATIS)

WSO and WSFO

AM WEATHER (on Public
Broadcast TV Stations)

Users

Pilots
• Preflight
• In-flight

Airline
dispatchers

Figure 9.1 The flow of weather
information to its users.

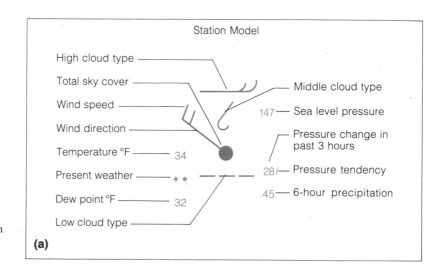

Station Model

High cloud type

Total sky cover

Wind speed

Wind direction

Temperature °F ——— 34

Present weather ——— * *

Dew point °F ——— 32

Low cloud type

Middle cloud type

147 — Sea level pressure

Pressure change in
past 3 hours

28/— Pressure tendency

.45 — 6-hour precipitation

(a)

Figure 9.2 **(a)** An annotated station
model. **(b)** *(opposite)* A typical
surface analysis chart.

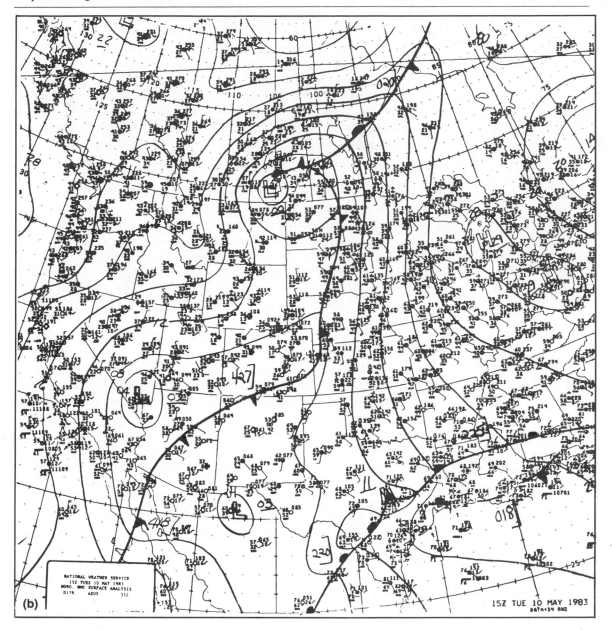

(b)

15Z TUE 10 MAY 1983
DATA=34 RM2

pressure patterns, fronts, surface winds, temperatures and dew points, restrictions to visibility, and more. Figure 9.2 shows a sample surface analysis chart and an annotated **station model**. The station model presents a large amount of data in an abbreviated format.

In the model shown, the sky is completely overcast, as revealed by the symbol at the center of the station model. Figure 9.3 presents a key for interpreting other possible sky cover codes, weather and cloud symbols, and the numerical values associated with visibility, cloud ceiling, precipitation, and barometric pressure. Types of clouds over the station are presented by special symbols and are placed in the same order as the clouds themselves: the lowest symbol for low-altitude clouds, the middle for medium-altitude clouds, and the uppermost for high-altitude clouds. Wind speed is determined by reference to the *wind arrow* attached to the model circle. Each full feather of the arrow represents 10 knots of wind, and each half-feather, 5 knots of wind. The arrow is always aligned with the wind direction, with the *tail* of the arrow showing the direction from which the wind is coming. If you see a pennant attached to the arrows instead of feathers, you know there are very high winds in the area; the pennant is worth five feathers—or 50 knots! A large number of weather symbols are used on the station model diagram. Fortunately, it is not necessary for you to memorize them. Data keys are presented in all facilities where these maps are displayed, and experienced personnel usually are available to help you.

The isobars on the surface analysis chart (Figure 9.2b) are labeled with the last two digits of their millibar pressure value and spaced at 4-millibar intervals. High- and low-pressure regions are labeled at their centers with an H or L, respectively. Fronts are shown using the familiar standard symbols shown in Figure 9.4.

A new surface analysis chart is issued every 3 hours. The valid time printed on the chart corresponds to the time of the plotted observations. The surface analysis chart represents a "snapshot" of the weather at the time of the observations. The data on a newly issued chart, however, may be an hour old, because of the time it takes to gather and process the observations.

Weather Depiction Charts

As useful as the surface analysis chart is, it is perhaps too detailed for the quick look you might want as a VFR pilot to determine the feasibility of a contemplated flight. Your primary concern is whether clouds and visibility meet VFR criteria. The **weather depiction chart** is designed to give such an overview of the weather. The weather depiction chart shades all regions where IFR was in effect—that is, visibility below 3 miles and/or ceiling less than 1000 feet. All regions of **marginal VFR (MVFR)**—that is, visibility 3 to 5 miles and/or a ceiling of 1000 to 3000 feet—are enclosed by a solid line. An abbreviated station model is provided that gives the visibility, obstruction to vision, and sky condition information for each reporting location (see Figure 9.5). This chart acts as your "eye in the sky" and provides much information of practical value to every flight.

Figure 9.6 shows a portion of a weather depiction chart. Suppose you are planning a flight from Tulsa, Oklahoma, to Minneapolis-St. Paul via Pierre, South Dakota. At a glance you can see that while Tulsa is VFR, both Pierre and Minneapolis are IFR. At Tulsa the sky is seven- to eight-tenths covered, the ceiling is 25,000 feet, and the visibility is greater than 6 statute miles. Pierre has a sky that is totally obscured, a ceiling that is 200 feet, and visibility of 1 statute mile due to light fog. Minneapolis is

Figure 9.3 *(opposite)* Key to the symbols and codes used on surface analysis charts.

Abbreviations of Cloud Types

Ac — Altocumulus
As — Altostratus
Cb — Cumulonimbus
Cc — Cirrocumulus
Ci — Cirrus
Cs — Cirrostratus
Cu — Cumulus
Fc — Fractocumulus
Fs — Fractostratus
Ns — Nimbostratus
Sc — Stratocumulus
St — Fs Stratus

Weather Symbols

*	Snow	▽	Showers
•	Rain	↻	Thunderstorm
↔	Ice needles	≡	Fog
˙,	Drizzle	⌇	Lightning
△	Sleet	V	Squalls
S	Dust	⑧	Dust devil
∞	Haze	][	Funnel cloud

Area Symbols

▽	Shower area
↻	Thunderstorm area

Color shading of
precipitation areas:

Solid Green = Continuous
Green Hatching = Intermittent
Solid Yellow = Fog
Solid Brown = Dust

Low Clouds (C$_L$)

Symbol	Description
⌒	Fair weather Cu
△	Towering Cu
⌂	CB with indistinct tops, but not cirriform or anvil-shaped
⌐⌐	Sc formed by spreading Cu
⌣	Sc not formed by spreading Cu
—	St or Fs or both, but no scud
– – –	FS and/or Fc (scud)
⌣⌣	Cu and Sc with bases at different levels
⋈	Cb having a cirriform, anvil-shaped top

Medium Clouds (C$_M$)

Symbol	Description
∠	Thin As layer
⫽	Thick As layer
⌣	Thin Ac
⌣	Thin, patchy Ac
∠	Thin Ac in bands
⋈	Ac formed by spreading Cu
⬱	Double-layered or a thick layer of Ac
⋔	Tufted Ac
⌇	Ac at different levels; patches of dense Ci

High Clouds (C$_H$)

Symbol	Description
⌐	Scattered Ci (mare's tails)
⌐	Dense or patchy Ci
⌐	Dense or anvil-shaped Ci
⌐	Hook-shaped Ci
∠	Bands of Ci and Cs, or Cs alone, below 45,000 feet altitude
∠	Bands of Ci and Cs, or Cs alone, above 45,000 feet altitude
⊃⊂	Cs covering the entire sky
⌐	Thinning Cs
∿	Cc only, or with some Ci or Cs

Code R$_t$	Time Precipitation Began or Ended
0	No precipitation
1	Less than 1 hour ago
2	1 to 2 hours ago
3	2 to 3 hours ago
4	3 to 4 hours ago
5	4 to 5 hours ago
6	5 to 6 hours ago
7	6 to 12 hours ago
8	More than 12 hours ago
9	Unknown

Code h	Altitude (Feet)
0	0 – 149
1	150 – 299
2	300 – 599
3	600 – 999
4	1,000 – 1,999
5	2,000 – 3,499
6	3,500 – 4,999
7	5,000 – 6,499
8	6,500 – 7,999
9	At or above 8,000 or no clouds

Symbol N	Sky Coverage
○	No clouds
◐	One-tenth or less
◕	Two-tenths or three-tenths
◕	Four-tenths
◑	Five-tenths
◒	Six-tenths
◕	Seven-tenths or eight-tenths
◕	Nine-tenths or overcast with openings
●	Completely overcast
⊗	Sky obscured

Figure 9.4 Key to air mass and pressure symbols found on surface analysis charts.

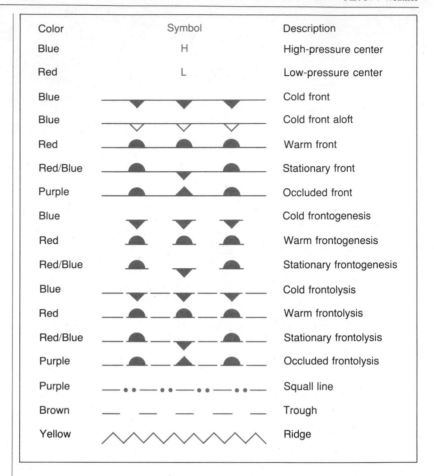

Color	Symbol	Description
Blue	H	High-pressure center
Red	L	Low-pressure center
Blue		Cold front
Blue		Cold front aloft
Red		Warm front
Red/Blue		Stationary front
Purple		Occluded front
Blue		Cold frontogenesis
Red		Warm frontogenesis
Red/Blue		Stationary frontogenesis
Blue		Cold frontolysis
Red		Warm frontolysis
Red/Blue		Stationary frontolysis
Purple		Occluded frontolysis
Purple		Squall line
Brown		Trough
Yellow		Ridge

completely overcast, with a ceiling of 1100 feet, and a visibility of 2½ statute miles due to drizzle.

Would a prudent, noninstrument-rated pilot proceed with the flight under these conditions? Probably not. We say *probably,* rather than definitely, because, as yet, we have seen no forecast data for these regions. Remember that weather is not a geographic fixture; it changes—sometimes for the better and sometimes for the worse. But prudent pilots do not begin any flight based on the mere *hope* of good weather. Even if terminal conditions at Pierre or Minneapolis were forecast to improve, the weather en route seems unsatisfactory for the VFR pilot.

Low-Level Prognosis Charts

Just how the weather conditions described on the surface analysis chart are expected to change, in the best estimation of the forecaster, is displayed on **significant weather prognosis charts**. A *prognosis,* or **prog** for short, is any studied estimate of the outcome of a certain situation—in other words, a forecast. Two charts are prepared for domestic flight planning, one for

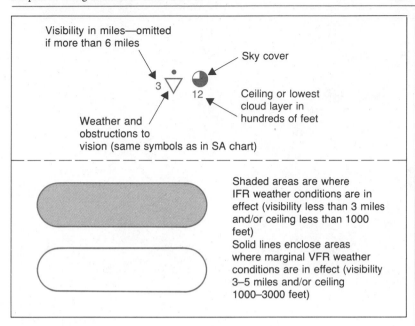

Visibility in miles—omitted
if more than 6 miles

Sky cover

Ceiling or lowest
cloud layer in
hundreds of feet

Weather and
obstructions to
vision (same symbols as in SA chart)

Shaded areas are where
IFR weather conditions are in
effect (visibility less than 3 miles
and/or ceiling less than 1000
feet)
Solid lines enclose areas
where marginal VFR weather
conditions are in effect (visibility
3–5 miles and/or ceiling
1000–3000 feet)

Figure 9.5 An abbreviated station model and area weather symbols found on weather depiction charts.

low-level flights (surface to 24,000 feet) and another for flights from 24,000 to 63,000 feet (high-level prog). This discussion is limited to the low-level charts. (The high-level charts will be covered when you progress to a more advanced course.)

Weather forecasting is an inexact science, to say the least, and the information on a prog chart can sometimes be wrong. Nonetheless, much can be learned from prog charts, especially when they are compared with other reported information. Valid data are selected using your own weather knowledge and judgment.

Figure 9.7 shows a typical prog chart. It is divided into two pairs of charts: the left-hand pair (the *12-hour prog*) shows different aspects of the overall weather estimated for a 12-hour period into the future; the right-hand pair (the *24-hour prog*) shows the same tendencies after an additional 12-hour period, or a total of 24 hours into the future. Both chart pairs may be used for domestic flight planning to 24,000 feet.

On the upper charts, solid lines enclose areas where IFR conditions are expected. Scalloped lines surround areas predicted to have marginal VFR conditions. Additionally, *broken line* areas show regions of greater turbulence, and *dotted line* areas depict surface freezing level. A *dashed line* represents the freezing level aloft, in altitude above MSL.

On the lower charts, the movement of high- and low-pressure centers is indicated by a small arrow and a number to specify the speed of movement in knots. Isobars (thin, solid lines marked with the last two digits of millibar pressures) may appear on some 24-hour progs. Unbroken lines enclose areas of expected persistent precipitation. Showery precipitation is shown by a *dot-dash line*. The type of precipitation is shown with standard symbols

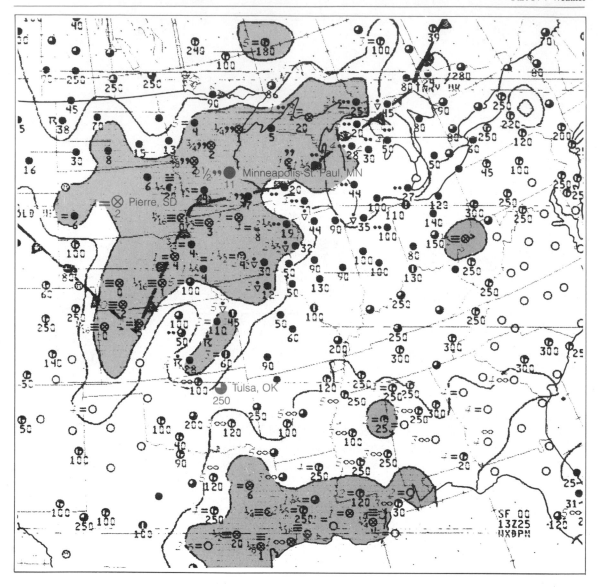

Figure 9.6 A portion of a typical weather depiction chart.

Figure 9.7 *(opposite)* Typical significant weather low-level and surface prognostic charts.

inside the area. If the precipitation is widespread enough—that is, if it covers more than half of the bounded area—the region of precipitation will be shaded.

A little time spent with the list of symbols while you read the chart will be very helpful for flight planning. For example, the lower panels in Figure 9.7 show a forecast for continuous snow in an area over the northern Rocky Mountain states. The shading indicates this precipitation should affect more than half the area within the boundaries of the line. On the central Gulf Coast, the same progs forecast showers and thunderstorms, but the lack of

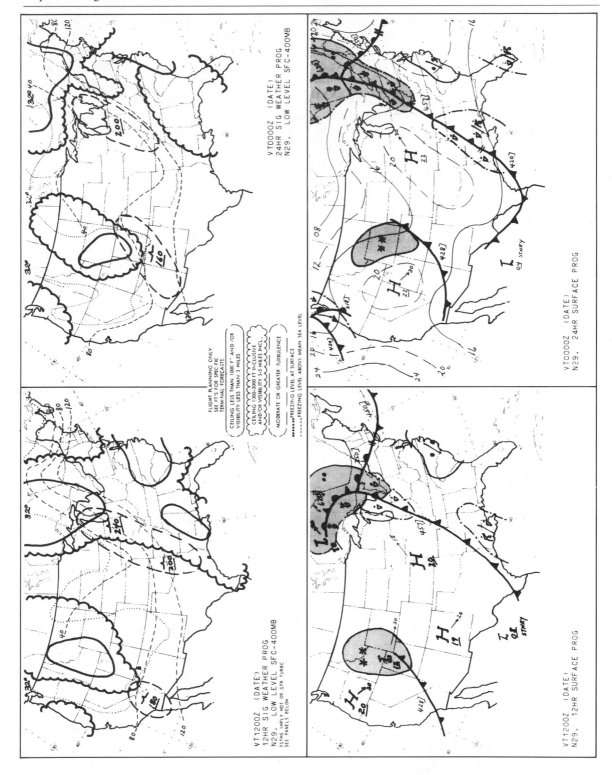

Figure 9.8 *(opposite)* **(a)** Typical radar summary chart. **(b)** Key to echo intensity on a radar summary chart. Numbers representing the intensity level do not appear on the chart. Beginning from the first contour line, the intensity level is 1–2; from the second contour line, the level is 3–4; and from the third contour line, 5–6. **(c)** Key to symbols and abbreviations used on a radar summary chart.

shading indicates this activity is expected to occur over less than half the bounded area.

Comparing the upper panels to the lower, we can make certain correlations. For example, thunderstorms depicted on the lower chart would easily generate enough turbulence to be shown on the upper chart in roughly the same area. But even if such regions are not intentionally circled, you should expect turbulence in any area displaying the thunderstorm symbol. The number between the lower (flat) and upper (spiked) lines on the prog chart represents the maximum altitude, in hundreds of feet, for the forecast turbulence; in the Gulf Coast example this would be from the surface to 20,000 feet. In this way you can visualize much important information about your route of flight: turbulence, icing, cloud cover—both terminal and en route—precipitation, and frontal disturbances.

Radar Summary Charts

Areas of precipitation appear on ground-based and airborne weather radars. When all of the weather service radar returns are collected, they are published on the **radar summary chart** and annotated with supplemental remarks of interest to pilots, such as direction and speed of echo (radar return) movements and precipitation trends and intensities.

An important thing to remember about the radar summary chart is that it shows *only* precipitation. That is, cloud cover may be, and probably is, more widespread than the areas depicted as radar echoes. Thus, the chart is primarily useful in pointing to areas of likely dangerous weather in and around the cloud regions shown on other weather charts. Figure 9.8 shows a typical radar summary chart and its associated symbology.

WEATHER REPORTS AND FORECASTS

Much weather information is passed along in coded text reports rather than in pictorial charts. Text data are easier and faster to assimilate and distribute than pictorial data and therefore can provide more up-to-date information. Furthermore, a textual description can be more specific and detailed than a pictorial form of the same information. A survey of aviation weather reports that are significant to light-aircraft pilots follows.

The Surface Aviation Weather Report

The **surface aviation weather report** is the backbone of flight planning. It contains a variety of specific aviation-related weather details that are provided in an abbreviated standard sequence, and the report is submitted by FAA/NWS reporting stations every hour, 24 hours a day. This format gives the report its common name: the *hourly sequence report,* or simply **sequence report.** It will contain some or all of the following information in this order:

1. Reporting station designator
2. Type of report
3. Time of report
4. Sky condition and ceiling

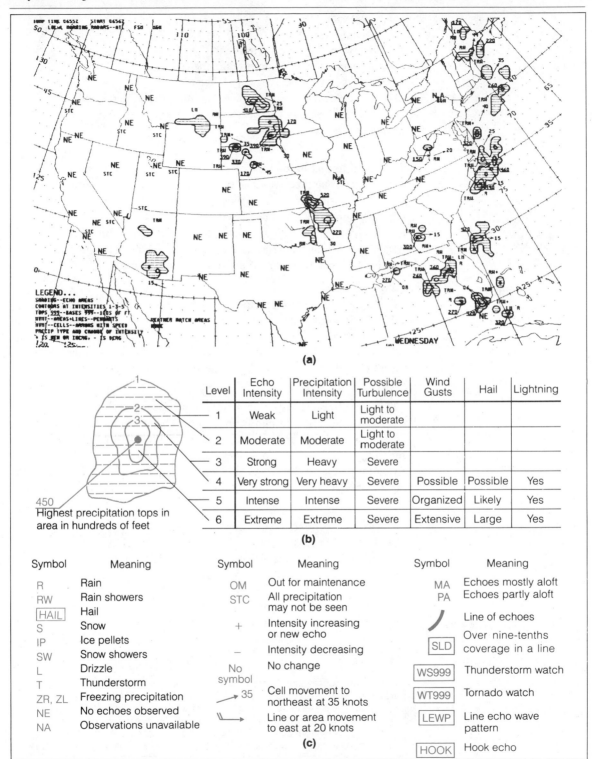

(a)

Level	Echo Intensity	Precipitation Intensity	Possible Turbulence	Wind Gusts	Hail	Lightning
1	Weak	Light	Light to moderate			
2	Moderate	Moderate	Light to moderate			
3	Strong	Heavy	Severe			
4	Very strong	Very heavy	Severe	Possible	Possible	Yes
5	Intense	Intense	Severe	Organized	Likely	Yes
6	Extreme	Extreme	Severe	Extensive	Large	Yes

450
Highest precipitation tops in area in hundreds of feet

(b)

Symbol	Meaning	Symbol	Meaning	Symbol	Meaning
R	Rain	OM	Out for maintenance	MA	Echoes mostly aloft
RW	Rain showers	STC	All precipitation may not be seen	PA	Echoes partly aloft
HAIL	Hail				Line of echoes
S	Snow	+	Intensity increasing or new echo		
IP	Ice pellets			SLD	Over nine-tenths coverage in a line
SW	Snow showers	−	Intensity decreasing		
L	Drizzle	No symbol	No change	WS999	Thunderstorm watch
T	Thunderstorm			WT999	Tornado watch
ZR, ZL	Freezing precipitation	35	Cell movement to northeast at 35 knots	LEWP	Line echo wave pattern
NE	No echoes observed		Line or area movement to east at 20 knots	HOOK	Hook echo
NA	Observations unavailable				

(c)

5. Visibility
6. Weather and obstructions to visibility
7. Sea level pressure (in millibars)
8. Temperature (in degrees Fahrenheit)
9. Dew point (in degrees Fahrenheit)
10. Wind direction and speed, including gusts, if applicable
11. Altimeter setting (in inches of mercury)
12. Remarks and coded data

The coded format used in these reports was developed to enable transmission of data using the fewest number of characters because teletype machines are relatively slow printing devices. (Newer computer-based equipment can probably support a more descriptive format, but the coded format is still used.) Figure 9.9 shows a typical sequence report and a "plain English" translation. Using the numbers shown in the figure, let us take a step-by-step look at how each part of the report is constructed.

1. Reporting station identifier. The report always begins by identifying the reporting station with a three-letter code, usually suggestive of the station's name. In the example, the reporting station is the Sacramento Metropolitan Field, located in Sacramento, California. A complete list of identifier codes is displayed in each FSS or NWS office.

2. Type of report. Normal hourly sequence reports are coded SA. Special reports dealing with significant weather changes at the station occurring since the last report are coded SP. These are the bulletins of the sequence reporting system. You should pay close attention to them if you will be flying into the area they cover. RS reports also indicate a change since the last report but one that is not significant enough for a special report.

3. Time of report. The time of the observation is always given in Coordinated Universal Time (UTC or zulu time). Remember, you must adjust UTC for time zone differences and possibly for daylight savings time differences too, depending on your area and time of year.

Figure 9.9 Typical surface aviation (hourly sequence) weather report and its interpretation.

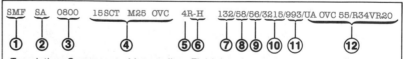

Translation: Sacramento Metropolitan Field: hourly sequence report; observation taken at 0800 UTC; 1500 feet scattered clouds; measured ceiling, 2500 feet overcast; visibility 4 statute miles because of light rain and haze; sea level pressure is 1013.2 millibars; temperature 58 degrees Fahrenheit; dew point 56 degrees Fahrenheit; wind from 320° at 15 knots; altimeter setting 29.93 inches of mercury; pilot reports top of overcast at 5500 feet MSL; runway 34 visual range 2000 feet.

CLR ———— Clear; less than one-tenth sky coverage

SCT ———— Scattered; one-tenth to one-half sky coverage

BKN ———— Broken; six-tenths to nine-tenths sky coverage

OVC ———— Overcast; more than nine-tenths sky coverage

X ———— Obscuration; sky hidden completely by some form of precipitation or obstruction to vision

−X ———— Partial obscuration; nine-tenths or less of sky hidden by precipitation or other obstructions to vision

− ———— Thin, when a prefix to the preceding contractions

Figure 9.10 Abbreviations used to indicate sky cover.

4. Sky condition and ceiling. Figure 9.10 shows the sky cover contractions used in sequence reports. Cloud base and obscuration information is presented in ascending order above the surface, as you would encounter those conditions while climbing out of the airport. The altitudes for the clouds are defined above ground level (AGL) and the last two zeros are omitted.

Recall from Chapter 8 that a *ceiling* is the lowest layer of clouds that is reported to be broken (BKN) or overcast (OVC). An obscuration (X) also constitutes a ceiling. If the sky cover descriptor is preceded by a minus sign (−X, −OVC, −BKN), this means a partial obscuration or thin clouds, and these do not constitute a ceiling.

To help you assess the reliability of ceiling information, its method of determination is also represented by a code letter that precedes the value:

M—measured. This means the ceiling was determined by a **ceilometer,** an electronic device that measures cloud bases.

E—estimated. This means the ceiling was estimated by a knowledgeable observer, such as a meteorologist tracking a balloon or a pilot flying at the base of the clouds.

W—indefinite. This is less a ceiling than a reference to vertical visibility from inside an obscuration. It is always estimated and usually less relevant to pilots than the slant range visibility, which is the over-the-nose visibility necessary to navigate the airplane by ground references or to land. Slant range visibility is usually less than the vertical visibility reported with a W symbol—so caution is in order.

If a ceiling is variable, the letter *V* will follow the ceiling height. For example, an hourly report from Redding, California, reporting an estimated 2000-foot overcast with varying ceilings in the general area, would read RDD E20 VOVC.

In our example, the Sacramento field reads scattered clouds at 1500 feet, but this does not constitute a ceiling. A ceiling was measured to be 2500 feet overcast. If the overcast clouds were reported to be thin, the report would read: 15 SCT 25 −OVC. (Note that since no ceiling exists, there is no ceiling determination code letter.)

5. Visibility.   Visibility is always given in statute miles and, where applicable, fractions of statute miles. The example shows Sacramento's visibility as 4 miles. The letter *V* appearing after this value would mean that the visibility at the station was variable.

6. Weather and obstructions to vision.   Figure 9.11 lists the kinds of weather and obstructions to vision that may be reported. In our example, Sacramento is experiencing light rain and haze.

7. Sea level pressure.   This is the station pressure, given in millibars, adjusted to equivalent sea level pressure. The initial 9 or 10 that you would expect to see has been deleted and must be added by the reviewer. The decimal point has also been deleted. If the first number in the pressure is 6 or greater, you would put a 9 before the number. For example, 985 means 998.5 millibars. An initial number less than 6 means putting the 10 in front: 351 translates to 1035.1 millibars. In our Sacramento example, the pressure is 132 or 1013.2 millibars.

8. Temperature.   The station temperature is given in degrees Fahrenheit. In our example, the temperature is 58 degrees Fahrenheit.

9. Dew point.   The dew point is given immediately after the temperature, separated by a slash. Remember, if the spread between these two numbers is in the range of 2 to 5 degrees, fog, low clouds, or some form of precipitation might be anticipated. In our example, it is not surprising to see rain and haze in conjunction with a 2-degree spread between temperature and dew point.

10. Wind.   The numbers after the dew point indicate the wind direction (rounded to the nearest 10°) and speed, given in knots. Sacramento's wind is from 320° true at 15 knots. (Meteorological winds are always given with respect to true north.) The letter *G* indicates that the winds are gusty (more

Figure 9.11 Abbreviations used to indicate present weather conditions.

A	Hail	IC	Ice crystals	S	Snow
BD	Blowing dust	IF	Ice fog	SG	Snow grains
BN	Blowing sand	IP	Ice pellets	SP	Snow pellets
BS	Blowing snow	IPW	Ice pellet showers	SW	Snow showers
D	Dust	K	Smoke	T	Thunderstorms
F	Fog	L	Drizzle	T+	Severe thunderstorm
GF	Ground fog	R	Rain	ZL	Freezing drizzle
H	Haze	RW	Rain showers	ZR	Freezing rain

Precipitation intensities are indicated by − for *light*; no sign for moderate; and + for heavy. *following the symbol.*

than 10 knots difference between the peaks and lulls in the wind). The value following the *G* is the peak wind speed, in knots. A *squall* is a sudden increase in speed of at least 15 knots that lasts at least one minute. The sustained wind speed must be at least 20 knots to be considered a squall. The letter *Q* indicates a squall, and the value following it is the peak wind speed (in knots, of course). Thus, 3627G35 tells you that the wind is from 360° true at 27 knots, gusting to 35 knots. A 0617Q37 report indicates that the wind is from 060° true at 17 knots with squalls causing winds of up to 37 knots. Four zeros (0000) indicate calm (no wind or wind less than 5 knots) conditions.

11. Altimeter setting.   After the winds reading comes the altimeter setting, which is given in its last three digits only, with the decimal point deleted. The first digit is either a 2 or a 3, whichever brings the decoded number closest to 30.00. In the example, Sacramento's altimeter is 29.93 inches of mercury. Since this is a barometric reading as well as an altimeter setting, it is a useful way of gauging pressure pattern changes from one station to another, as well as being more familiar to pilots than the millibar notation. When temperature and wind data (as well as general weather conditions) are correlated with this pressure value, the presence of frontal activity can often be inferred.

12. Remarks and coded data.   These always follow the altimeter setting, which is the last item of standard information shown. If remarks are given on a sequence report, they should never be overlooked, since they often contain extremely important information, such as PIREPs or other weather-related advisories. In our example, UA OVC 55/R34VR20 is such a case. The UA OVC 55 indicates a PIREP (UA) concerning a 5500-foot (MSL rather than AGL) overcast. The R34VR20 tells you that for runway 34, the visual range is 2000 feet. Other information frequently included with the sequence report remarks are *NOTAMs* (*not*ices *to* *a*ir*me*n), which are concerned with weather-related facilities, equipment, or procedural modifications, such as inoperative airport lighting, modified traffic patterns, unusable navigation or landing aids, and similar information. We will look more closely at these special advisories shortly.

Here are five more sequence reports for you to interpret. The stations reporting are: Wink, Texas (INK), Boise, Idaho (BOI), Los Angeles, California (LAX), Chicago Midway Airport, Illinois (MDW), and John F. Kennedy Airport, New York (JFK). The explanations for each report follow, but be sure you can read them without looking ahead.

INK CLR 15 106/77/63/1112G18/000
BOI 150 SCT 30 181/62/42/1304/015
LAX 7 SCT 250 SCT 6HK 129/60/59/2504/991 →LAX ↘ 6/38
MDW SP − X M7 OVC 1 1/2 R + F 990/63/61/3205/950/RF2 RB12
JFK SP W5 X 1/2F 180/68/64/1804/006/R04RVR22V30 TWR
   VSBY 1/4

INK CLR 15 106/77/63/1112G18/000
Wink, clear, visibility one five, pressure 1010.6 millibars, temperature seven seven, dew point six three, wind one one zero degrees at one two, peak gusts one eight, altimeter three zero zero zero.

BOI 150 SCT 30 181/62/42/1304/015
Boise, one five thousand scattered, visibility three zero, pressure 1018.1 millibars, temperature six two, dew point four two, wind one three zero degrees at four, altimeter three zero one five.

LAX 7 SCT 250 SCT 6HK 129/60/59/2504/991 → LAX ↘ 6/38
Los Angeles, seven hundred scattered two five thousand scattered, visibility six, haze, smoke, pressure 1012.9 millibars, temperature six zero, dew point five niner, wind two five zero degrees at four, altimeter two niner niner one. (Note that nothing past the arrow was read. The arrow indicates that *NOTAM* information follows and is not part of the *weather* report.)

MDW SP − X M7 OVC 1 1/2 R + F 990/63/61/3205/950/RF2 RB12
Chicago Midway, special, sky partially obscured, measured ceiling seven hundred overcast, visibility one and one-half, heavy rain, fog, pressure 999.0 millibars, temperature six three, dew point six one, wind three two zero degrees at five, altimeter two niner five zero, two-tenths sky obscured by rain and fog, rain began twelve minutes past the (previous) hour.

JFK SP W5 X 1/2F 180/68/64/1804/006/R04RVR22V30 TWR VSBY 1/4
New York Kennedy, special, indefinite ceiling five hundred sky obscured, visibility one-half, fog, pressure 1018.0 millibars, temperature six eight, dew point six four, wind one eight zero degrees at four, altimeter three zero zero six, runway four right visual range variable between two thousand two hundred feet and three thousand feet, tower visibility one quarter.

Pilot Reports

There are many weather observations that you, as a pilot, are better qualified to make than even the best ground-based meteorologist. Cloud tops can vary greatly in a given area and can change quickly from a "VFR on top" situation to one in which light airplanes can no longer keep pace with the vertical development of the clouds. While icing may be forecast, its severity seldom can be. Only IFR pilots encountering ice can make an accurate judgment as to the conditions prevailing inside the cloud. The list goes on to include turbulence (always a qualitative judgment); VFR corridors where pilots might make climbs, descents, or horizontal passage through the clouds; temperature inversions; and many other situations. It is your responsibility as a conscientious pilot to share your knowledge of any significant weather occurrences and any navigational factors that might affect the safe operation of other aircraft.

Required elements for all pilot reports (PIREPs) include message type (routine or urgent), location, time, altitude (MSL), type of aircraft, and at least one weather element—sky cover, cloud bases and/or tops, flight visibility, temperature, wind, turbulence, icing—encountered. To make a pilot report, call an FSS on the radio as soon as the unusual or changing situation is detected. If this is inconvenient because you are busy controlling the airplane or monitoring a busy ATC frequency, give your report to the controller to whom you may be talking. ATC personnel always relay weather reports to the appropriate weather authorities and frequently disseminate that information directly themselves. If you cannot remember standard phraseology or technical terms, it is better to go ahead with the report in plain English than deny the benefit of your observation to other pilots. Be aware, therefore, that some of the PIREPs you hear will be verbatim and sometimes amusing—but their content would not be aired if it was not significant to other traffic in the area. Here are a few examples:

1. UKI UA 222315 OVR WILLITS 1515 PST SVR CAT 100-115 C182
The sending station was the Ukiah, California, FSS on the twenty-second day of the month at 2315 Z (UTC). A pilot flying over Willits, California, at 1515 hours Pacific standard time encountered severe clear-air turbulence between the altitudes of 10,000 and 11,500 feet MSL. The type of aircraft was a Cessna 182. It is important to note the type of aircraft, because light airplanes react to turbulence differently from larger aircraft. "Severe" turbulence to a Cessna 182 might be "moderate" to a jetliner.

2. . . . PRETTY ROUGH AT 7500, VERY SMOOTH AT 9500 . . .
This is a verbatim report; while it is informative to a degree, it would have been more helpful if the pilot had used a standard reference term for the turbulence that was experienced, such as *light, moderate,* or *severe.* "Pretty rough" turbulence is subjective, and its interpretation would vary from pilot to pilot.

3. . . . 3 N SHASTA LARGE FLOCK OF GOOSEY-LOOKING BIRDS HDG GNLY NORTH MAY BE SEAGULLS, FORMATION LOUSY, COURSE IS VERY ERRATIC. . .
In this verbatim report, a rather important hazard to aerial navigation is reported in a jocular tone. The ability of the odd-looking birds to fly formation is secondary to the fact that pilots flying north of the Shasta, California, region ought to look out for a sizable flock of large birds, capable of inflicting considerable damage should it collide with an airplane.

4. . . . 50 E RNO LRG ISLTD TSTM DIAM 25 MOVG EWD CONTUS LTNG ALL TYPS TOP OF CB ESTD 400 CIRCUMNAVIGATED TO S . . .
In this very detailed report, a pilot alerted other fliers to a large, isolated, thunderstorm 50 miles east of Reno, Nevada. Continuous lightning of all types (cloud-to-cloud and cloud-to-ground) was observed. The top of the cumulonimbus (Cb) cloud was estimated to be 40,000 feet. The pilot successfully circumnavigated the storm to the south, suggesting to other pilots that a similar route might be advisable for them too.

Runway Visual Range

At airports equipped with instrument landing aids, a report of horizontal visibility at the runway's touchdown zone is made for a 10-minute period preceding observation time. This **runway visual range (RVR),** expressed in hundreds of feet, is a good indicator of slant range visibility. In the example of a sequence report we used (Figure 9.9), Sacramento was reporting an RVR of 2000 feet for runway 34, shown on the report as R34VR20.

Notices to Airmen

Notices to Airmen (NOTAMs) are released for a variety of aviation-related reasons by the FAA. They frequently include such information as closed runways, inoperative navigation or landing aids, runway or ramp construction hazards, bird hazards, unusual airspace use (such as an airshow), and other information that could affect aviation activities. These *NOTAMs* are teleprinted separately, in their own report, but their weather-related items are usually included in the remarks section of the sequence report. Good flying practice requires pilots to check both *NOTAMs* and weather information before a flight to make sure that no information is overlooked. Figure 9.12 shows a sample *NOTAM* identifier and its interpretation.

Figure 9.12 Sample *NOTAM* identifier and its interpretation.

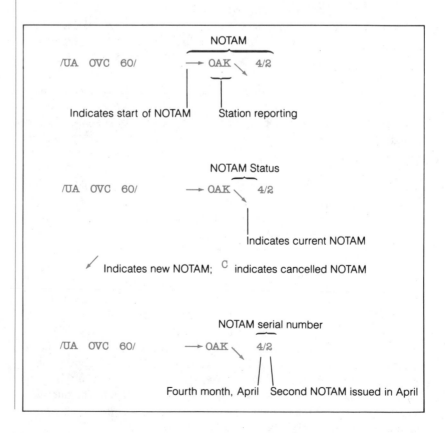

Terminal Forecasts

Three times daily, a 24-hour forecast is prepared for various large airports and teletyped throughout the weather information network. Figure 9.13 shows a typical **terminal forecast (FT)** and its interpretation. The information contained in a terminal forecast includes ceiling, cloud height, sky cover, visibility, weather, surface winds, and a classification of anticipated weather, called a **categorical outlook.** This last forecast deals specifically

Figure 9.13 Sample terminal forecast (FT) and its interpretation.

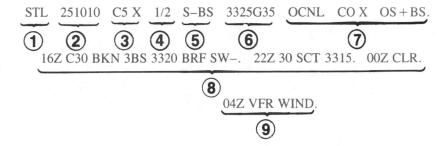

STL 251010 C5 X 1/2S-BS 3325G35 OCNL CO X OS + BS. 16Z C30 BKN 3BS 3320 BRF SW—. 22Z 30 SCT 3315. 00Z CLR 04Z VFR WIND.

STL 251010 C5 X 1/2 S–BS 3325G35 OCNL CO X OS + BS.

① ② ③ ④ ⑤ ⑥ ⑦

16Z C30 BKN 3BS 3320 BRF SW–. 22Z 30 SCT 3315. 00Z CLR.

⑧

04Z VFR WIND.

⑨

1 *Station identifier.* "STL" identifies St. Louis, Missouri. The forecast is for St. Louis.

2 *Date-time group.* "251010" is date and valid times. The forecast is valid beginning on the 25th date of the month at 1000Z valid until 1000Z the following day.

3 *Sky and ceiling.* "C5 X" means ceiling 500 feet, sky obscured. The letter "C" always identifies a *forecast* ceiling layer.

4 *Visibility.* "1/2" means visibility 1/2 mile. Visibility is in statute miles and fractions. Absence of a visibility entry specifically implies visibility more than 6 miles.

5 *Weather and obstructions to vision.* "S–BS" means light snow and blowing snow. These elements are in symbols identical to those used in SA reports and entered only when expected.

6 *Wind.* "3325G35" means wind from 330° at 25 knots gusting to 35 knots—the same as in SAs. Omission of a wind entry specifically implies wind less than 6 knots.

7 *Remarks.* "OCNL CO X 0S + BS" means occasional ceiling zero, sky obscured, visibility zero, heavy snow and blowing snow. Remarks may be added to more completely describe expected weather.

8 *Expected changes.* When changes are expected, preceding conditions are followed by a period and the time and conditions of the expected change. "16Z C30 BKN 3BS 3320 BRF SW–. 22Z 30 SCT 3315.   00Z CLR." means by 1600Z, ceiling 3,000 broken, visibility 3, blowing snow, wind 330° at 20 knots, brief light snow showers. By 2200Z, 3,000 scattered, visibility more than 6 (implied), wind 330° at 15 knots. By 0000Z sky clear, visibility more than 6, wind less than 10 knots (implied).

9 *6-hour categorical outlook.* The last 6 hours of the forecast is a categorical outlook as explained on page 35. "04Z VFR WIND . ." means that from 0400Z until 1000Z—the end of the forecast period—weather will be ceiling more than 3,000 and visibility greater than 5 (VFR); wind will be 25 knots or stronger. The double period (..) signifies the end of the forecast for the specific terminal.

Table 9.1 Categories Used in
Categorical Outlooks

Category	Description
LIFR (low IFR)	Ceiling less than 500 feet and/or visibility less than 1 mile.
IFR	Ceiling 500 feet to less than 1000 feet and/or visibility 1 mile to less than 3 miles.
MVFR (marginal VFR)	Ceiling 1000 to 3000 feet and/or visibility 3 to 5 miles, inclusive.
VFR	Ceiling greater than 3000 feet and visibility greater than 5 miles.
WIND	Winds or gusts over 25 knots are forecast.

with expected IFR or VFR conditions and pertains to the last 6 hours covered by the forecast. Table 9.1 gives the categories used and their descriptions. If winds or gusts of over 25 knots are forecast for this period, the word *wind* is included in the outlook. FT sky cover contractions and format are the same as those used for sequence reports except that a forecast ceiling is always preceded by the letter *C*.

Area Forecasts
Since pilots frequently fly into and out of airports not served by terminal weather forecasts, a forecast covering a large geographical area—sometimes the size of several large states—is prepared. **Area forecasts (FAs)** are issued three times a day and consist of a 12-hour forecast plus a 6-hour outlook. All times are given in UTC hours (with no fractions of hours); winds are given in knots from their true direction; and all distances, except visibilities, are given in nautical miles. Each area forecast consists of five sections:

1. Hazards/Flight Precautions (H)
2. Synopsis (S)
3. Icing (I)
4. Turbulence (T)—includes low-level wind shear if applicable
5. Significant Clouds and Weather (C)

Each section begins with a unique communications header that allows replacement of individual sections due to amendments or corrections. The header starts with the three-letter station identifier and the appropriate section character (H, S, I, T, or C). In the sample area forecast shown in Figure 9.14, note the use of the following headers:

1. DFWH FA 041040
This is the Dallas-Fort Worth (DFW) forecast area header for the Hazards and Flight Precautions (H) section. The "FA" identifies this as an area forecast report. The report was issued on the fourth day of the month at 1040Z. Each of the other sections (DFWS, DFWI, DFWT, and DFWC) was issued at the same time.

Hazards/Flight Precautions (H)	DFWH FA 041040 HAZARDS VALID UNTIL 042300 OK TX AR LA TN MS AL AND OSTL WTRS FLT PRCTNS. . .TURBC. . .TN AL AND CSTL WTRS . . .ICG. . .TN . . .IFR. . .TX TSTMS IMPLY PSBL SVR OR GTR TURBC SVR ICG AND LLWS NON MSL HGTS NOTED BY AGL OR CIG THIS FA ISSUANCE INCORPORATES THE FOLLOWING AIR- METS STILL IN EFFECT . . .NONE.
Synopsis (S)	DFWS FA 041040 SYNOPSIS VALID UNTIL 050500 AT LIZ RDG OF HI PRES ERN TX NWWD TO CNTRL CO WITH HI CNTR OVR ERN TX. BY 05Z HI CNTR MOVS TO CNTRL LA.
Icing (I)	DFWI FA 041040 ICING AND FRZLVL VALID UNTIL 042300 TN FROM SLK TO HAT TO MEM TO ORD TO SLK OCNL MDT RIME ICGIC ABV FRZLVL TO 100. CONDS ENDING BY 17Z. FRZLVL 80 CHA SGF LINE SLPG TO 120 S OF A IAH MAF LINE.
Turbulence (T)	DFWT FA 041040 TURBC VALID UNTIL 042300 TN AL AND CSTL WTRS FROM SLK TO FLO TO 90S MOB TO MEI TO BUF TO SLK OCNL MDT TURBC 250-380 DUE TO JTSTR. CONDS MOVG SLOLY EWD AND CONTG BYD 23Z.
Significant Clouds and Weather (C)	DFWC FA 041040 SGFNT CLOUD AND WX VALID UNTIL 042300 . . .OTLK 042300-050500 IFR. . .TX FROM SAT TO PSX TO BRO TO MOV TO SAT VSBY BLO 3F TIL 15Z. OK AR TX LA MS AL AND CSTL WTRS 80 SCT TO CLR EXCP VSBY BLO 3F TIL 15Z OVR PTNS S CNTRL TX. OTLK. . .VFR. TN CIGS 30-50 BKN 100 VSBYS OCNLY 3-5F BCMG AGL 40-50 SCT TO CLR BY 19Z. OTLK. . .VFR.

2. HAZARDS VALID UNTIL 042300

The hazards listed may be valid for the 12-hour forecast time period (11Z to 23Z). If a hazard has a specific time period, it will be stated in the appropriate subsequent section.

Figure 9.14 Sample area forecast.

3. OK TX AR LA TN MS AL AND CSTL WTRS

This identifies the states and geographical area that define the subject (DFW) forecast area. It is *not* an outline of the hazard area.

4. FLT PRCTNS . . . TURBC . . . TN AL AND CSTL WTRS . . . ICG . . . TN . . . IFR . . . TX

Turbulence (TURBC), icing (ICG), and IFR conditions are forecast for the listed states within the designated FA boundary. The actual forecasts are given in subsequent sections. If no hazards are expected, the report will read: "NONE EXPECTED."

5. TSTMS IMPLY PSBL SVR OR GTR TURBC SVR ICG AND LLWS

"Thunderstorms imply possible severe or greater turbulence, severe icing, and low-level wind shear." This reminder is put in all area forecasts. These thunderstorm-related hazards are not repeated within the body of the area forecast.

6. NON MSL HGTS NOTED BY AGL OR CIG

This statement (contained in all FAs) alerts the user that heights are, for the most part, given *above sea level*. The notation "CIG" denotes a ceiling that is, by definition, above ground. The contraction "AGL" denotes any other type of height reported above ground level. The absence of either CIG or AGL on a height automatically makes it MSL.

7. THIS FA ISSUANCE INCORPORATES THE FOLLOWING AIR-METS STILL IN EFFECT . . . NONE.

This is another statement contained in all FAs to note explicitly any **AIR-METs (WA)**—*air*men's *met*eorological advisories—that are incorporated into the forecast. Once this is done, the AIRMET is cancelled.

The Synopsis section in Figure 9.14 briefly summarizes the location and movement of fronts, pressure systems, and circulation patterns for an 18-hour period. The valid time in the header shows that this section covers an 18-hour period (the 12-hour forecast and the 6-hour outlook).

In this example, at 1100Z a ridge of high pressure is expected over eastern Texas extending northwest and west over central Colorado. By 0500Z the high-pressure center will move southward to central Louisiana.

The Icing section forecasts nonthunderstorm-related icing of light or greater intensity for up to 12 hours. If a trace or less of icing is expected, the remark "NO SGFNT ICING EXPCTD" is used. The location of each reported icing phenomenon is specified in a separate paragraph containing:

1. The affected states or areas within this FA's boundary

2. The radio navigation aid (VOR) points that outline the *entire* area of icing (extending into other FA areas if necessary)

3. The type, intensity, and heights of the icing expected

In Figure 9.14, Tennessee is the only state within the DFW forecast area to experience icing. Pilots should expect occasional moderate rime icing above the freezing level to 10,000 feet (MSL). Icing conditions are expected to end by 1700Z. The freezing level is at 8000 feet (MSL), on a line from

CHA (Chattanooga, TN) to SGF (Springfield, MO), sloping to 12,000 feet (MSL) south of a line from IAH (Humble, TX) to MAF (Midland, TX).

The Turbulence and low-level wind shear section forecasts nonthunderstorm-related turbulence of moderate or greater intensity and low-level wind shear. Unless "NO SGFNT TURBC EXPCTD" is stated, each location of turbulence is specified in a separate paragraph in the same format used to describe icing areas.

The example describes moderate turbulence from 25,000 to 38,000 feet due to the jet stream, with conditions moving slowly eastward. The conditions are expected to continue beyond the current forecast period. (Plotting the area where this turbulence is forecast is left as an exercise for the reader.)

The Significant Clouds and Weather section is a broadly stated 12-hour forecast of clouds and weather plus a 6-hour categorical outlook (as noted in the header). This section is usually several paragraphs in length, with each paragraph describing an area by states or well-known geographical features or by referring to the location and movement of a pressure system or front.

The example (Figure 9.14) forecasts IFR conditions in Texas, in an area bounded by the navaids noted, with visibilities below 3 miles due to fog until 1500Z. The next paragraph defines a multistate area that is expected to vary from 8000 (MSL) scattered clouds to clear conditions, except for visibilities below 3 miles in fog, until 1500Z over portions of south central Texas. The outlook period should be VFR. Tennessee is expected to have 3000 to 5000 (AGL) ceilings, broken clouds at 10,000 (MSL), with visibilities occasionally 3 to 5 miles in fog. By 1900Z conditions are expected to become 4000 to 5000 (AGL) scattered to clear, and the outlook is for VFR conditions.

Amended area forecasts.   Area forecasts are amended by transmitting only the affected segments. An amended FA is identified by "AMD." If a correction was issued, it is noted as a "COR," while delayed forecast is identified with "RTD."

Winds and Temperatures Aloft Forecast
One of the most important aids to planning your flight is the **winds and temperatures aloft forecast (FD).** The temperature aloft affects density-altitude and power plant performance, and winds affect ground speed and the headings required to hold a true navigational course. We will discuss all these factors again in the chapters on navigation and flight planning. Figure 9.15 shows a sample winds and temperatures aloft forecast and its interpretation.

Inflight Advisories
When impending weather conditions are such that it is unwise to wait for the next scheduled hourly report or forecast update, or if information merits separate attention to ensure pilot notice, FAA or NWS authorities issue one

```
①{    FDUS1 KWBC 180545
      DATA BASED ON 180000Z

②⌐   VALID 181200Z FOR USE 0600-1500Z. TEMPS NEG ABV 24000
```

FT	3000	6000	9000	12000	18000	24000	30000	34000	39000
BFF		2412+08	2715+04	2523−04	2536−20	2541−32	244544	246755	246862
CZI		2216+08	2619+02	2725−05	2531−23	2447−35	245047	256352	256762
DEN		2609+08	2717+03	2722−05	2630−19	2632−31	253543	236056	236262
RAP		2115+07	2415+03	2420−05	2431−21	2445−33	244745	244854	245561
RKS		2315+08	2517+03	2727−05	2439−20	2647−34	254346	237252	238160

① FD heading specifying date (eighteenth of month), GMT teletype transmission time (0545 Z), and day and time actual observation was made (the eighteenth day of the month at 0000 Z).

② Winds and temperatures will be as forecast at the "valid" time, however, they may be used during the "use" times indicated. "TEMPS NEG" means that the last two digits of the numbers listed under the columns above 24000 (that is, from 30000 upward) will always be negative.

③ The column heads represent altitude (3000 to 39,000 feet) with wind and temperature entries below for each station listed on the left. The first entry for any station must be at least 1500 feet AGL, hence the stations shown (all in the high terrain of the Rocky Mountain area) have no entry until the 6000-foot level. The first two digits of each entry represent the true (*not* magnetic) direction from which the winds are blowing, with the last digit deleted. The next two numbers represent the wind speed in knots. "9900" is printed when the winds for that level are light (below 5 knots) and variable. Winds of 100 to 199 knots can be read by *subtracting* 50 from the direction and *adding* 100 to the wind speed shown. Temperatures are given in degrees Celsius.

For example, the winds for BFF at 6000 feet are from 240° true at 12 knots. The temperature is 8 degrees Celsius. If BFF winds at 39,000 feet were not from 240° at 68 knots as shown, but from 240° at *168 knots*, the entry would read 7468 (74 − 50 = 24, or 240°. This code tells you to add 100 to any wind value shown). The temperature in this example would be − 62 degrees Celsius in both cases.

Figure 9.15 Typical winds and temperatures aloft forecast and its interpretation.

of several different kinds of **inflight advisories.** Which advisory is issued depends upon the nature of the situation and the category of aircraft affected.

Each advisory is identified by a phonetic letter, and each area issuing these reports numbers them sequentially as well. This results in identifiers like Alpha 1, Bravo 1, and Delta 3. When an area issues a new advisory, the previous one is cancelled. Therefore, when Kansas City issues Charlie 2, Charlie 1 is cancelled. Be aware that different reporting areas can use the same name. Both Kansas City and Fort Worth can issue advisories named Bravo, for example, and the two are not related, unless specifically stated.

SIGMET.   A **SIGMET (WS)** is a *sig*nificant *met*eorological advisory. It can affect all aircraft and refers to severe icing, severe or extreme turbulence, or sudden obstructions to visibility, such as dust or sand storms.

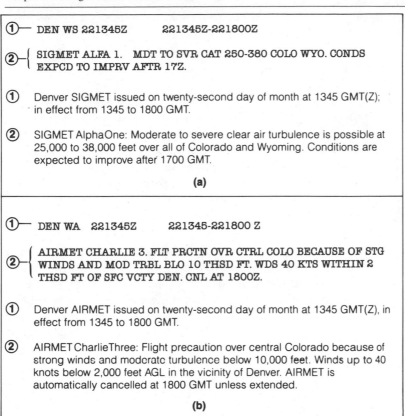

① — DEN WS 221345Z   221345Z-221800Z

② — SIGMET ALFA 1.   MDT TO SVR CAT 250-380 COLO WYO. CONDS
         EXPCD TO IMPRV AFTR 17Z.

①   Denver SIGMET issued on twenty-second day of month at 1345 GMT(Z);
        in effect from 1345 to 1800 GMT.

②   SIGMET AlphaOne: Moderate to severe clear air turbulence is possible at
        25,000 to 38,000 feet over all of Colorado and Wyoming. Conditions are
        expected to improve after 1700 GMT.

(a)

① — DEN WA   221345Z   221345-221800 Z

② — AIRMET CHARLIE 3. FLT PRCTN OVR CTRL COLO BECAUSE OF STG
         WINDS AND MOD TRBL BLO 10 THSD FT. WDS 40 KTS WITHIN 2
         THSD FT OF SFC VCTY DEN. CNL AT 1800Z.

①   Denver AIRMET issued on twenty-second day of month at 1345 GMT(Z), in
        effect from 1345 to 1800 GMT.

②   AIRMET CharlieThree: Flight precaution over central Colorado because of
        strong winds and moderate turbulence below 10,000 feet. Winds up to 40
        knots below 2,000 feet AGL in the vicinity of Denver. AIRMET is
        automatically cancelled at 1800 GMT unless extended.

(b)

Figure 9.16 Inflight advisories and their interpretations. **(a)** SIGMET. **(b)** AIRMET.

Convective SIGMETs (WST) pertain to thunderstorms and related severe weather, such as tornados, squall lines, embedded thunderstorms, unusually widespread thunderstorms, and hail with a diameter greater than ¾ inch. Since all thunderstorms presuppose severe turbulence, icing, and wind shear, do not wait for a convective SIGMET before avoiding them (see Figure 9.16a).

AIRMET.   Recall that an AIRMET (WA) is an airmen's meteorological advisory, applying primarily to light airplanes and pilots flying VFR. Conditions covered by AIRMETs can include moderate icing and turbulence, winds from the surface to 1000 feet AGL greater than 30 knots, widespread areas of visibility that are below VFR minimums, or extensive obscurations around high terrain. Figure 9.16b shows a sample AIRMET message and its interpretation.

Hurricane advisory.   A hurricane merits everyone's immediate attention. A hurricane is a massive cyclonic tropical storm whose winds exceed 70 knots. Although a wide variety of frontal and thunderstorm-type weather accompanies hurricanes, the primary concern of the **hurricane advisory**

(WH) is to dispatch immediate information on the storm's location, direction of movement, and maximum winds. Details such as station ceilings, visibilities, and other important but secondary effects are not included in the advisory.

Convective outlook.   This advisory estimates the potential for severe and general thunderstorms over a 24-hour period. The main value of the **convective outlook (AC)** is for planning flights that will pass through the threatened areas during the forecast period. As the storms materialize, severe weather watches and finally severe weather warnings may be issued. A severe thunderstorm is one with damaging surface winds with gusts in excess of 50 knots and hail with a diameter of ¾ inch or more and/or tornado activity.

Severe weather watch bulletin.   The National Severe Storms Forecast Center (NSSFC) in Kansas City, Missouri, issues a **severe weather watch bulletin (WW)** when severe thunderstorm conditions exist in a given area. A *tornado watch* implies that the severe storm area also contains ingredients favorable to tornado formation. A severe storm warning or tornado warning is issued when those phenomena have been confirmed to exist in the forecast area. Bulletins are canceled when the severe weather moves out of a given area or if the storms evolve into a less severe condition.

Special flight forecast.   When a given flight has an unusual route or is undertaken for unusual (and potentially hazardous) purposes—such as rescue missions in adverse weather or terrain, high-altitude photographic missions, flight record attempts, test flights, or special events such as air races or air tours—a *special forecast* may be requested through any FSS or NWS office, to be forwarded via teletype.

THE PREFLIGHT WEATHER BRIEFING

Since the bulk of your weather information for any given flight will come from your detailed interview with a weather specialist prior to your boarding the aircraft, the weather briefing procedure is worthy of elaboration.

FAR 91.5 requires you to familiarize yourself with all available weather reports and forecasts prior to any flight outside your local area. You can usually do this by phoning the nearest Flight Service Station or National Weather Service Office. It is important to be organized for this phone call, because you should write down all pertinent information and must be able to make sense of it later.

Whenever possible, visit the FSS or NWS office personally, so you can see the charts and other data firsthand. You may even be able to get copies of the textual reports. Unfortunately, most pilots seldom find themselves in the neighborhood of an FSS, but take advantage of the opportunity whenever you can. Make it a point to visit an FSS or NWS office at least once during your training.

How to request a briefing.   Since weather specialists often handle a great number of flights each day, efficiency and thoroughness are critical during the briefing. When you contact the facility (an FSS if one is available, or the NWS), you should give the weather briefer the following information, in this sequence:

1. Type of flight (VFR or IFR). If you are a student pilot, mention that at this time.

2. The full call sign of your aircraft, or your name.

3. The make and model of your aircraft.

4. Your departure point (the airport identifier, if known).

5. The planned route of flight.

6. Your destination (airport identifier, if known).

7. The planned cruising altitude.

8. Your estimated time of departure (ETD).

9. Either your estimated time en route (ETE) or the estimated time of arrival (ETA).

Armed with this information beforehand, your briefer can consult the appropriate charts, reports, and notices without wasting time relaying superfluous information or asking for additional details. You will probably jot down the weather briefing you receive on a form resembling that shown in Figure 9.17. Thus, you will want to learn the appropriate symbology and contractions—the meteorologist's shorthand—as quickly as possible.

Types of briefings.   There are three types of briefings that you can request, the **standard briefing** being the most complete. It begins with a "big picture" weather synopsis, with emphasis on any known hazardous weather that may cause you to reconsider attempting the flight. Next is the current weather at reporting points along and/or near your route of flight. Forecast weather for the appropriate time span is covered next, followed by winds aloft information. If applicable, alternate routes may then be suggested. Last, but certainly not least, *NOTAMs* are checked to see if any would possibly affect your flight.

You should request the **abbreviated briefing** when you want to do one of the following:

1. Supplement information obtained from other sources.

2. Update a previous briefing (tell the briefer what time you received the other briefing).

3. Obtain specific weather information.

This report will generally contain only the information you request.

The **outlook briefing** is useful when preparing for a flight 6 or more hours in the future. The briefer will provide only forecast data applicable for the proposed flight.

WEATHER BRIEFING

13Z SAT – 07Z SUN (0700 CST SAT – 0100 CST SUN)

① HI PRES OVR E US EXPCD TO RMN STNRY.
② MVFR SW OHIO, IFR REST OF OHIO.
③ S IND/KY 20-30 OVC V BEN

PILOT'S WEATHER "GO – NO GO" CHECKLIST

✓	AIRMETS	✓	ALTERNATE WX	✓	TOPS
✓	SIGMETS	✓	FORECASTS	✓	FREEZING LEVEL
✓	ENROUTE WX	✓	WINDS ALOFT	✓	TEMP/DEW PT (FOG)
✓	DESTINATION WX	✓	PIREPS	✓	BETTER WX AREA

TERMINAL FORECASTS 09-18 CST

LOCATION	15Z-00Z
SDF	1515 Z 20 SCT 250 SCT 5 H.
	20 Z C30 BEN 5H 1812 BEN V OVC, 01 Z
CVG	1515 Z C20 OVC CHC C2X IF TIL 16Z.
	19Z 25 SCT OCNL C25 BEN, 05 Z
CMH	1515 Z C25 OVC 2F CHC C8 OVC IF TIL 16Z.
	18Z C25 BEN OCNL 25 SCT, 04Z

WINDS ALOFT FORECASTS

LOCATION	30	60
IND	1906	2308-02

PIREPS/SIGNIFICANT WEATHER/NOTAMS

LOCATION	
OHIO & ADJ	AIRMET DELTA 3- CIGS AOB 1000'
GREAT LAKES	& VIS OCNL 3 MI OR LESS
CMH	1532 Z 10 OVC 40 CAVU ABV
30 SW CMH	1847 Z ENCOUNTERED IFR AT 15 TURNED BACK

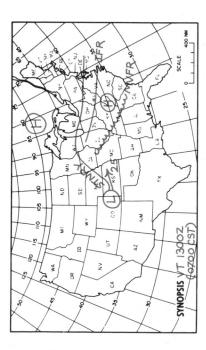

SYNOPSIS VT 1300Z (0700 CST)

ENROUTE WEATHER TREND

LOCATION	15Z (0900 CST)	17Z (1100 CST)	19Z (1300 CST)
EVV	250 SCT 7 43/39 1006 30.25	100 SCT 250 BEN 7 49/41 1610 30.18	
SDF	25 SCT 250-BEN 7 47/37 1205 30.25	25 SCT 250-BEN 7 50/38 1405 30.19	
CVG	M16 OVC 7 40/33 2204 30.26	M17 SCT 8 41/33 2105 30.22	
DAY	SPM 3 OVC 1½ F 40/39 0606 30.25	SPM 7 BEN 14 OVC 2F 39/37 1209 30.22	M9 BEN 20 OVC 2½F 39/36 1209 30.21
CMH	M6 BEN 10 OVC 3F 40/36 1506 30.29	M13 BEN 18 OVC 5 43/37 1306 30.25	M19 OVC 5 1306 30.25
OSU	E8 BEN 12 OVC 2F 1108 30.30	E10 BEN 200V C.5H 1008 30.27 BIN OVC	E 22 OVC 6 1305 30.25
MFD	M1 OVC ½F 35/35 0107 30.27	SPM 3 OVC 2F 34/34 0706 30.25	M3 OVC 1½ F 53/33 1607 30.24

The briefing itself.   In the upper right-hand corner of the form in Figure 9.17, you will note the general conditions of your flight. It is often helpful to sketch the information yourself on the map in the upper left-hand corner, as a quick visualization of the overall weather picture. In this case, a high-pressure area over the eastern United States is expected to remain stationary, with instrument flight rules in effect north of the high-pressure center and marginal VFR conditions south of it. Sky condition is also noted for southern Kentucky and Indiana, and the effective time of the synopsis (summary) weather chart noted in both zulu (Z, or UTC) and central standard time (CST).

The location boxes contain standard three-letter identifiers for reporting stations. The weather associated with each station is then listed for the times (UTC and local) noted above each column. Notice that three different times have been consulted. This allows you to have not only the weather forecast for the time of your anticipated arrival but enough information to diagnose a trend. The *terminal forecasts*, where available, cover the airports where you intend to land, and the *winds aloft forecast* is used to correct your initial assumptions about time en route after you have prepared a more detailed flight plan. In the example, two altitudes, 3000 and 6000 feet, are shown.

The lower right-hand corner contains advisory information—the latest bulletins or weather "news flashes" that might affect your trip. This information fills the gap between regular reports and forecasts until they are updated.

Getting the most from your briefing.   There is an old saying: "Knowledge is power." Ignorance of conditions along your route or at your destination leaves you literally powerless against nature's heat engine and all the forces it can summon in the form of adverse weather. Failure to obtain an adequate weather briefing—or even any weather briefing at all—has led to numerous aviation accidents that could easily have been avoided. At the earlier stages of your flying career, you may feel hesitant to deal with weather specialists because you are unsure of your own ability to understand their technical jargon, or because you have not had enough experience to ask the right questions. While both of these attitudes are understandable, neither of them is an acceptable reason for failing to obtain a comprehensive weather briefing. The weather briefers *assume* you understand what has been reported unless you tell them otherwise. According to common sense and your own best interest, the briefing is not complete until you understand it. If you do not grasp the meaning of the technical terms, request the information in plain English. The briefer wants you to be adequately prepared for the flight.

After you have collected all the data and listened to the briefer's analysis, review the material yourself with a critical eye. Question any information that seems to be out of place or contrary to the general trends you see developing in the rest of the data. An improper station report may have been read, or numbers may have been transposed. These mistakes are rare, but that is no reason to relax your vigilance.

Figure 9.17 *(opposite)* Sample pilot's weather briefing form.

Finally, you should never ask *any* weather specialist if you "should go or not." This decision is the pilot's alone, and no briefer would presume to make it for you, even if asked. If you feel so unsure about the situation that you are willing to let someone else make the decision for you, then you probably ought not to be acting as pilot-in-command of that particular flight. It is far wiser to cancel the trip and wait for better conditions than to flip a coin and rely on chance rather than your best judgment.

GETTING INFLIGHT WEATHER INFORMATION
The telephone or personal visit are not your only means to gather weather data. You also need to be able to update your information during your flight, especially if the weather is not CAVU (ceiling and visibility unlimited) along your route. On longer trips the weather may change significantly as well, and not always as predicted.

Flight Service Stations
Flight Service Stations provide the same services over the radio that you get over the phone. Your aeronautical chart will list the appropriate frequencies for you to use. Remember, an FSS is called "radio" when using the radio, and always mention the frequency on which you are listening.

Transcribed Weather Broadcasts (TWEB)
Meteorological and *NOTAM* information is recorded and broadcast continuously over certain low-frequency and VHF navigation stations. The stations that carry these **Transcribed Weather Broadcasts (TWEBs)** are noted on your aeronautical chart and in other aviation publications (discussed in the next chapter). When you tune the voice channel of these stations, you will hear the following information in this sequence:

1. The station identifier signal
2. General weather forecast for the area
3. PIREPs as applicable
4. Radar reports, when available
5. Winds aloft information
6. Supplemental weather information concerning selected locations within a 400-mile radius of the broadcasting station

As changes occur, the tapes are updated with new information.

En Route Flight Advisory Service (Flight Watch)
Pilots flying in a rapidly changing weather environment often need immediate information about the *current* weather. Even the hourly sequence reports are not timely enough. The **En Route Flight Advisory Service (EFAS),** also called **Flight Watch,** was created to fulfill this need. This service is provided by the FSSs shown in Figure 9.18 between 6 A.M. and 10 P.M., 7 days a week. A special radio frequency, 122.0 MHz, has been

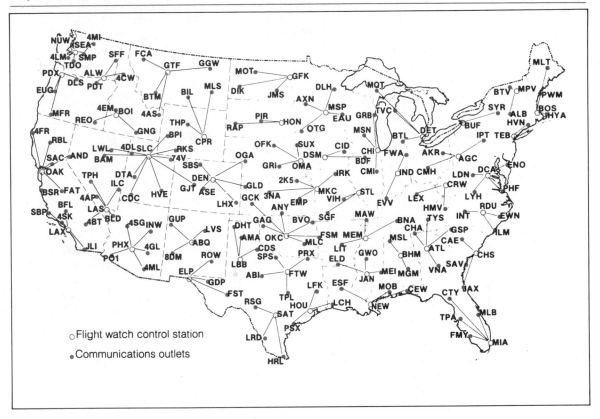

set aside for exclusive Flight Watch use. This frequency should not be used for any other FSS communications. The radio call "flight watch" replaces "radio" when calling an FSS for this service ("Saint Louis Flight Watch" instead of "Saint Louis Radio.")

Flight Watch is essentially a weather unicom. It was developed initially to help pilots during the summer thunderstorm season. The FSS person who responds to your call is a weather specialist who has access to the very latest weather data, including live radar. Pilots on the frequency report their current conditions (and location), which also keeps the data up to the minute. Use Flight Watch whenever you need to update your weather information, or if you observe any weather either better or worse than predicted.

USING WEATHER SERVICES: TWO SIMULATIONS

The purpose of gathering meteorological data in the form of maps or teletype and radio reports is to make it *useful*. That is why we have emphasized throughout this chapter *using* aviation weather services—not just classifying and describing these services. Let us put our knowledge of meteorological phenomena and weather services together now and "fly" two simulated cross-country flights under VFR conditions: the first toward a

Figure 9.18 En Route Flight Advisory Service (Flight Watch) stations. *Author's note:* Because of changes being made to the FSS system, this figure is out of date. Refer to the back cover of an appropriate, current *Airport/Facility Directory* for up-to-date information.

warm front and into a warm air mass, and the second toward a cold front and into a cold air mass. As we go, we will review some of the things we have learned in this and the previous chapter.

Approaching a Warm Front

All fronts have certain characteristics pilots can use to their advantage and others that are extremely hazardous. Helping you identify the positive and negative weather characteristics and use that information to conduct a safe, enjoyable flight is the goal of aviation weather services.

Let us assume you want to fly from El Paso, Texas, to Los Angeles, California, in a single-engine, general-aviation airplane. Because your airplane is neither pressurized nor supercharged, you will have to plan your flight for altitudes no higher than 10,000 to 12,000 feet.

As pilot-in-command, you decide to familiarize yourself with the overall weather conditions by calling a prerecording of weather information. (Chapter 10 tells you where you can find the phone numbers you will need.) You learn that there is a warm front moving eastward across your route of flight, with precipitation reported throughout many areas of southern California and western Arizona. Since you will be several hours en route, and the weather is good through New Mexico and Arizona, you elect to continue flight planning and pay a visit to the local FSS for a more detailed weather briefing. In preparation for that briefing, you work up a preliminary flight plan containing rough estimates for a VFR flight plan, including your estimated time of departure, time en route, and ETA for Los Angeles. You are particularly interested in terminal weather in Tucson, Arizona, and Blythe, California, since these seem like probable alternate airports should you have to divert your flight because of adverse weather.

Figure 9.19 shows the products of that briefing. Part a shows a pictorial cross-section of your route from a weather standpoint; part b shows the portion of the surface analysis chart appropriate to your flight; and part c shows the sequence reports (no remarks) for the major terminals en route, including your point of origin, destination, and designated alternate airports.

Let us summarize this information:

Los Angeles (LAX) has a measured overcast ceiling of 1000 feet, visibility of 1 mile in light rain. Temperature and dew point are the same with winds roughly from the south at 18 knots. The altimeter setting is 29.60 inches of mercury.

Blythe (BLH) has a measured ceiling of broken clouds at 400 feet and an overcast at 5000 feet with 3 miles visibility and rain. The winds are still generally from the south, and the barometric pressure (altimeter setting) is higher.

Tucson (TUS) has noticeably better weather, with an estimated ceiling of 6000 feet (overcast), visibility of 6 miles in haze, a dew point spread which is up to 6 degrees, and no precipitation, and the barometric pressure continues to rise in the direction of the high-pressure area.

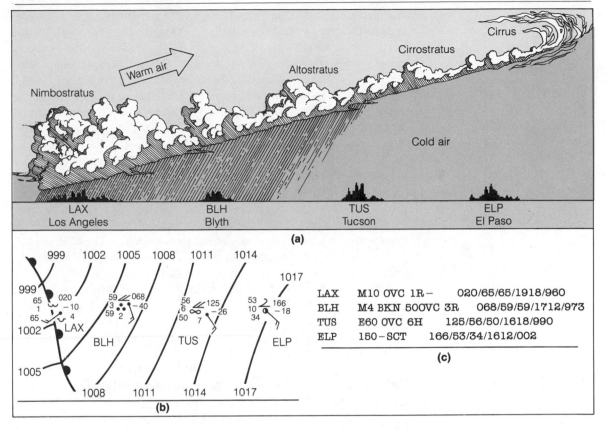

(a)

(b)

LAX	M10 OVC 1R−	020/65/65/1918/960
BLH	M4 BKN 500VC 3R	068/59/59/1712/973
TUS	E60 OVC 6H	125/56/50/1618/990
ELP	150−SCT	166/53/34/1612/002

(c)

El Paso (ELP) shows no ceiling, but a layer of thinly scattered clouds at 15,000 feet. The spread between temperature and dew point is 19 degrees Fahrenheit, indicating that El Paso has considerably drier air than the points farther west. The winds are more easterly than what the stations are reporting from California, and the barometric pressure is much higher as well, giving an altimeter setting of 30.02. Forecast information shows no appreciable changes at these stations over the next few hours.

Figure 9.19 Approaching a warm front. (a) Cross-section of weather conditions. (b) The corresponding portion of a surface analysis chart. (c) Weather conditions as given by a sequence report.

You elect to begin the flight, knowing that you will probably not be able to finish your flight but that a number of suitable alternate airports lie along your route of flight.

As you take off from El Paso, you notice high cirrus clouds and sunshine. It is a beautiful day to fly. Other pilots might have begun such a trip based on this evidence alone, but you recall that one of the first signs of an advancing warm front is an array of high cirriform clouds. Sure enough, as you progress westward, the array of "horsetails" begins to congeal, and you find yourself flying below a deck of cirrostratus clouds by the time you reach Tucson.

As you near the Arizona-California border outbound from Tucson, you contact Phoenix Flight Watch and learn of multilayered lower clouds and precipitation ahead. The clouds overhead have thickened and lowered appreciably, and you find that you have had to reduce your cruising altitude to stay below the clouds in VFR conditions. The bases of the clouds now appear dark and rain laden, and you correctly identify them as nimbostratus. Below the airplane, scattered stratiform clouds begin to appear. Finally, Blythe appears ahead, but with scattered precipitation now all around the airport. Beyond the town, a dark wall of clouds and precipitation makes continued flight westward unwise. You elect to land immediately at Blythe rather than continue your flight farther toward Los Angeles. At this point you face the classic VFR pilot's weather decision—"press on and hope for the best, or wait out the weather?"

You learn from the Blythe FSS that more intermediate and lower stratiform clouds cover the route into the Los Angeles Basin. Due to the relatively warm temperatures, some convective activity has occurred, and the radar summary chart shows isolated but growing echoes in and among the nimbostratus layers. Having seen some of the heavy precipitation from the air, you tend to believe the report without further clarification.

With frontal passage at Blythe and improving conditions noted on the terminal forecast for late tomorrow morning, you elect to invest in the airport's tie-down fee, a steak dinner, and a comfortable motel room. You go to sleep that night listening to the occasional rumble of the embedded Cbs as the worst of the storm passes overhead.

The next day, after a longer than usual takeoff run due to the warm, humid air, you continue beneath a high stratiform overcast into Los Angeles. Although you encounter no more rain along your route, the visibility is poor, and you land at Los Angeles very close to the visibility limits for VFR flight.

Approaching a Cold Front

Figure 9.20 shows a similar flight path, only this time the PATWAS tape informs you that a cold front lies between you and your destination. You elect to go ahead with a formal weather briefing at the El Paso FSS, as you did in our previous simulation. The results of that briefing are shown in parts b and c of Figure 9.20.

Again, we may summarize our available information as follows:

LAX is reporting an estimated ceiling of broken clouds at 5000 feet, another broken layer at 12,000 feet, visibility of 8 miles with light rain showers. The temperature–dew point spread is 13 degrees Fahrenheit, and the winds are from the northwest at 18 knots. The altimeter setting is 29.79 inches of mercury.

BLH is reporting a scattered layer of clouds at 2000 feet and an estimated broken ceiling at 10,000 feet with 7 miles visibility. The temperature–dew point spread has narrowed to 3 degrees Fahrenheit, and the winds have shifted radically to the southwest. The barometer has dropped 0.05 inch of mercury from the LAX reading to 29.74. At least you have located the cold front! It seems to be in the vicinity of Blythe, if not on top of it.

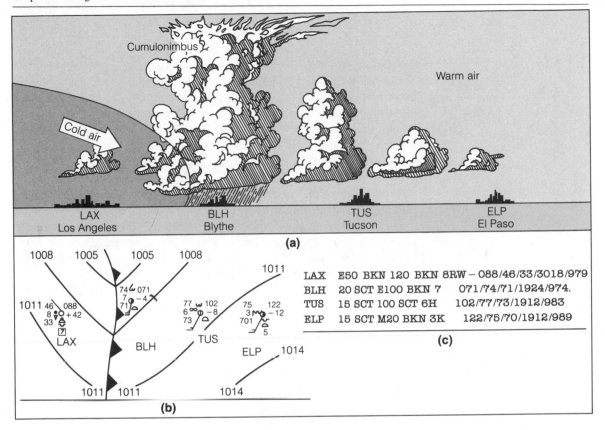

(a)

(b)

LAX	E50 BKN 120 BKN 8RW − 088/46/33/3018/979
BLH	20 SCT E100 BKN 7 071/74/71/1924/974.
TUS	15 SCT 100 SCT 6H 102/77/73/1912/983
ELP	15 SCT M20 BKN 3K 122/75/70/1912/989

(c)

TUS shows no ceiling, but there are scattered clouds at 1500 and 10,000 feet, with visibility limited to 6 miles with haze. The winds are holding from the southwest, and the barometric altimeter setting is up to 29.83.

ELP shows typical warm air mass weather: scattered clouds at 1500 feet and a measured ceiling of broken clouds at 2000 feet with smoke and visibility limited to 3 miles. The dew point spread is slightly greater than Tucson's, though the winds are the same. The altimeter setting is even higher at 29.89.

Looking at the SA, you confirm much of what you were beginning to suspect. The stations east of Blythe show classic warm air mass characteristics: warm surface temperatures, low visibility, trapped low-altitude obscurations. But they also show scattered cumuliform clouds and a sharp contrast from conditions in Los Angeles of cool, crisp, clearing weather.

You begin your flight by departing El Paso in VFR but decidedly poor conditions. As you near Tucson, the smooth air becomes a little bumpier. The stratocumulus layers of clouds now show more signs of vertical development. In the distance, to the west, you see several vaguely defined anvil-shaped clouds on the horizon.

Figure 9.20 Approaching a cold front. (a) Cross-section of weather conditions. (b) The corresponding portion of a surface analysis chart. (c) Weather conditions as given by a sequence report.

As you near the Arizona-California border, you find yourself in light turbulence as you dodge the progressively larger cumulus buildups. These have begun to combine into larger cloud masses, and you find your excursions from your planned course of flight are more extensive in order to avoid them. Since the anvil-head clouds are now plainly visible in a line intersecting your flight path (you count five of them before the line disappears to the north and south), and the western horizon seems dark and obscured all the way to the ground, you call the nearest Flight Watch.

The Flight Watch operator tells you that there is indeed a cold front lying approximately 75 miles to the west of Blythe. Radar shows intense precipitation all along the frontal zone from the Grand Canyon to the Mexican border. A PIREP from a light twin-engine airplane, cruising well above your altitude southbound toward Mexico, reports moderate to severe turbulence and cloud tops in excess of 23,000 feet all the way from the Grand Canyon. An airliner, cruising over the weather, reports the tops of the thunderstorms to be well past 45,000 feet and growing rapidly. You are also informed that a SIGMET has just been put into effect for all of western Arizona, southeastern California, and eastern Nevada until 0600 local time the next morning.

With no second thoughts, you decide to abort your flight to Los Angeles and let nature take its course. But as you descend toward Blythe, the FSS informs you that surface winds have increased to 30 knots with gusts to 45, with Cbs in the vicinity of the airport and locally heavy precipitation and cloud-to-ground lightning.

The front—or at least its squall line—seems to have beaten you to your primary alternate airport. Now you must make a quick decision: should you attempt an obviously risky landing at Blythe in an attempt to shave a few hours off your flying time tomorrow, or should you reverse course to a less threatened location behind you on the route you have already flown?

You attempt to contact the Blythe FSS again, but the frequency is full of traffic from other airplanes in the same situation. Static from the nearby lightning discharges is quite plain and annoying in your radio speaker, and the turbulence on your route of descent into Blythe is continuous, making it difficult for you to hold either a constant airspeed or heading. Without further consideration, you immediately reduce your airspeed to the airplane's maneuvering speed and begin a shallow 180-degree turn, clearing yourself between the buildups as you go. As you roll out on a reciprocal heading, you add power and climb several thousand feet to a new VFR cruising altitude, where the lateral development of the young Cbs has not consumed too much airspace.

When the Flight Watch frequency is clear, you state your intentions of diverting to an alternate airport farther east and request information about the nearest suitable airport. The operator tells you that Phoenix is showing a 15,000-foot ceiling, scattered clouds, with 8 miles visibility and haze. You "roger" this information and make the appropriate heading change to take you toward Phoenix and away from the storm. The FSS asks for a PIREP, and you inform them that the lower-altitude VFR corridors for the last 50 to 75 miles before the California border are closing rapidly due to convective cloud development and that you are cruising VFR on top at 9500 feet with scattered holes in the undercast. The turbulence is occasional now and light.

After cruising for 15 to 20 minutes on your new heading, the towering Cbs are behind you, and the deck of cumuliform clouds begins to break up into patches of scattered cumulus, now several thousand feet above you. You continue on into Phoenix and land without incident.

Near sunset, you glance out of the restaurant window to see a wide blanket of dust envelop the city from the west. The wind becomes stronger and rattles the windows, as the trees bend back and forth in the gusts. The sky is quite dark following the dust, and rain begins almost immediately, with more gusty wind and lightning. Though the temperature is still above 70 degrees, hail falls and collects on the ground for several minutes.

By nine o'clock local time that evening, however, you step outside your motel room and see stars blinking from behind patches of fast-moving cumulus. A quick call to the Phoenix PATWAS informs you that the SIG-MET has been lifted for western Arizona and California and now applies to eastern Arizona and western New Mexico. The weather for Phoenix is forecast to be the proverbial "clear and a million" (no clouds at all and visibility unlimited). You finish your trip into Los Angeles in crystal clear but moderately bumpy air with strong crosswinds (and a small headwind component) aloft.

Let us reflect a moment on the experience of our two simulations. In the first case, you noticed gradual deterioration of flying conditions associated with an approaching warm front. You found that you had more than enough time to check on the status of weather en route and to land at your primary alternate airport, or to reverse course if that had been your decision. Your preflight briefing and en route weather checks enabled you to accurately gauge actual weather conditions.

In our second simulated flight, weather conditions changed a little more quickly. Going from a warm air mass toward a cold front, visibility was poor and it was easier to "suddenly" find yourself in the region of convective activity. You found that this activity occurred with surprising speed and that the adverse weather associated with cold fronts really does occur well in advance of the front itself. You also found that by keeping calm and making your own safety decisions when you needed to make them, you were able to handle a potentially hazardous situation with a minimum of difficulty. Once again, the weather briefers before your departure and en route provided you with accurate weather information and made a good deal of valuable "real-time" information (PIREPs and radar reports) available to you when you needed it. In both instances, you were able to learn about severe and adverse weather from a private pilot's best classroom— *on the ground,* waiting out the storm.

KEY TERMS

abbreviated briefing

AIRMET (WA)

area forecast (FA)

En Route Flight Advisory Service
  (EFAS)

Flight Watch

inflight advisories

marginal VFR (MVFR)

National Weather Service (NWS)

Notices to Airmen (NOTAMs)

outlook briefing

pilot report (PIREP)

radar summary chart

runway visual range (RVR)

SIGMET (WS)

significant weather prognosis chart
  (prog)

standard briefing

station model

surface analysis chart (SA)

surface aviation weather (hourly
  sequence) report

terminal forecast (FT)

weather depiction chart

winds and temperatures aloft
  forecast (FD)

PROFICIENCY CHECK

1. What are the two primary sources of information for a pilot's weather briefings? In what order should they be used?

2. What is a station model? How is it used on a surface analysis chart?

3. What is the chief value to a pilot of a weather depiction chart?

4. What is a low-level prog chart? What kinds of information are found on it?

5. What is the value of a radar summary chart to a pilot?

6. Does a station report of VFR conditions guarantee VFR conditions en route? Explain.

7. What are the three ways of determining a station's ceiling, and how are they coded on the hourly sequence report?

8. What are PIREPs? How are they disseminated to the flying public?

9. In what ways are area forecasts different from terminal forecasts?

10. Why are winds aloft important to flight planning?

11. What is the En Route Flight Advisory Service (Flight Watch) and how is it used?

12. How is a SIGMET different from an AIRMET?

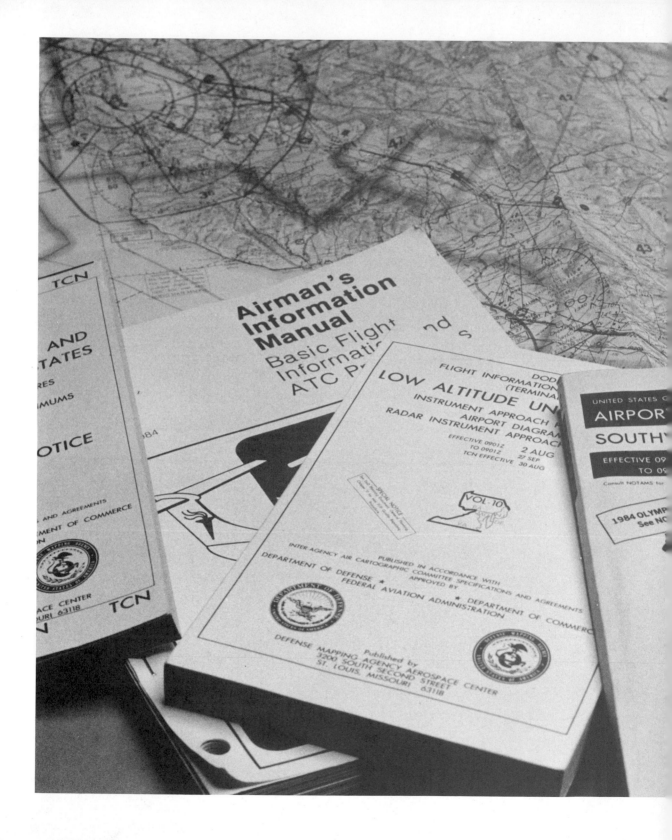

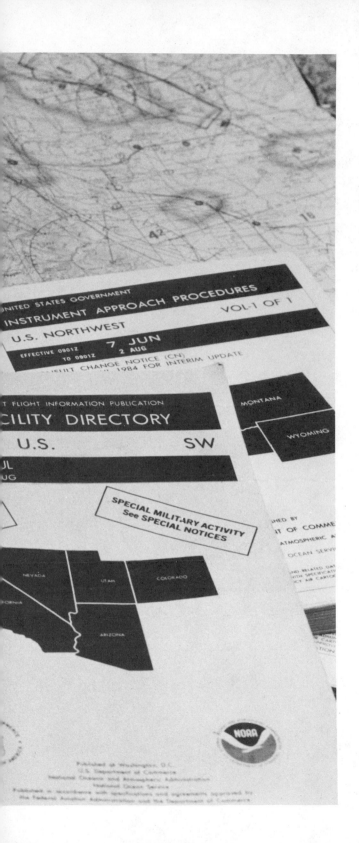

PART V
PUBLISHED MATERIAL

Knowledge is of two kinds: we know a subject ourselves, or we know where we can find information
upon it.

James Boswell
Life of Dr. Johnson

C H E C K P O I N T S

Where do pilots find the answers to flight planning questions? ✈ Which FAA documents
contain mandatory operating information? ✈ What educational material does the FAA
publish? ✈ What other agencies print and distribute flight information? ✈ Why is
the *Airman's Information Manual* considered the bible of general-aviation operations?
What information can be obtained from the *Airport/Facility Directory?* ✈ How can
pilots tell if their FAA publications are current?

FLIGHT INFORMATION PUBLICATIONS

Knowing where to look for accurate and complete flight information, and being able to find it quickly, will be among your most important piloting skills. Naturally, the FAA is the focal point of information acquisition and dissemination. It publishes or participates in the publication and distribution of over 5000 aviation-related documents per year. Documents that concern the private pilot are the materials we will discuss in this chapter.

You will find helpful and informative FAA publications in the areas of:

Federal Aviation Regulations
Pilot advisory information on safety and procedures
Technical documentation
Scientific studies on aeronautical phenomena
Administrative procedures
Educational and career materials for pilots and maintenance specialists
Operational information, including aeronautical charts and weather services

With so much information available, the FAA expects you to take seriously the job of maintaining yourself as a knowledgeable, well-informed pilot. FAA publications are distributed directly and also through a number of channels. The other government agencies involved in printing and distributing flight information documents are the National Technical Information Service, the Government Printing Office and its many official bookstores located nationwide, and the Department of Transportation, the parent agency of the FAA. You will find many FAA publications sold or reprinted for sale by aviation publishers at retail bookstores, flying schools, and many fixed-base operators (FBOs). Some FAA documents must be purchased, but many are free.

Aeronautical publications can become outdated as a result of new procedures and new regulations, obsolete facilities or radio frequencies, temporary or permanent deactivation of navigational aids or the installation of new aids, or changes to the structure or use of national airspace. Thus, the question of *currency* should be foremost in your mind whenever you use flight information publications. All FAA documents carry a date, and many also give the date on which the next edition will be published.

A complete list of FAA publications is printed in the *Guide to Federal Aviation Administration Publications,* which can be obtained free of charge from FAA-APA-PG-3, Department of Transportation, Publications Section, M-433.1, Washington, D.C. 20590. This guide classifies FAA documents into those performing a regulatory function and those conveying supplemental or nonregulatory information. As a well-informed pilot, you will be interested in both categories.

REGULATORY PUBLICATIONS

The documents published in this category cover a wide range, from aircraft manufacturing to repairs and operations. Those of interest to private pilots are introduced in the following paragraphs.

Federal Aviation Regulations (FARs) are the publications through which the FAA fulfills its statutory obligation to establish and enforce aviation safety standards. These regulations are treated at length in Chapter 11.

Airworthiness Directives (ADs) are notices of compulsory maintenance, repair, or inspection items issued with respect to a particular make and model of aircraft. While these are chiefly of concern to aircraft owners, pilots too should be aware of their existence, since an outstanding *AD* may ground an aircraft or limit its flight envelope until the appropriate action has been taken. *Airworthiness Directive* compliance records are kept with the airplane's maintenance logbooks.

FDC *NOTAMs* are distributed by the National Flight Data Center on occasions when some regulatory information must be disseminated. Examples of such information are amendments to current aeronautical charts, changes in instrument approach procedures, or added restrictions to flight. FDC *NOTAMs* are distributed to all air traffic facilities that have telecommunications access.

NONREGULATORY AND SUPPLEMENTAL PUBLICATIONS

Flight Standards Safety Pamphlets are distributed by the FAA's **Flight Standards District Offices (FSDOs)** as part of their aggressive campaign to promote safe flying. In addition to disseminating materials, safety representatives contact individual members of the flying public. The pamphlets deal with a wide range of operational problems affecting aviation safety and pilot judgment. They are available free at FSDOs and General Aviation District Offices.

The National Transportation Safety Board (NTSB), which compiles civil aviation safety statistics, publishes a number of informative accident and incident reports of interest to the general-aviation public. These publications can be obtained by contacting NTSB field offices or national headquarters at the addresses listed in Chapter 11.

AERONAUTICAL CHARTS

The **National Ocean Survey (NOS)** prepares and publishes a variety of marine and aeronautical charts used by civil and military operators around the world. A catalog of all NOS maps and charts is available from the Department of Commerce in Washington, D.C. As a private pilot, you will be interested mainly in the following charts:

Sectional aeronautical charts are the most widely used charts for VFR navigation. They have a scale of about 8 statute miles to the inch. It takes 37 sectional charts to cover the continental United States (see Figure 10.1). These charts are revised semiannually, except for several Alaskan sectionals, which are revised annually.

World aeronautical charts are smaller-scale charts (about 16 statute miles to the inch) designed for use by faster, high-performance aircraft. The United States can be covered by 12 of these charts, as shown in Figure 10.2. These charts are revised annually, except for several Alaskan charts and the Mexican/Caribbean charts, which are revised every two years.

Figure 10.1 Sectional and VFR terminal area charts available to pilots.

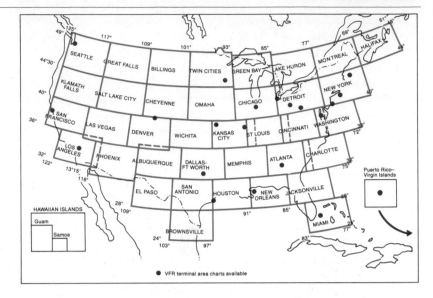

Figure 10.2 The world aeronautical charts (except Alaska) available to pilots.

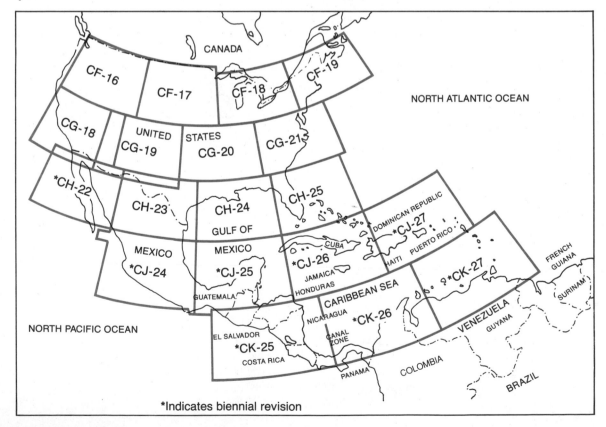

VFR terminal area charts are large-scale charts, about 4 statute miles to the inch. They show considerable detail about a small area around a heavily used air terminal. Figure 10.1 shows the locations that have published terminal charts.

Flight planning charts are small-scale charts of large size that show all of the continental United States (see Figure 10.3). These charts are extremely useful when planning a flight that spans several smaller charts. You will frequently see a VFR planning chart mounted on the wall of the flight planning room in most FBOs and flight schools.

Chapters 12 and 14 describe in detail how to read and use these charts. We mention them here to make you aware that they are a part of the total wealth of information available to you for the purpose of planning a safe, efficient flight.

OPERATIONAL PUBLICATIONS
Airman's Information Manual
The ***Airman's Information Manual (AIM)—Basic Flight Information and ATC Procedures*** is probably the most comprehensive document published by the FAA. The cover of each issue displays not only the publication

Figure 10.3 The VFR planning charts available to pilots.

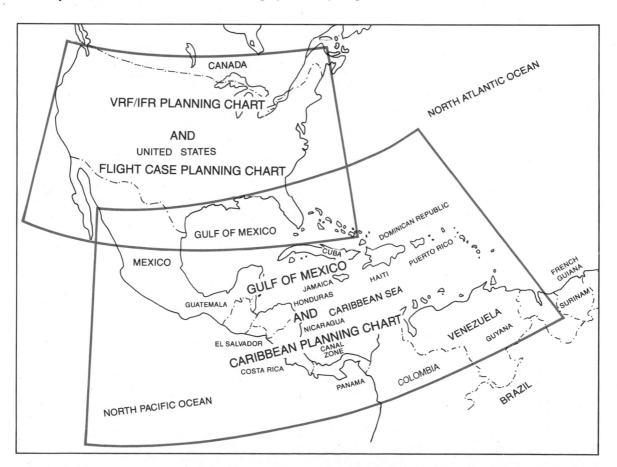

date of the current issue but also the date that the next issue will appear. The manual contains the fundamentals required to fly in the U.S. National Airspace System. It also contains items of interest to pilots concerning health and medical facts, factors affecting flight safety, a pilot/controller glossary, and information on safety, accident, and hazard reporting.

Figure 10.4 presents a sample contents list for this manual, to give you an idea of the range of information covered. The information is not discussed here because many of the data applicable to the VFR pilot are discussed in detail throughout this text. Notice that *AIM* also has a lot of information and procedures that apply to IFR operations (which are not covered in this text). Reading these procedures will not only increase your

Figure 10.4 Sample contents for an issue of *Airman's Information Manual (AIM)—Basic Flight Information and ATC Procedures.*

1. Navigation Aids
     Air Navigation Radio Aids
     Radar Services and Procedures
2. Airport, Air Navigation Lighting and Marking Aids
     Airport Lighting Aids
     Air Navigation and Obstruction Lighting
     Airport Marking Aids
3. Airspace
     General
     Uncontrolled Airspace
     Controlled Airspace
     Special Use Airspace
     Other Airspace Areas
4. Air Traffic Control
     Services Available to Pilots
     Radio Communications Phraseology and Techniques
     Airport Operations
     ATC Clearances/Separations
     Preflight
     Departure Procedures
     En route Procedures
     Arrival Procedures
     Pilot/Controller Roles and Responsibilities
     National Security and Interception Procedures
5. Emergency Procedures
     General
     Emergency Services Available to Pilots
     Distress and Urgency Procedures
     Two-way Radio Communications Failure
6. Safety of Flight
     Meteorology
     Altimeter Setting Procedures
     Wake Turbulence
     Bird Hazard and Flight over National Refuges, Parks,
     and Forests
     Potential Flight Hazards
     Safety, Accident, and Hazard Reports
7. Medical Facts for Pilots
8. Aeronautical Charts and Related Publications
9. Pilot/Controller Glossary

knowledge as a VFR pilot, it will help familiarize you with the IFR environment.

One of the most useful sections in *AIM* is the glossary of terms used by pilots and controllers for air-to-ground communications. While many of these terms are defined in this book, the *AIM* glossary includes a number of specialized words and phrases unique to air traffic control. If you review the glossaries of both publications, you should recognize most of the new words and phrases you will encounter during your flight training program and in reading other FAA publications.

In practice, all competent pilots become familiar with the material presented in the *Airman's Information Manual*, and the best pilots come to know it as well as they know FARs and the Pilot's Operating Handbook. You should make *AIM*'s acquaintance early in your flying career and review its pages routinely as you accumulate flying time and experience.

Airport/Facility Directory

The *Airport/Facility Directory* is an important aid to cross-country flying, listing airports, seaplane bases, heliports, communications and navigational facilities, and including special notices as appropriate. The *Directory* is issued every 56 days. It has seven volumes, one for each of seven geographic regions within the continental United States (see Figure 10.5). The

Figure 10.5 The geographic area covered by each volume of the *Airport/Facility Directory*.

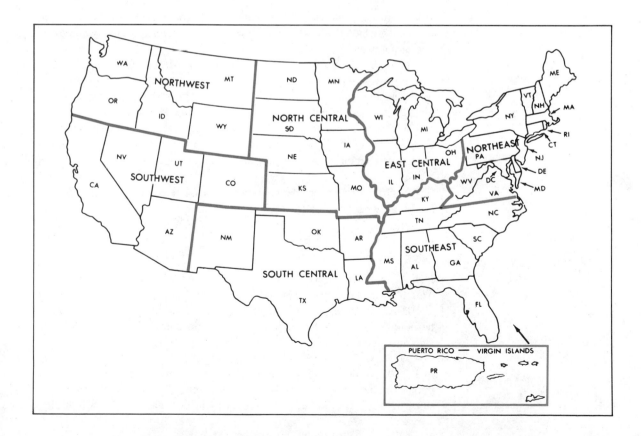

Figure 10.6 Contents of an *Airport/Facility Directory.* (Starred items are shown in this chapter.)

DIRECTORY LEGEND
Contents

volume on the southeast region contains information for Puerto Rico and the Virgin Islands. Alaska has its own *Airport/Facility Directory,* the *Alaskan Supplement*.

Figure 10.6 shows a table of contents for the *Airport/Facility Directory*. The information in this directory is also aimed at the needs of both the VFR and IFR pilot. A sample *Directory* entry is shown in Figure 10.7, along with its interpretation. A complete *Directory* legend appears at the end of this chapter for your review and study. (Note: When you take the FAA written exam, the test booklet has a copy of this legend, so there is no need to memorize these data, but it is important to become familiar with them.)

The *Directory* has a special section listing telephone numbers for all Flight Service Stations (FSS), recorded information, automated briefing facilities, and National Weather Service (NWS) offices. Figure 10.8 is a sample of this extremely useful information. (The written test booklet provides a legend for the symbols used.)

Notices to Airmen (NOTAMs)

NOTAMS contain up-to-date information that may deal with temporary alterations or procedures or with relatively sudden changes that airmen must be made aware of before normal publication dates of usual information channels. *NOTAMs* are classified into two types:

A *NOTAM-D* contains information that could affect a pilot's decision to make a flight. It includes information essential to planned en route, terminal, or landing operations—for example, primary runway or airport closure, navigational aid service interruptions, or radar service availability.

Figure 10.7 *(opposite)* A sample entry in the *Airport/Facility Directory* and its interpretation.

① ②
③ § ☐SAN CARLOS☐ (SQL)   1.7 NE   GMT −8(−7DT)   37°30′40″N 122°14′55″W   SAN FRANCISCO
  ~~02~~ ☐ B   S4 ☐   FUEL 80, 100, 100LL   OX 1, 3, 4   TPA— 802(800)   L-2F, A
④ RWY 12-30: H2600X75 (ASPH)   S-12   MIRL
⑤ RWY 12: VASI(V2L) — GA 3.0° TCH 25′. Road.
⑥ RWY 30: REIL. VASI(V2L) — GA 3.0° TCH 25′. Levee. Rgt tfc.
  AIRPORT REMARKS: Attended 1500-0600Z‡. Control Zone effective 1500-0600Z‡.
⑦ COMMUNICATIONS: ATIS 125.9 Opr 1500-0400Z‡   UNICOM 122.95
  OAKLAND FSS (OAK) LC 342-8626
⑧ Ⓡ BAY APP CON 133.95, 132.55, 134.5   Ⓡ BAY DEP CON 135.65
⑨ TOWER 119.0 Opr 1500-0400Z‡   GND CON 121.6
⑩ RADIO AIDS TO NAVIGATION:
  WOODSIDE (L) VORTAC 113.9   OSI   Chan 86   37°23′33″N 122°16′49″W   355° 7.3 NM to fld.
  2270/17E.

SAN CLEMENTE (NAVY) 33°01′38″N 118°34′14″W   LOS ANGELES
NDB (HW) 350   NUC   at San Clemente Island NALF (Frederick Sherman Fld)   L-3B
SAN CL⸱ ⸱ND Control Zone effe⸱⸱ ⸱500-0100Z‡ Mon-F⸱⸱

① — San Carlos Airport

② — Airport can be found on the San Francisco sectional chart.

③ B — There is a rotating beacon operating at the airport from dusk to dawn.
   S4 — Major airframe and power plant repairs are available.

④ RWY 12-30: — Following information pertains to runways 12 and 30:
   H — Is hard surfaced.
   2600 — Length is 2600 feet.
   X75 — Width is 75 feet.
   (ASPH) — Surface is asphalt.
   S-12 — Capable of supporting single-wheel landing gear airplanes with maximum gross weight capacity of 12,000 pounds.
   MIRL — Has medium-intensity runway lights.

⑤ VASI — A visual approach slope indicator system is available for runway 12.

⑥ REIL — Runway 30 has runway-end identifier lights.

⑦ ATIS — Information is available on frequency 125.9 MH.
   UNICOM — Advisories available on frequency 122.95 MH.

⑧ Ⓡ B BAY APP CON — Radar approach control is available on the listed frequencies.

⑨ TOWER — Tower control frequency is 199.0 MH.
   GND CON — Ground control frequency is 121.6 MH.

⑩ RADIO AIDS TO NAVIGATION — The airport is located on a 355° bearing, 7.3 nautical miles away from the Woodside VORTAC.

Figure 10.8 *(adjacent and opposite)*
Sample data from the *Airport/
Facility Directory.*

FAA AND NWS
TELEPHONE NUMBERS

Flight Service Station (FSS) numbers provide contact with an FAA pilot weather briefer.

Pilots Automatic Telephone Weather Answering Service (PATWAS) provides a recorded summary of weather conditions over a limited area in the vicinity of the associated facility.

Transcribed Weather Broadcast telephone numbers (TEL-TWEB) provide access to the transcribed weather broadcast on selected navigational facilities.

National Weather Service (WS) numbers will connect you with a national weather service pilot briefer.

Interim Voice Response System (IVRS), available in some metropolitan areas as listed at the end of this section, provides selected weather products via computer voice-generated system on touch-tone telephone.

Further information can be found in the Airman's Information Manual, Chapter 6.

★ PATWAS
■ TWEB
♦ Restricted Number for Aviation Weather Information
§§ Fast File (Flight Plan Filing Only)

Location and Identifier		Area Code	Telephone
	IOWA		
CEDAR RAPIDS CID	FSS	(319)	364-7127
INWATS	FSS	(800)	332-5241
		(800)	843-8553
Davenport (via Moline, Ill.)	WS	(309)	762-8347
Dubuque	WS	(319)	582-3171
Fort Dodge	FSS	(800)	WX-BRIEF ★§§
Mason City MCW	FSS	(515)	423-7512
INWATS	FSS	(800)	392-6690
Sioux City SUX	WS	(712)	255-3944 ♦
Omaha	FSS	(712)	258-4593
Waterloo	WS	(319)	234-1602 ♦

The *D* indicates that this information is distributed both locally and to distant air traffic facilities, according to predetermined address listings. All facilities have access to these data upon request.

A *NOTAM-L* contains information of an advisory, or nice-to-know, nature. It includes such information as taxiway closings, men or equipment near runways, and information on airports not annotated with the *NOTAM* service symbol in the *Airport/Facility Directory*. The *L* indicates that these data are maintained on file only at local air traffic facilities concerned with the operations at these airports. The information can be made available upon specific request to the local FSS having responsibility for the airport concerned.

Some *NOTAMs,* Class I, are distributed via telecommunications. Class II *NOTAMs* are published every 14 days and contain three basic parts:

1. *NOTAM-D* notices that are expected to remain in effect for an extended period. Once published, these notices are removed from the teletype circuit

Figure 10.8 (*continued*)

AIRPORT/FACILITY DIRECTORY

ALABAMA

---

§ **ANNISTON-CALHOUN CO** (ANB) 52 SW GMT 6(5DT) 33° 35′ 25″ N 85° 51′ 21″ W

                                                     ATLANTA

   611   B   S4   **FUEL** 100, JET A1 +   CFR Index A   **H-4G, L-14H**

  RWY 05-23: H5008X150 (ASPH) S-30, D-48, DT-75 L2 .34% up NE   **IAP**

    RWY 05: REIL, VASI G.A. 3.25° TCH 27′ Rgt tfc   **RWY 23:** VASI G.A. 3.75° TCH 25′

  AIRPORT REMARKS: Attended 1300 0300Z† For service and fuel after 0300Z† call (205)
    831-7941

  COMMUNICATIONS: UNICOM 1230

    ANNISTON FSS (ANB) on arpt 123.6 122.3 122.2 108 8T (205) 831-2303

    BIRMINGHAM APP/DEP CON 118 25

  RADIO AIDS TO NAVIGATION:

    ANNISTON NDB (BMH) 278 ANB 33 35 25 N 85 51 03 W at fld

    ILS 111 51 ANB rwy 05 BC unusable

---

§ **MUSCLE SHOALS** (MSL) 9 E GMT 6(5DT) 34°44′44″N 87°36′40″W   **ATLANTA**

   550   B   S4   **FUEL** 80, 100, JET A1 +   CFR Index A   **H-4G, L-14G**

  RWY 11-29: H6693X150 (ASPH) S-59, D-98, DT-160 HIRL   **IAP**

    RWY 11: VASI. Trees   **RWY 29:** MALSR. Tower

  RWY 18-36: H4000X150 (ASPH) S-30, D-50 MIRL

    RWY 18: Tree   **RWY 36:** Tree

  AIRPORT REMARKS: Attended dalgt hours, nights call (205) 383-1744 Night svc chg During
    calm winds pref rwy is RWY 29

  COMMUNICATIONS: UNICOM 123 G

    MUSCLE SHOALS FSS (MSL) on arpt 123.6 122.4 122.2 122 1R (205) 383-6541

   ® **HUNTSVILLE APP/DEP CON** 118.75 118.05

  RADIO AIDS TO NAVIGATOR: 123.0

    (L) BVORTAC 116.5 MSL Chan 112 34°42′24″N 87°29′29″W 291° 5 6 NM to arpt

    ILS 109 7 I MSL Rwy 29

---

to reduce congestion. *NOTAM-L* notices and special notices are included when they will contribute to flight safety.

2. FDC *NOTAMs* current at the time of publication. (Recall that these are regulatory notices.)

3. Notices that were not suitable for inclusion in the first section, either because of excessive length or because they concern a wide or unspecified geographical area.

Figure 10.9 shows some sample Class II *NOTAM* data. The notices are self-explanatory; however, many abbreviations are used to conserve space. Every *NOTAM* publication contains a list of abbreviations (as does the written test booklet).

Advisory Circulars

Advisory Circulars (ACs) are, as their name implies, informative and explanatory in nature, not regulatory (see Figure 10.10). Even so, they merit close study, largely because the regulations they describe are written in a legalistic and often terse style that can make it difficult to relate them to operational situations. *Advisory Circulars* are the FAA's attempt to sup-

Figure 10.9 Class II *NOTAM*
example.

NOTICES TO AIRMEN

THIS SECTION CONTAINS NOTICES TO AIRMEN THAT ARE EXPECTED
TO REMAIN IN EFFECT FOR AT LEAST SEVEN DAYS.
NOTE: NOTICES ARE ARRANGED IN ALPHABETICAL ORDER BY STATE
(AND WITHIN STATE BY CITY OR LOCALITY). NEW OR REVISED DATA.
NEW OR REVISED DATA ARE INDICATED BY BOLD ITALICIZING THE AIR-
PORT NAME.
NOTE: ALL TIMES ARE LOCAL UNLESS OTHERWISE INDICATED.

WEST VIRGINIA

BECKLEY, RALEIGH COUNTY MEML ARPT: MIRL rwy 1–19 6700 ft × 150 ft
    asphalt cmsnd. ILS LOM unusable beyond 10 NM below 6000 ft. Threshold rwy
    1 dsplcd 650 ft. (1/78)
BERKELEY SPRINGS POTOMAC AIRPARK: Twr 80 ft (AGL) located 900 ft W of
    apch end rwy 11 unmarked and unlighted. (6/76)
BLUEFIELD, MERCER COUNTY ARPT: ILS LOC rwy 23 OTS. (1/78)
CHARLESTON HUMMINGBIRD HELIPORT: Arpt closed.
LEWISBURG: CTLZ hours 0900–2100 daily. (2/78–3)
MARTINSBURG, EASTERN WEST VIRGINIA REGIONAL ARPT: Rwy 17–35 closed.
    (3/78)
MOUNDSVILLE MARSHALL COUNTY ARPT: Arpt open days VFR only. (11/77)
NEW CUMBERLAND, HERRON ARPT: TPA 775 ft. (11/77-2)
NEW MARTINSVILLE CIVIL AIR PATROL ARPT: TPA 1800 ft. (12/77-2)
WHEELING OHIO CO ARPT: 1570 ft chimney under const 3–1/2 NNW arpt lighted.
    (3/78–3)(3/78–3)

WYOMING

SPECIAL NOTICE: Coal mine blasting surface to 1000 ft AGL, 27 NM NNE of
    Sheridan. Blasting will continue indefinitely. (10/74)
SPECIAL NOTICE-YELLOWSTONE NATIONAL PARKS: Due to increasing low
    level flights over national parks, pilots are requested to maintain 2000 ft AGL when
    transiting Yellowstone National Parks unless aircraft capability is exceeded. (9/72)
CHEYENNE MUNI ARPT: Rwy lights rwy 16–34 OTS 2400–0600 daily. (1/78–
    3)
CODY MUNI ARPT: Tower 141 ft AGL 1320 ft NE apch end rwy 22. (1/78)
COWLEY/LOVEL/BYRON/BIG HORN COUNTY ARPT: VASI rwy 9 and rwy 27
    cmsnd, for VASI key freq 122.8 5 times. UNICOM freq 122.8 cmsnd. Rotating
    beacon RTS. MIRL rwy 9–27 comsnd, for rwy lights key freq 122.8 5 times. (10/
    77–2)
EVANSTON MUNI ARPT: Rwy lights 16–34 dcmend. (11/77–2)
LARAMIE, GENERAL BREES FIELD: VASI rwy 30 cmsnd. (2/78–2)
RIVERTON REGIONAL ARPT: VASI rwy 28 cmsnd. Rwy 10–28 now 8200 ft,
    HIRL cmsnd. Rwy 10–28 wt brg capacity −85000 lbs, D −110000 lbs, DT
    −165000 lbs. VASI rwy 10 cmsnd. Rwy 16–34 now 1000 ft. (3/78–2)

---

plement the letter of the law with some guidance in regard to its intent and
with techniques for operating safely within its framework. As such, *ACs*
can be an important addition to your aviation bookshelf.

    ACs are issued in a series of volumes corresponding to the topics covered
by the Federal Aviation Regulations. The series numbers match the FAR
subchapter numbers. The subject codes and topics are as follows:

    00 General

    10 Procedural Rules

    20 Aircraft

AC 90-48B

DATE 9/5/80

ADVISORY CIRCULAR

DEPARTMENT OF TRANSPORTATION
Federal Aviation Administration
Washington, D.C.

Subject: PILOTS' ROLE IN COLLISION AVOIDANCE

1. <u>PURPOSE</u>. This advisory circular is issued to <u>alert</u> all pilots to the midair collision and near midair collision hazard and to emphasize those basic problem areas of concern, as related to the human causal factors, where improvements in pilot education, operating practices, procedures, and techniques are needed to reduce midair conflicts.

2. <u>CANCELLATION</u>. AC 90-48A, Pilots' Role in Collision Avoidance, dated 7/24/79 is canceled.

3. <u>BACKGROUND</u>.

    a. During 1978, 34 midair collisions (MAC) occurred in the United States resulting in 190 fatalities. Of the 190 fatalities, 144 resulted from the collision between an airliner and a light plane and included fatal injuries to seven persons on the ground. Most of the midair collisions occurred in good weather during the hours of daylight. During the same period, there were 495 near midair collisions (NMAC); a 29 percent increase over 1977.

    b. The FAA has introduced significant programs designed to reduce the potential for midair and near midair collisions. This advisory circular is directed to pilots operating in the National Airspace System and emphasizes the need for all pilots to recognize the human factors associated with midair conflicts.

4. <u>ACTION</u>. The following areas warrant special attention and continuing action on the part of all pilots to avoid the possibility of their becoming involved in midair conflicts:

    a. "See and Avoid" Concept.

        (1) The flight rules prescribed in Part 91 of the Federal Aviation Regulations (FAR) set forth the concept of "See and Avoid." This concept requires that vigilance shall be maintained by each person operating an

Initiated by: AFO-820

Figure 10.10 A sample *Advisory Circular.*

   60 Airmen

   70 Airspace

   90 Air Traffic and General Operating Rules

 120 Air Carriers, Air Travel Clubs, and Operators for Compensation or Hire: Certification and Operations

 140 Schools and Other Certificated Agencies

 150 Airports

 170 Navigational Facilities

 180 Administrative Regulations

 190 Withholding Security Information; War-Risk Insurance; Aircraft Loan Guarantee Program

 210 Flight Information

Specific *ACs* within a series are further identified by their own serial numbers.

ACs tend to be a little longer-lived than other FAA publications, revised only when necessary to reflect changing concepts, the adoption of major new equipment or technology, or the approval of important new regulations. Each time an *AC* is revised, the letter at the end of the document identification number is changed. You can obtain an *Advisory Circular Checklist* (AC-00-2) giving *AC* titles, prices, and availability from the U.S. Department of Transportation, Publications Section M443.1, Washington, D.C. 20590.

Exam-O-Grams

Exam-O-Grams are prepared for both IFR and VFR pilots (see Figure 10.11). Since they are produced in response to feedback from the flying community (in the form of written test results, accident investigations, and violation reports), they have no regular publication schedule. Like *ACs,* they are educational in nature rather than directive; unlike *ACs,* they deal with specific questions and common misconceptions rather than with broad topics or general procedures. Because of their concise text and sometimes amusing style, they are popular and make easy reading. Nonetheless, they are not intended as substitutes for the full regulations or detailed procedures they pertain to.

Exam-O-Grams may be purchased as a set. You can also ensure that you receive the latest number by becoming a subscriber. *Exam-O-Grams* may be ordered from the Flight Standards National Field Office, Attn: AFO-590, P.O. Box 25082, Oklahoma City, OK 73125.

USING FLIGHT INFORMATION

To many novice fliers, the collected flight information publications seem like a dark forest of codes and numbers—especially when the information is needed to plan actual cross-country flights. It may help you to remember that even the bulkiest volume is made up of individual entries, or specific facts, and that you will need to research only a relatively small number of

Department of Transportation
FEDERAL AVIATION ADMINISTRATION
VFR PILOT EXAM-O-GRAM° NO. 26

COMMON MISCONCEPTIONS (Series 2)

Each question in FAA Airman Written Examinations offers the examinee a group of four
answers from which to select the answer he believes to be correct. Applicants' comments
and analyses of the answer sheets indicate that particular incorrect answers are frequently
being chosen because of a misconception regarding certain items of required aeronautical
knowledge. This Exam-O-Gram, as well as Exam-O-Gram No. 17, attempts to correct a
few of these preconceived ideas.

WHAT INDICATED AIRSPEED SHOULD BE USED FOR LANDING APPROACHES TO
FIELDS OF HIGHER ELEVATIONS? For all practical purposes, use the SAME indication
as you use at fields of lower elevations.

WILL THE SAME INDICATED APPROACH SPEED BE SAFE AT HIGH ELEVATIONS?
YES, in relatively smooth air. We all know that as altitude increases, the air becomes
less dense, and consequently with decreased drag the airplane travels faster through the
air. However, this faster speed creates no increase in impact pressure on the airspeed
pitot system because of the lesser air density. In other words, we get a higher True
Airspeed with the same Indicated Airspeed. Although the True Airspeed (TAS) at which

* Exam-O-Grams are non-directive in nature and are
issued solely as an information service to individuals
interested in Airman Written Examinations.

Figure 10.11 An example of a VRF pilot *Exam-O-Gram*.

these facts for a particular flight. Thus, the forest of flight documentation
may be thick, but you will have to penetrate only a little of it at a time.
You will also find that you will come to use the publications methodically,
letting the index of each volume guide you quickly to the information you
need. Figure 10.12 presents a matrix of typical aeronautical information
needs and the documents you should research to find your information.

The task of looking into all the documents will seem less onerous if you
keep a list of steps to follow in planning cross-country flights. This *flight
planning checklist* should be comprehensive enough to be serviceable for
the most ambitious flight you might undertake. You will not always have
to review everything listed, but before skipping an item you should consider
carefully whether it pertains to your flight. Chapter 14 presents an actual
flight planning history that can serve as a model for such a checklist. You
should add any items that you feel may help you become a safer and more
competent pilot.

In general, you will begin each flight by scanning a VFR planning chart
for a possible flight route. You will end with a completed flight plan form
that shows the navigational, operational, and performance information you
will need to conduct the flight safely. From beginning to end, you will
probably use documents in the following sequence:

Flight Information Publications

Type of Aeronautical Information Needed	Aeronautical charts	Advisory Circulars	Airman's Information Manual	Airport/Facility Directory	Airworthiness Directives	Exam-O-Grams	Federal Aviation Regulations	Flight Standards Safety Pamphlets	NOTAMs	NTSB reports
Accident reporting			●		●		●	●		●
Aeronautical glossary			●				●			
Aircraft systems		●			●	●	●			
Airplane performance		●				●				
Airport markings	●	●	●	●		●		●		
Airport procedures		●	●	●		●	●	●		
ATC procedures	●	●	●	●		●	●		●	
Aviation careers		●								
Aviation physiology		●	●			●	●	●		●
Aviation weather		●	●	●		●		●	●	●
Controlled airspace	●	●	●			●	●	●		
Emergencies		●	●			●	●	●		●
Flight instruments		●			●	●	●			
Flight planning	●	●	●	●		●	●		●	
Flight safety tips		●	●		●	●		●	●	●
General operating and flight rules	●	●	●			●	●	●		
Medical standards		●					●	●		●
Navigation aids	●	●	●	●		●	●		●	
Navigation procedures	●	●	●	●		●	●	●	●	●
Operating "bulletins"					●				●	
Pilot certificates		●				●	●			
Piloting techniques		●	●			●		●		●
Power plants		●			●	●				
Principles of flight		●	●			●				
Radio use		●	●			●	●			
Wake turbulence		●	●			●	●			●
Weather briefing information	●	●	●	●		●		●	●	
Weight and balance		●			●	●				

1. Inspect the VFR planning chart.

2. Lay out a detailed flight route on a sectional or, if appropriate, a world aeronautical chart.

3. Using the *Airport/Facility Directory,* research your destination, alternative airports, and the pertinent navigational aids.

4. Check the weather and see whether there are any *Notices to Airmen* that may affect your flight.

5. Refer to the *Airman's Information Manual* if you need to review or clarify any procedures or operating rules before takeoff.

If you are reviewing general concepts or procedures between flights, you may want to check the most comprehensive references before looking into the more specialized ones. Check *AIM* first, since it covers the widest range of general-aviation subjects. Check the Federal Aviation Regulations for final authority on allowed or prohibited activities. Check the appropriate *Advisory Circular* if you need a thorough refresher in a specific area. Check the VFR *Exam-O-Grams* if you are looking for a concise discussion of a common flying problem.

OTHER AVIATION READING

Numerous trade and technical publications have been written on the subject of aviation, ranging in topic from meteorology and pilot training to memoirs. Some publications, such as this textbook, can be used in home pilot-training courses. Other publications can be informative, but they are not necessarily appropriate aids for pilot certificate training. Read them for their enjoyment value.

A number of aviation publishers distribute and update (through paid revision services) commercial variations of the FAA documents described in this chapter. These publications often have additional features popular with many pilots, such as pictorial displays of airports and notes on the availability of rental cars or the hotels in the local area. If you use any publications other than those issued by the U.S. government, you must be doubly aware of their currency dates and of any other aspects that may limit their use for flight planning or navigation; often, they are excerpts from original government publications and often incomplete.

KEY TERMS

Advisory Circulars (ACs)

Airman's Information Manual (AIM)

Airport/Facility Directory

Airworthiness Directives (ADs)

Exam-O-Grams

FDC *NOTAMs*

National Transportation Safety Board (NTSB)

sectional aeronautical charts

VFR planning charts

VFR terminal area charts

world aeronautical charts

Figure 10.12 *(opposite)* Flight information publication matrix.

PROFICIENCY CHECK

1. FAA flight information publications are classified as either regulatory or nonregulatory. Indicate which of the following publications are regulatory.

    a. *Notices to Airmen*
    b. National Ocean Survey aeronautical charts
    c. *Airman's Information Manual*
    d. *Advisory Circulars*
    e. National Transportation Safety Board accident and incident reports
    f. *Airworthiness Directives*
    g. Federal Aviation Regulations
    h. *Airport/Facility Directory*
    i. *Exam-O-Grams*
    j. Flight Standards Safety Pamphlets

2. What are *Airworthiness Directives* and why should pilots be concerned with them?

3. Suppose you are interested in learning more about the special techniques and hazards of flying at night. What publication would you refer to?

4. What is the first thing you should check in a flight information publication before using it for flight planning or navigation?

5. In which document would you find a list of telephone numbers for an FAA flight service weather briefing?

6. Assume you are planning a twilight arrival at Beals Airport and you see the following *NOTAM* posted for Brule, Nebraska:

BRULE, BEALS ARPT: for rwy lights rwy 8-26 key
freq 121.7 (10/76-2)

Interpret the *NOTAM* and explain any operational procedure it contains that is relevant to your flight.

7. Refer to the entry from the *Airport/Facility Directory* at the bottom of Figure 10.8 on page 331 and answer the following questions about each airport:

    a. How would you obtain a weather briefing at this airport?
    b. Is fuel (100 octane) available for your airplane?
    c. What is the length of the longest runway? Does it have any approach aids or obstructions?
    d. Is the airport controlled or uncontrolled? What is its primary air-to-ground frequency?

DIRECTORY LEGEND
SAMPLE

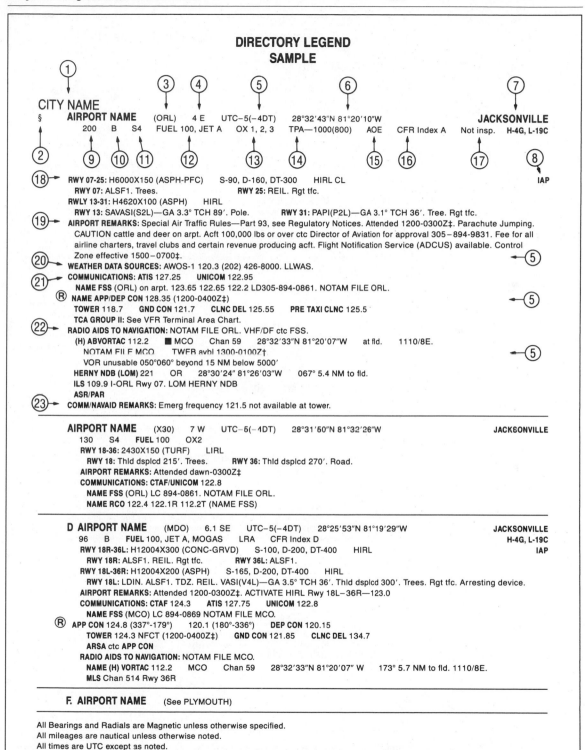

CITY NAME

§

AIRPORT NAME   (ORL)   4 E   UTC−5(−4DT)   28°32′43″N 81°20′10″W   **JACKSONVILLE**

200   B   S4   FUEL 100, JET A   OX 1, 2, 3   TPA—1000(800)   AOE   CFR Index A   Not insp.   **H-4G, L-19C**

IAP

RWY 07-25: H6000X150 (ASPH-PFC)   S-90, D-160, DT-300   HIRL CL
   RWY 07: ALSF1. Trees.   **RWY 25:** REIL. Rgt tfc.
RWLY 13-31: H4620X100 (ASPH)   HIRL
   RWY 13: SAVASI(S2L)—GA 3.3° TCH 89′. Pole.   **RWY 31:** PAPI(P2L)—GA 3.1° TCH 36′. Tree. Rgt tfc.
AIRPORT REMARKS: Special Air Traffic Rules—Part 93, see Regulatory Notices. Attended 1200-0300Z‡. Parachute Jumping. CAUTION cattle and deer on arpt. Acft 100,000 lbs or over ctc Director of Aviation for approval 305−894-9831. Fee for all airline charters, travel clubs and certain revenue producing acft. Flight Notification Service (ADCUS) available. Control Zone effective 1500−0700‡.
WEATHER DATA SOURCES: AWOS-1 120.3 (202) 426-8000. LLWAS.
COMMUNICATIONS: ATIS 127.25   UNICOM 122.95
  NAME FSS (ORL) on arpt. 123.65 122.65 122.2 LD305-894-0861. NOTAM FILE ORL.
® **NAME APP/DEP CON** 128.35 (1200-0400Z‡)
  TOWER 118.7   **GND CON** 121.7   **CLNC DEL** 125.55   **PRE TAXI CLNC** 125.5
  TCA GROUP II: See VFR Terminal Area Chart.
RADIO AIDS TO NAVIGATION: NOTAM FILE ORL. VHF/DF ctc FSS.
  (H) ABVORTAC 112.2   ■ MCO   Chan 59   28°32′33″N 81°20′07″W   at fld.   1110/8E.
   NOTAM FILE MCO   TWEB avbl 1300-0100Z†
   VOR unusable 050°060° beyond 15 NM below 5000′
  HERNY NDB (LOM) 221   OR   28°30′24″ 81°26′03″W   067° 5.4 NM to fld.
  ILS 109.9 I-ORL Rwy 07. LOM HERNY NDB
  ASR/PAR
COMM/NAVAID REMARKS: Emerg frequency 121.5 not available at tower.

AIRPORT NAME   (X30)   7 W   UTC−5(−4DT)   28°31′50″N 81°32′26″W   **JACKSONVILLE**

130   S4   **FUEL** 100   OX2
RWY 18-36: 2430X150 (TURF)   LIRL
  RWY 18: Thld dsplcd 215′. Trees.   **RWY 36:** Thld dsplcd 270′. Road.
AIRPORT REMARKS: Attended dawn-0300Z‡
COMMUNICATIONS: CTAF/UNICOM 122.8
  NAME FSS (ORL) LC 894-0861. NOTAM FILE ORL.
  NAME RCO 122.4 122.1R 112.2T (NAME FSS)

D AIRPORT NAME   (MDO)   6.1 SE   UTC−5(−4DT)   28°25′53″N 81°19′29″W   **JACKSONVILLE**
    H-4G, L-19C
96   B   **FUEL** 100, JET A, MOGAS   LRA   CFR Index D   **IAP**
RWY 18R-36L: H12004X300 (CONC-GRVD)   S-100, D-200, DT-400   HIRL
  RWY 18R: ALSF1. REIL. Rgt tfc.   **RWY 36L:** ALSF1.
RWY 18L-36R: H12004X200 (ASPH)   S-165, D-200, DT-400   HIRL
  RWY 18L: LDIN. ALSF1. TDZ. REIL. VASI(V4L)—GA 3.5° TCH 36′. Thld dsplcd 300′. Trees. Rgt tfc. Arresting device.
AIRPORT REMARKS: Attended 1200-0300Z‡. ACTIVATE HIRL Rwy 18L−36R—123.0
COMMUNICATIONS: CTAF 124.3   ATIS 127.75   UNICOM 122.8
  NAME FSS (MCO) LC 894-0869 NOTAM FILE MCO.
® **APP CON** 124.8 (337°-179°)   120.1 (180°-336°)   **DEP CON** 120.15
  TOWER 124.3 NFCT (1200-0400Z‡)   **GND CON** 121.85   **CLNC DEL** 134.7
  ARSA ctc **APP CON**
RADIO AIDS TO NAVIGATION: NOTAM FILE MCO.
  NAME (H) VORTAC 112.2   MCO   Chan 59   28°32′33″N 81°20′07″ W   173° 5.7 NM to fld. 1110/8E.
  MLS Chan 514 Rwy 36R

F. AIRPORT NAME   (See PLYMOUTH)

All Bearings and Radials are Magnetic unless otherwise specified.
All mileages are nautical unless otherwise noted.
All times are UTC except as noted.

Continued on page 340

ABBREVIATED DIRECTORY LEGEND

(1) CITY/AIRPORT NAME

Airports and facilities in this directory are listed alphabetically by associated city and state. When the city name is different from the airport name the city name will appear on the the line above the airport name. Airports with the same associated city name will be listed alphabetically by airport name and will be separated by a dashed rule line. All others will be separated by a solid rule line.

(2) NOTAM SERVICE

§—NOTAM "D" (Distant teletype dissemination) and NOTAM "L" (Local dissemination) service is provided for airport. Absence of annotation § indicates NOTAM "L" (Local dissemination) only provided to airport. See AIM. Basic Flight Information and ATC Procedures for detailed description of NOTAM.

(3) LOCATION IDENTIFIER

A three- or four-character code assigned to airports. These identifiers are used by ATC in lieu of the airport name in flight plans, flight strips and other written records and computer operations.

(4) AIRPORT LOCATION

Airport location is expressed as distance and direction from the center of the associated city in nautical miles and cardinal points, i.e., 4 NE.

(5) TIME CONVERSION

Hours of operation of all facilities are expressed in Coordinated Universal Time (UTC) and shown as "Z" time. The directory indicates the number of hours to be subtracted from UTC to obtain local standard time and local daylight saving time UTC − 5 (−4DT). The symbol ‡ indicates that during periods of Daylight Saving Time effective hours will be one hour earlier than shown. In those areas where daylight saving time is not observed that (−4DT) and ■ will not be shown. All states observe daylight savings time except Arizona and that portion of Indiana in the Eastern Time Zone and Puerto Rico and the Virgin Islands.

(6) GEOGRAPHIC POSITION OF AIRPORT

(7) CHARTS

The Sectional Chart and Low and High Altitude Enroute Chart and panel on which the airport or facility is located. Helicopter Chart locations will be indicated as, i.e., COPTER.

(8) INSTRUMENT APPROACH PROCEDURES

IAP indicates an airport for which a prescribed (Public Use) FAA Instrument Approach Procedure has been published.

(9) ELEVATION

Elevation is given in feet above mean sea level and is the highest point on the landing surface. When elevation is sea level it will be indicated as (00). When elevation is below sea level a minus (−) sign will precede the figure.

(10) ROTATING LIGHT BEACON

B indicates rotating beacon is available. Rotating beacons operate dusk to dawn unless otherwise indicated in AIRPORT REMARKS.

(11) SERVICING

S1:   Minor airframe repairs.
S2:   Minor airframe and minor powerplant repairs.
S3:   Major airframe and minor powerplant repairs.
S4:   Major airframe and major powerplant repairs.

NOTE: Starred items in this legend have been condensed. Refer to a current directory for complete information.

⑫ FUEL

CODE	FUEL
80	Grade 80 gasoline (Red)
100	Grade 100 gasoline (Green)
100LL	Grade 100LL gasoline (low lead) (Blue)
115	Grade 115 gasoline
A	Jet A—Kerosene freeze point − 40°C.
A1	Jet A-1—Kerosene, freeze point − 50° C.
A1 +	Jet A-1—Kerosene with icing inhibitor, freeze point − 50° C.
B	Jet B—Wide-cut turbine fuel, freeze point − 50° C.
B +	Jet B—Wide-cut turbine fuel with icing inhibitor, freeze point − 50° C.

⑬ OXYGEN

OX 1   High Pressure
OX 2   Low Pressure
OX 3   High Pressure—Replacement Bottles
OX 4   Low Pressure—Replacement Bottles

⑭ TRAFFIC PATTERN ALTITUDE

Traffic Pattern Altitude (TPA)—The first figure shown is TPA above mean sea level. The second figure in parentheses is TPA above airport elevation.

⑮ AIRPORT OF ENTRY AND LANDING RIGHTS AIRPORTS

AOE—Airport of Entry—A customs Airport of Entry where permission from U.S. Customs is not required, however, at least one hour advance notice of arrival must be furnished.

LRA—Landing Rights Airport—Application for permission to land must be submitted in advance to U.S. Customs. At least one hour advance notice of arrival must be furnished.

NOTE: Advance notice of arrival at both an AOE and LRA airport may be included in the flight plan when filed in Canada or Mexico, where Flight Notification Service (ADCUS) is available the airport remark will indicate this service. This notice will also be treated as an application for permission to land in the case of an LRA. Although advance notice of arrival may be relayed to customs through Mexico, Canadian, and U.S. Communications facilities by flight plan, the aircraft operator is solely responsible for insuring that Customs receives the notification. (See Customs, Immigration and Naturalization, Public Health and Agriculture Department requirements in the International Flight Information Manual for further details.)

* ⑯ CERTIFICATED AIRPORT (FAR 139)

Airports serving Civil Aeronautics board certified carriers and certified under FAR, Part 139, are indicated by the CFR index, i.e., CFR Index A, which relates to the availability of crash, fire, and rescue equipment.

⑰ FAA INSPECTION

All airports not inspected by FAA will be identified by the note: Not insp. This indicates that the airport information has been provided by the owner or operator of the field.

* ⑱ RUNWAY DATA

Runway information is shown on two lines. That information common to the entire runway is shown on the first line while information concerning the runway ends are shown on the second or following line. Lengthy information will be placed in the Airport Remarks.

Runway direction, surface, length, width, weight bearing capacity, lighting, gradient (when gradient exceeds 0.3 percent) and appropriate remarks are shown for each runway. Direction, length, width, lighting and remarks are shown for sealanes. The full dimensions of helipads are shown, i.e., 50 × 150.

⑲ AIRPORT REMARKS

LLWSAS—Indicated a Low Level Wind Sheer Alert System consisting of a centerfield and several field perimeter anemometers installed.

Landing Fee indicates landing charges for private or non-revenue producing aircraft; in addition, fees may be charged for planes that remain over a couple of hours and buy no services, or at major airline terminals for all aircraft.

Remarks—Data is confined to operational items affecting the status and usability of the airport.

Continued on page 342

* **WEATHER DATA SOURCES**

AWOS—Automated Weather Observing System

  AWOS-1—reports altimeter setting, wind data and usually temperature, dewpoint and density altitude.

  AWOS-2—reports the same as AWOS-1 plus visibility.

  AWOS-3—reports the same as AWOS-1 plus visibility and cloud/ceiling data.

  See AIM, Basic Flight Information and ATC procedures for detailed description of AWOS.

SAWRS—Identifies airports that have a Supplemental Aviation Weather Reporting Station available to pilots for current weather information.

LAWRS—Limited Aviation Weather Reporting Station where observers report cloud height, weather, obstructions to vision, temperature and dewpoint (in most cases), surface wind, altimeter and pertinent remarks.

LLWAS—Indicates a Low Level Wind Shear Alert System consisting of a center field and several field perimeter anemometers.

HIWAS—See RADIO AIDS TO NAVIGATION

* **COMMUNICATIONS**

 RADIO AIDS TO NAVIGATION

The Airport Facility Directory lists by facility name all Radio Aids to Navigation, except Military, TACANS, that appear on National Ocean Survey Visual or IFR Aeronautical Charts and those upon which the FAA has approved an Instrument Approach Procedure. All VOR, VORTAC and ILS equipment in the National Airspace System has an automatic monitoring and shutdown feature in the event of malfunction. Unmonitored, as used in this publication for any navigational aid, means that PSS or tower personnel cannot observe the malfunction or shutdown signal.

NAVAID information is tabulated as indicated in the following sample:

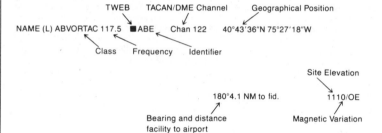

 COMM/NAVAID REMARKS

Pertinent remarks concerning communications and NAVAIDS.

The law is not an end in itself, nor does it provide an end. It is preeminently a means to serve what we think is right.

Justice William J. Brennan

C H E C K P O I N T S

What are the requirements to earn and maintain a pilot certificate? 🛩 What limitations are placed on student pilots? Private pilots? 🛩 What are the responsibilities of a pilot-in-command? 🛩 How often must an airplane be inspected? 🛩 What constitutes an aircraft accident?

FEDERAL AVIATION REGULATIONS

Aviation regulations, published by the FAA under its statutory obligations to promote aviation safety, are designed to make aircraft operations, manufacture, maintenance, and repair as safe and efficient as possible. FARs specifically cover flight situations and pilot activities that recur frequently, often with little time available for second-guessing or improvisation. They apply to everyone in the flying environment—from airline captains to the newest student pilots. In many ways they are comparable to the motor vehicle codes of your state and local governments. They stand as impersonal arbiters over the thousands of day-to-day decisions operators of highly technical equipment must make in a complex transportation system. Like our traffic laws, they work because they are willfully obeyed. The FAA needs few patrol officers in the sky as long as the flying public exercises common sense and keeps its own best interests in mind. Like the penalty for flying into a thunderstorm, the practical consequences of violating most aviation regulations are usually self-evident, unforgiving of careless infraction, and punishable on the spot by a near miss or accident.

This chapter presents the FARs pertinent to student and private pilots. Since the regulations are revised periodically, you should realize that those presented here may have been superseded by recent amendments. While we have made every effort to ensure that the text is up to date, it is *your* responsibility as a pilot to obtain the latest information from flight publications. Additionally, since the FARs in their entirety encompass some 11 volumes, we have selected only those FARs relevant to the needs of prospective private pilots. Any lack of continuity in the numbering of sections or letter labeling of subparagraphs is due to this selectivity we have exercised. You are encouraged to expand your aeronautical knowledge and review the other regulations as your flying career progresses.

For obvious legal reasons, the regulations are presented verbatim. Their wording sometimes makes them difficult to comprehend; however, the specified wording is necessary to make their meaning as indisputable as possible. Attempting to explain or interpret the regulations is best left to lawyers and courts, not to textbooks. Sample FAA written test questions are presented following selected regulations (answers to the sample questions appear at the end of the chapter). This procedure allows you to self-test your understanding of the regulation, and it also familiarizes you with the type of questions you will see on your FAA written test.

The regulations included in this chapter are selected portions of FARs Part 1, Definitions and Abbreviations; Part 61, Certification: Pilots and Flight Instructors; Part 67, Medical Standards and Certification; Part 91, General Operating and Flight Rules; and Part 830, National Transportation Safety Board (NTSB) Rules Pertaining to the Reporting of Aircraft Accidents or Incidents.

Although a number of aviation publishers distribute printed editions of selected FARs to local FBOs, flight schools, and retail bookstores, copies of the full regulations can be purchased from the Superintendent of Documents, U.S. Government Printing Office, Washington, D.C. 20402.

FAR PART 1:
DEFINITIONS AND ABBREVIATIONS

Aviation literature, like that of other modern technical fields, seems to be a veritable alphabet soup of acronyms, compound words, and abbreviations. But like any technological activity, its terminology must be precise and used with some standardization by its specialists. While we have given many of these terms working definitions elsewhere in this text, the FAA definitions are specifically linked to the use of those terms in the regulations. Thus, you must be familiar not only with the concepts these words represent, but their definitions under the law as well.

1.1 General Definitions

Administrator means the Federal Aviation Administrator or any person to whom he has delegated his authority in the matter concerned.

Aircraft means a device that is used or intended to be used for flight.

Aircraft engine means an engine that is used or is intended to be used for propelling aircraft. It includes turbosuperchargers, appurtenances, and accessories necessary for its functioning but does not include propellers.

Airframe means the fuselage, booms, nacelles, cowlings, fairings, airfoil surfaces (including rotors but excluding propellers and rotating airfoils of engines), and landing gear of an aircraft and their accessories and controls.

Airplane means an engine-driven fixed-wing heavier-than-air aircraft that is supported in flight by the dynamic reaction of the air against its wings.

Airport means an area of land or water that is used or intended to be used for the landing and takeoff of aircraft and includes its buildings and facilities, if any.

Airport traffic area means, unless otherwise specifically designated in Part 93, that airspace within a horizontal radius of 5 statute miles from the geographical center of any airport at which a control tower is operating, extending from the surface up to, but not including, an altitude of 3000 feet above the elevation of the airport.

Airship means an engine-driven lighter-than-air aircraft that can be steered.

Air traffic means aircraft operating in the air or on an airport surface, exclusive of loading ramps and parking areas.

Air traffic clearance means an authorization by air traffic control, for the purpose of preventing collision between known aircraft, for an aircraft to proceed under specified traffic conditions within controlled airspace.

Air traffic control means a service operated by appropriate authority to promote the safe, orderly, and expeditious flow of air traffic.

Alternate airport means an airport at which an aircraft may land if a landing at the intended airport becomes inadvisable.

Approved, unless used with reference to another person, means approved by the Administrator.

Area navigation (RNAV) means a method of navigation that permits aircraft operations on any desired course within the coverage of station-referenced navigation signals or within the limits of self-contained systems.

Area navigation low route means an area navigation route within the airspace extending upward from 1200 feet above the surface of the earth to, but not including, 18,000 feet MSL.

Balloon means a lighter-than-air aircraft that is not engine driven.

Brake horsepower means the power delivered at the propeller shaft (main drive or main output) of an aircraft engine.

Calibrated airspeed means indicated airspeed of an aircraft, corrected for position and instrument error. Calibrated airspeed is equal to true airspeed in standard atmosphere at sea level.

Category

(1) As used with respect to the certification, ratings, privileges, and limitations of airmen, means a broad classification of aircraft. Examples include: airplane, rotorcraft, glider, and lighter-than-air; and

(2) As used with respect to the certification of aircraft, means a grouping of aircraft based upon intended use or operating limitations. Examples include: transport, normal, utility, acrobatic, limited, restricted, and provisional.

Ceiling means the height above the earth's surface of the lowest layer of clouds or obscuring phenomena that is reported as "broken," "overcast," or "obscuration," and not classified as "thin" or "partial."

Civil aircraft means aircraft other than public aircraft.

Class

(1) As used with respect to the certification, ratings, privileges, and limitations of airmen, means a classification of aircraft within a category having similar operating characteristics. Examples include: single engine, multiengine, land, water, gyroplane, helicopter, airship, and free balloon; and

(2) As used with respect to the certification of aircraft, means a broad grouping of aircraft having similar characteristics of propulsion, flight, or landing. Examples include: airplane, rotorcraft, glider, balloon, landplane, and seaplane.

Commercial operator means a person who, for compensation or hire, engages in the carriage by aircraft in air commerce of persons or property, other than as an air carrier or foreign air carrier or under the authority of Part 375 of this Title. Where it is doubtful that an operation is for "compensation or hire," the test applied is whether the carriage by air is merely incidental to the person's other business or is in itself a major enterprise for profit.

Controlled airspace means airspace designated as a continental control area, control area, control zone, terminal control area, or transition area, within which some or all aircraft may be subject to air traffic control.

Critical engine means the engine whose failure would most adversely affect the performance or handling qualities of an aircraft.

Extended over-water operation means, with respect to aircraft other than helicopters, an operation over water at a horizontal distance of more than 50 nautical miles from the nearest shoreline.

Flight crewmember means a pilot, flight engineer, or flight navigator assigned to duty in an aircraft during flight time.

Flight level means a level of constant atmospheric pressure related to a reference datum of 29.92 inches of mercury. Each is stated in three digits that represent hundreds of feet. For example, flight level 250 represents a barometric altimeter indication of 25,000 feet; flight level 255, an indication of 25,500 feet.

Flight plan means specified information, relating to the intended flight of an aircraft that is filed orally or in writing with air traffic control.

Flight time means the time from the moment the aircraft first moves under its own power for the purpose of flight until the moment it comes to rest at the next point of landing ("block-to-block" time).

Flight visibility means the average forward horizontal distance, from the cockpit of an aircraft in flight, at which prominent unlighted objects may be seen and identified by day and prominent lighted objects may be seen and identified by night.

Glider means a heavier-than-air aircraft that is supported in flight by the dynamic reaction of the air against its lifting surfaces and whose free flight does not depend principally on an engine.

Ground visibility means prevailing horizontal visibility near the earth's surface as reported by the United States National Weather Service or an accredited observer.

Gyroplane means a rotorcraft whose rotors are not engine driven except for initial starting but are made to rotate by action of the air when the rotorcraft is moving and whose means of propulsion, consisting usually of conventional propellers, is independent of the rotor system.

Helicopter means a rotorcraft that for its horizontal motion depends principally on its engine-driven rotors.

IFR conditions means weather conditions below the minimum for flight under visual flight rules.

Indicated airspeed means the speed of an aircraft as shown on its pitot-static airspeed indicator calibrated to reflect standard atmosphere adiabatic compressible flow at sea level, uncorrected for airspeed system errors. [*Compressible flow* refers to that property of a gas such as air to compress or increase in density before a moving object, such as an airplane. At low speeds this compression is negligible but as the aircraft accelerates to a velocity close to the speed of sound, the compressibility effects become significant—not only on the pitot-static system but for the aircraft's power plant, wing, and control surfaces as well.]

Instrument means a device using an internal mechanism to show visually or aurally the attitude, altitude, or operation of an aircraft or aircraft part. It includes electronic devices that automatically control aircraft in flight.

Large aircraft means aircraft of more than 12,500 pounds, maximum certificated takeoff weight.

Lighter-than-air aircraft means aircraft that can rise and remain suspended by using contained gas weighing less than the air that is displaced by the gas.

Load factor means the ratio of a specified load to the total weight of the aircraft. The specified load is expressed in terms of any of the following: aerodynamic forces, inertia forces, or ground or water reactions.

Mach number means the ratio of the true airspeed to the speed of sound.

Major alteration means an alteration not listed in the aircraft, aircraft engine, or propeller specifications

(1) That might appreciably affect weight, balance, structural strength, performance, power plant operation, flight characteristics, or other qualities affecting airworthiness; or

(2) That is not done according to accepted practices or cannot be done by elementary operations.

Major repair means a repair

(1) That, if improperly done, might appreciably affect weight, balance, structural strength, performance, power plant operation, flight characteristics, or other qualities affecting airworthiness; or

(2) That is not done according to accepted practices or cannot be done by elementary operations.

Manifold pressure means absolute pressure as measured at the appropriate point in the induction system and usually expressed in inches of mercury.

Medical certificate means acceptable evidence of physical fitness on a form prescribed by the Administrator.

Minor alteration means an alteration other than a major alteration.

Minor repair means a repair other than a major repair.

Navigable airspace means airspace at and above the minimum flight altitudes prescribed by or under this chapter, including airspace needed for safe takeoff and landing.

Night means the time between the end of evening civil twilight and the beginning of morning civil twilight, as published in the *American Air Almanac,* converted to local time.

You should be aware that night flight experience [described in section 61.57(d)] begins 1 hour after sunset and ends 1 hour before sunrise.

Operate, with respect to aircraft, means use, cause to use, or authorize to use aircraft, for the purpose (except as provided in section 91.10 of this chapter) of air navigation including the piloting of aircraft, with or without the right of legal control (as owner, lessee, or otherwise).

Over-the-top means above the layer of clouds or other obscuring phenomena forming the ceiling.

Parachute means a device used to retard the fall of an object through air.

Pilotage means navigation by visual reference to landmarks.

Pilot in command means the pilot responsible for the operation and safety of an aircraft during flight time.

Pitch setting means the propeller blade setting as determined by the blade angle measured in a manner, and at a radius, specified by the instruction manual for the propeller.

Positive control means control of all air traffic, within designated airspace, by air traffic control.

Preventive maintenance means simple or minor preservation operations and the replacement of small standard parts not involving complex assembly operations.

Prohibited area means designated airspace within which the flight of aircraft is prohibited.

Propeller means a device for propelling an aircraft that has blades on an engine-driven shaft and that, when rotated, produces by its action on the air a thrust approximately perpendicular to its plane of rotation. It includes control components normally supplied by its manufacturer, but does not include main and auxiliary rotors or rotating airfoils of engines.

Rotating airfoils of engines *refers to the turbine and fan blades used in jet engines. While they are airfoils that rotate to produce thrust, they are not properly called propellers.*

Public aircraft means aircraft used only in the service of a government or a political subdivision. It does not include any government-owned aircraft engaged in carrying persons or property for commercial purposes.

Rating means a statement that, as a part of a certificate, sets forth special conditions, privileges, or limitations.

Reporting point means a geographic location in relation to which the position of an aircraft is reported.

Restricted area means airspace designated under Part 73 of this chapter within which the flight of aircraft, while not wholly prohibited, is subject to restriction.

RNAV way point (W/P) means a predetermined geographical position used for route or instrument approach definition or progress reporting purposes that is defined relative to a VORTAC station position.

Rotorcraft means a heavier-than-air aircraft that depends principally for its support in flight on the lift generated by one or more rotors.

Small aircraft means aircraft of 12,500 pounds or less, maximum certificated takeoff weight.

Standard atmosphere means the atmosphere defined in *U.S. Standard Atmosphere, 1962* (geopotential altitude tables).

The term geopotential altitude *refers to a fictitious model atmosphere used to describe geometric altitudes in terms of constant temperature layers or layers of constant temperature gradients.*

Takeoff power, with respect to reciprocating engines, means the brake horsepower that is developed under standard sea level conditions and under the maximum conditions of crankshaft rotational speed and engine manifold pressure approved for the normal takeoff, and limited in continuous use to the period of time shown in the approved specification.

Traffic pattern means the traffic flow that is prescribed for aircraft landing at, taxiing on, or taking off from an airport.

True airspeed means the airspeed of an aircraft relative to undisturbed air.

Type

(1) As used with respect to the certification, ratings, privileges, and limitations of airmen, means a specific make and basic model of aircraft, including modifications thereto that do not change its handling or flight characteristics. Examples include DC-7, 1049, and F-27, and

(2) As used with respect to the certification of aircraft, means those aircraft which are similar in design. Examples include DC-7 and DC-7C, 1049G and 1049H, and F-27 and F-27F.

(3) As used with respect to the certification of aircraft engines, means those engines which are similar in design. For example, JT8D and JT8D-7 are engines of the same type, and JT9D-3A and JT9D-7 are engines of the same type.

The aircraft used as examples tend to date the regulation and may be unfamiliar to contemporary student pilots. Modern aircraft requiring different airman type ratings would include the 707, 727, 747, DC-10, and L-1011, to name only a few.

Aircraft similar in design with respect to type *would be exemplified by the 747B and 747F.*

United States in a geographical sense means

(1) the States, the District of Columbia, Puerto Rico, and the possessions, including the territorial waters, and

(2) the airspace of those areas.

VFR over-the-top, with respect to the operation of aircraft, means the operation of an aircraft over-the-top under VFR when it is not being operated on an IFR flight plan.

1.2 Abbreviations and symbols

AGL means above ground level.

ALS means approach light system.

ASR means airport surveillance radar.

ATC means air traffic control.

CAS means calibrated airspeed.

DME means distance measuring equipment compatible with TACAN.

FAA means Federal Aviation Administration.

HIRL means high-intensity runway light system.

IAS means indicated airspeed.

ICAO means International Civil Aviation Organization.

IFR means instrument flight rules.

INT means intersection.

LFR means low-frequency radio range.

LMM means compass locator at middle marker.

LOM means compass locator at outer marker.

M means mach number.

MALS means medium-intensity approach light system.

MALSR means medium-intensity approach light system with runway alignment indicator lights.

MSL means mean sea level.

NDB (ADF) means nondirectional beacon (automatic direction finder).

PAR means precision approach radar.

RAIL means runway alignment indicator light system.

RBN means radio beacon.

RCLM means runway centerline marking.

RCLS means runway centerline light system.

REIL means runway end identification lights.

TACAN means ultra-high-frequency tactical air navigational aid.

TAS means true airspeed.

TVOR means very-high-frequency terminal omnirange station.

Under the designation of speeds, the capital letter V means velocity and is accompanied by a subscript denoting the particular speed in question.

V_A means design maneuvering speed.

V_B means design speed for maximum gust intensity.

V_C means design cruising speed.

V_F means design flap speed.

V_{FE} means maximum flap extended speed.

V_{LE} means maximum landing gear extended speed.

V_{NE} means never-exceed speed.

V_{NO} means maximum structural cruising speed.

V_S means the stalling speed or the minimum steady flight speed at which the airplane is controllable.

V_{SO} means the stalling speed or the minimum steady flight speed in the landing configuration.

V_{S1} means the stalling speed or the minimum steady flight speed obtained in a specified configuration.

V_X means speed for best angle of climb.

V_Y means speed for best rate of climb.

VFR means visual flight rules.

VHF means very high frequency.

VOR means very-high-frequency omnirange station.

VORTAC means collocated VOR and TACAN.

1.3 Rules of construction

    (1) Words importing the singular include the plural.

    (2) Words importing the plural include the singular.

    (3) Words importing the masculine gender include the feminine.

    (4) *Shall* is used in an imperative sense.

(5) *May* is used in a permissive sense to state authority or permission to do the act prescribed, and the words "no person may . . ." or "a person may not . . ." mean that no person is required, authorized, or permitted to do the act prescribed.

(6) *Includes* means "includes but is not limited to."

FAR PART 61:
CERTIFICATION: PILOTS AND FLIGHT INSTRUCTORS

The qualifications for becoming a pilot and the rules governing your progression from one certificate to another are contained in Part 61 of the FARs. It also contains requirements for medical certificates, pilots' logbooks, procedures for written and flight examinations, and such necessary matters as how to notify the FAA of any change of your name or address or the loss of your aviation records.

While we have included only those regulations pertinent to student and private pilots (the appropriate sections of Subparts A, B, C, and D), you will want to consult the entire regulation if you elect to seek advanced certificates such as commercial pilot, flight instructor, or airline transport pilot, or special operational endorsements such as instrument or multiengine ratings.

The following subparts and sections are included in this text:

Subpart A—General

Subpart A—General

61.1 Applicability

(a) This Part prescribes the requirements for issuing pilot and flight instructor certificates and ratings, the conditions under which those certificates and ratings are necessary, and the privileges and limitations of those certificates and ratings.

61.3 Requirements for certificates, ratings, and authorizations

(a) *Pilot certificate.* No person may act as pilot in command or in any other capacity as a required pilot flight crewmember of a civil aircraft of United States registry unless he has in his personal possession a current pilot certificate issued to him under this Part. However, when the aircraft is operated within a foreign country a current pilot license issued by the country in which the aircraft is operated may be used.

(c) *Medical certificate.* Except for free balloon pilots piloting balloons and glider pilots piloting gliders, no person may act as pilot in command or in any other capacity as a required pilot flight crewmember of an aircraft under a certificate issued to him under this Part, unless he has in his personal possession an appropriate current medical certificate issued under Part 67 of this chapter. However, when the aircraft is operated within a foreign country with a current pilot license issued by that country, evidence of current medical qualification for that license, issued by that country, may be used. In the case of a pilot certificate issued on the basis of a foreign pilot license under section 61.75, evidence of current medical qualification accepted for the issue of that license is used in place of a medical certificate.

(e) *Instrument rating.* No person may act as pilot in command of a civil aircraft under instrument flight rules or in weather conditions less than the minimum prescribed for VFR flight unless

    (1) In the case of an airplane, he holds an instrument rating or an
       airline transport pilot certificate with an airplane category rating on it.

(h) *Inspection of certificate.* Each person who holds a pilot certificate, flight instructor certificate, medical certificate, authorization, or license required by this Part shall present it for inspection upon the request of the Administrator, an authorized representative of the National Transportation Safety Board, or any Federal, State, or local law enforcement officer.

---

1. If you are a private pilot acting as pilot in command, or in any other capacity as a required pilot flight crewmember, you must have in your personal possession while aboard the aircraft

    (a) Your pilot logbook to show that you have met recent experience requirements to serve as pilot in command.

    (b) A current endorsement on your pilot certificate to show that you have satisfactorily accomplished a flight review.

    (c) Your current and appropriate pilot and medical certificates.

    (d) A current logbook endorsement to show that you have satisfactorily accomplished a flight review.

61.5 Certificates and ratings issued under this Part

(a) The following certificates are issued under this Part:

    (1) Pilot certificates:

        (i)   Student pilot.

        (ii)   Private pilot.

        (iii) Commercial pilot.

        (iv) Airline transport pilot.

    (2) Flight instructor certificates.

(b) The following ratings are placed on pilot certificates (other than student pilot) where applicable:

(1) Aircraft category ratings:
    (i)   Airplane.
    (ii)   Rotorcraft.
    (iii) Glider.
    (iv) Lighter-than-air.

(2) Airplane class ratings:
    (i)   Single-engine land.
    (ii)   Multiengine land.
    (iii) Single-engine sea.
    (iv) Multiengine sea.

(3) Rotorcraft class ratings:
    (i)   Helicopter.
    (ii)   Gyroplane.

(4) Lighter-than-air class ratings:
    (i)   Airship.
    (ii)   Free balloon.

(5) Aircraft type ratings are listed in Advisory Circular 61–1 entitled "Aircraft Type Ratings." This list includes ratings for the following:
    (i)   Large aircraft, other than lighter-than-air.
    (ii)   Small turbojet-powered airplanes.
    (iii) Small helicopters for operations requiring an airline transport pilot certificate.
    (iv) Other aircraft type ratings specified by the Administrator through aircraft type certificate procedures.

(6) Instrument ratings (on private and commercial pilot certificates only):
    (i)   Instrument—airplanes.
    (ii)   Instrument—helicopter.

(c) The following ratings are placed on flight instructor certificates where applicable:

(1) Aircraft category ratings:
    (i)   Airplane.
    (ii)   Rotorcraft.
    (iii) Glider.

(2) Airplane class ratings:
    (i)   Single-engine.
    (ii)   Multiengine.

(3) Rotorcraft class ratings:
    (i)   Helicopter.
    (ii)   Gyroplane.

(4) Instrument ratings:
    (i)   Instrument—airplane.
    (ii)   Instrument—helicopter.

61.11 Expired pilot certificates and reissuance

(a) No person who holds an expired pilot certificate or rating may exercise the privileges of that pilot certificate or rating.

(b) Except as provided, the following certificates and ratings have expired and are not reissued:

(2) A private or commercial pilot certificate or a lighter-than-air or free balloon pilot certificate issued before July 1, 1945. However, each of those certificates issued after June 30, 1945, and bearing an expiration date may be reissued without an expiration date.

(c) A private or commercial pilot certificate or a special purpose pilot certificate, issued on the basis of a foreign pilot license, expires on the expiration date stated thereon. A certificate without an expiration date is issued to the holder of the expired certificate only if he meets the requirements of section 61.75 of this Part for the issue of a pilot certificate based on a foreign pilot license.

61.13 Application and qualification

(a) Application for a certificate and rating, or for an additional rating under this Part is made on a form and in a manner prescribed by the Administrator.

(b) An applicant who meets the requirements of this Part is entitled to an appropriate pilot certificate with aircraft ratings. Additional aircraft category, class, type, and other ratings for which the applicant is qualified are added to his certificate. However, the Administrator may refuse to issue certificates to persons who are not citizens of the United States and who do not reside in the United States.

(c) An applicant who cannot comply with all of the flight proficiency requirements prescribed by this Part because the aircraft used by him for his flight training or flight test is characteristically incapable of performing a required pilot operation, but who meets all other requirements for the certificate or rating sought, is issued the certificate or rating with appropriate limitations.

(d) An applicant for a pilot certificate who holds a medical certificate under section 67.19 of this chapter with special limitations on it, but who meets all other requirements for that pilot certificate, is issued a pilot certificate containing such operating limitations as the Administrator determines are necessary because of the applicant's medical deficiency.

61.15 Offenses involving narcotic drugs, marijuana, and depressant or stimulant drugs or substances

(a) No person who is convicted of violating any Federal or State statute relating to the growing, processing, manufacture, sale, disposition, possession, transportation, or importation of narcotic drugs, marijuana, and depressant or stimulant drugs or substances is eligible for any certificate or rating issued under this Part for a period of 1 year after the date of final conviction.

(b) No person who commits an act prohibited by section 91.12 (a) of this chapter is eligible for any certificate or rating issued under this Part for a period of 1 year after the date of that act.

(c) Any conviction specified in paragraph (a) of this section or the commission of the act referenced in paragraph (b) of this section is grounds for suspending or revoking any certificate or rating issued under this Part.

61.17 Temporary certificate

(a) A temporary pilot or flight instructor certificate, or a rating, effective for a period of not more than 120 days, is issued to a qualified applicant pending a review of his qualifications and the issuance of a permanent certificate or rating by the Administrator. The permanent certificate or rating is issued to an applicant found qualified and a denial thereof is issued to an applicant found not qualified.

(b) A temporary certificate issued under paragraph (a) of this section expires

    (1) At the end of the expiration date stated thereon; or

    (2) Upon receipt by the applicant of

        (i) The certificate or rating sought; or

        (ii) Notice that the certificate or rating sought is denied.

61.19 Duration of pilot and flight instructor certificates

(a) *General*. The holder of a certificate with an expiration date may not, after that date, exercise the privileges of that certificate.

(b) *Student pilot certificate*. A student pilot certificate expires at the end of the 24th month after the month in which it is issued.

(c) *Other pilot certificates*. Any pilot certificate (other than a student pilot certificate) issued under this Part is issued without a specific expiration date. However, the holder of a pilot certificate issued on the basis of a foreign pilot license may exercise the privileges of that certificate only while the foreign pilot license on which that certificate is based is effective.

(e) *Surrender, suspension, or revocation*. Any pilot certificate or flight instructor certificate issued under this Part ceases to be effective if it is surrendered, suspended, or revoked.

(f) *Return of certificate*. The holder of any certificate issued under this Part that is suspended or revoked shall, upon the Administrator's request, return it to the Administrator.

---

2. In regard to the duration of Private Pilot Certificates, which statement is true?

    (a) They expire after a duration of 12 months.

    (b) They expire after a duration of 24 months.

    (c) They are issued without a specific expiration date.

    (d) When recency of experience requirements are not met, the certificates expire.

61.23 Duration of medical certificates

(a) A first-class medical certificate expires at the end of the last day of the 24th month after the month of the date of examination shown on the certificate, for operations requiring only a private or student pilot certificate.

(b) A second-class medical certificate expires at the end of the last day of the 24th month after the month of the date of examination shown on the certificate, for operations requiring only a private or student pilot certificate.

(c) A third-class medical certificate expires at the end of the last day of the 24th month after the date of examination shown on the certificate, for operations requiring a private or student pilot certificate.

---

3. Assume you were issued a Third-Class Medical Certificate 15 months ago. To act as pilot in command, this medical certificate
   (a) Has expired, therefore you cannot act as pilot in command, but you can serve as a crewmember.
   (b) Is current and can be used to exercise all the privileges of a private pilot.
   (c) Has expired, and you cannot exercise the privileges of a private pilot.
   (d) Is current but limits your flights to solo only.

61.25 Change of name

An application for the change of a name on a certificate issued under this Part must be accompanied by the applicant's current certificate and a copy of the marriage license, court order, or other document verifying the change. The documents are returned to the applicant after inspection.

61.27 Voluntary surrender or exchange of certificate

(a) The holder of a certificate issued under this Part may voluntarily surrender it for cancellation, or for the issue of a certificate of lower grade, or another certificate with specific ratings deleted. If he so requests, he must include the following signed statement or its equivalent:

   (1) This request is made for my own reasons, with full knowledge that my [insert name of certificate or rating, as appropriate] may not be reissued to me unless I again pass the tests prescribed for its issue.

61.29 Replacement of lost or destroyed certificate

(a) An application for the replacement of a lost or destroyed airman certificate issued under this Part is made by letter to the Department of Transportation, Federal Aviation Administration, Airman Certification Branch, P.O. Box 25082, Oklahoma City, Oklahoma 73125. The letter must

   (1) State the name of the person to whom the certificate was issued, the permanent mailing address (including zip code), social security number (if any), date and place of birth of the certificate holder, and any available information regarding the grade, number, and date of issue of the certificate, and the ratings on it; and

   (2) Be accompanied by a check or money order for $2.00, payable to the Federal Aviation Administration.

(b) An application for the replacement of a lost or destroyed medical certificate is made by letter to the Department of Transportation, Federal Aviation Administration, Aeromedical Certification Branch, P.O. Box 25082, Oklahoma City, Oklahoma 73125, accompanied by a check or money order for $2.00.

(c) A person who has lost a certificate issued under this Part, or a medical certificate issued under Part 67 of this chapter, or both, may obtain a telegram from the FAA confirming that it was issued. The telegram may be carried as a certificate for a period not to exceed 60 days pending his receipt of a duplicate certificate under paragraph (a) or (b) of this section, unless he has been notified that the certificate has been suspended or revoked. The request for such a telegram may be made by letter or prepaid telegram, including the date upon which a duplicate certificate was previously requested, if a request had been made, and a money order for the cost of the duplicate certificate. The request for a telegraphic certificate is sent to the office listed in paragraph (a) or (b) of this section, as appropriate. However, a request for both airman and medical certificates at the same time must be sent to the office prescribed in paragraph (a) of this section.

61.31 General limitations

(a) *Type ratings required*. A person may not act as pilot in command of any of the following aircraft unless he holds a type rating for that aircraft:

    (1) A large aircraft (except lighter-than-air).

    (2) A helicopter, for operations requiring an airline transport pilot certificate.

    (3) A turbojet-powered airplane.

    (4) Other aircraft specified by the Administrator through aircraft type certificate procedures.

(b) *Authorization in lieu of a type rating.*

    (1) In lieu of a type rating required under subparagraphs (a)(1), (3), and (4) of this section, an aircraft may be operated under an authorization issued by the Administrator, for a flight or series of flights within the United States, if

        (i) The particular operation for which the authorization is requested involves a ferry flight, a practice or training flight, a flight test for a pilot type rating, or a test flight of an aircraft, for a period that does not exceed 60 days;

        (ii) The applicant shows that compliance with paragraph (a) of this section is impracticable for the particular operation; and

        (iii) The Administrator finds that an equivalent level of safety may be achieved through operating limitations on the authorization.

    (2) Aircraft operated under an authorization issued under this paragraph

        (i) May not be operated for compensation or hire; and

        (ii) May carry only flight crewmembers necessary for the flight.

    (3) An authorization issued under this paragraph may be reissued for an additional 60-day period for the same operation if the applicant shows that he was prevented from carrying out the purpose of the particular operation before his authorization expired.

The prohibition of subparagraph (2)(i) does not prohibit compensation for the use of an aircraft by a pilot solely to prepare for or take a flight test for a type rating.

(c) *Category and class rating: Carrying another person or operating for compensation or hire*. Unless he holds a category and class rating for that aircraft, a person may not act as pilot in command of an aircraft that is carrying another person or is operated for compensation or hire. In addition, he may not act as pilot in command of that aircraft for compensation or hire.

(d) *Category and class rating: Other operations.* No person may act as pilot in command of an aircraft in solo flight in operations not subject to paragraph (c) of this section, unless he meets at least one of the following:

(1) He holds a category and class rating appropriate to that aircraft.

(2) He has received flight instruction in the pilot operations required by this Part, appropriate to the category and class of aircraft for first solo, given to him by a certificated flight instructor who found him competent to solo that category and class of aircraft and has so endorsed his pilot logbook.

(3) He has soloed and logged pilot-in-command time in that category and class of aircraft before November 1, 1973.

(e) *High performance airplanes.* A person holding a private or commercial pilot certificate may not act as pilot in command of an airplane that has more than 200 horsepower, or that has a retractable landing gear, flaps, and a controllable propeller unless he has received flight instruction from an authorized flight instructor who has certified in his logbook that he is competent to pilot an airplane that has more than 200 horsepower, or that has a retractable landing gear, flaps, and a controllable propeller, as the case may be. However, this instruction is not required if he has logged flight time as pilot in command in high performance airplanes before November 1, 1973.

(f) *Exception.* This section does not require a class rating for gliders or category and class ratings for aircraft that are not type certificated as airplanes, rotorcraft, or lighter-than-air aircraft. In addition, the rating limitations of this section do not apply to

(1) The holder of a student pilot certificate;

(2) The holder of a pilot certificate when operating an aircraft under the authority of an experimental or provisional type certificate;

(3) An applicant when taking a flight test given by the Administrator; or

(4) The holder of a pilot certificate with a lighter-than-air category rating when operating a hot air balloon without an airborne heater.

61.33 Tests: general procedure

Tests prescribed by or under this Part are given at times and places and by persons designated by the Administrator.

61.35 Written test: prerequisites and passing grades

(a) An applicant for a written test must

(1) Show that he has satisfactorily completed the ground instruction or home study course required by this Part for the certificate or rating sought;

(2) Present as personal identification an airman certificate, driver's license, or other official document; and

(3) Present a birth certificate or other official document showing that he meets the age requirement prescribed in this Part for the certificate sought not later than 2 years from the date of application for the test.

(b) The minimum passing grade is specified by the Administrator on each written test sheet or booklet furnished to the applicant. This section does not apply to the written test for an airline transport pilot certificate or a rating associated with that certificate.

61.37 Written tests: cheating or other unauthorized conduct

(a) Except as authorized by the Administrator, no person may

(1) Copy, or intentionally remove, a written test under this Part;

(2) Give to another, or receive from another, any part or copy of that test;

(3) Give help on that test to, or receive help on that test from, any person during the period that test is being given;

(4) Take any part of that test in behalf of another person;

(5) Use any material or aid during the period that test is being given;

(6) Intentionally cause, assist, or participate in any act prohibited by this paragraph.

(b) No person whom the Administrator finds to have committed an act prohibited by paragraph (a) of this section is eligible for any airman or ground instructor certificate or rating, or to take any test therefor, under this chapter for a period of 1 year after the date of that act. In addition, the commission of that act is a basis for suspending or revoking any airman or ground instructor certificate or rating held by that person.

61.39 Prerequisites for flight tests

(a) To be eligible for a flight test for a certificate, or an aircraft or instrument rating issued under this Part, the applicant must

(1) Have passed any required written test since the beginning of the 24th month before the month in which he takes the flight test;

(2) Have the applicable instruction and aeronautical experience prescribed in this Part;

(3) Hold a current medical certificate appropriate to the certificate he seeks or, in the case of a rating to be added to his pilot certificate, at least a third-class medical certificate issued since the beginning of the 24th month before the month in which he takes the flight test;

(4) Except for a flight test for an airline transport pilot certificate, meet the age requirement for the issuance of the certificate or rating he seeks; and

(5) Have a written statement from an appropriately certificated flight instructor certifying that he has given the applicant flight instruction in preparation for the flight test within 60 days preceding the date of application, and finds him competent to pass the test and to have satisfactory knowledge of the subject areas in which he is shown to be deficient by his FAA airman written test report. However, an applicant need not have this written statement if he

(i)   Holds a foreign pilot license issued by a contracting State to the Convention on International Civil Aviation that authorizes at least the pilot privileges of the airman certificate sought by him;

(ii) Is applying for a type rating only, or a class rating with an associated type rating; or

(iii) Is applying for an airline transport pilot certificate or an additional aircraft rating on that certificate.

61.41 Flight instruction received from flight instructors not certificated by FAA

Flight instruction may be credited toward the requirements for a pilot certificate or rating issued under this Part if it is received from

(a) An Armed Force of either the United States or a foreign contracting State to the Convention on International Civil Aviation in a program for training military pilots; or

(b) A flight instructor who is authorized to give that flight instruction by the licensing authority of a foreign contracting State to the Convention on International Civil Aviation and the flight instruction is given outside the United States.

61.43 Flight tests: general procedures

(a) The ability of an applicant for a private or commercial pilot certificate, or for an aircraft or instrument rating on that certificate to perform the required pilot operations is based on the following:

(1) Executing procedures and maneuvers within the aircraft's performance capabilities and limitations, including use of the aircraft's systems.

(2) Executing emergency procedures and maneuvers appropriate to the aircraft.

(3) Piloting the aircraft with smoothness and accuracy.

(4) Exercising judgment.

(5) Applying his aeronautical knowledge.

(6) Showing that he is the master of the aircraft, with the successful outcome of a procedure or maneuver never seriously in doubt.

(b) If the applicant fails any of the required pilot operations in accordance with the applicable provisions of paragraph (a) of this section, the applicant fails the flight test. The applicant is not eligible for the certificate or rating sought until he passes any pilot operations he has failed.

(c) The examiner or the applicant may discontinue the test at any time when the failure of a required pilot operation makes the applicant ineligible for the certificate or rating sought. If the test is discontinued, the applicant is entitled to credit for only those entire pilot operations that he has successfully performed.

61.45 Flight tests: required aircraft and equipment

(a) *General*. An applicant for a certificate or rating under this Part must furnish, for each flight test that he is required to take, an appropriate aircraft of United States registry that has a current standard or limited airworthiness certificate. However, the applicant may, at the discretion of the inspector or examiner conducting the test, furnish an aircraft of U.S. registry that has a current airworthiness certificate other than standard or limited, an aircraft of foreign registry that is properly certificated by the country of registry, or a military aircraft in an operational status if its use is allowed by an appropriate military authority.

(b) *Required equipment (other than controls)*. Aircraft furnished for a flight test must have

(1) The equipment for each pilot operation required for the flight test;

(2) No prescribed operating limitations that prohibit its use in any pilot operation required on the test;

(3) Pilot seats with adequate visibility for each pilot to operate the aircraft safely, except as provided in paragraph (d) of this section; and

(4) Cockpit and outside visibility adequate to evaluate the performance of the applicant, where an additional jump seat is provided for the examiner.

(c) *Required controls*. An aircraft (other than lighter-than-air) furnished under paragraph (a) of this section for any pilot flight test must have engine power controls and flight controls that are easily reached and operable in a normal manner by both pilots, unless after considering all the factors, the examiner determines that the flight test can be conducted safely without them. However, an aircraft having other controls such as nose-wheel steering, brakes, switches, fuel selectors, and engine air flow controls that are not easily reached and operable in a normal manner by both pilots may be used, if more than one pilot is required under its airworthiness certificate, or if the examiner determines that the flight can be conducted safely.

(d) *Simulated instrument flight equipment*. An applicant for any flight test involving flight maneuvers solely by reference to instruments must furnish equipment satisfactory to the examiner that excludes the visual reference of the applicant outside of the aircraft.

This requirement refers to a lightweight view-limiting hood [something like a bookkeeper's visor with an extended eye shade] worn by the pilot to simulate instrument meteorological conditions.

(e) *Aircraft with single controls*. At the discretion of the examiner, an aircraft furnished under paragraph (a) of this section for a flight test may, in the cases listed herein, have a single set of controls. In such case, the examiner determines the competence of the applicant by observation from the ground or from another aircraft.

(1) A flight test for addition of a class or type rating, not involving demonstration of instrument skills, to a private or commercial pilot certificate.

61.47 Flight tests: status of FAA inspectors and other authorized flight examiners

An FAA inspector or other authorized flight examiner conducts the flight test of an applicant for a pilot certificate or rating for the purpose of observing the applicant's ability to perform satisfactorily the procedures and maneuvers on the flight test. The inspector or other examiner is not pilot in command of the aircraft during the flight test unless he acts in that capacity for the flight, or portion of the flight, by prior arrangement with the applicant or other person who would otherwise act as pilot in command of the flight, or portion of the flight. Notwithstanding the type of aircraft used during a flight test, the applicant and the inspector or other examiner are not, with respect to each other (or other occupants authorized by the inspector or other examiner), subject to the requirements or limitations for the carriage of passengers specified in this chapter.

61.49 Retesting after failure

An applicant for a written or flight test who fails that test may not apply for retesting until after 30 days after the date he failed the test. However, in the case of his first failure he may apply for retesting before the 30 days have expired upon presenting a written statement from an authorized instructor certifying that he has given flight or ground instruction as appropriate to the applicant and finds him competent to pass the test.

61.51 Pilot logbooks

(a) The aeronautical training and experience used to meet the requirements for a certificate or rating, or the recent flight experience requirements of the Part must be shown by a reliable record. The logging of other flight time is not required.

(b) *Logbook entries.* Each pilot shall enter the following information for each flight or lesson logged:

    (1) *General.*
        (i)   Date.
        (ii)   Total time of flight.
        (iii) Place, or points of departure and arrival.
        (iv) Type and identification of aircraft.
    (2) *Type of pilot experience or training.*
        (i)   Pilot in command or solo.
        (ii)   Second in command.
        (iii) Flight instruction received from an authorized flight instructor.
        (iv) Instrument flight instruction from an authorized flight instructor.
        (v)   Pilot ground trainer instruction.
        (vi) Participating crew (lighter-than-air).
        (vii) Other pilot time.
    (3) *Conditions of flight.*
        (i)   Day or night.
        (ii)   Actual instrument.
        (iii) Simulated instrument conditions.

(c) *Logging of pilot time*

    (1) *Solo flight time.* A pilot may log as solo flight time only that flight time when he is the sole occupant of the aircraft. However, a student pilot may also log as solo flight time that time during which he acts as

the pilot in command of an airship requiring more than one flight crewmember.

(2) *Pilot in command flight time*

(i)   A private or commercial pilot may log as pilot in command time only that flight time during which he is the sole manipulator of the controls of an aircraft for which he is rated, or when he is the sole occupant of the aircraft, or when he acts as pilot in command of an aircraft on which more than one pilot is required under the type certification of the aircraft, or the regulations under which the flight is conducted.

(ii)   A certificated flight instructor may log as pilot in command time all flight time during which he acts as a flight instructor.

(3) *Second-in-command flight time*. A pilot may log as second-in-command time all flight time during which he acts as second in command of an aircraft on which more than one pilot is required under the type certification of the aircraft, or the regulations under which the flight is conducted.

(4) *Instrument flight time*. A pilot may log as instrument flight time only that time during which he operates the aircraft solely by reference to instruments, under actual or simulated instrument flight conditions. Each entry must include the place and type of each instrument approach completed, and the name of the safety pilot for each simulated instrument flight. An instrument flight instructor may log as instrument time that time during which he acts as instrument flight instructor in actual instrument weather conditions.

(5) *Instruction time*. All time logged as flight instruction, instrument flight instruction, pilot ground trainer instruction, or ground instruction time must be certified by the appropriately rated and certificated instructor from whom it was received.

(d) *Presentation of logbook*

(1)   A pilot must present his logbook (or other record required by this section) for inspection upon reasonable request by the Administrator, an authorized representative of the National Transportation Safety Board, or any State or local law enforcement officer.

(2)   A student pilot must carry his logbook (or other record required by this section) with him on all solo cross-country flights, as evidence of the required instructor clearances and endorsements.

61.53 Operations during medical deficiency

No person may act as pilot in command, or in any other capacity as a required pilot flight crewmember while he has a known medical deficiency, or increase of a known medical deficiency, that would make him unable to meet the requirements for his current medical certificate.

61.57 Recent flight experience: Pilot in command

(a) *Flight review*. After November 1, 1974, no person may act as pilot in command of an aircraft unless, within the preceding 24 calendar months, he has

(1) Accomplished a flight review given to him, in an aircraft for which he is rated, by an appropriately certificated instructor or other person designated by the Administrator; and

(2) Had his logbook endorsed by the person who gave him the review certifying that he has satisfactorily accomplished the flight review.

However, a person who has, within the preceding 24 months, satisfactorily completed a pilot proficiency check conducted by the FAA, an approved pilot check airman or a U.S. Armed Force for a pilot certificate, rating, or operating privilege, need not accomplish the flight review required by this section.

(b) *Meaning of flight review.* As used in this section, a flight review consists of

(1) A review of the current general operating and flight rules of Part 91 of this chapter, and

(2) A review of those maneuvers and procedures which in the discretion of the person giving the review are necessary for the pilot to demonstrate that he can safely exercise the privileges of his pilot certificate.

(c) *General experience.* No person may act as pilot in command of an aircraft carrying passengers, nor of an aircraft certificated for more than one required pilot flight crewmember, unless within the preceding 90 days, he has made three takeoffs and three landings as the sole manipulator of the flight controls in an aircraft of the same category and class and, if a type rating is required, of the same type. If the aircraft is a tailwheel airplane, the landings must have been made to a full stop in a tailwheel airplane. For the purpose of meeting the requirements of the paragraph, a person may act as pilot in command of a flight under day VFR or day IFR if no person or property other than as necessary for his compliance thereunder, are carried. This paragraph does not apply to operations requiring an airline transport pilot certificate, or to operations conducted under Part 135 of this chapter.

(d) *Night experience.* No person may act as pilot in command of an aircraft carrying passengers during the period beginning 1 hour after sunset and ending 1 hour before sunrise (as published in the *American Air Almanac*) unless, within the preceding 90 days, he has made at least three takeoffs and three landings to a full stop during that period in the category and class of aircraft to be used. This paragraph does not apply to operations requiring an airline transport pilot certificate.

61.59 Falsification, reproduction or alteration of applications, certificates, logbooks, reports, or records

(a) No person may make or cause to be made

(1) Any fraudulent or intentionally false statement on any application for a certificate, rating, or duplicate thereof, issued under this Part;

(2) Any fraudulent or intentionally false entry in any logbook, record, or report that is required to be kept, made, or used, to show compliance with any requirement for the issuance, or exercise of the privileges, or any certificate or rating under this Part;

4. To act as pilot in command of a single-engine nosewheel-equipped airplane, regulations require recent experience before carrying passengers. To meet this requirement you must, within the preceding

(a) 60 days, have made at least three takeoffs and three landings to a full stop in any single-engine airplane.

(b) 90 days, have made at least three takeoffs and three landings to a full stop in an aircraft of the same category, class, and type as the one you will be flying.

(c) 90 days, have made at least three takeoffs and three landings in an aircraft of the same category and class as the one you will be flying.

(d) 60 days, have made at least five takeoffs and five landings to a full stop in an aircraft of the same category as the one you will be flying.

5. If official sunset is 1830 MST and you do not meet the recency of experience requirements for a night flight carrying passengers, you must land at or before what time to comply with regulations?

(a) 1730 MST.

(b) 1830 MST.

(c) 1800 MST.

(d) 1930 MST.

6. Assume that your Private Pilot Certificate was issued on March 15, 1988. Unless you complete a proficiency check for another pilot certificate, rating, or operating privilege, to act as pilot in command of an aircraft you will be due for a flight review no later than

(a) March 15, 1989.

(b) March 31, 1990.

(c) March 31, 1989.

(d) March 15, 1990.

(3) Any reproduction, for fraudulent purpose, of any certificate or rating under this Part; or

(4) Any alteration of any certificate or rating under this Part.

(b) The commission by any person of an act prohibited under paragraph (a) of this section is a basis for suspending or revoking any airman or ground instructor certificate or rating held by that person.

61.60 Change of address

The holder of a pilot or flight instructor certificate who has made a change in his permanent mailing address may not, after 30 days from the date he moved, exercise the privileges of his certificate unless he has notified in writing the Department of Transportation, Federal Aviation Administration, Airman Certification Branch, Box 25082, Oklahoma City, OK 73125, of his new address.

---

7. If you have made a change in your permanent mailing address, you may not exercise the privileges of your pilot certificate after 30 days from the date you moved unless you

(a) Forward your certificate to the FAA Airman Certification Branch and request reissuance.

(b) Forward your certificate to the local General Aviation District Office (GADO) for a change of address.

(c) Notify the FAA Airman Certification Branch in writing of your change of address.

(d) Request your local General Aviation District Office (GADO) to issue you a temporary pilot certificate.

Subpart B—Aircraft Ratings and Special Certificates

61.61 Applicability

This subpart prescribes the requirements for the issuance of additional aircraft ratings after a pilot or instructor certificate is issued, and the requirements and limitations for special pilot certificates and ratings issued by the Administrator.

61.63 Additional aircraft ratings (other than airline transport pilot)

(a) *General*. To be eligible for an aircraft rating after his certificate is issued to him, an applicant must meet the requirements of paragraphs (b) through (d) of this section, as appropriate to the rating sought.

(b) *Category rating*. An applicant for a category rating to be added on his pilot certificate must meet the requirements of this Part for the issue of the pilot certificate appropriate to the privileges for which the category rating is sought. However, the holder of a category rating for powered aircraft is not required to take a written test for the addition of a category rating on his pilot certificate.

(c) *Class rating*. An applicant for an aircraft class rating to be added on his pilot certificate must

(1) Present a logbook record certified by an authorized flight instructor showing that the applicant has received flight instruction in the class of aircraft for which a rating is sought and has been found competent in the pilot operations appropriate to the pilot certificate to which his category rating applies; and

(2) Pass a flight test appropriate to his pilot certificate and applicable to the aircraft category and class rating sought.

A person who holds a lighter-than-air category rating with a free balloon class rating, who seeks an airship class rating, must meet the requirements of paragraph (b) of this section as though seeking a lighter-than-air category rating.

(d) *Type rating*. An applicant for a type rating to be added on his pilot certificate must meet the following requirements:

(1) He must hold, or concurrently obtain, an instrument rating appropriate to the aircraft for which a type rating is sought.

(2) He must pass a flight test showing competence in pilot operations appropriate to the pilot certificate he holds and to the type rating sought.

(3) He must pass a flight test showing competence in pilot operations under instrument flight rules in an aircraft of the type for which the type rating is sought or, in the case of a single pilot station airplane, meet the requirements of subdivision (i) or (ii) of this subparagraph, whichever is applicable.

(i)   The applicant must have met the requirements of this subparagraph in a multiengine airplane for which the type rating is required.

(ii)   If he does not meet the requirements of subdivision (i) of this subparagraph and he seeks a type rating for a single-engine airplane, he must meet the requirements of this subparagraph in either a single or multiengine airplane, and have the recent instrument experience set forth in section 61.57(e) of this Part, when he applies for the flight test under subparagraph (2) of this paragraph.

(4) An applicant who does not meet the requirements of subparagraphs (1) and (3) of this paragraph may only obtain a type rating limited to "VFR only." Upon meeting these instrument requirements or the requirements of section 61.73(e)(2), the "VFR only" limitation may be removed for the particular type of aircraft in which competence is shown.

(5) When an instrument rating is issued to the holder of one or more type ratings, the type ratings on the amended certificate bear the limitation described in subparagraph (4) for each airplane type rating for which he has not shown his instrument competency under this paragraph.

61.69 Glider towing: experience and instruction requirements

No person may act as pilot in command of an aircraft towing a glider unless he meets the following requirements:

(a) He holds a current pilot certificate (other than a student pilot certificate) issued under this Part.

(b) He has an endorsement in his pilot logbook from a person authorized to give flight instruction in gliders, certifying that he has received ground and flight instruction in gliders and is familiar with the techniques and procedures essential to the safe towing of gliders, including airspeed limitations, emergency procedures, signals used, and maximum angles of bank.

(c) He has made and entered in his pilot logbook

(1) At least three flights as sole manipulator of the controls of an aircraft towing a glider while accompanied by a pilot who has met the requirements of this section and made and logged at least 10 flights as pilot in command of an aircraft towing a glider; or

(2) At least three flights as sole manipulator of the controls of an aircraft simulating towing flight procedures (while accompanied by a

pilot who meets the requirements of this section), and at least three flights as pilot or observer in a glider being towed by an aircraft.

(d) If he holds only a private pilot certificate he must have had, and entered his pilot logbook at least

(1) 100 hours of pilot flight time in powered aircraft; or

(2) 200 total hours of pilot flight time in powered or other aircraft.

(e) Within the preceding 12 months he has

(1) Made at least 3 actual or simulated glider tows while accompanied by a qualified pilot who meets the requirements of this section; or

(2) Made at least 3 flights as pilot in command of a glider towed by an aircraft.

61.71 Graduates of certificated flying schools: Special rules

(a) A graduate of a flying school that is certificated under Part 141 of this chapter is considered to meet the applicable aeronautical experience requirements of this Part if he presents an appropriate graduation certificate within 60 days after the date he is graduated. However, if he applies for a flight test for an instrument rating, he must hold a commercial pilot certificate, or hold a private pilot certificate and meet the requirements of sections 61.65(e)(1) and 61.123 (except paragraphs (d) and (e) thereof). In addition, if he applies for a flight instructor certificate, he must hold a commercial pilot certificate.

(b) An applicant for a certificate or rating under this Part is considered to meet the aeronautical knowledge and skill requirements, or both, applicable to that certificate or rating, if he applies within 90 days after graduation from an appropriate course given by a flying school that is certificated under Part 141 of this chapter and is authorized to test applicants on aeronautical knowledge or skill, or both.

61.73 Military pilots or former military pilots: Special rules

(a) *General*. A rated military pilot or former rated military pilot who applies for a private or commercial pilot certificate, or an aircraft or instrument rating, is entitled to that certificate with appropriate ratings or to the addition of a rating on the pilot certificate he holds, if he meets the applicable requirements of this section. This section does not apply to a military pilot or former military pilot who has been removed from flying status for lack of proficiency or because of disciplinary action involving aircraft operation.

This section delineates the circumstances under which military pilots or former military pilots may be given credit for instruction received and flight time logged in the U.S. Armed Forces.

61.75 Pilot certificate issued on the basis of a foreign pilot license

(a) *Purpose*. The holder of a current private, commercial, senior commercial, or airline transport pilot license issued by a foreign contracting State to the Convention on International Civil Aviation may apply for a pilot certificate under this section authorizing him to act as pilot of a civil aircraft of U.S. registry.

Subpart C—Student Pilots

61.81 Applicability

This subpart prescribes the requirements for the issuance of student pilot certificates, the conditions under which those certificates are necessary, and the general operating rules for the holders of those certificates.

61.83 Eligibility requirements: general

To be eligible for a student pilot certificate, a person must

(a) Be at least 16 years of age, or at least 14 years of age for a student pilot certificate limited to the operation of a glider or free balloon;

(b) Be able to read, speak, and understand the English language, or have such operating limitations placed on his pilot certificate as are necessary for the safe operation of aircraft, to be removed when he shows that he can read, speak, and understand the English language; and

(c) Hold at least a current third-class medical certificate issued under Part 67 of this chapter, or, in the case of glider or free balloon operations, certify that he has no known medical defect that makes him unable to pilot a glider or a free balloon.

61.85 Application

An application for a student pilot certificate is made on a form and in a manner provided by the Administrator and is submitted to

(a) A designated aviation medical examiner when applying for an FAA medical certificate; or

(b) An FAA operations inspector or designated pilot examiner, accompanied by a current FAA medical certificate, or in the case of an application for a glider or free balloon pilot certificate, it may be accompanied by a certification by the applicant that he has no known medical defect that makes him unable to pilot a glider or free balloon.

61.87 Requirements for solo flight

(a) *General*. A student pilot may not operate an aircraft in solo flight until he has complied with the requirements of this section. As used in this subpart, the term *solo flight* means that flight time during which a student pilot is the sole occupant of the aircraft, or that flight time during which he acts as pilot in command of an airship requiring more than one flight crewmember.

(b) *Aeronautical knowledge*. He must have demonstrated to an authorized instructor that he is familiar with the flight rules of Part 91 of this chapter which are pertinent to student solo flights.

(c) *Flight proficiency training*. He must have received ground and flight instruction in at least the following procedures and operations:

    (1) *In airplanes*

        (i)   Flight preparation procedures, including preflight inspection and power plant operation;

        (ii) Ground maneuvering and runups;

        (iii) Straight and level flight, climbs, turns, and descents;

(iv) Flight at minimum controllable airspeeds, and stall recognition and recovery;

(v) Normal takeoffs and landings;

(vi) Airport traffic patterns, including collision avoidance precautions and wake turbulence; and

(vii) Emergencies, including elementary emergency landings.

Instruction must be given by a flight instructor who is authorized to give instruction in airplanes.

(d) *Flight instructor endorsements.* A student pilot may not operate an aircraft in solo flight unless the student pilot certificate is endorsed, and unless within the preceding 90 days the pilot logbook has been endorsed by an authorized flight instructor who

(1) Has given him instruction in the make and model of aircraft in which the solo flight is made;

(2) Finds that he has met the requirements of this section; and

(3) Finds that he is competent to make a safe solo flight in that aircraft.

61.89 General limitations

(a) A student pilot may not act as pilot in command of an aircraft

(1) That is carrying a passenger;

(2) That is carrying property for compensation or hire;

(3) For compensation or hire;

(4) In furtherance of a business; or

(5) On an international flight, except that a student pilot may make solo training flights from Haines, Gustavus, or Juneau, Alaska, to White Horse, Yukon, Canada, and return, over the province of British Columbia.

(b) A student pilot may not act as a required pilot flight crewmember on any aircraft for which more than one pilot is required, except when receiving flight instruction from an authorized flight instructor on board an airship and no person other than a required flight crewmember is carried on the aircraft.

61.91 Aircraft limitations: pilot in command

A student may not serve as pilot in command of any airship requiring more than one flight crewmember unless he has met the pertinent requirements prescribed in section 61.87.

61.93 Cross-country flight requirements

(a) *General.* A student pilot may not operate an aircraft in a solo cross-country flight, nor may he, except in emergency, make a solo flight landing at any point other than the airport of takeoff, until he meets the requirements prescribed in this section. However, an authorized flight instructor may allow a student pilot to practice solo landings and takeoffs at another airport within 25 nautical miles from the airport at which the student pilot receives instruction if he finds that the student pilot is competent to make those landings and takeoffs. As used in this section the term *cross-country flight* means a flight beyond a radius of 25 nautical miles from the point of takeoff.

(b) *Flight training.* A student pilot must receive instruction from an authorized instructor in at least the following pilot operations pertinent to the aircraft to be operated in a solo cross-country flight:

> (1) For solo cross-country in airplanes
>
>> (i)   The use of aeronautical charts, pilotage, and elementary dead reckoning using the magnetic compass;
>>
>> (ii)   The use of radio for VFR navigation and for two-way communication;
>>
>> (iii)   Control of an airplane by reference to flight instruments;
>>
>> (iv)   Short field and soft field procedures, and crosswind takeoffs and landings;
>>
>> (v)   Recognition of critical weather situations, estimating visibility while in flight, and the procurement and use of aeronautical weather reports and forecasts; and
>>
>> (vi)   Cross-country emergency procedures.

(c) *Flight instructor endorsements.* A student pilot must have the following endorsements from an authorized flight instructor:

> (1) An endorsement on his student pilot certificate stating that he has received instruction in solo cross-country flying and the applicable training requirements of this section and is competent to make cross-country solo flights in the category of aircraft involved.
>
> (2) An endorsement in his pilot logbook that the instructor has reviewed the preflight planning and preparation for each solo cross-country flight, and he is prepared to make the flight safely under the known circumstances and the conditions listed by the instructor in the logbook. The instructor may also endorse the logbook for repeated solo cross-country flights under stipulated conditions over a course not more than 50 nautical miles from the point of departure if he has given the student flight instruction in both directions over the route, including takeoffs and landings at the airports to be used.

Subpart D—Private Pilots

61.101 Applicability
This subpart prescribes the requirements for the issuance of private pilot certificates and ratings, the conditions under which those certificates and ratings are necessary, and the general operating rules for recipients.

61.103 Eligibility requirements: general
To be eligible for a private pilot certificate, a person must
(a) Be at least 17 years of age, except that a private pilot certificate with a free balloon or a glider rating only may be issued to a qualified applicant who is at least 16 years of age;
(b) Be able to read, speak, and understand the English language, or have such operating limitations placed on his pilot certificate as are necessary for the safe operation of aircraft, to be removed when he shows that he can read, speak, and understand the English language;
(c) Hold at least a current third-class medical certificate issued under Part 67 of this chapter, or, in the case of a glider or free balloon rating, certify

that he has no known medical defect that makes him unable to pilot a glider or free balloon, as appropriate;

(d) Pass a written test on the subject areas on which instruction or home study is required by section 61.105;

(e) Pass an oral and flight test on procedures and maneuvers selected by an FAA inspector or examiner to determine the applicant's competency in the flight operations on which instruction is required by the flight proficiency provisions of section 61.107; and

(f) Comply with the sections of this Part that apply to the rating he seeks.

61.105 Aeronautical knowledge

An applicant for a private pilot certificate must have logged ground instruction from an authorized instructor, or must present evidence showing that he has satisfactorily completed a course of instruction or home study in at least the following areas of aeronautical knowledge appropriate to the category of aircraft for which a rating is sought.

(a) *Airplanes*

(1) The Federal Aviation Regulations applicable to private pilot privileges, limitations, and flight operations, accident reporting requirements of the National Transportation Safety Board, and the use of the *Airman's Information Manual* and the FAA Advisory Circulars;

(2) VFR navigation, using pilotage, dead reckoning, and radio aids;

(3) The recognition of critical weather situations from the ground and in flight and the procurement and use of aeronautical weather reports and forecasts; and

(4) The safe and efficient operation of airplanes, including high density airport operations, collision avoidance precautions, and radio communication procedures.

61.107 Flight proficiency

The applicant for a private pilot certificate must have logged instruction from an authorized flight instructor in at least the following pilot operations. In addition, his logbook must contain an endorsement by an authorized flight instructor who has found him competent to perform each of those operations safely as a private pilot.

(a) *In airplanes*

(1) Preflight operations, including weight and balance determination, line inspection, and airplane servicing;

(2) Airport and traffic pattern operations, including operations at controlled airports, radio communications, and collision avoidance precautions;

(3) Flight maneuvering by reference to ground objects;

(4) Flight at critically slow airspeeds, and the recognition of and recovery from imminent and full stalls entered from straight flight and from turns;

(5) Normal and crosswind takeoffs and landings;

(6) Control and maneuvering an airplane solely by reference to instruments, including descents and climbs using radio aids or radar directives;

(7) Cross-country flying, using pilotage, dead reckoning, and radio aids, including one 2-hour flight;

(8) Maximum performance takeoffs and landings;

(9) Night flying, including takeoffs, landings, and VFR navigation; and

(10) Emergency operations, including simulated aircraft and equipment malfunctions.

61.109 Airplane rating: aeronautical experience

An applicant for a private pilot certificate with an airplane rating must have had at least a total of 40 hours of flight instruction and solo flight time which must include the following:

(a) Twenty hours of flight instruction from an authorized flight instructor, including at least

(1) Three hours of cross-country;

(2) Three hours at night, including 10 takeoffs and landings for applicants seeking night flying privileges; and

(3) Three hours in airplanes in preparation for the private pilot flight test within 60 days prior to that test.

An applicant who does not meet the night flying requirements in paragraph (a)(2) is issued a private pilot certificate bearing the limitation "Night flying prohibited." This limitation may be removed if the holder of the certificate shows that he has met the requirements of paragraph (a)(2).

(b) Twenty hours of solo flight time, including at least

(1) Ten hours in airplanes;

(2) Ten hours of cross-country flights, each flight with a landing more than 50 nautical miles from the original departure point. One flight must be at least 300 nautical miles with landings at a minimum of three points, one of which is at least 100 nautical miles from the original departure point; and

(3) Three solo takeoffs and landings to a full stop at an airport with an operating control tower.

61.111 Cross-country flights: pilots based on small islands

(a) An applicant who shows that he is located on an island from which the required flights cannot be accomplished without flying over water more than 10 nautical miles from the nearest shoreline need not comply with paragraph (b)(2) of section 61.109. However, if other airports that permit civil operations are available to which a flight may be made without flying over water more than 10 nautical miles from the nearest shoreline, he must show that he has completed two round trip solo flights between those two airports that are farthest apart, including a landing at each airport on both flights.

(b) The pilot certificate issued to a person under paragraph (a) of this section contains an endorsement with the following limitation which may be subsequently amended to include another island if the applicant complies with paragraph (a) of this section with respect to that island:

Passenger carrying prohibited on flights more than 10 nautical miles from [appropriate island].

(c) If an applicant for a private pilot certificate under paragraph (a) of this section does not have at least 3 hours of solo cross-country flight time, including a round trip flight to an airport at least 50 nautical miles from the place of departure with at least two full-stop landings at different points along the route, his pilot certificate is also endorsed as follows:

Holder does not meet the cross-country flight requirement of ICAO.

(d) The holder of a private pilot certificate with an endorsement described in paragraph (b) or (c) of this section, is entitled to a removal of the endorsement, if he presents satisfactory evidence to an FAA inspector or designated pilot examiner that he has complied with the applicable solo cross-country flight requirements and has passed a practical test on cross-country flying.

61.118 Private pilot privileges and limitations: pilot in command

Except as provided in paragraphs (a) through (d) of this section, a private pilot may not act as pilot in command of an aircraft that is carrying passengers or property for compensation or hire; nor may he, for compensation or hire, act as pilot in command of an aircraft.

(a) A private pilot may, for compensation or hire, act as pilot in command of an aircraft in connection with any business or employment if the flight is only incidental to that business or employment and the aircraft does not carry passengers or property for compensation or hire.

(b) A private pilot may share the operating expenses of a flight with his passengers.

(c) A private pilot who is an aircraft salesman and who has at least 200 hours of logged flight time may demonstrate an aircraft in flight to a prospective buyer.

(d) A private pilot may act as pilot in command of an aircraft used in a passenger-carrying airlift sponsored by a charitable organization, and for which the passengers make a donation to the organization, if

(1) The sponsor of the airlift notifies the FAA General Aviation District Office having jurisdiction over the area concerned at least 7 days before the flight and furnishes any essential information that the office requests;

(2) The flight is conducted from a public airport adequate for the aircraft used, or from another airport that has been approved for the operation by an FAA inspector;

(3) He has logged at least 200 hours of flight time;

(4) No acrobatic or formation flights are conducted;

(5) Each aircraft used is certificated in the standard category and complies with the 100-hour inspection requirement of section 91.169 of this chapter; and

(6) The flight is made under VFR during the day.

For the purpose of paragraph (d) of this section, a "charitable organization" means an organization listed in Publication No. 78 of the Department of the Treasury called the "Cumulative List of Organizations described in section 170(c) of the Internal Revenue Code of 1954," as amended from time to time by published supplemental lists.

---

8. Which statement is true regarding private pilot privileges and limitations? A pilot may

   (a) Act as pilot in command of an aircraft carrying property for hire only if the flight is in connection with a business.

   (b) Share the operating expenses of a flight with the passengers.

   (c) Act as pilot in command while demonstrating an aircraft to a prospective buyer if the private pilot has logged at least 100 hours of flight time in the aircraft being shown.

   (d) Act as pilot in command of an aircraft carrying passengers for compensation or hire if the flight is in connection with a business or employment.

61.120 Private pilot privileges and limitations: Second in command of aircraft requiring more than one required pilot

Except as provided in paragraphs (a) through (d) of section 61.118, a private pilot may not, for compensation or hire, act as second in command of an aircraft that is type certificated for more than one required pilot, nor may he act as second in command of such an aircraft that is carrying passengers or property for compensation or hire.

FAR PART 67:
MEDICAL STANDARDS AND CERTIFICATION

In addition to sections 61.3, 61.23, 61.83, and 61.103 in Part 61, Part 67 prescribes the medical standards for issuing medical certificates to pilots. The following section is of particular importance.

67.31 Medical records

Whenever the Administrator finds that additional medical information or history is necessary to determine whether an applicant for or the holder of a medical certificate meets the medical standards for it, he requests that person to furnish that information or authorize any clinic, hospital, doctor, or other person to release to the Administrator any available information or records concerning that history. If the applicant, or holder, refuses to provide the requested medical information or history or to authorize the release so requested, the Administrator may suspend, modify, or revoke any medical certificate that he holds or may, in case of an applicant, refuse to issue a medical certificate to him.

FAR PART 91:
GENERAL OPERATING AND FLIGHT RULES

FAR Part 91 is the FAA's rules of the road for the national airspace and airway system. It contains a considerable amount of information you will use daily as a student or private pilot. It also presents requirements for special operations as well, such as flights between the United States and Mexico or Canada or operations near the presidential party or space-flight recovery areas.

Subpart A deals with specific pilot actions that are allowed or prohibited by the FAA, ranging from limitations on the use of drugs and alcohol to participation in the Aviation Safety Reporting Program.

Subpart B presents pilot's general flight rules—the basis of aircraft operations—and, of particular interest to student and private pilots, the requirements for VFR operations.

Subpart C describes the requirements for maintenance, repairs, and alterations to aircraft, and the documentation for each relevant to pilots, owners, and operators.

While we have included just those regulations of interest to student and private pilots, Part 91 contains other sections detailing instrument flight rules, operation of large or turbine-powered multiengine airplanes, and aircraft operating noise limits. You should consult these sections as required when you study for future ratings.

The following subparts and sections are included in this text:

Subpart A—General

Subpart A—General

91.1 Applicability

(a) Except as provided in paragraph (b) of this section, this Part prescribes rules governing the operation of aircraft (other than moored balloons, kites, unmanned rockets, and unmanned free balloons) within the United States.

(b) Each person operating a civil aircraft of U.S. registry outside of the United States shall

    (1) When over the high seas, comply with Annex 2 (Rules of the Air) to the Convention on International Civil Aviation and with sections 91.70(c) and 91.90 of Subpart B;

    (2) When within a foreign country, comply with the regulations relating to the flight and maneuver of aircraft there in force;

    (3) Except for sections 91.15(b), 91.17, 91.38, and 91.43, comply with Subparts A, C, and D of this Part so far as they are not inconsistent with applicable regulations of the foreign country where the aircraft is operated or Annex 2 to the Convention on International Civil Aviation; and

    (4) When over the North Atlantic within airspace designated as Minimum Navigation Performance Specifications airspace, comply with section 91.20.

(c) Annex 2 to the Convention on International Civil Aviation, Sixth Edition–September 1970, with amendments through Amendment 20 effective August 1976, to which reference is made in this Part is incorporated into this Part and made a part hereof as provided in 5 U.S.C. 552 and pursuant to 1 CFR Part 51. Annex 2 (including a complete historic file of changes thereto) is available for public inspection at the Rules Docket, AGC-24, Federal Aviation Administration, 800 Independence Avenue SW, Washington, D.C. 20591. In addition, Annex 2 may be purchased from the International Civil Aviation Organization (Attention: Distribution Officer), P.O. Box 400, Succursale; Place de L'Aviation Internationale, 1000 Sherbrooke Street West, Montreal, Quebec, Canada H3A 2R2.

91.3 Responsibility and authority of the pilot in command

(a) The pilot in command of an aircraft is directly responsible for, and is the final authority as to, the operation of that aircraft.

(b) In an emergency requiring immediate action, the pilot in command may deviate from any rule of this subpart or of Subpart B to the extent required to meet that emergency.

(c) Each pilot in command who deviates from a rule under paragraph (b) of this section shall, upon the request of the Administrator, send a written report of that deviation to the Administrator.

9. If an inflight emergency requires immediate action, a pilot in command may
   (a) Deviate from Federal Aviation Regulations to the extent required to meet the emergency, but must submit a written report within 24 hours to the Administrator.
   (b) Not deviate from regulations unless permission is obtained from Air Traffic Control.
   (c) Deviate from any rule of Federal Aviation Regulations to the extent required to meet the emergency.
   (d) Not deviate from regulations unless prior to the deviation approval is granted by the Administrator.

91.5 Preflight action

Each pilot in command shall, before beginning a flight, familiarize himself with all available information concerning that flight. This information must include:

(a) For a flight under IFR or a flight not in the vicinity of an airport, weather reports and forecasts, fuel requirements, alternatives available if the planned flight cannot be completed, and any known traffic delays of which he has been advised by ATC.

(b) For any flight, runway lengths at airports of intended use, and the following takeoff and landing distance information:

(1) For civil aircraft for which an approved airplane or rotorcraft flight manual containing takeoff and landing distance data is required, the takeoff and landing distance data contained therein; and

(2) For civil aircraft other than those specified in subparagraph (1) of this paragraph, other reliable information appropriate to the aircraft,

10. In addition to other preflight action for a VFR cross-country flight, regulations specifically require the pilot in command to
    (a) Determine runway lengths at the airports of intended use.
    (b) Check each fuel tank visually to ensure that it is always filled to capacity.
    (c) File a flight plan for the proposed flight.
    (d) Perform a VOR equipment accuracy check prior to the proposed flight.

11. Preflight action as required by regulations for all flights away from the vicinity of an airport shall include a study of the weather, taking into consideration fuel requirements, and
    (a) An alternate course of action if the flight cannot be completed as planned.
    (b) The filing of a flight plan.
    (c) The designation of an alternate airport.
    (d) An operational check of your navigation radios.

relating to aircraft performance under expected values of airport elevation and runway slope, aircraft gross weight, and wind and temperature.

91.7 Flight crewmembers at stations

(a) During takeoff and landing, and while en route, each required flight crewmember shall

(1) Be at his station unless absence is necessary in the performance of his duties in connection with the operation of the aircraft or in connection with his physiological needs; and

(2) Keep his seat belt fastened while at his station.

(b) After July 18, 1978, each required flight crewmember of a U.S. registered civil airplane shall, during takeoff and landing, keep the shoulder harness fastened while at his station. This paragraph does not apply if

(1) the seat at the crewmember's station is not equipped with a shoulder harness; or

(2) the crewmember would be unable to perform his required duties with the shoulder harness fastened.

91.8 Prohibition against interference with crewmembers

No person may assault, threaten, intimidate, or interfere with a crewmember in the performance of the crewmember's duties aboard an aircraft being operated.

91.9 Careless or reckless operation

No person may operate an aircraft in a careless or reckless manner so as to endanger the life or property of another.

91.10 Careless or reckless operation other than for the purpose of air navigation

No person may operate an aircraft other than for the purpose of air navigation on any part of the surface of an airport used by aircraft for air commerce (including areas used by those aircraft for receiving or discharging persons or cargo), in a careless or reckless manner so as to endanger the life or property of another.

91.11 Liquor and drugs

(a) No person may act as a crewmember of a civil aircraft

(1) Within 8 hours after the consumption of any alcoholic beverage;

(2) While under the influence of alcohol; or

(3) While using any drug that affects his faculties in any way contrary to safety; or

(4) While having .04 percent by weight or more alcohol in the blood.

(b) Except in an emergency, no pilot of a civil aircraft may allow a person who is obviously under the influence of intoxicating liquors or drugs (except a medical patient under proper care) to be carried in that aircraft.

(c) A crewmember shall do the following:

(1) On request of a law enforcement officer, submit to a test to indicate the percentage by weight of alcohol in the blood, when

(i) The law enforcement officer is authorized under State or local law to conduct the test or to have the test conducted; and

(ii) The law enforcement officer is requesting submission to the test to investigate a suspected violation of State or local law governing the same or substantially similar conduct prohibited by paragraph (a)(1), (a)(2), or (a)(4) of this section.

(2) Whenever the Administrator has a reasonable basis to believe that a person may have violated paragraph (a)(1), (a)(2), or (a)(4) of this section, that person shall, upon request by the Administrator, furnish the Administrator, or authorize any clinic, hospital, doctor, or other person to release to the Administrator, the results of each test taken within 4 hours after acting or attempting to act as a crewmember that indicates percentage by weight of alcohol in the blood.

(d) Whenever the Administrator has a reasonable basis to believe that a person may have violated paragraph (a)(3) of this section, that person shall, upon request by the Administrator, furnish the Administrator, or authorize any clinic, hospital, doctor, or other person to release to the Administrator, the results of each test taken within 4 hours after acting or attempting to act as a crewmember that indicates the presence of any drugs in the body.

(e) Any test information obtained by the Administrator under paragraph (c) or (d) of this section may be evaluated in determining a person's qualifications for any airman certificate or possible violations of this chapter and may be used as evidence in any legal proceeding under section 602, 609, or 901 of the Federal Aviation Act of 1958.

---

12. Is it permissible for a pilot to allow a person who is obviously under the influence of intoxicating liquors or drugs to be carried aboard an aircraft? This is permitted
    (a) Only if the person does not have access to the cockpit or pilot's compartment.
    (b) Only if the person is a medical patient under proper care.
    (c) Only after a waiver has been obtained from the FAA.
    (d) Under no circumstances.

13. No person may act as a crewmember of a civil aircraft if that person has consumed any alcoholic beverages within the preceding
    (a) 8 hours.
    (b) 10 hours.
    (c) 16 hours.
    (d) 24 hours.

91.12 Carriage of narcotic drugs, marijuana, and depressant or stimulant drugs or substances
(a) Except as provided in paragraph (b) of this section, no person may operate a civil aircraft within the United States with knowledge that narcotic drugs, marijuana, and depressant or stimulant drugs or substances as defined in Federal or State statutes are carried in the aircraft.

(b) Paragraph (a) of this section does not apply to any carriage of narcotic drugs, marijuana, and depressant or stimulant drugs or substances authorized by or under any Federal or State statute or by any Federal or State agency.

91.13 Dropping objects

No pilot in command of a civil aircraft may allow any object to be dropped from that aircraft in flight that creates a hazard to persons or property. However, this section does not prohibit the dropping of an object if reasonable precautions are taken to avoid injury or damage to persons or property.

91.14 Use of safety belts

(a) Unless otherwise authorized by the Administrator

(1) No pilot may take off a U.S. registered civil aircraft (except a free balloon that incorporates a basket or gondola and an airship) unless the pilot in command of that aircraft ensures that each person on board is briefed on how to fasten and unfasten that person's safety belt.

(2) No pilot may take off or land a U.S. registered civil aircraft (except free balloons that incorporate baskets or gondolas and airships) unless the pilot in command of that aircraft ensures that each person on board has been notified to fasten his safety belt.

(3) During the takeoff and landing of U.S. registered civil aircraft (except free balloons that incorporate baskets or gondolas and airships) each person on board that aircraft must occupy a seat or berth with a safety belt properly secured about him. However, a person who has not reached his second birthday may be held by an adult who is occupying a seat or berth, and a person on board for the purpose of engaging in sport parachuting may use the floor of the aircraft as a seat.

(b) This section does not apply to operations conducted under Parts 121, 123, or 127 of this chapter. Subparagraph (a)(3) of this section does not apply to persons subject to section 91.7.

---

14. The use of safety belts during takeoffs and landings in airplanes of U.S. registry is
    (a) Required for crewmembers only.
    (b) Required by regulations in air carrier operations only.
    (c) Not required by regulations although their use is considered a good operating practice.
    (d) Required by regulations.

15. Safety belts in an airplane are required to be properly secured about the
    (a) Occupants during flights in moderate or severe turbulence only.
    (b) Crewmembers and passengers during the entire flight.
    (c) Occupants during takeoffs and landings.
    (d) Crewmembers only, during takeoffs and landings.

91.15 Parachutes and parachuting

(a) No pilot of a civil aircraft may allow a parachute that is available for emergency use to be carried in that aircraft unless it is an approved type and

(1) If a chair type (canopy in back), it has been packed by a certificated and appropriately rated parachute rigger within the preceding 120 days; or

(2) If any other type, it has been packed by a certificated and appropriately rated parachute rigger

(i) Within the preceding 120 days, if its canopy, shrouds, and harness are composed exclusively of nylon, rayon, or other similar synthetic fiber or materials that are substantially resistant to damage from mold, mildew, or other fungi and other rotting agents propagated in a moist environment; or

(ii) Within the preceding 60 days, if any part of the parachute is composed of silk, pongee, or other natural fiber, or materials not specified in subdivision (1) of this paragraph.

(b) Except in an emergency, no pilot in command may allow, and no person may make, a parachute jump from an aircraft within the United States except in accordance with Part 105.

(c) Unless each occupant of the aircraft is wearing an approved parachute, no pilot of a civil aircraft, carrying any person (other than a crewmember) may execute any intentional maneuver that exceeds

(1) A bank of 60 degrees relative to the horizon; or

(2) A nose-up or nose-down attitude of 30 degrees relative to the horizon.

(d) Paragraph (c) of this section does not apply to

(1) Flight tests for pilot certification or rating; or

(2) Spins and other flight maneuvers required by the regulations for any certificate or rating when given by

(i) A certificated flight instructor; or

(ii) An airline transport pilot instructing in accordance with section 61.169 of this chapter.

(e) For the purposes of this section, *approved parachute* means

(1) A parachute manufactured under a type certificate or a technical standard order (C-23 series); or

(2) A personnel-carrying military parachute identified by an NAF, AAF, or AN drawing number, an AAF order number, or any other military designation or specification number.

91.17 Towing: gliders

(a) No person may operate a civil aircraft towing a glider unless:

(1) The pilot in command of the towing aircraft is qualified under section 61.69 of this chapter.

There are many more regulations regarding the towing of gliders that appear as subparagraphs to section 91.17. If you plan to engage in this activity as a private pilot, you must be familiar with all of them, as well as meet the practical experience requirements of section 61.69.

91.18 Towing: other than under section 91.17

(a) No pilot of a civil aircraft may tow anything with that aircraft (other than under section 91.17) except in accordance with the terms of a certificate of waiver issued by the Administrator.

91.21 Flight instruction; simulated instrument flight and certain flight tests

(a) No person may operate a civil aircraft (except a manned free balloon) that is being used for flight instruction unless that aircraft has fully functioning, dual controls. However, instrument flight instruction may be given in a single-engine airplane equipped with a single, functioning throwover control wheel, in place of fixed, dual controls of the elevator and ailerons, when:

(1) The instructor has determined that the flight can be conducted safely; and

(2) The person manipulating the controls has at least a private pilot certificate with appropriate category and class ratings.

(b) No person may operate a civil aircraft in simulated instrument flight unless

(1) An appropriately rated pilot occupies the other control seat as safety pilot;

(2) The safety pilot has adequate vision forward and to each side of the aircraft, or a competent observer in the aircraft adequately supplements the vision of the safety pilot; and

(3) Except in the case of lighter-than-air aircraft, that aircraft is equipped with fully functioning dual controls. However, simulated instrument flight may be conducted in a single-engine airplane, equipped with a single, functioning, throwover control wheel, in place of fixed, dual controls of the elevator and ailerons, when

(i)   The safety pilot has determined that the flight can be conducted safely; and

(ii)   The person manipulating the control has at least a private pilot certificate with appropriate category and class ratings.

91.22 Fuel requirements for flight under VFR

(a) No person may begin a flight in an airplane under VFR unless (considering wind and forecast weather conditions) there is enough fuel to fly to the first point of intended landing and, assuming normal cruising speed,

(1) During the day, to fly after that for at least 30 minutes; or

(2) At night, to fly after that for at least 45 minutes.

(b) No person may begin a flight in a rotorcraft under VFR unless (considering wind and forecast weather conditions) there is enough fuel to fly to the first point of intended landing and, assuming normal cruising speed, to fly after that for at least 20 minutes.

91.24 ATC transponder and altitude reporting equipment and use

(a) *All airspace: U.S. registered civil aircraft.* For operations not conducted under Parts 121, 123, 127, or 135 of this chapter, ATC transponder equipment installed after January 1, 1974, in U.S. registered civil aircraft not previously equipped with an ATC transponder, and all ATC transponder equipment used in U.S. registered civil aircraft after July 1, 1975, must meet the performance and environmental requirements of any class of TSO-C74b or any class TSO-C74c as appropriate, except that the Administrator may approve the use of TSO-C74 or TSO-C74a equipment after July 1, 1975, if the applicant submits data showing that such equipment meets the minimum performance standards of the appropriate class of TSO-C74c and environmental conditions of the TSO under which it was manufactured.

(b) *Controlled airspace: all aircraft. . . .* No person may operate an aircraft in controlled airspace, after the applicable dates prescribed in subparagraphs (b)(1) through (b)(4) of this paragraph, unless that aircraft is equipped with an operable coded radar beacon transponder having a Mode 3/A 4096 code capability, replying to Mode 3/A interrogation with the code specified by ATC, and is equipped with automatic pressure altitude reporting equipment having a Mode C capability that automatically replies to Mode C interrogations by transmitting pressure altitude information in 100-foot increments. This requirement applies

(1) In Group I Terminal Control Areas governed by section 91.90(a);

(2) In Group II Terminal Control Areas governed by section 91.90(b), except as provided therein;

(3) In all controlled airspace of the 48 contiguous States and the District of Columbia, above 12,500 feet MSL, excluding the airspace at and below 2500 feet AGL.

(c) *Controlled airspace, all aircraft, transponder-on operation.* While in controlled airspace, each person operating an aircraft equipped with an operable ATC transponder maintained in accordance with section 91.172 of this Part shall operate the transponder, including Mode C equipment if installed, and shall reply on the appropriate code or as assigned by ATC.

(d) *ATC authorized deviations.* ATC may authorize deviations from paragraph (b) of this section

(1) Immediately, to allow an aircraft with an inoperative transponder to continue to the airport of ultimate destination, including any intermediate stops, or to proceed to a place where suitable repairs can be made, or both;

(2) Immediately, for operations of aircraft with an operating transponder but without operating automatic pressure altitude reporting equipment having a Mode C capability; and

(3) On a continuing basis, or for individual flights, for operations of aircraft without a transponder, in which case the request for a deviation must be submitted to the ATC facility having jurisdiction over the airspace concerned at least 1 hour before the proposed operation.

91.27 Civil aircraft: certifications required

(a) Except as provided in section 91.28, no person may operate a civil aircraft unless it has within it the following:

(1) An appropriate and current airworthiness certificate. Each U.S. airworthiness certificate used to comply with this subparagraph (except

a special flight permit, a copy of the applicable operations specifications issued under section 21.197(c) of this chapter, appropriate sections of the air carrier manual required by Parts 121 and 127 of this chapter containing that portion of the operations specifications issued under section 21.197(c), or an authorization under section 91.45), must have on it the registration number assigned to the aircraft under Part 47 of this chapter. However, the airworthiness certificate need not have on it an assigned special identification number before 10 days after that number is first affixed to the aircraft. A revised airworthiness certificate having on it an assigned special identification number, that has been affixed to an aircraft, may only be obtained upon application to an FAA Flight Standards District Office.

(2) A registration certificate issued to its owner.

(b) No person may operate a civil aircraft unless the airworthiness certificate required by paragraph (a) of this section or a special flight authorization issued under section 91.28 is displayed at the cabin or cockpit entrance so that it is legible to passengers or crew.

91.29 Civil aircraft airworthiness

(a) No person may operate a civil aircraft unless it is in an airworthy condition.

(b) The pilot in command of a civil aircraft is responsible for determining whether that aircraft is in condition for safe flight. He shall discontinue the flight when unairworthy mechanical or structural conditions occur.

91.31 Civil aircraft operating limitations and marking requirements

(a) Except as provided in paragraph (d) of this section, no person may operate a civil aircraft without compliance with the operating limitations for that aircraft prescribed by the certificating authority of the country of registry.

(b) No person may operate a U.S. registered civil aircraft

(1) For which an Airplane or Rotorcraft Flight Manual is required by section 21.5 unless there is available in the aircraft a current approved Airplane or Rotorcraft Flight Manual or the manual provided for in section 121.141(b); and

(2) For which an Airplane or Rotorcraft Flight Manual is not required by section 21.5, unless there is available in the aircraft a current approved Airplane or Rotorcraft Flight Manual, approved manual material, markings, and placards, or any combination thereof.

(c) No person may operate a U.S. registered civil aircraft unless that aircraft is identified in accordance with Part 45 of this chapter.

(e) The Airplane or Rotorcraft Flight Manual, or manual material, markings and placards required by paragraph (b) of this section must contain each operating limitation prescribed for that aircraft by the Administrator, including the following:

(1) Power plant (e.g., rpm, manifold pressure, gas temperature, etc.).

(2) Airspeeds (e.g., normal operating speed, flaps extended speed, etc.).

(3) Aircraft weight, center of gravity, and weight distribution, including the composition of the useful load in those combinations and ranges intended to ensure that the weight and center of gravity position will remain within approved limits (e.g., combinations and ranges of crew, oil, fuel, and baggage).

(4) Minimum flight crew.

(5) Kinds of operation.

(6) Maximum operating altitude.

(7) Maneuvering flight load factors.

(8) Rotor speed (for rotorcraft).

(9) Limiting height-speed envelope (for rotorcraft).

A convenient way to remember the aircraft documents required is by use of the acronym ARROW:

A—*Airworthiness certificate (section 91.27).*

R—*Registration (FAA and state requirement).*

R—*Radio Station License (FCC requirement).*

O—*Operating limitations (section 91.31).*

W—*Weight and balance data (section 91.31).*

---

16. Who is responsible for determining whether an aircraft is in condition for safe flight?
    (a) The pilot in command.
    (b) The owner of the aircraft.
    (c) The maintenance inspector.
    (d) The maintenance man who maintains the aircraft.

17. Choose those items that are required to be in the pilot's personal possession or aboard the aircraft during flight.
    A. Aircraft and engine logbooks.
    B. Airworthiness Certificate.
    C. Registration Certificate.
    D. Valid pilot certificate.
    E. Valid medical certificate.
    The required items are
    (a) A, B, C, D, E.
    (b) A, B, C.
    (c) B, C, D, E.
    (d) A, D, E.

18. During flight, which of these aircraft documents is required to be aboard?
    (a) Weight and Balance Handbook.
    (b) Owner's Manual.
    (c) Aircraft and engine logbooks.
    (d) FAA approved and current aircraft flight manual or aircraft operating limitations.

19. Where can the operating limitations of an aircraft be found?
    (a) In the Airplane Flight Manual, approved manual material, markings, and placards, or any combination thereof.
    (b) Only in the aircraft or engine logbooks.
    (c) On the Airworthiness Certificate.
    (d) Only in the Owner's Handbook published by the aircraft manufacturer.

20. No person may operate a civil aircraft unless the Airworthiness Certificate, or special flight permit or authorization required by regulations, is
    (a) On file in the owner's operation office where the aircraft is based.
    (b) Filed with the other required certificates or documents within the aircraft to be flown.
    (c) Displayed at the cabin or cockpit entrance so that it is legible to passengers or crew members.
    (d) Included in the approved logbooks for the aircraft.

91.32 Supplemental oxygen

(a) *General.* No person may operate a civil aircraft of U.S. registry
    (1) At cabin pressure altitudes above 12,500 feet (MSL) up to and including 14,000 feet (MSL), unless the required minimum flight crew is provided with and uses supplemental oxygen for that part of the flight at those altitudes that is of more than 30 minutes duration;
    (2) At cabin pressure altitudes above 14,000 feet (MSL), unless the required minimum flight crew is provided with and uses supplemental oxygen during the entire flight time at those altitudes; and
    (3) At cabin pressure altitudes above 15,000 feet (MSL), unless each occupant of the aircraft is provided with supplemental oxygen.

(b) *Pressurized cabin aircraft*
    (1) No person may operate a civil aircraft of U.S. registry with a pressurized cabin
        (i)   At flight altitudes above flight level 250, unless at least a 10-minute supply of supplemental oxygen, in addition to any oxygen required to satisfy paragraph (a) of this section, is available for each occupant of the aircraft for use in the event that a descent is necessitated by loss of cabin pressurization.

21. Unless each occupant is provided with supplemental oxygen, no person may operate a civil aircraft of U.S. registry above a cabin pressure altitude of
    (a) 10,000 feet MSL.
    (b) 12,500 feet MSL.
    (c) 14,000 feet MSL.
    (d) 15,000 feet MSL.

91.33 Powered civil aircraft with standard category U.S. airworthiness certificates; instrument and equipment requirements

(a) *General*. Except as provided in paragraphs (c)(3) and (e) of this section, no person may operate a powered civil aircraft with a standard category U.S. airworthiness certificate in any operation described in paragraphs (b) through (f) of this section unless that aircraft contains the instruments and equipment specified in those paragraphs (or FAA approved equivalents) for that type of operation, and those instruments and items of equipment are in operable condition.

(b) *Visual flight rules (day)*. For VFR flight during the day the following instruments and equipment are required:

(1) Airspeed indicator.

(2) Altimeter.

(3) Magnetic direction indicator.

(4) Tachometer for each engine.

(5) Oil pressure gauge for each engine using pressure system.

(6) Temperature gauge for each liquid-cooled engine.

(7) Oil temperature gauge for each air-cooled engine.

(8) Manifold pressure gauge for each altitude engine.

(9) Fuel gauge indicating the quantity of fuel in each tank.

(10) Landing gear position indicator, if the aircraft has a retractable landing gear.

(11) If the aircraft is operated for hire over water and beyond power-off gliding distance from shore, approved flotation gear readily available to each occupant and at least one pyrotechnic signaling device.

(12) Except as to airships, an approved safety belt for all occupants who have reached their second birthday. After December 4, 1981, each safety belt must be equipped with an approved metal-to-metal latching device. The rated strength of each safety belt shall not be less than that corresponding with the ultimate load factors specified in the current applicable aircraft airworthiness requirements considering the dimensional characteristics of the safety belt installation for the specific seat or berth arrangement. The webbing of each safety belt shall be replaced as required by the Administrator.

(13) For small civil airplanes manufactured after July 18, 1978, an approved shoulder harness for each front seat. The shoulder harness must be designed to protect the occupant from serious head injury when the occupant experiences the ultimate inertia forces specified in section 23.561 (b)(2) of this chapter. Each shoulder harness installed at a flight crewmember station must permit the crewmember, when seated and with his safety belt and shoulder harness fastened, to perform all functions necessary for flight operations. For purposes of this paragraph

(i)   The date of manufacture of an airplane is the date the inspection acceptance records reflect that the airplane is complete and meets the FAA Approved Type Design Data; and

(ii)   A front seat is a seat located at a flight crewmember station or any seat located alongside such a seat.

(c) *Visual flight rules (night)*. For VFR flight at night the following instruments and equipment are required:

   (1) Instruments and equipment specified in paragraph (b) of this section.

   (2) Approved position lights.

   (3) An approved aviation red or aviation white anticollision light system on all U.S. registered civil aircraft. Anticollision light systems initially installed after August 11, 1971, on aircraft for which a type certificate was issued or applied for before August 11, 1971, must at least meet the anticollision light standards of Parts 23, 25, 27, or 29, as applicable, that were in effect on August 10, 1971, except that the color may be either aviation red or aviation white. In the event of failure of any light of the anticollision light system, operations with the aircraft may be continued to a stop where repairs or replacement can be made.

   (4) If the aircraft is operated for hire, one electric landing light.

   (5) An adequate source of electrical energy for all installed electrical and radio equipment.

   (6) One spare set of fuses, or three spare fuses of each kind required.

91.52 Emergency locator transmitters

(a) Except as provided in paragraphs (e) and (f) of this section, no person may operate a U.S. registered civil airplane unless it meets the applicable requirements of paragraphs (b), (c), and (d) of this section.

(b) To comply with paragraph (a) of this section, each U.S. registered civil airplane must be equipped as follows:

   (1) For operations governed by the supplemental air carrier and commercial operator rules of Part 121 of this chapter, or the air travel club rules of Part 123 of this chapter, there must be attached to the airplane an automatic type emergency locator transmitter that is in operable condition and meets the applicable requirements of TSO-C91;

   (2) For charter flights governed by the domestic and flag air carrier rules of Part 121 of this chapter, there must be attached to the airplane an automatic type emergency locator transmitter that is in operable condition and meets the applicable requirements of TSO-C91;

   (3) For operations governed by Part 135 of this chapter, there must be attached to the airplane an automatic type emergency locator transmitter that is in operable condition and meets the applicable requirements of TSO-C91; and

   (4) For operations other than those specified in subparagraphs (1), (2), and (3) of this paragraph, there must be attached to the airplane a personnel type or an automatic type emergency locator transmitter that is in operable condition and meets the applicable requirements of TSO-C91.

(c) Each emergency locator transmitter required by paragraphs (a) and (b) of this section must be attached to the airplane in such a manner that the probability of damage to the transmitter, in the event of crash impact, is minimized. Fixed and deployable automatic type transmitters must be attached to the airplane as far aft as practicable.

(d) Batteries used in the emergency locator transmitters required by paragraphs (a) and (b) of this section must be replaced (or recharged, if the battery is rechargeable)

(1) When the transmitter has been in use for more than one cumulative hour; or

(2) When 50 percent of their useful life (or, for rechargeable batteries, 50 percent of their useful life of charge), as established by the transmitter manufacturer under TSO-C91, paragraph (g)(2), has expired.

The new expiration date for the replacement (or recharge) of the battery must be legibly marked on the outside of the transmitter and entered in the aircraft maintenance record. Subparagraph (d)(2) does not apply to batteries (such as water-activated batteries) that are essentially unaffected during probable storage intervals.

(e) Not withstanding paragraphs (a) and (b) of this section, a person may

(1) Ferry a newly acquired airplane from the place where possession of it was taken to a place where the emergency locator transmitter is to be installed; and

(2) Ferry an airplane with an inoperative emergency locator transmitter from a place where repairs or replacement cannot be made to a place where they can be made.

No person other than required crewmembers may be carried aboard an airplane being ferried pursuant to paragraph (e) of this section.

(f) Paragraphs (a) and (b) of this section do not apply to

(1) Turbojet-powered aircraft;

(2) Aircraft while engaged in scheduled flights by scheduled air carriers certificated by the Civil Aeronautics Board;

(3) Aircraft while engaged in training operations conducted entirely within a 50-mile radius of the airport from which such local flight operations began;

(4) Aircraft while engaged in flight operations incident to design and testing;

(5) New aircraft while engaged in flight operations incident to their manufacture, preparation, and delivery;

(6) Aircraft while engaged in flight operations incident to aerial application of chemicals and other substances for agricultural purposes;

(7) Aircraft certificated by the Administrator for research and development purposes;

(8) Aircraft while used for showing compliance with regulations, crew training, exhibition, air racing, or market surveys;

(9) Aircraft equipped to carry not more than one person; and

(10) An aircraft during any period for which the transmitter has been temporarily removed for inspection, repair, modification, or replacement, subject to the following:

(i) No person may operate the aircraft unless the aircraft records contain an entry which includes the date of initial removal, the make, model, serial number, and reason for removal of the transmitter, and a placard is located in view of the pilot to show "ELT not installed."

(ii) No person may operate the aircraft more than 90 days after the ELT is initially removed from the aircraft.

---

22. In order to determine when the battery of an Emergency Locator Transmitter (ELT) will need replacement, regulations require that the expiration date be
    (a) Listed on the Airworthiness Certificate.
    (b) Marked on the aircraft instrument panel placard.
    (c) Marked on the outside of the transmitter.
    (d) Listed in the engine logbook.

23. When are Emergency Locator Transmitter (ELT) batteries required to be replaced or recharged?
    (a) Every 6 months.
    (b) After 100 cumulative hours of use.
    (c) After 30 cumulative minutes of use.
    (d) After 1 cumulative hour of use.

91.57 Aviation Safety Reporting Program: prohibition against use of reports for enforcement purposes
The Administrator of the FAA will not use reports submitted to the National Aeronautics and Space Administration under the Aviation Safety Reporting Program (or information derived therefrom) in any enforcement action, except information concerning criminal offenses or accidents which are wholly excluded from the Program.

The Aviation Safety Reporting Program is a voluntary program in which a pilot committing or observing a violation of FARs may report it to a neutral third party (NASA), which then compiles the information for use by the FAA and NTSB in assessing FARs and safety programs.

Subpart B—Flight Rules: General

91.61 Applicability
This subpart prescribes flight rules governing the operation of aircraft within the United States.

91.63 Waivers
(a) The Administrator may issue a certificate of waiver authorizing the operation of aircraft in deviation of any rule of this subpart if he finds that the proposed operation can be safely conducted under the terms of that certificate of waiver.
(b) An application for a certificate of waiver under this section is made on a form and in a manner prescribed by the Administrator and may be submitted to any FAA office.
(c) A certificate of waiver is effective as specified in that certificate.

91.65 Operating near other aircraft

(a) No person may operate an aircraft so close to another aircraft as to create a collision hazard.

(b) No person may operate an aircraft in formation flight except by arrangement with the pilot in command of each aircraft in the formation.

(c) No person may operate an aircraft carrying passengers for hire in formation flights.

(d) Unless otherwise authorized by ATC, no person operating an aircraft may operate his aircraft in accordance with any clearance or instruction that has been issued to the pilot of another aircraft for radar Air Traffic Control purposes.

91.67 Right-of-way rules; except water operations

(a) *General.* When weather conditions permit, regardless of whether an operation is conducted under Instrument Flight Rules or Visual Flight Rules, vigilance shall be maintained by each person operating an aircraft so as to see and avoid other aircraft in compliance with this section. When a rule of this section gives another aircraft the right of way, he shall give way to that aircraft and may not pass over, under, or ahead of it, unless well clear.

(b) *In distress.* An aircraft in distress has the right of way over all other air traffic.

(c) *Converging.* When aircraft of the same category are converging at approximately the same altitude (except head-on, or nearly so), the aircraft to the other's right has the right of way. If the aircraft are of different categories

    (1) A balloon has the right of way over any other category of aircraft;

    (2) A glider has the right of way over an airship, airplane, or rotorcraft;

    (3) An airship has the right of way over an airplane or rotorcraft.

However, an aircraft towing or refueling other aircraft has the right of way over all other engine-driven aircraft.

(d) *Approaching head-on.* When aircraft are approaching each other head-on, or nearly so, each pilot of each aircraft shall alter course to the right.

(e) *Overtaking.* Each aircraft that is being overtaken has the right of way and each pilot of an overtaking aircraft shall alter course to the right to pass well clear.

(f) *Landing.* Aircraft, while on final approach to land, or while landing, have the right of way over other aircraft in flight or operating on the surface. When two or more aircraft are approaching an airport for the purpose of landing, the aircraft at the lower altitude has the right of way, but it shall not take advantage of this rule to cut in front of another which is on final approach to land, or to overtake that aircraft.

(g) *Inapplicability.* This section does not apply to the operation of an aircraft on water.

91.69 Right-of-way rules; water operations

(a) *General.* Each person operating an aircraft on the water shall, insofar as possible, keep clear of all vessels and avoid impeding their navigation,

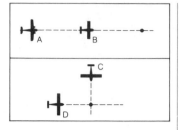

24. Airplane A (left) is overtaking airplane B, and both are at the same altitude. What action should be taken?
    (a) Airplane A should descend on course and pass well below airplane B.
    (b) Airplane A should alter course to the right and pass well clear of airplane B.
    (c) Airplane A should alter course to the left and pass well clear of airplane B.
    (d) Airplane A should climb on course and pass well above airplane B.

25. Airplanes C and D above are converging at the same altitude. Which statement is true?
    (a) Airplane C should gain 500 feet and airplane D should lose 500 feet of altitude.
    (b) The airplane that is flying on an airway has the right-of-way.
    (c) Airplane D should alter course since airplane C is to its left.
    (d) Airplane C should alter course since airplane D is to its right.

26. Approaching a VORTAC while headed westward at 6500 feet MSL, you see a multiengine airplane converging from your right; it is at the same altitude headed southwest. According to regulations, which pilot should give way and why?
    (a) You should give way since your airplane is smaller, slower, and more maneuverable than the multiengine airplane.
    (b) The pilot of the multiengine airplane should give way since this airplane is not flying at a proper VFR cruising altitude.
    (c) The pilot of the multiengine airplane should give way since your airplane is to its left and you have the right-of-way.
    (d) You should give way since the other airplane is on your right and has the right-of-way.

27. When two aircraft are approaching each other head-on or nearly so, which aircraft should give way?
    (a) Regardless of the aircraft categories, a glider has the right-of-way over all engine-driven aircraft.
    (b) If the aircraft are of different categories, an airship would have the right-of-way over a helicopter.
    (c) Regardless of the aircraft categories, the pilot of each aircraft shall alter course to the right.
    (d) If the aircraft are of different categories, an airship would have the right-of-way over an airplane.

and shall give way to any vessel or other aircraft that is given the right of way by any rule of this section.

(b) *Crossing*. When aircraft, or an aircraft and a vessel are on crossing courses, the aircraft or vessel to the other's right has the right of way.

(c) *Approaching head-on*. When aircraft, or an aircraft and a vessel, are approaching head-on or nearly so, each shall alter its course to the right to keep well clear.

(d) *Overtaking*. Each aircraft or vessel that is being overtaken has the right of way, and the one overtaking shall alter course to keep well clear.

(e) *Special circumstances*. When aircraft, or an aircraft and a vessel, approach so as to involve risk of collision, each aircraft or vessel shall proceed with careful regard to existing circumstances, including the limitations of the respective craft.

91.70 Aircraft speed

(a) Unless otherwise authorized by the Administrator, no person may operate an aircraft below 10,000 feet MSL at an indicated airspeed of more than 250 knots (288 mph).

(b) Unless otherwise authorized or required by ATC, no person may operate an aircraft within an airport traffic area at an indicated airspeed of more than

    (1) In the case of a reciprocating engine aircraft, 156 knots (180 mph); or

    (2) In the case of a turbine-powered aircraft, 200 knots (230 mph).

Paragraph (b) does not apply to any operations within a Terminal Control Area. Such operations shall comply with paragraph (a) of this section.

(c) No person may operate an aircraft in the airspace underlying a terminal control area, or in a VFR corridor designated through a terminal control area, at an indicated airspeed of more than 200 knots (230 mph).

However, if the minimum safe airspeed for any particular operation is greater than the maximum speed prescribed in this section, the aircraft may be operated at that minimum speed.

---

28. When operating an aircraft equipped with a reciprocating engine within an airport traffic area, the maximum indicated airspeed permitted is
    (a) 109 knots (125 mph).
    (b) 156 knots (180 mph).
    (c) 200 knots (230 mph).
    (d) 250 knots (288 mph).

29. Unless otherwise authorized, no person may operate an aircraft below 10,000 feet MSL at an indicated airspeed of more than
    (a) 156 knots (180 mph).
    (b) 200 knots (230 mph).
    (c) 250 knots (288 mph).
    (d) 300 knots (345 mph).

91.71 Acrobatic flight

No person may operate an aircraft in acrobatic flight

(a) Over any congested area of a city, town, or settlement;

(b) Over an open air assembly of persons;

(c) Within a control zone or Federal airway;

(d) Below an altitude of 1500 feet above the surface; or

(e) When flight visibility is less than three miles.

For the purposes of this section, acrobatic flight means an intentional maneuver involving an abrupt change in an aircraft's attitude, an abnormal attitude, or abnormal acceleration not necessary for normal flight.

---

30. According to Federal Aviation Regulations, which of the following are true statements?

A. Parachutes are required when a private pilot carrying a passenger executes an intentional maneuver that exceeds a 30° nose-up attitude relative to the horizon.

B. All acrobatic maneuvers must be completed at least 2000 feet above the surface.

C. Parachutes are always required for all occupants of an aircraft when spins are practiced.

D. An intentional maneuver, not necessary for normal flight, involving an abrupt change in the aircraft's attitude is considered acrobatic flight.

The true statements are:

(a) A, B, C, D.

(b) A, D.

(c) B, C, D.

(d) A, B, C.

31. An aircraft should not be operated in acrobatic flight when

(a) The flight visibility is less than 5 miles.

(b) Below 3000 feet AGL.

(c) The flight visibility is less than 10 miles.

(d) Over any congested area.

32. An aircraft should not be operated in acrobatic flight when

(a) Supplemental oxygen equipment is aboard.

(b) Flight visibility is less than 10 miles.

(c) Below 3000 feet AGL.

(d) Within a control zone.

33. Acrobatic flight should not be performed unless

(a) A normal category airplane is used.

(b) An instructor is aboard.

(c) The flight visibility is at least 5 miles.

(d) The aircraft is more than 1500 feet AGL.

91.73 Aircraft lights

No person may, during the period from sunset to sunrise (or, in Alaska, during the period a prominent unlighted object cannot be seen from a distance of three statute miles or the sun is more than six degrees below the horizon)

(a) Operate an aircraft unless it has lighted position lights;

(b) Park or move an aircraft in, or in dangerous proximity to, a night flight operations area of an airport unless the aircraft

    (1) Is clearly illuminated;

    (2) Has lighted position lights; or

    (3) Is in an area which is marked by obstruction lights.

(c) Anchor an aircraft unless the aircraft

    (1) Has lighted anchor lights; or

    (2) Is in an area where anchor lights are not required on vessels; or

(d) Operate an aircraft, required by section 91.33(c)(3) to be equipped with an anticollision light system, unless it has approved and lighted aviation red or aviation white anticollision lights. However, the anticollision lights need not be lighted when the pilot in command determines that, because of operating conditions, it would be in the interest of safety to turn the lights off.

---

34. Aircraft operating at night, in the air or on the surface, must display lighted position lights during the period from
    (a) 1 hour before sunset to 1 hour after sunrise.
    (b) Sunset to sunrise.
    (c) 30 minutes after sunset to 30 minutes after sunrise.
    (d) 30 minutes before sunset to 30 minutes after sunrise.

91.75 Compliance with ATC clearances and instructions

(a) When an ATC clearance has been obtained, no pilot in command may deviate from that clearance, except in an emergency unless he obtains an amended clearance. However, except in positive controlled airspace, this paragraph does not prohibit him from canceling an IFR flight plan if he is operating in VFR weather conditions. If a pilot is uncertain of the meaning of an ATC clearance, he shall immediately request clarification from ATC.

---

35. Suppose that you had an inflight emergency and found it necessary to deviate from previous ATC instructions, and then you were given landing priority at a controlled airport. If requested by ATC, a report must be submitted within 48 hours to the Chief of the
    (a) Appropriate Search and Rescue Unit.
    (b) Air Traffic Control facility.
    (c) Nearest National Transportation Safety Board Field Office.
    (d) Nearest General Aviation District Office.

(b) Except in an emergency, no person may, in an area in which air traffic control is exercised, operate an aircraft contrary to an ATC instruction.

(c) Each pilot in command who deviates, in an emergency, from an ATC clearance or instruction shall notify ATC of that deviation as soon as possible.

(d) Each pilot in command who (though not deviating from a rule of this subpart) is given priority by ATC in an emergency, shall, if requested by ATC, submit a detailed report of that emergency within 48 hours to the chief of that ATC facility.

91.77 ATC light signals

ATC light signals have the meaning shown in the following table:

Color and type of signal	Meaning with respect to aircraft on the surface	Meaning with respect to aircraft in flight
Steady green	Cleared for takeoff	Cleared to land
Flashing green	Cleared to taxi	Return for landing (to be followed by steady green at proper time)
Steady red	Stop	Give way to other aircraft and continue circling
Flashing red	Taxi clear of runway in use	Airport unsafe—do not land
Flashing white	Return to starting point on airport	Not applicable
Alternating red and green	Exercise extreme caution	Exercise extreme caution

36. If you are on the final approach for landing and notice a flashing red light directed at you from the control tower, what action should you take?

    (a) Continue to the airport and land because this signal applies only to airplanes taxiing on the surface.

    (b) You should give way because there is another aircraft on final approach.

    (c) You should not land because the airport is unsafe for landing.

    (d) Continue to the airport and land, exercising extreme caution.

37. A "steady red" ATC light signal directed to an aircraft on the surface is a signal to the pilot of that aircraft to

    (a) Return to the starting point on the airport.

    (b) Taxi clear of the runway in use.

    (c) Exercise extreme caution.

    (d) Stop taxiing.

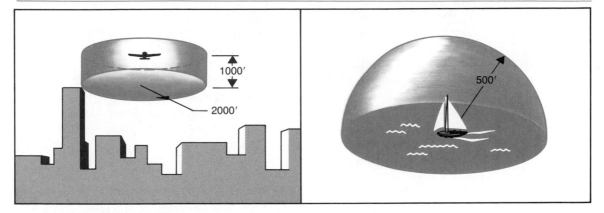

91.79 Minimum safe altitudes; general

Except when necessary for takeoff or landing, no person may operate an aircraft below the following altitudes:

(a) *Anywhere.* An altitude allowing, if a power unit fails, an emergency landing without undue hazard to persons or property on the surface.

(b) *Over congested areas.* Over any congested area of a city, town, or settlement, or over any open air assembly of persons, an altitude of 1000 feet above the highest obstacle within a horizontal radius of 2000 feet of the aircraft. (See Figure 11.1.)

(c) *Over other than congested areas.* An altitude of 500 feet above the surface, except over open water or sparsely populated areas. In that case, the aircraft may not be operated closer than 500 feet to any person, vessel, vehicle, or structure. (See Figure 11.2.)

Figure 11.1 *(left)* Minimum safe altitude over congested areas.

Figure 11.2 *(right)* Over uncongested areas, an aircraft may not be operated closer than 500 feet to any person, vehicle, or vessel.

38. Over sparsely populated areas an aircraft may not be operated, except when necessary for takeoff or landing, closer than what distance from any person, vehicle, or structure?
    (a) 100 feet.
    (b) 500 feet.
    (c) 1000 feet.
    (d) 2000 feet.

39. Except when necessary for takeoff or landing, to operate an airplane over a congested area of a city, the minimum altitude for flight directly above the highest obstacle is
    (a) 500 feet.
    (b) 1000 feet.
    (c) 1500 feet.
    (d) 3000 feet.

91.81 Altimeter settings

(a) Each person operating an aircraft shall maintain the cruising altitude or flight level of that aircraft, as the case may be, by reference to an altimeter that is set, when operating

(1) Below 18,000 feet MSL, to

(i)   The current reported altimeter setting of a station along the route and within 100 nautical miles of the aircraft;

(ii)   If there is no station within the area prescribed in subdivision (i) of this subparagraph, the current reported altimeter setting of an appropriate available station; or

(iii) In the case of an aircraft not equipped with a radio, the elevation of the departure airport or an appropriate altimeter setting available before departure; or

(2) At or above 18,000 feet MSL to 29.92 inches of mercury.

More information is given in section 91.81 about altimetry above 18,000 feet MSL. Since flight at those altitudes requires an instrument rating, you must review this section in its entirety before applying for instrument pilot privileges.

---

40. To maintain the proper cruising altitude, if your airplane is not equipped with a radio, the altimeter should be set to

(a) The elevation of the airport of departure, or appropriate altimeter settings available prior to departure.

(b) The density altitude at the airport of departure.

(c) 29.92″ Hg at the airport of departure and whenever below 18,000 feet MSL.

(d) Zero.

91.83 Flight plan; information required

(a) Unless otherwise authorized by ATC, each person filing an IFR or VFR flight plan shall include in it the following information:

(1) The aircraft identification number and, if necessary, its radio call sign.

(2) The type of the aircraft or, in the case of a formation flight, the type of each aircraft and the number of aircraft in the formation.

(3) The full name and address of the pilot in command or, in the case of a formation flight, the formation commander.

(4) The point and proposed time of departure.

(5) The proposed route, cruising altitude (or flight level), and true airspeed at that altitude.

(6) The point of first intended landing and the estimated elapsed time until over that point.

(7) The radio frequencies to be used.

(8) The amount of fuel on board (in hours).

(9) In the case of an IFR flight plan, an alternate airport, except as provided in paragraph (b) of this section.

(10) The number of persons in the aircraft, except where that information is otherwise readily available to the FAA.

(11) Any other information the pilot in command or ATC believes is necessary for ATC purposes.

(d) *Cancellation*. When a flight plan has been activated, the pilot in command, upon canceling or completing the flight under the flight plan, shall notify an FAA Flight Service Station or ATC facility.

---

41. Closing a VFR flight plan at the completion of a flight is
    (a) Accomplished by any government agency through teletype service.
    (b) Advisable, but is not required by regulations.
    (c) Required by regulations.
    (d) Automatically accomplished by the control tower or FSS personnel when the aircraft lands at its destination.

91.84 Flights between Mexico or Canada and the United States
Unless otherwise authorized by ATC, no person may operate a civil aircraft between Mexico or Canada and the United States without filing an IFR or VFR flight plan, as appropriate.

91.85 Operating on or in the vicinity of an airport; general rules
(a) Unless otherwise required by Part 93 of this chapter, each person operating an aircraft on or in the vicinity of an airport shall comply with the requirements of this section and of sections 91.87 and 91.89.
(b) Unless otherwise authorized or required by ATC, no person may operate an aircraft within an airport traffic area except for the purpose of landing at, or taking off from, an airport within that area. ATC authorizations may be given as individual approval of specific operations or may be contained in written agreements between airport users and the tower concerned.

91.87 Operation at airports with operating control towers
(a) *General*. Unless otherwise authorized or required by ATC, each person operating an aircraft to, from, or on an airport with an operating control tower shall comply with the applicable provisions of this section.
(b) *Communications with control towers operated by the United States*. No person may, within an airport traffic area, operate an aircraft to, from, or on an airport having a control tower operated by the United States unless two-way radio communications are maintained between that aircraft and the control tower. However, if the aircraft radio fails in flight, he may operate that aircraft and land if weather conditions are at or above basic VFR weather minimums, he maintains visual contact with the tower, and he receives a clearance to land. If the aircraft radio fails while in flight under IFR, he must comply with section 91.127.
(c) *Communications with other control towers*. No person may, within an airport traffic area, operate an aircraft to, from, or on an airport having a non-United States operated control tower unless
    (1) If that aircraft's radio equipment so allows, two-way radio communications are maintained between the aircraft and the tower; or
    (2) If that aircraft's radio equipment allows only reception from the tower, the pilot has the tower's frequency monitored.

(d) *Minimum altitudes*. When operating to an airport with an operating control tower, each pilot of (3) an airplane approaching to land on a runway served by a visual approach slope indicator, shall maintain an altitude at or above the glide slope until a lower altitude is necessary for a safe landing. However, subparagraphs (2) and (3) of this paragraph do not prohibit normal bracketing maneuvers above or below the glide slope that are conducted for the purpose of remaining on the glide slope.

(e) *Approaches*. When approaching to land at an airport with an operating control tower, each pilot of

(1) An airplane, shall circle the airport to the left; and

(2) A helicopter, shall avoid the flow of fixed-wing aircraft.

(f) *Departures*. No person may operate an aircraft taking off from an airport with an operating control tower except in compliance with the following:

(1) Each pilot shall comply with any departure procedures established for that airport by the FAA.

(2) Unless otherwise required by the departure procedure or the applicable distance from the clouds criteria, each pilot of a turbine-powered airplane and each pilot of a large airplane shall climb to an altitude of 1500 feet above the surface as rapidly as practicable.

(g) *Noise abatement runway system*. When landing or taking off from an airport with an operating control tower, and for which a formal runway use

---

42. Unless otherwise authorized, two-way radio communications with ATC are required for landings or takeoffs

(a) At tower-controlled airports within control zones only when weather conditions are less than VFR.

(b) At all tower-controlled airports only when weather conditions are less than VFR.

(c) At all tower-controlled airports regardless of the weather conditions.

(d) Within control zones regardless of the weather conditions.

43. As you prepare to taxi out for takeoff, you receive the following clearance:

"BIRDCRAFT CLEARED TO RUNWAY 3. TAXI SOUTHWEST ON THE RAMP. . ."

Select the true statement that describes the action you should take.

(a) Taxi to Runway 3, cross runways that intersect the taxi route but hold clear of active Runway 3.

(b) Taxi on the ramp but hold clear of any runway that intersects a taxiway.

(c) Taxi to Runway 3 and hold in position on the runway until the tower clears you for takeoff.

(d) Wait for further clearance before leaving the ramp.

program has been established by the FAA, each pilot of a turbine-powered airplane and each pilot of a large airplane, assigned a noise abatement runway by ATC, shall use that runway. However, consistent with the final authority of the pilot in command concerning the safe operation of the aircraft as prescribed in section 91.3(a), ATC may assign a different runway if requested by the pilot in the interest of safety.

(h) *Clearances required.* No person may, at an airport with an operating control tower, operate an aircraft on a runway or taxiway, or take off or land an aircraft, unless an appropriate clearance is received from ATC. A clearance to "taxi to" the takeoff runway assigned to the aircraft is not a clearance to cross that assigned takeoff runway, or to taxi on that runway at any point, but is a clearance to cross other runways that intersect the taxi route to that assigned takeoff runway. A clearance to "taxi to" any point other than an assigned takeoff runway is a clearance to cross all runways that intersect the taxi route to that point.

91.88 Airport radar service areas

(a) *General.* For the purposes of this section, the primary airport is the airport designated in Part 71, Subpart L, for which the airport radar service area is designated. A satellite airport is any other airport within the airport radar service area.

(b) *Deviations.* An operator may deviate from any provision of this section under the provisions of an ATC authorization issued by the ATC facility having jurisdiction of the airport radar service area. ATC may authorize a deviation on a continuing basis or for an individual flight, as appropriate.

(c) *Arrivals and overflights.* No person may operate an aircraft in an airport radar service area unless two-way radio communication is established with ATC prior to entering that area and is thereafter maintained with ATC while within that area.

(d) *Departures.* No person may operate an aircraft within an airport radar service area unless two-way radio communication is maintained with ATC while within that area, except that for aircraft departing a satellite airport, two-way radio communication is established as soon as practicable and thereafter maintained with ATC while within that area.

(e) *Traffic patterns.* No person may take off or land an aircraft at a satellite airport within an airport radar service area except in compliance with FAA arrival and departure traffic patterns.

91.89 Operation at airports without control towers

Each person operating an aircraft to or from an airport without an operating control tower shall

(a) In the case of an airplane approaching to land, make all turns of that airplane to the left unless the airport displays approved light signals or visual markings indicating that turns should be made to the right, in which case the pilot shall make all turns to the right;

(b) In the case of a helicopter approaching to land, avoid the flow of fixed-wing aircraft; and

(c) In the case of an aircraft departing the airport, comply with any FAA traffic pattern for that airport.

---

44. In regard to the correct traffic pattern departure procedure to use at a noncontrolled airport, which statement is true?
    (a) Depart as prearranged with other pilots using the airport.
    (b) Comply with any FAA traffic pattern established for the airport.
    (c) Make all turns to the left.
    (d) Depart in any direction consistent with safety, after crossing the airport boundary.

91.90 Terminal control areas
(a) *Group I terminal control areas*
   (1) *Operating rules.* No person may operate an aircraft within a Group I terminal control area designated in Part 71 of this chapter except in compliance with the following rules:
      (i)   No person may operate an aircraft within a Group I terminal control area unless he has received an appropriate authorization from ATC prior to the operation of that aircraft in that area.
   (2) *Pilot requirements.* The pilot in command of a civil aircraft may not land or take off that aircraft from an airport within a Group I terminal control area unless he holds at least a private pilot certificate.
   (3) *Equipment requirements.* Unless otherwise authorized by ATC in the case of in-flight VOR, TACAN, or two-way radio failure; or unless otherwise authorized by ATC in the case of a transponder failure occurring at any time, no person may operate an aircraft within a Group I terminal control area unless that aircraft is equipped with
      (i)   An operable VOR or TACAN receiver (except in the case of helicopters);
      (ii) An operable two-way radio capable of communicating with ATC on appropriate frequencies for that terminal control area; and
      (iii) The applicable equipment specified in section 91.24.
(b) *Group II terminal control areas*
   (1) *Operating rules.* No person may operate an aircraft within a Group II terminal control area designated in Part 71 of this chapter except in compliance with the following rules:
      (i)   No person may operate an aircraft within a Group II terminal control area unless he has received an appropriate authorization from ATC prior to operation of that aircraft in that area, and unless two-way radio communications are maintained within that area between that aircraft and the ATC facility.
      (ii) Unless otherwise authorized by ATC, each person operating a large turbine-engine-powered airplane to or from a primary airport shall operate at or above the designated floors while within the lateral limits of the terminal control area.

(2) *Equipment requirements*. Unless otherwise authorized by ATC in the case of in-flight VOR, TACAN, or two-way radio failure; or unless otherwise authorized by ATC in the case of a transponder failure occurring at any time, no person may operate an aircraft within a Group II terminal control area unless that aircraft is equipped with

(i)   An operable VOR or TACAN receiver (except in the case of helicopters);

(ii) An operable two-way radio capable of communicating with ATC on the appropriate frequencies for that terminal control area; and

(iii) The applicable equipment specified in section 91.24. A transponder is not required for IFR flights operating to or from an airport outside of but in close proximity to the terminal control area, when the commonly used transition, approach, or departure procedures to such airport require flight within the terminal control area.

---

45. Which of the following statements are true regarding the requirements for operating within a Group I Terminal Control Area (TCA)?
    A. The pilot must hold at least a Commercial Pilot Certificate.
    B. Authorization from ATC is required prior to operating in the area.
    C. The pilot must be instrument rated and he must be operating on an instrument flight plan.
    D. The airplane must have an operable VOR receiver, two way communications radio, and a radar beacon transponder.
    E. The pilot in command must hold at least a Private Pilot Certificate to take off or land within the TCA.
    The true statements are:
    (a) A, C, D.
    (b) C, D, E.
    (c) B, D, E.
    (d) A, B, C, D.

91.91 Temporary flight restrictions

(a) Whenever the Administrator determines it to be necessary in order to prevent an unsafe congestion of sight-seeing aircraft above an incident or event which may generate a high degree of public interest, or to provide a safe environment for the operation of disaster relief aircraft, a *Notice to Airmen* will be issued designating an area within which temporary flight restrictions apply.

(b) When a *Notice to Airmen* has been issued under this section, no person may operate an aircraft within the designated area unless

(1) That aircraft is participating in disaster relief activities and is being operated under the direction of the agency responsible for relief activities;

(2) That aircraft is being operated to or from an airport within the area and is being operated so as not to hamper or endanger relief activities;

(3) That operation is specifically authorized under an IFR ATC clearance;

(4) VFR flight around or above the area is impracticable due to weather, terrain, or other considerations, prior notice is given to the Air Traffic Service facility specified in the *Notice to Airmen,* and en route operation through the area is conducted so as not to hamper or endanger relief activities; or

(5) That aircraft is carrying properly accredited news representatives, or persons on official business concerning the incident or event which generated the issuance of the *Notice to Airmen;* the operation is conducted in accordance with section 91.79 of this chapter; the operation is conducted above the altitudes being used by relief aircraft unless otherwise authorized by the agency responsible for relief activities; and further, in connection with this type of operation, prior to entering the area the operator has filed with the Air Traffic Service facility specified in the *Notice to Airmen* a flight plan that includes the following information:

  (i)   Aircraft identification, type, and color.
  (ii) Radio communications frequencies to be used.
  (iii) Proposed times of entry and exit of the designated area.
  (iv) Name of news media or purpose of flight.
  (v)   Any other information deemed necessary by ATC.

91.93 Flight test areas

No person may flight test an aircraft except over open water, or sparsely populated areas, having light air traffic.

91.95 Restricted and prohibited areas

(a) No person may operate an aircraft within a restricted area (designated in Part 73) contrary to the restrictions imposed, or within a prohibited area, unless he has the permission of the using or controlling agency, as appropriate.

(b) Each person conducting, within a restricted area, an aircraft operation (approved by the using agency) that creates the same hazards as the operations for which the restricted area was designated, may deviate from the rules of this subpart that are not compatible with his operation of the aircraft.

91.100 Emergency air traffic rules

(a) This section prescribes a process for utilizing Notices to Airmen (NOTAMs) to advise of the issuance and operations under emergency air traffic rules and regulations and designates the official who is authorized to issue NOTAMs on behalf of the Administrator in certain matters under this section.

(b) Whenever the Administrator determines that an emergency condition exists, or will exist, relating to the FAA's ability to operate the Air Traffic Control System and during which normal flight operations under this chapter cannot be conducted consistent with the required levels of safety and efficiency

(1) The Administrator issues an immediately effective Air Traffic rule or regulation in response to that emergency condition, and

(2) The Administrator, or the Director, Air Traffic Service, may utilize the Notice to Airmen (NOTAM) system to provide notification of the issuance of the rule or regulation.

Those NOTAMs communicate information concerning the rules and regulations that govern flight operations, the use of navigation facilities, and designation of that airspace in which the rules and regulations apply.

(c) When a NOTAM has been issued under this section, no person may operate an aircraft, or other device governed by the regulation concerned, within the designated airspace, except in accordance with the authorizations, terms, and conditions prescribed in the regulation covered by the NOTAM.

91.102 Flight limitation in the proximity of space flight recovery operations
No person may operate any aircraft of United States registry, or pilot any aircraft under the authority of an airman certificate issued by the Federal Aviation Administration within areas designated in a *Notice to Airmen (NOTAM)* for space flight recovery operations except when authorized by ATC, or operated under the control of the Department of Defense Manager for Manned Space Flight Support Operations.

91.104 Flight restrictions in the proximity of the presidential and other parties
No person may operate an aircraft over or in the vicinity of any area to be visited or traveled by the President, the Vice President, or other public figures contrary to the restrictions established by the Administrator and published in a *Notice to Airmen (NOTAM)*.

Subpart B—Flight Rules: Visual Flight Rules

91.105 Basic VFR weather minimums
(a) Except as provided in section 91.107, no person may operate an aircraft under VFR when the flight visibility is less, or at a distance from clouds that is less, than that prescribed for the corresponding altitude in the table at the top of page 412.
(b) When the visibility is less than 1 mile, a helicopter may be operated outside controlled airspace at 1200 feet or less above the surface if operated at a speed that allows the pilot adequate opportunity to see any air traffic or other obstruction in time to avoid a collision.
(c) Except as provided in section 91.107, no person may operate an aircraft, under VFR, within a control zone beneath the ceiling when the ceiling is less than 1000 feet.
(d) Except as provided in section 91.107, no person may take off or land

Altitude	Flight visibility	Distance from clouds
1200 feet or less above the surface (regardless of MSL altitude)		
Within controlled airspace	3 statute miles	{ 500 feet below 1000 feet above 2000 feet horizontal
Outside controlled airspace	1 statute mile except as provided in section 91.105(b)	Clear of clouds
More than 1200 feet above the surface but less than 10,000 feet MSL		
Within controlled airspace	3 statute miles	{ 500 feet below 1000 feet above 2000 feet horizontal
Outside controlled airspace	1 statute mile	{ 500 feet below 1000 feet above 2000 feet horizontal
More than 1200 feet above the surface and at or above 10,000 feet MSL	5 statute miles	{ 1000 feet below 1000 feet above 1 mile horizontal

an aircraft, or enter the traffic pattern of an airport, under VFR, within a control zone

    (1) Unless ground visibility at that airport is at least 3 statute miles; or

    (2) If ground visibility is not reported at that airport, unless flight visibility during landing or take off, or while operating in the traffic pattern, is at least 3 statute miles.

(e) For the purposes of this section, an aircraft operating at the base altitude of a transition area or control area is considered to be within the airspace directly below that area.

---

46. To conduct a VFR flight in controlled airspace, at an altitude that is less than 10,000 feet MSL, you should have at least

    (a) 3 miles visibility and remain at least 1,000 feet below or 500 feet above and 1 mile horizontally from all clouds.

    (b) 1 mile visibility and remain "clear of clouds."

    (c) 3 miles visibility and remain at least 500 feet below or 1000 feet above and 2000 feet horizontally from all clouds.

    (d) 1 mile visibility and remain at least 500 feet below or 1000 feet above and 2000 feet horizontally from all clouds.

47. During operations *outside controlled airspace* at altitudes of more than 1200 feet AGL, but less than 10,000 feet MSL, the minimum "distance below clouds" requirement for VFR flight is
    (a) 500 feet.
    (b) 1000 feet.
    (c) 1500 feet.
    (d) 2000 feet.

48. During VFR operations *outside controlled airspace* at altitudes of less than 1200 feet AGL, the minimum flight visibility requirement when operating airplanes is
    (a) 1 statute mile.
    (b) 3 statute miles.
    (c) 5 statute miles.
    (d) Not specified by regulations.

49. During operations *within controlled airspace* at altitudes of less than 1200 feet AGL, the minimum "distance above clouds" requirement for VFR flight is
    (a) 500 feet.
    (b) 1000 feet.
    (c) 1500 feet.
    (d) 2000 feet.

50. During operations at altitudes of more than 1200 feet above the surface and at or above 10,000 feet MSL, the minimum "horizontal distance from clouds" requirement for VFR flight is
    (a) 1000 feet.
    (b) 2000 feet.
    (c) ½ mile.
    (d) 1 mile.

51. The minimum ceiling and visibility to operate an airplane VFR in a control zone are
    (a) 500 feet and 1 mile.
    (b) 1000 feet and 3 miles.
    (c) 1400 feet and 2 miles.
    (d) 2000 feet and 3 miles.

91.107 Special VFR weather minimums
(a) Except as provided in section 93.113, when a person has received an appropriate ATC clearance, the special weather minimums of this section

instead of those contained in section 91.105 apply to the operation of an aircraft by that person in a control zone under VFR.

(b) No person may operate an aircraft in a control zone under VFR except clear of clouds.

(c) No person may operate an aircraft (other than a helicopter) in a control zone under VFR unless flight visibility is at least 1 statute mile.

(d) No person may take off or land an aircraft (other than a helicopter) at any airport in a control zone under VFR

    (1) Unless ground visibility at that airport is at least 1 statute mile; or

    (2) If ground visibility is not reported at that airport, unless flight visibility during landing or takeoff is at least 1 statute mile.

(e) No person may operate an aircraft (other than a helicopter) in a control zone under the special weather minimums of this section, between sunset and sunrise (or in Alaska, when the sun is more than six degrees below the horizon) unless:

    (1) That person meets the applicable requirements for instrument flight under Part 61 of this chapter; and

    (2) The aircraft is equipped as required in section 91.33(d).

---

52. A *special* VFR clearance authorizes the pilot of an airplane to operate VFR while within a control zone

    (a) At or below cloud base with a flight visibility of 1 mile or less, provided he remains below 1000 feet above the surface.

    (b) With no minimum visibility requirements if clear of the clouds.

    (c) If clear of clouds and the visibility is at least 1 mile.

    (d) When the ceiling is less than 1000 feet and visibility less than 1 mile if he does not exceed maneuvering speed.

53. A special VFR clearance applies to what kind of controlled airspace?

    (a) Transition Area.

    (b) Control Area.

    (c) Control Zone.

    (d) Airport Traffic Area.

54. No person may operate an airplane within a control zone at night under special VFR unless

    (a) The flight visibility is at least 3 miles.

    (b) The airplane is equipped for instrument flight, and pilot is instrument rated.

    (c) An instructor is aboard.

    (d) The flight can be conducted 500 feet below the clouds.

91.109 VFR cruising altitude or flight level

Except while holding in a holding pattern of 2 minutes or less, or while turning, each person operating an aircraft under VFR in level cruising flight more than 3000 feet above the surface shall maintain the appropriate altitude or flight level prescribed below, unless otherwise authorized by ATC:

(a) When operating below 18,000 feet MSL and

    (1) On a magnetic course of zero degrees through 179 degrees, any odd thousand-foot MSL altitude + 500 feet (such as 3500, 5500, or 7500); or

    (2) On a magnetic course of 180 degrees through 359 degrees, any even thousand-foot MSL altitude + 500 feet (such as 4500, 6500, or 8500). (See Figure 11.3.)

(b) When operating above 18,000 feet MSL to flight level 290 (inclusive), and

    (1) On a magnetic course of zero degrees through 179 degrees any odd flight level + 500 feet (such as 195, 215, or 235); or

    (2) On a magnetic course of 180 degrees through 359 degrees, any even flight level + 500 feet (such as 185, 205, or 225).

(c) When operating above flight level 290 and

    (1) On a magnetic course of zero degrees through 179 degrees, any flight level, at 4000-foot intervals, beginning at and including flight level 300 (such as flight level 300, 340, or 380); or

    (2) On a magnetic course of 180 degrees through 359 degrees, any flight level, at 4000-foot intervals, beginning at and including flight level 320 (such as flight level 320, 360, or 400).

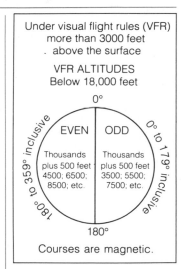

Figure 11.3 VFR cruising altitudes below 18,000 feet MSL.

---

55. You are cruising VFR on a magnetic heading of 174° and making good a magnetic course of 185°—and wish to maintain an altitude of more than 3000 feet above the surface, but less than 18,000 feet MSL. Of the following altitudes listed, which would be appropriate in this situation?

    (a) 5500 feet MSL.

    (b) 6000 feet MSL.

    (c) 6500 feet MSL.

    (d) 7000 feet MSL.

Subpart C—Maintenance, Preventive Maintenance, and Alterations

91.161 Applicability

(a) This subpart prescribes rules governing the maintenance, preventive maintenance, and alteration of U.S. registered civil aircraft operating within or without the United States.

(b) Section 91.165, 91.169, 91.171, 91.173, and 91.174 of this subpart do not apply to an aircraft maintained in accordance with a continuous airworthiness maintenance program as provided in Part 121, 127, or Subpart 135.411(a)(2) of this chapter.

(c) Section 91.165, 91.169, 91.171, and Subpart D of this Part do not apply to an airplane inspected in accordance with Part 125 of this chapter.

91.163 General

(a) The owner or operator of an aircraft is primarily responsible for maintaining that aircraft in an airworthy condition, including compliance with Part 39 of this chapter.

(b) No person may perform maintenance, preventive maintenance, or alterations on an aircraft other than as prescribed in this subpart and other applicable regulations, including Part 43 of this chapter.

(c) No person may operate an aircraft for which a manufacturer's maintenance manual or Instructions for Continued Airworthiness has been issued that contains an Airworthiness Limitations section unless the mandatory replacement times, inspection intervals, and related procedures specified in that section or alternative inspection intervals and related procedures set forth in an operations specification approved by the Administrator under Parts 121, 123, 127, or 135, or in accordance with an inspection program approved under Subpart 91.217(e), have been complied with.

---

56. The responsibility for ensuring that an aircraft is maintained in an airworthy condition is *primarily* that of the
(a) Certified mechanic who signs the aircraft maintenance records.
(b) Maintenance shop.
(c) Owner or operator of the aircraft.
(d) Pilot in command of the aircraft.

91.165 Maintenance required

Each owner or operator of an aircraft shall have that aircraft inspected as prescribed in Subparts 91.169, 91.171, and 91.172 and shall, between required inspections, have discrepancies repaired as prescribed in Part 43 of this chapter. In addition, each owner or operator shall ensure that maintenance personnel make appropriate entries in the aircraft maintenance records indicating that the aircraft has been approved for return to service.

91.167 Operation after maintenance, preventive maintenance, rebuilding, or alteration

(a) No person may operate any aircraft that has undergone maintenance, preventive maintenance, rebuilding, or alteration unless
    (1) It has been approved for return to service by a person authorized under Subpart 43.7 of this chapter; and
    (2) The maintenance record entry required by Subpart 43.9 or 43.11, as applicable, of this chapter has been made.

(b) No person may carry any person (other than crewmembers) in an aircraft that has been maintained, rebuilt, or altered in a manner that may have appreciably changed its flight characteristics or substantially affected its operation in flight until an appropriately rated pilot with at least a private pilot certificate flies the aircraft, makes an operational check of the maintenance performed or alteration made, and logs the flight in the aircraft records.

(c) The aircraft does not have to be flown as required by paragraph (b) of this section if, prior to flight, ground tests, inspections, or both show conclusively that the maintenance, preventive maintenance, rebuilding, or alteration has not appreciably changed the flight characteristics or substantially affected the flight operation of the aircraft.

---

57. If an alteration or repair may have appreciably changed an airplane's flight characteristics, the airplane must be test flown and approved for return to service by an appropriately rated pilot prior to being operated
    (a) Away from the vicinity of the airport.
    (b) By anyone who is not at least a commercial pilot.
    (c) With passengers aboard.
    (d) For compensation or hire.

91.169 Inspections

(a) Except as provided in paragraph (c) of this section, no person may operate an aircraft unless, within the preceding 12 calendar months, it has had
>   (1) An annual inspection in accordance with Part 43 of this chapter and has been approved for return to service by a person authorized by Subpart 43.7 of this chapter; or
>   (2) An inspection for the issue of an airworthiness certificate.

No inspection performed under paragraph (b) of this section may be substituted for any inspection required by this paragraph unless it is performed by a person authorized to perform annual inspections, and is entered as an "annual" inspection in the required maintenance records.

(b) Except as provided in paragraph (c) of this section, no person may operate an aircraft carrying any person (other than a crewmember) for hire, and no person may give flight instructions for hire in an aircraft which that person provides, unless within the preceding 100 hours of time in service it has received an annual or 100-hour inspection and been approved for return to service in accordance with Part 43 of this chapter, or received an inspection for the issuance of an airworthiness certificate in accordance with Part 21 of this chapter. The 100-hour limitation may be exceeded by not more than 10 hours if necessary to reach a place at which the inspection can be done. The excess time, however, is included in computing the next 100 hours of time in service.

(c) Paragraphs (a) and (b) of this section do not apply to
>   (1) An aircraft that carries a special flight permit, a current experimental certificate, or a provisional airworthiness certificate;
>   (2) An aircraft inspected in accordance with an approved aircraft inspection program under Part 123, 125, or 135 of this chapter and so identified by the registration number in the operations specifications of the certificate holder having the approved inspection program; or
>   (3) An aircraft subject to the requirements of paragraph (d) or (e) of this section.

58. An aircraft shall not be flown unless it has been given an "annual inspection"
   (a) Within the preceding 100 hours of logged flight time.
   (b) Within the preceding 12 calendar months.
   (c) Upon change of ownership.
   (d) Within the preceding 365 days, only if it is flown for hire.

59. To determine the expiration date of the last annual aircraft inspection, you should refer to the
   (a) Owner-Operator Manual.
   (b) Aircraft maintenance records.
   (c) Registration Certificate.
   (d) Airworthiness Certificate.

60. The Airworthiness Certificate of your airplane remains valid
   (a) As long as the airplane is maintained and operated as required by Federal Aviation Regulations.
   (b) As long as the aircraft has not had major damage.
   (c) As long as the aircraft has a current Registration Certificate.
   (d) From the date of its issuance.

61. The records of the airplane you plan to fly show that the last annual inspection was performed on November 15, 1984. The next *annual* inspection will be due no later than
   (a) 100 hours of flying time following the last annual inspection.
   (b) October 31, 1985.
   (c) 12 calendar months after the date shown on the Airworthiness Certificate.
   (d) November 30, 1985.

91.171 Altimeter system and altitude reporting equipment tests and inspections

(a) No person may operate an airplane in controlled airspace under IFR unless

   (1) Within the preceding 24 calendar months, each static pressure system, each altimeter instrument, and each automatic pressure altitude reporting system has been tested and inspected and found to comply with Appendices E and F of Part 43 of this chapter;

   (2) Except for the use of system drain and alternate static pressure valves, following any opening and closing of the static pressure system, that system has been tested and inspected and found to comply with paragraph (a), Appendix E, of Part 43 of this chapter; and

   (3) Following installation or maintenance on the automatic pressure altitude reporting system or the ATC transponder where data corre-

spondence error could be introduced, the integrated system has been tested, inspected, and found to comply with paragraph (c), Appendix E, of Part 43 of this chapter.

(b) The tests required by paragraph (a) of this section must be conducted by

(1) The manufacturer of the airplane on which the tests and inspections are to be performed;

(2) A certified repair station properly equipped to perform those functions and holding

(i)   An instrument rating, Class I;

(ii) A limited instrument rating appropriate to the make and model of appliance to be tested;

(iii) A limited rating appropriate to the test to be performed;

(iv) An airframe rating appropriate to the airplane to be tested; or

(v)   A limited rating for a manufacturer issued for the appliance in accordance with Subpart 145.101(b)(4) of this chapter; or

(3) A certified mechanic with an airframe rating (static pressure system tests and inspections only).

(c) Altimeter and altitude reporting equipment approved under Technical Standard Orders are considered to be tested and inspected as of the date of their manufacture.

(d) No person may operate an airplane in controlled airspace under IFR at an altitude above the maximum altitude at which all altimeters and the automatic altitude reporting system of that airplane have been tested.

91.172 ATC transponder tests and inspections

(a) No person may use an ATC transponder that is specified in Part 125, Subpart 91.24(a), Subpart 121.345(c), Subpart 127.123(b) or Subpart 135.143(c) of this chapter unless, within the preceding 24 calendar months, that ATC transponder has been tested and inspected and found to comply with Appendix F of Part 43 of this chapter; and

(b) Following any installation or maintenance on an ATC transponder where data correspondence error could be introduced, the integrated system has been tested, inspected, and found to comply with paragraph (c), Appendix E, of Part 43 of this chapter.

(c) The tests and inspections specified in this section must be conducted by

(1) A certified repair station properly equipped to perform those functions and holding

(i)   A radio rating, Class III;

(ii) A limited radio rating appropriate to the make and model transponder to be tested;

(iii) A limited rating appropriate to the test to be performed;

(iv) A limited rating for a manufacturer issued for the transponder in accordance with Subpart 145.101(b)(4) of this chapter; or

(2) A holder of a continuous airworthiness maintenance program as provided in Part 121, 127, or Subpart 135.411(a)(2) of this chapter; or

(3) The manufacturer of the aircraft on which the transponder to be tested is installed, if the transponder was installed by that manufacturer.

91.173 Maintenance records

(a) Except for work performed in accordance with Subpart 91.171, each registered owner or operator shall keep the following records for the periods specified in paragraph (b) of this section:

(1) Records of the maintenance and alteration, and records of the 100-hour, annual, progressive, and other required or approved inspections, as appropriate, for each aircraft (including the airframe) and each engine, propeller, rotor, and appliance of an aircraft. The records must include

(i)   A description (or reference to data acceptable to the Administrator) of the work performed;

(ii)   The date of completion of the work performed; and

(iii)   The signature and certificate number of the person approving the aircraft for return to service.

(2) Records containing the following information:

(i)   The total time in service of the airframe, each engine and each propeller.

(ii)   The current status of life-limited parts of each airframe, engine, propeller, rotor, and appliance.

(iii)   The time since last overhaul of all items installed on the aircraft which are required to be overhauled on a specified time basis.

(iv)   The identification of the current inspection status of the aircraft, including the times since the last inspections required by the inspection program under which the aircraft and its appliances are maintained.

(v)   The current status of applicable airworthiness directives (AD) including, for each, the method of compliance, the AD number, and revision date. If the AD involves recurring action, the time and date when the next action is required.

(vi)   Copies of the forms prescribed by Subpart 43.9(a) of this chapter for each major alteration to the airframe and currently installed engines, rotors, propellers, and appliances.

(b) The owner or operator shall retain the following records for the periods prescribed:

(1) The records specified in paragraph (a)(1) of this section shall be retained until the work is repeated or superseded by other work or for 1 year after the work is performed.

(2) The records specified in paragraph (a)(2) of this section shall be retained and transferred with the aircraft at the time the aircraft is sold.

(3) A list of defects furnished to a registered owner or operator under Subpart 43.11 of this chapter, shall be retained until the defects are repaired and the aircraft is approved for return to service.

(c) The owner or operator shall make all maintenance records required to be kept by this section available for inspection by the Administrator or any authorized representative of the National Transportation Safety Board (NTSB).

62. You can determine if an aircraft has had an annual inspection and has been returned to service by referring to the
   (a) Issuance date of the Airworthiness Certificate.
   (b) Appropriate notation in the aircraft maintenance records.
   (c) Relicensing date on the Airworthiness Certificate.
   (d) Appropriate notation on a Repair and Alteration Form.

63. After aircraft inspections have been made and defects repaired, who is responsible to ensure that maintenance personnel make appropriate entries in the aircraft and maintenance records indicating that an aircraft has been released to service?
   (a) Pilot in command of the aircraft.
   (b) Owner or operator of the aircraft.
   (c) FAA certificated repair station.
   (d) FAA certificated mechanic with inspection authorization.

64. Which record or document shall the owner or operator of an airplane keep to show compliance with an applicable Airworthiness Directive?
   (a) The aircraft Owner's Handbook.
   (b) The aircraft maintenance records.
   (c) The aircraft Airworthiness Certificate.
   (d) The aircraft Registration Certificate.

91.174 Transfer of maintenance records
Any owner or operator who sells a U.S. registered aircraft shall transfer to the purchaser, at the time of sale, the following records of that aircraft, in plain language form or in coded form at the election of the purchaser, if the coded form provides for the preservation and retrieval of information in a manner acceptable to the Administrator.
(a) The records specified in Subpart 91.173(a)(2).
(b) The records specified in Subpart 91.173(a)(1) which are not included in the records covered by paragraph (a) of this section, except that the purchaser may permit the seller to keep physical custody of such records. However, custody of records in the seller does not relieve the purchaser of his responsibility under Subpart 91.173(c), to make the records available for inspection by the Administrator or any authorized representative of the National Transportation Safety Board (NTSB).

91.175 Rebuilt engine maintenance records
(a) The owner or operator may use a new maintenance record, without previous operating history, for an aircraft engine rebuilt by the manufacturer or by an agency approved by the manufacturer.
(b) Each manufacturer or agency that grants zero time to an engine rebuilt by it shall enter, in the new record
   (1) A signed statement of the date the engine was rebuilt;

(2) Each change made as required by Airworthiness Directives; and

(3) Each change made in compliance with manufacturer's service bulletins; if the entry is specifically requested in that bulletin.

(c) For the purposes of this section, a rebuilt engine is a used engine that has been completely disassembled, inspected, repaired as necessary, reassembled, tested, and approved in the same manner and to the same tolerances and limits as a new engine with either new or used parts. However, all parts used in it must conform to the production drawing tolerances and limits for new parts or be of approved oversize or undersized dimensions for a new engine.

FAR PART 830:
NATIONAL TRANSPORTATION SAFETY BOARD RULES PERTAINING TO THE NOTIFICATION AND REPORTING OF AIRCRAFT ACCIDENTS OR INCIDENTS AND OVERDUE AIRCRAFT, AND PRESERVATION OF AIRCRAFT WRECKAGE, MAIL, CARGO, AND RECORDS

The National Transportation Safety Board (NTSB) is charged with the investigation and analysis of civil aviation accidents and incidents in the United States. It enjoys a close working relationship with the FAA and requires the participation of all members of the civil aviation industry in its programs to improve air safety. While you must begin the search for an overdue aircraft or report an incident or accident to the FAA first, there are instances of injury or damage where the NTSB must be involved. Part 830 provides guidance for these required actions.

Forms used for accident or incident reporting can be obtained from the Board field offices (listed under U.S. Government listings in telephone directories) in Anchorage, Alaska; Chicago, Illinois; Denver, Colorado; Fort Worth, Texas; Kansas City, Missouri; Los Angeles, California; Miami, Florida; New York, New York; Oakland, California; Seattle, Washington; and Washington, D.C., or by contacting the National Transportation Safety Board, Washington, D.C. 20594, or FAA Flight Standards District Offices.

The following subparts and sections are included in this text:

Subpart A—General

830.1   *Applicability*
830.2   *Definitions*

Subpart B—Initial Notification of Aircraft Accidents, Incidents, and Overdue Aircraft

830.5   *Immediate notification*
830.6   *Information to be given in notification*

Subpart C—Preservation of Aircraft Wreckage, Mail, Cargo, and Records

830.10   *Preservation of aircraft wreckage, mail, cargo, and records*

Subpart D—Reporting of Aircraft Accidents, Incidents, and Overdue Aircraft

830.15   Reports and statements to be filed

Subpart A—General

830.1 Applicability

This part contains rules pertaining to:

(a) Providing notice of and reporting aircraft accidents and incidents and certain other occurrences in the operation of aircraft when they involve civil aircraft of the United States wherever they occur, or foreign civil aircraft when such events occur in the United States, its territories, or possessions.

(b) Preservation of aircraft wreckage, mail, cargo, and records involving all civil aircraft in the United States, its territories, or possessions.

830.2 Definitions

As used in this part the following words or phrases are defined as follows:

Aircraft accident means an occurrence associated with the operation of an aircraft which takes place between the time any person boards the aircraft with the intention of flight until such time as all such persons have disembarked, and in which any person suffers death or serious injury as a result of being in or upon the aircraft or by direct contact with the aircraft or anything attached thereto, or in which the aircraft receives substantial damage.

Fatal injury means any injury which results in death within 30 days of the accident.

Operator means any person who causes or authorizes the operation of an aircraft; such as the owner, lessee, or bailee of an aircraft.

Serious injury means any injury which (1) requires hospitalization for more than 48 hours, commencing within 7 days from the date the injury was received; (2) results in a fracture of any bone (except simple fractures of fingers, toes, or nose); (3) involves lacerations which cause severe hemorrhages, nerve, muscle, or tendon damage; (4) involves injury to any internal organ; or (5) involves second- or third-degree burns, or any burns affecting more than 5 percent of the body surface.

Substantial damage:

(1) Except as provided in subparagraph (2) of this paragraph, substantial damage means damage or structural failure which adversely affects the structural strength, performance, or flight characteristics of the aircraft, and which would normally require major repair or replacement of the affected component.

(2) Engine failure, damage limited to an engine, bent fairings or cowling, dented skin, small punctured holes in the skin or fabric, ground damage to rotor or propeller blades, damage to landing gear, wheels, tire, flaps, engine accessories, brakes, or wing tips are not considered "substantial damage" for the purpose of this part.

Subpart B—Initial Notification of Aircraft Accidents, Incidents, and Overdue Aircraft

830.5 Immediate notification

The operator of an aircraft shall immediately, and by the most expeditious means available, notify the nearest National Transportation Safety Board, Bureau of Aviation Safety field office when:

(a) An aircraft accident or any of the following listed incidents occur:

(1) Flight control system malfunction or failure;

(2) Inability of any required flight crewmember to perform his normal flight duties as a result of injury or illness;

(3) Turbine engine rotor failures excluding compressor blades and turbine buckets;

(4) In-flight fire; or

(5) Aircraft collide in flight.

(b) An aircraft is overdue and is believed to have been involved in an accident.

830.6 Information to be given in notification

The notification required in section 830.5 shall contain the following information, if available:

(a) Type, nationality, and registration marks of the aircraft;

(b) Name of owner, and operator of the aircraft;

(c) Name of the pilot in command;

(d) Date and time of the accident;

(e) Last point of departure and point of intended landing of the aircraft;

(f) Position of the aircraft with reference to some easily defined geographical point;

(g) Number of persons aboard, number killed, and number seriously injured;

(h) Nature of the accident, the weather and the extent of damage to the aircraft, so far as is known; and

(i) A description of any explosives, radioactive materials, or other dangerous articles carried.

Subpart C—Preservation of Aircraft Wreckage, Mail, Cargo, and Records

830.10 Preservation of aircraft wreckage, mail, cargo, and records

(a) The operator of an aircraft is responsible for preserving to the extent possible any aircraft wreckage, cargo, and mail aboard the aircraft, and all records, including tapes of flight recorders and voice recorders, pertaining to the operation and maintenance of the aircraft and to the airmen involved in an accident or incident for which notification must be given until the Board takes custody thereof or a lease is granted pursuant to section 831.17.

(b) Prior to the time the Board or its authorized representative takes custody of aircraft wreckage, mail, or cargo, such wreckage, mail, or cargo may not be disturbed or moved except to the extent necessary:

(1) To remove persons injured or trapped;

(2) To protect the wreckage from further damage; or

(3) To protect the public from injury.

(c) Where it is necessary to disturb or move aircraft wreckage, mail, or cargo, sketches, descriptive notes, and photographs shall be made, if possible, of the accident locale including original position and condition of the wreckage and any significant impact marks.

(d) The operator of an aircraft involved in an accident or incident as defined in this part, shall retain all records and reports, including all internal documents and memoranda dealing with the accident or incident, until authorized by the Board to the contrary.

Subpart D—Reporting of Aircraft Accidents, Incidents, and Overdue Aircraft

830.15 Reports and statements to be filed

(a) *Reports*. The operator of an aircraft shall file a report as provided in paragraph (c) of this section on Board form 6120.1 or Board form 6120.2 within 10 days after an accident, or after 7 days if an overdue aircraft is still missing. A report on an incident for which notification is required by section 830.5(a) shall be filed only as requested by an authorized representative of the Board.

(b) *Crewmember statement*. Each crewmember, if physically able at the time the report is submitted, shall attach thereto a statement setting forth the facts, conditions, and circumstances relating to the accident or incident as they appear to him to the best of his knowledge and belief. If the crew-

---

65. Certain incidents require immediate notification to the nearest National Transportation Safety Board Field Office. Which of the following incidents would require this action?
    (a) Substantial aircraft ground fire with no intention of flight.
    (b) Inability of any required crewmember to perform normal flight duties due to inflight injury or illness.
    (c) Landing gear damage, due to a hard landing.
    (d) A forced landing due to engine failure.

66. Notification requirements pertaining to aircraft accidents, incidents, and overdue aircraft are covered in
    (a) Department of Transportation Regulations, Part 300, Emergency Procedures.
    (b) National Transportation Safety Board regulations, Part 830.
    (c) Federal Aviation Regulations, Part 91, General Operating and Flight Rules.
    (d) Federal Aviation Regulations, Part 13, Enforcement Procedures.

67. Suppose an aircraft is involved in an accident that results in substantial damage to the aircraft but no injuries to the occupants. When must the pilot or operator of the aircraft notify the nearest National Transportation Safety Board Field Office of the occurrence?
    (a) Within 10 days.
    (b) Within 48 hours.
    (c) Immediately.
    (d) Within 1 week.

68. Of the following incidents, which would require an immediate notification to the nearest National Transportation Safety Board Field Office?
    (a) Minor damage to an aircraft with no intention of flight, sustained during ground operations with the engine functioning.
    (b) Damage to a landing gear as a result of a hard landing.
    (c) An inflight generator failure.
    (d) Flight control system malfunction or failure.

69. Which of these incidents would require that an immediate notification be made to the nearest National Transportation Safety Board Field Office?
    (a) Inflight hail damage.
    (b) An inflight generator or alternator failure.
    (c) An inflight radio (communication) failure.
    (d) An overdue aircraft that is believed to be involved in an accident.

70. Of the following incidents, which would necessitate an immediate notification to the nearest National Transportation Safety Board Field Office?
    (a) Ground damage to the propeller blades.
    (b) An inflight loss of VOR receiver capability.
    (c) An inflight fire.
    (d) An inflight generator/alternator failure.

member is incapacitated, he shall submit the statement as soon as he is physically able.

(c) *Where to file the reports.* The operator of an aircraft shall file with the field office of the Board nearest the accident or incident.

VIOLATION OF FARs

The sixteenth-century French philosopher Montaigne wrote that "there is no man so good who, were he to submit all his thoughts and actions to the laws, would not deserve hanging ten times in his life." In a later age, the screen star Mae West agreed that it was "okay to *crack* a few laws now and then so long as you don't break any."

While these conclusions may be a little extreme, the point they make is quite important. It is difficult to operate in a highly technical, highly regulated environment without "nudging" the rules a little bit, albeit inadvertently. For example, just how does one measure "2000 feet horizontally" from a cloud, or "500 feet laterally" from an object on a remote field where one is practicing simulated forced landings? While no conscientious pilot ever sets out intentionally to break the rules, even with the best intentions, violations do sometimes occur.

The FAA considers all pilot actions subject to review. Violations not witnessed by the FAA or other pilots are frequently reported by the public, particularly instances of real or apparent buzzing or acrobatics in unusual areas. Even deviations to FARs made under a pilot's so-called emergency authority provisions may have to be defended, but only on request by the FAA.

Violations of FARs are in no sense taken lightly by regulatory agencies. Penalties for infractions can range from warnings or reprimands (which are made part of your permanent flying records) to fines of up to $1000 per violation (with higher limits contemplated). In severe cases, the offending pilot's license may be suspended or revoked. Certain violations may carry criminal penalties as well; and, as is the case with your automobile, you may be liable under civil codes for damage done to other persons or property as the result of a flying accident or incident, in the air or on the ground.

Your study of FARs will not end with the completion of this chapter. Aviation journals and pilots' magazines print many columns and feature articles about FARs—their interpretation and implementation—and other regulatory issues. The FAA informs the flying public about its intentions to modify aviation regulations by publishing Notices of Proposed Rule-Making (NPRMs). No regulation is ever added, changed, or deleted without the opportunity for thorough scrutiny by those being regulated.

The FARs are specific, frequently complex, and always important. But until engineers devise a way to build common sense into a machine, conformance to regulations and aviation safety will be left largely up to you—the pilot.

ANSWERS TO SAMPLE QUESTIONS

No.	Answer	FAR	No.	Answer	FAR
1.	c	61.3 a, b	36.	c	91.77
2.	c	61.19 c	37.	d	91.77
3.	b	61.23 c	38.	b	91.79 c
4.	c	61.57 c	39.	b	91.79 b
5.	d	61.57 d	40.	a	91.81 a-1-iii
6.	b	61.57 a	41.	c	91.83 d
7.	c	61.60	42.	c	91.87 b
8.	b	61.118 b	43.	a	91.87 h
9.	c	91.3	44.	b	91.89 c
10.	a	91.5 b	45.	c	91.90 a
11.	a	91.5 a	46.	c	91.105 a
12.	b	91.11 b	47.	a	91.105 a
13.	a	91.11 a	48.	a	91.105 a
14.	d	91.14 a	49.	b	91.105 a
15.	c	91.14 a	50.	d	91.105 a
16.	a	91.29 b	51.	b	91.105 c, d
17.	c	61.3 c, 91.27 a	52.	c	91.107 b, c
18.	d	91.31 b, e	53.	c	91.107 a
19.	a	91.31 b, e	54.	b	91.107 e
20.	c	91.27 a	55.	c	91.109 a
21.	d	91.32 a	56.	c	91.163 a
22.	c	91.52 d	57.	c	91.167 b
23.	d	91.52 d	58.	b	91.169 a
24.	b	91.67 e	59.	b	91.169 a
25.	d	91.67 c	60.	a	91.169, 91.27
26.	d	91.67 c	61.	d	91.169 a
27.	c	91.67 d	62.	b	91.173 a
28.	b	91.70 b	63.	b	91.165
29.	c	91.70 a	64.	b	91.173 a
30.	b	91.15 c, 91.71	65.	b	NTSB Part 830.5 a2
31.	d	91.71 a	66.	b	NTSB Part 830
32.	d	91.71 c	67.	c	NTSB Part 830.5
33.	d	91.71 d	68.	d	NTSB Part 830.5 a1
34.	b	91.73	69.	d	NTSB Part 830.5 b
35.	b	91.75 d	70.	c	NTSB Part 830.5 a4

PART VI
NAVIGATION

But whereof does the navigator think as he threads his
way across the sky? Of what is the needle that guides
the thread? . . . Navigation is a pursuit of truth.

Guy Murchie
Song of the Sky

C H E C K P O I N T S

What are the principles of air navigation? ✈ How do pilots interpret aeronautical charts
and use them for planning and conducting VFR flights? ✈ What is pilotage and what
are its limitations? ✈ What are the basic steps in dead reckoning navigation? ✈ How
do pilots use basic navigational tools—the chart, plotter, and computer—to solve navigation problems quickly and accurately?

BASICS OF AIR NAVIGATION

Human beings are born navigators. We take to navigation as instinctively as migrating animals or birds that follow the seasons from one part of the earth to another. We survey our territories carefully, learning first the boundaries of our home, then our neighborhood and city, and sometimes our state and nation and even more distant places.

The world can seem a pretty big place when viewed from its surface, on which mountain ranges and seas act as natural boundaries and restrict vision and mobility. The age of flight has changed our perspective, however. As Saint-Exupéry wrote in *Wind, Sand, and Stars,* "The airplane has unveiled for us the true face of the earth." Airplanes, like their predecessors, ocean-going ships, have stimulated our basic desire "to go and to know." Aviation technology, together with the instinct to explore, has made navigation a distinctive human art—combining science and intuition, skill and common sense, audacity and perseverance. Ancient sailors who demonstrated these traits were called *navigators,* for "those who set the course of ships *(navis)*." Today, NASA has updated this definition for those who ply the ocean of air, calling **air navigation** "the art of determining the geographic position, and maintaining the desired direction, of an aircraft relative to the earth's surface." Today, all pilots are navigators.

All navigational problems, whether marine or aerial, have certain things in common. Before you can go someplace else, you must know where you are. Determining your location with respect to the earth's surface is called *fixing* a position, or simply determining a fix. A **fix** is made wherever two or more **lines of position (LOPs)** cross. Suppose, for example, you telephone a taxicab company and ask the dispatcher to send a cab to Walnut Street. This information limits your whereabouts to a line of possible locations as long as the stretch of blocks known as Walnut Street, but it would be difficult and time consuming for the cab driver to search the entire length of the street looking for you. If you add that you are also on Third Street, you will be specifying a unique point on both streets—the place where they cross. You will have made a fix using the two LOPs Walnut Street and Third Street. With this knowledge in hand, the dispatcher is now in a position to send a cab to your location so that you can go to another fixed position across town.

Determining LOPs and fixes is at the heart of all navigational problems. With this information it is possible to calculate the headings you must follow in order to arrive at your destination.

METHODS OF NAVIGATION

There are five basic methods of navigation:

1. **Pilotage** is navigation by reference to visible landmarks.
2. **Dead reckoning (DR)** is navigation along a predetermined course, based on time, speed, and distance calculations. The effects of wind are included in these calculations.
3. **Radio navigation** utilizes airborne radios in conjunction with ground-based equipment to establish lines of position.

4. Celestial navigation uses observations of the planets and stars and almanac data to establish position on the earth's surface.

5. Inertial navigation uses extremely sensitive motion sensors and a computer to monitor displacement from a known position. The computer is set with the aircraft's exact position before takeoff. Then the sensors report every motion of the airplane, and the computer continually updates its position information.

Of these methods, pilotage and dead reckoning are considered fundamental and are the subject of this chapter. Knowledge of these fundamentals is essential to any navigation method.

Radio navigation is covered in the next chapter. Most practical air navigation involves a combination of pilotage, DR, and radio techniques.

Celestial and intertial navigation represent, respectively, the oldest and one of the newest navigation methods. Both require special equipment and training. It is unlikely that you will encounter either one as a private pilot, so these methods are not covered in this text.

LONGITUDE AND LATITUDE—A NAVIGATOR'S FRAME OF REFERENCE

The taxicab example that opened this chapter made use of a set of streets to define a location within a city. The streets provide both a means to get from place to place and a *coordinate system,* which is used to describe locations. This system works fine for its specific purpose, but general navigation to *any* point on earth requires a more general coordinate system.

The Geographic Coordinate System

To construct a coordinate system on the earth's surface, we idealize the earth as a sphere. Fortunately, the earth is a *spinning* sphere. The axis of rotation provides fixed reference points (the North and South Poles) from which to build a system of global lines of position (see Figure 12.1). First, we extend straight lines from pole to pole called **lines of longitude,** or **meridians.** These meridians are then divided evenly into intersecting **lines of latitude,** or **parallels**—so called because they, unlike meridians, do not converge at any point but run parallel to one another, forming a grid (pattern of intersections) with the lines of longitude.

The first meridian we draw runs north and south through Greenwich, England, and is known as the **prime meridian.** All other meridians are positioned either to the east or the west of this first meridian. They are formally referred to as east or west lines of longitude and are numbered in angular degrees, from 0° to 180° until "east meets west" on the reverse side of the earth. Lines of latitude, on the other hand, are identified by their position either north or south of the **equator,** the line that bisects the earth into Northern and Southern Hemispheres. Parallels are also numbered in angular degrees, from 0° at the equator to 90° at the poles, both north and south (see Figure 12.2a). For both latitude and longitude the areas between whole degrees are subdivided into 60 arc minutes per degree and

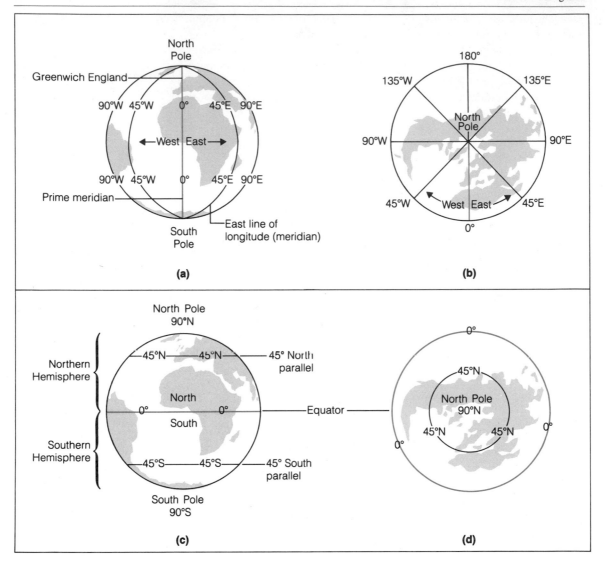

Figure 12.1 Basics of the geographic coordinate system. (a) The lines of longitude or meridians, side view. (b) Lines of longitude, top view. (c) The lines of latitude or parallels, side view. (d) Lines of latitude, top view.

60 arc seconds per minute. Since a degree of latitude is the same size anywhere on earth, we can use it as a measure of distance—the **nautical mile (NM),** which is equal to one minute of latitude marked off vertically, north and south, on a meridian. Minutes of longitude, marked off horizontally on parallels east and west, show no such relationship, since they converge and become smaller at the poles. One minute of longitude equals one nautical mile only at the equator.

The places where meridians and parallels cross are called **coordinates,** and the complete network of intersecting longitudinal and latitudinal LOPs, precisely defined by degrees and subunits of degrees, is called the **geographic coordinate system.** Every natural feature or constructed object

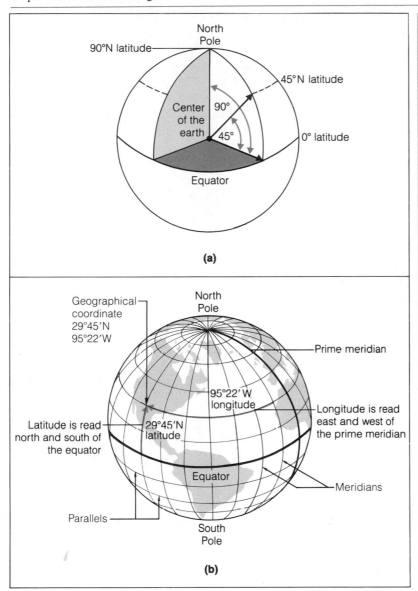

on the surface of the earth has a coordinate as its own unique address (see Figure 12.2b). Furthermore, any object moving over the earth's surface can claim a coordinate as a navigational fix for the instant of time during which the coordinate was beneath it.

Great and Small Circles
The grid pattern we have just described is really a set of circles, some running north and south, converging at the poles and of equal size; others running east and west, parallel to each other and diminishing in size from

the largest at the equator to the smallest at the poles. The circles whose planes run through the center of the earth are known as **great circles,** and they have special significance to a navigator. An arc of a great circle represents the shortest distance between any two points on the earth's surface connected by that arc (see Figure 12.3). To express it another way, if a pilot wished to fly between two cities by the shortest possible route, the pilot would pick a great circle for the airplane's course. There is simply no shorter way to get from one point to another on the surface of a sphere other than to burrow into the sphere.

All meridians are great circles, but the only parallel that is a great circle is the equator. Why? Because it is the only parallel whose plane passes through the center of the earth. All the other parallels are **small circles,** so called because their planes do not run through the center of the earth. A line drawn on the surface of a sphere that is the arc of a small circle is called a **rhumb line.** Such a line connecting any two cities would *not* represent the shortest surface distance between them. Unless the navigator had a particular objective in mind, rhumb lines would not be the most efficient navigational courses.

Figure 12.3 Great and small circles. (a) A comparison of distance covered by a great circle and rhumb line. (b) Classifications.

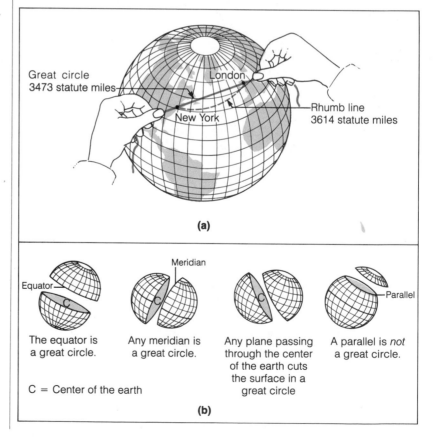

(a)

Meridian

Equator

C

C

C

Parallel

The equator is a great circle.

Any meridian is a great circle.

Any plane passing through the center of the earth cuts the surface in a great circle

A parallel is *not* a great circle.

C = Center of the earth

(b)

Great circle 3473 statute miles

London

New York

Rhumb line 3614 statute miles

Time Zones

We all expect the sun to rise in the morning, be directly overhead about noon, then set in the evening. In other words, we synchronize our local time with the sun. Obviously, the sun cannot be directly overhead everywhere at the same time, so local time is a function of location on the earth. The earth rotates 360° in 24 hours. If we divide 360 by 24, we see that the earth rotates 15° per hour. Therefore, **time zones** have been established every 15° around the earth. The exact boundaries between time zones are established locally, for economic and political purposes. The continental United States has four time zones, shown in Figure 12.4.

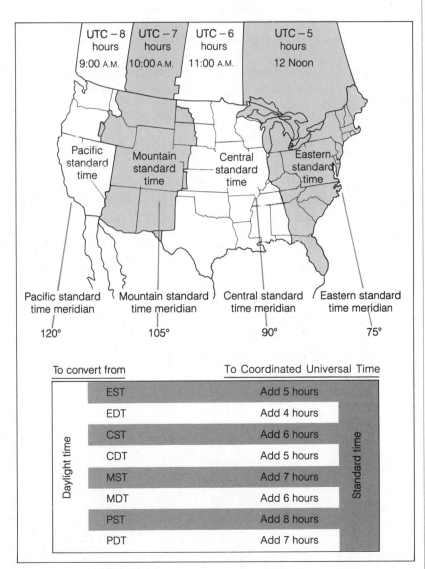

Figure 12.4 Continental United States' time zones.

To convert from	To Coordinated Universal Time
EST	Add 5 hours
EDT	Add 4 hours
CST	Add 6 hours
CDT	Add 5 hours
MST	Add 7 hours
MDT	Add 6 hours
PST	Add 8 hours
PDT	Add 7 hours

Most communities (but not all) further adjust local time according to the season of the year. When this is done, the local time is advanced 1 hour in the spring, and *daylight savings time* is in effect. In the fall the clocks are set back to *standard time*.

As you can see, knowing what time it is can be complicated. To eliminate any ambiguity about time, navigators need one worldwide standard time so that there is no confusion when traveling across many local time zones. This standard time is also necessary when reporting weather data, which is time dependent but applies across many time zones simultaneously. Therefore, the time in Greenwich, England, has been established as the international standard time for navigational and weather reporting purposes. Recall that this is known as **coordinated universal time (UTC),** or **zulu time.** Figure 12.4 lists the conversions from local times in the United States to UTC time. [Note: UTC used to be called *Greenwich mean time (GMT).*]

The 24-hour clock.   Converting local time to UTC and back can be confusing if you have to worry whether it's 1:00 A.M. or 1:00 P.M. To eliminate this ambiguity, times are usually expressed in a 24-hour format rather than the 12-hour format we use in everyday affairs. Figure 12.5 shows a clock with both sets of markings. In the 24-hour format, time is expressed as four digits. The first two are hours, the last two are minutes past the hour. Thus, midnight (the start of the day) is 0000; 1:00 A.M. is 0100; 2:00 A.M. is 0200; and so on up to 1200. Then the clock does strike 13! In the 24-hour format, 1:00 P.M. is 1300, and it continues, 1400, 1500, and so on. One minute before midnight is 2359, then the clock strikes 0000 again to start another day.

Figure 12.5 Time in 12- and 24-hour notation.

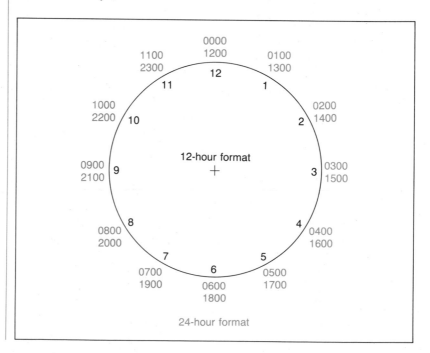

From Circular Coordinates to Flat Maps

Since the geographic coordinate system is so essential, you might expect to see a globe at the pilot's station of every ship and airplane. But using a globe for daily navigation would be impractical—and even undesirable, given the great scale of the earth's sphere and the size of the surface details of interest to navigators. Thus, much thought has been given over the years to projecting the earth's spherical outline onto a two-dimensional field. In this way the detail on the earth's surface may be expanded or condensed as necessary, spread out to be studied on a table, and rolled or folded to be carried easily from place to place.

To be useful for navigation, a projection must have three important characteristics:

1. The shapes of the globe's physical features must be preserved, including their angular relationships.

2. Zones of equal area must be represented in their correct relative proportions.

3. The distance between any two points on the map must be the same distance you would get measuring it on the globe.

It is also important to have great circles represented as straight lines on the map. Navigators are usually interested in the most direct route between two points.

There are a variety of projection methods for maps because no one projection is capable of meeting all of these objectives over the earth's entire surface. However, one projection has proved to be the most useful for aeronautical charts: the Lambert projection.

The *Lambert conformal conic projection,* or **Lambert projection** for short (see Figure 12.6), is based on mathematical formulas rather than graphic geometry for its proportions. This representation provides the best flat-map accuracy for distances and angular directions and thus is widely used for aeronautical charts.

The secret of the Lambert projection's accuracy is that it represents a small section of a giant cone superimposed on the spherical earth, bounded by an upper and lower *standard parallel.* Only the top and bottom edges of the conical section, when flattened out, are subject to significant distortion. The bar scale describing distances on a Lambert chart represents an average of the upper and lower distances and can be used anywhere on the chart with reasonable accuracy. A straight line drawn on a Lambert chart is an approximate great circle on a globe and represents the shortest distance between any two points depicted.

AERONAUTICAL CHARTS

The purpose of any chart is to show the relationship between the geographical coordinate system and the details of the earth's surface. These surface features are particularly important when you are planning low-altitude flights, since they may affect safety.

Figure 12.6 The Lambert conformal conic projection.

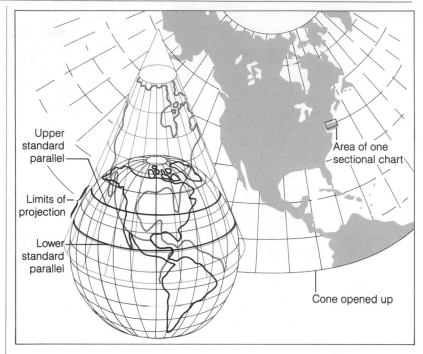

Upper standard parallel

Limits of projection

Lower standard parallel

Area of one sectional chart

Cone opened up

The National Oceanic and Atmospheric Administration (NOAA) publishes many types of charts for VFR navigation. The three most commonly used inflight charts are the following:

1. VFR terminal area charts. These are large-scale charts (1:250,000; roughly 4 statute miles to the inch) that show considerable detail around a busy air terminal.

2. Sectional charts. These are the most commonly used aeronautical charts. They have a scale of 1:500,000, which is about 8 statute miles to the inch.

3. World aeronautical charts (WACs). Pilots who fly higher-performance airplanes often prefer a smaller-scale chart. WACs have a scale of 1:1,000,000 or about 16 statute miles to the inch.

The information on these charts is grouped into three categories:

1. *Topographical data,* describing the features of the earth's surface, both natural and man-made.

2. *Aeronautical data,* information about airports, radio navigation aids, communications, and airspace.

3. *The legend,* explaining all the symbols and colors used on the chart. Take some time and review the legend of one of these charts carefully. A sample chart is included with the text for this purpose.

The legend of each chart also explains the effective dates for the data it contains (see Figure 12.7). You are responsible, as pilot-in-command, for using current data when planning a flight, and this responsibility includes using current charts. Remember also that both the *Airport/Facility Directory* and *NOTAMs* may contain changes to charts made after the chart was published.

Figure 12.7 shows the topographical and obstruction symbols used on these charts (refer to the sample sectional for an actual color example). Notice the following:

1. Roads and highways that can be distinguished from the air are shown in magenta. Major highways may be identified.

2. Railroads are shown as black lines with small, evenly spaced crossbars. Sets of double crossbars means two tracks, three crossbars together means three tracks, and so on.

3. Drainage features, such as streams, lakes, rivers, and canals, are shown in blue. The high-water level of perennial lakes and streams is shown with dashed blue lines.

4. Bridges and viaducts are shown in magenta or black.

5. Power lines are shown with a black line and symbols resembling power line towers.

6. Mines and quarries are shown by a set of crossing pickaxe symbols.

7. Lookout towers are identified with both their site number and (MSL) elevation of the base of the tower.

8. Coast Guard stations are shown by a black diamond and a *CG*.

9. Racetracks and outdoor theaters are shown by symbols resembling those items.

10. Tall obstructions (1000 feet AGL and higher) are shown with a stretched, inverted *V* symbol. A normal inverted V indicates an obstruction lower than 1000 feet AGL. Every obstruction is marked with the MSL elevation of its top in bold numbers. The nonbold number in parentheses is the height above ground.

11. Within each block bounded by lines of longitude and latitude is a bold blue figure (see Figure 12.7). This is the *maximum elevation figure* within that area, represented in thousands and hundreds of feet above MSL. This altitude will put you above the highest known feature, natural or manmade, in that block.

These charts are color coded to aid in representing elevation and contours (refer to the sample sectional for the actual colors).

Figure 12.8 presents the symbols used to identify the various types of airports and the airport data key. Your attention is directed to the following details:

1. An open circle indicates an airport without paved runways or a paved runway that is less than 1500 feet long.

Figure 12.7 Sectional chart excerpts. *Clockwise from top:* effective dates; maximum elevation figure; color data and obstruction symbols; and topographical information.

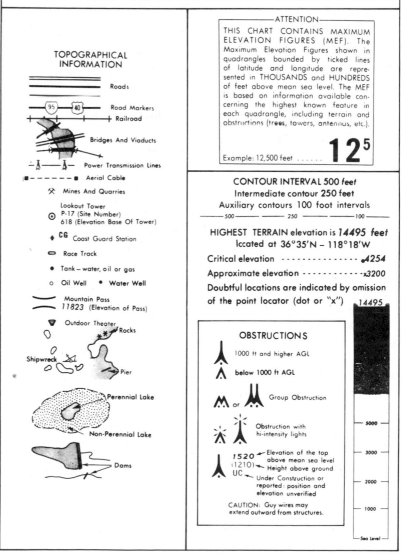

SAN FRANCISCO
SECTIONAL AERONAUTICAL CHART
SCALE 1:500,000

Lambert Conformal Conic Projection Standard Rarallels 33°20′ and 38°40′
Topographic data corrected to January 19

32 ND EDITION   *April 12, 19*
Includes airspace amendments effective   *March 15, 19*
and all other aeronautical data received by   *February 23, 19*
Consult appropriate NOTAMs and Flight Information
Publications for supplemental data and current information.
This chart will become *OBSOLETE FOR USE IN NAVIGATION* upon publication of
the next edition scheduled for   *OCTOBER 25, 19*

PUBLISHED IN ACCORDANCE WITH INTER-AGENCY AIR CARTOGRAPHIC COMMITTEE
SPECIFICATIONS AND AGREEMENTS APPROVED BY
DEPARTMENT OF DEFENSE ★ FEDERAL AVIATION ADMINISTRATION ★ DEPARTMENT OF COMMERCE

TOPOGRAPHICAL INFORMATION

Roads
Road Markers   95   40
Railroad
Bridges And Viaducts
Power Transmission Lines
Aerial Cable
Mines And Quarries
Lookout Tower
P-17 (Site Number)
618 (Elevation Base Of Tower)
CG   Coast Guard Station
Race Track
Tank – water, oil or gas
Oil Well   ● Water Well
Mountain Pass
11823 (Elevation of Pass)
Outdoor Theater
Rocks
Shipwreck
Pier
Perennial Lake
Non-Perennial Lake
Dams

— ATTENTION —
THIS CHART CONTAINS MAXIMUM ELEVATION FIGURES (MEF). The Maximum Elevation Figures shown in quadrangles bounded by ticked lines of latitude and longitude are represented in THOUSANDS and HUNDREDS of feet above mean sea level. The MEF is based on information available concerning the highest known feature in each quadrangle, including terrain and obstructions (trees, towers, antennas, etc.).

Example: 12,500 feet **12⁵**

CONTOUR INTERVAL 500 feet
Intermediate contour 250 feet
Auxiliary contours 100 foot intervals
— 500 —   — 250 —   — 100 —

HIGHEST TERRAIN elevation is *14495 feet*
located at 36°35′N – 118°18′W

Critical elevation - - - - - - - - - - - - - - ▲4254
Approximate elevation - - - - - - - - - - - ×3200
Doubtful locations are indicated by omission of the point locator (dot or "x")

14495

OBSTRUCTIONS

1000 ft and higher AGL
below 1000 ft AGL
or   Group Obstruction
Obstruction with hi-intensity lights
1520 ← Elevation of the top above mean sea level
(1210) ← Height above ground
UC ← Under Construction or reported: position and elevation unverified

CAUTION: Guy wires may extend outward from structures.

5000
3000
2000
1000
Sea Level

2. A circle symbol that shows the runway pattern is used for airports with paved runways from 1500 to 8000 feet long. Airports with runways longer than 8000 feet have a noncircular symbol showing the runway pattern. Note that runways not in use may show up in these patterns for visual identification of the airport.

3. Airports with services (with attendants and with fuel available during normal working times) have four square "tick marks" sticking out from the circle symbol. No tick marks on a circle symbol means that, generally, no services are available. Large airports (with noncircular symbols) do not show the availability of services on the symbol. The *Airport/Facility Directory* must be consulted to obtain that information.

4. A star on the airport symbol indicates a rotating beacon in operation from sunset to sunrise.

5. An airport data key always has at least two lines: the name line and the elevation line.

6. If the airport has a control tower, the tower frequency is given on the name line. An asterisk after the frequency indicates part-time tower operation.

7. The airport elevation is given in full, no abbreviations. (In Figure 12.8 the airport is at 3 feet MSL.)

8. Notice the various kinds of lighting an airport may have. The use of pilot-controlled lighting is explained in the *Airport/Facility Directory*.

9. The length of the longest runway is given in *hundreds of feet* (add two zeros).

Figure 12.8 Sectional chart excerpt: aeronautical data legend.

Figure 12.9 Sectional chart excerpt: airport and airspace data legend.

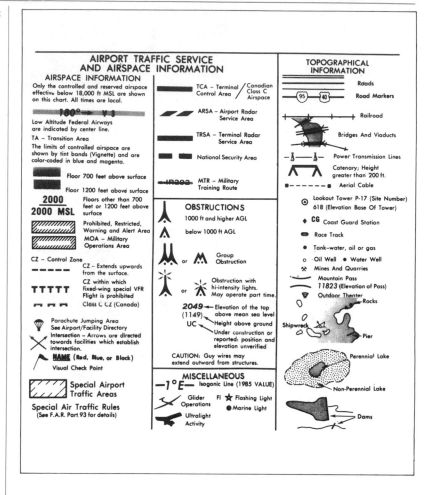

Figure 12.9 illustrates the details of the symbols used to identify various kinds of airspace. Again, refer to the sample sectional for the correct colors.

1. A feathered magenta band bounds areas where controlled airspace begins at 700 feet AGL. A feathered blue band indicates that controlled airspace begins at 1200 feet AGL.

2. Areas where controlled airspace begins at an altitude other than 700 or 1200 feet AGL are shown in bold blue numbers.

3. Prohibited, restricted, warning, and alert areas are bounded by a blue crosshatch.

4. Military operations areas (MOAs) are bounded by a magenta crosshatch.

5. Control zones are bounded by a blue dashed line. If no special VFR is allowed in the control zone, it is bounded by *T*s.

6. Terminal Control Areas (TCAs) are outlined by a solid blue line. Terminal radar service areas (TRSAs) are outlined in magenta.

7. Airport radar service areas (ARSAs) are outlined by a broken magenta line.

8. A blue symbol indicates airports with a control tower operating at least part of the time. Magenta circles mean the airport is uncontrolled.

Be sure to familiarize yourself with *all* the symbols on the chart. The outline provided here is intended to *supplement* a thorough review of the legend. The symbols for radio aids and communication are discussed in Chapter 13.

THE ART OF PILOTAGE

Pilotage is the simplest method of navigation. It consists of fixing your position over the earth's surface and directing the airplane to its next navigational fix by reference to visible landmarks. To navigate by pilotage, you need little more than a clear day, a sectional chart for determining position, and a straightedge for drawing straight lines.

Flight Planning by Pilotage

Navigating by pilotage is similar to picking your way through the fields on a cross-country hike by watching for a particular hill, a neighbor's barn, or "three dead oaks by the fork in the road." Obviously, pilotage is possible only if you can see the ground. In navigational terms, this means that you must mentally calculate lines of position (LOP) (with the assistance of a chart) that fix your airplane over the ground in relation to known landmarks, and then determine new headings as required to reach each successive landmark and your final destination. Since you do not want to be selecting landmarks hurriedly in flight, you will have to do some preflight planning even to use this simplest navigational method safely.

Flight planning based on pilotage is carried out in the following steps:

1. *Choosing the correct chart.* Select the aeronautical chart suitable for your flight. Make sure it is a valid, current issue. Turn the chart so that north is at the top, directly away from you.

2. *Picking a general route.* Make a general inspection of the terrain between your departure point and destination. Determine whether there are any surface features or special-use airspace you would choose to avoid.

3. *Determining a course line.* Let us assume that you elect to use a direct route. Lay a straightedge over the centers of both your departure airport symbol and destination airport symbol. Connect the two points with a pencil line. Do not mark through the airport symbol or its data block, to avoid obliterating any data. This is your **course** line, and it represents a great circle route on the Lambert conformal chart. Your objective is to make the airplane's **track** (the actual path it flies over the ground) match this course line as closely as possible.

4. *Measuring the total distance.* Using the mileage scale on the chart, measure the distance from the departure airport to your destination. You must check the performance data in your Pilot's Operating Handbook to be sure you have adequate fuel for the trip.

5. *Adding mileage reminders.* With the mileage scale still in place, divide your true course line into equal intervals by placing tick marks every 10 to 20 miles. These marks will help you locate landmarks, quickly measure distances to other features or airports, and monitor progress en route.

6. *Selecting checkpoints.* The real test of good pilotage is the ability to select prominent landmarks that can serve as **checkpoints** for your flight. In pilotage, you determine LOPs by imagining yourself on a line extending between the aircraft and a landmark. When you "draw" such a line for at least two landmarks and compare the results with the features on your chart, you should have a reasonable intersection of two LOPs, and thus a fix. If the fix confirms that the airplane's track is following the course line, you may continue on the same heading. If it indicates that the airplane's track is off the course line, you will have to change the airplane's heading in order to resume your desired course. It is important to correct your course before you are scheduled to pass over your next checkpoint. Otherwise, you will risk missing the checkpoint and increase your chances of getting lost.

The first landmark you look for after takeoff should be close enough to the airport to be readily distinguishable, but not so close that you are still busy dealing with the airport traffic pattern or other terminal procedures when you pass it. After that you will often be able to determine LOPs easily by picking several major and a number of minor landmarks and comparing their positions quickly. As a general rule, landmarks that make the best checkpoints have the following characteristics:

1. They are prominent enough to be easily distinguished from other surface features.

2. They are oriented or formed in such a way as to suggest direction. Examples would be a row of radio towers aligned at a particular angle to your route, a fork or prominent bend in an otherwise straight length of river, a long ridge standing by itself, or a small town with a large grain silo positioned directly north of it.

3. The landmarks should be located on both sides of the course line, whenever possible, and be visible from one another. This arrangement is known as **bracketing** the course line. Its purpose is to compensate for the fact that, even with visibility well above VFR minimums, it can be difficult to immediately identify a landmark and to place your airplane in relation to it. If you have selected landmarks that bracket your route, you can immediately relate the LOPs derived from them to your airplane's track.

Limitations of Pilotage

Pilotage is limited primarily by visibility. Hazy conditions can obscure or distort even the most prominent feature. You must have suitable landmarks too, and these are not always available. Many classic "town-highway-tower" combinations look alike. Moreover, pilots trained in mountainous regions can become disoriented over the flat Midwest, and pilots from flat regions are sometimes confused by the Far West's seemingly endless array of mountain peaks and valleys. Thus, pilotage is best used on short flights over familiar terrain. While it is an excellent supplement to more advanced techniques of navigation, it is seldom a completely suitable replacement for them. Let us now consider a method of navigation that solves many of the problems of pilotage—dead reckoning.

DEAD RECKONING NAVIGATION

Dead reckoning is a more scientific approach to navigation than pilotage. With DR, you can set a compass heading from one point to another, correcting for wind effects and variations in the earth's magnetic field, and then monitor the progress of the flight with calculations relating time, speed, and distance. Thus, the more serious limitations of landmark navigation are disposed of, and you can follow longer routes and have better control over flight planning variables. Regardless of the means of determining LOPs, the flight planning techniques used in preparing for DR navigation and the related computations are central to nearly all other forms of navigation. It will benefit you many times over to become as proficient as possible in the concepts and applications of DR.

Measuring True Course

The first step in a DR problem is to draw the course line on the chart, using the procedure explained in the pilotage discussion. The course line direction is measured using a **navigational plotter,** shown in Figure 12.10.

Using the plotter.   A plotter is a combination straightedge, mileage scale, and protractor. The mileage scales have both statute and nautical markings for both sectional charts and WACs. Be careful to use the correct mileage scale for the type of chart you are using, and to use the same unit of measurement consistently.

Refer to Figure 12.10a. Find a meridian as near as possible to the center of your course line. A centrally located meridian is used because meridians near the beginning or end of your flight would give slightly different angular values, since they converge toward the pole. They would thus bias the overall direction of your flight. Place the small hole at the center of your plotter over the point where your course line intersects the meridian. Align the top edge of your plotter with your course line, making sure that the small hole stays in position over the intersection. (You may want to insert a sharp pencil point into the hole to anchor the plotter.) Now read the number of degrees shown on the protractor, using the meridian itself as your index line. If your destination lies east of the meridian, read the outer scale. If it lies west of the meridian, read the inner scale. This value is your **true course (TC),** from your departure point to your destination, expressed as degrees relative to true north.

What if your course line is nearly north-south and does not cross any meridians? Figure 12.10b shows such a case, and the technique for solving the problem. The course direction is measured against a parallel, using the small auxiliary scale on the plotter. The hole in the plotter is placed over

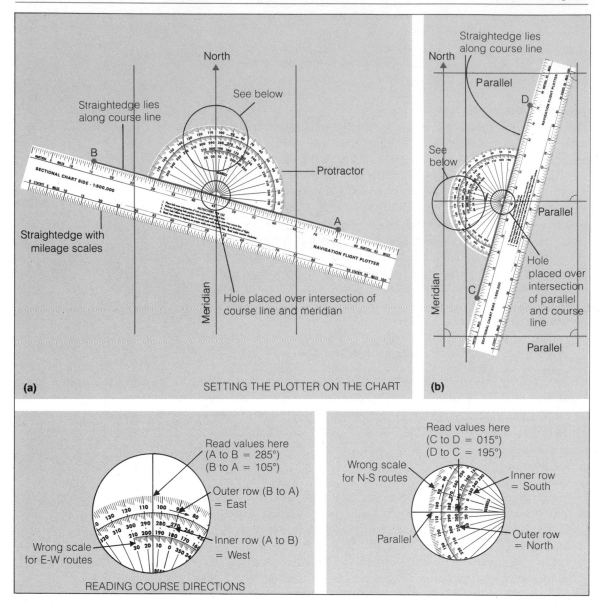

Figure 12.10 How to use a navigational plotter. **(a)** East-west courses that intersect a meridian. **(b)** North-south courses using a parallel.

the intersection of the course line and the parallel, and the course direction is read where the parallel crosses the auxiliary scale.

Determining the Effect of Wind

Once your aircraft leaves the ground, it becomes part of the local air mass. *Wind* is defined as a mass of air moving over the surface of the earth in a definite direction. Recall from Chapter 9 that winds-aloft forecasts report the wind direction with respect to true north. Wind direction is always given as the direction *from which the wind is blowing*. We can now accurately calculate any effects of the wind, since our course direction is also measured with respect to true north.

The motion of your airplane over the ground is the combination of two things: (1) its motion through the air, and (2) the motion of the air over the ground.

Any component of the wind that is directly opposite your flight path is a **headwind.** Wind acting in the same direction as your flight path is a **tailwind.** Figure 12.11 shows that headwinds and tailwinds affect the airplane's **ground speed.** You need to be able to calculate ground speed in order to determine how long it will take you to reach your destination. Note that true airspeed (the speed of the airplane *through the air*) is not affected by winds.

Any component of wind that is not a headwind or tailwind is a **crosswind.** Figure 12.12 illustrates that, in a crosswind, the airplane's *track (the direction it is traveling over the ground)* is not the same as its **heading** *(the direction the airplane is pointed)*. It is important to understand the difference between a heading and a track.

Your objective is to fly the airplane along the course line you drew on the chart. To correct for crosswinds, you must fly the airplane on a heading that is angled into the wind just enough to counteract the effects of the

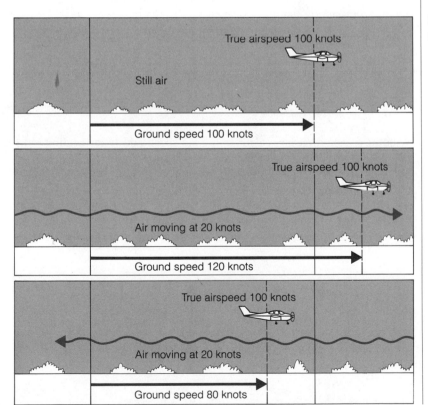

Figure 12.11 Effects of wind on ground speed.

Figure 12.12 Effect of crosswind on flight path.

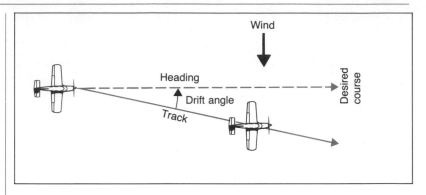

crosswind (see Figure 12.13). That is, you must calculate a **wind correction angle (WCA).** Knowing the WCA, you can find the heading that will give you a ground track that is the same as your desired course.

Constructing a wind triangle.   A *wind triangle* is a graphic illustration of the effect of wind on a flight. It is one method to determine ground speed and WCA for a given set of flight conditions. Even though you will learn to use a flight computer to solve the same type of problem later in this chapter, an understanding of the graphic wind triangle will be very helpful in mastering that technique.

   Solving the wind triangle problem by any method requires that you have the following information:

1. Wind speed and direction
2. The desired true course direction
3. The airplane's true airspeed

With these data, you can calculate ground speed and **true heading**—the true course plus or minus a wind correction angle. Figure 12.14 illustrates the steps to take in creating a wind triangle. The wind in this example is from 45° at 40 knots; the true course is 90°; and the airplane cruises at 120

Figure 12.13 Establishing a wind correction angle that will counteract the crosswind and maintain the desired course.

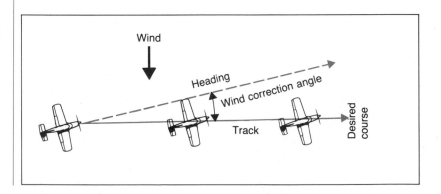

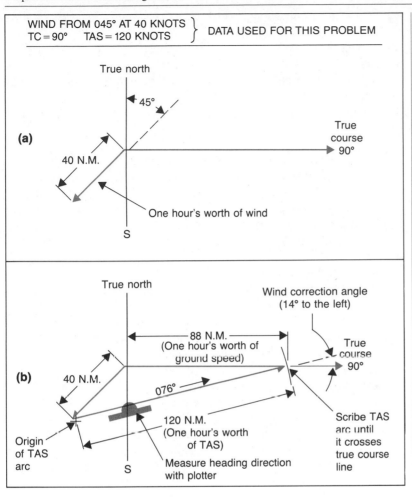

WIND FROM 045° AT 40 KNOTS }
TC = 90°   TAS = 120 KNOTS } DATA USED FOR THIS PROBLEM

(a)

True north

45°

True course 90°

40 N.M.

One hour's worth of wind

S

(b)

True north

Wind correction angle (14° to the left)

88 N.M. (One hour's worth of ground speed)

True course 90°

40 N.M.

076°

120 N.M. (One hour's worth of TAS)

Scribe TAS arc until it crosses true course line

Origin of TAS arc

Measure heading direction with plotter

S

Figure 12.14 The graphic wind triangle. **(a)** The true course line and wind vector. **(b)** Adding the TAS-heading line.

knots TAS. We will draw lines that represent the movement of the wind and the airplane for *1 hour*.

1. The first step is to draw the true course line. (For a real flight, you would probably do this right on the chart.) See Figure 12.14a.

2. Next, draw the wind direction line, at the correct angle, through the course line at the departure point. The line will be 40 nautical miles long (one hour's worth). It will start at the departure point and extend *from* a direction of 45° (Figure 12.14a). The end of this line is where the airplane would be after one hour if it were suspended in the air, like a balloon.

3. From the end of the wind line, we will scribe an arc that is 120 nautical miles long (one hour of flying time in the airplane). Note the point where the arc crosses the true course line. Connecting this point with the end of the wind line completes the triangle (Figure 12.14b).

4. The distance flown in 1 hour is the length of the third leg of the triangle (the leg formed by the true course line). In this example, the third leg is 88 nautical miles long, which means that your ground speed is 88 knots.

5. Using your plotter, measure the true direction of the line connecting the wind line and the true course line (the one that is 120 miles long). This line represents the true heading required to fly the desired course. In this example, the true heading is 76°. The wind correction angle is the difference between the true course and the true heading—14 degrees to the left in this case.

To summarize, you would take off and fly a true heading of 76° at a TAS of 120 knots. Because of the wind (40 knots from 45°), you would actually track 90° at a ground speed of 88 knots (see Figure 12.15). This method is rather cumbersome to use in practice, which is why navigation computers are discussed later. Nevertheless, the method does clearly illustrate the principles involved.

Magnetic Heading

Unfortunately, the earth's magnetic pole does not coincide with its geographic pole. **Magnetic north** is actually located near geographical coordinates 71° N, 96° W, which is about 1300 miles from the geographic North Pole. Since the magnetic compass points to the magnetic north rather than to the earth's true North Pole, you must account for this discrepancy before you can fly your desired course. This difference between true north and magnetic north is called **magnetic variation,** or simply **variation (VAR). Magnetic course (MC)** is thus the true course of an aircraft corrected for magnetic variation.

The magnetic lines radiating between north and south magnetic poles are very much like meridians. A compass will always try to align itself with them and thereby provide you with a continuous reading of **magnetic headings.** These "magnetic meridians," if we may call them that, are referred to as **isogonic lines,** or lines of equal variation. While you are flying along

Figure 12.15 How the wind triangle information applies to a flight.

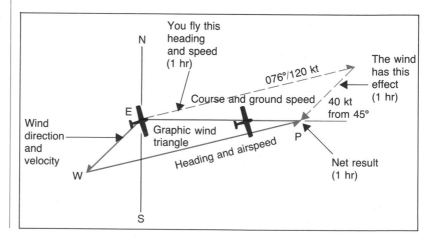

one of them toward the north or south magnetic pole, or while you are flying within a certain limited range of one, the angular variations between true north and magnetic north will be constant.

On one particular isogonic line, the magnetic line of force exactly coincides with the geographic meridian lying beneath it. This is called the **agonic line** (meaning line of no variation). In its vicinity there is no need to correct for variation. As you move away from the agonic line, progressively larger correction factors must be applied (see Figure 12.16). East of the agonic line—for example, in Boston—the magnetic compass would point 16° *west* of true north, since that is the variation between the north geographic and north magnetic poles in that area. To compute a magnetic heading from a previously computed true heading, you would have to *add* the westerly variation for that area (given in degrees) to the true heading. West of the agonic line—for example, in San Jose, California—the magnetic compass would point 16° *east* of true north, and you would have to *subtract* the easterly variation to obtain a proper magnetic heading from a computed true heading. A good way to remember this convention is by the pilot's rhyme, "East is least and west is best"—"least" denoting a minus sign and "best" a plus sign. Easterly variation is subtracted from true headings to obtain magnetic headings; westerly variation is added.

Isogonic lines are shown on all WACs and sectional charts as a dashed magenta line. Unlike geographic meridians, which are straight, isogonic lines trace an irregular path between the north and south magnetic poles. If your course line extends far enough, you will have to account for changes in variation.

Compass heading.   You have now provided for all possible errors to your true course except for the installation effects of the magnetic compass itself. **Compass deviation**—the error in compass readings caused by radio interference and the airplane's metal parts, ignition system, and similar equipment—was discussed in the chapter on instrumentation. To compute the **compass heading** you will need to hold in order to fly a desired track, you must consult the compass correction card mounted in the cockpit (see Figure 12.17). Since all installations are unique, it is not possible to generalize about the size or direction of the compass corrections you will have to make in a given aircraft. Simply consult the card and add or subtract the values shown in order to adjust your computed magnetic heading to a final compass heading. For a magnetic heading falling between published deviation values, interpolate a new value as required.

Figure 12.18 illustrates how all these corrections are organized. You will always start with true course, apply wind correction, then variation, and finally deviation. The result is the compass heading for your airplane, under the existing conditions.

A Sample Problem
Let us see how these concepts work together by using them to solve a sample flight planning problem. Suppose you are planning a flight within

Figure 12.16 Magnetic variation.

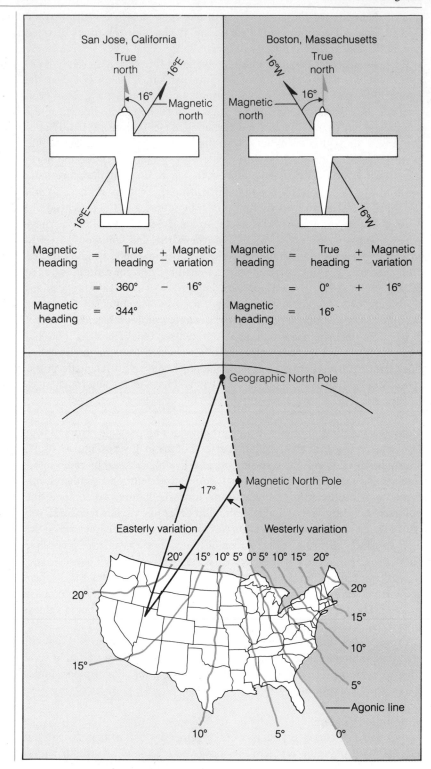

FOR (Magnetic)	N	30	60	E	120	150	S	210	240	W	300	330
STEER (Compass)	0	27	55	84	114	147	180	213	246	278	305	334
Correction	0	−3	−5	−6	−6	−3	0	+3	+6	+8	+5	+4

Figure 12.17 Example of a compass correction card.

Figure 12.18 Determining compass heading.

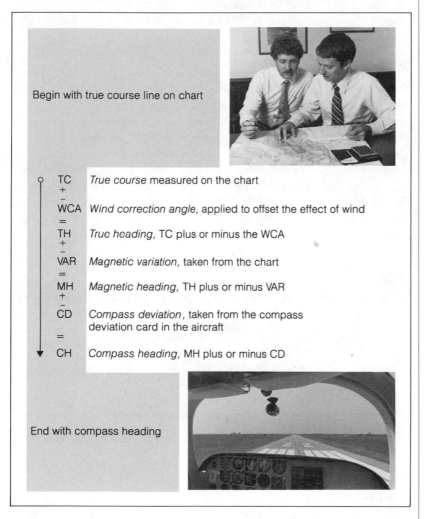

Begin with true course line on chart

TC — *True course* measured on the chart
+
−
WCA — *Wind correction angle*, applied to offset the effect of wind
=
TH — *True heading*, TC plus or minus the WCA
+
−
VAR — *Magnetic variation*, taken from the chart
=
MH — *Magnetic heading*, TH plus or minus VAR
+
−
CD — *Compass deviation*, taken from the compass deviation card in the aircraft
=
CH — *Compass heading*, MH plus or minus CD

End with compass heading

California, from the San Jose Municipal Airport to the Modesto City-County Airport.

1. Select a chart and draw a line between the center points of the two airports. Measure true course by reference to a meridian at the midpoint of the course line—in this case, 071°.

2. Check the winds-aloft forecast. Let us say that you plotted a wind triangle for practice and determined that the wind correction angle required is 7° to the right. This gives you a true heading of 078° (071 + 7 = 078).

3. Consulting your chart, you find that the isogonic line near the midpoint of your flight is 16° east. Since "east is least," you subtract the magnetic variation from your true heading to obtain a magnetic heading of 062° (078 − 016 = 062).

4. Now check the compass correction card (see Figure 12.17). To steer 60° you would steer 55° (− 5° correction). Applying this correction to your magnetic heading, you end up with a compass heading of 057° (062 − 005 = 057).

FLIGHT COMPUTERS

Dead reckoning navigation involves estimating the effects of the forecast winds on your flight path, as discussed earlier. It also means checking these estimates in flight, against your real progress, and revising the initial estimates accordingly. The purpose of a navigation **flight computer** is to allow you to do these calculations, plus a few others, easily and accurately.

Figure 12.19 shows a commonly used style of computer, called the E6B. This mechanical device has a calculator side (Figure 12.19a), a wind side (Figure 12.19b), and a sliding grid (which is used with the wind side). There are other styles of mechanical computers, but they are not discussed in this text.

Time-Speed-Distance Relationships

A good many of the calculations you will perform as a pilot deal with the fundamental relationship between time, speed, and distance. Speed is the *rate* at which distance changes with time, expressed in statute miles per hour (mph) or nautical miles per hour (knots). This relationship is expressed by the formula:

$$\text{Speed} = \frac{\text{Distance}}{\text{Time}}$$

This formula can be rearranged to solve for distance or time also:

$$\text{Time} = \frac{\text{Distance}}{\text{Speed}} \quad \text{or} \quad \text{Distance} = \text{Speed} \times \text{Time}$$

Fuel Consumption

Fuel computations use the same formula but name some variables differently. Gallons of fuel are the commodity used (instead of miles), and fuel flow is the rate of fuel used, expressed in gallons per hour (replacing speed). The basic fuel flow equation is:

$$\text{Fuel flow} = \frac{\text{Gallons}}{\text{Time}}$$

This formula can also be rearranged to solve for gallons or time, as demonstrated in the time, speed, and distance formulas.

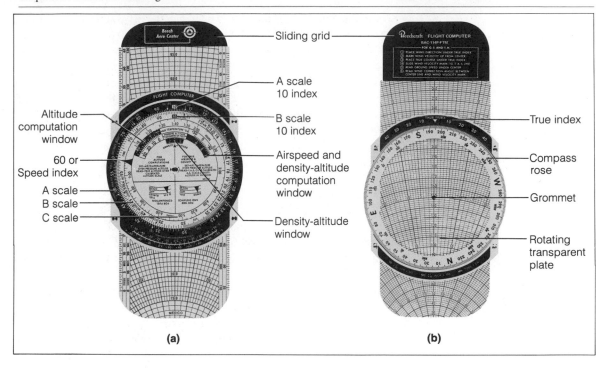

(a)   **(b)**

Computer face. To accommodate calculations such as these, the DR computer face has a circular slide rule with special indexes that can be used to solve simple proportion problems; to multiply and divide numbers; to convert between equivalent units of measure, such as statute and nautical miles; and to convert hours and minutes to hours and tenths, and vice versa. The slide rule consists of a fixed outer scale, or *A scale;* a movable inner scale, the *B scale;* and a third scale, the *C scale,* which is another version of scale B. By adjusting these scales appropriately, you can set the mathematical ratios depicted on the computer to solve any of the above problems. Depending on the calculation at hand, the A scale represents nautical miles or statute miles traveled, gallons of fuel used, and true airspeed or true altitude. It also contains an index of 10 that marks the beginning of the scale. The large arrow covering the 60 on the B and C scales is the "per hour" index, which is used to calculate speed and fuel flow.

Reading the scales. If you align the indexes of 10 of the A and B scales, you will notice that both scales are the same numerically. The 10 can stand for any combination of zeros and ones that you need, such as 0.01, 1, 10, 100, or 1000. Reading to the right, the scale progresses in tenths, with the value of each increment dependent upon the value of the number being used in the problem. If, for example, the number of interest on the A scale

Figure 12.19 The E6B type computer. **(a)** The calculator side. **(b)** The wind face and slide.

is 12, each increment beyond 12 will be worth 0.1. If you wished the same region of the scale to be 120, each increment beyond 120 (or the 12 position) would be worth 1, and so on.

When you reach 15, however, the scale increments are reduced from 10 between each major increment to 5. Thus, each tick mark represents two digits instead of one. The A and B scales are not numbered between 25 and 30, although they are still divided into 5 increments and are numbered in major increments of 5, each divided further into 2 increments to the 60 position. From there they are numbered to the point where the scale begins again at the index of 10. The numerical values for the higher areas of the scale will therefore be a little less precise than those for the lower areas, regardless of the size of the number involved.

The C scale begins at the index of 60 (speed) and is read just as it appears, in hours and minutes—in 5-minute intervals from the index to the 2:00 point and in 10-minute intervals from there to the end of the scale, 10:00. The space between each interval decreases gradually as it nears the index of 60.

To place the decimal point in your answer, you will have to apply your knowledge of the values used in the problem. The time needed to fly 210 miles at a ground speed of 140 mph, for example, would be 210 divided by 140, or 1.5 hours. A practical grasp of the problem would prevent you from thinking the correct answer could be 15 hours or 0.15 hours. When you set up other problems on the computer, you will need to apply the same reasoning.

Proportional Problems
Let us begin by working a simple proportional problem. The A and B scales can be set to show the proportional relationship between any two sets of numbers. Suppose we want to solve the expression:

$$\frac{30}{90} = \frac{12}{x}$$

To find x:

1. Find 30 on the A scale and 90 on the B scale. Set 30 opposite 90.
2. Find 12 on the A scale and read the value for x on the B scale.

The answer is 36. The 36 on the B scale *could* represent 3.6 or 36 or 360 (etc.), but, of these, only 36 is a reasonable answer.

Speed and Fuel Calculations
The calculations involving speed or fuel flow are also proportional problems. Since speed and fuel flow are expressed "per hour," the computer has a heavy arrowhead identifying one hour on the B scale.

To solve rate problems with the computer, remember that:

The B scale always represents time.
The A scale always represents distance or fuel (depending on the problem).

Knowing this, solve the following problem:

1. Your airplane has traveled 21 nautical miles in 12 minutes. What is its ground speed?

    a. Establish the proportion

$$\frac{21 \text{ nautical miles}}{12 \text{ minutes}} = \frac{x}{\blacktriangle \text{ (hour index)}} \quad x = \text{Speed (knots)}$$

    b. Set the 21 on the A scale over the 12 on the B scale and read 105 knots over the index arrow (see Figure 12.20).

2. Given the same ground speed as above, how far will your airplane go in 40 minutes?

    a. Leave the computer set where it is because you have already

Figure 12.20 Solving a ground speed problem.

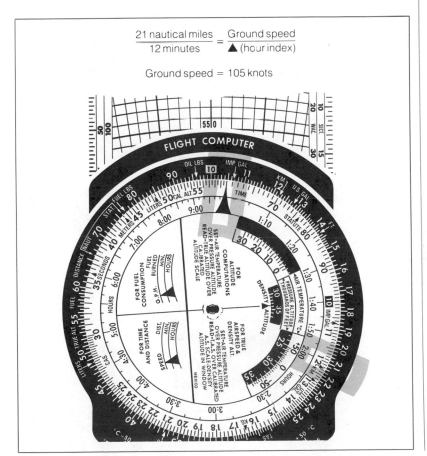

Figure 12.21 Solving a distance problem.

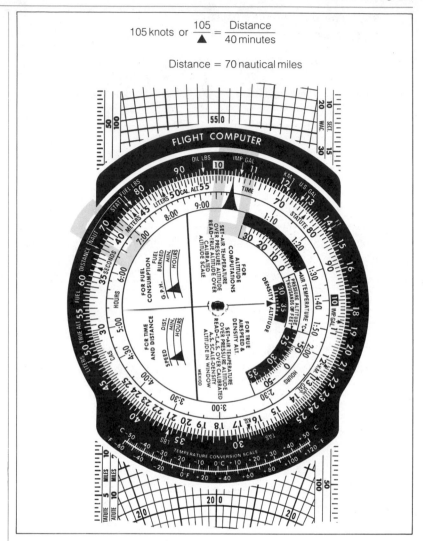

$$105\,\text{knots} \quad \text{or} \quad \frac{105}{\blacktriangle} = \frac{\text{Distance}}{40\,\text{minutes}}$$

$$\text{Distance} = 70\,\text{nautical miles}$$

located the ground speed above the index arrow, a necessary step in solving a distance problem.

b. Find the 40 on the B scale and read the value above it on the A scale: 70 nautical miles (see Figure 12.21).

3. If your ground speed is 90 miles per hour, how long will it take you to travel 300 miles?

a. Again, set the proportion

$$90\,\text{mph} \quad \text{or} \quad \frac{90\,\text{miles}}{\blacktriangle\,(\text{hour index})} = \frac{300\,\text{miles}}{x\,\text{time traveled}}$$

b. Move the index arrow under 90 and find 300 on the A scale. Below it is 20, but you know that 20 minutes would be a non-sensical answer. Thus, you would add a decimal place to the 20, making your answer 200 minutes.

c. But 200 minutes is not a convenient value, since minutes over 60 are usually given as hours. For your final answer, drop down to the C scale and read 3:20, or 3 hours and 20 minutes (see Figure 12.22). (You can verify the agreement of the B and C time scales by dividing 200 by 60.)

4. Your airplane has a fuel consumption rate of 11 gallons per hour and you have been flying for 4 hours and 30 minutes (4:30). How much fuel has the airplane consumed?

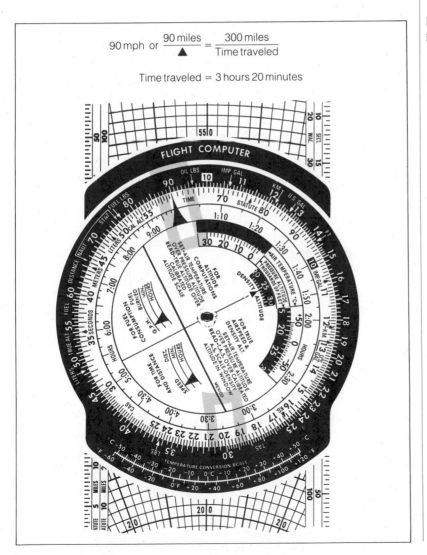

$$90\,\text{mph or } \frac{90\,\text{miles}}{\blacktriangle} = \frac{300\,\text{miles}}{\text{Time traveled}}$$

Time traveled = 3 hours 20 minutes

Figure 12.22 Solving a time problem.

a. Establish the proportion

$$11 \text{ gph} \quad \text{or} \quad \frac{11 \text{ gallons}}{\blacktriangle \text{ (hour index)}} = \frac{\text{Fuel consumed}}{4:30 \text{ hours:minutes}}$$

b. Set the index arrow under the 11 and find the 4:30 position on the C scale. Your answer will be directly above it, approximately 49.5 gallons (see Figure 12.23).

5. You have been flying for 2 hours and the fuel gauge indicates that the airplane has consumed 15 gallons of fuel. What was your fuel consumption rate during this period?

Figure 12.23 Solving a fuel-consumed problem.

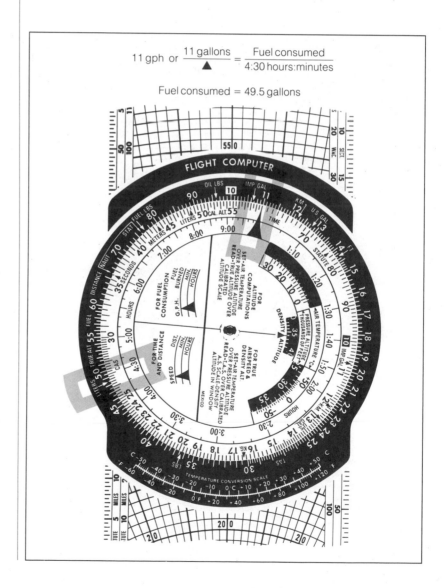

a. Establish the proportion

$$\text{Fuel flow (gph)} \quad \text{or} \quad \frac{x}{\blacktriangle \text{(hour index)}} = \frac{15 \text{ gallons}}{2{:}00 \text{ hours}}$$

b. Set the 15 on the A scale over the 2:00 on the C scale and read your answer over the index arrow: 7.5 gallons per hour (see Figure 12.24).

6. Your airplane's fuel flow for maximum endurance is 8.5 gallons per hour and your tank currently holds 34 gallons of usable fuel. How long can you remain in the air before running out of fuel?

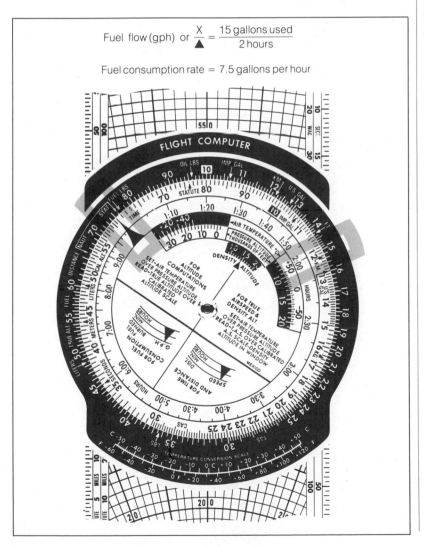

Figure 12.24 Solving a fuel consumption rate problem.

a. Establish the proportion

$$8.5 \text{ gph} \quad \text{or} \quad \frac{8.5 \text{ gallons}}{\blacktriangle \text{ (hour index)}} = \frac{34 \text{ gallons}}{\text{Endurance (time)}}$$

b. Set the index arrow on the B scale at 8.5 on the A scale. Then read your answer beneath the 34: 240 minutes on the B scale or 4 hours on the C scale (see Figure 12.25).

True Airspeed Problems

As you will recall from the chapter on flight instruments, there are several airspeeds of interest to pilots. *Indicated airspeed* is the airspeed read directly from the instrument in the cockpit. This is the airspeed that reflects the

Figure 12.25 Solving an endurance problem.

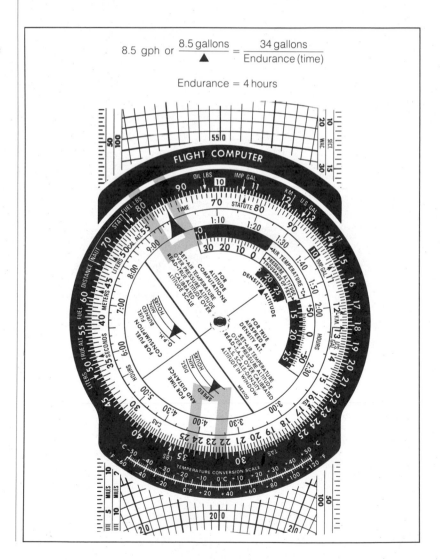

$$8.5 \text{ gph} \quad \text{or} \quad \frac{8.5 \text{ gallons}}{\blacktriangle} = \frac{34 \text{ gallons}}{\text{Endurance (time)}}$$

Endurance = 4 hours

aerodynamic conditions of flight experienced by the aircraft. *Calibrated airspeed* is indicated airspeed corrected for errors in the pitot-static system. In the interest of simplicity, we will assume that calibrated airspeed is the same as indicated airspeed. (To be truly accurate, you should refer to your Pilot's Operating Handbook for the IAS to CAS conversion. Our simplification is not baseless, however, since manufacturers strive to make the difference between the two minimal at cruise speed.) *True airspeed* is calibrated airspeed corrected for the effects of altitude and temperature on air density. Since true airspeed represents the actual rate at which the airplane is moving through the air, it is of key importance for navigation.

To determine true airspeed using the flight computer, you must know the following: *pressure-altitude,* which may be read from the altimeter in flight with 29.92 set in the Kollsman window or estimated before takeoff; *temperature in degrees Celsius,* which may be read in flight from the OAT gauge or during flight planning from the winds-aloft forecast; and *indicated airspeed,* which may be read from the airspeed indicator in flight.

Solving for true airspeed.   In computing your true airspeed, note the following steps:

1. Locate the window on the computer face that is labeled For True Airspeed & Density Altitude.

2. Rotate the scale until the OAT in degrees Celsius (shown as minus on left, plus on right) appears above the desired pressure-altitude (shown in thousands of feet).

3. Find the indicated airspeed on the B scale; the true airspeed will appear above it on the A scale.

A sample problem.   Assume that you are flying at an indicated airspeed of 120 miles per hour with a pressure-altitude of 5500 feet and an OAT of + 10 degrees Celsius. What is your true airspeed?

Go to the airspeed computations window on the computer face and set + 10 over the 5500-foot position. (In dealing with fractions of thousands of feet, as in this problem, you will have to estimate the scale positions carefully.) Above the 12 (representing 120 miles per hour) on the B scale, read your answer: 132 miles per hour (see Figure 12.26).

True Altitude Problems

Recall that indicated or pressure-altitude can be misleading when nonstandard temperatures prevail at a given altitude. True altitude is your actual height above MSL, corrected for these nonstandard conditions. To find true altitude on the computer, locate the altitude window on the left side of the computer face. Set pressure-altitude below the current OAT for that altitude, in degrees Celsius. Now locate your pressure-altitude on the B scale. Immediately above this value on the A scale is the true altitude for that condition.

For example, assume that you are flying at 7000 feet with an OAT of

Figure 12.26 Solving a true airspeed problem.

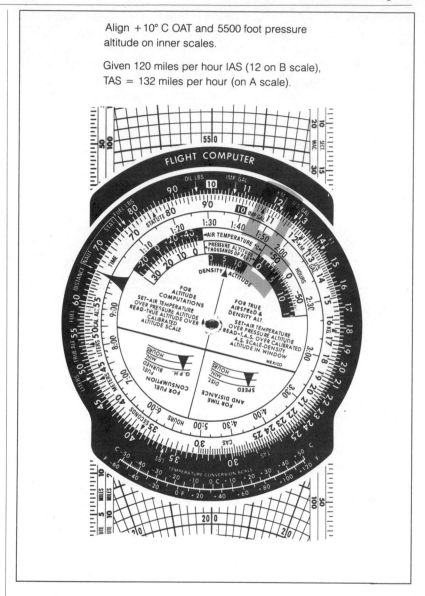

Align +10° C OAT and 5500 foot pressure altitude on inner scales.

Given 120 miles per hour IAS (12 on B scale), TAS = 132 miles per hour (on A scale).

+20 degrees Celsius. Set +20 over the 7000-foot point in the altitude window and find the numeral 7 on the B scale. If you have set the scale carefully, you will read approximately 7475 feet on the A scale just above it (see Figure 12.27).

Periodically checking true altitude when you detect nonstandard temperatures aloft can give you an indication of your actual clearance above surface obstructions en route. This information can be important if the temperature trend during a flight shows an increasing difference between pressure-altitude and true altitude—particularly if the flight is conducted at low altitudes over high terrain and air temperature is lower than standard.

Pressure altitude = 7000 feet (on lower scale of altitude computation
window)

OAT = +20°C (on upper scale of altitude computation window)

True altitude = 7475 (on A scale above 7000-feet mark on B scale)

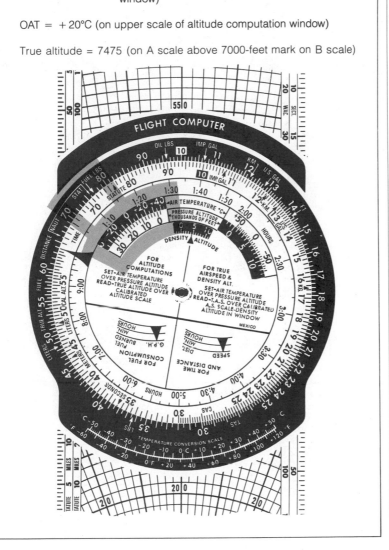

Figure 12.27 Computing true altitude.

Density-Altitude Problems

At times you may have to determine density-altitude without reference to the conversion charts available in the Pilot's Operating Handbook. This is easily accomplished on the computer face (see Figure 12.28).

1. Locate the window labeled For True Airspeed & Density Altitude.

2. Set the OAT in degrees Celsius over the appropriate pressure-altitude value.

3. The density-altitude may then be read over the index in the density-altitude window beneath the B scale.

Figure 12.28 Computing density-altitude using data from the true airspeed problem.

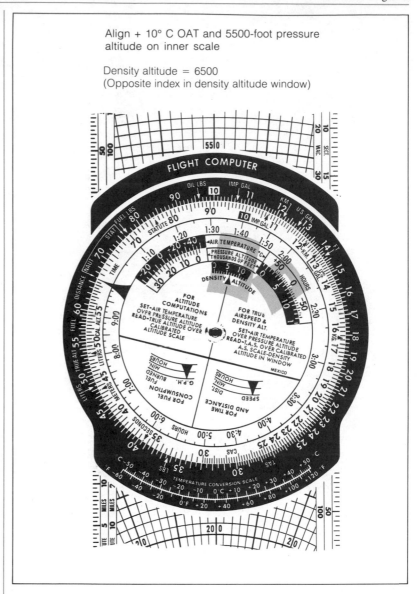

Align + 10° C OAT and 5500-foot pressure altitude on inner scale

Density altitude = 6500
(Opposite index in density altitude window)

Conversions

Sometimes you may have to convert certain standard units of measure to their equivalent value in another system. Most frequently, you will have to convert statute miles to nautical miles and vice versa. But you may also have to convert degrees Fahrenheit to degrees Celsius, gallons to pounds of fuel, miles to kilometers, or U.S. gallons to imperial gallons. Most flight computers include special indexes that allow you to perform these conversions quickly.

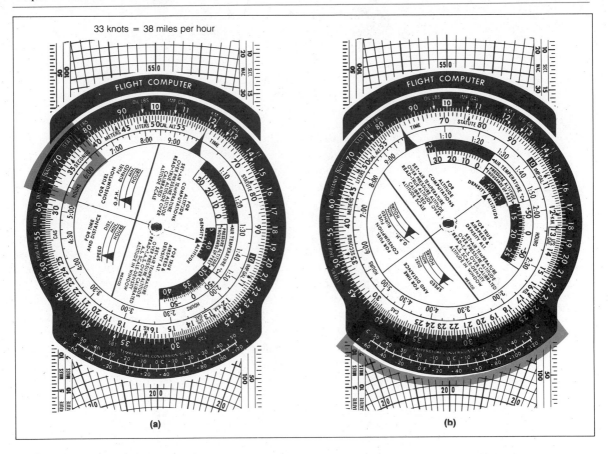

33 knots = 38 miles per hour

(a)   (b)

Conversion of nautical and statute miles. Place the statute mile value under the A scale arrow marked Stat. The equivalent nautical mile value may then be read under the A scale arrow marked Naut.

Suppose, for example, you learned in the winds-aloft forecast that the winds at your cruising altitude would be 33 knots, but your airspeed references were all in miles per hour. To convert this value to statute miles, you would rotate the B scale until the 33 appeared under the Naut arrow. The statute mile equivalent, 38 miles per hour, could then be read under the Stat arrow (see Figure 12.29a).

Conversion of Fahrenheit and Celsius. There are a number of uses for temperature information, many of which require the temperature to be given in a certain unit of measure (TAS computations require degrees Celsius, for example). Most computers have a fixed Celsius-Fahrenheit conversion scale printed on them (see Figure 12.29b).

Figure 12.29 **(a)** Converting from nautical miles to statute miles. **(b)** Converting from degrees Fahrenheit to degrees Celsius.

Computing Wind Effects with the Computer

As mentioned earlier, the flight computer can calculate the effects of wind on your flight path. Using the computer is simpler and less involved than the graphical method discussed earlier.

The side of the computer opposite the calculator face is called the *wind face*. It features a rotating transparent plate with a **compass rose,** and a sliding grid, visible through the transparent section.

Using the wind face.   On the rim of the computer's wind face you will find an arrow labeled True Index in the middle of a series of angles marked off to either side (up to 45°) in 1° increments. The wind face itself is a rotating transparent plate edged with a 360° compass rose that can be aligned with any value on the true index. Cardinal points of the compass are labeled N, S, E, and W. The center of the rotating plate is marked with a small circle, called the **grommet.** The transparent surface has a mat finish to allow repeated pencil markings and erasures to be made. Under the transparent plate the sliding grid has a centerline marked with numbers representing miles, or speed. On the low-speed side, these numbers range from 50 to 280 in intervals of 10, with increments of 2 miles (miles per hour or knots) in between. On the opposite, high-speed side, the grid has similar markings, but the numbers range from 70 to 820, with the angle scale compressed at the lower end of the slide. The low-speed side offers slightly more accurate computations than the high-speed side because of this scale difference.

To compute the effects of wind on any given flight, you must first decide on the range of speed that applies to your aircraft. Since most of your flights will be below 250 knots, you will be using the low-speed grid most of the time. With the slide in place (the speed numbers visible beneath the transparent plate and the true index at the top of your hand), you are ready to solve for true heading and ground speed.

A sample problem.   Let us suppose the winds aloft are from 240° at 30 *26 kts* miles per hour. (Note: The winds-aloft forecasts report the wind speed in knots. Do not forget to convert this value to statute miles if you are working the problem in statute miles per hour. Your true course, measured on a sectional chart, is 195°, and your true airspeed (TAS) is 120 knots. *138 MPH*

1. *Convert all speeds and distances to the same units.*
2. Set the wind direction, 240°, under the true index (see Figure 12.30a).
3. Center the grommet on any convenient speed line (in our example, 180) and place a pencil dot on the centerline 30 knots "up" from the grommet toward the true index.
4. Now rotate the compass rose until your true course, 195°, is under the true index (see Figure 12.30b).
5. Reposition the slide until the TAS, 120 knots, is directly beneath the

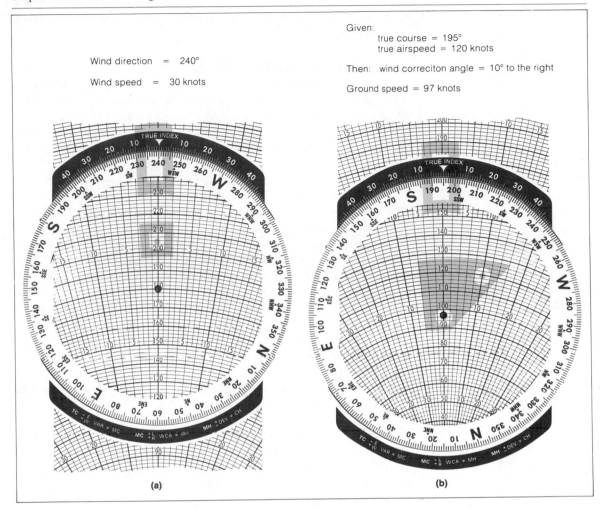

Wind direction = 240°

Wind speed = 30 knots

Given:
    true course = 195°
    true airspeed = 120 knots

Then: wind correciton angle = 10° to the right

Ground speed = 97 knots

(a)   (b)

wind dot. This wind dot will be to the right of the centerline on the 120 knot line.

6. The wind correction angle is the number of degrees the wind dot is displaced from the centerline, in this case 10° to the right.

7. Add this 10° to the true course to obtain a true heading, in this case 205°.

8. With the wind dot still in place on the 120 knot TAS arc, read your ground speed, which appears directly beneath the grommet. In this case, it is 97 knots, since you are facing both headwind and right crosswind components in the winds aloft.

Having determined a true heading, you can now finish your corrections for a cockpit compass heading. Use the ground speed figure to finish your flight

Figure 12.30 Using the wind face. (a) Setting wind direction and wind speed. (b) Determining the wind correction angle and ground speed.

planning computations by calculating time en route and the corresponding fuel requirements.

ELECTRONIC FLIGHT CALCULATORS

Electronic calculators are available to pilots in a wide range of prices and with many special features, some of which go well beyond the capabilities of the manual E6B. In addition to the basic dead reckoning functions, these calculators can compute weight and balance data, convert center of gravity to moments and vice versa, calculate rate of climb, time to climb, and other performance problems, and provide automatic conversions of many standard units of measure. On the other hand, no E6B ever failed because of low batteries or baffled its operator because of a mispunched button. The speed and accuracy of electronic calculations brings with them the need for greater operator awareness.

The exact numerical results obtained will vary from one electronic calculator model to another. The results between a manual computer and a calculator will also differ, depending upon the operator's skill in the case of the computer and programming in the case of the calculator. Also, the many-decimal-place precision of electronic calculators can be misleading. It can produce a false sense of security about the many variables affecting airplanes in flight—the accuracy of winds-aloft forecasts, the ways in which an aircraft may deviate from the handbook data, the effects of individual piloting techniques, and so on. Nonetheless, if you remember that their results offer only approximate descriptions of real conditions, you may find that electronic calculators are useful tools.

FAA Restrictions on Using Calculators During Written Tests

While the choice between a manual flight computer and an electronic calculator is a personal one, you should be aware that the FAA has placed certain restrictions on the use of electronic calculators during written exams for pilot certificates. The FAA will allow applicants to use electronic calculators during written exams provided these calculators have permanently inscribed or printed instructions that pertain *only* to their operation and not to formulas or conversions related to written test subject matter. Any information about regulations, ATC signals, weather data, radio frequencies, weight and balance formulas, and so forth must be obscured by tape or other masking material.

Use of the calculator during the exam is subject to the following additional limitations:

1. Prior to and on completion of the test, the test monitor will instruct the applicant to push the On/Off switch and will watch to ensure erasure of any data stored in the memory circuits.

2. If the calculator has a tape printout, it must be turned over to the monitor at the end of the test.

3. Use of any operating booklet or manual during the test is not permitted.

4. Electronic calculators equipped with permanent or continuous memory circuits that lack erasure capability may not be used.

5. Also prohibited is the use of magnetic cards, tapes, modules, or other devices upon which prewritten programs or information related to the written test can be stored and retrieved.

PILOTS AS PLANNERS—A REVIEW

If student pilots are not careful planners when they enter their ground- and flight-school programs, they will become careful planners by virtue of their navigational training. The reason so many flights are routine and uneventful is that the pilots planned all the relevant details carefully—like chess players plotting their moves well in advance. When you know the rules and the variations to be expected in different situations, flying will hold few surprises for you. Let us review the steps in planning a flight by dead reckoning navigation:

1. Plot your course line on the appropriate chart, and measure the total distance of the flight.

2. Measure your *true course* using the meridian that is closest to the halfway point of the flight.

3. Determine your *true airspeed* from the performance information in your Pilot's Operating Handbook.

4. Obtain the *winds-aloft* information applicable to your flight from a Flight Service Station or National Weather Service Office.

5. Compute your *ground speed* and *true heading* with a flight computer or electronic flight calculator.

6. Adjust your true heading for *magnetic variation* to obtain your *magnetic heading*.

7. Apply the appropriate *deviation* to your magnetic heading to compute your *compass heading*.

8. Use the ground speed and total distance, obtained in the steps above, to compute your *estimated time en route*.

9. Determine the anticipated *fuel flow* from the performance data in your handbook. Calculate the *maximum endurance* of your airplane under these conditions, using the *fuel on board*. Calculate the amount of *fuel required* for this trip. From these data, calculate the *fuel reserve* in terms of gallons and time.

There are other necessary steps to the flight planning process. For example, you have to select checkpoints. You must also make use of the Pilot's Operating Handbook to obtain takeoff, climb, en route, and landing data. We will discuss ways of integrating these techniques in the chapter on composite navigation. In the next chapter we will discuss radio navigation, which you will use to supplement the basic techniques learned in this chapter.

KEY TERMS

air navigation   Lambert projection
bracketing   lines of latitude (parallels)
checkpoints   magnetic variation (VAR)
compass deviation (CD)   nautical mile (NM)
compass heading (CH)   navigational plotter
compass rose   pilotage
coordinated universal time (UTC)   prime meridian
course   radio navigation
dead reckoning navigation (DR)   time zones
equator   track
fix   true airspeed (TAS)
flight computer   true course (TC)
geographic coordinate system   true heading (TH)
great circle   wind correction angle (WCA)
ground speed (GS)   zulu time
heading

PROFICIENCY CHECK

1. Explain the relationship between a line of position (LOP) and a fix.

2. What are the three methods of navigation most commonly used by private pilots?

3. What does the expression "45°30′N, 96°40′W" refer to and how would it be interpreted by a pilot or navigator?

4. How are surface obstructions and terrain relief depicted on sectional charts? What information about these features would you expect to find on a sectional chart?

5. What are the two main limitations to pilotage as a primary means of air navigation?

6. Why is dead reckoning considered a means of coordinating other methods of navigation?

7. Find (a) magnetic heading and (b) ground speed given the following conditions:

True course:	030°
Variation:	5° west
Cruising altitude:	7500 feet MSL
Wind at 7500 feet:	340° at 45 knots
True airspeed:	180 miles per hour

8. Suppose you plan a flight of 95 statute miles at an anticipated ground speed of 120 miles per hour. The airplane has 30 gallons of fuel on board and a fuel consumption rate of 8 gallons per hour. What will be the maximum flying time available to you with the fuel remaining when you arrive at your destination?

9. Assume you depart an airport in Ohio at 0945 EDT for a 2-hour flight to an airport in Illinois. When would you land (in zulu hours)?

All things considered, that closetful of navaids is a
pretty good deal.

"I Learned about Flying from That"
Flying

C H E C K P O I N T S

What is the role of radio aids in VFR navigation? 🛩 What radio navigation aids do pilots use? 🛩 How do VOR stations work and how are their signals used for navigation? 🛩 What is distance measuring equipment and how does it complement VOR navigation? 🛩 To what extent are commercial broadcast stations suitable for radio navigation? 🛩 What are some of the latest cockpit navaids a private pilot might encounter? 🛩 How do pilots base their flight plans on radio navaids?

RADIO NAVIGATION

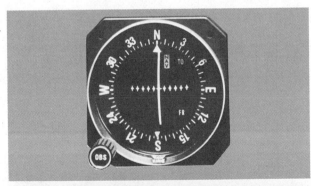

The fundamental problem of any navigation is to find credible lines of position (LOPs) with which to determine fixes. Pilotage is acceptable as long as visibility is good and suitable landmarks are available. Dead reckoning is a valuable tool for planning and monitoring progress during a flight, but it provides only an *estimation* of position, based on time, speed, and distance. Actual fixes are still made by visual reference to landmarks. But visual landmarks are not always available, even when the weather is good. Flying over water or sparsely populated land or at night, you are unlikely to have landmarks to refer to.

Radio navigation provides the means to establish LOPs that do not depend on visibility or the availability of landmarks. Radio receivers on board the airplane process signals from ground-based transmitters to establish a fix. In the near future, navigation transmissions may be coming from satellites in space.

AN OVERVIEW OF RADIO NAVIGATION AIDS

A variety of types of radio navigation aids **(navaids)** are in use today. The basic difference between them is the radio frequency spectrum each uses. There are also differences in the cockpit instrumentation used to display their data.

VHF Omnidirectional Ranges (VORs)

VHF omnidirectional ranges (VORs) are navaids that use the very-high-frequency (VHF) portion of the radio spectrum. The word *omnidirectional* signifies that these radios broadcast directional signals in all directions. VORs are the most commonly used navaids and are discussed in great detail in this chapter.

UHF Navigation

Navigation stations using the ultrahigh frequency (UHF) portion of the radio spectrum are called **tactical air navigation** stations, or **TACAN** for short. The bearing information broadcast by these facilities is used primarily by the military. Most VHF and UHF airway stations have been combined to form a single nationwide airway system shared by all users of the national airspace. VOR and TACAN facilities in the same location and operating simultaneously are called **VORTAC** stations.

Like VOR, TACAN supplies bearings for all 360°, and it has an additional feature called **distance measuring equipment (DME).** This complements bearing transmissions by providing information on the aircraft's distance from the station. The DME portion of TACAN can be picked up by civilian aircraft furnished with the appropriate airborne equipment.

LF/MF Navigation

The low-frequency (LF) **nondirectional radio beacon (NDB)** was one of the earliest electronic navigation aids available to pilots. The radio receiver that uses these signals employs a directional antenna to determine the bearing from the receiver to the transmitting station, a process known as **radio direction finding (RDF).** The airborne radio equipment that continuously displays this bearing information is called an **automatic direction finder (ADF).** Most modern ADFs receive both the low- and medium-frequency (LF/MF) radio bands, which means they will receive commercial AM broadcasts in addition to NDB signals. Although NDBs have long since been replaced by the VOR for en route navigation in the United States, they are still used for certain types of IFR approaches to airports.

Long-Range Navigation (LORAN)

LORAN is a long-range, low-frequency radio navigation system developed for the military during World War II. Low-frequency transmissions travel great distances over the earth's surface, which allows reception of LORAN signals from "over the horizon" and behind most obstructions. LORAN is the primary marine navigation system and is now becoming popular for aviation use as well.

Until the advent of modern microprocessors, LORAN receivers were large, heavy, and complex to use. In recent years, new technology has produced a virtual explosion of airborne LORAN receivers. These new radios enable pilots to fly a direct great circle route to any destination, specified by longitude and latitude, with continuous ground speed, bearing, and distance data available en route. Many of these units contain digital databases of airport locations—the pilot simply enters the airport's three- or four-letter identifier, and the airport's coordinates are loaded from the radio's computer memory. Some of these digital wizards will display minimum safe altitudes, warn you when you approach special-use airspace, or even find the nearest airports to your present location!

All of this good news must be tempered by the knowledge that currently there are gaps in LORAN signal coverage in the middle of the continental United States. Since LORAN historically has been a marine system, coverage was necessary only along the coasts and major inland waterways. The tremendous growth in aviation's use of LORAN will, no doubt, eventually force the closing of this "mid-continental gap." Until such time, however, LORAN users must be aware of this limitation.

The popularity and impact of LORAN on aerial navigation cannot be ignored. An in-depth discussion of these systems, however, is beyond the scope of this text.

VOR NAVIGATION

VOR stations transmit on frequencies from 108.00 to 117.95 megahertz (MHz). These frequencies are just below those used for aeronautical voice communication.

A VOR station transmits two signals. One is an omnidirectional pulse, like a flashing light visible from all directions. The other is a rotating unidirectional signal, similar to the light from a rotating beacon. The two are in phase (the flash from both lights comes simultaneously) in the direction of *magnetic* north. As you move clockwise around the station, the phase of the signals changes one degree for each degree you are away from magnetic north.

The signals can be received by appropriate airborne equipment and displayed as *radio lines of position* in the cockpit. These bearings are called **radials** because they radiate from the station like the spokes of a wheel. Each radial is named for its magnetic course, 000 through 359, one for each degree of the compass.

Radials represent courses *from* the station. Thus, if you were using a radial as your magnetic course, you would be flying *away* from the station. If you wished to fly *to* the station, you would set your magnetic course to the radial's reciprocal value. If you continued *past* the station, the outbound radial would be the course that brought you to the station. Figure 13.1 illustrates this concept.

In practice, an airplane's actual magnetic heading and the radial (or its reciprocal) rarely match because of winds. We will have more say about tracking VOR radials later in this chapter. For the time being, simply remember that the magnetic course and the VOR radial are the same only when you are flying away from the station. When you are inbound, the magnetic course is the reciprocal of the VOR radial that you are following to the station.

Chart Depiction

On aeronautical charts, a VOR station can be depicted by one of three symbols: one for a VOR only; one for a VORTAC; and one for a VOR with

Figure 13.1 VOR radials and courses.

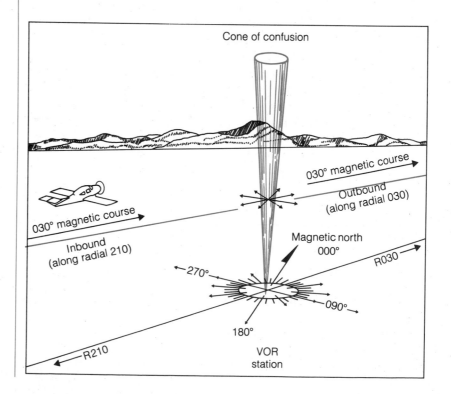

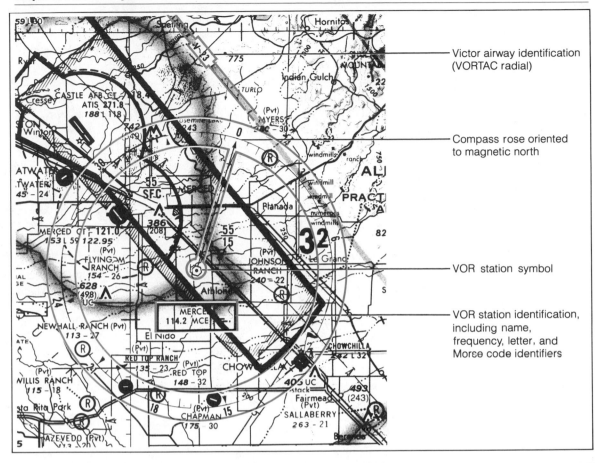

Victor airway identification (VORTAC radial)

Compass rose oriented to magnetic north

VOR station symbol

VOR station identification, including name, frequency, letter, and Morse code identifiers

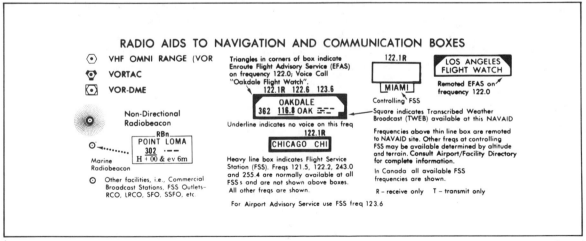

DME capability (but no TACAN). These symbols are shown in Figure 13.2. A VOR located on an airport is depicted by a small white circle inside the airport symbol, and a nearby data box (discussed later) describes the type

Figure 13.2 Example of a VOR station shown on a sectional chart along with a legend that explains navaid and communication symbols.

of navaid. Most VORs are shown with the appropriate symbol surrounded by a compass rose, or azimuth circle, aligned with magnetic north. Low-power terminal class VORs usually do not have a compass rose. Measuring course directions using a VOR compass rose eliminates the need to correct for local variation.

Certain radials running between VORs are marked by a light blue shaded line and are identified by the letter V and a number (for example, V 23). These are called **victor airways** (*victor* standing for the letter V). Victor airways were established to provide en route controlled airspace corridors for IFR traffic. They are marked on the charts because they are one form of controlled airspace (see Chapter 7).

Near every VOR symbol is a blue box containing the radio station name and frequency. Each station also lists a three-letter identifier and the Morse code for those three letters.

Radio Communication Information

All VORs are controlled by a Flight Service Station, and typically each FSS controls a number of VORs. Most FSSs have one primary VOR, which has the same name as the FSS. This VOR-FSS identity is indicated by a VOR data box with heavy lines (see Figure 13.2). Above the box are the frequencies that FSS has available for communication. The FSS frequencies are given above a communication box that contains only the FSS name when there is no VOR with the same name. A heavy line box means that frequencies 121.5 (the emergency frequency) and 122.2 are available even though they are not shown above the box.

A Flight Service Station's satellite VORs have data boxes with normal weight lines, which means that only the frequencies shown are available for communication. The name of the controlling FSS is in brackets below the box. Many VORs act as remote communications outlets for their controlling FSSs. This is indicated by a 122.1R above the data box, which means that the FSS can *receive* (hence the R) through the VOR on frequency 122.1. The FSS will respond on the VOR frequency. In the airplane, you will transmit on 122.1 and will listen on the VOR frequency. This technique allows you to communicate with an FSS well beyond the range of direct radio contact.

Airborne VOR Equipment

VOR radio receivers and indicators come in many designs, but they all have certain features in common. As shown in Figure 13.3, most installations have two functional units. One has the controls for On/Off, frequency selection, and volume; the other is the display unit, often called the **VOR head.** Some designs package both units together, but, in any case, they function the same. The display unit has four parts:

1. The **course card,** which displays the selected course.
2. The **omni bearing selector (OBS)** knob, which rotates the course card and is used to select a course.

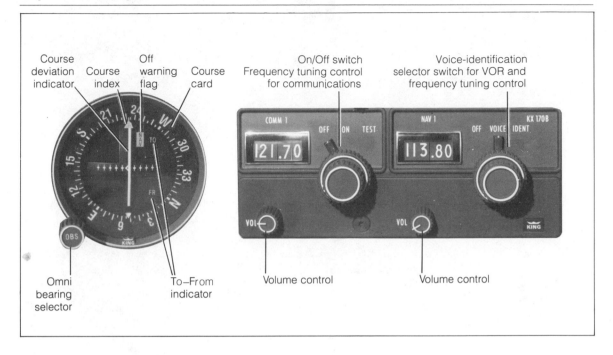

Course deviation indicator, Course index, Off warning flag, Course card, On/Off switch Frequency tuning control for communications, Voice-identification selector switch for VOR and frequency tuning control

Omni bearing selector, To–From indicator, Volume control, Volume control

3. The needle, or **course deviation indicator (CDI).**

4. The **To-From indicator.**

Figure 13.3 A typical VOR cockpit control unit and display.

When the station signal is too weak for reliable navigation, an **Off flag** will appear in front of the CDI, warning you not to rely on its course information. This flag normally appears in one of the following situations:

1. When the station is not broadcasting at all

2. When you are out of range of the station

3. When you are passing directly over the top of the station, inside an area known as the **cone of confusion** because the phased signals cannot be correctly interpreted there

4. When you are located on a radial that is at a 90° angle to the radial that you have selected on the OBS

5. When the radio has failed, or its power source has failed

6. When the radio is turned off

Interpreting VOR indications. The VOR allows you to determine your *position* with respect to the VOR, but provides *no information about heading*. Interpreting the VOR starts by visualizing the selected course line drawn through the VOR and pointing away from you. Figure 13.4 illustrates how this would look. The selected radial can be any value you like. If you were drawing this diagram on a chart, you would rotate the chart until the course arrow was oriented like the one in Figure 13.4. The CDI needle is centered when your position is anywhere along the course line. If your

Figure 13.4 The relationship
between selected course and needle
(CDI) deflection. The indication is
independent of aircraft heading.

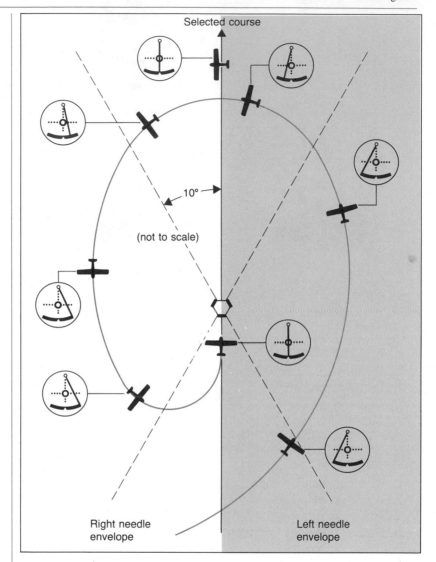

position is to the left of the course line (oriented as described), the needle
will deflect to the right. This is illustrated by the unshaded half of Figure
13.4, marked "right needle envelope." A position to the right of the course
line would produce a left needle deflection, illustrated by the shaded half
of Figure 13.4. Notice that the direction the airplane is pointed (its heading)
has no effect whatsoever on the position of the needle. Only the aircraft's
position relative to the selected course is reflected by the needle.

The further you are from the course, the greater the needle deflection.
It is important to know that the VOR needle represents an *angular* displacement from the selected course. A full-scale deflection (a pegged needle)
occurs when you are 10° off the selected course. Of course, once the needle

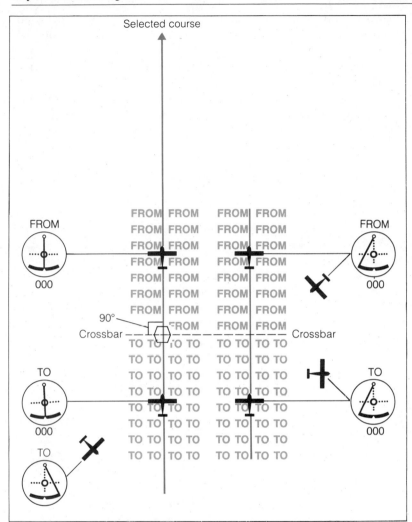

Figure 13.5 The relationship between selected course and To-From indication. The indication is independent of aircraft heading.

pegs, its usefulness is limited because all you know is that you are *at least* 10° off course. The *distance* you are off course, for a given partially deflected needle, is a function of how far you are from the station. At a distance of 60 miles from the station, you are displaced 1 mile for each degree you are off course. You can use this relationship to estimate your displacement, in miles, from your selected course for other angles and distances from the station. For instance, when you are 30 miles from the station, you are displaced a half mile for each degree off course. The closer you are to the VOR station, the smaller the displacement for each degree away from the selected course.

Figure 13.5 illustrates the meaning of the *To-From indicator.* If following the course line, from your present position, would take you from the station, the flag says *From*. If your position is such that following the course line would take you to the station, the flag indicates *To*. Notice that the dividing line between *to* and *from* is a line perpendicular to the selected course. A position anywhere along this dividing line, called the *crossbar,* will cause the warning flag to appear.

Figure 13.6 combines the data from the CDI needle and the To-From indicator into one composite picture. This illustration shows the eight possible combinations the CDI and To-From indicator can have and correlates each with a position relative to the VOR.

Tuning and identifying a VOR.   Every operating VOR broadcasts a Morse code identifier, which is repeated ten times every minute. Many stations have a voice identifier as well, stating the name of the VOR in English. Even though the cockpit frequency display may show that the receiver is set for the desired station's frequency, you cannot be certain that you are receiving that station unless you hear its audio identifier. Thus, you should never merely *tune* the VOR; you must always *tune and identify* the appropriate station. The Morse code station identifier (and voice identifier, if applicable) will not be heard if the station is not operating correctly for any reason, including periods when scheduled maintenance is being performed and navigational signals continue to be broadcast.

Figure 13.6 VOR indications for various positions versus selected course.

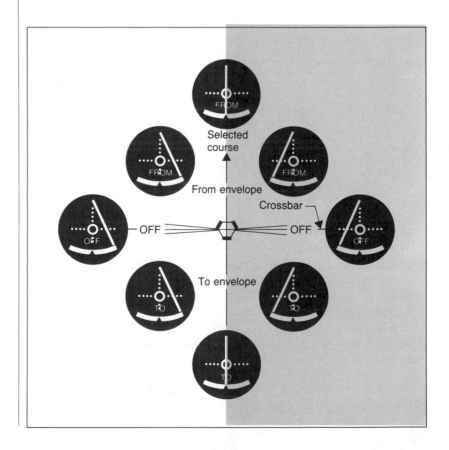

Advantages and Disadvantages of VOR

The 360° coverage of the omnidirectional bearing system allows great flexibility in course selection and such other navigational benefits as two-station fixes and verification of ground speed. Unlike the low-frequency systems, VOR, which uses VHF signals, is relatively free of atmospheric interference. Additionally, VOR radials provide radio lines of position and hence ready-made magnetic courses suitable for flight planning and compass navigation. They are also quite accurate, furnishing bearing information that is within ± 1° of the actual magnetic course the radials represent.

The major shortcoming of any VHF radio system is that its signals operate only on a line-of-sight basis. That is, signals can be blocked by intervening terrain or by the curvature of the earth (see Figure 13.7). Each VOR station therefore has a limited range, and the complete VOR navigational network is made up of hundreds of separate stations. Even so, aircraft operating at low altitudes or in mountainous areas may be out of range of any VOR station for part of their flight. Finally, VOR, like most radio systems, can function properly only if both ground and airborne equipment are in good working order.

VOR NAVIGATIONAL PROCEDURES

To avoid errors of commission or omission, it is advisable to follow a step-by-step procedure in using a navigational system. In this section we will look at the following VOR operations: tuning and identifying, proceeding

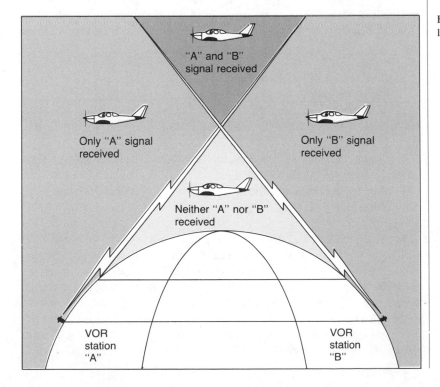

Figure 13.7 VOR reception limitations.

direct to the station, inbound and outbound course interceptions, station passage, two-station fixes, and navigation receiver checks.

Tuning and Identifying

Tuning the VOR receiver and positively identifying the station you are receiving constitute the important first step in using the VOR system. To tune the VOR receiver and positively identify your station, follow this procedure:

1. Be sure that your VOR receiver is turned on and that circuit breakers or fuses are in place.

2. Select the desired frequency from a current aeronautical chart or *Airport/Facility Directory.*

3. Adjust the volume and identify the VOR station. Positively match the three-letter Morse code identifier signal to the symbols on the chart.

4. Turn down the signal volume but continue to monitor the station as long as you are using it. If the identifier fails, the station's signal must be considered unreliable.

5. Check to be sure the Off flag is not showing. If it is, change the selected course by about 90° with the OBS knob (in case you happen to be on the crossbar of the original course). If the Off flag is still showing, either your equipment or the VOR is not operating correctly.

Proceeding Direct

The most efficient way of going to a station is with a technique called **proceeding direct.** This is the procedure you should follow if an ATC controller clears you "direct" to a certain station from your current position (see Figure 13.8).

1. Tune and identify the station.

2. Adjust the OBS until the To-From indicator reads To.

3. Continue turning the OBS until the course deviation indicator is centered. You will then have the magnetic course from the aircraft to the station.

4. Taking the shortest direction, turn the aircraft to place this heading under the index of the directional gyro.

5. Maintain this course to the station, keeping the course deviation indicator centered.

You will probably find that after flying this heading for a while, the CDI will begin to drift to one side of the case or the other. This is because the wind is blowing you off the selected course. If the CDI drifts to the left of center, for instance, you have a crosswind from the left that is displacing the aircraft to the right of the course. To correct, simply turn the aircraft to the left (no more than 30° or so) and fly this heading until the needle centers again. When the CDI is centered, ease off of your heading change somewhat, though not completely, since you will need some wind correc-

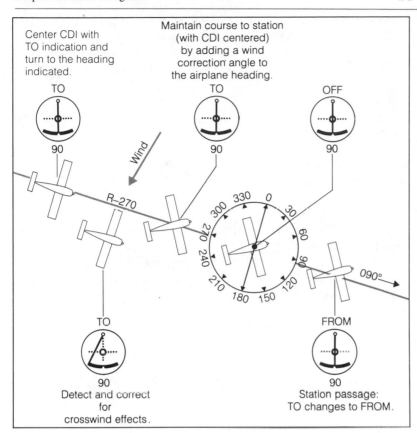

Center CDI with TO indication and turn to the heading indicated.

Maintain course to station (with CDI centered) by adding a wind correction angle to the airplane heading.

TO

90

Wind

R-270

TO

90

OFF

90

300 330 0
270   30
240   60
210   90
180 150 120

090°

TO

90

Detect and correct for crosswind effects.

FROM

90

Station passage: TO changes to FROM.

Figure 13.8 Proceeding direct. Adding a wind correction angle to your heading allows you to stay on course.

tion angle to hold the course with the current crosswind. By trial and error you will eventually find a constant compass heading by which to maintain the course.

Course Interception

One of the measures of a skilled pilot is the smoothness with which VOR radial interceptions are made. An **interception** is any maneuver that has as its end the collocation of an aircraft with a desired target—in this case, a VOR radial.

There are a few special terms associated with the technique of interception. The heading that the aircraft must take in order to reach the desired radial (or course) is called the **intercept heading.** The **angle of interception** is the angle the aircraft's intercept heading makes with the desired course. A large or steep angle of interception will bring you to a radial quickly, but it may also carry you past the radial unless you turn quickly to avoid overshooting. With a small or shallow angle of interception, you may take a little longer to reach your course, but the transition between your intercept heading and the desired course will be smoother. You will use your own best judgment in picking an intercept angle in any given situation, taking into account the winds aloft, your airspeed, the radial location, and your distance from the station.

Rate of interception is the term used to describe how rapidly you meet the desired course. It is indicated in the cockpit by the movement of the course deviation indicator. If the CDI moves quickly from the side of the VOR head toward the center, a high rate of interception is indicated. Rate of interception is influenced by your ground speed, intercept angle, and distance from the station.

Inbound course interceptions.   Figure 13.9 shows the procedure for making inbound course interceptions.

1. Tune and identify the station.

2. Set the OBS for the desired inbound course and check the To-From indicator for a To reading.

3. Turn the shortest distance to the heading that will parallel the inbound course selected on the OBS. As long as you parallel the inbound course, you will be pointed in the same general direction as the desired course.

Figure 13.9 Inbound course interception.

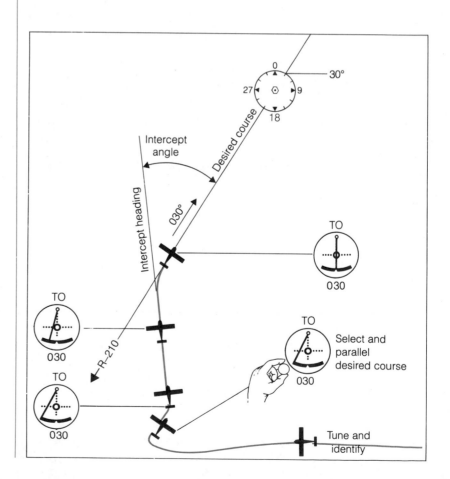

4. Note whether the CDI lies to the right or the left side of center. Turn toward the needle to establish an intercept angle. The greater the distance from the station, the larger the intercept angle should be.

$$\text{Intercept heading} = \text{Course selected} \begin{array}{l} - \text{ a left intercept angle or} \\ + \text{ a right intercept angle} \end{array}$$

5. Maintain the intercept heading until the CDI begins to leave the side of the VOR head. If it moves slowly, maintain the intercept heading until the needle is nearly to the center position, then begin turning gradually to the desired course. If the CDI moves quickly away from the side of the VOR head, cut the angle of the intercept heading by half or as required to provide a smooth transition to the inbound course.

Outbound course interceptions. The procedure for outbound course interceptions is intended for use immediately after the aircraft passes a station, but it will work for any outbound interception (see Figure 13.10).

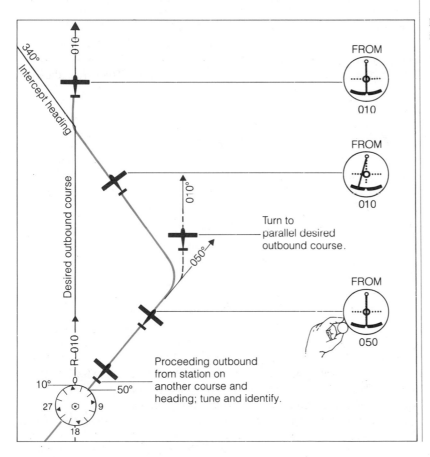

Figure 13.10 Outbound course interception.

1. Tune and identify the station.

2. Set the OBS for the desired course. Check the To-From indicator for a From reading.

3. Turn the shortest distance to the heading that will parallel the outbound course selected on the OBS. As long as you parallel the outbound course, you will be pointed in the same general direction as the desired bearing.

4. Turn the shortest distance to an intercept heading. The size of the intercept angle will depend upon your distance from the station and/or the selected radial. The angle can be as small as 15° if you are close to the station. Normally, an intercept angle of greater than 45° should not be used.

5. Maintain the intercept heading until the CDI comes away from the side of the VOR head and complete the interception based on the speed with which the CDI moves toward the center of the instrument.

Station Passage

The *cone of confusion*—the area above the station that is blocked by the physical geometry of the station itself—is fairly narrow at low altitudes and fairly wide at higher altitudes. The time spent in the cone depends, of course, upon the aircraft's ground speed. You will know you have entered the cone when the CDI begins to swing from one side of the VOR head to the other. Frequently, too, the Off flag will appear or pop in and out of view. You will know you have passed the station when the To-From indicator makes its first positive change from To to From. Thereafter, the CDI should resume its normal indications.

Two-Station VOR Fixes

As you already know, you cannot establish your position with certainty without reference to the intersection of at least two lines of position. If you are flying within range of two VOR stations, you can determine a fix quickly and accurately.

Tracking a radial.   If you are proceeding inbound or outbound on a known course or radial, you already have half the problem solved. On an aeronautical chart plot your course line to or from the VOR, using the printed VOR compass rose as your protractor. Remember, if you are proceeding outbound, the number of degrees of the OBS course will be the same as your radial. If you are proceeding inbound, the OBS course will be the reciprocal of the radial on which you are flying. The *bearing,* or "radio LOP," that you are tracking covers the same track either way, which is why you can use it in determining your fix (see Figure 13.11).

Now, holding the heading you have established, correcting for the effects of wind if necessary, tune and identify a second station within range. Rotate the OBS until the CDI is centered with a From indication. Read the course selected and plot it as you did your first course line, using the second

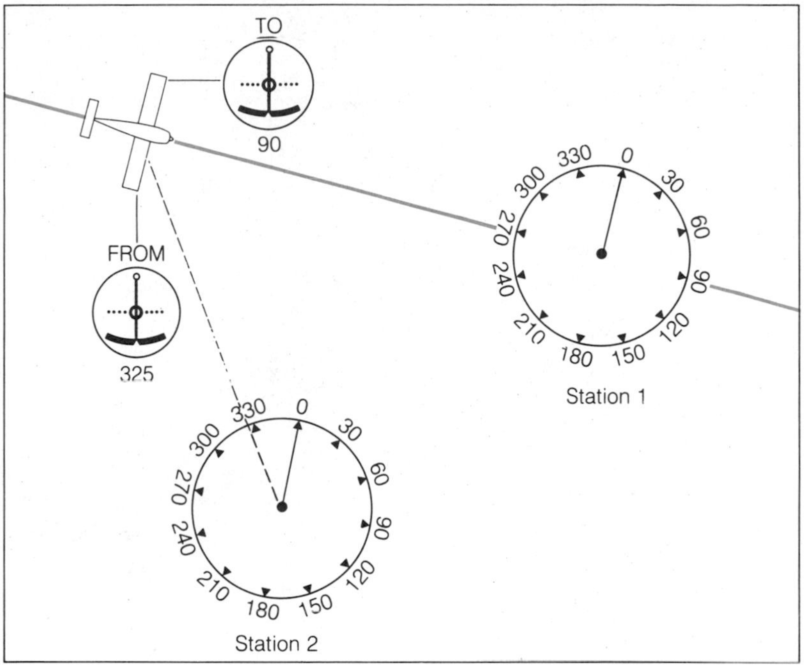

Figure 13.11 Performing a two-station VOR fix tracking a radial.

station's compass rose. Remember, in this case the OBS course selected and the radial are the same, since the To-From indicator registers From. The point at which the two lines cross is the fix—your actual location at the moment your aircraft was on track to station one and collocated on the radial from station two.

If necessary, you could use this fix to replan your flight or you could perform a number of useful navigational checks—for example, verifying ground speed. If you have only one VOR receiver, do not forget to retune and identify station one and reposition your OBS if you intend to proceed with your original flight plan.

Operating between radials. If your course line is taking you between two nearby stations rather than to or from a station, you can carry out the same procedure. Tune and identify the first station, then adjust the OBS until the CDI is centered and the To-From indicator registers From. Take note of the radial. Then tune and identify the second station and record the radial from that station in the same manner. Plot both radials on your chart (see Figure 13.12). You will now have a pair of intersecting LOPs, but you may not have an exact fix. If you compare the radio fix to your original course line, you will probably find that the fix lies to one side. There was a delay when you retuned and identified the second station, rotated the OBS, and waited for the needle to center. Obviously, the airplane continued

Figure 13.12 Performing a two-station VOR fix between radials.

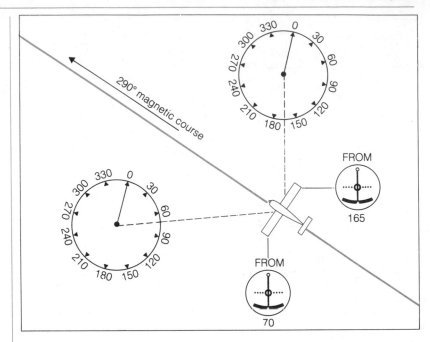

to move during that time. If your true airspeed (or ground speed) was high, the discrepancy in your two-station fix may have been marked. Conversely, if your true airspeed was relatively low, the fix was probably a fairly accurate representation of your location. To be useful in determining a fix, the LOPs must be established *simultaneously,* or as near to simultaneously as you can manage.

The built-in error in this procedure can be minimized in several ways. First, you should measure your bearing from the second station as quickly as possible. Next, you might consider proceeding direct toward one of the stations temporarily. This keeps one LOP constant and allows a more accurate reading, if that is important. Of course, the best way (and the easiest) to take a two-station fix is to use two VOR receivers simultaneously.

Navigation Receiver Checks

Some airports that are located close enough to a VOR have a predetermined VOR checkpoint on the airport. This location is usually marked with a circle on the ground and a sign showing the VOR frequency and the radial to be used. Once located in the circle, you tune and identify the VOR, then center the needle. If the course indicated on the VOR head is within $\pm 4°$ of the certified radial, your radio is within acceptable tolerances. The *Airport/Facility Directory* lists the airports having VOR receiver checkpoints.

At many airports you will not be able to pick up the nearest VOR station until you are airborne and have cleared surface obstructions or terrain.

Fortunately, some airports have an FAA **VOR test (VOT) facility** that can be used to check the operation and accuracy of your equipment before you take off. Airports so equipped are identified in the *Airport/Facility Directory*.

To use the VOT, tune and identify the appropriate published test frequency. The VOT aural signal is a steady series of dots or a continuous tone. Turn the OBS until the needle is centered. The bearing selected should be 000° with a From indication or 180° with a To indication. If the ground test error is more than ±4°, the source of the error should be investigated by a maintenance technician before the equipment is used for navigation.

If a ground check is not available, refer to the *Airport/Facility Directory* for the locations of authorized air checkpoints. These are certified radials that should be received over specific landmarks, at the specified altitude. The acceptable tolerance for airborne VOR checks is ±6°. The larger tolerance is allowed because an airborne position is less precise than either of the ground check methods.

DISTANCE MEASURING EQUIPMENT

Distance from a station can be used as a line of position, since it defines a circle of a known radius. When such a circle is intersected with a straight line of position, such as a radial, a fix is defined.

As mentioned earlier, the military TACAN system allows aircraft equipped with *distance measuring equipment (DME)* to do what that name implies: to measure the distance to the station. There are also some VOR installations that have DME capability but no TACAN. To a civilian aircraft, these VOR-DME facilities are identical to VORTACs. DME uses the UHF frequency band for its transmissions, but you will simply select the VOR frequency on your airborne equipment. Every VOR frequency is paired with a DME channel, so the equipment will automatically set the appropriate DME frequency.

DME measures the time it takes for a signal broadcast from the aircraft to reach the station, trigger a transponder, and receive the return signal (see Figure 13.13). Since the speed of the radio wave is precisely known, any

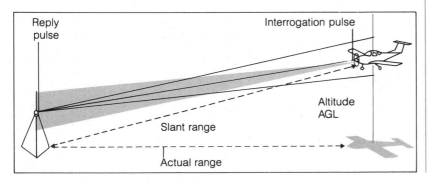

Figure 13.13 The principle of distance measuring equipment.

Figure 13.14 A typical DME indicator.

time delay between the sending of the first signal and the receipt of the second can be attributed to distance and displayed as miles and tenths of miles on an indicator in the cockpit (see Figure 13.14). The important thing to remember is that DME measures **slant range distance**—not linear distance between the station and a point on the ground under the aircraft. Thus, an airplane passing over the station at 12,000 feet AGL would show a distance of 2 miles on its range indicator. This slant range error, however, is negligible at distances beyond 10 miles from the station.

Like the VOR system, DME has a few operating peculiarities. It is subject to line-of-sight restrictions, and its signal may be interrupted by airplane maneuvers that block the DME antenna from the station. Loss of the DME signal "unlocks" the indicator readout and renders it temporarily unusable. The DME counter will stop its downward readings when the slant range distance to the station reaches its minimum (the moment you are directly over the station) and will gradually begin building up again as you draw away from the station. Station passage occurs at the moment the indicator stops decreasing (see Figure 13.15). Some DME equipment also offers ground speed readouts and/or time-to-station, supplementing the distance readout. These values are valid only when flying directly to or from the sending station and not flying close to it.

AUTOMATIC DIRECTION FINDING (ADF)

Recall that before the development and implementation of VOR radios, the primary method of radio navigation was based on low- and medium-frequency radio beacons. These radios emit a nondirectional signal and are

Figure 13.15 DME station passage.

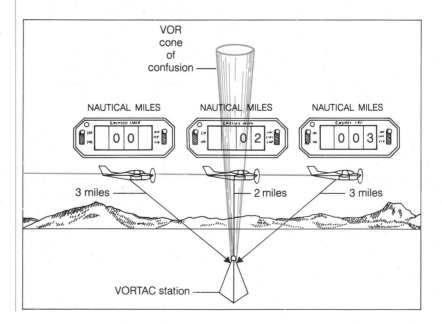

appropriately named **nondirectional beacons (NDBs).** The complementary airborne equipment consists of a radio that receives signals on the medium- and low-frequency band and automatically senses the direction from which the signals are transmitted—thus the name **automatic direction finding (ADF).**

The ADF system has two basic advantages: low cost and low maintenance. It also has some disadvantages. The low- and medium-frequency signals can be reflected and/or refracted (bent) by a number of natural phenomena. These disturbances cause erratic and erroneous indications. Thunderstorms also produce low-frequency radio activity, which can cause the ADF to sense the storm rather than the radio station being used.

Ground Facilities and Chart Depictions

Nondirectional beacons are classified by their power output and usage. NDBs broadcast continuously with a three-letter Morse code identifier. Low-power NDBs that are part of an instrument landing system are called **compass locators** and use a two-letter Morse code identifier. All aeronautical NDBs are depicted on sectional charts by a magenta circle of dots and information box (see Figure 13.16a).

Commercial AM radio stations operate in the frequency range received by ADF radios and therefore could be used for supplemental VFR navigation. They have all of the advantages and disadvantages of nondirectional beacons, plus a few of their own. For example, many pilots enjoy tuning in on commercial stations because the modulated signal contains music, news, and other programs passengers find entertaining on longer flights. (Good pilots, of course, never allow themselves to be distracted by such en route entertainment.) Many AM transmitters are also located on natural prominences so that their range is extended; they broadcast with considerable power and so can easily be received from far away. On the other hand, commercial stations sometimes overlap with other stations' frequencies, causing erratic cockpit indications. Moreover, as permitted by FCC

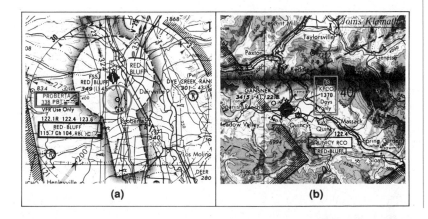

(a)   **(b)**

Figure 13.16 Identifying ADF ground stations on sectional charts. **(a)** A nondirectional beacon. **(b)** A commercial broadcast state. (Legend excerpt is shown in Figure 13.2.)

Figure 13.17 Typical automatic direction finding cockpit instrumentation.

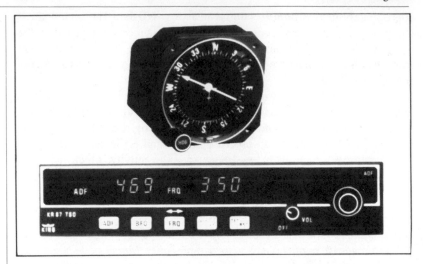

rules, these stations need not identify themselves as often as FAA-approved navaids do, leaving a considerable margin for uncertainty when you initially tune a station. Obviously, these stations are not suitable for primary navigation, but they are often useful as secondary information. AM stations are depicted on the chart as a small blue circle and an information box (see Figure 13.16b).

Cockpit Instrumentation

Figure 13.17 shows the typical cockpit components of an ADF radio. The control unit houses the On/Off, volume, and frequency selection knobs. ADFs also have a switch that selects one of several modes of operation. The ANT (for antenna) position will usually provide the clearest audio signal for station identification, but direction sensing is only active in the ADF mode. The ADF display (or ADF head) has a **bearing indicator** in the form of a rotating pointer. Behind the pointer is an azimuth card, which may or may not be manually rotatable.

ADF orientation.   The rotating pointer in the ADF head displays the **relative bearing (RB)** of the station being received. Relative bearing is the direction of the station *relative to the nose of the airplane*. A fixed azimuth card, with 0° set to the straight-ahead position, illustrates this concept (see Figure 13.18): 0° RB is always straight ahead; 180° RB means directly behind; 90° RB is to the right; and so on. If the azimuth card in the ADF head is set with 0° at the top of the dial, the pointer indicates RB directly.

The ADF allows you to calculate the **magnetic bearing (MB)** to the station being received. This magnetic bearing is the magnetic heading that

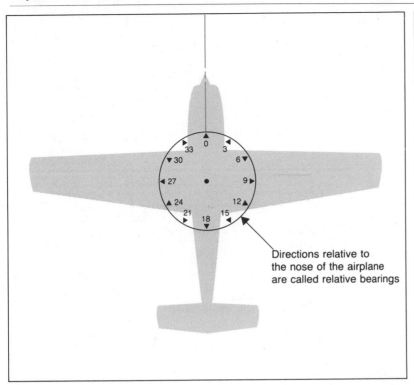

Directions relative to
the nose of the airplane
are called relative bearings

Figure 13.18 The definition of
relative bearing.

would point the airplane directly toward the station. This value can be calculated with the following formula:

Magnetic heading + Relative bearing = Magnetic bearing to the station
(MH)   +   (RB)   =   (MB)

Figure 13.19 illustrates this formula graphically. If the resulting number is greater than 360, then subtract 360. For example, if MH = 270 and RB = 110, use of the formula gives us:

$$270 + 110 = 380 - 360 = 020$$

The magnetic bearing to the station is 020° (see Figure 13.20).

The reciprocal of the bearing to the station can be drawn *from* the station on the chart to form a line of position. Any other LOP, from a VOR or from another NDB, can be used to establish your position (see Figure 13.21).

Tracking to and from an NDB is considerably more complicated than it is with a VOR. Since you will rarely, if ever, use the ADF for primary navigation as a private pilot, these procedures are not discussed in this text. ADF tracking will be covered thoroughly when you train for your instrument rating.

Figure 13.19 Determining magnetic
bearing.

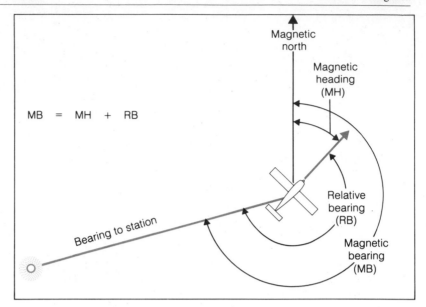

Figure 13.20 Sample ADF problem.

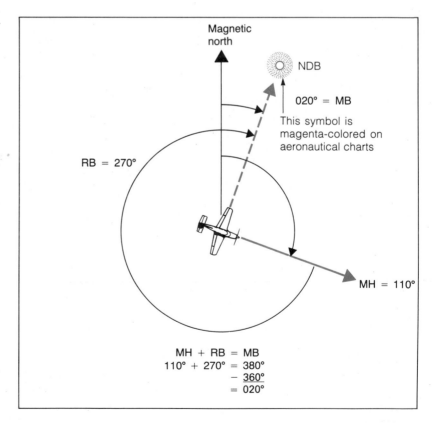

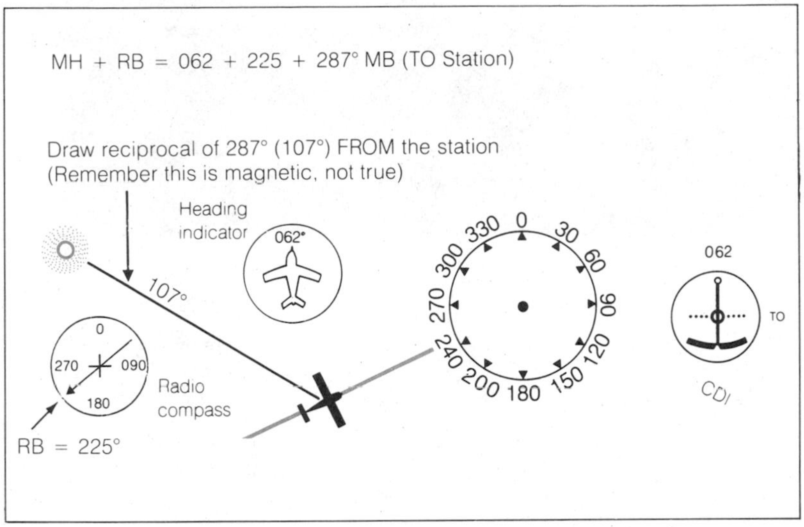

Figure 13.21 Performing a fix using an NDB and a VOR station.

MH + RB = 062 + 225 + 287° MB (TO Station)

Draw reciprocal of 287° (107°) FROM the station
(Remember this is magnetic, not true)

Heading indicator   062°

107°

Radio compass

0
270 — 090
180

RB = 225°

062

TO

CDI

AREA NAVIGATION

A rapidly growing alternative to airways navigation is a system called **area navigation (RNAV).** You may already have spotted one or two shortcomings concerning the use of VOR airways. One is that routes are limited to courses that run between stations, and these routes do not always represent the shortest distance between two destinations. Second, these radio fixes are natural points of congestion as many different aircraft converge over the station on many different bearings. Although FAA regulations regarding cruising altitudes minimize the danger of collision for aircraft on opposite courses (FAR 91.109), VFR aircraft with similar headings can sometimes converge at potentially dangerous angles. Extra vigilance is required any time you operate in the vicinity of a radio navigation station.

These two factors—route inflexibility and congestion—have given rise to area navigation. RNAV makes use of new technology and existing ground facilities and procedures.

RNAV equipment allows you to establish a **waypoint,** which is defined by a radial and distance from any VORTAC or VOR-DME within range (see Figure 13.22). A computer, which is part of the RNAV equipment, then makes the VOR and DME displays react as if the VOR were located at the waypoint. You can select any course to or from the waypoint, and respond to needle deflections as if the waypoint were a real VOR. The DME distance (and any other readouts your equipment may have, such as ground speed and/or time-to-station) will also react as if the VOR were located at the waypoint. The needle deflection for RNAV represents a *linear offset* from the selected course (not an angular offset, as the raw VOR signal gives). This means that the offset is constant for a particular needle deflec-

Figure 13.22 Definition of an RNAV waypoint.

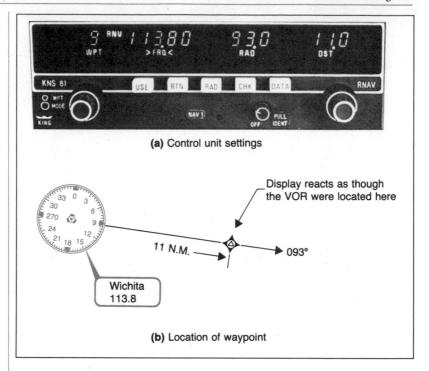

(a) Control unit settings

Display reacts as though the VOR were located here

11 N.M. ⟶ 093°

Wichita 113.8

(b) Location of waypoint

tion, regardless of your distance from the station. A full-scale deflection of the needle represents a displacement of 10 nautical miles on most systems.

RADAR ASSISTANCE AVAILABLE TO VFR PILOTS

In Chapter 7 we described terminal control areas (TCAs), airport radar service areas (ARSAs), and terminal radar service areas (TRSAs), which provide radar services for particular local areas. Within a TCA or ARSA, communication with controllers is *mandatory,* whereas participation in TRSA services is optional (but highly recommended).

If you are in the local area of a TCA or TRSA but not inside the defined airspace, or outside the outer area of an ARSA, you can often obtain similar radar services, on request. This extra service is offered on a "workload-permitting basis," which means that as long as the controllers' primary duties are light enough, you will get radar service. This is a valuable aid, and many VFR pilots take advantage of it.

During the en route portion of a flight, you may be able to obtain radar services from an Air Route Traffic Control Center (called Centers for short). Again, VFR services are provided on a workload-permitting basis.

In order to take advantage of these services, your airplane should be equipped with a **transponder.** A transponder is a radio that can receive special "interrogation" signals from ATC radar and send back a special coded reply. This signal allows the radar to "see" a small aircraft as easily as a large airliner. Without a transponder, the radar relies on the metal components of the airframe to reflect its signal back. Small aircraft and aircraft made largely of nonmetallic components may not provide a reply signal strong enough to be identified. (Use of the transponder is discussed in the paragraphs following.)

The primary benefit of radar for the VFR pilot is that it allows controllers to monitor the flight paths of aircraft and to see potential conflicts before the pilots could notice each other visually. Pilots talking to the controller can be warned and, if desired, can be given a heading to eliminate the possibility of conflict.

Radar can also be used as a means of navigation. The controller can give pilots vectors (headings) toward their destination or toward navaids or around other traffic.

The Limitations of Radar Services

Radar advisories and vectors make it easy for a pilot to become complacent about navigating and knowing his or her exact position. To guard against this, you should be acquainted with both your own and the controller's responsibilities and limitations.

Controller vectors do not in any way relieve the pilot-in-command of navigational responsibility for the aircraft. Your transponder may fail in flight, leaving you without an adequate radar return for controller headings, or, at low altitudes, you may fall below the coverage of the radar antenna. VFR pilots' radar services may be terminated if the IFR traffic workload becomes too great. When flying vectors, therefore, you should keep the VOR receiver, VOR-DME, and ADF tuned to an appropriate station and regularly note your position by pilotage on your chart. In this way you will always be prepared to resume primary navigation of the aircraft in an instant.

Additionally, even though the controller may be giving you vectors and traffic advisories, you are still responsible for seeing and avoiding other traffic, maintaining VFR clearances from clouds, and observing safe altitudes above the terrain and other surface obstructions.

Most controllers are more than willing to provide radar services to VFR pilots when their workload permits. Occasionally, however, their workload picks up and they can no longer continue the service. The problem is that *often the pilot is not informed that radar services are no longer being provided.* It is not mandatory for the controller to inform you that he or she is too busy to continue voluntary services. Most will attempt to do so, but never assume that you will be told.

Using the Transponder

Much of the terminology describing present-day radar systems originated in the time when radar was first employed—as a tool for aerial warfare. The unit itself is sometimes referred to as the **IFF,** for "Identification Friend or Foe"; its transponder codes told radar operators which aircraft were friendly and not to be fired upon and which were hostile.

Figure 13.23 Typical transponder.

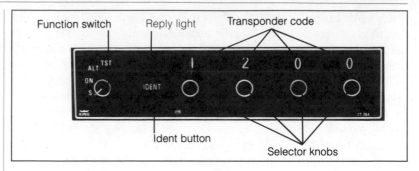

Figure 13.23 shows a typical transponder. The transponder code is a four-digit number, and each number can be a value from 0 to 7 (8 and 9 are not used). The function switch has either four or five positions:

1. *Off.*

2. *Standby,* which activates the unit but allows no transmissions.

3. *On,* which activates Mode A operation. This mode does not send altitude information, even if the aircraft is equipped with an encoding altimeter.

4. *Alt,* which activates Mode C operation. If the aircraft is equipped with an encoding altimeter, this mode sends altitude information as part of the coded reply to the radar.

5. *Test* may or may not be present. If it is, refer to the manufacturer's data for its use.

The *ident button* causes the unit to transmit a special identification code, which causes a distinctive symbol to appear on the controller's screen. One momentary push of this button will transmit the signal for the appropriate length of time.

The *reply light* will blink whenever the unit responds to a radar signal. This feedback lets you know that the unit is operating. When the ident button is pushed, the reply light will remain on while the ident signal is being sent.

Transponder instructions. Some of the more familiar instructions you will receive from controllers are the following:

1. *Squawk (code).* The term **squawk** refers to any transmission of the airborne transponder. An instruction to squawk a particular code means that you should enter that code at once with the unit's code selector knobs. The controller will give you the numerical values to use.

2. *Squawk ident.* The controller wants you to push the Ident button.

3. *Squawk standby.* You should move the function knob to Standby at once, since your aircraft is probably close to the radar antenna and possibly blocking the returns of other aircraft.

4. *Squawk altitude.* You should move the function knob to Alt if your airplane has a functioning altitude-encoder altimeter. If it does not, inform the controller that no altitude-reporting function is available on your aircraft.

5. *Stop squawk.* You should turn off your transponder. If the instruction to "Stop squawk" is followed by a four-digit code, you should stop transmitting that particular code and switch either to a code assigned by ATC or to a general code, as described next.

General transponder codes.   In the absence of specific ATC instructions, you should squawk whichever of the following codes is appropriate:

1200: For VFR flight
7500: For aerial hijacking in progress
7600: For loss of two-way radio communications
7700: For an airborne emergency

Obviously, the last three codes are for use only during the appropriate emergency. You should take special care never to set them by mistake, even momentarily.

FAR 91.24 now requires all transponder-equipped aircraft flying in controlled airspace to have the transponder on and set to 1200 (or the code assigned by ATC), even if you do not intend to use any radar services. If altitude-encoding equipment is installed, it must also be used. Your transponder will allow controllers to point you out as traffic to other aircraft in the area.

Emergency Use of Radar Services
On rare occasion, *as an emergency procedure only,* ATC controllers have aided VFR pilots down through an overcast sky to a visual landing, when poor judgment or poor planning put their aircraft above the airport with IFR conditions underneath. Because of this possibility, you should be aware of the facilities at which radar approach assistance is available, but you should *never* let this knowledge lead you into violating FARs or common sense by intentionally putting your airplane in a situation in which instrument flight is the only alternative to an accident.

OTHER AVIONIC AIDS AND DISPLAYS
Like the automobile, the private airplane can come "stripped to the essentials" or "loaded with extras." Nearly every manufacturer of aviation electronics, called **avionics,** has top-of-the-line and (comparatively speaking) bargain-basement equipment, as well as many peripheral devices that complement the basic functions of radio or DR navigation.

Most aircraft that have more than one nav/com radio are equipped with an **audio panel** (see Figure 13.24). This unit allows the pilot to direct the audio output from any radio to the aircraft speaker or to the headphones,

Figure 13.24 An audio control panel.

or to turn it off. It usually also has a switch that selects the active communication radio and automatically mutes the other(s).

Nicknamed "George" by its early users, the **automatic pilot** has been both boon and bane to transport pilots for many years. Developed to relieve pilots of the laborious job of holding constant headings for long periods of time, autopilots have been improved to include constant-altitude functions and, finally, vertical speed functions as well (see Figure 13.25). Some modern autopilots can also guide the aircraft from bearing to bearing, make course interceptions, and control the throttles to command any airspeed desired by the pilot for the current phase of flight. In short, autopilots can do almost anything pilots can do—except complain about the food in the flight-line snack bar and exercise good, old-fashioned human judgment. On the negative side, autopilots must be maintained to close tolerances because they interact with the flight control system. In case of malfunction, therefore, it must be possible to override them manually or deactivate them in an instant.

Of course, common sense dictates that you know and understand how to operate *all* equipment on board the airplane before you act as pilot-in-command. A thorough checkout with the appropriate instructor will answer your questions and give you experience using the equipment. Your passengers, and the pilots you share the sky with, deserve a knowledgeable, competent pilot at the controls.

Figure 13.25 Typical autopilot control panel.

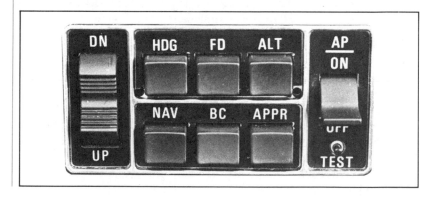

FLIGHT PLANNING WITH RADIO NAVAIDS

Radio aids to navigation extend the capabilities of nearly all aircraft, and the demands they make on pilots by way of extra procedural knowledge are more than made up for by the safety and flexibility they add to each flight. The cost of these benefits is a little extra care in flight planning and the consideration of a few extra details that go beyond the minimum requirements of pilotage and DR.

Since VOR signals are limited to line-of-sight transmissions, you will have to exercise some care in assuring that terrain features or range do not render your navaid unusable during critical segments of your flight. Be sure to complete a thorough DR flight plan for each route segment so that you will be able to continue your flight in an orderly manner should your primary radio aid become unusable.

Published data. Flight information publications are printed to be used. A dog-eared, soiled *Airport/Facility Directory* probably says more for a pilot's flight planning habits than any written test the FAA can devise. Check the status of all en route navaids you intend to use, just as you would check your destination and alternate airports. Be sure you have obtained all of the latest *NOTAMs*.

Equipment check. Even if you are planning a VFR trip, it is always a good idea to check the functions of your radio navaids before you take off. If a VOT facility or designated ground or airborne checkpoint is available, use it.

Shortcuts. There are a few shortcuts built into the world of radio navigation as well. VOR radials (and their reciprocals) make fine magnetic courses for flight planning. Simply plot your course line using the printed compass rose around the station and adjust for winds aloft to obtain your magnetic heading. If your airplane is equipped with DME, use the indicator to confirm or update your estimated ground speed en route.

Finally, radio aids tend to make each flight more enjoyable, since they allow you to spread the navigational duties among a variety of different methods—making chart reading and pilotage a sight-seeing pleasure as well as a responsibility and DR a rewarding exercise in deductive thinking rather than merely a tedious task for flight computer and plotter.

The use of one method of navigation to complement another is called **composite navigation.** Understandably, most flights are conducted in this way, regardless of the aircraft's performance or the sophistication of its systems. The skill and judgment brought to bear in choosing one technique over another or in knowing which indication is most reliable or best in a given situation is the real experience of piloting. You will put all you have learned in the previous chapters to work when you conduct your first composite navigation flight in the next chapter.

KEY TERMS

area navigation (RNAV)

automatic direction finding (ADF)

avionics

bearing indicator

compass locators

composite navigation

course deviation indicator (CDI)

distance measuring equipment
   (DME)

nondirectional beacon (NDB)

Off flag

omni bearing selector (OBS)

proceeding direct

radar

radial

radio navigation

rate of interception

squawk

To-From indicator

transponder

VHF omnidirectional ranges
   (VORs)

victor airways

VORTAC

VOR test (VOT)

PROFICIENCY CHECK

1. A fix is any intersection between two (or more) lines of position. Name a way in which a fix can be made by reference to a single VORTAC station.

2. What is the VOR procedure for proceeding direct to the station?

3. Name two advantages and two disadvantages of VOR as a navigational aid.

4. What is the cockpit indication that you have passed a VOR station?

5. Refer to the following figure. Match the correct VOR indication with the airplanes shown in flight around a typical VOR station. Assume the

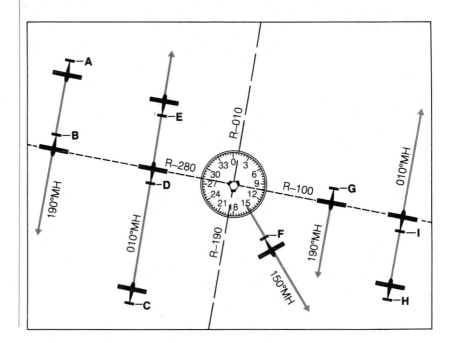

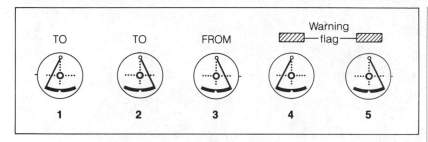

omni bearing selector in all aircraft is set to read 010°. (*Hint:* All indicators are used twice except for one, which is used once.)

6. What one major advantage does a low-frequency automatic direction finder navaid have over a VOR station? What is a low-frequency station's biggest disadvantage?

7. What are a pilot's chief navigational duties when following radar vectors?

CHAPTER FOURTEEN

Flight takes us out of the pressure and anxiety of today and into another world, not a dream-world of fantasy . . . but a world of new and strong reality, of freer spaces and wider vision. And we return rich in impressions of the eye and the mind.

Peter Supf
Airman's World

CHECKPOINTS

What are the reasons for planning a cross-country flight? ✈ What is a flight log and how is it used to plan and conduct a cross-country flight? ✈ How do pilots and the FAA work together to monitor the progress of airplanes flying cross-country? ✈ Why might a pilot replan a flight en route, and what are the established procedures for inflight revisions? ✈ What special responsibilities does a pilot have after a cross-country flight?

COMPOSITE NAVIGATION: GOING CROSS-COUNTRY

J ust as a contractor would never begin building a house without blue-
prints, a pilot should never begin a cross-country flight without a
flight plan. The flight plan is the technical specification for your trip.
It is the means by which you foresee problems and the scale against which
you measure the progress of your flight. When it is filed with a Flight
Service Station, it becomes the FAA's official record of the flight and your
own "insurance policy" against emergencies that could jeopardize the safe
completion of the flight. For these and other reasons—such as compliance
with FAR 91.5—flight planning is a good idea.

Flight documentation is also an old idea—as old as the first cross-country
flights. Figure 14.1 shows probably the earliest cross-country flight record,
a 1909 hand-drawn map used by aviation pioneer Louis Blériot to document
the first heavier-than-air flight across the English Channel. Of course, Blériot had no radio aids to navigation. He did not even have a compass, so
the chart is very simple. Nonetheless, the chart has obvious value: by
recording his progress during the flight, the French aviator was able to
measure his airplane's position and replan his route in response to changing

Figure 14.1 Aviation's first flight
record. The sketch was prepared and
annotated by Louis Blériot on his
flight across the English Channel on
July 25, 1909. His annotations
translate as follows: (1) Spotted ship
after takeoff from Calais; (2) ten
minutes without seeing anything;
(3) I distinguish the English coast;
(4) the west wind prevents me from
flying over the cliffs.

BLERIOT AND PLANE AFTER CHANNEL CROSSING 1909

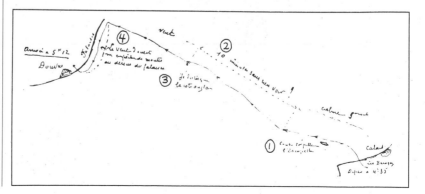

conditions—for instance, the high winds he encountered near the cliffs of Dover.

This chapter describes the process of gathering and using information to plan and execute a cross-country flight safely and efficiently. In doing this, you will apply the knowledge you have gained about airplane instruments, weight and balance, performance, flight information publications, and navigation. By combining these elements to solve actual flight planning and cross-country problems, you will gain confidence in your abilities as a pilot.

OVERVIEW OF FLIGHT PLANNING PROCEDURES

A **flight plan** is simply a summary of details about an intended cross-country flight. A more complete compilation of flight information, called a **flight log,** includes route and checkpoint information, DR computations, communications and facility information, and any special remarks about operating conditions, weather, and so on that might be useful to the pilot.

A conscientiously prepared flight plan reduces cockpit workload once the trip is under way. It allows the pilot to follow the flight's progress in an orderly manner and minimizes the psychological stress of dealing with unusual flight situations.

Although each cross-country trip is unique in its details, the method of flight planning is standard. In this section we will review the different phases of planning involved in a cross-country flight, and in the following section we will conduct a simulated cross-country flight using actual locations and situations in order to demonstrate the principles of flight planning and composite navigation. The phases we will examine are general planning, preflight planning, airplane preflight inspection, departure, en route navigation, replanning a route segment en route, arrival, and postflight activities.

General Planning

You begin planning a flight by checking your probable flight route, usually on a VFR planning chart. In this initial, strategic inspection you will learn whether refueling stops will have to be made, whether adverse terrain or special-use airspace must be flown over or avoided, and whether any limitations of a general nature—including your own medical or physiological condition—will apply to the flight. A call to the FAA's nearest **Pilot's Automatic Telephone Weather Answering Service (PATWAS)** will inform you of weather conditions in the area and of any frontal activity or other significant weather that could affect or delay your flight. If all of these preliminary questions are answered satisfactorily, you can begin planning your flight in more detail.

Preflight Planning

The first step in this phase is to select the current aeronautical chart appropriate to your flight. For light airplanes, this will usually be a sectional chart.

Using a plotter, draw your course line and measure your true course for each leg of the flight, as described in Chapter 12. You will need *magnetic course* information in order to comply with the FARs concerning choice of a VFR cruising altitude. Inspect the chart for appropriate landmarks and radio navigation aids. If a navaid such as a VOR is located near your destination airport, you may want to draw a course line direct to the station to simplify your en route and arrival navigation. Similarly, if a navaid lies just off what might otherwise be a direct pilotage/DR route, you may want to plan your route directly between VORs. The ease of tracking directly to and from VORs, and the security of continuous position information, offsets the added distance flown.

Call the local Flight Service Station (FSS) or the National Weather Service and obtain an aviation weather briefing, as outlined in Chapter 9. If necessary, take a moment now to review the form and content of this briefing.

Altitude selection is probably the next item to consider. How do you select the appropriate altitude for a given flight? Unfortunately, there is no magic formula, but there are plenty of considerations:

1. Terrain will obviously establish the minimum altitude to consider. FAR 91.79 specifies the minimum safe altitudes you *must* observe. Any flight conducted at low altitudes must be planned, and flown, very carefully because of the inherent risks involved. Marginal weather sometimes forces VFR pilots to fly at low altitudes, in order to stay out of the clouds and maintain visual contact with the ground. Risks, then, are increased because obstructions are harder to see, yet the low altitude exposes you to more of them. FAR 91.79 requires that you always be able to make an emergency landing without undue hazard to persons or property on the ground. Common sense requires that you be able to make an emergency landing with minimal risk to *you*! The lower you fly, the fewer are the suitable landing sites of either type. Low-altitude flying can be safe, and fun, if you take the time to plan carefully and if you fly the same way.

2. Clouds will often establish the maximum altitude available to the VFR pilot. Remember that FAR 91.105 requires you to stay at least 500 feet below the clouds. Sometimes it is possible to climb above a cloud layer, in which case you must remain at least 1000 feet above them. Beware when climbing above a cloud layer because it is always possible for the openings between clouds to close up, trapping you on top with no VFR way to get down. Get down below the clouds while there are plenty of big openings. The regulation requires 2000 feet of horizontal separation from clouds, which means a "hole" must be more than a mile wide to be legal. All these numbers apply *below 10,000 feet*. At and above that altitude, even larger separation criteria apply (see FAR 91.105).

3. Wind speed tends to increase with altitude. If you are flying *against* the wind, lower altitudes will minimize the detrimental effects. Conversely, tailwinds tend to favor choice of a higher altitude. The penalty for climbing (slow airspeed, high fuel consumption) must be balanced against the benefit of the tailwind (faster ground speed, engine leaned). The length of the trip is a factor here also, because the more time you spend cruising at altitude, the greater the benefit of climbing. Unfortunately, there is no simple formula that will yield the most efficient altitude to use. You must do performance calculations to determine total time en route for a variety of altitudes and expected winds. To be complete, you should also consider various cruise power settings as well. The airlines use computer programs to help their pilots select the most fuel-efficient altitudes. These aircraft burn hundreds of gallons per hour, and the wrong altitude can cost thousands of dollars of extra fuel. The differences will not be that dramatic for a light airplane, but careful flight planning may mean the difference between going nonstop and making a fuel stop on a long trip (and still having adequate reserves on landing).

4. As previously noted, FAR 91.109 specifies cruising altitudes for VFR flight. These altitudes apply when flying over 3000 feet above the surface (we will only discuss the regulations that apply below 18,000 feet). The appropriate altitude is based on your *magnetic course*. Recall that this is true course, corrected for magnetic variation but *without any wind corrections applied*. This is the magnetic direction you are actually traveling (not your heading). When your magnetic course is from 0° to 179°, inclusive, you must fly at odd thousand-foot altitudes plus 500 feet (i.e., 3500, 5500, 7500, etc.). Magnetic courses from 180° to 359°, inclusive, require even thousand-foot altitudes plus 500 feet (4500, 6500, 8500, etc.). (Note: IFR aircraft are assigned even and odd thousand-foot altitudes by the same method, so VFR aircraft should never fly at those altitudes.) This simple scheme separates aircraft flying in opposite directions by altitude. Since all aircraft at the same altitude are going in the same general direction, there is more time to see and avoid potential collisions. There is still plenty of opportunity to encounter aircraft *crossing* your path at the same altitude, so the need for vigilance is not reduced. This rule simply gives you a fighting chance to see a collision hazard in time to do something about it.

You are now ready to prepare a detailed flight log. Figure 14.2 shows some typical flight log forms, or you can organize the data your own way. The purpose of any flight log is to record the data you will use to check the progress of your flight. The items of primary interest are checkpoints, headings, distances, and estimated times. Your predicted times are the basis for determining the fuel required for the trip. En route, you will compare actual ground speed and time against your prediction and determine if a change in plans is necessary to complete the flight with adequate fuel reserves.

You may want to annotate your flight log and chart with relevant weather or *NOTAM* information received during your briefing. If necessary, replot certain legs in order to avoid adverse conditions or unusable facilities. When the flight log is complete, transfer the details, as specified, to an FAA flight

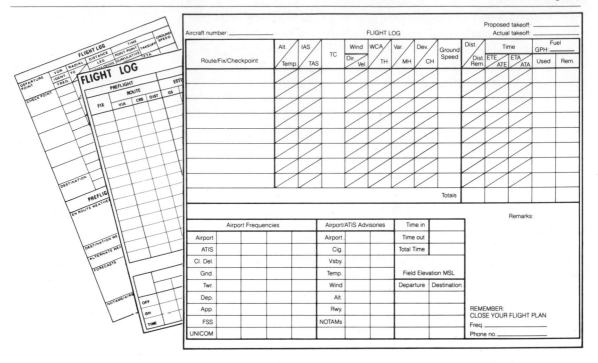

Figure 14.2 Typical
flight log forms.

Figure 14.2 Typical
flight log forms.

plan form, shown in Figure 14.3, and file the plan with the local FSS. Ask for a last check on *NOTAMs*, AIRMETs, SIGMETs, and pilot reports (PIREPs).

Since you are dealing with both composite navigation and the practical aspects of getting into and out of a number of different terminal areas, you will want to record on your flight log all frequencies needed to communicate with ATC centers, control towers, UNICOMs, Flight Service Stations, and approach and departure controllers. Also make note of the radio navigation frequencies of stations along your route. For legs flown along a VOR radial, the magnetic course to record will be the appropriate inbound and outbound bearings. Look up each airport and navaid of interest in the *Airport/Facility Directory* in order to learn of any operating limitations that may affect your flight. Remember, too, that *NOTAMs* apply to navaids as well as airports.

Since you cannot count on the FSS briefer to automatically check every facility that may be of interest to you, be sure to mention each airport and navaid you plan to use.

Your preflight activities must also include weight and balance calculations. You may be loading more aboard the airplane for a cross-country flight than you have for local hops, so this step cannot be ignored. Rather than estimate weights for baggage, use your bathroom scale to get actual weights. While you have the airplane's handbook out, check takeoff performance under the current conditions and compare that against the runways you intend to use.

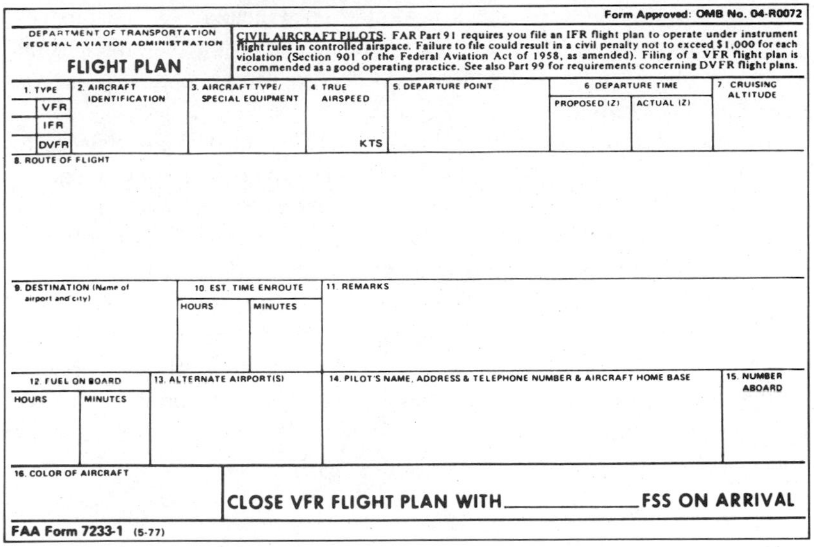

Form Approved: OMB No. 04-R0072

DEPARTMENT OF TRANSPORTATION
FEDERAL AVIATION ADMINISTRATION

FLIGHT PLAN

CIVIL AIRCRAFT PILOTS. FAR Part 91 requires you file an IFR flight plan to operate under instrument flight rules in controlled airspace. Failure to file could result in a civil penalty not to exceed $1,000 for each violation (Section 901 of the Federal Aviation Act of 1958, as amended). Filing of a VFR flight plan is recommended as a good operating practice. See also Part 99 for requirements concerning DVFR flight plans.

1. TYPE: VFR / IFR / DVFR
2. AIRCRAFT IDENTIFICATION
3. AIRCRAFT TYPE/ SPECIAL EQUIPMENT
4. TRUE AIRSPEED — KTS
5. DEPARTURE POINT
6. DEPARTURE TIME — PROPOSED (Z) / ACTUAL (Z)
7. CRUISING ALTITUDE
8. ROUTE OF FLIGHT
9. DESTINATION (Name of airport and city)
10. EST. TIME ENROUTE — HOURS / MINUTES
11. REMARKS
12. FUEL ON BOARD — HOURS / MINUTES
13. ALTERNATE AIRPORT(S)
14. PILOT'S NAME, ADDRESS & TELEPHONE NUMBER & AIRCRAFT HOME BASE
15. NUMBER ABOARD
16. COLOR OF AIRCRAFT

CLOSE VFR FLIGHT PLAN WITH ____________ FSS ON ARRIVAL

FAA Form 7233-1 (5-77)

Figure 14.3 The FAA flight plan form.

Airplane Preflight Inspection

Every flight, local or cross-country, must begin with a thorough inspection of the airplane. Be sure all the required papers are on board the aircraft (remember the mnemonic AROW mentioned after FAR 91.31). You should also check the aircraft maintenance logs to verify that the required inspections are current (see subpart C of FAR 91).

Departure

Chapter 7 details most of the activities involved in VFR departures from small, UNICOM-supported fields and major terminals. Departing a large airport, for example, you may have to change communications frequencies a number of times: from Automatic Terminal Information Service (ATIS) to ground control, to tower and/or departure control, and then to the FSS to open your flight plan.

En Route Navigation

As soon as practical, you will want to turn to the heading you expect will keep you on course. If you depart from a large airport, you may be vectored off course initially to conform with the controller's needs; eventually, however, you will be freed to "resume normal navigation." Once you have reached your cruising altitude, carefully set your power and lean the engine (in accordance with the Pilot's Operating Handbook, of course).

Your first order of business is to determine your actual cruising ground speed. You should select your first couple of checkpoints with this in mind. Checking ground speed early allows you to proceed with confidence, or to begin considering your alternate plan. Unless fuel reserves are unusually tight, a ground speed that is slower than you expected is not a concern; it simply changes your arrival time. If fuel reserves *are* tight, you know immediately that a fuel stop is probably necessary.

Your first ground speed check is simply an indicator. As you proceed and as subsequent speed calculations are averaged together, the results become more accurate. Continually update your estimated time of arrival (ETA) at your destination.

By following your flight log, you virtually eliminate your chances to become disoriented. If you have been able to positively identify your checkpoints and to accurately predict arrival over the next one, you must know where you are and which way and how fast you are going. The only real "secret" to flying cross-country is to *hold your heading*. You will adjust the heading, based on your actual ground track, but once you have the right one, maintain it. Every once in a while, if you are flying over terrain that has few recognizable features, you may entertain feelings of doubt. This is normal. If you are holding your heading, your next checkpoint will arrive on schedule. You can always use two VORs to get a position fix and set your mind at ease.

Replanning En Route

There are many reasons to depart from a preplanned flight route. Adverse weather, mechanical malfunctions, a higher rate of fuel consumption than expected, a change in facility status—any of these situations may compel you to change your route. But you may also have an urge to go sight-seeing, to visit a nearby city or airport, just as you might spontaneously take a side trip while driving an automobile cross-country.

In general, unless you are facing a problem requiring an immediate change, such as adverse weather, it is best to replan your flight by picking a point ahead on your present route where the change will take effect. Simply turning to a heading that you think will take you to your new goal will probably get you lost rather than save time. Pick a spot far enough away that you can make some quick DR calculations, but not so far that you waste time and fuel getting there. Replot your new course line on your chart. Obviously, to replan in-flight you must have the minimum tools for flight planning you would use on the ground, such as a flight computer or calculator and plotter. Be sure to divide your attention between sky and cockpit while you do your figuring; you are still responsible for flying your airplane, for VFR navigation, and for keeping away from other aircraft.

Your main interests in replanning the flight are your new heading, ETE and ETA, and the adequacy of your fuel reserve. When you are satisfied that the change in plan is feasible and the FSS has informed you of any *NOTAMs* or weather affecting your new route and destination, revise your plan with the FSS, providing new information in the same format as your original flight plan.

Keep these points in mind as you replan your flight:

1. Know where you are at all times. Do not get into an area of adverse weather or low visibility while you are concentrating on your new flight plan.

2. Continue to fly the airplane while replanning. Be sure the airspace around you is clear, and maintain control of the airplane.

3. Satisfy yourself that the detour or side trip can be conducted safely.

Arrival

The arrival phase begins when you start your descent into the airport area. You must prepare yourself mentally for this phase, since it is demanding and is often preceded by several relatively relaxed hours of cruising. If you have not flown into an area before, you will probably have to work hard picking out the local landmarks. There is a saying that you must "fly the last mile as well as the first." You must not let the confidence built up during an uneventful trip become overconfidence or complacency on landing, especially when you are returning to your home airport. The arrival is neither complete nor successful until the airplane is parked safely on the ramp. You must close your flight plan either by radioing the nearest FSS while you are still in the air or by telephoning them once on the ground. You may also ask the control tower to close your flight plan for you, although not all airports provide this service.

Postflight Activities

If you did not do so in the air, you must close your flight plan as soon as possible after landing, usually by telephone at the destination airport. Since the airplane will probably have to be refueled, either for the return trip or to wait overnight, you must ensure that the right grade of fuel is available and that the airplane is properly serviced. Relay any maintenance concerns to the appropriate repair technicians as well. Maintenance services for transient aircraft can usually be obtained from the local fixed-base operator.

Finally, never leave the ramp until the airplane has been fully secured. This means that it has been properly tied down, with wheel chocks and pitot (and other intake) covers installed. For safety as well as security, the cockpit and luggage compartments should also be locked.

GOING CROSS-COUNTRY

General advice and hypothetical situations are fine, but getting into an airplane and flying is even better. With our factual knowledge and concepts at hand, let us climb into a real airplane (albeit in our imagination) and find out what composite navigation is all about.

Preflight Briefing

Assume that you, a student pilot, in consultation with your instructor, are planning a morning solo cross-country flight in the area south of San Francisco, California. Your flight school and airplane are based at San Carlos Airport in San Mateo County, about 10 miles south of San Francisco International Airport. Your airplane is a Beechcraft Skipper Model 77, identification number 37259. In the course of the flight, you are to use as many as possible of the flight planning and navigation techniques discussed in this and previous chapters. Your instructor also asks that you return to San

Carlos by the early afternoon, so you tentatively select an 8:00 A.M. takeoff time and agree to limit your flight to within 100 miles of the San Francisco Bay Area. You decide in principle on a multilegged, round-robin flight with at least one full-stop landing en route.

General Planning

After scanning the VFR planning chart on the wall of the flight planning room, you decide that the picturesque Monterey Peninsula, located an hour or so south of the Bay Area, would make a pleasant intermediate stop, with a second leg made into the San Joaquin Valley, and a third back into the San Francisco area, for a total trip of 200 miles. From a call to the PATWAS line at the Oakland FSS, you learn that the Bay Area is expected to remain clear all day but to have reduced visibilities inland because of trapped obscurations from a high-pressure center over northern California. Late afternoon coastal fog is predicted, together with orographic thunderstorms inland along the Sierra Nevada. Turbulence is forecast in the vicinity of the higher elevations in the state, but VFR conditions are expected to prevail throughout. Aside from local obscurations in the San Joaquin Valley, weather should not be a factor in the flight, you decide. Selecting a San Francisco sectional chart, you begin your preliminary flight planning activities (see Figure 14.4).

Terminal area.   You immediately notice that San Carlos is located next to the San Francisco terminal control area, and that you will have to take special precautions on departure and arrival in order not to fly into it. You also notice that a straight line drawn from the San Carlos Airport to the Monterey Peninsula Airport crosses a portion of Monterey Bay. Even without measuring the distance from your course line to shore, you can see that your proposed flight route will take you 5 to 10 miles out over the water. Your instructor asks you if this is acceptable.

First modification of the plan.   In the Pilot's Operating Handbook you read that the Skipper will glide 1.3 nautical miles for every 1000 feet of altitude in a no-wind condition. At a cruising altitude of 6500 feet, your chances of gliding 8.5 miles back to the coast and then finding a suitable forced landing site would be slight. You therefore elect to alter your proposed course so that the airplane remains over the coast. Your instructor congratulates you on this decision, reminding you that the airplane is not equipped with flotation gear and a pyrotechnic device (required equipment for commercial flights) and that you, as a student pilot, are not trained for emergency water landings (called **ditching**). You draw your course line from the San Carlos Airport to the Watsonville Airport, located near the head of the bay, and from there you draw a second course line (leg number two) into the Monterey Peninsula Airport, where you will land.

Using radio navaids.   Next you look for a likely course inland from Monterey. Since the Salinas VORTAC provides bearing information both into

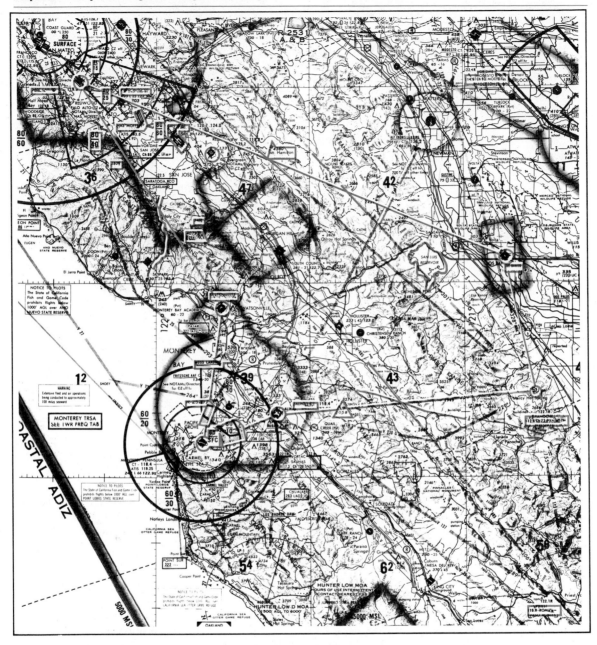

Figure 14.4 The proposed round-robin flight route for Skipper 37259.

and out of the Monterey area, you draw a short course line (leg number three) inland to the station. Then you add a fourth course line outbound, the Salinas 068° radial, which will take you toward the Panoche VORTAC, another prominent radio aid, located on the edge of the San Joaquin Valley. You note that the outbound 068° radial from Salinas becomes the 070° course inbound to Panoche (the reciprocal of the Panoche 250° radial). This realignment of magnetic courses is due to changes in magnetic variation.

Second stopover.   You will probably be ready for a mid-morning coffee break after passing over Panoche. As there is no airport in the vicinity of the VORTAC, you will make a second landing at the Los Banos Municipal Airport, about 21 nautical miles northwest of the station. You plot this course line, noting that it overlays the 332° radial outbound from the station.

Home stretch.   You decide to proceed from Los Banos directly back to San Carlos, the longest leg of the trip. You plot the course line, a stretch of 71 nautical miles. Although there are no radio navaids located directly on this segment of your route, there are several on either side, and you mentally make a note of them for use in future one- and two-station fixes. The last third of this leg is also rich in pilotage landmarks, and you will be passing over four separate airport traffic areas as you proceed inbound through the TCA to San Carlos. Your entire route is plotted on the excerpt of the San Francisco sectional shown in Figure 14.4.

Appraising the flight.   To obtain a briefing from the FSS weather briefer, you will have to furnish some tangible information about your flight route, such as anticipated cruising altitudes and arrival times at your points of landing. You therefore inspect the features along your course lines more closely now, looking for terrain elevations and surface obstructions en route. (The large boldface numbers on the chart followed by smaller bold-face numbers show the highest elevations in thousands and hundreds of feet, respectively.)

After ensuring that the highest features in the vicinity of each leg will be either below your desired altitude or well away from your line of flight, you tentatively decide upon 5500 feet to Watsonville, 5500 feet to Monterey, 5500 feet to Panoche, 4500 feet to Los Banos, and 6500 feet inbound to San Carlos.

Although a precisely estimated ETA is not mandatory to receive a weather briefing, many pilots (especially for longer flights) believe it is helpful to compute a preliminary zero-wind ETA so that the briefer will give them the terminal forecast for their arrival time. In this case, the Skipper handbook shows an average true airspeed of around 97 knots for these altitudes at medium cruise rpm (2500 rpm), which with no wind would give a ground speed of 97 knots as well. Carefully measuring the length of each leg, you add up a total distance of 207 miles for the trip. With a ground speed of 97 knots, your flying time will be 2 hours and 8 minutes. You make your calculations on your flight computer using the formulas presented in Chapter 12. You figure in an hour's delay between the time you file the flight plan and the time you take off from San Carlos and an additional hour or so for your intermediate landings (a half-hour stopover at each airport). This gives you a total time in which to complete the trip of 4 hours, 8 minutes, starting immediately. You also figure an estimated arrival time for the airports at Monterey and Los Banos, based on their incremental time en route. Armed with this information, you are now ready to obtain a detailed weather briefing for the flight.

Preflight Planning

A telephone call to the pilot's weather briefing line at the Oakland FSS puts you in touch with an FSS weather specialist. You inform her of your airplane's identification number, your name, and your route—a round robin from San Carlos Airport via Watsonville, Monterey, Salinas, Panoche, and Los Banos, with landings at Monterey and Los Banos. Cruising altitudes will be between 4500 and 6500 feet, and the flight will be VFR. You state that you plan to depart San Carlos at 0800 PST, or 1600 UTC, arriving at Monterey at 1640 UTC, Los Banos at 1800 UTC, and San Carlos at 1908 UTC. You ask for winds-aloft and terminal forecasts for your destination airports, information about any significant weather in the area, and *NOTAMs*. You respond to her "stand by one" with your pencil and weather briefing form ready (see Figure 14.5).

Figure 14.5 Sample weather briefing form.

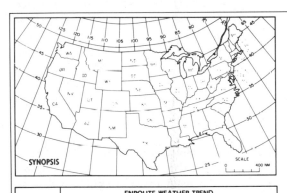

WEATHER BRIEFING

SYNOPSIS

PILOT'S WEATHER "GO — NO GO" CHECKLIST		
AIRMETS	ALTERNATE WX	TOPS
SIGMETS	FORECASTS	FREEZING LEVEL
ENROUTE WX	WINDS ALOFT	TEMP/DEW PT (FOG)
DESTINATION WX	PIREPS	BETTER WX AREA

LOCATION	ENROUTE WEATHER TREND	

LOCATION	TERMINAL FORECASTS

LOCATION	WINDS ALOFT FORECASTS		

LOCATION	PIREPS/SIGNIFICANT WEATHER/NOTAMS

Weather briefing.   Within a few minutes the weather briefer returns with
the following information:

*Northern California synopsis, 1400 to 2300 zulu: A high-pressure area
continues to dominate the state's weather pattern, holding clear skies and
haze over much of the northern part of the state. Skies are clear with light,
variable winds along the Pacific coast and northern San Joaquin Valley,
with low-altitude obscurations and local fog in some locations. Freezing
level is at 8000 feet over California and most of Oregon, increasing to
12,000 feet south of Bakersfield to the Mexican border. The Bay Area will
be clear with winds light and variable becoming generally northwest at 10
knots, with late afternoon and evening fog locally near the coast. San
Carlos forecast: clear with surface winds from 300° at 12 gusting to 15
knots. Monterey forecast: clear, winds 300° at 10 with local fog in late
afternoon and evening. Los Banos forecast: clear, visibility 6 miles in haze
with chance of light to moderate turbulence afternoons in the vicinity of
high terrain. Convective activity forecast for the Sierra region with a SIG-
MET in effect for the central San Joaquin Valley for moderate turbulence
in the vicinity of high terrain and thunderstorms. San Carlos winds and
temperatures-aloft forecast: 3000 feet, 270° at 10, plus 10; 6000 feet, 290°
at 10, plus 5; 9000 feet, 310° at 12, plus 2. Los Banos: 3000 feet, 280° at
10, plus 10; 6000 feet, 290° at 12, plus 5; 9000 feet, 300° at 12, plus 2.
Notice to Airmen for the Monterey Peninsula Airport: North parallel taxiway is closed for construction until further notice.*

You record this information on your weather briefing form, as shown in
Figure 14.6. After reviewing it quickly, you decide that you have no further
questions and you thank the briefer, promising to call back shortly in order
to file your flight plan. You review the weather with your instructor and
find nothing that would disturb or delay your flight, provided you return to
the San Carlos area before the late afternoon convective activity begins in
the central San Joaquin Valley or fog a can penetrate the coastal hills to the
Bay Area airports.

Flight log.   You are now ready to work out a DR flight plan and record
it on one of the many flight planning logs or forms published by suppliers
of aeronautical materials. Most of these forms allow you to work step by
step through DR computations for every leg of a flight. You will be using
the form shown in Figure 14.2. Remember that you will need a separate
DR computation for any change in winds, altitude, course, or true airspeed.
If your flight carries you into a region of different magnetic variation, you
will have to compute a new magnetic course and magnetic heading for these
legs as well.

Begin your flight log by filling in the identification number of your airplane. Each line of the column headed Route/Fix/Checkpoints represents
the beginning and ending fix for each navigational leg. You will complete

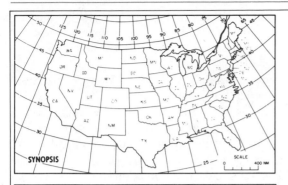

WEATHER BRIEFING

1400 Z - 2300Z
① HI PRESS OVR NCAL
② FRZ LVL: 8Ø OVR CAL & ORE
        12Ø OVR SO CAL

PILOT'S WEATHER "GO — NO GO" CHECKLIST					
✓	AIRMETS	✓	ALTERNATE WX	✓	TOPS
✓	SIGMETS	✓	FORECASTS	✓	FREEZING LEVEL
✓	ENROUTE WX	✓	WINDS ALOFT	✓	TEMP/DEW PT (FOG)
✓	DESTINATION WX	✓	PIREPS	✓	BETTER WX AREA

SYNOPSIS   SCALE 0 400 NM

LOCATION	ENROUTE WEATHER TREND	
SQL	CLR VRB 5 BCMG NW 12 G15 LCL FOG LATE PM	
MRY	CLR 30 10 LCL FOG LATE PM	
LSN	VFR H, Cbs East of ARPT ALONG SIERRAS LATE PM	

LOCATION	TERMINAL FORECASTS
MRY	CLR 30 10
LSN	CLR VIS 6H
SQL	CLR 30 12 G15

LOCATION	WINDS ALOFT FORECASTS			
	3Ø	6Ø	9Ø	
SQL	2710+10	2910+5	3112+2	
LSN	2810+10	2912+5	3012+2	

LOCATION	PIREPS/SIGNIFICANT WEATHER/NOTAMS
CEN CAL VALLEY	SIGMET MOD TURB VCTY HI TERRAIN & CONVECTIVE ACTIVITY ALG SIERRAS
COAST	LCL FOG LATE PM
MRY	NOTAM: N PARALLEL TAXIWAY CLOSED FOR CNSTN

a separate DR computation for each route segment, ending with time en route, arrival time, and fuel calculations.

First, enter the checkpoints marking the beginning and end of each of the six legs, using the location identifier code from the *Airport/Facility Directory:* San Carlos (SQL), Watsonville (WVI), Monterey (MRY), Salinas (SNS), Panoche (PXN), Los Banos (LSN), and San Carlos again. You will also use the VOR station identifiers to indicate VOR radials that you intend to use as course lines. Between the identifiers of the checkpoints of the first two legs, you enter the symbol for proceeding direct—a capital *D* with an arrow through it. This symbol is one of a number of flight planning symbols used primarily for instrument flight clearances; they constitute a kind of aviation shorthand. Although private pilots do not need to know these symbols, a few, such as the proceed direct symbol, are useful when copying the ATC clearances issued to VFR pilots departing a terminal control area. The proceed direct symbol on your VFR flight plan indicates that you are flying the leg directly from one fix or station to another by

Figure 14.6 Completed weather briefing form.

reference to radio navaids or by DR and pilotage techniques. For legs that you will fly on VOR radials, record the inbound and outbound courses, as shown on the compass rose around the station, or the victor airway designator depicted on your chart.

From this point on, there are basically two ways of filling out the form. You may work each column vertically, filling in the relevant altitudes for all legs, then recording the temperature information for all legs, the IAS for all legs, and so on. This method has the advantage of permitting you to do all DR computations of a particular kind at once (for example, TAS values, magnetic headings, and ground speeds). Many pilots find this method quicker, since they need not refer to the chart or weather briefing so often, and more accurate, since their flight computer or wind face is set for similar calculations.

The second method is to compute each leg completely before starting the next. This method has the advantage of lending continuity to your calculations and of revealing errors or transpositions in numbers that can be overlooked when filling out the form vertically. Whichever way you choose (or your instructor suggests), use it consistently to avoid confusion and mistakes. We will assume that you use the vertical method for this flight. Figure 14.7 shows the completed flight log for the trip.

In the altitude (Alt.) column, you enter the VFR cruising altitudes chosen earlier. We will discuss the temperature entry in a moment.

The next column provides space for entering your indicated airspeed (IAS) and true airspeed (TAS) for each leg of the flight. You must now make a firm decision about your power setting and cruising airspeed. When you estimated the flight characteristics before requesting weather, you based your calculations on 2500 rpm, which gave you a true airspeed of around 97 knots for the range of altitudes envisioned. Now you refer to the handbook chart again (see Figure 14.8) and decide upon a lower power setting of 2400 rpm in order to conserve fuel. You then calculate a revised IAS and TAS for each altitude based on this power setting and enter these values on your log.

In the next column enter the true course for each leg of the flight, which you previously measured on your chart.

In the column labeled Temp. you enter the outside air temperatures (OAT) given in the winds-aloft forecast. You will notice that your VFR cruising altitudes do not match the altitude increments in which the winds and temperatures are reported. Unless you file an IFR flight plan, this will always be so. (Even then, cruising altitudes frequently fall somewhere other than on one of the even altitudes given in the forecast.) You must simply interpolate a new wind and temperature value proportional to your cruising altitude. Additionally, since you were given forecasts for only two locations (San Carlos and Los Banos) rather than for all your checkpoints, you will have to gauge the winds and temperatures for each leg according to how close the leg is to each of these locations. It is handy to compute and enter values for wind direction and wind velocity at the same time as you figure temperatures since the same proportions are involved.

Aircraft number: _N 37259_

FLIGHT LOG

Proposed takeoff: _0800/1600 Z_

Actual takeoff: _____

Fuel GPH: _5.5_

Route/Fix/Checkpoint	Alt. / Temp.	IAS / TAS	TC	Wind Dir. / Vel.	WCA / TH	Var. / MH	Dev. / CH	Ground Speed	Dist. / Dist. Rem.	Time ETE / ATE	Time ETA / ATA	Used	Rem.
SQL ↦ WVI	5500 / +5	85 / 92	148	290 / 10	+4R / 152	-16E / 136	-2 / 134	100	41 / 166	25	0825	2.3	22.7
WVI ↦ MRY	4500 / +7	87 / 93	190	280 / 10	+6R / 196	-16E / 180	0 / 180	92	21 / 145	14	0839	1.3	21.4
MRY ↦ SNS (117.3)	5500 / +5	85 / 92	069	290 / 10	-4L / 065	-16E / 049	-3 / 046	99	13 / 132	8	0847	.7	20.7
SNS V230 PXN (112.6)	5500 / +5	85 / 92	084	290 / 12	-3L / 081	-16E / 065	+3 / 067	103	40 / 92	23	0910	2.1	18.6
PXN ↦ LSN	4500 / +7	87 / 93	348	285 / 11	-6L / 342	-16E / 326	+2 / 328	87	21 / 71	15	0925	1.4	17.2
LSN ↦ SQL	6500 / +5	84 / 92	293	290 / 11	0 / 293	-16E / 277	+4 / 281	81	71 / 0	53	1018	4.9	12.3
							Totals		207	2+18		12.7	12.3

Airport Frequencies				Airport/ATIS Advisories			Time in	
Airport	SQL	MRY	LSN	Airport	MRY	LSN	Time out	
ATIS	125.9	119.25		Cig.			Total Time	
Cl. Del.				Vsby.				
Gnd.	121.6	121.9		Temp.			Field Elevation MSL	
Twr.	119.0	118.4		Wind			Departure	Destination
Dep.	135.65	120.8		Alt.			SQL 2	MRY 244
App.	133.95	127.15		Rwy.				LSN 119
FSS	OAK 122.5	SNS 122.6	FAT 122.3	NOTAMs				
UNICOM	122.95	122.95	122.8					

Remarks:
Stopover MRY: 30 min.
Stopover LSN: 30 min.

REMEMBER:
CLOSE YOUR FLIGHT PLAN
Freq. _122.5_
Phone no. _668-0925_

Wind and temperature values for the first leg of the flight, for example, are relatively straightforward. The OAT drops from 10 degrees to 5 degrees Celsius between 3000 and 6000 feet. Since your cruising altitude is 5500 feet, very close to the 6000-foot level, you can safely use the 6000-foot forecast at San Carlos for your values. On the fourth leg, you are again cruising near the 6000-foot altitude forecast, but since you are now much closer to Los Banos than to San Carlos, you will use the forecast for Los Banos. You can find the wind and temperature values for the other legs of the flight in a similar manner.

On this particular form, you are called upon next to calculate a wind correction angle (WCA) on your flight computer or electronic calculator, using the wind direction, velocity, and true course recorded previously. If you have forgotten how to work the wind face of your computer, review the procedure in Chapter 12. Remember that winds in the winds-aloft forecast are always given in relation to true north, and you must therefore use the true course values from your flight log. At this time it is also convenient

Figure 14.7 Completed flight log.

Figure 14.8 Cruise performance chart.

CRUISE PERFORMANCE*
STANDARD DAY
AVERAGE CRUISE WEIGHT = 1600 POUNDS

ALTITUDE FEET	THROTTLE SETTING RPM	FUEL FLOW GPH	IAS KNOTS	TAS KNOTS
2500	2700	8.0	101	105
	2500	6.4	94	97
	2400	5.7	90	93
	2300	5.2	85	88
3500	2700	7.8	100	105
	2500	6.3	92	97
	2400	5.7	88	93
	2300	5.2	84	88
4500	2700	7.7	99	105
	2500	6.3	91	97
	2400	5.6	87	93
	2300	5.1	82	88
5500	2700	7.6	97	105
	2500	6.2	89	97
	2400	5.5	85	92
	2300	5.0	81	87
6500	2700	7.4	96	105
	2500	6.1	88	97
	2400	5.4	84	92
	2300	5.0	79	87
7500	2500	6.0	86	96
	2400	5.3	82	91
	2300	4.9	77	86
8500	2500	5.8	85	96
	2400	5.3	80	91
	2300	4.9	76	85
9500	2500	5.7	83	95
	2400	5.2	79	90
	2300	4.8	74	85
10500	2500	5.6	81	95
	2400	5.1	77	90
	2300	4.7	72	84
11500	2500	5.5	80	94
	2400	5.0	75	89
	2300	4.7	70	82

*Cruise performance is based on best power mixture. Lean to maximum rpm for best performance.

to record your ground speed (GS) for each leg, since you will find it as part of your computation of the wind correction angle. Enter all of these values on the log.

You must now make some simple additions and subtractions. You may complete the true heading (TH) portion of the form simply by adding or subtracting the wind correction angle, whichever is appropriate, to the true course. From the sectional chart, you can then record the number of degrees of magnetic variation (VAR) for each leg of the flight. Since our imaginary flight is in a relatively small area, the magnetic variation is a constant −16°E for all legs. By adding or subtracting the magnetic variation from the true heading, you arrive at the value of the magnetic heading (MH). Also record, from your airplane's compass correction card, the deviation values (Dev.) of your magnetic compass. By applying these values to your magnetic heading, you can derive your magnetic compass heading (CH). This applies only to operations using the magnetic compass, however. Once the heading indicator has been aligned for flight, you will find it far more convenient to fly a magnetic heading using this instrument even though you must check it regularly.

Next you enter the distances of each leg, which you measured on your chart. Add them up and enter this number beside Totals at the bottom of the form. Now subtract the distance of the first leg from the total distance and enter the result in the first space headed Rem., for "distance remaining." Subtract the distance of the next leg from this value, and so on, until the distance remaining is zero. This computation will help you assess the impact of any subsequent changes in the flight plan.

Using your electronic calculator or flight computer again, calculate the time it will take to fly each leg at the ground speed shown for that leg and enter the values in minutes in the spaces headed ETE. Then total the minutes (138 or 140, depending upon the method of calculation—computer or electronic calculator) and divide by 60. This will give you the number of hours your flight will take, in this case 2 hours, with either 18 or 20 minutes left over. Enter this value in the Totals space at the bottom of the Time column, writing the number of hours plus the number of minutes—that is, 2 + 18 or 2 + 20. This represents your estimated cruising time in the air. Notice that time on the ground for anticipated intermediate landings is not included.

Write your expected departure time in the blank provided at the top of the Time column. Specify local (L) or zulu (Z or UTC) hours. Now add your cumulative ETEs to your departure time to derive successive ETAs at your various checkpoints. Be sure to add in time for your expected ground delays at each intermediate airport. Write reminders about your expected stopover times in the Remarks section of the form. Leave the spaces for actual time en route (ATE) and actual time of arrival (ATA) vacant for now; you will complete them when you update your plan.

Now look at the cruise performance table in the Pilot's Operating Handbook (see Figure 14.8). As described in Chapter 6, look up the fuel flow, in gallons per hour (GPH), for the cruise conditions you have chosen. Take an average value, weighted for the approximate cruising time you will spend at each condition, and enter it in the GPH space. If extreme accuracy is required, use actual GPH for each leg's cruise condition. Using the formula described in Chapter 12, compute fuel consumption for each leg (based on GPH and estimated time en route). Enter this value for each leg in the Fuel Used column. Since your Skipper will be fully serviced to its 29-gallon maximum capacity, giving you 25 gallons of usable fuel, subtract the amount of fuel consumed during leg one from 25 gallons and enter the remainder beside it in the Fuel Remaining (Rem.) column. Subtract the next fuel consumption value from this answer, and so on, until you have computed your fuel remaining upon landing. For this flight, as you can see, you will have approximately half a tank remaining. For longer flights, or flights involving delays, you will want to keep a close eye on this value.

Although the DR portion of the flight log is comprehensive, it does not show everything. For example, the distances covered and fuel used in climbing to cruising altitude from airport field elevation are not shown, and the lower ground speed normally associated with a takeoff or en route climb is not accounted for. Some pilots enter the takeoff climb separately in the flight log; this practice is followed in the military and by pilots of high-performance aircraft climbing to very high cruising altitudes. One technique is to add some extra time, based on your cruising altitude. Initially add 1 minute per 1000 feet to account for climbing. This value can be adjusted as necessary, based on your experience. Other pilots point to the unknown factors involved in terminal radar vectors, which can expedite or delay the completion of a flight, depending upon traffic and terminal weather. A good compromise is to prepare a flight log and, based on fuel remaining, decide whether a more detailed evaluation of airplane performance is necessary.

Look up the airports at which you will be landing and taking off in the *Airport/Facility Directory* and record the appropriate communications frequencies in the Airport Frequencies section of the log. At this time you should also review each of the airports and facilities you will be using during the flight. The sequence of this review and the entries for each are shown in the figures accompanying our simulation of the flight.

The Airport/ATIS Advisories section is left blank until the information is received over the radio during the flight.

Flight plan. You now transfer the data on the completed flight log to a flight plan form, such as the one shown in Figure 14.9. A flight plan form is much simpler than the flight log. This is because it is concerned primarily with your flight route, true airspeed, estimated time en route, and total fuel on board—in other words, those variables that define the intended flight and the airplane's capability of flying on should you fail to arrive at your destination. With this information, the FSS can work out alternative flight paths should the need arise.

Since the nearest FSS is in Oakland, you file your completed flight plan by telephone, reading the flight plan to the FSS specialist. Simply *filing* a flight plan does not mean that the FSS will expect to see you at your destination airport at your ETA, however. Your flight plan will not be activated (put on the FAA teletype) until you *open* it after becoming air-

Form Approved: OMB No. 04-R0072

DEPARTMENT OF TRANSPORTATION
FEDERAL AVIATION ADMINISTRATION
FLIGHT PLAN

CIVIL AIRCRAFT PILOTS. FAR Part 91 requires you file an IFR flight plan to operate under instrument flight rules in controlled airspace. Failure to file could result in a civil penalty not to exceed $1,000 for each violation (Section 901 of the Federal Aviation Act of 1958, as amended). Filing of a VFR flight plan is recommended as a good operating practice. See also Part 99 for requirements concerning DVFR flight plans.

1. TYPE	2. AIRCRAFT IDENTIFICATION	3. AIRCRAFT TYPE/ SPECIAL EQUIPMENT	4. TRUE AIRSPEED	5. DEPARTURE POINT	6. DEPARTURE TIME PROPOSED (Z)	ACTUAL (Z)	7. CRUISING ALTITUDE
✓ VFR / IFR / DVFR	N37259	BE 77/u	92 KTS	SQL	1600		5500

8. ROUTE OF FLIGHT
D→ WVI D→ MRY D→ SNS V230 PXN D→ LSN D→ SQL

9. DESTINATION (Name of airport and city)	10. EST. TIME ENROUTE HOURS	MINUTES	11. REMARKS
San Carlos Airport San Carlos	3	18	Stopovers at MRY (+30), LSN (+30)

12. FUEL ON BOARD HOURS	MINUTES	13. ALTERNATE AIRPORT(S)	14. PILOT'S NAME, ADDRESS & TELEPHONE NUMBER & AIRCRAFT HOME BASE	15. NUMBER ABOARD
4	30	N/A	J. Jackson 329 Elm St. San Carlos 595-1111	1

16. COLOR OF AIRCRAFT: Blue

CLOSE VFR FLIGHT PLAN WITH Oakland FSS ON ARRIVAL

Figure 14.9 A completed FAA flight plan form.

borne, usually by making a radio call to the same FSS at which the plan was filed. The FAA only keeps flight plans on file for 1 hour past the proposed departure time. If your departure will be delayed more than 1 hour, you must update your planned ETD with the FSS or refile the flight plan.

Some Flight Service Stations offer a fast-file flight plan system by which pilots can file a flight plan in accordance with prerecorded instructions. This service is described in the *Airport/Facility Directory*.

In our example, you identify your airplane with its model designator and provide the special equipment suffix *U*, which indicates that you have a 4096 code transponder with an altitude encoder (Mode C). The true airspeed you enter is an average of the TASs calculated in your flight log. After specifying your departure point and proposed time of departure, enter your *initial* cruising altitude. The rest of the form is self-explanatory until space 11, Remarks. In this space you state that you desire a **stopover flight plan,** naming the airports and giving your estimated time on the ground at each. These ground delays are then added to your estimated time en route, entered in space 10. An alternative but more laborious method would be to prepare and file a new flight plan after each landing. Fuel on board (space 12) is based on your takeoff load (25 gallons usable fuel consumed at your cruising fuel flow, 5.5 gallons per hour). You write "N/A" in space 13 to indicate that an alternative airport will not be needed owing to the favorable weather en route.

Airplane Preflight Preparations

Weight, balance, and performance checks.   After you file your flight plan, you inspect the airplane. Figure 14.10 shows your weight and balance card for this flight, assuming a load of one occupant at 170 pounds weight, 15 pounds of baggage, and 25 gallons of fuel. The method for determining component weights, positioning them on the aircraft, and converting them to moments is described in Chapter 5.

You check the takeoff performance chart in the Pilot's Operating Handbook, which confirms that the San Carlos runway is more than adequate in length for your airplane. You refer to the *Airport/Facility Directory* in order to check runway and approach conditions at Monterey and Los Banos; these, too, appear to be more than adequate for your airplane given the weather forecast for your trip. Finally, you check all conditions against your landing performance chart. Short fields, fields at high density-altitudes, soft fields, or fields with approach or departure obstructions are all considered sound reasons for caution, and in these cases you should make detailed takeoff and landing calculations. Although fuel should not be a factor on this flight, you will carry the Pilot's Operating Handbook charts for fuel consumption, range, and endurance with you in the cockpit.

Preflight inspection.   Taking your kit of materials (chart, plotter, flight computer or electronic calculator, Pilot's Operating Handbook, abbreviated checklist, and flight log, including the FAA flight plan and weather brief-

Figure 14.10 Weight and balance computations for the flight.

ITEM	WEIGHT	MOM/100
BASIC EMPTY CONDITION	1190	1023
OCCUPANT - LEFT	170	158
OCCUPANT - RIGHT	0	0
BAGGAGE	15	18
SUB TOTAL ZERO FUEL CONDITION	1375	1199
FUEL LOADING (25 gal.)	150	122
SUB TOTAL RAMP CONDITION	1525	1321
*LESS FUEL FOR START, TAXI AND RUNUP	−5	−4
SUB TOTAL TAKEOFF CONDITION	1520	1317
LESS FUEL TO DESTINATION	−23	−20
LANDING CONDITION	1497	1297

ing), you walk to the airplane and begin the preflight inspection, as described in Chapter 7. When you have confirmed that the airplane is airworthy and that no outstanding maintenance write-ups remain, you buckle yourself into the pilot's seat. It is 10 minutes before your scheduled takeoff time of 8:00 A.M.

Departing San Carlos

The Skipper's engine starts normally, and you run through your pretaxi checklist. You tune the San Carlos ATIS and record the required departure details on your flight log. You tune San Carlos Ground Control on 121.6.

"San Carlos Ground, Skipper three seven two five niner, with bravo, taxi, VFR Monterey, over."

"Skipper two five niner, San Carlos Ground, taxi runway three zero, over."

"Skipper two five niner, roger."

You make your engine runup in the engine runup area short of runway 30. You reenter the taxiway, number two for the active runway behind a light twin. Thoughts of wake turbulence automatically run through your mind, and you correctly decide that it will not be a factor on this takeoff, unless traffic from nearby San Francisco International is encountered during your climb.

A light trainer similar to yours floats across the threshold and touches down. The twin takes its position on the active runway and holds while the trainer pulls out and turns off onto a taxiway. You tune in tower frequency.

"San Carlos Tower, Skipper three seven two five niner's ready for takeoff, over."

"Skipper two five niner hold short."

"Skipper two five niner, roger."

"Baron eight five whiskey cleared for takeoff."

The propellers on the twin become gray disks as its engines come up to takeoff rpm. The airplane bobs on its nose gear as the pilot presses the brakes and reaches up in the cockpit to turn his transponder from Standby to On.

"Baron eight five whiskey, roger." As the pilot answers, he lifts his toes from the brakes and the twin's nose comes up quickly. The engines' noise subsides as the airplane moves down the runway, and then the twin is gone, leaving two vortices of dust at the sides of the asphalt.

"Skipper two five niner, taxi into position and hold."

"Two five niner, roger." You acknowledge automatically. Releasing the brakes, you scan the approach end of the runway for any unannounced traffic on final approach, taxi into takeoff position on the runway, and wait for further instructions.

"Skipper two five niner, climb to one thousand, five hundred, maintain runway heading to the Bay Meadows racetrack, cleared for takeoff."

"Two five niner, roger."

You advance the throttle to takeoff rpm. All engine instruments read in the green. The runway is clear ahead of you. You note the time, 7:58 local. Your feet come off the brakes, right hand covering the throttle, left hand applying a small amount of left aileron to compensate for a light quartering headwind. The airplane gathers speed quickly. The cabin noise drops away and you find yourself unconsciously feeding more and more right rudder to keep the runway centerline directly beneath the spinner. The airspeed indicator passes 50 knots, and at about 57 knots the nose begins to rise in response to your light backward pull on the control wheel. As the airplane leaves the ground, you make minor trim adjustments so that it stabilizes in its climb attitude. You adjust the pitch to hold the airspeed for best rate of climb, which is 68 knots. Scanning the horizon quickly from wing tip to wing tip, you see traffic that was invisible from the ground.

Departing the San Carlos Airport traffic area, you turn toward the outbound heading of your first leg and prepare to open your flight plan with the FSS. Your first pilotage checkpoint is Stanford University, with its large stadium and many distinctive red-roofed buildings (see Figure 14.11). Your chart, which you have turned so that your course line is parallel to the airplane's centerline, indicates that this landmark should be off to the right. The buildings are already visible some 2 or 3 miles in the distance. You turn the airplane so as to pass them on the proper compass heading, 134°. You then reach over to dial in the Oakland FSS on 122.5.

"Oakland Radio, Skipper three seven two five niner."

"Skipper two five niner, this is Oakland Radio, go ahead."

Figure 14.11 Chart showing a
portion of the departure leg with
pilotage checks.

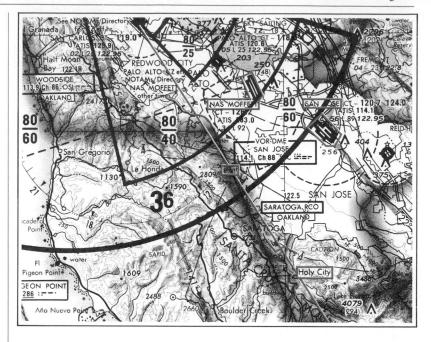

"Oakland Radio, Skipper two five niner would like to open its flight plan, airborne San Carlos at five eight past the hour, VFR round robin with stopovers at Monterey and Los Banos."

"Skipper two five niner, Oakland Radio, roger, copied all. Give Salinas Flight Service a call when airborne, Monterey. San Jose altimeter two niner, niner eight. Have a nice flight."

"Skipper two five niner, altimeter two niner, niner eight; roger, thank you."

En Route Navigation

You now level off at 5500 feet and set your cruising rpm, opening the Pilot's Operating Handbook to carry out the tasks on the cruise checklist, including leaning the fuel mixture. You survey the sky from left to right, pausing briefly to take in each sector of sky as you pass it. The air is relatively smooth, and the airplane is holding its heading nicely. On your chart you see that the 20-mile ring of the TCA intersects your course where it crosses a freeway (Interstate 280); at this point the Santa Cruz Mountains are close by on your right, and a cement plant is about 2½ miles farther along your route (see Figure 14.11). About 5 miles to the left is Moffett Naval Air Station. Its parallel runways and huge airship hangars make it a conspicuous landmark even from many miles away.

As you fly over the cement plant, you see the multiple runway pattern of San Jose Municipal Airport drawing closer on the left. You are very near the 25-mile limit of the San Francisco TCA. You continue making your pilotage checks—a transmission line and a highway that cross your track just before you fly over the town of Holy City in the Santa Cruz hills (see Figure 14.11). Farther on and to your left, Mount Umunhum (3486 feet) is very prominent.

Leg number two. Flying over the Watsonville Airport (see Figure 14.12), you note your time and record it on your flight log under ATA. Your time en route was 27 minutes, but because of your early departure (2 minutes), your ATA is exactly on schedule. You are not sure whether your delay en route was caused by your northerly takeoff heading or by an error in your winds-aloft calculations. However, you do not have time right now to spend on the log. You turn at once to your outbound magnetic heading of 180°. You confirm your outbound course by checking the position of the California coastline as it passes by to your left (see Figure 14.13).

The Monterey Peninsula is already clearly visible as a green finger of land extending across the airplane's nose ahead of you on course. Your attention turns to your chart, on which Monterey is marked as a stage III terminal radar service area (TRSA). You notice too that your flight path will take you over a restricted area, R-2529, which you must clear by 1000 feet above the surface (see Figure 14.14). Since you are nearing Moss Landing, you dial in the Monterey ATIS, looking up the frequency on your flight log. You receive the transmission halfway through its cycle:

. . . *east of State Highway One to the airport. Maintain one thousand five hundred feet traffic pattern altitude until reaching the downwind leg.* Notice to Airmen: *North parallel taxiway, runway two eight and one zero, closed for construction until further notice. VFR arrivals advise Monterey approach control or the tower on initial contact if you are transponder equipped, and that you have received information charlie.*

The automated signal beeps, and the transmission begins again after a short pause.

This is Monterey Peninsula Airport information charlie. Monterey Peninsula weather: clear, visibility two five miles, wind three zero zero degrees at eight, temperature four three degrees, altimeter two niner, niner six; inbound traffic landing runway two eight, fly east of State Highway One to the airport. Maintain one thousand five hundred feet traffic pattern altitude until reaching the downwind leg. Notice to Airmen . . .

§ **WATSONVILLE MUNI** (WVI) 2.6 NW GMT−8(−7DT) 36°56'09''N 121°47'19''W **SAN FRANCISCO**
160 B S4 **FUEL** 100LL TPA—1160(1000) H-2E, L-2F
RWY 01-19: H4500X150 (ASPH) S-80, D-96, DT-167 MIRL .38% up N **IAP**
RWY 01: Tree.   **RWY 19:** Thld dsplcd 600'. Poles.
RWY 08-26: H4000X150 (ASPH) S-50, D-70, DT-110 .67% up W
RWY 08: Tree.   **RWY 26:** Fence.
AIRPORT REMARKS: Attended 1600-0300Z‡. Rwy 08-26 poor condition.
COMMUNICATIONS: UNICOM 122.8
    SALINAS FSS (SNS) Toll free (800) 688-0750.
Ⓡ **MONTEREY APP/DEP CON** 127.15

Figure 14.12 Information about Watsonville Municipal Airport from the *Airport/Facility Directory*.

Figure 14.13 Chart showing leg number two.

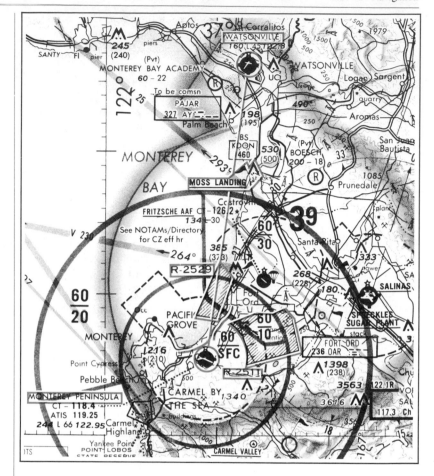

You reset your altimeter and switch the VHF communications radio to 133.0. As you make these adjustments, a power plant with billowing smokestacks located at the mouth of the Salinas River passes off to your left—Moss Landing.

"Monterey Approach Control, Skipper three seven two five niner, Moss Landing, four thousand five hundred squawking one two, zero zero with charlie, requesting stage III services for landing, Monterey Peninsula, over."

"Skipper two five niner, Monterey Approach, squawk one four, zero zero, ident."

"Skipper two five niner, one four, zero zero." You perform the required actions.

"Skipper two five niner, radar contact. Descend to and maintain one thousand five hundred; enter right traffic for runway two eight, Monterey Peninsula Airport. Report the shoreline freeway, this frequency, over."

"Skipper two five niner, out of four thousand five hundred for one thousand five hundred."

You cross the coastal highway, a prominent pilotage landmark, and begin planning your turn to a downwind, right-hand pattern. The airport is about

§ **MONTEREY PENINSULA**   (MRY)   2.6 SE   GMT−8(−7DT)   36°35'17"N 121°50'53"W   SAN FRANCISCO
    244   B   S4   **FUEL** 100, JET A   OX 2, 4   LRA   CFR Index C   TPA— 1744(1500)   H-2E, L-2E
    RWY 10-28: H6597X150 (ASPH)   S-100, D-160, DT-300   HIRL   1.4% up E   IAP
    RWY 10: SSALR. Tree.   **RWY 28:** REIL. VASI(V4R)— GA 3.5° TCH 47.3'. Trees. Rgt tfc.
    RWY 06-24: H4001X150 (ASPH)   S-60, D-110, DT-200   MIRL
    RWY 06: Tree.   **RWY 24:** Thld dsplcd 469'. Tree. Rgt tfc.
    AIRPORT REMARKS: Attended continuously. Rwy 24 closed to ngt ldg; lights have not been removed. Overngt tiedown
       fee at FBO. Ldg fee for acft over 8000 pounds. Flight Notification Service (ADCUS) available.
    COMMUNICATIONS: ATIS 119.25   **UNICOM** 122.95
       SALINAS FSS (SNS) LC 372-6050 NOTAM FILE MRY
    ® **APP/DEP CON** 120.8 (360°-096°) 133.0, 127.15 (096°-360°)
       TOWER 118.4   **GND CON** 121.9
       STAGE III SVC ctc **APP CON** within 30 NM
    RADIO AIDS TO NAVIGATION:
       SALINAS (H) ABVORTAC 117.3   ■ SNS   Chan 120   36°39'50"N 121°36'08"W   232° 12.7 NM to fld.
          80/17E.
       MUNSO NDB (LOM) 385   MR   36°37'15"N 121°56'15"W   096° 4.3 NM to fld
       FREYA NDB (LMM) 370   RY   36°35'41"N 121°51'56"W   096° 0.5 NM to fld
       ILS 110.1 I-MRY Rwy 10 LOM MUNSO NDB LMM FREYA NDB
          Glide Slope coupled approaches unusable 5.5-2 NM inbound.

(a)

PROHIBITED, RESTRICTED, WARNING, AND ALERT AREAS
ON SAN FRANCISCO SECTIONAL CHART

NO.	NAME	ALTITUDE	TIME	APPROPRIATE AUTHORITY
R-2511	Fort Ord, California	To 5,000	Continuous	† FAA, Monterey Approach Control C.G., Fort Ord, California
R-2513	Hunter-Liggett, California	To FL 240	Continuous	† FAA, Oakland ARTC Center * Area FSS. C.G., Fort Ord, California
R-2529	Fort Ord West, Calif.	To 1,000	30' before sunrise to 30' after sunset	† FAA, Monterey Approach Control C.G., Fort Ord, California
R-2531A	Tracy, Calif.	To but not incl. 3000	1000 to 1800 Mon. thru Fri.	† FAA Oakland ARTC Center * Area FSS. U.S., Energy Research and Development Administration San Francisco Operations, Calif.
R-2531B	Tracy, Calif.	3000 to 4000	1000 to 1800 Mon thru Fri.	† FAA, Oakland ARTC Center * Area FSS. U.S., Energy Research and Development Administration San Francisco Operations, Calif.

(b)

Figure 14.14 Monterey published information. **(a)** For Monterey Peninsula Airport from the *Airport/Facility Directory*. **(b)** Restricted areas near Monterey from the San Francisco sectional chart.

4 miles away and is easily distinguishable against the high terrain to the southwest and east (see Figure 14.15). Another single-engine airplane, a red Cessna Centurion, passes in front of you, right to left, already established on the downwind leg. You are somewhat surprised that the approach controller has not called out this traffic, but you recall that controllers are not always able to report all traffic. You turn to enter a downwind pattern at a comfortable distance behind the other airplane.

"Skipper two five niner's over the highway, turning downwind."

"Skipper two five niner, contact the tower now, one one eight point four, radar service terminated."

"Skipper two five niner, roger."

You change frequencies quickly, scanning the traffic pattern as you roll out on your downwind course at 1500 feet. The light plane ahead of you is just turning base leg as the tower frequency comes alive.

" . . . base," the pilot ahead of you says, concluding her base-turn transmission.

Figure 14.15 An aerial view of
Monterey Peninsula Airport.

"Three zero tango, report short final. Golden Gate eight five eight cleared for takeoff." The tower controller's voice sounds harried.

"Eight five eight's rolling."

You spot a large, twin-engine STOL (short takeoff and landing) airliner moving slowly forward over the numbers of runway 28.

"Skipper three seven two five niner, downwind," you interject quickly.

The tower controller comes back at once. "Skipper two five niner, follow the red Centurion, call base."

"Skipper two five niner, roger."

You run through the before-landing checklist quickly but thoroughly. As the red airplane passes your right wing tip, descending toward the runway in the opposite direction, you retard the throttle, adding nose-up trim and lowering your flaps to approach position. You bank right in a normal descending turn.

"Skipper two five niner, turning base."

"Skipper two five niner, continue. Cessna three zero tango, cleared to land."

"Three zero tango, roger," comes the reply from the airplane ahead of you.

"Golden Gate eight five eight, contact Departure one three three point zero."

"Golden Gate, eight five eight, one three three point zero, good day."

"Good day, sir."

You roll out on a long final approach behind the Cessna, now approaching the threshold, flaps lowered, tripod landing gear reaching down toward its shadow. The Golden Gate airliner is in the air and turning out of traffic like an ungainly, cream-colored seabird. You glance at the visual approach slope indicator (VASI) bracketing the runway. It shows you pink over white—slightly high on the glide path. You retard the throttle a little farther and put down the rest of your flaps. The VASI bars turn red over white, and you continue on your final descent with a slight crab to the right to compensate for the gentle onshore breeze. The Centurion has already touched down and is halfway down the 6600-foot runway.

"Three zero tango, contact Ground Control one two one point niner when clear. Skipper two five niner cleared to land."

"Three zero tango, roger," the Centurion's pilot says.

"Two five niner," you reply, "roger, cleared to land."

Your touchdown is normal, though a little "hot" (fast), which you chalk up to the natural excitement of your first solo landing at a strange field. As you clear the active runway, you note your landing time and call Ground Control. You begin noticing details of the airport buildings and its surroundings, which were unnoticed from the air because your attention was devoted to such things as general topography, landmarks, beacons, airborne traffic, runway geometry and markings, and instrument indications. Taxiing south of the active runway, you see the construction on the north taxiway for the first time, exactly as reported in the *NOTAM*. You park at the transient aircraft ramp in front of the executive terminal. Since no tie-downs are available, you chock the wheels before leaving the airplane.

In the flight planning room, you review your next two legs into Los Banos, observing that you will be flying over another restricted area, R-2511, which extends from the surface to 5000 feet (see Figure 14.14b), and you doubt that your airplane will top the required altitude as you climb on course. You place a call to the published controlling agency (in this case, Monterey Approach Control) and obtain permission to fly through the area at a lower altitude while you climb on course.

During your stopover at Monterey Peninsula Airport, you bring your flight log up to date, recording your actual time en route (ATE) for leg two and your actual ground speed (see Figure 14.16). You flew leg two, a distance of 21 miles, in 13 minutes, a minute faster than predicted, giving you an effective ground speed for the leg of 97 knots. To keep to your schedule, however, you must be airborne at 9:09. You enter the flight in your log book and return to the airplane on the hour.

Leg number three.   After starting the engine, you tune the Monterey ATIS again and record information delta, which specifies a new, higher altimeter setting, 29.97. Then you switch to Monterey Ground Control. This leg of your trip, you recall, will take you into another restricted area, R-2511.

"Monterey Ground, Skipper three seven two five niner at the executive ramp, VFR eastward, ready to taxi with delta."

"Skipper two five niner, this is Monterey Ground Control. Taxi to runway two eight; after takeoff maintain runway heading to the freeway interchange one-half mile east of the airport, turn left to one one zero degrees, maintain VFR. Climb as soon as possible to one thousand, five hundred for noise abatement, departure end of runway two eight. Contact Departure Control on one two zero point eight after takeoff, squawk zero one one three."

Figure 14.16 The updated flight log
for legs number one and two.

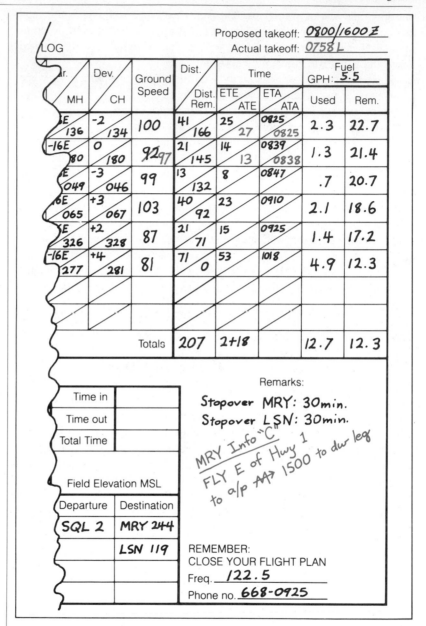

Proposed takeoff:	0800/1600 Z
Actual takeoff:	0758 L
GPH:	5.5

| Var. | | Dev. | | Ground Speed | Dist. | Time | | Fuel | |
MH		CH			Dist. Rem.	ETE ATE	ETA ATA	Used	Rem.
E 136		-2 134		100	41 166	25 27	0825 0825	2.3	22.7
-16E 80		0 180		92 97	21 145	14 13	0839 0838	1.3	21.4
E 049		-3 046		99	13 132	8	0847	.7	20.7
6E 065		+3 067		103	40 92	23	0910	2.1	18.6
E 326		+2 328		87	21 71	15	0925	1.4	17.2
-16E 277		+4 281		81	71 0	53	1018	4.9	12.3
Totals					207	2+18		12.7	12.3

Time in	
Time out	
Total Time	

Field Elevation MSL

Departure	Destination
SQL 2	MRY 244
	LSN 119

Remarks:

Stopover MRY: 30 min.
Stopover LSN: 30 min.

MRY Info "C"
FLY E of Hwy 1
to a/p AA→ 1500 to dwr leg

REMEMBER:
CLOSE YOUR FLIGHT PLAN
Freq. 122.5
Phone no. 668-0925

You read back the clearance, taxi to the active runway, perform your
engine runup check, and make a normal takeoff, noting your departure
time. When you are past the end of the runway, the tower clears you to the
departure control frequency.

"Monterey Departure Control, Skipper three seven two five niner's over
the interchange, heading one one zero, at eight hundred feet climbing to
one thousand five hundred."

"Skipper two five niner, this is Monterey Departure Control, radar contact, traffic at two o'clock inbound, expedite turn."

You look out and see the traffic, a light twin.

"Skipper two five niner, contact," you respond, meaning that you have the traffic in sight.

"Skipper two five niner, maintain VFR, proceed on course, the Salinas VOR; transit approved Romeo two five one one, below five thousand; squawk one two zero zero; radar service terminated; good day."

"Skipper two five niner, roger, good day."

Crossing the Monterey Airport at 3500 feet, you turn the airplane to a magnetic heading of 049° and set the inbound course to the Salinas VOR on your omni bearing selector. With the station tuned and identified, the course deviation indicator is slightly to the right of center with a To flag showing. You roll in a small intercept angle to the right, centering the needle, then roll back to your magnetic heading of 049° in order to maintain the 051° course inbound to the station.

You level at 5500 feet a few miles from the Salinas VORTAC, which is collocated with the Salinas Municipal Airport (see Figure 14.17). You confirm your position by pilotage reference to the large Spreckels sugar plant 3 miles southwest of the airport. As you pass over the Salinas Airport the needle on the VOR begins to swing from side to side, and the Off flag flickers into view. A moment later, the To flag switches to From, and you turn the airplane to a magnetic heading of 064° for the fourth leg of the flight.

Leg number four. You note the time of station passage and record it on your flight log, turning the omni bearing selector to the outbound course, the 068° radial. The needle stabilizes again, this time to the left of the case. You turn the airplane left, in the direction indicated by the course deviation indicator, and the needle quickly begins to move to the center of the case— much more quickly than it did over Monterey when you intercepted the inbound course. You realize that the course deviation indicator is always more sensitive when you are close to a station, as you are now, because the distance separating VOR radials from each other is less. As the needle centers, you roll back onto your computed magnetic heading, maintaining your desired track, and dial the frequency of the Salinas FSS on the VHF communications radio.

"Salinas Radio, Skipper three seven two five niner position report on a VFR flight plan over Salinas at two two, five thousand, five hundred, VFR to Panoche, with a stop at Los Banos, then to San Carlos, over."

"Skipper two five niner, roger, copied your position report, Salinas altimeter, two niner, niner seven. How's the visibility up there this morning?"

"Skipper two five niner, roger, Salinas altimeter two niner, niner seven. It's a beautiful day. I'd estimate the visibility to be over twenty miles, though there seems to be a pretty good haze over the San Joaquin Valley this morning, with some towering cumulus to the northeast. I'm showing an OAT of plus one degree Celsius at this altitude, with smooth air."

Figure 14.17 Salinas Municipal
Airport, end of leg number three.

§ **SALINAS MUNI**   (SNS)   2.6 SE   GMT−8(−7DT)   36°39′45″N 121°36′20″W   **SAN FRANCISCO**
    84   B   S4   **FUEL** 80, 100, 100LL, JET A   TPA−884(800)   **H-2E, L-2F**
    RWY 08-26: H4995X200 (ASPH)   S-25, D-32, DT-62   MIRL   IAP
        RWY 08: VASI(V4L)— GA 3.0° TCH 50.3′. Tower. Rgt tfc.   RWY 26: VASI(V4L)— GA 3.0° TCH 52.9′.
    RWY 13-31: H4825X150 (ASPH)   S-65, D-100, DT-170   HIRL
        RWY 13: REIL. VASI(V4L)— GA 3.0° TCH 50.3′. P-line.   RWY 31: MALSR. Rgt tfc.
    RWY 14-32: H1899X50 (ASPH)   S-30, D-45, DT-75.
        RWY 14: Tree.
    RWY 03-21: H1200X150 (ASPH)   S-50, D-75, DT-125   .42% up N
        RWY 21: P-line.
    AIRPORT REMARKS: Attended continuously. Rwy 14-32 floods in heavy rains. Rwys 03-21 & 14-32 restricted to
        agriculture opr.
    COMMUNICATIONS: UNICOM 122.95
        SALINAS FSS (SNS) on arpt 122.6, 122.2, 121.1R (408) 443-2195 FSS provides AAS on 119.4 when tower
        closed.
    ® MONTERREY APP/DEP CON 133.0, 120.8
        TOWER 119.4 opr 1400-0600Z‡   GND CON 121.7
    RADIO AIDS TO NAVIGATION:
        (H) ABVORTAC 117.3   ■ SNS   Chan 120   36°39′50″N 121°36′08″W   at fld. 80/17E
            VOR unusable 010°-080° beyond 20 NM below 8000′   150°-170° beyond 8 NM below 10,000′
            DME unusable 010°-080° beyond 22 NM below 8000′   150°-200° beyond 22 NM below 11,000′
        ILS 108.5 I-SNS Rwy 31

     "Skipper two five niner, thank you for the PIREP. Notify Fresno Radio
on departure, Los Banos."
     "Skipper two five niner, roger."

With the airplane trimmed to hold its course and airspeed, you examine your chart for an off-airway VOR station with which you might practice radio navigation position-fixing and verify your ground speed. You notice that although the Big Sur VORTAC lies well to the south of your course, it is probably in range for these checks (see Figure 14.18).

After checking once again that you are trimmed to hold the 068° radial from Salinas, you retune your VOR radio to Big Sur and identify the station. Next you turn the omni bearing selector until the course deviation indicator is centered with a From indication on 000°. You note the time and set the omni bearing selector 15° in advance of the reading (from 000° to 015°)—enough to provide an adequate single-station check. The course deviation indicator moves to the right-hand side of the case, but the To-From indicator continues to register From. After several minutes, the needle begins to move again. When it centers, you check the clock, which shows an elapsed time of 6 minutes, 4 seconds from radial to radial. Using the Big Sur compass rose as a protractor and your plotter as a straightedge, you draw these radials onto your chart. Next, you use the sectional side of the plotter's mileage scale to measure the distance between the intersection points—10 miles. With your flight computer or electronic calculator, you set up a ground speed problem with factors of 10 miles and 6 minutes. The ground speed you compute is 100 knots—somewhat slower than the 103 knots predicted in your flight log.

By this time you are about halfway between Salinas and Panoche, so you tune and identify Panoche on 112.6 and reset the omni bearing selector to 070° (the reciprocal of 250°) to better maintain the centerline of the airway, V-230.

When the course deviation indicator swings, indicating station passage, you note the time and turn left to magnetic heading for Los Banos, resetting the omni bearing selector to the 332° radial. Since the station is located in a remote area, a pilotage check is made by observing the distinctively shaped facility itself.

After a few minutes of flight outbound from the station, an airplane in the Los Banos traffic pattern calls your attention to the airport itself (see Figure 14.19). You set Los Banos UNICOM (122.8) on your communications radio and report your position, stating your intention to land and requesting landing advisories. Although the UNICOM operator responds with active runway information, you know that traffic is uncontrolled, so you decide to exercise even more caution than usual for your landing on runway 32. You fly over the field, observing the landing direction indicator and wind sock, descending with clearing turns to the traffic pattern altitude of 919 feet MSL. At lower altitudes, you notice that the visibility in the San Joaquin Valley has deteriorated to perhaps 5 miles. Your landing is uneventful, and you taxi to the transient parking area southwest of the runway.

Arrival Procedures

Before leaving Los Banos, you place a toll-free call to the Fresno FSS in order to update the Bay Area terminal weather, which remains as forecast.

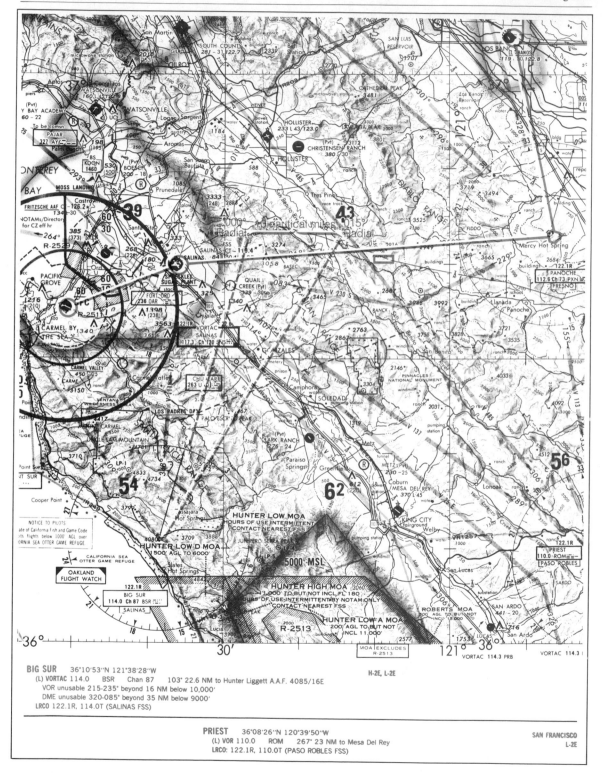

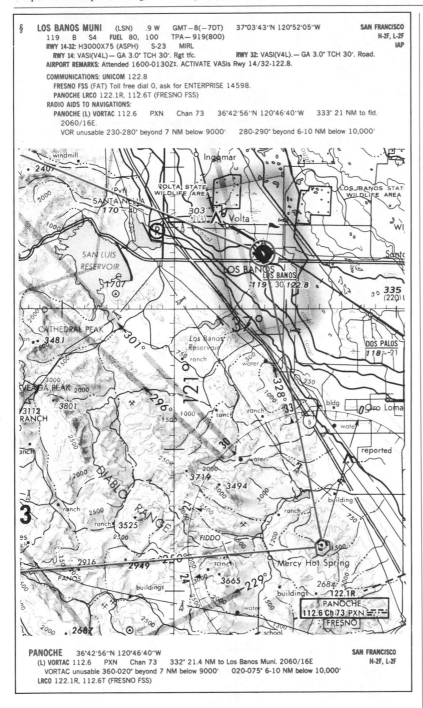

Figure 14.18 *(opposite)* Chart showing leg numbers three, four, and five with ground speed check and change of course.

Figure 14.19 Los Banos Municipal Airport, end of leg number three.

As the Los Banos Airport is uncontrolled, you are particularly careful to be well clear of other traffic before taking off on runway 32. You turn immediately to your outbound magnetic heading of 277° and climb on

Figure 14.20 Position check using
Modesto VOR radial.

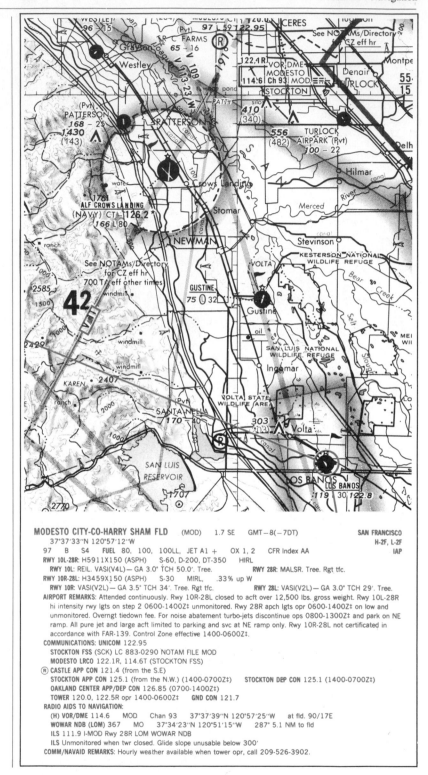

MODESTO CITY-CO-HARRY SHAM FLD   (MOD)   1.7 SE   GMT−8(−7DT)   SAN FRANCISCO
37°37'33"N 120°57'12"W   H-2F, L-2F
97   B   S4   FUEL 80, 100, 100LL, JET A1 +   OX 1, 2   CFR Index AA   IAP
RWY 10L-28R: H5911X150 (ASPH)   S-60, D-200, DT-350   HIRL
   RWY 10L: REIL. VASI(V4L) — GA 3.0° TCH 50.0'. Tree.   RWY 28R: MALSR. Tree. Rgt tfc.
RWY 10R-28L: H3459X150 (ASPH)   S-30   MIRL   .33% up W
   RWY 10R: VASI(V2L) — GA 3.5° TCH 34'. Tree. Rgt tfc.   RWY 28L: VASI(V2L) — GA 3.0° TCH 29'. Tree.
AIRPORT REMARKS: Attended continuously. Rwy 10R-28L closed to acft over 12,500 lbs. gross weight. Rwy 10L-28R
   hi intensity rwy lgts on step 2 0600-1400Z‡ unmonitored. Rwy 28R apch lgts opr 0600-1400Z‡ on low and
   unmonitored. Overngt tiedown fee. For noise abatement turbo-jets discontinue ops 0800-1300Z‡ and park on NE
   ramp. All pure jet and large acft limited to parking and svc at NE ramp only. Rwy 10R-28L not certificated in
   accordance with FAR-139. Control Zone effective 1400-0600Z‡.
COMMUNICATIONS: UNICOM 122.95
   STOCKTON FSS (SCK) LC 883-0290 NOTAM FILE MOD
   MODESTO LRCO 122.1R, 114.6T (STOCKTON FSS)
Ⓡ CASTLE APP CON 121.4 (from the S.E)
   STOCKTON APP CON 125.1 (from the N.W.) (1400-0700Z‡)   STOCKTON DEP CON 125.1 (1400-0700Z‡)
   OAKLAND CENTER APP/DEP CON 126.85 (0700-1400Z‡)
   TOWER 120.0, 122.5R opr 1400-0600Z‡   GND CON 121.7
RADIO AIDS TO NAVIGATION:
   (H) VOR/DME 114.6   MOD   Chan 93   37°37'39"N 120°57'25"W   at fld. 90/17E
   WOWAR NDB (LOM) 367   MO   37°34'23"N 120°51'15"W   287° 5.1 NM to fld
   ILS 111.9 I-MOD Rwy 28R LOM WOWAR NDB
   ILS Unmonitored when twr closed. Glide slope unusable below 300'
COMM/NAVAID REMARKS: Hourly weather available when tower opr, call 209-526-3902.

course to your cruising altitude of 6500 feet, completing your checklists as required and notifying Fresno FSS of your departure time.

You check your position by the Modesto 191° radial (V-111); you are on track (see Figure 14.20). Farther along is a pilotage checkpoint, Mount Hamilton, a 4380-feet peak located to the right of your course (see Figure 14.21). Within a few more minutes, the Santa Clara Valley opens up to reveal Reid-Hillview Airport, San Jose Municipal Airport, and Moffett NAS airship hangars (see Figure 14.22).

As you skirt the top of the San Jose Airport traffic area, you notice on your chart that the floor of the San Francisco TCA requires a gradual descent, starting below 6000 feet at the 25-mile limit, to below 4000 feet passing Moffett, to 2500 feet passing Palo Alto, to 1500 feet around San Carlos Airport.

Although your airplane clears the Moffett NAS ATA above 3000 feet, you decide to make radio contact with the Palo Alto Tower on 118.6 in order to obtain clearance through its ATA (see Figure 14.23). As you dial in the frequency, you adjust your cockpit air vent to refresh yourself for the approach and landing. Sitting in an airplane for several hours can be fatiguing, and extra vigilance is needed on arrival into a busy terminal area.

"Palo Alto Tower, Skipper three seven two five niner is five miles southeast of the airport, two thousand, five hundred, VFR to San Carlos."

"Skipper two five niner, proceed on course, maintain VFR, Palo Alto altimeter three zero, zero one."

"Skipper two five niner, altimeter three zero, zero one, roger."

You reset your altimeter, continuing to scan the area for traffic. A large airliner is descending into San Francisco International parallel to your course, flaps lowered to the approach position. After advising the Palo Alto Tower that you are leaving its ATA, you dial in the San Carlos ATIS and record information Golf.

Five miles from the airport, nearly aligned with the final approach course for runway 30, you tune the San Carlos Tower. Your altitude is 1500 feet, and the VASI on runway 30 shows you red over red at this distance. Wisps of fog appear at the crest of the hills to the west.

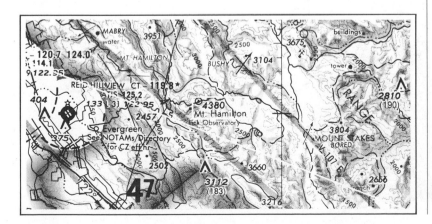

Figure 14.21 Mount Hamilton pilotage check.

"San Carlos Tower, Skipper three seven two five niner is five miles southeast of the airport, VFR for landing with Golf."

"Skipper two five niner, this is San Carlos Tower, you are cleared for a straight-in approach, runway three zero, winds are three zero zero at one zero zero gust to one five knots. San Carlos altimeter three zero, zero one. Maintain one thousand two hundred feet until passing Kaiser Hospital left of course, over."

"Skipper two five niner, roger; altimeter three zero, zero one."

As you approach to within 2 miles, the VASI begins to show red over pink. Kaiser Hospital slides by your left window as the VASI changes to red over white. You ease back on the throttle and complete your before-landing checklist. The airplane begins to react slightly to the turbulent surface winds.

"Skipper two five niner's cleared to land."

Figure 14.22 Chart showing portion of leg number six and pilotage checks.

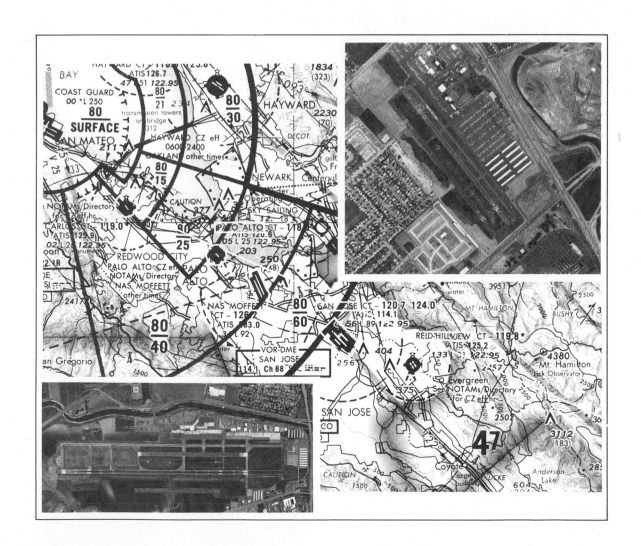

"Skipper two five niner, roger."

Your touchdown is just past the numbers, and you complete a short rollout, positioning the ailerons against the wind as you turn off the active runway.

"Skipper two five niner, contact Ground on one two one point six."

"Skipper two five niner, roger—and Tower, Skipper two five niner requests you close my flight plan, please."

"Skipper two five niner, roger, will do."

Postflight Activities

You park the airplane and shut down the engine and equipment according to your checklist. The time on your cockpit clock is 11:26 local. Allowing 5 minutes for taxiing after landing, parking, and shutting down the airplane,

Figure 14.23 Palo Alto Airport.

§ **PALO ALTO OF SANTA CLARA CO** (PAO)   0 E   SAN FRANCISCO
   GMT—8(—7DT)   37°27'40"N 122°06'50"W   L-2F, A
   05   B   S4   **FUEL** 80, 100   OX 2, 4   TPA— See Remarks
   RWY 12-30: H2500X65 (ASPH)   S-5   MIRL
      RWY 12: Lighted dike.
      RWY 30: REIL. VASI(V2L)— GA 4.0° TCH 28.7'. Lighted poles. Rgt ttc.
   AIRPORT REMARKS: Attended 1500-0700Z‡. P-line SE. Flocks of birds feeding in garbage dumps & along shoreline,
      adjacent to arpt. TPA— 1005(1000) SW, and 805(800) NE. Control Zone effective 1500-0600Z‡.
   COMMUNICATIONS: ATIS 120.6 (415) 858-0606 opr 1500-0600Z‡   **UNICOM** 122.95
      OAKLAND FSS (OAK) LC 326-2941
      WOODSIDE LRCO 122.1R 113.9T (OAKLAND FSS)
   ® **BAY APP CON** 120.1, 133.95, 134.5
      TOWER 118.6 opr 1500-0600Z‡.   **GND CON** 125.0
   ® **BAY DEP CON** 121.3
   RADIO AIDS TO NAVIGATION:
      WOODSIDE (L) VORTAC 113.9   OSI   Chan 86   37°23'33"N 122°16'49"W   046° 9.0 NM to fld.
      2270/17E.

you calculate that you landed within 3 minutes of your ETA. You find yourself convinced that with care in planning and conscientious execution, DR and radio navigation make a powerful, accurate combination.

Before leaving the airplane, you ensure that it is tied down at all three points (left wing, right wing, and tail) and that the chocks and gust locks are installed. Back in the flight planning room, you reflect on the events of your flight and their implications. You have learned, for instance, that:

1. Extra vigilance is required during terminal operations when traffic is dense.

2. Visibility may have deteriorated below VFR minimums in the central San Joaquin Valley. The value of keeping in contact with the local FSS for relevant *NOTAM* and weather information cannot be overemphasized.

3. A flight log is a valuable aid both in planning and in monitoring a flight.

4. Following well-established procedures and navigational methods will help you keep track of your location, monitor fuel consumption and flying time, and, in general, maintain control of the flight.

5. You should be aware of the accessibility of airports at every stage of your flight in case of an emergency, and you should also know the direction of open areas should an emergency or precautionary landing be required where a regular facility is not available.

GENERAL TIPS FOR CROSS-COUNTRY FLYING

Nearly everything you will learn about airplanes and flying will make your cross-country flights safer and more efficient, but there are a few general habits you should cultivate in flying outside of your local area.

Always plan to arrive at your destination at least an hour before the published time for sunset. Flights often leave late and have delays en route, and an arrival after dark at an unfamiliar field can be perplexing even to experienced pilots.

Plan altitudes en route that are at least 500 feet higher than the highest nearby obstructions in sparsely populated areas and 1000 feet higher in densely populated areas. When flying near mountains, stay at least 2000 feet above the highest peaks.

Before taking off, work out ETAs for all checkpoints. Good pilotage landmarks are of little value if you do not know when to look for them, just as DR computations have limited use if you do not have some way (pilotage or radio) of confirming the fixes they represent. In flight, always read your aeronautical chart by aligning the course line on the chart with your actual flight path. Landmarks must be used directionally, and it is an added task to try to turn your chart mentally to match the airplane's heading. Remember, too, to reset the heading indicator periodically to compensate for gyroscopic precession.

If your calculations show that you will have less than 45 minutes of fuel left when you arrive at your destination, land as soon as practicable and refuel. As you will probably need more fuel rather than less to complete the anticipated flight, why take chances, especially if weather is a factor?

If you think you are lost, do not change course at random as you look for landmarks, which will probably add to your confusion and draw you farther away from your last known position. Hold your original course while you reorient yourself or ask for assistance. In either case, slow down to low cruise or slow flight airspeeds while you take appropriate action.

In these days of reliable two-way communications, transponders, and radio navaids, it is unlikely that you will ever lose your way or, having strayed off course, be unable to reorient yourself. Nonetheless, if either of these unlikely events does occur, you must never let pride or stubbornness come between you and a safe landing. Being lost is an emergency, as anyone who has experienced it will confirm. Your first responsibility is to let air traffic control or other aircraft in your vicinity know of your condition. Remember, safety is the pilot's first and last commandment.

KEY TERMS
flight log
flight plan

PROFICIENCY CHECK

1. What is the difference between an FAA flight plan and a pilot's flight log?

2. Why do pilots make a general review of a proposed flight before beginning detailed flight planning?

3. What preliminary information should you have on hand before requesting a weather briefing?

4. How long does the FSS keep unopened flight plans on file?

5. What are a pilot's primary duties when navigating en route?

6. What are the three main rules to remember about replanning a flight en route?

7. What is the meaning of the saying that you must "fly the last mile as well as the first"?

8. Name three ways of closing a flight plan at the end of a flight.

9. What is the most effective placement for your chart when you are looking up pilotage landmarks en route?

10. What is the first responsibility of any pilot who becomes lost?

PART VII
MEDICAL ASPECTS AND EMERGENCIES

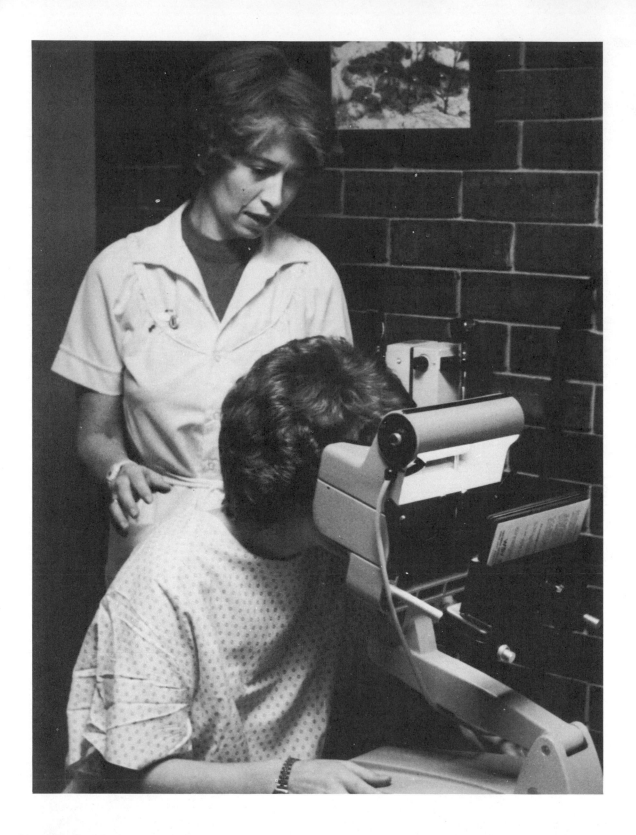

Oh, the mysteries of this machine called man.

Charles Dickens

C H E C K P O I N T S

What are the concerns of aviation physiology? ➤ How does the human body's respiration and circulation system work? ➤ What effects do altitude and motion have on the human body? ➤ What contributes to stress and how can it influence pilot performance? ➤ What are the restrictions on the use of drugs and medications prior to flight? ➤ How should pilots respond to symptoms of oxygen-related or motion-related physiological disorders? ➤ Why is mental fitness frequently as important as physical health to pilots? ➤ What are a pilot's responsibilities in determining his or her fitness to fly?

THE PHYSIOLOGY OF FLIGHT

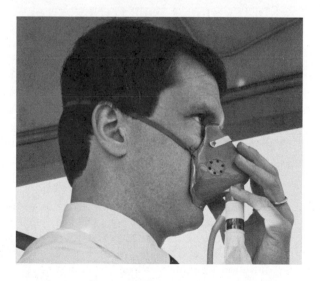

Airplanes are asked to do many things: to endure extremes of temperature and pressure, to withstand G forces and engine vibrations, and to cover long distances in daylight or darkness safely and efficiently. In all respects, flying is a demanding test for any machine. Pilots too must experience conditions and forces not encountered by those who remain on the ground. Machines can be redesigned for unique environments, but human beings do not enjoy that option. There are two primary means by which pilots can overcome or accommodate the sometimes inhospitable environment of flight: by knowledge of **aviation physiology,** the science that deals with the processes, activities, and phenomena of human life in the aviation environment; and through the use of special physiological support equipment that extends the range of normal human functions into conditions not encountered on the surface of the earth.

Aerospace medicine is the branch of medicine that deals with the application of aviation physiology. It is a wide-ranging field that calls for specialized knowledge not normally included in the training or experience of most physicians. That is why the FAA selects only physicians who receive additional specialized training to act as *Aviation Medical Examiners (AMEs)*. As a private pilot you should also supplement your knowledge of biology and health care with the medical facts unique to the flying environment.

In this chapter you will learn how training, mental well-being, and good physical habits go hand in hand with safe piloting. In general, anything that can affect the alertness, reaction time, or decision-making capability of the pilot is of concern to aviation physiology—and of concern to *you,* as a student or private pilot. Further readings on aerospace medicine may be found in FAA Advisory Circular 67-2, *Medical Handbook for Pilots*, and in the *Airman's Information Manual,* "Medical Facts for Pilots."

DETERMINING YOUR FITNESS TO FLY

General good health is all that is required to pass an FAA medical exam. Serious, potentially incapacitating diseases such as epilepsy, heart disease, diabetes mellitus (not controlled by diet alone), and sickle cell disease will prevent you from receiving a medical certificate. A certificate will also be denied temporarily if you are suffering from an acute infection at the time of your examination or because of disorders such as anemia or peptic ulcers. Beyond these conditions, persons with handicaps, such as artificial limbs, have learned to fly safely and skillfully. It is a good idea, though, to check with an Aviation Medical Examiner before committing time and money to a flying program if you have any condition that you think may disqualify you.

FAR 61.53 prohibits you from acting as pilot-in-command of any flight when you know that you have a medical deficiency that would prevent you from meeting all requirements of your current medical certificate. Thus, you should not act as a pilot when suffering from a head cold or any local infection requiring self-medication or a physician's care. It is wise to use your energy to get well rather than to try to fly in a marginal physical condition.

EFFECTS OF ALTITUDE ON THE HUMAN BODY
Respiration
Commonly known as breathing, respiration is the exchange of gases between your body and the environment (see Figure 15.1). Your body's cells need oxygen (O_2) to burn the "fuel" you consume as food; in turn, cells give off carbon dioxide (CO_2) as waste material in this process. The cells are served by an intricate network of arteries, veins, and capillaries that shuttle fresh oxygen to each cell and pick up the CO_2 for disposal. When the circulating blood reaches your lungs, it passes next to very small, thin air sacs called **alveoli** (singular, *alveolus*; see Figure 15.2). Inhaling fills the alveoli with fresh air containing O_2 from outside your body. The high pressure within the lungs forces the oxygen through the alveoli into the bloodstream, where it is carried by the **hemoglobin** in the blood. When you exhale, or let air out of your lungs, the carbon dioxide moves out of the bloodstream into the alveoli and is expelled from your body along with the mixture of nitrogen and other inert gases that make up the atmosphere. This entire cycle normally takes place 12 to 16 times per minute. That speed can be altered voluntarily or involuntarily by your brain, depending on your level of activity and conscious desire to control your rate of respiration.

Breathing and Atmospheric Pressure
The earth's atmosphere is a mixture of gases, primarily nitrogen and oxygen. The ratio of these gases, shown in Figure 15.3, is essentially constant

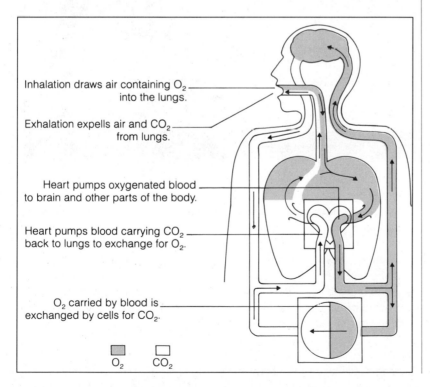

Inhalation draws air containing O_2 into the lungs.

Exhalation expells air and CO_2 from lungs.

Heart pumps oxygenated blood to brain and other parts of the body.

Heart pumps blood carrying CO_2 back to lungs to exchange for O_2.

O_2 carried by blood is exchanged by cells for CO_2.

O_2 CO_2

Figure 15.1 Respiration: the exchange of gases between the body and the atmosphere.

Figure 15.2 Exchange of oxygen
and carbon dioxide in the lungs.

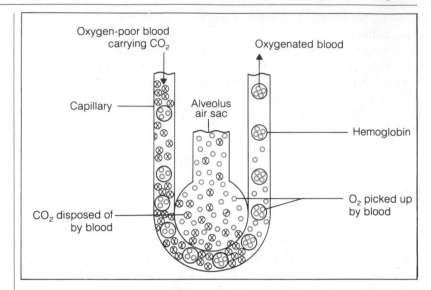

Figure 15.3 The percentage of
gases that make up our atmosphere.

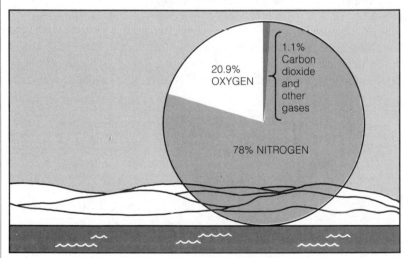

throughout the atmosphere. The ability of the alveoli to transfer oxygen to
the blood is a function of both the percentage of oxygen in the air and the
atmospheric pressure. These two factors (percentage and total pressure)
combined form the *partial pressure* of a gas. As altitude increases and
atmospheric pressure decreases, the result is a decrease in the partial pressure of oxygen available to the lungs. Above 10,000 feet, the partial pressure of oxygen quickly declines to the point of not being sufficient to fully
supply your body with the oxygen it requires. The higher you go, the less
oxygen your blood can absorb.

Hypoxia

Oxygen deficiency in the body tissues great enough to cause impairment
of function is called **hypoxia.** Hypoxia is a progressive condition rather

than a single event. The onset of hypoxia is insidious in that its effects may not be immediately noticed. Left unheeded, the warning signs of hypoxia progress toward eventual unconsciousness and possibly death. The time available to a pilot or passenger from the time oxygen deficiency begins to the loss of ability to function is called the **time of useful consciousness (TUC).**

The point at which oxygen deficiency begins differs from individual to individual, as do the symptoms exhibited. A person's ability to detect his or her own symptoms also varies. Oxygen deficiency manifests itself through any combination of these reactions:

Impairment of vision
Euphoria (a sense of well-being, like the giddiness associated with intoxication)
Lightheadedness or dizziness
Hot and cold flashes
Breathlessness
Reasoning difficulties, often characterized by repetitive thought patterns
Headache
Poor motor coordination or slowed responses
A tingling sensation in the extremities
Increased perspiration

If exposure to the oxygen-deficient environment continues, the symptoms become more pronounced, to the point of allowing objective diagnosis by the subject or by other occupants of the aircraft. These progressive symptoms are:

1. A marked increase in the rate and depth of respiration.
2. Cyanosis, or the bluing of the skin. This first appears beneath the fingernails or around the lips and may appear very early in some individuals.
3. Obvious deterioration of mental and motor faculties, often to the point of inability to perform simple calculations or use a pencil.
4. Unconsciousness.

Rate of onset.   Altitude makes a difference in the severity and rate of onset of hypoxia. At lower altitudes the onset is slower and less pronounced. At higher altitudes all symptoms may occur quite rapidly, reducing the TUC to a matter of minutes, or even seconds at very high altitudes.

As a general rule, flights below 10,000 feet MSL without the use of supplemental oxygen are considered safe; however, night vision is particularly critical, and impairment of sight can occur above 5000 feet, especially in smokers. Anything that decreases the amount of oxygen available to the brain also decreases TUC. Substances such as alcohol, carbon monoxide (discussed shortly), and many drugs, even in small amounts, reduce the TUC when they are present in the body.

Hypoxia is a more serious problem for pilots of high-performance airplanes. In trainer airplanes you will probably not cruise high enough or for long enough periods of time for any serious oxygen deficiencies to develop. Your susceptibility to hypoxia, or need for supplemental oxygen, can be increased by the effects of stress or chronic fatigue, by dietary deficiencies, or by the presence of alcohol in the blood. Chronic smokers and people in poor cardiovascular health also experience these symptoms more readily. Therefore, you should always be aware of your physical condition while flying. Flights of more than 1 or 2 hours at 8000 to 10,000 feet without supplemental oxygen, for example, may lead to symptoms such as slowed reactions, diminished motor coordination, and difficulty in concentrating or solving ordinary problems. Higher flights up to 15,000 feet, even for less than an hour, may cause headaches, a narrowed field of vision, rapid pulse, and impaired mental and motor faculties.

Countermeasures.   If any of the symptoms of hypoxia are experienced, you should descend at once to a lower altitude. Recovery from hypoxic symptoms is quite rapid once an oxygen-rich environment is provided. FAR 91.32 *requires* pilots to use oxygen when above 12,500 feet for more than 30 minutes, and at all times above 14,000 feet (these are cabin pressure altitudes). Passengers must be provided supplemental oxygen above 15,000 feet. The recommendations made below are more conservative than these requirements, but if you follow them, you will virtually eliminate the risk of your developing hypoxia.

If oxygen is carried aboard the aircraft, its use is recommended on flights of over 10,000 feet during the day and flights of over 5000 feet at night. It is also a good idea to spend the last 30 minutes of a night flight at or below 5000 feet cabin altitude to increase your alertness and improve your night vision before landing. Passengers should be provided with supplemental oxygen for flights above 10,000 feet (see Figure 15.4). In order to conserve it, passengers typically use oxygen intermittently rather than continuously, since their alertness is not as vital as that of the pilot. A few breaths every 15 minutes is usually sufficient.

Figure 15.5 shows a typical supplemental oxygen system used on general-aviation airplanes. The system, which may be permanently installed or portable, consists of a supply tank with a master valve and a number of outlets into which oxygen masks can be plugged. The mask assembly consists of a flow restrictor (to control the flow of oxygen), an accumulator bag, and the mask itself. Oxygen is fed into the bag and is mixed with the gases you exhale. When you next inhale, you receive this oxygen-rich mixture. These systems usually provide a special mask for the pilot, which has a larger orifice in the restrictor to provide more oxygen. When you are pilot-in-command, be sure you use the correct mask. Of course, you must familiarize yourself thoroughly with the operation of such equipment and the procedures recommended by the manufacturer before using it in flight.

Hyperventilation

With respiration such a vital physiological activity, you may wonder how your body determines the involuntary rate of breathing. The key to the

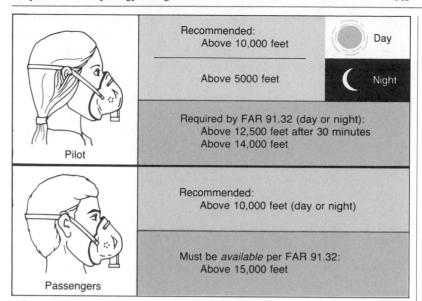

Figure 15.4 The recommended and required use of oxygen.

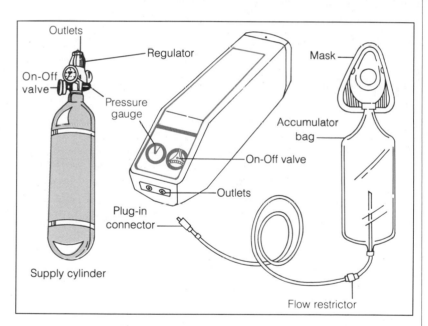

Figure 15.5 Typical oxygen system for a general-aviation aircraft.

entire process is not the amount of oxygen in the bloodstream but the amount of carbon dioxide. There are many instances, such as during and after periods of physical exertion, when normal respiration will not allow the lungs to exchange enough carbon dioxide for oxygen. As a result, the amount of carbon dioxide in the blood increases. The body responds with rapid breathing to replenish its supply of oxygen. Respiration returns to normal when the correct level of CO_2 returns.

Hyperventilation results when breathing is too rapid and deep for the current level of activity, so that there is an abnormal loss of carbon dioxide from the blood. Stress and hypoxia are the two most common causes of this excessive rate of breathing. Sometimes a pilot concentrating on a critical flight situation or whose senses are dulled by hypoxia is not even aware that he or she is starting to hyperventilate (see Table 15.1).

The effects of hyperventilation illustrate how the body's defense mechanisms respond. Prolonged overbreathing can lead to a severe CO_2 shortage in the blood (*alkalosis*), which causes the larger blood vessels in the brain to contract, starving the voluntary respiration centers of the brain of oxygen and causing the individual to pass out. This allows the autonomic nervous system (which governs the body's involuntary responses) to take over and restore the blood's proper chemical balance. It is an effective response, but one of little comfort to pilots controlling airplanes in flight.

Symptoms. Obviously, it is important for all pilots to recognize the early symptoms of hyperventilation before the body's defense mechanisms take over. The most frequent symptoms of hyperventilation, besides a rapid rate of breathing, are:

Lightheadedness or dizziness
Tingling sensations in hands and feet
Nausea
Muscle spasms
Coolness

If countermeasures are not taken, symptoms can progress to lack of coordination, disorientation or incapacitation, and finally to unconsciousness. This progression can occur in a few minutes. Notice that many of the symptoms of hyperventilation are also common to hypoxia and airsickness.

Table 15.1 The causes, symptoms, and relief of hyperventilation

Anxiety-producing situations	Reaction	Producing	Relieved by
Unfamiliar flight situations		Inadequate CO_2 level in blood	
Claustrophobia		**Symptoms**	Relaxing
Emergencies			Controlled, slow rate of breathing
Emotional worries	Increased breathing rate	Nausea	
Physical discomfort		Muscle spasms	Breathing deoxygenated air
Personal discomfort		Dizziness	
Recovery from hypoxia		Tingling sensations	

Countermeasures.   If you suspect the onset of hyperventilation, you should first consciously reduce your rate of breathing by forcing an unusually long exhalation followed by a slow, measured intake of air. At first the rate of inhalation will seem inadequate, but the urge to gasp will quickly pass as your respiratory system slows to the new voluntary rate. If the symptoms are particularly acute and you feel as though you are going to pass out (or if an afflicted passenger is about to lose consciousness), breathe into an enclosed space, such as a paper bag or—in an emergency—even one's own shirt or blouse. This will allow you to inhale a certain amount of CO_2-rich air and will allow the CO_2 content of the blood to rise. Talking aloud is another simple way to consciously regulate one's breathing rate. Symptoms will usually subside within a few minutes after breathing is brought under control.

Hypoxia or Hyperventilation?

Since hyperventilation is one of the body's normal responses to hypoxia and since the symptoms of both are similar, you may have trouble deciding which malady is affecting you. If oxygen is available, there is a simple test: take a couple of breaths of oxygen-rich air. If the symptoms disappear, you had hypoxia and should continue to use oxygen. If, however, no change is apparent after just a few breaths, you are under the influence of hyperventilation. You should immediately use one of the procedures described above to consciously slow your breathing rate.

If oxygen is *not* available, you should probably assume that *both* respiration problems are present. Descend to a lower altitude immediately *and* consciously control your breathing. The lower altitude will not adversely affect a case of hyperventilation, since breathing rate is the problem. Controlled breathing will not affect hypoxia, because lack of oxygen is the culprit.

Carbon Monoxide Poisoning

Carbon monoxide (CO) is always present in the exhaust gases of an internal combustion engine, as a result of the incomplete combustion of the fuel. Although CO itself is an odorless and colorless gas, exhaust gases also contain other particles and gases that often—but not always—can be detected by their odor.

Symptoms.   Carbon monoxide represents a special danger to people because hemoglobin (the agent in the blood that carries oxygen) has a *much* greater attraction to CO than to oxygen (see Figure 15.6). In fact, once hemoglobin is contaminated with CO, it becomes incapable of carrying oxygen. Carbon monoxide poisoning is therefore similar to hypoxia and has similar symptoms. The differences are that an excess of CO will cause:

A feeling of vague uneasiness (rather than euphoria)
Dizziness (usually without lightheadedness)
Mental confusion
A more severe and faster-building headache

Figure 15.6 Hemoglobin has a much higher affinity for carbon monoxide than for oxygen.

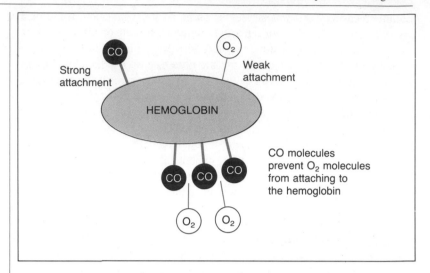

If the source of CO is not eliminated, the gas will cause unconsciousness and eventually death. The unconsciousness caused by CO is not a defense mechanism of the body (as it is with hyperventilation) but is the result of the poisoning of the blood.

Countermeasures.   Since carbon monoxide decreases the ability of the blood to carry oxygen, it is a more serious problem than the lack of oxygen in the air. Even when a source of oxygen is supplied, the effects of CO poisoning will persist for days. The best defense is to always mix fresh outside air with heated air used in the cockpit. If CO poisoning is suspected, turn off the heater (the most common source of CO) and flood the cabin with fresh air by opening outside air vents. If oxygen equipment is available, use it immediately. Naturally, you should land at the nearest field practicable.

Carbon monoxide detectors are available. Low-cost devices are usually a plastic card with a brown chemical spot on them. The spot darkens in the presence of CO. These devices are reliable, but they must be replaced regularly because, after 1 or 2 months, their sensitivity to CO begins to decline steadily. Electronic CO detectors are also available; they do not lose sensitivity but are much more expensive.

Altitude and Trapped Gas

You may be familiar with the physics of the weather balloon. A balloon is released from the surface of the earth with a certain volume of lighter-than-air gas, such as helium. The balloon then floats aloft, displacing the heavier air around it. As it rises into regions of decreasing pressure, the gas contained inside the elastic balloon skin tries to expand to fill the less dense area around it.

The human body contains many pockets of trapped gases: in the stomach and intestines, where gas is a by-product of digestion, and in the sinus cavities, ears, and teeth. From sea level to 18,000 feet, for example, the volume of a quantity of gas expands to twice its former size. If there is no way to vent, or eliminate, this expanding gas, physiological problems, such as gastrointestinal pains, earaches, toothaches, and headaches could be felt. Flatulence is nature's way of helping the body adjust to this pressure change, and it is no source for embarrassment among knowledgeable pilots.

Air trapped in the middle ear and **eustachian tube** (the tube that connects the middle ear to the throat) can be extremely painful (see Figure 15.7). The ears usually clear themselves on ascent but may require some assistance when descending, such as yawning deeply or chewing gum. One method for clearing the ears that usually works if yawning fails is the **Valsalva technique.** To use this method, simply pinch your nostrils and blow *gently* through your nose. Unless your eustachian tube is blocked with congestion, your ears should clear (or "pop") normally. Severe ear pain on descent should always be regarded as a potentially serious condition, since the eardrum may rupture if the descent is too quick. In these cases, slow the rate of descent to allow the afflicted pilot or passenger to clear the blockage. If pain persists after landing, a physician should be consulted at once.

Altitude and scuba diving.   Many pilots also enjoy aquatic sports such as snorkeling and scuba diving and use the freedom the airplane gives them to take quick trips to places where these pastimes can be pursued. Just as the ratio of ambient air pressure to the pressure of the gases in the blood declines in flight, the process reverses itself when diving beneath the surface of the sea (see Figure 15.8). Excess nitrogen, always present in the blood, is absorbed into the tissues and may rapidly evolve again as bubbles in the muscles, should you decrease the pressure around your body too quickly. The symptoms of this reaction are called **decompression sickness,** or the **bends,** since the body is frequently doubled over by pain. Most divers take care to avoid the bends by ascending slowly to the surface after a dive. However, some forget that the same process continues during flights in an airplane. Thus, it is recommended that you wait at least 24 hours between a dive and takeoff in an aircraft—even for flights at modest altitudes.

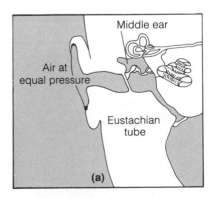
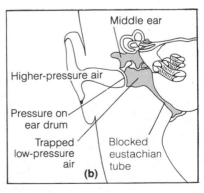

Figure 15.7 Air pressures on the eardrum. **(a)** Balanced pressures. **(b)** Descent with a blocked eustachian tube.

Figure 15.8 Climbing to altitude in an aircraft aggravates decompression after scuba diving.

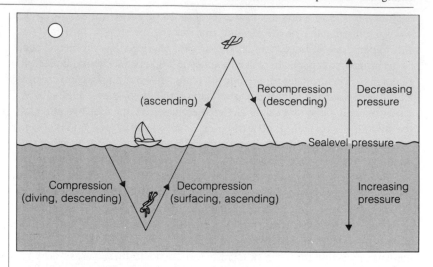

EFFECTS OF MOTION

Whenever your body is traveling in a constant direction and at a constant speed, you have no sensation of motion or reaction to the motion. In contrast, your body is very sensitive to *changes* to both speed and direction. The term **velocity** is defined as a magnitude of speed that acts in a linear direction. **Acceleration** is the rate of change of velocity and is caused by a force in the same direction. Accelerations can be measured in **gravity level equivalents,** or **Gs.**

An acceleration is named for the direction in which the change takes place. As Figure 15.9 illustrates, the airplane coordinate system is the basis for the naming convention. The force of gravity causes a constant 1G positive acceleration, which keeps us on the earth's surface. *Positive* accel-

Figure 15.9 The axes used to describe acceleration correspond to the aircraft coordinate system.

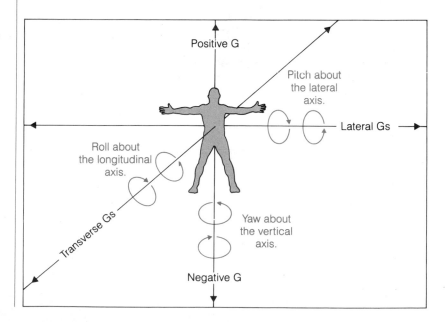

eration (in excess of 1G) is felt when the body experiences an upward force. You feel positive acceleration as a force that pushes you down into your seat. *Negative* acceleration acts in the opposite direction, causing you to strain against your seat belt and allowing loose items to float around in the cockpit. Negative Gs may be induced by gusts or by pushing forward on the control wheel. A negative acceleration that exactly matches the gravitational force puts you in a *zero G* condition. Forward and aft Gs, which are the result of changing forward speed, are called **transverse Gs.** Forces that cause the airplane to move sideways cause **lateral Gs.** Naturally, forces operating in parallel but opposite directions, such as positive and negative Gs, can never be experienced simultaneously, although they may occur in rapid succession.

Gs and Circulation

As you increase the intensity and duration of G-loads—say, by establishing a constant altitude turn—the volume of blood pumped to the upper extremities declines while blood begins to pool in the lower extremities (see Figure 15.10a). During the shallow banked turns used in normal flying, which usually last just a short time, the change is not significant enough to be noticed. However, if the positive G level becomes high enough or is sustained for a prolonged period, this pooling of blood will affect the brain and, in particular, your vision. Because there is a lack of oxygen-bearing blood to the brain, your eyes begin to lose their acuity and your field of vision becomes narrowed. This condition is called **grayout.** Vision is still possible but is limited, as details, colors, and contrast fade away.

If more than 4 or 5 sustained positive Gs are experienced, the field of view is lost completely. The brain is still conscious and capable of sending commands to the limbs and reasoning problems, but there is no vision. This condition is known as **blackout.** If the Gs persist at or beyond this level, the brain loses the volume of blood necessary for conscious processes and lapses into unconsciousness. Involuntary life-sustaining processes continue, but awareness, reasoning, and purposeful action are impossible.

Negative Gs have the opposite effect (see Figure 15.10b). Blood pools in the upper extremities, and the face rapidly begins to feel full and flushed. Continued negative Gs result in a definite reddening of the vision, called **redout,** followed by the *sensation* of the eyeballs popping out.

These extremes of circulatory distress are seldom reached, even by pilots performing aerobatics. Most individuals dislike the physical discomfort of such maneuvers and so either limit their exposure to them or avoid them altogether.

Motion Sensing and Spatial Orientation

It is important to understand how the human body senses motion and how it can be deceived by the dynamics of flight. We maintain our orientation in space and our equilibrium by means of clues received from:

1. The eyes. Visual cues are processed by the logic centers of the brain based on our cumulative experience with similar sights and their significance.

Figure 15.10 The effects of
sustained Gs on the circulatory
system. **(a)** Positive Gs.
(b) Negative Gs.

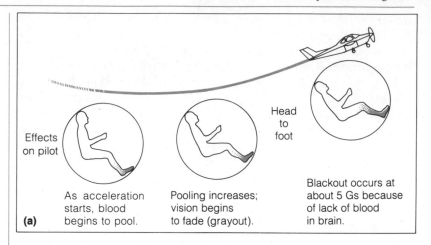

(a)

Effects on pilot

As acceleration starts, blood begins to pool.

Pooling increases; vision begins to fade (grayout).

Head to foot

Blackout occurs at about 5 Gs because of lack of blood in brain.

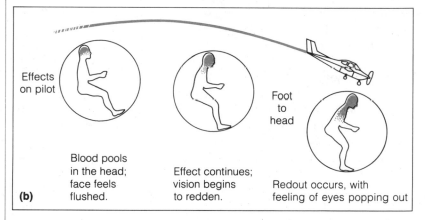

(b)

Effects on pilot

Blood pools in the head; face feels flushed.

Effect continues; vision begins to redden.

Foot to head

Redout occurs, with feeling of eyes popping out

2. The motion-sensing semicircular canals in the inner ear (*vestibular organ*) and the gravity-seeking organs of the inner ear (*otoliths*).

3. The senses for postural detection and verification (called *proprioception*), such as touch, pressure, and tension.

With any action we take, we constantly weigh and use sensations received from our eyes, inner ear, and postural system (see Figure 15.11). Like a fail-safe electronics system, if any one of these systems fails us or causes us to suspect that it is providing unreliable information, we use the signals of the other two systems for guidance. Unfortunately, as we will see later, deceptive signals can make the selection of a proper course of action more difficult.

The three-dimensional movements of an aircraft in flight bombard the pilot's sensory organs with an enormous volume of signals. For example, a normal motion in the cockpit, such as bending over to retrieve a fallen chart, may be compounded by other motions of the airplane simultaneously sensed by the body. As a result, the brain must try to make sense of all of

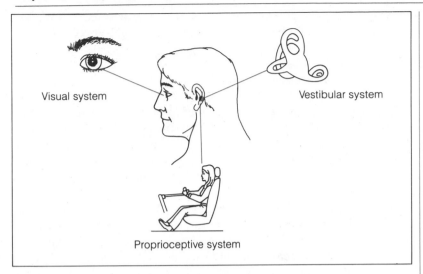

Figure 15.11 The senses that report motion and spatial orientation.

this information—to sort out one motion from another—and retain a valid three-dimensional orientation in space. The human mind is conditioned to use and trust visual cues above all others. Therefore, even a momentary disorientation will be quickly resolved when you glance outside the airplane and see the natural horizon. This visual information instantly overrides any contrary information provided by the vestibular or postural sensors.

Vertigo

Unfortunately, if valid visual data are not available, as can happen during flights in poor visibility, the confusion caused by conflicting data from the various motion-sensing systems can be debilitating. Under these circumstances you simply are unable to tell "which way is up." This condition is called **spatial disorientation** or **vertigo.**

Many hours of flying time is no defense against spatial disorientation; it is a physiological disorder, not a training shortcoming. It can strike airline captains as well as student pilots. The effects and severity of vertigo, however, *can* be cut short by training and an understanding of the phenomenon.

Overcoming vertigo.   Spatial disorientation is usually a problem only when the natural horizon is *not* visible. Under these circumstances you must rely on instrument indications, primarily the artificial horizon, to provide the necessary visual cues. *You must learn to believe your instruments and to react correctly to their indications.* The biggest problem, as mentioned before, is the confusion caused by conflicting signals from the various senses. *Develop the self-discipline to act according to your instrument indications and to overcome the strong conflicting urges that may accompany periods of disorientation.* Your flight training will expose you to these feelings and give you the chance to recover from them; however, this training is for emergency use only. (Your skills will be fully developed when you train for an *instrument rating*.)

Motion-Related Disorientations

Although the more dangerous physiological reactions to flight will occur only in special circumstances, a number of specific kinds of disorientation do result from commonly encountered flight situations. These are discussed in the following paragraphs to demonstrate the various ways our senses can cause disorientation. This knowledge makes it easier for you to consciously make correct decisions in the face of conflicting sensory inputs.

The inner ear.   The motion-sensing system located in our **inner ears** consists of three tubes arranged at right angles to one another and connected to a sac (see Figure 15.12). The *semicircular canals* contain fluid and sensory hairs that detect movement of the fluid. This part of the system senses angular accelerations around the pitch, roll, and yaw axes. The sensory organ in the sac detects gravity and linear accelerations (up, down, left, right, forward, backward).

The graveyard spiral.   When an aircraft *enters* a constant-rate turn, it disturbs the fluid, giving you the sensation of turning (see Figure 15.12b). However, if an *inadvertent* turn is entered very gradually, or while your attention is on another matter (navigation, communication, or the like), you may not notice the turning sensation. Once the turn is constant for more than a few seconds, the fluid is no longer disturbed and the vestibular system reports that the turn has stopped, even though it has not (see Figure 15.12c).

Eventually, you will notice either the altitude loss (due to the unplanned bank angle) or the turn indications on your instruments. If you react to the altitude loss, you will, of course, pull back on the control yoke. Unfortunately this will tend to tighten the turn, aggravating the situation. If you notice the bank angle and level the wings, the fluid in your ears will report the change as the start of a turn in the opposite direction, as illustrated in Figure 15.12d. (Remember, the fluid was motionless prior to your reaction.) The result is that even though your instruments will correctly indicate wings-level flight, your brain will be receiving signals that say you are turning. If you believe the turning sensation, you will (incorrectly) try to stop it by banking away from the sensation, which means that you will reenter the original turn.

Naturally, the airplane is constantly descending because of the banked flight, so either of these two untrained actions will make the situation worse. The airplane will end up in a steep descending turn, named the **graveyard spiral** because of the tragic result that typically ends such a situation (see Figure 15.13). The correct action is to ignore the turning sensation (much easier said than done) and to level the wings by visual reference to your instruments.

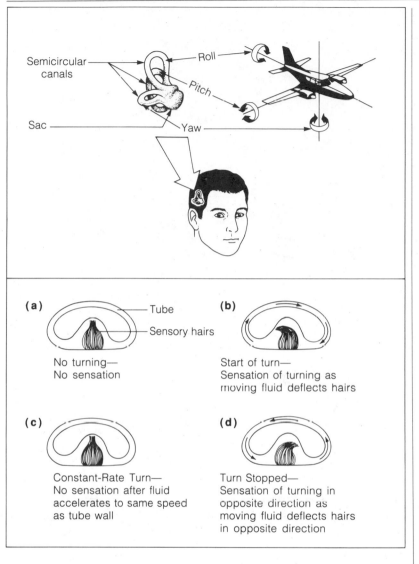

Figure 15.12 The design and workings of the inner ear.

(a) — Tube
— Sensory hairs

No turning—
No sensation

(b) Start of turn—
Sensation of turning as
moving fluid deflects hairs

(c) Constant-Rate Turn—
No sensation after fluid
accelerates to same speed
as tube wall

(d) Turn Stopped—
Sensation of turning in
opposite direction as
moving fluid deflects hairs
in opposite direction

Semicircular canals
Roll
Pitch
Sac
Yaw

Coriolis illusion.   As we have seen in the graveyard spiral, the vestibular systems can correctly sense an initial acceleration, but then they quickly stabilize. If you are in a stabilized constant turn, moving your head to one side or the other, leaning forward, looking up, or any combination of these movements will cause a sense of rotation in the vestibular systems that is illusory and is called the **Coriolis illusion.** It is your head that has made the motion, not the aircraft. This may cause you to experience strong sensations of unusual airplane attitudes (see Figure 15.14). If you act upon this illusory sensation, you may actually maneuver the aircraft into a dangerous or undesirable attitude. This is why it is important to "ride with the airplane" when maneuvering rather than to maintain an upright posture.

Figure 15.13 The graveyard spiral.

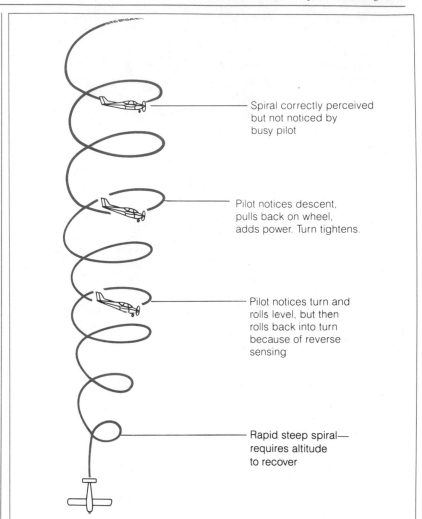

Spiral correctly perceived
but not noticed by
busy pilot

Pilot notices descent,
pulls back on wheel,
adds power. Turn tightens.

Pilot notices turn and
rolls level, but then
rolls back into turn
because of reverse
sensing

Rapid steep spiral—
requires altitude
to recover

Figure 15.14 Coriolis illusion.

The head should be turned slowly when flying by reference to cockpit instruments or during flight without a definite outside horizon.

Acceleration illusion. This occurs when the aircraft experiences transverse G forces during acceleration or deceleration. Inertia causes the otoliths in the inner ear to move, resulting in a climbing sensation. Your natural reaction as a pilot would be to lower the nose. If this sensation is experienced on takeoff, particularly a takeoff at night with an indefinite horizon, the climb rate may be diminished to the point that obstacles no longer can be cleared. The aircraft might actually be directed into a shallow dive. Technically, this condition is called **oculogravic illusion.** You can prevent any ill effects from its occurrence by monitoring your attitude indicator, altimeter, and vertical speed indicator.

Autokinesis. During night flight a stationary light such as a beacon or ground light that you stare at for several seconds may appear to move. This is caused by eye movements, resulting in a sense of relative motion, or **autokinesis.** This effect has been diminished by designing lights used for aeronautical purposes that are large, intense, and arranged in patterns or to flash on and off.

Postural illusion. The "seat of the pants" perception, or **postular sensations**—the feeling of your weight on the seat, the pressure of the seat belt, the push and pull of side forces due to yawing moments—provides motion cues and illusions to the brain. During a coordinated turn, for example, gravity is always sensed at the floor of the aircraft and is a false cue for distinguishing up from down (see Figure 15.15). Although postural

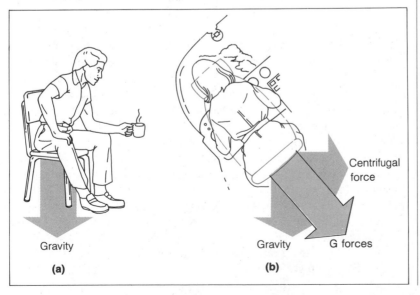

(a)   (b)

Figure 15.15 Postural illusion.

sensations are more easily disregarded than visual or vestibular inputs, they can add to the confusion when conflicting illusions are experienced.

Airsickness

Airsickness, like seasickness, is a physiological disorder unrelated to physical conditioning, skills as a pilot, or even the desire to fly. It is caused by a sympathetic reaction by the stomach to the conflicting vestibular, visual, and postural sensations experienced by some people when they are removed from their usual one positive-G environment. Additionally, a person's emotional state can contribute to the occurrence and severity of motion sickness.

Any motion that can induce spatial disorientation can induce airsickness. Also, any factors that may exaggerate disorientation once it begins (such as a head cold, medication, hypoxia, or fatigue) may increase the probability of airsickness. An individual's comfort in the flying environment is also a factor. A warm cockpit with a lack of fresh air, coupled with uncomfortable seating, seats that lack a view of the horizon, turbulence, or vibration, can also trigger any tendencies toward motion sickness.

As with spatial orientation, the brain is the key to preventing or to minimizing most motion sickness. For many passengers, flying is an unusual and anxiety-producing situation, sometimes coupled with apprehension about safety. These feelings of stress can be manifested by airsickness. Sometimes the mere anticipation of the *possibility* of airsickness is enough to bring on an attack. Some pilots may occasionally experience bouts of airsickness as a reaction to stress. It is important to realize that airsickness is no cause for self-recrimination and by itself is no indicator of fear of flying.

Combating airsickness.   Preventing airsickness is easier and more effective than trying to cure it after it begins. Passengers who have a history of motion sickness ought to consult a physician for a prescription or over-the-counter remedy. Pilots should never take any medication for airsickness or any other disorder without consulting an AME. Student pilots who are prone to airsickness should inform their instructors at once. CFIs are understanding of this problem and will take extra time to brief students before flights. This minimizes the source of stress that may be prompting uneasiness.

Flights with a passenger who is prone to airsickness should begin with a complete briefing of what will happen during the flight. Since surprises are anxiety producers, keep them to an absolute minimum. Turbulence, which is both uncomfortable and unpredictable, should be avoided if at all possible. All maneuvers must be gentle, with pitch and bank angles kept to a minimum. Keep the cabin temperature a bit cool if possible and provide plenty of fresh air. Remind your friend to keep visual contact with the natural horizon. Plan a flight of short duration, as short as once around the traffic pattern if necessary, so that you can land *immediately* when the first signs of uneasiness occur. It is very important to land *before* illness occurs if you wish to increase resistance to this disorder. Of course, be sure you have a ready supply of sealable airsickness bags available, but keep them out of sight until needed. Do not even mention that you have them, since that is a subconscious suggestion that you expect problems.

If one of your passengers does become ill in flight, the following actions will minimize the effects:

1. Have the person scan the horizon rather than anything inside the airplane. This will help minimize the effect of conflicting sensory signals.

2. Administer fresh air as directly as possible. If oxygen is available, a few breaths may prove refreshing.

3. Keep the sick person cool rather than warm. Loosen any tight-fitting clothing.

4. Recline the seat back as far as possible. This reduces the effects of any up-and-down motions.

5. Land as soon as practicable.

NIGHT VISION

Our eyes function best in daylight, but that does not mean we are entirely disadvantaged at night. The human eye adapts quite well to low levels of illumination, but that physical adaptation is easily disturbed by bright lights and can be fooled by illusions.

Adaptation Period

Think about the sensations you experience when entering a darkened motion picture theater from a bright city street. Your eyes need time to adapt to the new, lower level of illumination. Once that adaptation has taken place, it must be preserved. Give yourself plenty of time to develop your night vision before the flight; 20 minutes to half an hour in a room with lowered lights should be the minimum.

Rods and Cones

The part of the eye that senses light is the **retina,** at the back of the eye. It is made up of two kinds of nerves called **rods** and **cones.** These nerves are connected to the cells of the optic nerve, which transmits messages directly to the brain. The cones are located in the center of the retina, and the rods are concentrated in a ring around the cones (see Figure 15.16).

The function of the cones is to detect color, details, and distant objects. The rods function when something is seen out of the corner of the eye by means of **peripheral vision,** the off-center portion of the field of vision. They do not give detail or color and are most effective in detecting moving objects. Both the rods and cones are used for vision during daylight. Although there is no clear-cut division of function, the rods are more important in making night vision possible.

The fact that the rods are distributed in a band around the cones and do not lie directly behind the pupils makes peripheral vision important during night flight. You may not be able to see objects at night if you stare directly

Figure 15.16 The relative location of the rods and cones in the eye.

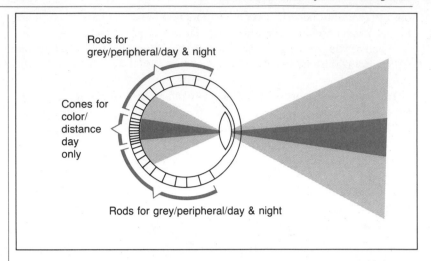

at them, but if you gaze indirectly, they will appear in the "corner of your eye" (see Figure 15.17).

As mentioned previously, visual acuity at night begins to decrease at altitudes as low as 5000 feet, because less oxygen is available to the body. Staying below that altitude for at least the last 30 minutes of a night flight will help your night vision—and will also minimize the other effects of hypoxia.

THE EFFECTS OF NOISE

Your ears respond to sound waves in the air. The outer ear funnels the vibrations to strike the eardrum, which then transmits them through the

Figure 15.17 Comparison between day and night vision.

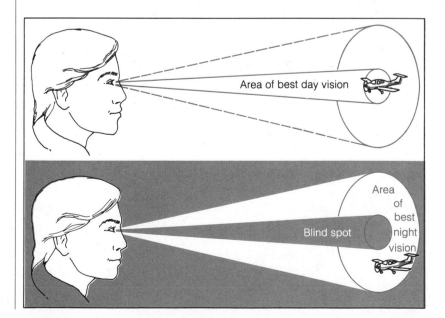

middle ear through three tiny bones to the spiral-shaped *cochlea*. This part of the inner ear is filled with fluid (see Figure 15.18). The motion of the fluid in the cochlea is registered by tiny hair-like cells that translate the motion into an auditory nerve signal, which the brain interprets as an audible sound.

Sound levels are measured in terms of **decibels (db).** Your reaction to sound depends on both its level and the duration of your exposure to it. Exposure to high levels of sound, even for a short time, will usually result in a noticeable degradation in your hearing for a short time afterward. Such exposures may also cause an unnoticeable permanent degradation in hearing. If you experience repeated exposure (over a number of years) to high sound levels, the permanent hearing degradation will eventually become noticeable.

Exposure to high sound levels also induces fatigue, resulting from constant stimulation of the body's nervous system. The longer you are in a high db environment, the more the sound literally "grates" on your nerves. Even moderate sound levels become irritating after a long enough period of time.

Unfortunately, the cabin of a general-aviation airplane in flight easily qualifies as a high-noise environment. After a flight you will undoubtedly notice some short-term hearing loss. Permanent hearing loss is not uncommon in pilots who have been flying regularly for a number of years. If the hearing loss becomes acute enough, you could be refused a medical certificate.

Protection from Noise

Earplugs or noise-attenuating headsets provide effective protection from high noise levels. These devices reduce the total decibel level that reaches your eardrum. Earplugs tend to block higher-pitch noises (like aerodynamic noise and propeller and power plant noises) more effectively than lower-pitch sounds (such as human voices). Communication with passengers and controllers may therefore become clearer and more understandable while wearing earplugs. Noise-attenuating headsets, on the other hand, block out all ranges of external noise (including voice) while providing unrestricted radio audio reception. The choice of which one to use is a personal one,

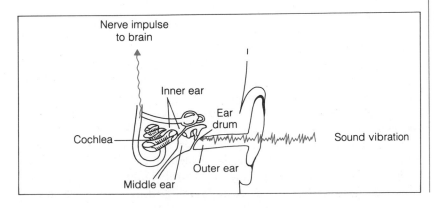

Figure 15.18 The mechanism of hearing.

but it is highly recommended that you always use some form of hearing protection while flying.

DRUGS

The ingestion of drugs or alcohol can have significant effects on your ability to pilot an airplane. By drugs we do not necessarily mean just "street drugs" or fashionable recreational drugs such as marijuana but any substance that is introduced into the system for purposes other than nourishment. Some of these purposes may be acceptable, such as self-medication with drugstore cold remedies or pain relievers. Nonpilots can consume these over-the-counter drugs with no apparent ill effects. For pilots, however, such drugs may affect reaction time and alertness or may have other side effects due to the high-altitude environment. For many years aspirin was thought to be a neutral agent in the flying environment, but now there is controversy even about it. Aspirin or any over-the-counter pain reliever may mask symptoms of a more serious condition and can have unwanted side effects. You should discuss your own practices with an Aviation Medical Examiner before using the medications while flying. Allergy or cold remedies may cause drowsiness or reduced motor coordination and should not be used for a period of 24 hours prior to a flight. Certain cough syrups or decongestants may cause rapid heart rates and general nervous behavior. These side effects can impair judgment and make a pilot susceptible to altitude-related disorders. Obviously, tranquilizers will result in slowed reflexes and a placid attitude that may run contrary to safety. All medications should be approved by an AME before you select them or use them before or during a flight.

Alcohol is a depressant drug in medical terms, and it should be avoided 24 hours prior to a flight, even though FARs only require 8 hours "from bottle to throttle" (FAR 91.11). The effects of alcohol may include reduced judgment, reduced sense of responsibility, loss of coordination, shorter attention span, increased reaction time, loss of visual acuity, diminished tactile sensitivity, poorer reasoning capacity, *and*—what makes those effects even more dangerous—a *false* sense of capability, self-confidence, and well-being. Additionally, high altitude lowers the body's tolerance for alcohol. Two ounces in the blood at 10,000 feet has the effect of 6 ounces at sea level. The higher you get, the "higher" you get.

Alcohol is metabolized by the body at a fixed rate. There is no known way to speed up this process. Some people mistakenly believe that drinking coffee, breathing oxygen, taking cold showers, or swallowing aspirin can make you sober up quicker. These activities will tend to stimulate the body, counteracting the depressant properties of alcohol for a short period, but they will not make you sober.

FAR 91.11 also specifically prohibits you from flying "while under the *influence* of alcohol." This means not only while you are drunk but also while you are recovering from any subsequent effects, such as a hangover. In order to provide a legal definition of "under the influence," this regulation prohibits flying (or even attempting to do so) if you have 0.04 percent by weight or more alcohol in your blood. In comparison, most states define

0.10 percent as legally drunk for drivers. Furthermore, when you exercise the privileges of your pilot certificate, you implicitly agree to submit to tests for drugs and/or alcohol in your blood, upon the reasonable request of any law enforcement officer or FAA official. This provision is called *implied consent* (see FAR 91.11c for more details).

Smoking is a well-known health hazard for reasons both related and unrelated to flying. In the short term smoking adds to the risk of oxygen-related disorders by diminishing the elasticity of the lungs and reducing the O_2-CO_2 exchange by coating large portions of the lungs with the inhaled products of combustion. Additionally, about 4 percent of cigarette smoke is carbon monoxide. FAA and Air Force research indicates that someone who smokes a pack a day will experience the symptoms of hypoxia as much as 5000 feet lower than a nonsmoker.

EFFECTS OF STRESS ON THE HUMAN BODY

Stress, or psychological or bodily tension, is a by-product of living. In a way, it is as much a vital sign as respiration, since it reflects much of our internal composition and the balance of forces that confront us in daily life. Contrary to popular belief, not all stress is bad or the result of negative forces. Significant life events, such as the death of a loved one or loss of a job, are acknowledged stress producers, but so are marriages, promotions, and learning new skills such as flying airplanes. If we had no stress in our lives, we would lead a very boring existence. Stress compels us to resolve (or avoid) certain situations and propels us to new accomplishments. Thus, you must accept a certain amount of stress as necessary to productive life but learn to recognize excess stress and to resolve it.

The Mechanisms of Stress

Generally, there are three sources of stress: the environment, the body, and psychological processes.

Environmental stress.   For a pilot, and particularly for student pilots, environmental stress can come from many directions. As human beings, we share many common stress-producing activities—living, loving, going to the dentist, earning a living, and so on. It is not our intent here to provide a treatise on the causes of stress in everyday life, but you should be aware that virtually no one is exempt from it and that stress from one area of your life can affect other areas of concern. Trouble on the job frequently results in trouble at home or difficulties with interpersonal relationships. Similarly, domestic problems can make it hard to concentrate at work or school, and so on. Sometimes the interplay and interaction of stress-producing agents can make one feel as though one's life is "unraveling at the seams."

Common sources of stress shared by both fliers and nonfliers are:

1. *Apprehension* related to a natural fear of the unknown.
2. *Anxiety* based on feelings such as a desire to perform well in an unfamiliar area or doubts about one's own abilities.

3. *Frustration* stemming from failure to progress as fast as one might desire.

Each of these stress-producing elements has a positive side. Without a normal, healthy respect for the dangers of bad weather, pilots might fly into conditions exceeding their capabilities. Without some fear of failure, many people might become lax about learning safety rules or proper procedures. Without an element of pride in one's accomplishments, there would be little incentive to practice more refined piloting techniques.

Body stress.   Stressful feelings can come directly from the body as feedback to the brain over maltreatment, from injury, or from disease. Your medical examination will probably detect any pathological sources of stress, such as a debilitating disease or handicap. But these constitute only a minority of sources of stress among pilots. More common sources are lack of sleep (fatigue), poor diet, or the effects of drugs and alcohol.

Most mature human beings have a nominal rhythm established in their daily habits. While short-term changes in these patterns can occur, in the long run they tend to normalize into a predictable sequence of work, play, and sleep—all of which are necessary for a healthy life. When one of these activities begins to take precedence over the others, stress can develop. One of the first things busy people decide they can do without is sleep. When you are trying to crowd an important activity like learning to fly into a crowded schedule, a few nights with little sleep can easily occur. This practice can lead to **acute fatigue.**

One or two instances of "late to bed and early to rise" can probably be accepted by the body without distress. But continued functioning in a fatigued condition (**chronic fatigue**) can result in inattention to detail, slowed reactions, and a generally ambivalent attitude—even when it comes to safety. Physiologically, the blood reflects this condition through the buildup of lactic acid. FAA or NTSB officials investigating an aircraft accident or near miss will frequently take blood samples from the pilots involved. If the blood is found to contain lactic acid in abnormally large amounts, pilot fatigue is often cited as a contributing factor.

Most people are raised with a knowledge of which foods will result in an adequate diet. Usually, foods consumed in a balanced manner promote general good health and a positive attitude. When one type or category of food begins to dominate the others, deficiencies can develop. Your diet can definitely influence your ability to fly safely, and a reasonable amount of attention to maintaining a balanced diet is required.

The Relaxation Response

The key to stress management is to learn to recognize your own particular reaction to excess stress. You should honestly evaluate your own psychological responses to stress and use them as early warning signals of possible adverse reactions. Let us review the first easily detectable indicators of excess stress: increased heartbeat, increased perspiration, increased breathing rate, and muscular tension. You can detect these symptoms almost as soon as they begin. When you do notice them, program yourself to take immediate countermeasures. For example:

1. Take a deep breath or sigh.
2. Follow this with regular, even breathing.
3. Reposition your arms and legs or feet and hands briefly. Wiggle your fingers and toes to help dissipate muscular tension.
4. Let stressful thoughts dissipate and allow new, relaxed, and confident thoughts to enter your mind.

This **relaxation response** can be augmented by other stress-reducing techniques recommended by psychologists and physicians, such as meditation, exercise, biofeedback, and breathing-control programs. If you take the time to develop your own methods of reducing stress, these techniques will be ready whenever signs of excess stress are detected—at home, on the job, in the classroom, or in the cockpit. In this way the pilot's worst enemy—panic—can be permanently avoided.

The Physiology of Panic

Panic is defined as sudden, overpowering, and unreasoning fright. The key word here is not *fear* but *overpowering* or *unreasoning*. Fear is a natural protective response to a threatening situation. Truly fearless people exist only in fiction. Fear, like ambition or pride, can be an effective spur to acts of good judgment. Unreasoning fear is abnormal, and it places the body in greater jeopardy, not less. Panic hinders a person's ability to make clear judgments and implement previously learned emergency procedures. It also blocks sensory information that could be essential to solving the problem and prompts the individual to waste time trying fruitless or repetitive solutions. By learning and employing the relaxation response and other techniques to reduce stress, you will limit your susceptibility to panic.

Knowing your airplane and its procedures—normal and emergency—is a great deterrent to panic. Most people find that the most stressful situations are those for which they are least prepared. By constantly expanding your base of aviation facts, principles, and concepts, you should be able to keep flying relaxing, rewarding, and full of healthful challenges.

The Get Home Syndrome

There is a special combination of fatigue and stress that sometimes clouds the judgment of even the most conscientious and skilled pilots. Some pilots who exercise every caution and careful procedure outbound on a cross-country flight—departing, say, on a Friday afternoon or Saturday morning—become veritable kamikazes Sunday evening, when time is short for the return flight. Sadly, the newspapers following a holiday weekend frequently report missing or overdue aircraft—often victims of *get-home-itis*: the irrational desire to get home regardless of wind, weather, mechanical conditions, or physiological needs.

One of the disciplines you will learn early as a competent pilot is the knowledge of when to say "No, I won't fly today." It is not that you "can't" or "couldn't if you had to," but simply that, in your best judgment, it would be foolish to try—despite the protests of friends and relatives or the imaginary wrath of employers, spouse, or others at home base.

Perhaps Richard Collins said it best in his book *Flying Safely*:

Managing fatigue and not flying when ill or when under the influence of medicine is pure common sense. . . . As we explore . . . the various things that are related to flying safely, it is continually noted that the pilot, the complex human being, is the strength, the weakness, and the determiner of success.

A mnemonic aid that many pilots have added to their preflight checklist to determine their fitness to fly is the I'M SAFE check:

I̲llness: Do not fly when you are feeling less than your best.
M̲edication: Be sure that any medication you take is approved by an AME before your flight.
S̲tress: Know the signs of stress and cultivate your own relaxation response.
A̲lcohol: If you drink, allow for recovery time.
F̲atigue: When in doubt, sleep on it.
E̲motions: Keep yours as healthy as possible. Remember that you are participating in one of life's greatest pleasures, the joy of piloting.

KEY TERMS

acute fatigue
aviation physiology
blackout
carbon monoxide poisoning
chronic fatigue
Coriolis illusion
decompression sickness
graveyard spiral
grayout

hyperventilation
hypoxia
redout
relaxation response
spatial disorientation
stress
Valsalva technique
vertigo

PROFICIENCY CHECK

1. How does the blood's chemistry act as the body's "telegraph" to the brain to regulate normal respiration?

2. What are the symptoms of hypoxia? What countermeasures can you take?

3. What is hyperventilation? How is it related to stress?

4. You are pilot-in-command on a cross-country flight at 9500 feet MSL. Several minutes after leveling off at this altitude, a passenger begins to complain of a severe headache. Inquiring further, you find that the passenger was suffering from a mild cold before entering the airplane. What physiological disorder might you suspect? What action should you take?

5. Explain the effect of positive and negative G forces on the human circulatory system.

6. Name the three systems the body uses to establish its orientation in space and to establish its equilibrium.

7. What two general rules can minimize the occurrence and effects of spatial disorientation?

8. You are at the midpoint of a cross-country flight at 4500 feet on a hot summer day. A passenger begins to complain of nausea. What physiological disorder do you suspect? What action should you take?

9. What are the three sources of stress? What special kinds of flight-related stress may be encountered by student pilots?

10. What is the difference between acute and chronic fatigue? Which is more dangerous?

11. What is the FAA regulation about the time between consuming alcohol and acting as pilot-in-command of an aircraft?

12. What are the common early warning signs of stress?

C H A P T E R   S I X T E E N

Nothing is as good as holding on to safety.

Euripides
The Phoenician Women

C H E C K P O I N T S

How do pilots differentiate between an actual emergency and a suspected or potential emergency? ✈ What are compound emergencies and how do pilots respond to them? ✈ How does preparing, filing, and following a flight plan contribute to safety on a cross-country flight? ✈ How do pilots safely make emergency landings? ✈ What procedures should pilots follow if they become lost? ✈ What special communications procedures should be employed during an airborne emergency? ✈ What precautions can pilots take to prevent aviation accidents?

HANDLING AIRBORNE EMERGENCIES

Many of us tend to dismiss or ignore unpleasant possibilities—such as airborne emergencies—in the hope that doing so will somehow prevent them from happening. It is true that emergency situations are rare. However, the possibility exists that you may be confronted with an emergency on any given flight. Pilots of high-performance military and commercial airplanes spend many hours training for unusual situations that they have little likelihood of encountering in flight. Your private-pilot training will also include practicing emergency procedures you hope never to use. This effort is not misspent. A pilot who is well prepared for all foreseeable problems is likely to be capable of handling actual problems when they occur.

This chapter has been prepared with this philosophy in mind. Although normal and emergency procedures are presented separately in your Pilot's Operating Handbook and in this text, they are both integral parts of your aeronautical knowledge. An actual airborne emergency is no place to *begin* to learn your emergency procedures.

Before we survey emergency situations, let us review the three general rules that apply to any airborne emergency:

1. Maintain control of the aircraft.
2. Analyze the situation and take proper action.
3. Land as soon as conditions permit.

MAINTAINING EMERGENCY SKILLS

You will practice simulated emergencies throughout your flight training. These experiences develop the *habits* you will exhibit when a real emergency occurs. Reviewing emergency procedures on a regular basis is the most effective way to ensure that the correct habits are developed and reinforced. The FAA considers regular refresher training *essential* for pilots who fly the paying public. Airline and charter pilots are required to take training every 6 months. The regulations for private pilots are considerably less restrictive, requiring a review of piloting skills only every 2 years (the Biennial Flight Review). Conscientious pilots, especially those who fly infrequently, refresh their skills with an instructor *at least* once a year.

Common Causes of Emergencies

Weather causes pilots more problems than any other single aspect of flying. This is true no matter how much experience a pilot has had. Both students and airline captains, both instrument-rated and noninstrument-rated pilots, experience weather-related troubles. Historically, about one-half of all aviation accidents are weather related. The other causes of accidents cover the entire spectrum of possibilities, from pure mechanical failures to careless and reckless flying to flying while intoxicated. In addition, the following three factors are commonly cited as contributing to aviation accidents:

1. Inadequate preflight preparations or planning, or both.
2. Failure to obtain or maintain flying speed (another way of saying failure to maintain control of the airplane).

3. Improper inflight decision making or planning.

The unfortunate and tragic aspect of most accidents is that they are *preventable*. Good judgment and emergency procedures can be taught to pilots. Pilots who use the former rarely need the latter. Pilots who learn both can usually handle the unpreventable emergency that may confront even the most careful pilot.

Compound Emergencies

A single problem or malfunction rarely constitutes an emergency; however, when a number of simple problems occur simultaneously, or in rapid succession—a **compound emergency**—the situation changes drastically. A pilot can usually retain control of the situation until three or more problems confront him or her. At that point, judgment and performance are affected by stress. The more stress you are experiencing, the poorer your judgment and performance. When the situation demands decisions and/or actions that are beyond your current level of capability, an accident is likely to be the result.

Unfortunately, the appearance of one problem often leads to others, especially when one of the problems is weather. In good weather, your position and fuel situation are probably monitored constantly, and the symptoms of carburetor ice would be noticed as soon as they occurred. A pilot distracted by a deteriorating weather situation is more likely to become disoriented or to allow carburetor ice to develop or to overlook a diminishing fuel supply. The stress caused by marginal weather can also cause poor performance—even outright errors—when an emergency requiring immediate action occurs. If unnoticed carb ice is allowed to develop into power loss, will the pilot react correctly and put on the carb heat?

The solution to such dilemmas is never to let more than two problems confront you at one time. In essence, this means that as soon as a second thing goes wrong during a flight, either request assistance to solve the problems or land as soon as practicable. The whole idea is either to find solutions or to get you on the ground before stress can erode your performance and judgment to critical levels.

As pilots gain experience, many become overconfident in their power to handle "anything." They do not consider a couple of problems significant and tend to let the list grow before acknowledging that an emergency exists. Some may attempt to nurse an ailing airplane back to health in flight; some may postpone a sensible precautionary landing because it is not their final destination. A pilot receives no bonus points from anyone for "nearly making" the destination when a suitable diversionary field was available en route.

EMERGENCY LANDINGS

For many people, the term *emergency landing* evokes the image of a barnstormer asking for directions (or a wrench) in a farmer's field or a disabled airliner sliding to a stop on a bed of foam. In reality, most emergency landings take less dramatic forms. In only rare instances do they meet the stereotype of an immediate forced landing as depicted in movies. Throughout this chapter we recommend various actions in response to certain emergency situations, such as "land as soon as possible" or "land immediately." The following are definitions of the relative urgency of these recommendations:

1. *Land as soon as practicable* means to land at the nearest airport with suitable facilities for your airplane and emergency condition. It implies that you are capable of continued flight and navigation until such a facility can be reached.

2. *Land as soon as possible* means that you should locate the nearest airport and land at once, without regard for facilities. Safety requires that the airplane be put on the ground as soon as possible, although it is not necessary to make an off-airport landing.

3. *Land immediately,* sometimes called a **precautionary forced landing,** means that continued flight—even to the nearest airport—might not be possible and that an attempt to do so might result in an uncontrollable condition. However, it does imply that power is available to the airplane and some maneuvering is possible. With this latitude, a superior forced landing site can be selected and a nearly normal approach and landing made.

4. A **forced landing** is usually associated with the complete failure of the engine. Under these circumstances the airplane will land very soon whether the pilot wishes it or not. Unlike the precautionary landing, there is no power available for a go-around should one be necessary. The selection of the landing site and the approach to it are critically important.

RECOGNIZING AND HANDLING AN EMERGENCY

Your knowledge of your airplane and its systems is the most important factor in recognizing problems. Your skill, experience, and judgment will determine how the problem is handled. As you will see, not every problem is an emergency; however, every problem has the potential of contributing to an emergency.

When faced with a serious threat, the human mind often reacts by invoking powerful defense mechanisms. There is, at first, a period of denial, a refusal to acknowledge that the threat is real. This is not the same as not believing the information being shown on a gauge. Denial begins when you realize that the situation is real: your mind says "No!—this is not really happening to me." Eventually, the reality of the situation will be accepted.

The next stage is anger. It is normal to experience anger whenever your authority is challenged and this threat is overwhelming your control over your flight. Even though the anger is justifiable, getting angry will not solve the problem.

Soon after the rush of anger, there may be some confusion or indecision: "What do I do now?" Even if you know very well what to do, your mind may be processing so many perceptions and feelings at this point that no useful decisions come out. An observer might perceive your state as inaction, or "freezing at the controls." In reality, the problem is too much action—all of it mental, none of it physical. You can count on your training and habits to take over and control your actions, regardless of your mental state, so you can see why it is so important to develop and maintain these habits and skills.

Everyone experiences these feelings to some extent whenever threatened. Every individual reacts differently. The purpose of discussing them is to point out that they are normal, in fact an unavoidable part of being human. In general, these first feelings will pass quickly if you are prepared. If not, you may tend to dwell on one of them, wasting valuable time.

Verifying Instrument Indications

Your flight training will teach you how to respond correctly when the engine loses power in flight. These procedures are also discussed later in this chapter. But what do you do when the engine seems to be running fine, yet you notice unusual engine instrument indications? For instance, you notice that the oil pressure gauge suddenly reads zero! You realize, of course, that if this gauge is accurate, engine failure is imminent. But perhaps it is just a malfunctioning gauge.

The general rule in a situation like this is to check the reading from one instrument with other, verifying indications. In this example, you should check oil temperature and cylinder head temperature. If they also indicate a problem, land as soon as possible. If you are convinced that engine failure is in progress, or if the confirming indication is a partial power loss, then land immediately. Unusual vibrations, sounds, or smells in the cockpit may be enough to confirm a problem. *Any* other indication that a problem exists should be cause for action. Of course, if your survey reveals nothing unusual, then continue to monitor the situation and (for now) assume that the gauge is wrong.

Fuel gauges are notoriously inaccurate and undependable in general-aviation airplanes. This undependability is one of the reasons your instructor will teach you how to monitor your fuel use based on time, not the gauge. Familiarity with the particular airplane you are flying is essential, in order to correlate the fuel gauge indications to your time-based calculations. How can you confirm or dispel an unexpected low-fuel indication? A large fuel leak may leave enough evidence to be noticed, but a small leak may not. If you had just refueled, you may have a loose fuel cap. Be aware that on some fuel systems (primarily those that have a *Both* position on the fuel selector), one loose fuel cap can cause *both* tanks to lose fuel. Select the apparently unaffected tank, if you can. If you are convinced that you may actually be losing fuel, land as soon as possible.

Radio Malfunctions

For most VFR flights, failure of any of the radios—navigation or communication—should present nothing more than an inconvenience to you. However, when flying in airspace where communications are required, such as an Airport Traffic Area (ATA) or TCA, or while participating in a TRSA, the situation gets more complex. (The following discussion assumes that radio failure is the only problem at hand.)

The procedures to use following radio failure within an ATA were discussed in Chapter 7. To refresh your memory: in this situation, enter the traffic pattern currently in use and wait for the tower to signal you with a light gun. The signals and their meaning are explained in FAR 91.77. You will rock your wings or flash your lights to indicate that you understand and will comply. Since you probably will not remember the signals when you really need them, it is not unusual to find a sticker in training airplanes listing the signals for quick reference. Many pilot supplies (clipboards, chart holders, and the like) also have the light signals listed for similar reasons. If you fly into controlled airports regularly, it is probably a good idea to have this type of reference available.

While flying within any radar service area (TCA or TRSA), the general rule is to maintain VFR and land as soon as practicable. If your destination is a large congested airport, it may be wise to land at another, less busy, local airport instead. The controller will observe your actions on the radar screen and may surmise the problem, but after you have landed always call the facility by phone to explain. The controller deserves this courtesy. It may also save a needless search and rescue operation, if the controller is not assured of the outcome of your flight.

Transponder-equipped aircraft have more options available to them, especially if you can still *receive* radio transmissions. First, set code 7700 for one minute, then change to code 7600 (the failed radio code). The controller will then ask you to "ident if you hear this transmission." If you ident, then two-way communications have been reestablished. You should also turn up the volume on your navigation radios because ATC will attempt to transmit on *all* frequencies you could or should be using. This nonstandard method (they talk; you ident if you understand and will comply) will usually allow the flight to continue to landing in a nearly normal manner.

If you cannot receive at all, continue to squawk 7600 for 15 minutes or until landing, whichever occurs first. If you are still airborne after 15 minutes, repeat code 7700 for one minute, then 7600 for 15 minutes. This procedure is necessary because some ARTCCs are not equipped to read code 7600 automatically. Again, it is probably wise to land at a less busy airport, if one is available.

Inflight Fires

An inflight fire is one of the most dangerous situations you can encounter. The source of the fire could be the power plant or fuel system, the electrical system, or the inside of the cabin. You must determine the source before you can attempt to extinguish the fire.

If the fire is in the engine compartment, you must, of course, shut off the fuel supply to the engine compartment—using both the fuel selector shutoff and mixture control. The goal of this procedure is to deprive the fire of fuel, so you can concentrate on the forced landing. If the oil system is on fire, this procedure will probably reduce the fire but will not eliminate it.

Shut off all heater vents. Some airplanes have a control that closes off all airflow into the cabin from the engine compartment. Smoke inside the cabin is usually difficult to eliminate or control. The fresh air vents may help, but if there is a fire in the cabin, they can easily make matters worse; the extra air may help feed the flames. There are no textbook answers, just your best judgment and experimentation (if time permits).

If smoke or flames outside the cabin interfere with visibility, it may help to put the airplane into a sideslip, probably to the left. This will help direct the smoke and/or flames away from the cockpit and the pilot's windshield. The slip will also help you lose altitude quickly, which is important. It is vital to get on the ground as quickly as possible before the fire spreads or causes structural failure.

Electrical fires can often be detected by a pungent acid-like odor in the cockpit. The odor may actually be detected before the fire breaks out. The first thing to do when an electrical overload or fire is suspected is to turn off the master switch. (Remember, this will not affect the engine.) If the indications of fire subside, you can proceed to investigate the problem further and continue the flight if you desire. If turning the master switch has no effect, you must make an immediate landing.

With the master switch off, you can troubleshoot electrical problems in the following manner: first, turn off each electrical component individually. Now turn the master switch back on. If the smoke, smell, or other indications of a problem return, turn it off and leave it off. If not, begin to turn components on, one at a time. Wait a few minutes after each item is activated. Eventually, you will identify the equipment causing the trouble. This technique allows you to use unaffected components for the remainder of your flight and may allow you to complete the flight as planned.

Any time fire is used in the cockpit—smoking being the most common use—there is a danger of a cabin fire. If an accident does produce fire in the cabin, douse it with liquids (coffee, soda, or the like) if they are on hand, unless the liquid might penetrate the electrical system. A portable fire extinguisher is the best solution here.

Fire Extinguishers

Many aircraft owners put a portable fire extinguisher aboard their aircraft. It should be permanently mounted in a position the pilot can reach without any unusual contortions. It must be secure and at the same time capable of being unlatched quickly and easily. Activation of the extinguisher must be simple and obvious. The device must be inspected regularly and recharged as necessary.

You should be aware, however, that the activation of a fire extinguisher within the confines of a cockpit can *cause* problems as well as solve them. It may be difficult to discharge the chemical at the source of the fire, so there is no guarantee that an extinguisher will solve the problem at all. Extinguishers that use carbon dioxide or certain dry chemicals can fill the cockpit with a chemical cloud, making it difficult to see or even to breathe. Therefore, the decision to use these types of devices is not automatic or straightforward. Extinguishers that use a chemical called *halon* are considered the best to use on an aircraft because the material comes out as a liquid mist, and there is no visible cloud.

THINKING SAFETY: FROM THE GROUND UP

The well-worn slogan "Safety is no accident" contains an important gem of truth. Safety in the skies is in large part the result of organized and conscientious efforts on the ground in flight planning rooms across the nation.

The Value of a Filed Flight Plan

Whenever you go flying, either locally or cross-country, it makes good sense to leave the details of your intended flight with someone on the ground. The idea, of course, is to be missed as soon as possible if you fail to arrive at your destination on time. If you have the misfortune to be involved in an accident, the sooner help arrives, the greater are your chances for survival.

The chapters on navigation explain how to plan a flight and file a VFR flight plan with a Flight Service Station. A filed flight plan is the FAA's record of your *intended* movements. A VFR flight plan must be activated by radio after takeoff.

On longer flights, especially when traversing relatively open country, it is a good idea to supplement your flight plan with **position reports** every 45 minutes to an hour. Simply call the nearest FSS, stating that you are on a VFR flight plan and reporting your current position.

In the unlikely event that your airplane fails to reach its destination as scheduled, the FAA reconstructs your probable path over the ground on the basis of your flight plan and any position reports you have made.

Forced Landing Procedures

There are two general kinds of forced landing: those that occur immediately after takeoff and those that occur after the airplane has gained a reasonable amount of altitude. (Note: the definition of *reasonable* is a judgment call by the pilot.)

The recommended action for power failure on the takeoff leg of the traffic pattern is to *land straight ahead*. It is acceptable to make a turn that is less than 90° in order to avoid obstacles or to select the best site that is basically ahead. However, *do not attempt to turn back to the runway*. Remember that maintaining control of the airplane is absolutely essential. A controlled arrival at a poor landing site is a better risk than arriving anywhere out of control.

A sudden failure of the power plant should trigger an almost automatic set of reactions. Whatever altitude you have gained will be your biggest asset, since the more altitude you have, the more time you will be allowed to choose a suitable landing site or to restart the engine, if that is possible. We will divide the forced landing procedure into five phases and look at each in turn (see Figure 16.1): immediate actions required, choosing a

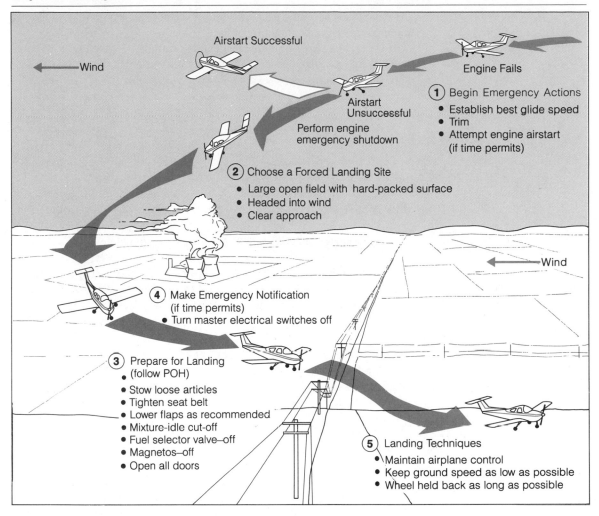

Wind

Airstart Successful

Engine Fails

(1) Begin Emergency Actions
- Establish best glide speed
- Trim
- Attempt engine airstart
  (if time permits)

Airstart
Unsuccessful

Perform engine
emergency shutdown

(2) Choose a Forced Landing Site
- Large open field with hard-packed surface
- Headed into wind
- Clear approach

Wind

(4) Make Emergency Notification
(if time permits)
- Turn master electrical switches off

(3) Prepare for Landing
(follow POH)
- Stow loose articles
- Tighten seat belt
- Lower flaps as recommended
- Mixture-idle cut-off
- Fuel selector valve—off
- Magnetos—off
- Open all doors

(5) Landing Techniques
- Maintain airplane control
- Keep ground speed as low as possible
- Wheel held back as long as possible

landing site, preparation for landing, emergency notification, and landing techniques.

Immediate actions.   Your Pilot's Operating Handbook will give you the specific procedures to follow for any type of engine malfunction. Not all power plant malfunctions necessitate a forced landing, and not all power losses are total. Most modern airplane engines are quite rugged even when damaged internally, and they may run for a considerable period of time before failing completely.

In general, the procedure outlined in your Pilot's Operating Handbook will probably be something like this:

Establish the best gliding speed. Any variation from this speed will significantly degrade your gliding distance, so trim the airplane to hold it.

Figure 16.1 Forced landing procedures.

Trimming is important because your attention will be divided among a number of other activities.

If smoke, flames, or oil are seen coming from the engine compartment, you should take the appropriate actions. Otherwise, the following actions should be taken immediately, and from memory (this is only an example; refer to your Pilot's Operating Handbook for the exact procedures to follow):

1. Carburetor heat—ON. (Carb ice is the most common cause of power loss.)

2. Mixture—RICH.

3. Fuel selector—Fullest tank, or Both (depending on the type of aircraft).

4. Check magnetos. Select all three positions: L, R, Both. If there is a difference, leave the switch on the best one. If not, leave it on Both.

These actions should take only a few seconds to complete.

Choose a landing site. You should try to look for and choose a site while taking the immediate actions just outlined, especially if you are at a low altitude. What is important to look for? First, select a site within easy gliding distance. Trying to stretch your glide is usually unwise. Remember, arriving *under control* is your highest priority. Next, do your best to land into the wind. This will reduce your ground speed as much as possible, reducing the energy you must dissipate while stopping. Finally, select the best surface available. A hard and smooth surface, like a lightly traveled highway, is ideal. A good surface makes wind direction less critical. Avoid soft ground if possible, because the airplane tends to dig into the soft surface and stop abruptly or flip over. Do not be concerned with damage to the airplane. Airplanes can be replaced; *you* cannot.

Preparations for landing. At this point you should secure the engine if this has not already been done. This means shutting off the fuel supply to the engine with both the fuel selector and mixture control and turning the magneto switch to OFF. (Leave the airplane master switch ON so that you can continue to use the radios, transponder, and flaps, if they are electric.)

Since you may be landing on an unpaved surface, the airplane will decelerate more quickly than on a normal runway. Be sure that your seat belt and your passengers' are fastened securely (the tighter the better), and if shoulder harnesses are available, be sure they are worn. Many harnesses have an inertial reel that automatically locks when transverse Gs are sensed (that is, when the body leans forward suddenly). Some installations recommend that the pilot lock the harness manually as an added precaution. Stow any loose items that may be lying around the cockpit, such as flight computers, calculators, plotters, thermoses, or flight publications. These can become projectiles during a forced landing. Also, if you wear sunglasses or eyeglasses, it may be best to remove them as you cross the landing threshold unless you cannot see without them. If your emergency locator transmitter (ELT) has an activation switch in the cockpit, turn it on. Some airplane manufactuers recommend that you lower the flaps once the landing is assured. This will reduce your stalling speed and allow a lower ground speed at touchdown. Follow the Pilot's Operating Handbook procedures for your airplane. At this point you should turn off the airplane's master electrical switch, securing the rest of your airplane's systems. Last, unlatch all doors. To ensure that the doors cannot jam shut, it is also a good idea to stick a map or coat sleeve (or anything) in the door opening.

Emergency notification.   If time permits, you should set code 7700 on your transponder and broadcast your predicament over the appropriate communication frequency. You may already be tuned into a tower, ARTCC, FSS, approach or departure control, or a nearby UNICOM. If so, use that frequency since it may well bring immediate response. If you are not tuned in, use the standard emergency frequency—121.5. (Emergency communications procedures are discussed later in this chapter.) Remember, do this only if it does not interfere with the preparation and execution of the forced landing.

Landing techniques.   Since you will have practiced landings with and without engine power, you can expect the forced landing flare and touchdown to be similar to landing without power. While it is important to obtain the slowest possible forward speed prior to touchdown, it is crucial that the airplane be controlled and controllable throughout the landing maneuver. This means that it is far better to touch down a little bit fast than to stall prematurely. Premature stalling is a major cause of unsuccessful forced landings. Sometimes the stall is precipitated by a last-minute decision to change fields. You must remember that banking the aircraft causes the wings to lose some of their vertical lift, and as a result your vertical speed (rate of descent) will increase. If you try to check this increased rate of descent with back pressure on the control wheel, you will simply lose airspeed and risk a stall. It is far better to continue into the field in a controlled, well-prepared approach that to improvise at the last minute. After touchdown, hold the control wheel well back to keep the airplane's weight off the nosewheel (with tricycle gear airplanes) for as long as possible.

Emergency Locator Transmitter

Most general-aviation aircraft are required to carry a functional **emergency locator transmitter (ELT)** on all flights. These devices broadcast a distinctive signal on emergency channels and are used as homing beacons by rescue aircraft. If the battery is fully charged, your ELT will broadcast for 48 hours in a wide range of climatic conditions. ELTs are constructed to withstand considerable G forces and so should operate regardless of any damage done to the airframe during the landing. They also have a G-sensing switch that activates the transmitter automatically, though you should play it safe and use the manual switch if possible.

ELT signals are now monitored worldwide, by special satellites. These extremely sensitive receivers pick up virtually all ELT signals and relay position information to the Search and Rescue Coordination Center (SARCC) at Scott Air Force Base in Illinois.

One of the unfortunate facts about ELTs is that the vast majority of activations are inadvertent. The SARCC personnel waste a huge amount of time and effort tracking down false ELT signals. The satellites have increased their workload because they receive signals previously unnoticed by ground stations. As pilots, we can prevent most, if not all, of this wasteful effort. After each flight, tune in 121.5 on your Comm radio and listen for a minute. An ELT signal is an unmistakable warbling tone. If you hear one, check *your* ELT by turning the switch to the OFF position. If the signal ceases, your transmitter was inadvertently transmitting. Always place the switch back to the ARM position after such a test. The tone should not return. If it does, turn it off again and have the unit repaired. If your ELT is not the source of the transmissions, report your findings to the airport manager or to the nearest FSS.

Of course, you should also verify on a regular basis that your ELT works. Regulations permit the activation of an ELT for testing during the first 5 minutes of every hour. The test must be limited to one or two "sweeps" of the transmitted tone.

Ground-to-Air Visual Signals

If your forced landing site is remote, your approach may not have been witnessed by any bystanders and you may have to wait for aerial search-and-rescue aircraft. If the terrain is exceptionally rugged, you may face a further delay while ground rescuers make their way to your location. Since you will probably be spotted by a rescue aircraft first, you may want to inform them of your party's needs or condition. Figures 16.2 and 16.3 show the standard ground-to-air codes for this communication.

Survival Procedures and Equipment

Unless you have some reason to believe that your airplane will not be found by search aircraft—for example, if it is hidden by trees or snow—you should plan to stay near it until you are rescued. Although a single airplane is a small object in a remote area of wilderness, a human being is smaller still. Your aircraft has many reflective surfaces (as well as its ELT) that can attract a searcher's attention. If there is no danger of fire from spilled fuel, the airplane also makes a convenient shelter from the elements. Many survivors of successful forced landings only delay their rescue by setting out to find help on their own. Unless you can see a source of assistance and are certain of your own physical capacity to make the trek, you should wait for help to come to you. It is easy to underestimate distances in wilderness areas, to overestimate one's own physical abilities, and to lose one's bearings in rough terrain.

Several good survival manuals are published commercially and by the government. Any pilot planning flights in a single-engine airplane over remote areas should obtain one of these manuals and carry it on each

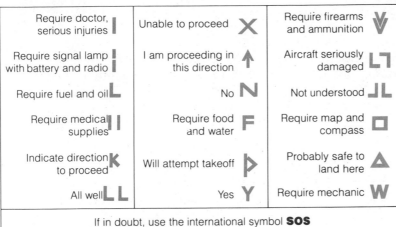

Figure 16.2 Ground-to-air visual emergency codes.

Require doctor, serious injuries **I**	Unable to proceed **X**	Require firearms and ammunition **V**
Require signal lamp with battery and radio **II**	I am proceeding in this direction **↑**	Aircraft seriously damaged **L⌐**
Require fuel and oil **L**	No **N**	Not understood **⌐L**
Require medical supplies **II**	Require food and water **F**	Require map and compass **□**
Indicate direction to proceed **K**	Will attempt takeoff **▷**	Probably safe to land here **△**
All well **LL**	Yes **Y**	Require mechanic **W**

If in doubt, use the international symbol **SOS**

1. Lay out symbols by using strips of fabric or parachutes, pieces of wood, stones, or any other available material.
2. Provide as much color contrast as possible between material used for symbols and background against which symbols are exposed.
3. Symbols should be at least 10 feet high or larger. Care should be taken to lay out symbols exactly as shown.
4. In addition to using symbols, every effort should be made to attract attention by means of radio, flares, smoke, or other available means.
5. On snow-covered ground, signals can be made by dragging items through the snow, shoveling, or tramping. Depressed areas forming symbols will appear black from the air.
6. A pilot should acknowledge a message by rocking wings from side to side.

appropriate flight. Survival kits are also available (see Figure 16.4). These kits are lightweight and compact. They contain the minimum equipment necessary for signaling rescue aircraft and supporting short-term survival in the wild. More elaborate kits contain drinking water, condensed food-stuffs, and shelter material, but these kits are correspondingly heavier and require more space. Pilots can put together their own kits inexpensively. Survival manuals suggest items that should be included.

Parachutes

New student pilots and nonpilots frequently misunderstand the functions of parachutes in general aviation. Most modern parachutes are used for sport and are somewhat different from the safety parachutes carried by military and aerobatic pilots. Like any other piece of flying gear, a parachute should never be carried by someone who has not been properly trained in its use. Without training, complications can arise in exiting an aircraft in flight; injuries due to opening shock and rough landings can occur; and parachute landings in high surface winds can be hazardous. Parachutes must be carried on aerobatic flights because there is a greater chance that the airplane may assume an unrecoverable flight attitude or may experience structural failure (due to excessive G-loads) that could preclude a controlled

Wave one arm overhead.

All ok; do not wait

Make throwing motion.

Use drop message

Wave both arms across face.

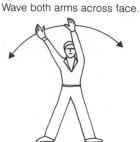

Do not attempt to land here

Cup hands over ears.

Our receiver is operating

Both arms forward
horizontally, squatting and
point in direction
of landing; repeat.

Land here

White cloth waved
vertically

Yes

White cloth waved
horizontally

No

Both arms vertical

Pick us up;
plane abandoned

Use only when a life
is at stake.

Need medical
assistance; urgent

One arm horizontal

Can proceed shortly;
wait if practicable

Both arms horizontal

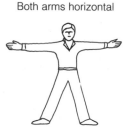

Need mechanical help
or parts; long delay

Fishtail plane.

No

Pilot Responses

Dip nose of plane
several times.

Yes

- Stand in the open when you make the signals.
- Be sure that the background, as seen from the air, is not confusing.
- Go through the motions slowly and repeat each signal until you are positive
  that the pilot understands you.

Figure 16.3 *(opposite)* Ground-to-air visual emergency signals.

Figure 16.4 Typical survival kit.

landing. In such cases, the pilot is better off using a parachute for a safe descent. For all other flights, however, these G forces are not experienced, and the chance of structural damage or uncontrollable unusual attitudes is minimal. Therefore, pilots are almost always better off staying with their airplane.

ASSISTANCE FOR LOST PILOTS

Being lost is an emergency condition. It means that you have tried but are unable to fix your location by reference to visual or radio checkpoints. At this point, every minute you delay by *not* considering the situation an emergency and asking for assistance is one less minute of fuel available or another few miles flown farther off course. It is helpful to remember the pilot's **"four Cs,"** which are useful reminders for actions required in many other kinds of emergencies as well: *climb, communicate, confess, comply* (see Figure 16.5).

1. *Climb* when possible to improve your radio reception and the range of your transmissions. Sometimes this alone will put you within range of a radio aid and allow you to proceed direct or establish a fix. It will also increase the likelihood of your airplane being picked up on ATC radar, especially in areas of high terrain. Obviously, you do not want to change your altitude if doing so would take you out of VFR conditions.

2. *Communicate* over the appropriate radio channel, explaining your situation as concisely as possible. If other conditions that might compound your emergency seem imminent, such as flight into instrument conditions or a low level of fuel, relay that information too. A format for emergency communications is provided in the next section of this chapter.

3. *Confess* your predicament. Many pilots feel chagrined about failing to make regular position checks or being uncertain of VOR orientation

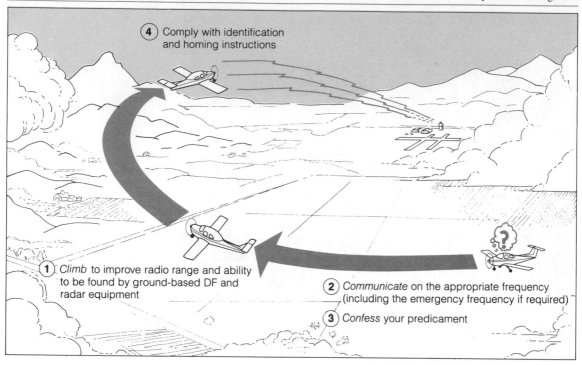

④ Comply with identification
and homing instructions

① Climb to improve radio range and ability
to be found by ground-based DF and
radar equipment

② Communicate on the appropriate frequency
(including the emergency frequency if required)

③ Confess your predicament

Figure 16.5 The "four Cs" for lost
pilots.

procedures. This chagrin is usually justified, and if the episode results in
a safer, more conscientious pilot (instead of an accident), then it might be
considered a regrettable but valuable learning experience. But feelings of
embarrassment and chagrin must not prevent a pilot from seeking help. It
is better to ask for assistance in haste and repent at leisure, with the airplane
safely on the ground.

4. *Comply* with instructions you receive. This sounds obvious, but in a
stressful situation it will take real concentration. Assistance from the ground
is useless unless you act upon it. You will be given headings to fly and
probably asked to describe indications from your navigation radios. A transponder code may be issued if radar service is possible. Remember that
you are still pilot-in-command and must remain clear of clouds, ground
obstructions, and other airplanes at all times.

Direction-Finding Steers

Many FSS and ATC facilities are equipped with radios that can home in
on your radio transmissions. This **direction-finding (DF) steer** can be
considered a ground-based ADF able to indicate the relative bearing from
the ground station to you. The DF operator will direct you to "key your
mike" (depress the microphone switch) for a specified number of seconds
or will ask you to count. This action provides a suitable signal to detect.

This single line of position must be crossed with another to establish
your location. This is usually done by one of the following methods:

1. The DF operator will obtain a bearing from another DF station that can receive your transmissions.

2. You will be asked to tune in a nearby VOR, center the needle using the OBS knob, and relay the resulting bearing.

3. You will be asked to describe any prominent landmarks or terrain features and their relative position to your heading.

The DF operator will locate you, and give you headings to the nearest appropriate airport (often the one assisting you). Your progress will be monitored by the same method used to locate you.

Feelings About Being Lost

Getting lost in flight is not ascribable to bad luck but rather to your own carelessness or oversight. The anger, fear, and contrition you may feel about it, however, do not solve the problem or lessen the danger. Fear of ridicule or even punishment is insufficient grounds to continue trying to orient yourself in a steadily deteriorating situation. Ask for emergency assistance as soon as you realize that your own efforts will not be successful. Do not wait until you are dangerously low on fuel or until the clouds around you or below you have no openings.

COMMUNICATIONS DURING EMERGENCIES

It is a rare emergency that will leave you without a calm, knowledgeable, and empathetic voice at the other end of the radio. Since normal communications frequencies may be saturated with traffic, emergency frequencies have been established for both VHF and UHF radio bands. These frequencies are always monitored by most control towers, Air Route Traffic Control Centers, and FSS facilities. Because of this constant surveillance, emergency channels are frequently referred to as **guard frequencies.** The VHF emergency frequency is 121.5; the UHF emergency frequency is 243.0.

These frequencies have been set aside for the exclusive use of aircraft in distress and should not be used for any other purpose. If you declare an emergency on another communications frequency, you may be asked to switch to guard for further communications in order to free the normal channel for routine traffic. If your airplane is equipped with dual receivers, it is a good practice on cross-country flights to tune one of them to 121.5 while you are using the other for normal communications. That way you can assist the FAA by listening for aircraft in distress or ELT signals or have the channel available for immediate use yourself if the necessity arises.

The Content of an Emergency Message

Rather than delay your message to figure out the proper wording, you should transmit your distress call at once, in plain English. In order to be useful, the message should have at least the following elements:

1. Who you are (your aircraft number).

2. Where you are (to the best of your knowledge).

3. What your problem is and the kind of assistance you need.

If you do not receive an immediate response, you may want to repeat **mayday, mayday, mayday** before restating your message. This is the international distress call, derived from the French expression *m'aidez,* "aid me," and should only be used when you are declaring an emergency. If you want assistance but do not consider your situation an emergency, use the words **pan, pan, pan** instead. Any aircraft or ground station that receives either of these phrases will offer assistance immediately.

Clarity is essential for *any* communication, and it is especially important during an emergency, where time is precious. Your message must be coherent and understandable if anyone is to assist you. You must be capable of receiving, understanding, and acting on radioed instructions. Obviously, all of this takes time, which is why it is so important to enlist help as soon as you realize you have a problem.

The Role of the Transponder

If you have established radio contact with ATC or FSS, you may be given a transponder code to verify your position with radar. If you are unable to communicate with anyone on the ground, set code 7700 on your transponder (when time permits). This special code triggers an immediate alarm on any ATC radar receiving the signal. Furthermore, the recorded path of that signal can be used by search and rescue personnel to help locate you, if necessary.

GENERAL RULES FOR FLYING SAFELY

Throughout this book we have referred to "safe and efficient" operations. This is because there may be times when you, as pilot-in-command, may feel pressured to forgo a safer procedure in favor of a less laborious and seemingly more expedient action. After a while, this sort of compromise becomes ingrained in a pilot's flying habits. It becomes impossible for the individual to tell where conscious expediency leaves off and carelessness begins. These are the pilots who are apt to be surprised, confounded, and eventually panicked by airborne emergencies. If flying safety is to have any meaning at all—and it does for most pilots—it must be learned as any other flying skill is learned and practiced in the course of every flight. If safety becomes an unused skill, you will be unable to use it to rescue yourself from a potentially serious situation.

The FAA Accident Prevention Program offers this short checklist as a daily guide for safe piloting:

Know your limits, physiologically and technically. Expand your skills and broaden your experience in a rational manner. Experience is the best teacher only when you have initially received the appropriate training.

Use a checklist. Human memory is fallible, particularly when performing routine tasks. It is easy to allow your concentration to be broken momentarily and to forget a necessary step. During an emergency, perform the actions required immediately from memory and then refer to your emergency procedures checklist as time permits.

Preplan your flight. Prepare a thorough flight plan, file the flight plan, open the flight plan with the FSS, fly the plan, communicate any changes as they occur, and close the plan on arrival at your destination.

Thoroughly check your airplane. A thorough check should be made *before every flight.* Many equipment malfunctions that occur in flight could have been detected on the ground.

Know your airplane's systems. An imminent emergency is no time to begin to take an interest in how your airplane works. Take pride in your knowledge of its systems and equipment and keep that knowledge sharp by frequent study and review. Use the required Biennial Flight Reviews to brush up on subject areas that are dim in your memory.

Know your airplane's performance limits. Do not expect your airplane to do things it was not designed to do. Respect its limitations and use its strengths to maximum advantage. Fly the airplane according to its Pilot's Operating Handbook data—not too timidly and not to aggressively, but properly.

Perhaps the best advice for ensuring a long career of safe and enjoyable flying is to cultivate a personal *challenge and response system.* Learn to ask yourself: "Am I doing the reasonable or required thing in a reasonable and proper way?" If you can answer this question affirmatively each time it is asked, then you are probably managing the risks of flying in a competent, professional manner. With such a positive attitude toward flying safety, you should always be pleased with your decision to accept our *invitation to fly.*

Congratulations on becoming a pilot!

KEY TERMS

compound emergency

direction-finding (DF) steer

emergency locator transmitter
  (ELT)

forced landing

four Cs

guard frequency

mayday

pan

precautionary forced landing

PROFICIENCY CHECK

1. What are the three general rules for handling any airborne emergency?

2. What factors are most frequently cited by the NTSB in aviation accidents?

3. What is a compound emergency? How can pilots cause their own compound emergencies?

4. While proceeding outbound from a VOR station you notice that the Off flag suddenly appears and the identification signal falls silent. Do you have a VOR malfunction? How would you begin to troubleshoot this situation?

5. Describe the four kinds of emergency landings and give examples of situations that might lead to each.

6. What are the three immediate actions you should take in the event of an engine failure?

7. What are the criteria for choosing an appropriate forced landing site?

8. Some pilots refuse to believe that being lost is an emergency condition until they compound the situation by flying into adverse weather, by allowing themselves to be caught by darkness, or by continuing until they reach a low fuel condition. What are the "four Cs" and how do they help a lost pilot become reoriented?

9. What is the VHF emergency frequency? What are the ATC transponder codes to use in case of (a) a general emergency and (b) communications radio failure?

10. What are the international radio code words for (a) an aircraft in distress and (b) a suspected or probable emergency?

11. Pilot A is a very confident pilot who passed the private pilot's check ride with high marks and compliments. Pilot A is also comfortable about skipping many flight planning details, though the weather and the airplane's preflight condition are always checked before a flight. Pilot A believes real experience comes from flying, not from books. Pilot B enjoys flying but has less natural talent at the controls and had to work hard to pass the private pilot's flight check. Pilot B is cautious about responding to potential emergencies, spends a great deal of time studying the airplane's manuals, and always files a flight plan. Who is the safer pilot, pilot A or pilot B? Explain your answer.

DICTIONARY
Aeronautical Terms

In this section all technical words, phrases, and concepts that appear in **boldface** type in the text are defined. This includes all key terms listed at the end of each chapter. In addition, certain terms that are frequently encountered by private pilots have also been included. Terms within definitions that are **boldface** appear elsewhere in the Dictionary.

AAS See **Aeronautical Advisory Station**.

abbreviated briefing A preflight weather briefing through which a pilot may supplement information obtained from other sources, update a previous briefing, and/or obtain specific weather information.

absolute altitude The altitude of an airplane above ground level (AGL).

AC See **convective outlook**.

accelerated stall An aerodynamic **stall** encountered during flight maneuvers of greater than one positive G load factor. The stalling airspeed is *higher* than that encountered during a wings-level, unaccelerated stall.

acceleration The time rate of change of velocity. Since velocity includes the elements of both speed and direction, a change in either results in an acceleration.

acceleration-deceleration error The deflection of the **magnetic compass** card from the horizontal caused by aircraft acceleration or deceleration and the vertical component of the earth's magnetic field. This error is most apparent when an aircraft is flying on an easterly or westerly heading, resulting in an apparent *northward* turn during accelerations and an apparent *southward* turn during decelerations.

acceleration illusion See **oculogravic illusion**.

accessory drive pad A cluster of interlocking gears and component mounting structure located at the aft end of the **crankcase**. The accessory drive pad provides a source of rotary motion for a variety of engine-driven equipment (fuel, oil, and vacuum pumps) as well as electrical generators, instrument signal generators, and other key components used by the aircraft's support systems.

active runway The runway(s) at an airport that are currently being used for takeoffs and landings.

acute fatigue The result of several nights with little sleep.

ADF See **automatic direction finder**.

adiabatic lapse rate The rate of temperature decrease in the atmosphere as air rises. The lapse rate for dry, unsaturated air is 3 degrees Celsius per 1000 feet. The lapse rate for moist or saturated air varies from 1.1 degrees to 2.8 degrees Celsius per 1000 feet. The average or standard lapse rate is 2 degrees Celsius (3.5 degrees Fahrenheit) per 1000 feet.

advection fog Fog formed when warm, moist air moves over a colder surface, cooling the air to its **dew point**, causing **condensation** and fog.

adverse yaw The **yawing** of the airplane's nose away from the direction of turn caused by the excess asymmetrical drag of the depressed **aileron** on the upraised wing.

Advisory Circulars (ACs) A series of FAA books, booklets, and flyers of a nonregulatory nature dealing with a variety of specialized aeronautical topics.

aerodynamics That branch of science and engineering dealing with the motion of the air and other gaseous fluids and with the forces acting on bodies in motion relative to such fluids.

aerodynamic twist A wing design technique that incorporates a gradual change in the wing **chord line** such that the airfoil sections near the tip are continually flying at a *lower* **angle of attack** than those near the root. This tends to produce a wing with gentler stalling characteristics and improved handling at low speeds.

Aeronautical Advisory Station (AAS) A radio facility (often operated by a **fixed-base operator**) chartered by the FAA to provide pilots with advice and information about safe aircraft flight and ground operations in and around that facility. See also **UNICOM**.

aerospace medicine That branch of medical science that deals with **aviation physiology**.

AFOS See **Automated Field Observing System**.

AGL   Above ground level.

agonic line   The **isogonic line** that indicates no magnetic **variation**.

ailerons   Primary aerodynamic control surfaces usually located on the outboard trailing edge of the wing, hinged to move up and down, producing a rolling **moment** about the airplane's **longitudinal axis**.

air   The major constituent of the earth's **atmosphere**, composed of a mechanical mixture of gases: nitrogen (78 percent), oxygen (21 percent), argon (.9 percent), and other gases (0.1 percent).

aircraft   A weight-carrying structure, supported by its own buoyancy or by the dynamic action of the air against its surfaces, intended for navigation in the air.

Air Defense Identification Zone (ADIZ)   The area of airspace over land or water, extending upward from the surface, within which the ready identification, location, and control of the aircraft are required in the interest of national security.

airfoil   Any member or surface of an aircraft whose major function is a dynamic interaction with the airflow to accomplish a specific purpose.

airframe   The structure of an aircraft (excluding the power plant).

airframe and power plant (A&P) mechanic   An FAA-certified specialist who repairs and maintains aircraft.

air induction system   A system of ducts and filters that draws air into the engine compartment from the atmosphere.

airline transport pilot   A pilot certified to act as **pilot-in-command** of flights involving airline operations.

Airman's Information Manual (AIM)   A publication containing basic flight information and air traffic control procedures for pilots operating in the national airspace system (conterminous United States only).

air mass   An extensive body of air having uniform properties of moisture and temperature in a horizontal plane. Air masses can be identified and described according to their source regions: *continental*, those that form over land; *maritime*, those that form over water; and *arctic*, *polar*, *tropical*, or *equatorial*. Air masses are further categorized as *hot* or *cold* depending on their temperature relative to the surface over which they are moving.

air mass thunderstorm   See **thunderstorm**.

AIRMET (WA)   Literally, airmen's meteorological advisories released by the NWS and FAA as an inflight weather advisory service. These short-term forecasts deal with weather that could be hazardous to light aircraft, such as moderate icing; moderate turbulence; extensive areas where visibilities are less than 2 miles and/or ceilings are less than 1000 feet, including mountain ridges and passes; and winds exceeding 40 knots within 2000 feet of the surface.

air navigation   The art of determining the geographic position and maintaining the desired direction of an aircraft relative to the earth's surface.

airplane   An engine-driven, fixed-wing (heavier-than-air) aircraft that is supported in flight by the dynamic reaction of air against its wings.

Airport/Facility Directory   An FAA publication containing all airports, seaplane bases, and heliports open to the public, including communications data, navigation facilities, and certain special notices and procedures. The *Directory* is issued in seven volumes according to geographic area.

Airport Radar Service Area (ARSA)   Controlled airspace surrounding designated airports extending upward from the surface to approximately 4000 feet AGL for a 5-nautical-mile radius, and from about 1200 feet AGL to 4000 feet AGL from a 5-to-10-nautical-mile radius area. All other airspace out to a 20-mile radius is part of the ARSA's Outer Area. Exact limits vary depending on local radar coverage. These areas are depicted on aeronautical charts.

airport surveillance radar (ASR)   Approach control radar used to detect and display an aircraft's position in the terminal area, with a range of 60 miles. ASR provides range and azimuth information but does not provide elevation (or **glide slope**) data.

airport traffic area (ATA)   Unless otherwise specifically designated in FAR Part 93, that airspace within a horizontal radius of 5 statute miles from the geographical center of any airport at which a control tower is operating, extending from the surface up to, but not including, an altitude of 3000 feet above the altitude of the airport.

Air Route Traffic Control Center (ARTCC)   A facility established to provide air traffic control service to aircraft operating on IFR flight plans within controlled airspace and principally during the en route phase of flight. When equipment capabilities and controller work loads permit, certain advisory and assistance services may be provided to VFR traffic. There are currently 21 ARTCCs in the United States.

airship   A lighter-than-air aircraft that is powered and that has controls to direct its movements, such as a blimp or a dirigible.

airspeed   The speed of an aircraft relative to its surrounding **air mass**. See also **calibrated airspeed (CAS), indicated airspeed (IAS), true airspeed (TAS)**.

airspeed indicator   The cockpit instrument that tells a pilot how fast the airplane is moving through the air.

Air Traffic Control Radar Beacon System (ATCRBS)   A system consisting of an interrogator, an airborne **transponder**, and the controller's radarscope; also called *secondary surveillance radar*. The ground-based radar interrogator triggers a reply from the aircraft's transponder, which is displayed as a "target" on the radarscope, allowing positive identification and separation of transponder-equipped aircraft in the controller's sector.

air traffic control tower   A terminal facility that uses air/ground communications, visual signaling, and other devices to provide ATC services to airborne aircraft operating in the vicinity of an airport. The tower also controls aircraft on the ground operating in the airport's movement area.

airway   A control area or portion thereof established in the form of a corridor, the centerline of which is defined by **radio navigation** aids.

Airworthiness Directives (ADs)   Notices of compulsory maintenance, repair, modifications, or inspection issued against a particular type of design and model of aircraft. *AD* compliance records are kept with the aircraft's maintenance **logbooks**.

alert area   Airspace that may contain a high volume of pilot training activities or an unusual type of aerial activity—neither of which is hazardous to aircraft. Alert areas are depicted on aeronautical charts.

alternating current (AC)   Electric current that reverses its direction at regularly recurring intervals.

alternator   An electrical generator that produces **alternating current**.

altimeter The cockpit instrument that measures the height of the aircraft above a given reference plane, such as **mean sea level (MSL)**.

altimeter setting The barometric pressure reading used to adjust a pressure altimeter for variations in existing atmospheric pressure.

altostratus cloud A middle-altitude cloud with a sheetlike appearance whose base is between 6500 and 16,500 feet.

alveoli The tiny air sacs of the lungs through which gases are exchanged during **respiration**.

amber light A flashing light in the segmented circle, on top of the control tower, or on an adjoining building that indicates a right-hand traffic pattern is in effect.

ambient air The air surrounding the aircraft, the characteristics of which are not disturbed by its passage.

ambient temperature The temperature of the local **air mass** through which the aircraft is moving.

AME See **Aviation Medical Examiner**.

ammeter The cockpit instrument that displays **alternator** output in amps.

AMOS See **automatic meteorological observation stations**.

amperes (A) See **electric current**.

Amphibian An aircraft that can take off and land on either land or water.

ANDS The mnemonic (memory-assisting) device used by pilots to correct for **magnetic compass acceleration-deceleration error:** *Accelerate—North, Decelerate—South.*

angle of attack The acute angle measured between the **chord line** of an airfoil and the **relative wind**.

angle of incidence The angle between the mean **chord line** of the wing and the airplane's **longitudinal axis;** the angle (or "tilt") at which the wing is attached to the **fuselage** with respect to its leading and trailing edges. The angle of incidence is usually set to minimize **drag due to lift** at cruising airspeeds.

angle of interception The angular difference between the heading of the aircraft and the desired course.

anticollision light A flashing red or white light fixed to the **fuselage** of an aircraft to facilitate traffic separation under **visual meteorological conditions**.

anticyclone An area of high pressure whose winds are circulating in a clockwise direction.

antiknock value See **octane number**.

apparent precession See **precession**.

approved flight school See **FAA-approved flying school**.

area forecast (FA) Forecasts issued every 8 hours by several NWS offices serving the 50 states. The forecast includes expected weather for a 12-hour period and a more general outlook for an additional 6 hours. It describes areas of clouds and significant weather, ceilings, height of cloud bases and tops, surface visibilities, and the movement of major weather disturbances such as **thunderstorms** and **squall lines**. It also gives the heights of the freezing level and zones of expected icing and turbulence.

area navigation (RNAV) A method of navigation that permits aircraft operations on any desired course within the coverage of station-referenced navigation signals or within the limits of self-contained system capabilities. The aircraft proceeds from waypoint to waypoint, bypassing ground-based navigation facilities.

arm The distance from the datum of an item, measured along an aircraft's **longitudinal axis**. More generally, any distance over which a mass applies a force from a fulcrum.

ARTCC See **Air Route Traffic Control Center**.

artificial horizon See **attitude indicator**.

ashless dispersant (AD) oil The most widely used oil for general aviation aircraft engines.

ASR See **airport surveillance radar**.

asymmetric Gs Any combination of positive or negative and transverse or lateral Gs. They are most commonly encountered when rolling the airplane while pulling positive Gs.

ATA See **air traffic area**.

ATCRBS See **Air Traffic Control Radar Beacon System**.

ATIS See **Automatic Terminal Information Service**.

atmosphere The blanket of **air** and particulate matter that surrounds the earth.

atmospheric pressure The weight of the **atmosphere** measured in force per unit area taken at any height from the surface to its outer limits.

atomization The reduction of a liquid into a spray of fine particles; specifically, the atomization of liquid fuel into a combustible mixture of fuel and air.

attitude The position of an aircraft's axes with respect to the horizon.

attitude indicator A **gyroscopic instrument** that provides the pilot with a visual representation of the aircraft's attitude with respect to the horizon; also referred to as the *artificial horizon* or *gyro horizon*.

audio panel An integrated communications and navigation control panel.

autokinesis A sensory illusion that occurs when a stationary light, such as a beacon or ground light, is stared at for several seconds. The illusion is caused by eye movements themselves, resulting in a sense of relative motion.

Automated Field Observing System (AFOS) A system for distributing weather information using television screens to provide clear, easy-to-read displays at virtually the same time the information is released from the submitting station. AFOS will eventually be available at pilot weather briefing facilities throughout the NWS and FAA system, replacing older, slower teletype machines.

automatic direction finder (ADF) A radio receiver and directional (loop) and sense antennas that automatically receive low-frequency signals and display (on a **bearing indicator**) the bearing of the receiver relative to the transmitter.

automatic pilot (autopilot) A gyroscopic device that operates the aircraft's controls without attention from the pilot. Autopilots range from simple wing-leveler devices to fully coupled systems capable of flying the aircraft from takeoff to touchdown.

Automatic Terminal Information Service (ATIS) A continuous broadcast of prerecorded terminal area information of a noncontrol nature. ATIS provides arriving and departing pilots with essential but routine information (such as weather conditions, active runway, altimeter setting) without congesting controller frequencies. ATIS is usually broadcast over its own frequency and is available only at selected airports.

automatic weather observation stations (AWOS) Robot weather observation stations located in remote areas of land and sea. Their periodic transmission of meteorological data supplements other National Weather Service observations.

avgas See **aviation gasoline**.

aviation fuel A general term referring to all fuels refined for aeronautical use, including **aviation gasoline** and jet fuel (kerosene).

aviation gasoline (avgas)   Fuel refined specially for use in aeronautical internal combustion engines. Avgas is assigned an **octane number** and **performance number** and is identified at the pump as one of several fuel grades, which are color coded to prevent improper fueling. On occasion, a higher grade of avgas may be used in a particular engine, but a lower grade should never be used.

Aviation Medical Examiner (AME)   A physician trained in **aerospace medicine** empowered by the FAA to issue **medical certificates** to flight crews.

aviation physiology   The science that deals with the processes, activities, and phenomena of human life in the flying environment.

avionics   A contraction for the words *aviation electronics*; a general term used for electrically powered cockpit instruments, controls, and radio receiver/transmitter systems.

axis   See **lateral axis, longitudinal axis, vertical axis**.

azimuthal projection   A method of chart making in which the earth is viewed from the pole, with **lines of longitude** radiating outward like the spokes of a wheel.

azimuth card   A display of horizontal angular direction, beginning with 0 degrees and ending with 360 degrees.

baffles   Close-fitting, molded plates installed over aircraft engine **cylinders** to direct the air more efficiently over the cylinder's cooling **fins**.

balloon   A lighter-than-air aircraft that depends on air currents for movement.

bank   To roll the airplane about its **longitudinal axis** for the purpose of making a turn. In a level turn, the steeper the bank angle, the faster the rate of heading change and the higher the **load factor** placed on the airplane.

bank angle   The angle of the aircraft's lateral axis relative to the horizon.

barometer   An instrument that measures **atmospheric pressure**.

base leg   That portion of the airport **traffic pattern** flown at right angles to the landing runway off its approach end. The base leg normally extends from the **downwind leg** to the intersection of the extended runway centerline.

basic empty weight   The weight of the airplane with all listed equipment, hydraulic fluid, full engine oil (total amount of oil in the engine, sump, filter, cooler, and lines, with a full reading on the dipstick), and unusable fuel.

basic empty weight form   A form prepared by the manufacturer at the time the aircraft is delivered.

basic runway   A runway used for operations under Visual Flight Rules (VFR) consisting of centerline marking and runway direction numbers (with left, right, or center runway identifier letters as required).

basic T   The arrangement of flight instruments in most modern airplanes, with the **attitude indicator** at the center of the T, **airspeed indicator** to the left, **altimeter** to the right, and **heading indicator** below. This arrangement allows the pilot to check and correct the airplane's attitude while cross-checking the readings on the other flight instruments.

bearing   The horizontal direction to or from any point, usually measured clockwise from true north, magnetic north, or some other reference point, through 360 degrees. See also **azimuth card**.

bearing indicator   A cockpit instrument for use in **radio nav**igation, primarily with an **automatic direction finder (ADF)**. It consists of an **azimuth card** and rotating bearing pointer. The azimuth card may or may not be capable of rotating, with 0 degrees usually set under the instrument's top index. On some instruments, the azimuth card is slaved to a remote gyrocompass system and displays the aircraft **magnetic heading** under the top index. In either system, the bearing pointer always points to the station. See also **radio magnetic indicator**.

bends   See **decompression sickness**.

Bernoulli's Principle   The principle of physics that states that as the air velocity increases, the pressure decreases, and that as velocity decreases, pressure increases. This principle has been used to explain how a portion of aerodynamic **lift** is developed over the upper surface of an **airfoil**.

best angle of climb (V_x)   The **flight path** of an airplane that will give a maximum increase in altitude over a given horizontal distance.

best rate of climb (V_y)   The **flight path** of an airplane that will give a maximum increase in altitude for a given unit of time.

biplane   An airplane with two wings mounted one above the other, usually with some amount of "stagger," or overlap.

blackout   A physiological condition in which the volume of blood to the brain is reduced due to the presence of positive G forces to the point at which vision is not possible. Although vision is "blacked out," the brain is still conscious and capable of reasoning and sending commands to the limbs and other parts of the body.

blade elements   The different cross-sectional **airfoils** of a **propeller** blade.

blimp   An inflatable/deflatable **lighter-than-air aircraft** with engines for propulsion and **airfoils** for stabilization and control. See also **dirigible**.

boost pump   An electrically driven auxiliary pump in the fuel or oil system that provides additional pressure when needed, most commonly during takeoffs and landings.

bracketing   Choosing and following selected pairs of **pilotage** landmarks that fall on either side of the desired course line, making it virtually impossible to deviate from the intended route of flight.

buffet   Turbulent airflow over an aerodynamic surface that causes the controls affected to "shake"; usually accompanied by a pronounced rise in general **airframe** noise. Buffeting is most commonly associated with a developing airplane **stall** or a configuration inappropriate for a given airspeed, such as accelerating the airplane past the limiting airspeed for wing **flaps, cowl flaps,** and so on.

burble   Turbulent airflow across the top of an **airfoil** that has exceeded its maximum, or **critical angle of attack**, warning of an incipient **stall**. The burble is perceived in the cockpit as a high-frequency vibration in the **elevator** control system and is often audible above the general **airframe** noise. Wing burble commonly leads to general airframe **buffet** as the stall develops.

bus   The power distribution point to which a number of electrical circuits may be connected; also called **bus bar**.

butterfly valve   See **throttle valve**.

calibrated airspeed (CAS)   **Indicated airspeed (IAS)** corrected for installation errors, mechanical losses within the instrument itself, and position error; sometimes called *true indicated airspeed (TIAS)*. See also **airspeed**.

call sign The aircraft type and identification numbers (and letters) used for communications over the voice radio, such as "Skipper 37259."

camber The mean curvature of an **airfoil** from the leading edge to the trailing edge. Both upper and lower surfaces may have camber to some degree.

camshaft A rotating shaft driven through gears by the engine **crankshaft** that controls the sequence and timing of **intake** and **exhaust valve** movements.

carbon monoxide poisoning A physiological disorder caused by breathing air containing carbon monoxide (CO), a product of combustion found in engine exhaust gases. Effects are insidious and can lead to unconsciousness and death. Countermeasures include breathing fresh air or oxygen and landing immediately. Since the CO sticks to the oxygen-carrying **hemoglobin** in the blood, its effects can last for hours after the onset of symptoms.

carburetor The power plant component that mixes fuel and air together to form a combustible mixture. Most light airplane engines use a float-type carburetor that depends on a positive G environment for proper operation (hence such carburetors are generally not used on acrobatic airplanes). Carburetor subsystems include: accelerating system, **economizer system, idling system,** and **mixture control system.** These subsystems, plus the **throttle valve,** are the pilot's primary means of controlling the engine.

carburetor heat system The system that directs heated air into the carburetor to combat or prevent the formation of carburetor ice.

carburetor ice Ice on the walls and throttle valve of the carburetor that chokes off the flow of air and reduces power.

cardinal headings The cardinal points labeled on a compass using the initial for the first letter of each: N, S, E, and W.

CAS See **calibrated airspeed.**

CAT See **clear air turbulence.**

categorical outlook A classification of anticipated weather that may appear at the end of a **terminal forecast (FT).** It deals specifically with expected IFR, MVFR, VFR, or wind conditions and pertains to the last 6 hours covered by the forecast.

category (of aircraft) The broadest classification of aircraft. The FAA currently recognizes four categories: lighter-than-air, rotorcraft, glider, and airplane.

CD See **compass deviation.**

CDI See **course deviation indicator.**

ceiling (aircraft) The maximum altitude an aircraft is capable of attaining under specified operating conditions.

ceiling (weather) The height above ground of the lowest layer of clouds or obscuring phenomena that is reported as "broken," "overcast," or "obscuration," and not classified as "thin" or "partial."

ceilometer An electronic device that measures the height of cloud bases above the ground.

celestial navigation The determination of geographic position by reference to celestial bodies, usually accomplished by using a sextant, a celestial almanac, and an accurate clock.

cell (of circulation) See **three-cell circulation.**

center of gravity (CG) The point within an aircraft through which, for balance purposes, the force of gravity is assumed to act. The forward and aft travel of the CG (as determined by aircraft loading, servicing, and modification) is extremely important in determining aircraft performance and flying characteristics.

center of gravity envelope The set of weight and balance limitations assigned to an aircraft by its designers.

Certified Flight Instructor (CFI) A pilot who is certificated by the FAA to instruct students and other pilots.

CG See **center of gravity.**

CH See **compass heading.**

checklist A sequential list of steps to be accomplished in the operation of an aircraft and its equipment.

checkpoints Predetermined points in a flight where geographic positions are noted to confirm the proper progress of the flight.

chocks Durable wood or metal wedges placed under the wheels of an airplane to prevent its movement.

chord line A straight line drawn directly across the cross-section of an **airfoil** from leading edge to trailing edge. This imaginary line is the reference line from which the upper and lower contours (**camber**) of the wing are measured. The **angle of attack** is the acute angle between the chord of an airfoil and the **relative wind.**

chronic fatigue The continued functioning in a fatigued condition that can result in inattention to detail, slowed reactions, and a generally ambivalent attitude—even in regard to safety.

circuit Electrical components connected with a conductive material to form one or more complete electrical paths. When a source of electromotive force (voltage differential) is introduced, current flows in the circuit, allowing the electrical components to operate.

circuit breaker A protective device that opens a circuit automatically in the event that the current flow exceeds a preestablished limit.

cirriform cloud Any form of high cloud, including *cirrocumulus, cirrostratus,* and **cirrus,** whose base is above 16,500 feet.

cirrus clouds The main type of **cirriform clouds,** shaped like long, wispy horsetails. The average height of these clouds is 20,000 feet, but they can range higher.

class (of aircraft) Subdivision of category of aircraft based on similar operating characteristics.

clear air turbulence (CAT) Turbulence encountered in air when no clouds are present. The term is most commonly used to describe high-altitude **turbulence** associated with **wind shear** and operations near the **jet stream.**

clear ice Airframe ice formed when large, supercooled water droplets freeze on impact with the airplane's structure, building a blanket of colorless ice that conforms to the shape beneath it. Clear ice is most likely to form at temperatures between 0 degrees Celsius and -15 degrees Celsius, and in clouds with much vertical development. It can deform airfoils, damage highly stressed parts (such as propellers), and add considerable weight to the aircraft.

cloud Condensed water vapor visible in the air as an accumulation of minute water droplets suspended at low, medium, or high altitudes or in clouds of vertical development built through the process of convection. In subfreezing temperatures, clouds are composed of ice crystals.

col The neutral area between two highs and two lows; the intersection of a **trough** and a **ridge.**

cold front The boundary between two masses of air that indicates the place where cold air is replacing warmer air.

commercial aviation   That branch of aviation encompassing scheduled airline operations.

commercial pilot   A pilot certificated by the FAA to carry passengers and/or cargo for hire.

Common Traffic Advisory Frequency (CTAF)   The radio frequency to be used for airport advisory information at uncontrolled airports.

compass   See **magnetic compass**.

compass correction card   A cockpit placard showing the correct **magnetic compass headings** to "steer" to obtain a desired **magnetic heading** corrected for **compass deviation** errors.

compass deviation (CD)   Small errors in **magnetic compass headings** due to the influence of magnetized metal and electrical components within the aircraft. Magnetic compass headings are calibrated for each aircraft installation and placarded on a **compass correction card** or compass deviation card.

compass heading (CH)   The **magnetic heading** plus or minus the **compass deviation** correction value.

compass locator   A **nondirectional beacon (NDB) radio** facility operating in the 200 to 415 kHz band. When collocated with an **instrument landing system (ILS)** outer marker, the compass locator is called *LOM* (locator outer marker). When collocated with an ILS middle marker, it is called *LMM* (locator middle marker). Compass locators are given two letter aural identifiers and are frequently used with automatic direction finding (ADF) equipment.

compass rose   An azimuth circle aligned with magnetic north depicted on aeronautical charts or painted onto an airport ramp for use in setting or calibrating **magnetic compass** equipment.

compass variation   The fundamental error of all **magnetic compasses**: they point to magnetic rather than true north; also, the angular difference between true and magnetic north.

composite flying   The process of controlling an aircraft's attitude by cross-checking the flight instrument readings inside the cockpit with the real horizon outside; also known as *integrated flying*.

composite navigation   A practical combination of **pilotage** (visual or landmark), **dead reckoning** (computational), and **radio** (ground-based signal) **navigation**.

compound emergency   A situation in which more than one emergency condition is being experienced. Most compound emergencies are precipitated by pilot inaction or by preoccupation with one condition at the expense of others, such as flying into an area of poor weather while troubleshooting a mechanical problem.

condensation   The re-forming of water vapor into water.

condensation nuclei   Small particles suspended in the air onto which water vapor molecules adhere to form visible moisture, such as **clouds, fog,** or **precipitation**.

cone of confusion   The area above a **VOR** or **TACAN** station where the phased signals (radial or bearing) cannot be received due to the geometry of the station itself. The cone is fairly narrow at low altitudes and grows wider as altitude increases. Inside the cone, the **course deviation indicator (CDI)** swings from one side of the instrument case to the other (or "pegs out" and does not move at all), and the Off flag may appear, indicating a weak signal. VOR station passage over the cone is confirmed by the first positive change from To to From on the **To-From indicator**. Aircraft equipped with **DME** crossing VORTAC or TACAN stations note station passage at the time the indicator stops decreasing and begins increasing.

cones   Light sensors in the eye's retina that report color information to the brain. Cones are concentrated directly behind the iris, in the center of the retina. See also **retina** and **rods**.

configuration   The relative arrangement of an aircraft's parts. Configuration can be changed by design (such as by lengthening the **fuselage** and adding more passenger seats) or by the pilot (such as by removing existing passenger seats). The airplane's configuration also changes when the flaps and landing gear are lowered, since the "relative arrangement" of the airplane's parts is changed. Flight characteristics, performance, and weight and balance data are usually all affected by configuration changes.

connecting rod   The link that transmits the force from the **piston** to the **crankshaft** in a **reciprocating engine**. The unique, free-swinging connection of the piston end and the crankpin end allows for the conversion of the piston's up-and-down motion to the rotary motion of the crankshaft.

constant-speed propeller   A variable-pitch **propeller** that is controlled by a speed governor to maintain a selected engine rpm. Increased engine power (increased manifold pressure) during flight causes the propeller blade angle to be increased by the governor to absorb the additional power, while the rpm remains constant. The governor is controlled by the rpm lever in the cockpit.

continental control area (CCA)   The airspace of the 48 contiguous stages, the District of Columbia, and Alaska, excluding the Alaska Peninsula west of longitude 160°00′00′′W, at and above 14,500 feet MSL. The continental control area does not include the airspace less than 1500 feet above the surface of the earth or prohibited and restricted areas, other than the restricted areas listed in FAR Part 71.

control area   Airspace designated as colored federal airways, VOR federal airways, **terminal control areas**, additional control areas, and control area extensions, but not including the **continental control area**. Unless otherwise designated, control areas also include the airspace between a segment of a main VOR **airway** and its associated alternate segments. The vertical extent of the various categories of airspace contained in control areas are defined in FAR Part 71.

controlled airport   An airport with an operating control tower that supervises and coordinates the flow of ground and air traffic.

controlled airspace   Airspace designated as **continental control area, control area, control zone, terminal control area, transition area,** or **positive control area** within which some or all aircraft may be subject to air traffic control.

control zone   Controlled airspace that extends upward from the surface and terminates at the base of the **continental control area**. Control zones that do not underlie the continental control area have no upper limit. A control zone may include one or more airports and is normally a circular area with a radius of 5 statute miles and any extensions necessary to include instrument approach and departure paths.

convective current   An ascending or descending current of air.

convective outlook (AC)   An advisory that assesses the potential for severe and general thunderstorms for a 24-hour period.

convective SIGMET (WST)   A type of significant meteorological advisory (**SIGMET**) that pertains to **thunderstorms** and related severe weather, such as tornadoes, **squall lines**, embedded thunderstorms, unusually widespread thunderstorms, and hail with a diameter of more that ¾ inch. Convective SIGMETs affect all aircraft.

conventional landing gear   See **tail-wheel aircraft**.

coordinated flight   The result of the proper use of ailerons and rudder.

coordinated turn   A turn in which the **ailerons** and **rudder** are used together to prevent airplane **yaw**; a turn during which the ball in the cockpit **inclinometer** remains centered.

coordinated universal time (UTC)   The time measured at the **prime meridian**, or 0° **line of longitude**; also called **zulu** or **Z time**. The prime meridian passes through the Royal Observatory, Greenwich, England, and serves as the basis for navigational and astronomical almanac time measurements. Many aviation operational and weather data bulletins and reports are referenced to UTC. See also **time zones**.

coordinates   The location of a point on the earth described by the intersection of two or more lines of position. The term *geographic coordinates* refers to the intersection of **lines of latitude** and **lines of longitude**.

Coriolis force   A deflective force acting on a body of air in motion above the earth due to the rotation of the earth on its axis. Bodies of air in the Northern Hemisphere are deflected to the right of their course, while bodies of air in the Southern Hemisphere appear to be deflected to their left. The amount of apparent deflection depends on the body's velocity and its latitude. Above the ground **friction level**, air tends to move parallel to pressure isobars due to the Coriolis effect.

Coriolis illusion   A physiological illusion that causes the sensation of unusual airplane attitudes when the pilot's head is moved abruptly while engaged in a prolonged turn.

course card   The part of a VOR receiver cockpit display that shows the selected course.

course deviation indicator (CDI)   The cockpit instrument that tells the pilot the aircraft's location relative to the **VOR radial** selected with the **omnibearing selector**; also called the *left-right needle*.

course (course line)   The intended or actual path traveled across the ground.

cowl   The streamlined aircraft structure used to protect the engine installation and to channel cooling air to its components. On wing-mounted engines, the cowling is incorporated into a larger structural member called the **nacelle**.

cowl flaps   Movable, shutterlike **airfoils** located on the aircraft's **cowling** that can be opened or closed from the cockpit to regulate engine cooling. Cowl flaps are generally used only on higher-horsepower engines.

crab (or crabbing)   A flight maneuver in which the nose of the aircraft is angled into a **crosswind** in order to offset **drift** effects. Crabbing is a technique used to maintain a desired track across the ground in an airport **traffic pattern** as well as during en route navigation.

crankcase   The housing that encloses the **crankshaft** and its mechanisms, providing a tight enclosure for lubricating oil, bearing support for the crankshaft, support for the **cylinders**, and a place for mounting the **accessory drive pad** and associated equipment.

crankshaft   A shaft composed of a number of cranks, or "throws," which receive power from the reciprocating **piston** and **connecting rods** to produce the rotary motion necessary to turn the **propeller**.

critical angle of attack   The **angle of attack** at which the airflow over the top of the wing separates and becomes turbulent, resulting in aerodynamic **burble** or **buffet** and **stall**.

cross check   The process of methodically scanning the aircraft's flight instruments to maintain or change the aircraft's flight condition. The two key components of a cross check are the proper division of attention among the instruments and the proper interpretation of each instrument's reading.

cross-country flight   A flight of more than 50 **nautical miles** from a pilot's home airport.

crosswind   A wind blowing across the desired course of an aircraft. All winds other than direct **headwinds** or **tailwinds** have a crosswind component that pilots must account for to maintain a desired course.

crosswind leg   A **flight path** at right angles to the landing runway made by turning from its **upwind** (takeoff) **leg**. The crosswind leg is terminated by a turn onto the **downwind leg**.

cumuliform cloud   Any cloud exhibiting a dome-shaped upper surface, frequently with billowing protuberances, whose base is generally flat or horizontal. Most cumuliform clouds appear separated from one another and may exhibit considerable vertical development.

cumulonimbus clouds (CB)   A significant **cumuliform** cloud type, the classic **thunderstorm** clouds, showing massive towers and anvil-shaped tops in their later phases of development; also called *thunder bumpers* and *thunder heads*. Cbs can spawn many types of severe weather, including lightning, thunder, hail, and occasional tornadoes.

cumulus clouds (Cu)   The principal **cumuliform** cloud type, characterized by puffy domes or towers and flat, nearly horizontal bases. Precipitation, if it occurs, is usually showery.

cyanosis   Bluing of the skin resulting from a lack of oxygen in the bloodstream. A physiological symptom associated with **hypoxia**, cyanosis usually begins beneath the fingernails or around the lips.

cyclogenesis   The creation of a **cyclone** or region of low pressure with counterclockwise circulation of winds.

cyclone   An area of low **atmospheric pressure** with counterclockwise circulation of winds, some of them violent. Tropical cyclones may be the most violent storms in nature, except for tornadoes. Tropical cyclones are also called *hurricanes* if spawned in the Atlantic, *typhoons* if spawned in the Pacific, or *baguios* if they occur in the Philippines. Cyclones that occur in the higher latitudes (extratropical) are usually called *lows* or *depressions*, and they generally bring about a marked change in weather, frequently stormy, due to the presence of weather **fronts** that may follow the pattern of circulation around the low.

cylinder   The juglike vessel mounted on the **crankcase** of an internal combustion engine in which the chemical energy of fuel is released (combustion chamber) and translated by the **piston** into mechanical energy. See also **four-stroke cycle**.

cylinder head temperature (CHT) gauge   The cockpit instrument that gives a direct measurement of fuel mixture temperature effects during combustion within the **cylinder**. The measurement is usually made on the engine's hottest running cylinder.

datum   Any numerical or geometrical quantity or set of such quantities that can serve as a reference or base for the measurement of other quantities; also called *datum line*. In airplane design, the datum refers to the arbitrary line from which the location of components are measured along the airplane's axes. For weight and balance purposes, the datum falls at or near the nose of the airplane. **Fuselage stations** measured aft of the datum have a positive value; those forward of the datum have a negative value.

dead reckoning (DR)   A method of navigation beginning with a **true course** line drawn on a map and to which corrections are made for magnetic **variation**, winds aloft, aircraft **true airspeed**, and **compass deviation** to compute headings that will take the aircraft from one desired position to another. An integral part of DR computations is the estimation of a **ground speed**, which is then used to compute fuel required and estimated time en route. DR is not so much a separate form of navigation as a means of complementing other methods, such as **pilotage** and **radio navigation**. See also **flight log**.

decibel (db)   A unit for measuring the relative loudness of sounds detectable to the human ear, beginning with 1 for the faintest audible sound to about 130, after which physical damage to the ear prevents further discrimination of sound.

decompression sickness   The acute pain in the muscular tissue and joints resulting from the evolution of nitrogen bubbles in the body's tissues, together with other biological gases, caused by exposure to rapidly reduced pressure; also called the *bends*. The possibility of encountering the bends at high altitude can be greatly reduced by breathing 100 percent oxygen at ground level before ascent and by avoiding flight too soon after activities involving pressure changes on the body, such as scuba diving.

density-altitude   **Pressure-altitude** corrected for nonstandard temperature. High density-altitude means thinner air (due to high temperatures, humidity, or lower barometric pressures). Low density-altitude means denser air (due to lower temperatures, dry air, or higher barometric pressures). Airplane performance usually decreases with increased density-altitude.

Designated Flight Examiner   A highly qualified civilian flight instructor empowered by the FAA to administer flight checks.

Designated Medical Examiner   See **Aviation Medical Examiner (AME)**.

detonation   An explosion, specifically a gasoline explosion in the combustion chamber of an internal combustion engine. Normal combustion involves an even burning of the fuel-air mixture. Detonation creates excessive pressures and temperatures within the **cylinders**, which in turn create hot spots on the cylinder wall or **piston** head and can result in loss of power and eventual engine damage.

deviation errors   See **compass deviation (CD)**.

DEWIZ   Distant Early Warning Identification Zone. An ADIZ over the coastal waters of the state of Alaska. See also **ADIZ**.

dew point   The temperature to which air must be cooled (at a constant pressure and **humidity**) for **saturation** to occur. If the air is cooled beyond the dew point, condensation occurs, resulting in clouds, fog, or precipitation.

differential pressure instruments   Cockpit instruments that measure the difference between moving air and still air, or the difference between these values and the air trapped inside the instrument itself. Examples of differential pressure instruments are the **airspeed indication**, the **altimeter**, and the **vertical speed indicator**.

dihedral   The angle at which the airplane's wing attaches to the **fuselage**. A positive angle (between 0 and 90 degrees to the vertical) tends to enhance the airplane's lateral **stability**, automatically raising a wing that may have been lowered in a gust. A wing attachment angle of greater than 90 degrees (or a downward-sloping wing) is called *anhedral*. Anhedral wings may be used to enhance high-speed stability (as in the Lockheed F-104 Starfighter) or to achieve other design requirements, such as propeller clearance (as in the Chance-Vought F-4C Corsair World War II fighter).

dipstick   A metal rod inserted into the engine to measure the oil level.

direct current (DC)   Electric current that flows continuously in one direction.

directional gyro (DG)   See **heading indicator**.

directional stability   See **stability (airplane)**.

direction-finding (DF) steer   A procedure whereby a controller with direction-finding equipment furnishes a pilot requesting assistance with headings that will bring the aircraft to a suitable airport or **pilotage** landmark where normal navigation can be resumed.

dirigible   A **light-than-air aircraft** similar in configuration to a **blimp** but with a rigid internal structure.

displaced threshold   A **threshold** that is located at a point on the runway other than the designated beginning of the runway.

distance measuring equipment (DME)   A UHF navigational aid that measures the slant range distance between an airborne interrogator and a ground-based **transponder**. The distance from the aircraft to the station is displayed as nautical miles and tenths of nautical miles on a cockpit range indicator. All **TACAN** and **VORTAC** stations are equipped with DME transponders. The aircraft's interrogator is automatically tuned to this transponder when the appropriate TACAN or VOR station frequency is tuned and identified.

Distant Early Warning Identification Zone   See **DEWIZ**.

distribution system   That part of the engine **ignition system** that routes ignition voltage from the **magneto** to the various **cylinders** in the sequence necessary to develop smooth, continuous power at all throttle settings and rpms. See also **distributor**.

distributor   A component in the **ignition system** that is mechanically timed to rotate in synchronization with the **crankshaft**, providing voltage to the **cylinders** in the correct intervals and sequence.

ditching   A forced landing in the water.

DME   See **distance measuring equipment**.

doghouse   The left and right index marks found on the older-style *turn and slip indicators*. When the needle is on the doghouse, a **standard rate turn** of 3 degrees per second is established.

downwash   The downward rush of air from the upper surface of a wing that contributes a portion of total lift through the action-reaction principle. Downwash has two negative characteristics: It contributes to total drag due to an **induced drag** component, and it results in **wing tip vortices**. The vortices can be extremely dangerous to following aircraft when they are produced by large airplanes.

downwind leg   The **flight path** parallel to the landing runway flown in the direction opposite to landing. The downwind leg normally extends between the **crosswind leg** and the **base leg**.

DR   See **dead reckoning**.

drag   The force opposing the motion of the aircraft as it moves through the air. Total drag has two major components: *drag due to lift* (**induced drag**) and **parasite drag**, which includes drag caused by all other sources.

drag due to lift   See **induced drag**.

drift   The deflection of the aircraft from its intended course by the action of the wind.

drift correction angle (DCA)   See **wind correction angle (WCA)**.

drizzle A fine misty rain from **stratus clouds**.

dual ignition system The principle of redundancy used in aircraft engine ignition systems. Each system contains two **magnetos**, both of which generate voltage used by one of two **spark plugs** in every **cylinder**. Thus failure of one magneto will not result in the loss of ignition or the loss of any cylinder, though total power available from the engine will be reduced. In addition, the use of two spark plugs in each cylinder promotes cleaner, more even combustion.

dual instruction A flight by a student pilot (or any other pilot) with a **Certified Flight Instructor** in an aircraft with two sets of flight controls for the purpose of instruction.

dynamic pressure The difference between total pressure and static pressure; the measure of an aircraft's forward speed.

dynamic stability See **stability (airplane)**.

economizer system A valve in the **carburetor** designed to be closed at cruising speeds but to open as the throttle is advanced for high-speed operations. The economizer enables the pilot to obtain a **lean mixture** during cruise while enriching the mixture for full-throttle operations.

electric current The flow of electrons, measured in amperes (A), or amps.

electronic flight calculator A hand-held calculator that performs the functions of a circular (slide rule type) manual **flight computer**, plus other calculations (such as weight and balance computations) helpful to pilots.

elevator Hinged control surface attached to the trailing edge of the **horizontal stabilizer** used to move the airplane about its **lateral axis**. The elevator controls the airplane's **pitch**.

emergency locator transmitter (ELT) An emergency radio transmitter attached to the aircraft's structure. The ELT operates from a self-contained power source to broadcast a downward sweeping audible tone on both 121.5 and 243.0 MHz (**guard frequencies**) two to four times per second. Although it may be activated from the cockpit in most installations, it is designed to broadcast automatically in case of an accident.

emergency procedures Those procedures recommended by the aircraft's manufacturer and approved by the FAA for use during an emergency situation. The **Pilot's Operating Handbook** contains both normal and emergency procedure checklists. Although certain emergency procedures should be committed to memory and performed at once when the emergency situation develops, the pilot should refer to the emergency procedures checklist as soon as time permits thereafter to ensure that no steps have been overlooked.

empennage The tail of the airplane, including both **horizontal** and **vertical stabilizers** and their control surfaces.

empty weight See **licensed empty weight**.

encoder A device linking the aircraft's **altimeter** to its **transponder**, allowing ground-based ATC radar to detect and display the aircraft's altitude (mode C function of the airborne transponder).

engine instruments Those cockpit instruments used to monitor and control the power plant, including engine rpm (tachometer), oil temperature, oil pressure (and, where applicable, manifold pressure), cylinder head temperature, and fuel flow.

engine primer A cockpit control and power plant device used to inject raw fuel directly into the engine **cylinder** for use during engine starts, particularly in cold weather or when the engine has not recently been operated. Priming is necessary on most aircraft engines since the float-type **carburetor** does not function efficiently until the engine is running.

En Route Flight Advisory Service (EFAS) An FSS service providing timely weather information about a pilot's route of flight, altitude, and other operating conditions; also called **flight watch**. FSSs providing EFAS services are listed in the *Airport/Facility Directory*.

equator The **line of latitude** (parallel) that bisects the earth into Northern and Southern Hemispheres; the 0° line of latitude on the geographic coordinate system. The equator is the only line of latitude that is a **great circle**.

estimated time en route (ETE) The estimate of the time required to complete a flight (total or between two **checkpoints**); a **dead reckoning (DR)** computation based on the aircraft's **ground speed** and the distance to be traveled.

eustachian tube The channel that connects the space behind the eardrum to the throat, used to equalize the pressure differences between these areas. If the eustachian tube becomes blocked due to a head cold and these pressures cannot be equalized in flight (particularly on descent), the eardrum may be ruptured.

Exam-O-Grams FAA circulars written in an informal, easy-to-read style that analyze areas of aeronautical knowledge frequently missed on FAA written examinations.

exhaust valve A device located on the top of an engine **cylinder** that opens at the end of the power stroke to allow exhaust gases to escape the combustion chamber. See also **four-stroke cycle**.

FA See **area forecast**.

FAA See **Federal Aviation Administration**.

FAA-approved flying school A flying school that has been granted an Air Agency Certificate by the FAA. Since it operates under the provisions of FAR Part 141, it is also known as a "part 141 school."

FAA Designated Medical Examiner See **Designated Medical Examiner**.

FAA Flight Inspector An FAA pilot-specialist who acts as a flight check pilot for all other certificated pilots.

FAA flight plan See **flight plan**.

FAA Flight Service Station See **Flight Service Station**.

FAA medical certificates Documents attesting to the minimum physical condition required of all individuals who wish to use the privileges of their flight certificates or perform other flight crew duties. The **First Class Medical Certificate** is required for airline pilots; the **Second Class Medical Certificate** is the minimum required for commercial pilots; and the **Third Class Medical Certificate** is required for all student and private pilots. The Third Class Medical Certificate usually serves as the **Student Pilot Certificate**. A higher-level medical certificate may be used with a lower-level pilot certificate.

FAA medical examiner See **Aviation Medical Examiner (AME)**.

fairing A structural member (usually not load carrying), the primary function of which is to smooth the airflow around the aircraft, reducing **drag**.

FARs See **Federal Aviation Regulations**.

fast file flight plan system A system whereby a pilot files a flight plan via telephone that is tape-recorded and transcribed for transmission to the appropriate ATC facility. Locations with fast file capability are listed in the *Airport/Facility Directory*.

FBO See **fixed-base operator**.

FCC See **Federal Communications Commission**.

FD   See **winds and temperatures aloft forecast**.

FDC NOTAMs   Regulatory publications, distributed to all air traffic facilities that have telecommunications access, covering such topics as amendments to current aeronautical charts, changes in instrument approach procedures, and added restrictions to flight.

Federal Aviation Administration (FAA)   That branch of the Department of Transportation responsible for all civil aeronautical activities in the United States *except* economic regulation of airlines (Civil Aeronautics Board, CAB) and investigation of airline and certain other aviation-related accidents (National Transportation Safety Board, NTSB).

Federal Aviation Regulations (FARs)   The body of regulations established and administered by the FAA that governs civil aviation and aviation-related activities in the United States.

Federal Communications Commission (FCC)   That branch of government charged by law to assign and regulate the use of the public broadcast spectrum.

fin   Term occasionally used for the **vertical stabilizer**.

final approach   A **flight path** in the direction of landing along the extended runway centerline. The final approach normally extends from the **base leg** to the runway. An aircraft making an extended straight-in approach VFR is also considered to be on final approach. *Short final* is the term applied to that portion of the final approach flight path approaching the runway **threshold**.

fins   Ridges found on the **cylinder** of an internal combustion engine that increase the conductive surface area of the cylinder, allowing more heat to be carried away in the passing airflow.

fire wall   A protective structural barrier made of fireproof material designed to isolate all combustion equipment (engines, auxiliary power units, combustion heaters, and so on) from the rest of the aircraft.

First Class Medical Certificate   The **medical certificate** required to exercise the privileges of an Airline Transport Pilot Certificate; expires at the end of the sixth calendar month from the date of issue.

fix   The intersection of two or more **lines of position**.

fixed-base operator (FBO)   An airport facility that caters to the needs of the general aviation community, usually offering new and used aircraft sales and service and/or flight and ground school instruction.

fixed-distance marker   Provides a fixed-distance mark for landing turbojet aircraft on other than a **precision** instrument **runway**. This marking is similar to the fixed-distance marking on a precision instrument and is located 1000 feet from the **threshold**.

fixed-pitch propeller   A one-piece **propeller** that cannot change its design blade angle.

flaps (wing)   A movable appendage to an **airfoil**, usually a wing, that changes the airfoil's lift characteristics, generally to achieve slower takeoff and landing speeds. Flaps can be simple (plain or split) arrangements or complex, many-slotted devices supplemented in their action by bleed air from the aircraft's systems routed over their upper surfaces. High-performance airplanes sometimes feature flaps on the leading as well as trailing edges to achieve the same effects. However they are arranged, flaps are always lowered and raised in unison and symmetrically.

flare (landing)   A maneuver to round out the **flight path** prior to touchdown. This involves raising the airplane's nose, increasing wing **angle of attack**, as airspeed is lost. The object of the flare is to touch down safely on the airplane's main landing gear at the lowest possible forward speed short of an airplane **stall**.

flat-plate drag   Also called *frontal drag* or *form drag*. See **parasite drag**.

flight check   A flight conducted for the purpose of ascertaining a pilot's competence to obtain or renew a pilot certificate; also called a *check ride*, *flight test*, or *flight examination*.

flight computer   A hand-held, circular slide rule composed of a wind face and slide rule face used for solving **dead reckoning (DR)** and other flight-related problems.

flight following   The service provided by **Flight Service Stations** to monitor and assist a pilot over the course of a cross-country flight. Flight following requires a filed **flight plan** activated upon departure by the pilot, and occasional position reports en route. In return, the pilot's progress is monitored by FSS personnel, and in-flight advisories are routinely made available.

Flight Information Publications (FLIP)   Department of Defense flight information publications used by military pilots for flight planning, en route operations, and terminal approaches. FLIP en route charts, supplementary airport/facility directory, and terminal approach procedure books are distributed and revised through Department of Defense channels and should not be used by civilian pilots, who may be unfamiliar with certain symbols and terminology and may not have access to updated material.

flight instruments   Those instruments used to monitor and control an aircraft's attitude and **flight path**, including the **attitude indicator, airspeed indicator, altimeter, vertical speed indicator, turn coordinator,** and **heading indicator**.

flight level (FL)   A level of constant atmospheric pressure related to a reference datum of 29.92 inches of mercury set into the altimeter's **Kollsman window**. Each flight level is stated in three digits representing hundreds of feet. For example, flight level 250 represents a barometric altimeter indication of 25,000 feet with 29.92 set in the Kollsman window; FL 255 represents 25,500 feet, and so on. Flight levels are used to denote all altitudes above 18,000 feet MSL, or flights in the **positive control area (PCA)**.

flight log   A comprehensive compilation of information related to planning and conducting a flight, including route and **checkpoint** information, **dead reckoning (DR)** computations, communications and navigation aid frequencies, *NOTAMs*, and any other special information useful to the pilot. The flight log is used as the basis for preparing and filing an FAA **flight plan**.

flight path   A line, course, or track (in three dimensions) along which an aircraft is flying or is intended to be flown. See also **relative wind**.

flight plan   Specified information, usually summarized from the **flight log**, relating to the intended flight of an aircraft filed orally or in writing with an FSS or ATC facility. A standardized FAA form is available for summarizing and organizing this information. See also **fast file flight plan system**.

flight planning charts   Small-scale charts of large size that show all of the continental United States, useful when planning a flight that spans several smaller charts.

Flight Service Station (FSS)   Air traffic facilities that provide pilot briefing and en route communications and VFR search and rescue services, assist lost aircraft and aircraft in emergency situations, relay ATC clearances, originate *NOTAMs*, broadcast aviation weather and NWS information, receive and process VFR and IFR flight plans, and monitor **navaids**. In addition, at selected locations FSSs provide **En Route Flight Advisory Service (flight watch)**, take weather observations, issue airport advisories, and advise customs and immigration officials of transborder flights.

Flight Standards District Office (FSDO)   An FAA field office that serves a designated geographical area and is staffed with flight standards personnel who serve the aviation industry and the general public on matters relating to the certification and operation of air carrier and general-aviation aircraft. Activities include general surveillance of operational safety, certification of air crews and aircraft, accident prevention, investigation, enforcement, and so on.

Flight Standards Safety Pamphlets   Flight Standards District Office publications dealing with a wide range of operational problems affecting aviation safety and pilot judgment. Safety pamphlets fall somewhere between *Advisory Circulars* and *Exam-O-Grams* in technical content and tone and are available to pilots and the public through FSDO and GADO facilities.

Flight Watch   Term used to identify the **Flight Service Station** providing **En Route Advisory Service**, usually via radio contact on frequency 122.0 MHz—for example, Oakland Flight Watch.

float-type carburetor   See **carburetor**.

fog   A general term used for a cloud forming at or very near the earth's surface. Fog consists of numerous water droplets so small that they cannot be readily distinguished by the human eye. Technically, visibility inside such a low-lying cloud must be less than 1 kilometer to be classified as fog. If the visibility is greater than this, the cloud is classified as mist or thin fog. True fogs are categorized according to their method of formation: **advection fog, frontal fog, radiation fog, upslope fog**.

forced landing   A type of emergency landing usually associated with complete failure of the power plant. In general, forced landings occur either immediately after takeoff (on the **upwind leg**) or after some maneuvering altitude has been gained (**traffic pattern** altitude or above). Forced landings from the upwind leg should usually be made straight ahead to avoid airplane **stall**. Forced landings from traffic pattern or en route altitudes should be made in accordance with **Pilot's Operating Handbook** procedures, with special consideration for immediate actions required: choice of a forced landing site, emergency notification, preparation for landing, and touchdown techniques.

form drag   See **parasite drag**.

four Cs   The general procedure for coping with an airborne emergency, particularly being lost: *climb, communicate, confess, comply*. Climb to improve radio reception and clear dangerous terrain, communicate over the appropriate frequency, confess your predicament, and comply with ground instruction.

four-stroke cycle   The cycle of movements made by the **piston** inside the **cylinder** of an internal combustion engine. The cycle begins with the *intake stroke*, during which the piston moves down the cylinder, drawing the air-fuel mixture in through the **intake valve**. The *compression stroke* begins when the piston moves back up again, compressing the air-fuel charge into a very small area known as the combustion cham-

ber. Near the top of the compression stroke, the air-fuel mixture is ignited by the spark plugs (or by compression heating in the case of diesel engines). The *power stroke* is the descending movement of the piston after combustion, during which the chemical energy of the burning charge is transformed into mechanical energy that rotates the **crankshaft**. The *exhaust stroke* ends the cycle as the piston moves back up the cylinder to expel the burned gases through the **exhaust valve**.

friction level   The lowest level of the **atmosphere**, below which friction with the earth's surface features affect its flow; also called *friction layer*. Although the friction level varies with changing conditions, it usually extends to about 2000 feet above the surface.

front   A zone of transition extending between two **air masses** of different characteristics. See also **cold front, occluded front, stationary front, warm front**.

frontal fog   Fog associated with **air mass** movement and frontal zones in which warm rain or drizzle falling through cooler air evaporates, saturating the cool air to form low-lying clouds or fog; also called *precipitation fog*.

frontal area   See **parasite drag**.

frontal thunderstorm   See **thunderstorm**.

frontal wave   See **cyclogenesis**.

frontogenesis   The creation of a **front**, generally caused by the horizontal encounter of two different **air masses** containing widely different characteristics.

frontolysis   The dissipation of a **front**, generally caused by the horizontal mixing of the two **air masses**.

FSDO   See **Flight Standards District Office**.

FSS   See **Flight Service Station**.

FT   See **terminal forecast**.

fuel flow   The amount of fuel used by an aircraft engine in a given period of time, usually measured in gallons per hour (gph) or pounds per hour (pph). Some aircraft have a cockpit fuel flow indicator that allows for very precise fuel use measurements for desired engine power settings.

fuel injectors   A system for injecting fuel directly into the induction system or combustion chambers of an engine without using a conventional float-type **carburetor**; also called a *fuel injection system*. Injector systems have several advantages over float-type carburetion, including delivery of a more uniform air-fuel charge into the **cylinder**, better control over the air-fuel ratio, improved engine acceleration, avoidance of complex maintenance procedures required for float-type carburetors, and avoidance of certain operational hazards such as **carburetor ice**.

fuel pressure gauge   A cockpit instrument that displays fuel system pressure used by aircraft featuring engine-driven and fuel boost pumps. A sudden drop in the fuel pressure reading usually means that the boost pump, if it is on, has failed, or that the engine-driven pump has failed and that the boost pump, if off, should be turned on and a landing made as soon as practicable.

fuel pump   An engine-driven pump that provides fuel under pressure to the **carburetor**. Commonly used by low-wing airplanes or aircraft whose geometry does not permit gravity feeding of the fuel to the engine or by aircraft with fuselage auxiliary fuel tanks.

fuel quantity gauge   A cockpit instrument activated by a tank-mounted, float-type sensor that transmits fuel quantity information proportional to the float's displacement in the tank.

fuel reserve   Fuel on board the aircraft less the amount of fuel required for the flight. The fuel reserve should always be adequate for unforeseen contingencies, such as diversion to an alternate airport.

fuel selector valve   A cockpit switch used to select the appropriate fuel tank to feed the engine; sometimes called the *fuel cock*. Usual settings including Left (wing tank), Right (wing tank), Both (tanks), or Auxiliary (tank). The Off setting is used to isolate the engine from the fuel system in case of fire and to help prevent fuel leakage through the system when the engine is not in use.

fuel strainer   A filter located in or near the lowest part of the fuel system used to trap water and sediment that may have collected or condensed inside the tanks. The *fuel sump drain*, which is usually located in the engine compartment, allows condensation to be drained off.

fuel vent   A passage to the atmosphere from the fuel tank that allows air to displace the volume of fuel as it is used. Fuel vents should always be unobstructed to ensure safe, adequate servicing and to avoid possible fuel system malfunctions in flight.

fuse   A small piece of metal that melts when overheated by excessive electric current, breaking the circuit and protecting other components in the system. Unlike a **circuit breaker**, a fuse cannot be reused (or "reset") after tripping; it must be replaced by a new fuse with the same power rating.

fuselage   The body of the aircraft; that portion of the **airframe** usually housing the pilot, passengers, and baggage compartment and to which the engine, wings, landing gear, and **empennage** are usually attached. Structurally, most modern airplane fuselages are of *semimonocoque* construction, using a framework of vertical and longitudinal members (*frames* and *stringers*) to stiffen the metal skin and carry the bulk of the fuselage structural load.

fuselage station (FS) number   The design reference system for locating any point along the aircraft's **fuselage** in inches forward or aft of the **datum**. For weight and balance purposes, the FS represents an item's **moment arm** (the location along the fuselage where it will concentrate its weight).

GADO   See **General Aviation District Office**.

general aviation   That branch of aviation encompassing all flying that is not a part of **commercial** or **military aviation**.

General Aviation District Office (GADO)   An FAA field office that serves a designated geographic area and is staffed by flight standards personnel who serve the aviation industry and the general public on matters relating to the certification and operation of general aviation aircraft.

generator   See **alternator**.

geographic coordinate system   The system of **lines of latitude** (parallels) and **longitude** (meridians) used to locate any particular point on the earth's surface. See also **coordinates**.

glide path   See **glide slope**.

glider   A heavier-than-air aircraft supported in flight by wings, the free flight of which does not depend principally on an engine.

glide slope   The descent profile determined for vertical guidance during a **final approach**; also called the *glide path* (although *glide path* additionally implies certain terminology used by ATC for aircraft conducting **precision approach radar (PAR)** landings). In general, the glide slope consists of electronic components emitting signals that provide vertical guidance by reference to airborne instruments, such as the **instru-**

ment landing system (ILS), or visual ground aids such as a **visual approach slope indicator (VASI)**, which provides vertical guidance for VFR approaches.

GMT   See **coordinated universal time**.

gnomonic projection   A chart or map projection on which all straight lines are **great circles** and all geographic great circles (**meridians** and the **equator**) are represented as straight lines.

go-around   A missed approach; an aborted landing attempt from the **final approach** phase of flight.

governor   A device controlled by the cockpit rpm lever that adjusts the pitch of a variable or **constant-speed propeller**. The governor uses the hydraulic pressure of engine oil or electrical power to reposition the propeller blades.

gradient   The increase or decrease of a measured value with respect to distance. *Runway gradient* refers to the runway's horizontal slope; *pressure gradient* refers to the change of atmospheric pressure over a given horizontal distance. A "steep" pressure gradient usually indicates the presence of strong winds.

Graphic Notices and Supplemental Data (GNSD)   A publication designed primarily as a pilot's operational manual containing a tabulation of parachute jump areas, special notice area graphics, terminal radar service area graphics, civil flight test areas, military refueling tracks and areas, and other data not requiring frequent change.

graveyard spiral   An inadvertent flight maneuver resulting from pilot disorientation. The aircraft enters a constant-rate, descending turn, and the pilot's semicircular canals stabilize, reducing or eliminating the sensation of turn. Sensing straight and level flight, the pilot may then pull back on the wheel, noting the altitude being lost, and aggravate the situation. Even if the pilot correctly rolls out of the turn, a false sensation of a turn in the other direction may be stimulated, and the pilot may reestablish the spiral in an attempt to "level" the wings. Proper use of the aircraft's flight instruments is the only way to avoid or recover from the maneuver.

gravity level equivalents (Gs)   Units of measure of **acceleration**. One G is equal to the earth's gravity.

grayout   The fading of the field of vision due to pooling of blood in the lower extremities while pulling positive Gs. Vision is still possible but is limited.

great circle   Any circle on the earth's surface whose plane extends through the center of the earth's sphere—that is, any circle about the earth whose diameter is equal to the earth's diameter. A great circle arc (segment) drawn between two points on the surface represents the shortest distance between those points.

Greenwich mean time (GMT)   See **coordinated universal time**.

grommet   The small reference circle drawn at the center of the rotating transparent plate on the wind face of the **flight computer**; also, the small reference hole located at the center of the protractor portion of a **navigational plotter**.

gross weight   The total weight of an aircraft before deductions are made for specific conditions. The *maximum gross weight* of an aircraft is certificated by the FAA and includes the basic weight of the aircraft, pilot and passengers, usable fuel, and baggage.

ground effect   The apparent gain in lift due to an airplane's flight at or below one wing span's height above the ground. The ground effect is caused by the sudden reduction in **induced**

drag caused by diffusion of the **downwash** from the upper surface of the wing as it meets the ground.

ground fog   See **radiation fog**.

grounding   In refueling, the connection of the aircraft to the earth by means of a conducting material. In aircraft electrical systems, grounding refers to the procedure of using the aircraft's metal structure as the means of completing the electrical circuit, saving the weight of additional "return" wiring. See also **grounding wire**.

ground instruction   Any nonflying pilot training.

grounding wire   A conducting wire that grounds the aircraft to earth during refueling. This allows for a static electricity discharge path and minimizes the chance for an electrical spark in the vicinity of the fueling nozzle.

ground speed (GS)   The speed of the aircraft over the ground. Ground speed is **true airspeed** corrected for wind effects.

ground speed indicator   A cockpit instrument that converts changes in **Distance Measuring Equipment (DME)** indications to a **ground speed** equivalent, sometimes with an additional time-to-station (TTS) calculation and display.

ground waves   That portion of a transmitted radio wave that travels along the ground. This is the type of wave most commonly received by airborne radios. Ground waves are blocked by the curvature of the earth. See also **sky waves**.

Gs   See **gravity level equivalents**.

guard frequencies   The frequencies—VHF 121.5 MHz and UHF 243.0 MHz—over which ATC, FSS, and military facilities keep a constant surveillance for aircraft distress calls.

G units (gravity units)   Units used to express **load factor,** where one G is the normal force of gravity. See also **gravity level equivalents.**

gust locks   Mechanical braces installed on movable control surfaces to prevent movement and damage due to high winds.

gyro horizon   See **attitude indicator**.

gyroplane   A rotorcraft whose rotors are not engine driven (except for initial starting) but are made to rotate by the forward motion of the gyroplane itself. The gyroplane's means of propulsion is usually a conventional aircraft internal combustion engine with tractor or pusher propeller.

gyroscope   A relatively heavy mass spinning about an axis that is free to rotate in one or both of two other axes perpendicular to the spin axis and to each other.

gyroscopic instruments   Cockpit instruments using a **gyroscope** or the principles of gyroscopic action in their operation, including the **attitude indicator, turn coordinator**, and **heading indicator**.

Handbook   See **Pilot's Operating Handbook**.

heading   The direction in which an aircraft's nose is pointed.

heading indicator   A gyroscopic flight instrument, vacuum or electrically driven, that indicates the aircraft's heading with respect to a 360-degree compass azimuth card. Outdated terms for the heading indicator include *directional gyro*, or *DG*, and *gyrocompass*. The heading indicator displays only a gyro-stabilized aircraft heading and must be periodically aligned to a **magnetic compass** to be used for navigation.

headwind   Any wind that approaches the aircraft from a frontal direction and acts opposite to its course. A direct headwind approaches the aircraft "on the nose." A wind approaching from any other direction to either wing tip will have both headwind and **crosswind** components. A headwind or headwind component always reduces the aircraft's **ground speed**.

helicopter   A rotorcraft that depends principally on its engine-driven rotors for horizontal motion.

hemoglobin   The oxygen-bearing, iron-containing protein in vertebrate red blood cells.

high frequencies (HF)   Frequencies on the band between 3 and 30 MHz.

hold   A predetermined maneuver that keeps the aircraft within a specified airspace while awaiting further clearance from ATC; also used during ground operations to keep aircraft within a specified area or at a specified point while awaiting further clearance from ATC.

holding lines   Lines painted across a taxiway not less than 100 feet from the intersection of a runway (and farther in the case of a category II instrument landing runway, so indicated by a pair of holding lines joined by bars; the tower will inform the pilot any time category II equipment is in use). No aircraft my cross a holding line onto an **active runway** without specific clearance to do so from the tower.

homing   Flight toward a **navaid** without correcting for wind, accomplished by adjusting the aircraft's heading to maintain a relative bearing of 0°—that is, keeping the bearing pointer under the top index, or "on the nose." In the presence of a **crosswind**, the resulting **flight path** will leave a curved track across the ground.

homolosine projection   An equal-area map projection that is interrupted over the oceans so that the continental masses are depicted without significant distortion.

horizontal stabilizer   The fixed **airfoil** in the empennage group that resists airplane displacement about the **lateral axis**, or changes in **pitch**. The **elevator** is usually attached to the trailing edge of the **horizontal stabilizer**, and, by its movements, it changes the airfoil characteristics of the stabilizer such that desired pitch changes occur. See also **stabilator**.

horsepower   A unit of measurement of engine power output; the power required to raise 550 pounds 1 foot in 1 second.

hourly sequence report   See **surface analysis chart**.

humidity   The amount of water vapor in the air.

hurricane advisory (WH)   An inflight weather advisory regarding hurricane location, direction of movement, and maximum winds. Although a wide variety of other adverse and aviation-related weather occurs in and around the hurricane system, these details are usually left to other reports and advisories.

hyperventilation   A physiological disorder caused by a rate of respiration that is excessively fast for the current level of body activity. Symptoms include light-headedness, tingling sensations in the extremities, and coolness. Countermeasures call for controlling and slowing the rate of respiration and may be aided by breathing deoxygenated air.

hypoxia   A physiological disorder defined as the state of oxygen deficiency in the body tissues great enough to cause impairment of function. Symptoms include euphoria, light-headedness, hot and cold flashes, breathlessness, reasoning difficulties, impairment of motor coordination, and, in advanced cases, **cyanosis** (bluing of the skin), inability to perform simple motions or calculations, unconsciousness, and eventual death. At extreme altitudes, the **time of useful consciousness** can be a matter of minutes. Countermeasures include breathing supplemental oxygen as required by FARs. If symptoms occur, the pilot should descend at once to a lower altitude and use supplemental (100 percent) oxygen immediately.

hysteresis   The delay or "lag" in an altimeter's indications due to the elastic properties of the materials used in the aneroids; also called *hysteresis error*. Hysteresis error is most noticeable after the aircraft has flown at a constant altitude for some time and then makes a large, rapid altitude change.

IAS   See **indicated airspeed**.

ICAO   See **International Civil Aviation Organization**.

idling system   That subsystem of a float-type **carburetor** that automatically provides fuel to keep the engine running with the throttle nearly closed (at "idle").

IFF   "Identification Friend or Foe," a term derived from the military and sometimes applied to the **ATCRBS** transponder. In the early days of radar, transponders were carried by warplanes with signals coded to identify the aircraft as "friend" or "foe."

IFR   See **Instrument Flight Rules**.

IFR en route charts   Special aeronautical charts published and updated for instrument pilots, showing **navaids, airways**, and other IFR information. Since terrain features (other than obstructions near airways) are not displayed, these charts are not suitable for VFR navigation.

ignition   The production of a spark between the center electrode and ground electrode of the **spark plugs** in the combustion chamber of an internal combustion engine. The spark ignites the air-fuel mixture, which releases the chemical energy of the fuel. The ignition event occurs just before the **piston** reaches its top-dead-center position on the compression stroke. See also **four-stroke cycle**.

ignition control switch   A cockpit rotary switch, labeled Off, Right, Left, Both, and Start, used to energize the starting system and to select a source of voltage for the ignition system when the engine is running; also called *magneto switch*.

ignition system   A system to provide voltage in proper sequence to the **spark plugs** in each **cylinder**. The ignition system consists of **magnetos**, or special generators that provide high-voltage pulses for ignition; a timing device to ensure that the voltage pulse reaches the cylinder at the right time to develop smooth engine power; a distribution system to provide the correct sequence of voltage pulses for continuous engine power; spark plugs to ignite the air-fuel mixture in the combustion chamber; a control switch to energize the system for starts and to select magnetos; and a shielding system to prevent high-voltage pulses in the ignition wiring from interfering with other aircraft systems. Aircraft ignition systems operate on the design principle of *duality*, providing dual spark plugs for each cylinder and dual magnetos to power one plug in each cylinder, ensuring that a failed magneto or spark plug will not result in a dangerous loss in engine power.

ILS   See **instrument landing system**.

IMC   See **instrument meteorological conditions**.

incidence   See **angle of incidence**.

inclinometer   A component of the **turn coordinator**; a metal ball suspended in a curved, liquid-filled tube similar to a carpenter's spirit level. A positive **load factor** keeps the ball centered in the tube, while asymmetrical loads (such as the centrifugal force encountered in an uncoordinated turn) tend to move the ball to the edge of the tube. A **coordinated turn** (angle of bank appropriate to rate of turn) keeps the ball centered between its index lines and is the result of the proper use of **ailerons** and **rudder**.

indefinite ceiling   A condition that occurs when the ceiling height cannot be distinguished by surface vertical observation due to the presence of a surfaced-based atmospheric obscuration.

indicated airspeed (IAS)   The **airspeed** displayed on the **airspeed indicator**.

indicated altitude   The altitude displayed on the **altimeter**. To display the correct height of the aircraft above **mean sea level**, the indicated altitude must be corrected for installation and scale errors and for nonstandard atmospheric conditions.

induced drag   That portion of total airplane aerodynamic drag caused by the rearward component of the **lift** vector created by the wing; also called *drag due to lift*. The more lift the wing produces, the higher lift-induced drag becomes. At low airspeeds, when the wing is flying at a high **angle of attack**, induced drag contributes the largest share of total airplane drag. At higher airspeeds, where the airplane operates at a reduced angle of attack, lift-induced drag becomes minimal, and the other component of total drag, **parasite drag**, becomes significant.

inertial navigation   Computation of fixes and headings based on precision airborn **gyroscopes** that have been aligned with a known position on the earth's surface before flight, and motion sensors (accelerometers) that keep track of displacements from that original position.

inflight advisories   Weather advisories issued to pilots en route of possible hazardous flying conditions that may not have been known and communicated during preflight briefings. Significant meteorological advisories (**SIGMETs**) are of interest to all aircraft, while airmen's meteorological advisories (**AIRMETs**) are of interest primarily to pilots of light aircraft.

inner ear   The sensory organs, located behind the ear, that provide motion and balance information to the brain.

Instrument Flight Rules (IFR)   Rules governing the procedures for instrument flight; also a term used by pilots and controllers to indicate a type of flight plan. Instrument Flight Rules prevail when weather conditions are less than those required for VFR, or as prescribed for using certain airspace, regardless of weather conditions. See also **instrument meteorological conditions**.

instrument flying   Controlling the aircraft solely by reference to the cockpit instruments.

instrument landing system (ILS)   A **precision** instrument **approach** system that normally consists of the following electronic components and visual aids: localizer, **glide slope**, outer marker, middle marker, and approach lights. The VHF localizer beam provides lateral (course) guidance; the UHF glide slope provides vertical (rate of descent) guidance; and the VHF markers provide position fixes along the approach path. A low-frequency compass locator is situated at one of the markers for terminal area guidance to the **final approach** course.

instrument meteorological conditions (IMC)   Meteorological conditions expressed in terms of visibility, distance from clouds, and **ceiling** that is less than the minimum specified for **visual meteorological conditions**; conditions where outside visual references are not continuously available to the pilot, requiring instrument flying.

instrument routes (IR)   Low-altitude, high-airspeed military training routes where operations may be conducted under both VFR and IFR conditions.

intake valve   The valve on the **cylinder** of an internal combustion engine that admits the air-fuel charge to the combustion chamber during the intake stroke. See also **four-stroke cycle**.

intercept, angle of   See **angle of interception**.

intercept, rate of   See **rate of interception**.

intercept heading   The heading determined by the pilot as being necessary to intercept the desired course. The intercept heading flown must take into account the aircraft's distance from the station and the number of of degrees the aircraft is displaced from the desired course.

interception   Any maneuver that has as its end the collocation of the aircraft with a desired target. In civil **radio navigation**, that end is a VOR **radial** or ADF **bearing**.

interference drag   See **parasite drag**.

International Civil Aviation Organization (ICAO)   A specialized agency of the United Nations whose objective is to develop the principles and techniques of international air navigation and to foster planning and development of international air transport. Although ICAO's standards and procedures touch nearly every aspect of aviation, their final implementation is left to the discretion of the sovereign nations.

international date line   The 180° meridian; the **line of longitude** that marks the beginning of the 24-hour calendar day.

International Standard Atmosphere (ISA)   See **standard atmosphere**.

intersection takeoff   A departure or takeoff from the intersection of two runways or the intersection of a runway and a taxiway. Intersection takeoffs may be conducted in the interest of expediting air traffic, provided safety of flight is not adversely affected.

inversion   See **temperature inversion**.

ionosphere   One of the more distant layers of the earth's **atmosphere**; a shell of ionized gas (charged particles) lying from between 40 to 200 miles in altitude. The unique electrical properties of the ionosphere account for a number of phenomena, including the propagation of radio **sky waves** and the aurora borealis.

IR   See **instrument routes**.

ISA   See **International Standard Atmosphere**.

isobar   A line of constant barometric pressure drawn on a weather map.

isogonic lines   Lines of equal magnetic **variation**.

jet blast   Turbulent airflow following jet engine exhaust.

jet charts   Aeronautical charts used for IFR navigation above 18,000 feet MSL.

jet stream   A migrating stream, or "tunnel," of winds moving at velocities of greater than 50 knots amid the normal air flow aloft, at altitudes between 20,000 and 40,000 feet. A factor in high-altitude weather and navigation.

knot (Kt)   One nautical mile per hour, the equivalent of 1.15 statute miles per hour.

Kollsman window   The small rectangular "window" on the right side of a barometric **altimeter** through which barometric pressure correction values can be set and displayed. A change of .01 inch of mercury on the barometric scale inside the window results in a 10-foot change in **indicated altitude**.

Lambert projection   The projection used for many aeronautical charts, including **sectional** and **world aeronautical charts**. On this projection, straight lines approximate **great circle** arc segments and hence represent the shortest navigational route

between the two points that connect. Distances measured along the segment are very accurate.

laminar airflow   A smooth, layered flow of air, such as the lift-producing airflow on the upper surface of a wing.

land breeze   See **offshore wind**.

land flow turbulence   A turbulent airflow set up by low-altitude winds passing around surface obstructions such as trees, buildings, and hills.

landing direction indicator   A device located near the center of the airport in the vicinity of the runway that visually indicates the direction in which landings and takeoffs should be made. The landing direction indicator is usually in the form of a **tetrahedron** that must be manually repositioned to show a change in landing direction.

landing flare   See **flare**.

landing lights   Bright lights analogous to an automobile's headlights, installed near the wing leading edge or landing gear, and used to illuminate the runway for takeoff and landing operations.

lapse rate   See **adiabatic lapse rate**.

lateral axis   An imaginary reference line running from wing tip to wing tip through the airplane's **center of gravity**. Movement about the airplane's lateral axis is called **pitch**.

lateral Gs   Load factors encountered along the lateral axis; side-force Gs.

lateral stability   See **stability (airplane)**.

latitude   See **lines of latitude**.

leaning (the mixture)   The process of setting and resetting the fuel mixture control knob so as to restrict fuel flow at altitude such that the sea level ratio of air to fuel is approximately restored. Most light aircraft require leaning above a **density-altitude** of 5000 feet MSL.

lean mixture   See **mixture control system**.

leans   A physiological illusion caused by vestibular stabilization during a prolonged turn. When the pilot rolls out of the turn, the semicircular canals may perceive straight and level flight to be a turn in the opposite direction, causing the pilot to lean in the direction of the assumed vertical. The leans may also be induced by differential roll rates—that is, by rolling slowly into a turn and rolling out of it rapidly. This is one of the most common vestibular illusions and one of the easiest to offset, though the pilot may unconsciously lean toward the assumed vertical for a short while afterward.

lenticular clouds   A stationary cloud having a shape roughly analogous to a double-convex lens or almond. Lenticular clouds are frequently formed at the crest of standing waves of air currents such as those associated with **mountain waves**.

licensed empty weight   Term used to describe airplane with all installed equipment, hydraulic fluid, and all *unusable* fuel and oil.

lift   The aerodynamic force generated by the action of air moving over an **airfoil**. Lift offsets gravity and allows the airplane to fly. When the wing is banked, the same force allows the airplane to turn, though more lift must be generated if the airplane is to sustain both the turn and flight at a constant altitude.

lighter-than-air (LTA) aircraft   Aircraft that rise and maintain flight by displacing a mass of heavier air with a contained mass of lighter air or a gas, such as helium or hydrogen. LTAs include hot-air balloons and airships, the latter category composed of **blimps** and **dirigibles**.

lines of latitude   The distance north or south of the **equator**, measured in degrees, minutes, and seconds of arc; also called *parallels*. The equator is the only line of latitude that is a **great circle**.

lines of longitude   The distance measured in degrees, minutes, and seconds of arc along the equator from the **prime meridian** (or *Greenwich meridian*), to a point below a given **line of latitude**; also called *meridians*. All lines of longitude are **great circles** and converge at the geographic poles.

line of position (LOP)   A general term for any line of constant navigational values. Examples are VOR **radials**, DME arcs, ADF **bearings**, and **lines of latitude** and **longitude**. A navigational **fix** occurs wherever two or more LOPs intersect.

load (electrical)   One or more useful components requiring electrical current to operate. The more electrical components operating on a given circuit, the heavier the load.

load factor   The ratio of total lift being produced, by an aircraft, to the weight of the aircraft, expressed in gravity units, or **Gs**.

loading chart   Any one of a series of charts carried in an aircraft that show the proper location for the payload as referenced by checklists, balance records, and weight and balance limits.

load meter   Gauge that indicates the electrical load (in amperes) being placed on the **alternator** or **generator**.

local flying area   The area within 50 nautical miles of an airport.

logbook   A permanent, bound record of a pilot's flight experience. Logbooks are also kept by maintenance technicians for the **airframe** and power plant.

longitude   See **lines of longitude**.

longitudinal axis   An imaginary reference line that runs from nose to tail through the aircraft's **center of gravity**. Movement about the aircraft's longitudinal axis is called **roll**.

longitudinal stability   See **stability (airplane)**.

LOP   See **line of position**.

LORAN   Contraction for long-range navigation; an electronic **navaid** using slaved station pairs to broadcast low-frequency signals usable over long distances.

magnetic bearing (MB)   The **magnetic heading** of the aircraft plus the number of degrees (**relative bearing**) to the station. For example, an aircraft with a magnetic heading of 300° and a relative bearing on its ADF indicator of 020° would have a magnetic bearing to the station of 320°.

magnetic compass   A cockpit instrument containing a suspended, liquid-dampened magnetic element that senses the lines of the earth's magnetic field; sometimes called a *"whiskey" compass*.

magnetic course (MC)   The **true course** of the aircraft (or its intended course with respect to true north) corrected for magnetic **variation**.

magnetic heading (MH)   The **true heading** (**true course** plus or minus the **wind correction angle**) plus or minus magnetic **variation**.

magnetic north   The northward direction of the earth's magnetic lines of force, converging at the earth's north magnetic pole (as opposed to the geographic North Pole).

magnetic variation (VAR)   See **variation**.

magneto   A special engine-driven electrical generator that produces a high-voltage pulse for use in the aircraft's **ignition system**.

magneto check   An important preflight procedure that verifies whether or not both magnetos are operating as part of the

dual ignition system; colloquially termed the *mag check*. The procedure involves setting a recommended engine rpm and alternately grounding out the left magneto, then the right one. If the engine begins to lose more than the required number of rpm when one magneto is selected, that magneto is probably faulty.

magneto switch   See **ignition control switch**.

main metering system   A subsystem of a float-type **carburetor** that controls the amount of fuel used in all power settings above the idle range.

maneuvering speed (V_a)   The highest speed at which airloads cannot damage the **airframe**. This is the maximum speed to fly in turbulent air or during maneuvers requiring abrupt control movement.

manifold   A pipe or duct with many interconnections; in aircraft power plants. Manifold systems are used for both air induction and exhaust.

manifold pressure (MP) gauge   A cockpit instrument that measures and displays (in inches of mercury) the pressure in the intake manifold that carries the air-fuel charge to the engine. Higher manifold pressure indicates greater engine power.

marginal VFR (MVFR)   A ceiling of 1000 to 3000 feet and/or visibility of 3 to 5 miles, inclusive.

marshaler   See **signaler**.

master switch   A two-position switch that must be in the On position in order to activate any of the aircraft's electrical components. The master switch also provides a convenient way to deactivate the aircraft's electrical components in case of emergency.

maximum endurance   The longest time an aircraft can remain aloft at a given **gross weight**.

maximum endurance airspeed   That **airspeed** yielding the best ratio of fuel consumed per unit of time.

maximum landing weight   The maximum weight approved by the FAA for touchdown on landing.

maximum ramp weight   The maximum weight approved by the FAA for ground maneuvering. It includes fuel used for start, taxi, and engine runup.

maximum range   The greatest distance an aircraft can fly at a given **gross weight**.

maximum range airspeed   That **airspeed** yielding the best ratio of nautical miles per gallon of fuel consumed.

maximum takeoff weight   The maximum weight approved by the FAA for the start of the takeoff run.

mayday   From the French *m'aidez* ("Aid me!"), the international radiotelephone distress signal.

MB   See **magnetic bearing**.

MC   See **magnetic course**.

mean sea level (MSL)   The standard reference plane used for measuring elevations throughout the United States.

megahertz (MHz)   Formerly cycles per second, or CPS, now replaced by *hertz* (the prefix *mega* refers to one million, or one million cycles per second); the band of radio frequencies used for VHF and UHF communications and navigation.

Mercator projection   A chart projection frequently used for nautical (marine) charts, on which **great circles** appear as curved lines and **rhumb lines** appear as straight lines. This projection is not especially useful for aeronautical purposes.

meridians   See **lines of longitude**.

meteorology   The science of the **atmosphere**, particularly weather patterns and phenomena.

MH   See **magnetic heading**.

MHz See **megahertz**.

military aviation That branch of aviation encompassing all flights by the armed forces, including their aircraft, bases of operation, and special training areas.

Military Operations Area (MOA) An airspace of defined vertical and lateral dimensions established outside **positive control areas** to separate certain military activities from IFR traffic and to identify for VRF traffic where these activities are conducted.

Military Training Routes (MTR) Areas designated by the FAA and the Department of Defense in which military aircraft conduct low-altitude, high-speed training.

millibar (mb) A unit of atmospheric pressure equal to 1000 dynes per square centimeter, or 1/1000th of a *bar*. Standard atmospheric pressure at sea level is 1013.25 mb or 29.92 inches of mercury. One inch of mercury is equivalent to approximately 34 millibars.

mineral oil Lubricant typically used only during the break-in period of a new engine.

missed approach See **go-around**.

mixed icing Ice that forms when the water drops vary in size or when liquid drops are intermingled with snow or ice particles. A combination of clear and rime icing.

mixture control system A power plant and cockpit control system that allows the pilot to manually increase the air-fuel ratio to a leaner mixture for cruising flight at altitude. Combustible air-fuel ratios range from 8:1 to as high as 18:1, with best power for most engines generated in the area of 12:1 to 16:1. **Lean mixtures** fall on the high side of this range, while **rich mixtures** fall on the lower side.

MOA See **military operations area**.

mode A See **transponder**.

mode C See **transponder**.

moment A force acting in a given direction. In weight and balance, a moment is the object's weight times its **arm**.

monoplane An airplane with only one wing.

Morse code Named for its inventor, Samuel B. Morse, a code consisting of either dots and dashes or long and short tones used for transmitting alphanumeric characters. In aviation, the Morse code is used primarily in the automatic station identification signals broadcast by radio **navaids**.

mountain wave A meteorological condition that occurs when wind velocities perpendicular to a mountain range exceed 35 knots, causing a region of updrafts and downdrafts that can extend as far as several times the height of the mountains themselves, sometimes even beyond the **tropopause**. The mountain wave is sometimes identified by the presence of **lenticular clouds** above the mountain and a line of **rotor**, or roll, **clouds** on the downwind, or lee, side. The effects of the wave can sometimes be experienced as far as 100 miles downwind from the mountain range itself.

MSL See **mean sea level**.

MULTICOM The VHF frequency of 122.9 MHz used for air-to-air and air-to-ground radio communications during certain general aviation operations, such as crop dusting, skydiving, and fire fighting. If **UNICOM** or tower facilities are not available, the MULTICOM frequency should be used by pilots for traffic coordination.

multiengine land A class of aircraft in the airplane category. See also **category, class**.

multiengine water A class of aircraft in the airplane category. See also **category, class**.

MVFR See **marginal VFR**.

nacelle See **cowl**.

National Ocean Survey (NOS) A branch of the National Oceanic and Atmospheric Administration (NOAA) in the Department of Commerce. The NOS prepares and publishes a variety of marine and aeronautical charts used by civil and military operators around the world. NOS charts of greatest importance to the private pilot are **sectional charts, VFR planning charts, VFR terminal control area charts,** and **world aeronautical charts (WAC)**.

National Transportation Safety Board (NTSB) An agency of the Department of Transportation that is the custodian of aviation safety statistics. The NTSB investigates accidents involving publicly chartered carriers and publishes a number of accident and incident reports of interest to the general aviation public.

National Weather Service (NWS) The civilian agency that coordinates all weather services in the United States. The NWS is a branch of the National Oceanic and Atmospheric Administration (NOAA) in the Department of Commerce. NWS facilities gather meteorological data from throughout the United States, Alaska, and Puerto Rico and on several islands in the Pacific, and the agency disseminates weather information to the flying public through FAA facilities. If an FSS is not available to provide the pilot with weather services, the NWS will do so directly.

nautical mile (NM) The standard unit of distance measurement used for marine and air navigation. One nautical mile equals 1.15 statute miles or 6,076.1 feet and is approximately equal to one minute of latitude (measured from a **great circle meridian**).

navaids Contraction for *navigational aids*. The term commonly refers to radio aids to navigation, such as **VOR, distance measuring equipment (DME),** and **automatic direction finders (ADF)**.

navigation instruments Those cockpit instruments used to participate with ground-based **navaids**. Typical instruments include the **VOR** indicator, the ADF **bearing indicator**, and the **radio magnetic indicator (RMI)**.

navigational plotter A device used by pilots and navigators to plot and measure courses, consisting of a straightedge, mileage scales, and a protractor.

NDB See **nondirectional radio beacon**.

Newton's Third Law of Motion The law that states: For every action there is an equal and opposite reaction. This law has been used to explain a portion of aerodynamic **lift** resulting from the **downwash** of airflow from the upper surface of an **airfoil**.

NM See **nautical mile**.

nondirectional radio beacon (NDB) Radio navigation station that broadcasts in the low- or medium-frequency range of 200 to 415 kHz; also called a *homing beacon*.

nonprecision approach A standard instrument approach procedure in which no electronic **glide slope** is provided. **Navaids** commonly used for nonprecision approaches include **VOR, NDB,** localizer only approaches, and **airport surveillance radar (ASR)** approaches.

nonstandard traffic pattern An airport traffic pattern in which all turns within the pattern are made to the right.

northeast trades In the Northern Hemisphere, northeast trade winds that blow from the subtropical belts of high pressure to the low-pressure area at the **equator**.

northerly-southerly turning error The **magnetic compass** error encountered in northern latitudes when flying on northerly and southerly headings. When an aircraft heading north begins a turn to a new heading, the compass gives a brief indication of a turn in the opposite direction. When turning from a southerly heading, the compass tends to anticipate the turn by moving in the proper direction and at a more rapid rate than the turn itself. This is caused by the magnet's tendency to follow the vertical as well as horizontal component of the earth's magnetic field, and by the mounting system used in the compass.

NOS See **National Ocean Survey**.

NOTAMs (notices to airmen) Notices containing information (not known sufficiently in advance to publish by other means) concerning the establishment, condition, or change of any facility, service, or procedure of or hazard in the national airspace system, the timely knowledge of which is essential to personnel concerned with flight operations. The publication *Notices to Airmen* is designed primarily as a pilot's operational manual containing current *NOTAM* information considered essential to the safety of flight as well as supplemental data to other aeronautical publications.

N prefix Aircraft identification prefix signifying the aircraft bearing such identification is registered in the United States.

NWS See **National Weather Service**.

OBS See **omni bearing selector**.

obscuration A condition in which a surface-based particulate phenomenon obscures visibility from the surface to a ceiling height that may be reported as definite or indefinite. Although there are a number of natural causes for surface obscurations, many are caused by industrial pollutants and automobile exhaust (smog).

occluded front A front that has been overtaken by another and forced aloft.

octane number The measure of a gasoline's ability to suppress detonation while delivering a high level of energy per unit weigh; also called the *antiknock value* of the gasoline. A fuel with an octane number of 80, for example, has as 80 percent of its mixture an ingredient that resists detonation.

oculogravic illusion A physiological condition in which acceleration of the aircraft causes the otolithic membrane in the inner ear to move (due to inertia); also called *acceleration illusion*. The result is a sensation of climbing that may cause the pilot to dive in an attempt to compensate for the illusory change in attitude. This can be especially dangerous when encountered after accelerating on takeoff at night or under conditions of low visibility.

oculogyral illusion A physiological illusion caused by stimulation of the semicircular canals. Objects in the field of vision appear to move when in fact they are stationary. Oculogyral illusion can occur as a complication to the **graveyard spiral** and the **Coriolis illusion**.

Off flag A component of airborn **VOR** receiver equipment. The Off flag comes into view on the cockpit instrument whenever the VOR signal is too weak for reliable navigation or when crossing a radial that is 90° to the radial selected on the **omni bearing selector**.

offshore wind An airflow related to the **convective currents** set up over land and water due to diurnal heating. At night land cools more quickly than water. The warmer water transfers its heat to the air, establishing rising air currents, while the cooling air descends over the land. The horizontal move-

ment of cooler air to feed the rising column of warmer air over the water is called an offshore wind or a *land breeze*. See also **onshore wind**.

oil filter A component of the power plant's oil system that traps contaminants.

oil pressure gauge A cockpit instrument that displays the pressure of the oil being sent to lubricate the engine, measured in pounds per square inch (psi).

oil temperature gauge A cockpit instrument that displays the temperature of the engine oil, measured in degrees Fahrenheit and/or Celsius.

OMEGA A network of eight VLF stations located throughout the world that provide navigational signals for long-distance flights over remote areas.

omni bearing selector (OBS) The control knob on the **VOR** receiver's cockpit display used to select the desired **radial** or course.

ONC See **operational navigation chart**.

onshore wind An airflow related to the **convective currents** set up over land and water due to diurnal heating. During the day land heats more rapidly than water, transferring its heat to the lower layers of air, which rise. The cooled air descends over the water and is transferred horizontally onto the land to feed the rising thermals, creating an onshore wind, or *sea breeze*.

operational navigational chart (ONC) Charts used for navigating long-range routes outside the United States. ONCs are prepared to the same scale as **world aeronautical charts (WAC)** but cover an area four times their size and so are printed on oversized sheets.

opposed cylinder arrangement The most common arrangement of **cylinders** used today in **reciprocating engines** for light aircraft. The cylinders are attached horizontally on the **crankcase** opposing each other.

orographic thunderstorm See **thunderstorm**.

oscillation errors Erroneous but transient readings on a **magnetic compass** caused by flight through rough air or rapid flight maneuvers.

outlook briefing A preflight weather briefing that provides only forecast data applicable to the proposed flight.

outside air temperature (OAT) gauge A cockpit instrument similar in construction to a home thermometer that reads the temperature outside the aircraft (free air temperature) in degrees Fahrenheit and Celsius. In addition to its usefulness in calculating temperature effects on aircraft performance, the OAT gauge should be consulted whenever subfreezing (icing) or **temperature inversion** conditions are suspected.

overrun area Any surface or area extending beyond the usable runway that appears to be usable but is not due to the nature of its construction.

pan The international radiotelephone urgency signal. When the word is repeated three times it indicates uncertainty or alert, followed by the nature of the urgent condition.

PAR See **precision approach radar**.

parallels See **lines of latitude**.

parasite drag That portion of total aerodynamic drag that is caused by everything other than lift-induced drag. Parasite drag includes *frontal* (or *flat-plate*) *drag*, which is related to the aircraft's cross-sectional area; *form drag*, which is a function of the shape of the aircraft's components; *skin-friction drag*, which is related to smoothness or roughness of the aircraft's surface finish; and *interference drag*, which is the result of airflows mixing at the wing root, strut intersections, door handles, and so on. At low airspeeds, the main component of total drag is drag due to lift (**induced drag**), since the wing is operating at a high **angle of attack**. At higher airspeeds, the angle of attack is lower, and the main component of total drag is parasite drag.

partial obscuration A condition similar to **obscuration** except that only a portion of the sky is obscured.

pattern altitude The published or broadcast altitude (MSL) at which a VFR airport traffic pattern is to be flown.

payload The useful load of an aircraft, including passengers, baggage, cargo, and so forth. The minimum flight crew required to operate the aircraft (such as the pilot) is usually not included in the specified payload.

PCA See **positive control area**.

performance As generally used in aviation, the takeoff, climb, cruise, and landing characteristics of an aircraft. Low performance aircraft tend to be aircraft with a low *wing loading* (low ratio of **gross weight** to wing area), short takeoff and landing runs, low rate of climb, and slower cruising speeds. High-performance aircraft tend to be aircraft with higher wing loading (higher ratio of gross weight to wing area), longer takeoff and landing runs, more rapid rates of climb, and higher cruising speeds. *Short takeoff and landing (STOL) aircraft* tend to have higher cruise and payload capabilities than would otherwise be expected from their short runway performance; this is usually achieved through such special design features as elaborate flap systems.

performance number The gasoline rating that indicates how much *beyond* a 100 percent **octane number** the fuel is capable of protecting an engine against **detonation**.

peripheral vision The ability of the eye to detect objects to the side of the center of vision. Using peripheral vision correctly is one of the keys to safe night flying, since the eye's daylight receptors are less efficient and the night receptors have a large blind spot in their center.

P-factor Abbreviation for *propeller factor*; a condition of asymmetric thrust from the disk of a loaded **propeller** operating at a high airplane **angle of attack**. On clockwise-rotating tractor engines, the ascending blade elements have a lower local angle of attack than do the descending blade elements, resulting in more thrust being generated on the right side of the propeller disk than on the left, resulting in airplane **yaw** to the left.

phonetic alphabet An alphabet adopted by the **International Civil Aviation Organization (ICAO)** that is used by FAA personnel when communications conditions are such that the information required cannot be readily received without their use. Pilots should use the phonetic alphabet when identifying their aircraft during initial contact with ATC or when aircraft with similar-sounding call signs are using the same frequency. The phonetic alphabet should also be used for single letters or to spell out groups of letters or difficult words during adverse communications conditions. As in most spoken languages, there is a "vernacular" associated with phonetic alphabet use that most pilots acquire with experience.

pilotage Navigating by reference to visible landmarks.

pilot balloon A small, unmanned hydrogen- or helium-filled balloon whose buoyancy is precisely controlled so that a known ascension rate results. The balloon is then tracked by ground observers to determine the wind velocity at various levels.

pilot-in-command A pilot properly certified to conduct a flight as sole operator of the aircraft's controls; the pilot responsible for operation and safety of an aircraft during flight time. After earning a **Private Pilot Certificate**, pilot-in-command time may be logged solo or with passengers, with other pilots in the aircraft (even those with higher pilot certificates), or in the company of a CFI.

Pilot's Automatic Telephone Weather Answering Service (PATWAS) A continuous telephone recording containing current and forecast weather information for pilots. PATWAS supplements the dissemination of initial weather information in busy terminal areas, although FSS weather briefers should still be consulted for a detailed route briefing. PATWAS locations are found in the *Airport/Facility Directory* under the FSS-CS/T Weather Service Telephone Numbers section.

Pilot's Operating Handbook The manual published by the aircraft's manufacturer containing operating limitations, procedures, normal and emergency checklist, performance charts, systems descriptions, and other important information necessary for the safe operation of the aircraft. Major sections of the handbook are reviewed and verified by the FAA during aircraft certification. This FAA-Approved Flight Manual may be integrated with the basic handbook or appear as a separate document.

pilot report (PIREP) A report of meteorological phenomena encountered by an aircraft in flight. PIREPs may be solicited by an FSS or controlling agency or may be volunteered by the pilot. They are the only source of information about certain weather data, such as actual icing conditions or height of cloud tops.

PIREP See **pilot report**.

piston A durable, moving "plunger" that precisely fits the interior of a **cylinder** on a **reciprocating engine**. The piston forms a nearly airtight seal for the area above it (the combustion chamber), and is connected to the throw (crankpin) of the **crankshaft** by a **connecting rod**. The burning air-fuel charge in the combustion chamber transmits its energy to the piston head, which then moves down the cylinder. The action of the connecting rod transforms this reciprocating motion to rotation of the crankshaft. See also **four-stroke cycle**.

pitch (attitude) Movement of the aircraft about its **lateral axis**. Pitch is controlled primarily by the **elevators**.

pitch (propeller) The blade angle of a **propeller**.

pitot air Ram air or impact air measured by the **pitot-static system**. Pitot air pressure is composed of two elements, static and dynamic; hence the pressure of the pitot air is said to represent "total pressure."

pitot head See **pitot tube**.

pitot-static (P-S) instruments Those cockpit instruments that require total and/or static pressure for operation. P-S instruments include the **airspeed indicator, altimeter,** and **vertical speed indicator.**

pitot-static (P-S) system A system of ports and receptacles and associated tubing to capture total and static pressure and route it to the **pitot-static instruments**. The P-S system normally includes a **pitot tube, static ports,** the pitot heat control, and an alternate static air source.

pitot tube A device for capturing pitot air, usually placed well clear of the propeller slipstream or other disturbed airflow; also called *pitot head*. The pitot tube may be heated electrically to prevent ice blockage during flight, and it usually has some protective covering that must be removed before flight.

planform The shape, form, or outline of an object as seen from above. The planform of an airplane includes its wing, tail, and fuselage geometry.

plotter See **navigational plotter**.

polar easterlies Winds circulating in a clockwise direction from the high-pressure region of the North Pole, coming from the east.

position lights Lights installed on an aircraft to form a directional triangle: red on the left wing, green on the right wing, and white on the tail; also called *navigation lights*. The orientation of these lights will always indicate an airplane's direction of flight.

position report A radiotelephone flight progress report given over a predetermined point on the ground or as directed by ATC. A complete VFR position report should include (in the following order): (1) aircraft identification, (2) position, (3) time (in minutes after the hour), (4) altitude, (5) VFR flight plan, and (6) destination.

positive control area (PCA) Airspace designed in FAR Part 71 in which aircraft are required to be operated under Instrument Flight Rules (IFR). The vertical extent of the PCA is from 18,000 feet to and including flight level 600 throughout most of the conterminous United States. Rules for operating in the PCA are found in FARs 91.97 and 91.24.

postural sensation The "seat-of-the-pants" sense resulting from the normal pressure of the seat, floor, armrests, and so forth on the pilot's body. Since positive load factors always work through the floor of the aircraft (the direction of normal gravity), these postural sensations can be erroneous indicators of the outside horizon.

precautionary forced landing An immediate landing made when the pilot determines that continued flight, even to the nearest airport, might not be possible and that an attempt to do so would put the aircraft into an uncontrollable situation.

precession Movement of the spin axis of a **gyroscope** with respect to its original alignment. *Apparent precession* is the movement of the earth's surface below the gyroscope, whose spin axis otherwise remains fixed in its original orientation. *Real precession* is the actual "tilting" of the spin axis due to some external force. Apparent precession is the result of the gyroscope's transportation over the earth's surface, or the earth's rotation below an airborne gyroscope. Real precession can be either inadvertent, caused by rotor imbalance or friction (called *gyro drift*), or intentional, such as the application of the gyro erection mechanism to realign the spin axis to a new position over the earth's surface.

precipitation The condensation and discharge of water vapor in the **atmosphere**. Precipitation can be in liquid form, such as rain or drizzle, or solid, such as snow or hail.

precision approach A standard instrument approach procedure in which an electronic **glide slope** is provided. **Navaids** commonly used for precision approaches are the **instrument landing system (ILS)** and **precision approach radar (PAR)**.

precision approach radar (PAR) Radar equipment in some ATC facilities (primarily serving military airports) that is used to detect and display the azimuth, range, and elevation of an aircraft on the **final approach** course to a runway. During PAR approaches the controller issues headings to the aircraft and informs the pilot when to begin the descent from **pattern altitude**. Subsequent instructions include the small heading changes necessary to maintain the final approach course and advice about the aircraft's distance above or below the **glide**

slope. The approach is terminated at the *decision height*, where the pilot either takes over visually and lands or misses the approach.

precision runway A runway served by nonvisual precision approach aids. Markings include nonprecision runway marking, **touchdown zone** marking, **fixed-distance marking**, plus **side stripes**.

preferred IFR routes Routes established between busier airports to increase ATC system efficiency and capacity. Preferred IFR routes are listed in the *Airport/Facility Directory*.

preflight inspection The examination of the aircraft's external structure, control surfaces, lighting, landing gear, pitot-static ports, and power plant before flight; also called the *walk-around inspection*. The preflight inspection should always be accomplished in accordance with the **Pilot's Operating Handbook checklist**.

preignition Ignition inside the combustion chamber of an internal combustion engine before the **spark plug** has fired, spoiling engine timing, reducing power available, and adding stress to engine components. Preignition is caused by incomplete burning of fuel that leaves hot carbon particles floating in the **cylinder** or by hot spots on the cylinder head or wall. Preignition that occurs after the ignition system has been turned off is sometimes called *dieseling* (after the diesel engine, which uses the heat of high compression within the cylinder, rather than spark plugs, to obtain normal ignition).

pressure-altitude The altitude above the standard datum plane, where the air pressure is 29.92 inches of mercury. Pressure-altitude may be read from the **altimeter** by setting 29.92 into the **Kollsman window**. Above 18,000 feet MSL, all aircraft use this altimeter setting.

pressure gradient See **gradient**.

prevailing visibility The greatest horizontal visibility equaled or exceeded throughout at least half of the horizon circle; it need not be continuous.

prevailing westerlies Winds circulating in a clockwise direction blowing toward the poles from a position of 30° North and South latitudes.

primary controls The flight controls essential to controlling the movements of an airplane about its three axes of motion: the **elevator, ailerons,** and **rudder**.

prime meridian The **line of longitude** that passes through the Royal Observatory at Greenwich, England; the 0° line of longitude in the **geographic coordinate system**. See also **coordinated universal time**.

primer See **engine primer**.

private pilot In general, a pilot certified by the FAA to operate an aircraft in the national airspace system for private purposes—that is, for reasons other than for compensation or hire. FAR Part 61 specifies the privileges and responsibilities of private pilots.

Private Pilot Certificate The certificate issued by the FAA to a private pilot specifying the kinds of flying (ratings and limitations) in which that pilot may engage. The certificate and a current **medical certificate** (third class or higher) must be carried each time the individual exercises the privileges of the certificate. Requirements for issuance, renewal, and replacement of Private Pilot Certificates are described in FAR Part 61.

proceeding direct A flight maneuver that involves leaving an aircraft's current position and traveling directly to a specified point, usually a radio **navaid** such as a **VOR**. Proceeding direct is not the same as **homing**, since homing does not guarantee a straight line track across the ground.

prog See **significant weather prognosis chart**.

prohibited area Designated airspace within which the flight of an aircraft is prohibited.

propeller A special **airfoil**, attached to the engine **crankshaft**, that rotates in a plane roughly 90 degrees to the aircraft's **fight path**, producing thrust in that direction.

propeller control Device in cockpit that controls the governor, which controls engine RPM.

propeller blade pitch See **pitch.**

propeller hub The point where the **propeller** blades converge; their attachment point to the **crankshaft.**

protractor A device for measuring angles, particularly for measuring course lines relative to true north on a navigational chart. See also **navigational plotter.**

pusher-type aircraft An aircraft whose power plant faces aft, "pushing" the aircraft through the air rather than pulling it.

radar Contraction for *radio detection and ranging;* a system using a pulsed beam of radio energy to scan for, detect, and return information about a target to the radar operator. Nonmilitary uses of radar include ATC (primary target scanning and ATCRBS), **airport surveillance radar (ASR)** and **precision approach radar (PAR)** instrument approaches, radar altimetry, collision-avoidance systems, and airborne weather radar.

radar summary chart A weather chart prepared hourly from special **National Weather Service** weather radars. The chart displays areas of precipitation heavy enough to show up as radar "echoes," annotated with supplemental information such as direction and speed of echo movements, precipitation trends and intensities, and tops of severe weather cells. The radar summary chart is primarily useful in picking out areas of dangerous weather in and around the cloud regions shown in other charts.

radial The **magnetic bearing** from a **VOR** station.

radial cylinder arrangement An arrangement in which the **cylinders** encircle a round or cylindrical **crankcase.** Radial arrangements are most frequently seen on large, piston-engine transports or vintage aircraft.

radiation fog Fog caused by the radiational cooling of the air above the ground at night; also called *ground fog* or *tule fog*. Radiation fog is most common under clear skies with calm winds just before and after sunrise.

radio compass General term for low- or medium-frequency **radio direction finding** and **automatic direction finding (ADF)** equipment, particularly the cockpit **bearing indicator** instrument.

radio direction finding (RDF) An alternate means of low- or medium-frequency **radio navigation** similar to the **automatic direction finder (ADF)**, except that the loop antenna used for signal reception must be positioned manually by locating the aural null, or area of minimum signal strength.

radio magnetic indicator (RMI) A cockpit navigational instrument that displays aircraft heading and bearing data. The instrument consists of a rotating compass card and two bearing pointers. The aircraft's **magnetic heading** is displayed under the top index, while the pointers display **automatic direction finding (ADF)** or **VOR magnetic bearings** as selected by the navigation receiver controls.

radio navigation Navigation accomplished by observing the aircraft's **bearings** (radio **lines of position**) from one or more ground-based stations. Radio navigation methods include **VOR, ADF, TACAN**, and **DME.**

radiosondes Miniature meteorological observation units lofted into the atmosphere via balloon or rocket that make a parachute descent to the earth, transmitting pressure, temperature, and humidity data as they return. Since these units cannot always be readily recovered after landing, the National Weather Service offers a reward for each probe returned to their facilities.

ram air Air impacting the **pitot tube.**

ramp condition The weight of the airplane ready to taxi.

rate of climb indicator See **vertical speed indicator (VSI)**.

rate of interception How fast the aircraft encounters the desired course (**radial** or **bearing**), as indicated in the cockpit by the rate of movement of the VOR **course deviation indicator** or the ADF bearing pointer. The rate of intercept is influenced by the aircraft's **ground speed**, intercept angle, distance from the station, and whether or not the aircraft is proceeding to or from the station. Rapid movement of the CDI or bearing pointer indicates a high rate of intercept.

RCC See **Rescue Coordination Center**.

RDF See **radio direction finding**.

real precession See **precession**.

reciprocal heading A direction 180° opposite to the given heading or course.

reciprocating engine An internal combustion engine in which the rotary motion of the **crankshaft** is obtained by linkage to the movement of a **piston** within a **cylinder**.

rectifier An electrical device that transforms alternating current into direct current.

redout A physiological condition in which the blood pools in the head and upper extremities due to the presence of negative G forces. This pooling causes a saturation of tissues with blood around the optic nerve, causing a definite reddening of the vision and the feeling that one's eyeballs are popping out.

redundancy The concept used in the design of critical or safety-related systems in aviation; the use of backup or independent systems to perform the same key functions.

relative bearing The **bearing** of a station or object relative to the aircraft's heading, measured clockwise in degrees. For an aircraft passing the station off the right wing tip, for example, the relative bearing is 90°.

relative humidity The ratio of the amount of moisture in the air to the amount of moisture that the air could hold at the same temperature. Relative humidity is usually expressed as a percent.

relative wind The direction of airflow parallel and opposite to the flight path of the aircraft.

relaxation response A method of personal stress management that involves "programming" oneself to take immediate and automatic countermeasures at the first signs of excessive stress. Response techniques include taking a deep breath or sighing, breathing evenly and regularly, repositioning the arms and legs (feet and hands), wiggling the fingers and toes to release muscular tension, and letting go of stressful, nonproductive thoughts.

Rescue Coordination Center (RCC) A search and rescue (SAR) facility equipped and manned to coordinate and control SAR operations in an area designated by the SAR plan. The

U.S. Coast Guard and the U.S. Air Force have responsibility for the operation of RCCs.

respiration   Breathing; the exchange of gases between the lungs and the atmosphere.

restricted area   Airspace designated under FAR Part 73 within which the flight of an aircraft, while not wholly prohibited, is subject to restriction. Most restricted areas are designated joint use, and IFR/VFR operations in the area may be authorized by the controlling ATC facility when it is not being used by the operating agency. Restricted areas are depicted on **sectional** and **world aeronautical charts**. Where joint use is authorized, the name of the ATC controlling facility is also shown.

retina   The light-sensitive portion of the eyeball where the visual image is formed. See also **rods** and **cones**.

rhumb line   An arc segment of a **small circle**—that is, any curved line on the earth's surface. Rhumb lines cross all **meridians** at a constant angle and thus have some utility in marine navigation, though they usually make poor course lines in aviation, since they do *not* represent the shortest distance between the two points they connect.

rich mixture   See **mixture control system**.

ridge   An elongated area of high pressure.

rime ice   A deposit of milky, opaque, granular ice particles usually formed on the **airframe** leading edges during flight through visible moisture at subfreezing temperatures. Rime ice is most likely to form at temperatures of -10 degrees to -40 degrees Celsius. While rime ice is less dangerous than **clear ice**, it is three times more common.

rings   Precision objects that fit into grooves in the pistons and form a tight seal against the cylinder walls.

RMI   See **radio magnetic indicator**.

RNAV   See **area navigation**.

rods   Light sensors in the eye's retina that report only black and white information to the brain. Rods are located in the peripheral vision portion of the retina. See also **retina** and **cones**.

roll   The movement of an airplane about its **longitudinal axis**, controlled by the **ailerons**.

rotation   On takeoff, the change of pitch accomplished to assume the proper airplane attitude for liftoff. This action is accomplished because the airplane will accelerate more quickly in a level attitude (with the nose wheel in contact with the runway) than if the takeoff attitude is established too early, exacting a higher than necessary penalty in lift-induced drag during the takeoff roll. See also **rotation speed**.

rotation speed   The airspeed at which you establish the airplane's takeoff attitude by raising the nose. See also **rotation**.

rotor (of a gyroscope)   The spinning mass that gives a **gyroscope** its rigidity in space.

rotor cloud   A turbulent altocumulus cloud sometimes found in the lee of a mountain range in the presence of a **mountain wave**; also known as a *roll cloud*.

rotorcraft   An aircraft that generates lift through the rotation of a long, thin "wing" (rotor) above the fuselage. **Helicopters** and **gyroplanes** are examples of rotorcraft.

rough engine   An engine that "misses" (due to mistiming of ignition, fouled **spark plugs**, or a deal **cylinder**), causing an uneven engine noise and airplane vibration.

round-robin flight   A **cross-country flight**, the final destination of which is the airport of initial departure.

rudder   The primary control surface that controls **yaw**, or the movement of the airplane about its **vertical axis**.

runway gradient   See **gradient**.

runway identification number   The means of identifying a runway, labeled for the runway's magnetic direction rounded off to the nearest 10°. For example, a runway with a magnetic direction of 250° would be numbered 25. Parallel runways are further identified with a letter indicating their relative position on the airport: L (left), R (right), and C (center).

runway visual range (RVR)   An instrumentally derived value, based on standard calibrations, that represents the horizontal distance a pilot will see down the runway from the approach end based either on the sighting of high-intensity runway lights or on the visual contrast of other targets, whichever yields the greater visual range. RVR, in contrast to prevailing or runway visibility, is based on what the pilot of a moving aircraft should see looking down the runway. RVR is the horizontal visual range, not the slant visual range. It is based on the measurement of a transmissometer made near the touchdown point of the instrument runway and is reported in hundreds of feet.

SA   See **surface analysis chart**.

sailplane   See **glider**.

saturation   The condition of 100 percent relative humidity; air that contains the maximum amount of water vapor possible for the current pressure and temperature.

scale error   A characteristic of most **altimeters** in which the aneroids do not assume the exact size designed for a particular pressure difference. Typical scale errors might be a reading of 970 feet at a reference altitude of 1000 feet, or 10,050 feet at a level of 10,000 feet. Scale error is sometimes combined with installation error on an altitude correction card in the cockpit.

sea breeze   See **onshore wind**.

Second Class Medical Certificate   The medical certificate required to exercise the privileges of a commercial pilot. This certificate expires at the end of the twelfth month after the date of issue.

sectional aeronautical chart   The largest-scale aeronautical chart commonly used, with a scale of 8 miles to the inch. Based on the Lambert conformal conic projection and designed primarily for pilotage navigation by low-performance aircraft flying at low to medium altitudes, the charts feature topographical details chosen for their relevance to visual navigation, aeronautical data (such as airports and **navaids**), and supplemental legends and notes that are often as informative as the graphic depictions.

segmented circle   A system of visual indicators designed to provide **traffic pattern** information at airports without operating control towers. The circle frequently contains the **landing direction indicator**, wind sock, and L-shaped markers (**traffic pattern indicators**) arranged to show the base to final turn portions of the usable runways.

self-contained instruments   Those cockpit instruments that do not rely on outside power sources to operate, such as the **magnetic compass** (powered by the earth's magnetic field) and the **outside air temperature (OAT) gauge** (powered by a temperature probe).

sequence report   See **surface aviation weather report**.

servo motors   Actuating devices that receive control signals, perform a required action, and then send back a signal confirming that the action has taken place; also called **servos**.

severe weather watch bulletin (WW) An inflight advisory issued by the National Severe Storms Forecast Center (NSSFC) in Kansas City, Missouri, whenever severe **thunderstorm** conditions exist in a given area.

shielding Insulating of high-voltage wiring to minimize electromagnetic interference with aircraft radios and other equipment.

short circuit An undesired electrical path somewhere in the electrical system.

short field For performance purposes, a runway with an obstacle at the approach end (if landing), or the departure end (if taking off).

short field landing A landing made with fully lowered flaps during which the airplane uses maximum allowable braking to achieve a minimum total landing distance and ground roll.

side stripes (runway) Markings added to a runway's edges to facilitate landing surface identification during **precision** instrument **approaches**.

SIGMET (WS) Literally, significant meteorological information; a weather advisory about weather significant to the safety of all aircraft. SIGMETs cover severe and extreme turbulence, severe icing, and widespread dust or sandstorms that reduce visibility to less than 3 miles.

signaler An airport ground crew employee authorized to guide aircraft into and out of parking spots on the ramp using a standard set of hand and arm signals.

significant weather prognosis chart (prog) A four-panel chart forecasting expected changes to the current weather described on the **surface analysis** and **weather depiction charts**. The left-hand pair show a 12-hour prognosis and the right-hand pair a 24-hour prognosis. Upper charts use weather depiction symbols, while the lower charts show the movement of high- and low-pressure areas and precipitation. The charts assist pilots in extrapolating movements of weather patterns and detecting development or decay of significant weather that might affect their flights.

single-engine land A class of aircraft in the airplane category. See also **category, class**.

single-engine water A class of aircraft in the airplane category. See also **category, class.**

sink rate Vertical speed in a descent, especially on **final approach** at low airspeeds.

skid Sideward motion of an airplane in flight produced by centrifugal force.

skin friction drag See **parasite drag**.

sky cover The extent of clouds, whether or not they form a ceiling. *Clear* (CLR) means that less than one-tenth of the sky is covered. *Scattered* (SCT) means that the sky is one-tenth through one-half covered. *Broken* (BKN) means that six-tenths through nine-tenths is covered. *Overcast* (OVC) means more than nine-tenths coverage. See also **obscuration** and **partial obscuration**.

sky obscured See **obscuration**.

sky partially obscured See **partial obscuration**.

sky waves Radio signals reflected by the **ionosphere** back to the earth's surface. The range of sky waves is limited only by the power available to the transmitter.

slant range distance The distance from an aircraft to a given object on the ground; the *hypotenuse* of a right triangle formed by the aircraft's altitude and the linear (ground) distance to the object from a point directly beneath the aircraft. **Distance measuring equipment (DME)** measures slant range distance rather than ground distance. The error between slant range and ground distances becomes more significant with increased altitude and a shorter distance from the object or station.

slant range visibility The "over-the-nose" visibility necessary to fly an airplane to the runway, as opposed to ground visibility, **prevailing visibility**, or horizontal flight visibility, all of which may be above minimum criteria for landing but not representative of slant range visibility.

slip The controlled flight of an airplane in a direction not in line with its **longitudinal axis.**

slipstream The rotating current or air driven aft by the **propeller.**

slow flight Flight at minimum controllable airspeed.

slow routes (SR) Low-altitude, low-airspeed (below 250 knots) military training routes. SRs are depicted on aeronautical charts, and their status can be ascertained by contacting the nearest **Flight Service Station.**

small circle A curved line on the surface of a sphere caused by the intersection of the sphere and the line's plane, the extension of which does not pass through the center of the sphere. All **lines of latitude** (except the **equator**) are small circles. See also **rhumb line**.

soaring An aviation sport using special **gliders**, called **sailplanes**, to ride the natural **convective currents** in the air.

soft field For airplane performance purposes, any runway without a hard surface—for example, dirt, gravel, grass, or sod runways.

solo flight A flight in which the pilot is the sole occupant of the aircraft. *Supervised solos* are the student's initial solo flights, in which the instructor "supervises" the student's takeoffs and landings from a position near the runway.

spark plug That part of the **ignition system** that converts the magneto's high-voltage current to a spark within the combustion chamber.

spatial disorientation A physiological disorder in which the pilot cannot readily orient the aircraft to the natural horizon. Caused by a number of sensory illusions, spatial disorientation is sometimes referred to as *vertigo*.

special-use airspace Airspace of defined dimensions identified by an area of the surface of the earth to which activities must be confined because of their nature and/or in which limitations may be imposed upon aircraft operations that are not a part of those activities. See also **alert area, military operations area, prohibited area, restricted area, warning area.**

special VFR clearance Weather conditions in a control zone that are less than basic VFR and in which some aircraft are permitted flight under Visual Flight Rules. Such operations must be requested by the pilot and approved by ATC.

spin A prolonged stall in which the airplane rotates about its **center of gravity** while it descends, usually with its nose well down below the horizon line. A *flat spin* is one in which the nose is raised closer to level flight attitude during rotation.

spinner A cone-shaped **fairing** fitted over the hub of a **propeller**. The spinner helps direct cooling air into the engine, reduce total airplane drag, and, on **constant-speed propellers**, protect the propeller governor assembly.

spoiler A flaplike device usually installed on the upper surface of a wing to "spoil" lift and increase drag when it is thrust up into the airflow.

squall line A relatively narrow line of active **thunderstorms** usually preceding, but not a part of, a weather **front**. The instability associated with squall lines and the resulting severe weather are among the most violent of all storms.

squawk An instruction by an air traffic controller to activate specific modes, codes, or functions on the aircraft's transponder—for example, "Squawk one two, zero, zero." The term derives from colloquial reference to early transponders as parrots.

squelch A control on the aircraft's voice radio transceiver that blocks static noise when no desired signal is being received.

stabilator A tail plane component used on some aircraft that combines the functions of **horizontal stabilizer** and **elevator** in a single, movable structure.

stability (airplane) Composed of two elements: *static stability*, the initial tendency for the airplane to return to its original trimmed condition after a displacement, and *dynamic stability*, the motions of the airplane in response to its static stability tendencies over a short period of time. An airplane may exhibit *positive, negative,* or *neutral* stability, depending on whether the responses after displacement are self-dampening, self-reinforcing, or continuous, respectively. Most modern airplanes are designed for both positive static and positive dynamic stability about all axes. Stability about the **longitudinal (roll) axis** is called *lateral stability*. Stability about the **vertical (yaw) axis** is called *directional stability*. Stability about the **lateral (pitch) axis** is called *longitudinal stability*. See also **dihedral**.

stability (atmospheric) The tendency of a parcel of air to return to its original condition after being displaced. Atmospheric *instability* is usually manifested by convective activity, **cumuliform clouds**, and **thunderstorms**.

stabilized area (of a runway) Certain areas around some runways and taxiways that are not designed to support aircraft, even though they are hard surfaced. Stabilized areas are marked with a distinctive chevron pattern.

stall A flight maneuver or condition in which the wing's **angle of attack** for maximum **lift** has been exceeded, resulting in turbulent airflow, **buffeting**, and abrupt loss of lift. Although pilots are accustomed to think of stalls in relation to "flying speed," a stall is a function of angle of attack *only* and can occur at any attitude or airspeed.

stall speed The speed at which an airplane wing stalls in level flight; the minimum speed possible for level flight.

stall warning device A sensor on the wing's leading edge, as well as a light or horn (or both) to warn that a stall is near; required by FAA on most certified planes.

standard atmosphere A statistical average of atmospheric values calculated for a number of important variables and set to a "typical" *standard day* at sea level of 59 degrees Fahrenheit (15 degrees Celsius) and 29.92 inches of mercury (1013.2 millibars); officially known as *U.S. Standard Atmosphere* or *International Standard Atmosphere (ISA)*.

standard briefing The most complete preflight weather briefing, consisting of a "big picture" weather synopsis, a current weather report for the particular flight route, a weather forecast and winds aloft information, suggestions for alternate routes (if applicable), and a review of *NOTAMs*.

standard conditions See **standard atmosphere**.

standard day See **standard atmosphere**.

standard lapse rate See **adiabatic lapse rate**.

standard rate of turn Three degrees of heading change per second, or a 360-degree turn in 2 minutes; also called *standard rate of turn*.

standard traffic pattern A visual **traffic pattern** in which all turns within the pattern are made to the left.

starter motor A device usually combined with an electric generator used to rotate the engine initially (on start) and disengaged thereafter; sometimes called *starter-generator*.

static More specifically, *static electricity*, or electrical charges at rest. Static is an electrical disturbance caused by static charges jumping across insulated joints in the airplane. When static conditions are present in the air *bonding* is the process of providing channels in the **airframe** through which these charges may pass without causing sparks and the resulting "pop and crackle" in the radio equipment. All aircraft pick up a certain static electrical charge while moving through the air. This charge could cause electrical shock upon landing if it were not discharged in some manner. Static discharge wires, static-conducting tires, and trailing-edge static-discharge "wicks" are all devices for removing static electricity from aircraft. See also **grounding wire**.

static air Still air, or that portion of total pressure resulting from **atmospheric pressure** at a given altitude; also called *static pressure*.

static ports Receptacles mounted in a region of relatively undisturbed airflow on the **fuselage** to allow pressure changes in static air to enter the aircraft's **pitot-static system**. The ports are normally aligned at right angles to the flight path (fuselage) to minimize erroneous readings due to dynamic pressure effects.

static stability See **stability (airplane)**.

stationary front A frontal zone along which one **air mass** does not move to replace the other; a **front** that moves less than 5 miles per hour.

station model A grouping of weather symbols and information around a station circle on a **surface analysis chart** that marks the geographic location of the reporting station.

station pressure The **atmospheric pressure** reported at an airport or other geographical location converted to sea level. This pressure is used for **altimeter** setting corrections when operating in the vicinity of the station.

stopover flight plan A **flight plan** that includes two or more separate en route flight segments with a stopover at one or more intermediate airports.

stopway See **overrun area**.

stratosphere The layer of **atmosphere** between the **troposphere** and the mesosphere where the air is characterized by constant, cold temperatures and a lack of vertical currents.

stratus clouds A principal cloud type of the stratoform group, appearing as a uniform sheet, low lying and gray in color. When precipitation is present, it is sparse (drizzle or light snow). Stratus clouds, which can cover a widespread area, are usually associated with a stable **air mass**.

stress Bodily or mental tension resulting from exertion or psychological factors. Some stress is necessary for productive activity, but excessive stress can lead to a variety of physical and psychological disorders. See also **relaxation response**.

student pilot A pilot certified to operate an aircraft for purposes of dual instruction or practice solo flight, subject to the limitations noted and endorsed in the student's logbook.

Student Pilot Certificate A document that bears the Student Pilot Certificate on one side and a current, properly endorsed **medical certificate**—third class or above—on the other.

sublimation The physical process by which matter in the solid state changes directly to a gas (or a gas directly into a solid) without passing through the liquid state.

sump (fuel system) A small drain at a local low point in the fuel system.

sump (oil) A reservoir containing engine lubricating oil located on the lower portion of an engine.

supercharger A device for increasing the manifold pressure of an internal combustion engine that operates by compressing the air-fuel charge delivered to the **cylinders**, developing more engine power and allowing the aircraft to operate at higher altitudes; also called a *turbosupercharger*.

surface analysis chart (SA) A weather chart issued every 3 hours showing pressure patterns, **fronts**, surface winds, temperatures and **dew points**, restrictions to visibility, and other information. See also **station model**.

surface aviation weather report A report containing a variety of specific aviation-related weather details in an easy-to-read, standard sequence, every hour, 24 hours a day; also called *hourly sequence report*, or simply *sequence report*. The report contains some or all of the following information in the order presented: station designator; type of report; time of report; sky ceiling and condition; visibility; weather and obstructions to visibility; sea level pressure in millibars; temperature; dew point; wind direction and speed, including gusts, if applicable; altimeter setting; and remarks and coded data.

TACAN See **tactical air navigation**.

tachometer A cockpit instrument that measures and displays engine **crankshaft** revolutions per minute (rpms).

tactical air navigation (TACAN) A UHF electronic **navaid** that provides suitably equipped aircraft (normally military) with a continuous indication of **bearing** and distance to the TACAN station.

tail assembly See **empennage**.

tail-wheel aircraft Aircraft with an undercarriage arrangement consisting of two main landing gear and a tail wheel; also called *conventional gear* aircraft.

tailwind Any wind that approaches the aircraft from a rearward direction and acts in conjunction with its course. A direct tailwind approaches the aircraft "from the tail." A wind approaching from any other direction to either wing tip will have both tailwind and **crosswind** components. A tailwind or tailwind component always acts to increase the aircraft's **ground speed**.

takeoff condition The weight condition of the airplane ready for takeoff. The takeoff condition is derived by subtracting the **moment** and weight of fuel allowed for start, taxi, and runup from airplane ramp weight.

takeoff leg A **flight path** parallel to the landing runway in the direction of takeoff; also called the *upwind leg*.

TAS See **true airspeed**.

TC See **true course**.

TCA See **terminal control area**.

temperature A measure of thermal energy.

temperature inversion A momentary reversal of the normal **adiabatic lapse rate**; a layer of warm air overlying a layer of cooler air.

terminal approach procedure booklets Published low- and high-altitude instrument approach procedures for airports served by **VOR, VORTAC, ILS,** and **NDB navaids**.

terminal areas Airspace in which approach control or airport traffic control service is provided. See also **airport traffic area, terminal control area**.

terminal control area (TCA) Controlled airspace extending upward from the surface or higher to specified altitudes, within which all aircraft are subject to operating rules and pilot and equipment requirements specified in FAR Part 91. TCAs are depicted in **sectional charts, world aeronautical charts,** en route low-altitude charts, Department of Defense FLIP charts, and TCA charts.

terminal forecast (FT) Twenty-four-hour forecasts prepared three times daily for various large airports and teletyped throughout the National Weather Service network. F T information includes ceiling, cloud height, sky cover, visibility, weather, surface winds, and a classification of anticipated weather called a **categorical forecast**, which deals specifically with expected VFR or IFR conditions associated with the last 6 hours of the forecast.

terminal radar service area (TRSA) Airspace surrounding designated airports in which ATC provides radar vectoring, sequencing, and separation on a full-time basis for all IFR and participating VFR aircraft. Service provided in a TRSA is called *Stage III service*. Graphics depicting TRSA layout and communications frequencies are shown in *Graphic Notices and Supplemental Data*. Pilot participation is urged but is not mandatory. See also **Terminal Radar Service Program**.

Terminal Radar Service Program A national program instituted to extend the terminal radar services provided to IFR and VFR aircraft. Pilot participation in the program is urged but is not mandatory. The progressive stages of the program are referred to as basic radar service (formerly Stage I), Stage II, and Stage III. *Basic radar service* provides traffic information and limited vectoring to VFR aircraft as workloads permit. *Stage II service* provides, in addition to Stage I service, vectoring and sequencing on a full-time basis to arriving VFR traffic. The purpose is to adjust the flow of arriving IFR and VFR aircraft into the traffic pattern in a safe and orderly manner and to provide traffic advisories to departing VFR traffic. *Stage III service* provides, in addition to Stage II services, separation between all participating aircraft. The purpose is to provide separation between all VFR and all IFR aircraft operating within the airspace defined as a **terminal radar service area (TRSA)**.

tetrahedron A wind direction indicator consisting of four triangular-shaped sides.

TH See **true heading**.

thermal See **convective current**.

Third Class Medical Certificate The **medical certificate** required to exercise the privileges of a student or private pilot. Expires at the end of the twenty-fourth calendar month after the date of issue.

three-cell circulation The three basic zones of weather operating in each hemisphere of the earth: the *equator to 30° latitude*, with warm air rising from a permanent low-pressure area; *30° latitude to 60° latitude*, the belt of prevailing westerlies, with air mixing from both north and south and frequent storms; and *60° latitude to the pole,* building a permanent low-pressure area at the 60° zone from northward-

and southward-moving air, the vertical column rising to descend again at the cold polar region to form a permanent high, from which southerly flow recommences.

threshold A line perpendicular to the runway centerline designating the beginning of the portion of a runway that is usable for landing.

throttle control The cockpit control that regulates the movement of the **throttle** (or butterfly) **valve** of the **carburetor**, allowing more or less of the vaporized air-fuel mixture to enter the **cylinders**, increasing or decreasing engine speed.

throttle valve An oval metal ("butterfly" type) disc located in the throttle shaft of the **carburetor**, activated by a mechanical linkage to the **throttle** in the cockpit. When the valve is in its closed position, the suction in the carburetor's venturi is reduced, and less air-fuel mixture is delivered to the engine. Conversely, a fully opened throttle delivers maximum power from the engine.

throw Crankpin displacement from the **crankshaft**.

thrust The forward pushing or pulling force developed by an aircraft engine.

thunderstorm A storm accompanied by lightning and thunder; **cumulonimbus (Cbs)**. Thunderstorms are of several types: *air mass thunderstorms* are caused by the heating of the air at the earth's surface by convection. *Orographic thunderstorms* are the product of moist air approaching and being uplifted by mountain ranges. *Frontal thunderstorms* are formed by a similar vertical motion, though the impetus for development comes from the mechanical lifting of one air mass by the other. The life cycle of a thunderstorm follows three definite stages of development, each with special characteristics and hazards: *cumulus stage*, characterized by rapid vertical development with convection currents in and around the clouds; *mature stage*, a mixture of convective currents in and around certain sectors of the cloud, with heavy downdrafts near the center; appearance of first rain at the surface, some of it quite heavy, considered the storm's most dangerous phase; *dissipating* or *"anvil" stage*, identified by the formation of the anvil-shaped cirroform clouds at the top of the storm, blown by high-altitude winds in the general direction of the storm's movement; generally a decrease of rain at the surface, though hail and other precipitation, including severe airframe icing and turbulence, can still be experienced aloft.

time of useful consciousness (TUC) The time available to a pilot or passenger from the moment oxygen deficiency begins to loss of consciousness.

time zone A geographical area measured every 15° of longitude (1 hour) from the Greenwich **meridian** in which all local times are the same. Local time may be corrected to **coordinated universal time** by adding 1 hour for every time zone in between (to the west), or subtracting 1 hour for every time zone if the local point is to the east of Greenwich. Due to local preferences, not all time zones have boundaries exactly coincident with their appropriate east and west meridians, and some locations do not adjust from standard to daylight savings time.

To-From indicator A component of the **VOR** cockpit indicator that shows whether the course selected will take the aircraft to or from the station at its present position; also called *To-From Flag*.

torque The twisting moment or "rotary power" produced by an engine turning a **crankshaft**. The term is also applied to

the rolling moment experienced by an aircraft in response to this rotation. The larger the **propeller**, the greater the torque effects.

touch-and-go landing A flight maneuver designed to increase pilot proficiency in which a normal touchdown is followed by an immediate application of power and another takeoff, without the airplane braking or taxiing clear of the runway.

touchdown zone The first 3000 feet of the runway beginning at the **threshold**.

track The actual **flight path** of an aircraft over the surface of the earth.

traffic pattern The traffic flow that is prescribed for aircraft landing at, taxiing on, or taking off from an airport. See also **base leg, crosswind leg, downwind leg, final approach, nonstandard traffic pattern, standard traffic pattern, upwind leg**.

traffic pattern indicators See **segmented circle**.

transceiver A combination voice radio transmitter and receiver.

Transcribed Weather Broadcast (TWEB) A continuous recording of meteorological and aeronautical information broadcast on L/MF and **VOR** facilities for pilots. The message includes station identification, general weather forecast, **PIREPs**, radar reports (when available), winds aloft data, and weather reports for selected locations within a 250-mile radius of the central point.

transition area Controlled airspace extending upward from 700 feet or more above the surface of the earth when designated in conjunction with an airport for which an approved instrument approach procedure has been prescribed or from 1200 feet or more above the surface of the earth when designated in conjunction with airway route structures or segments. Unless otherwise indicated, transition areas terminate at the base of the overlying controlled airspace. Transition areas are designed to contain IFR operations in controlled airspace during portions of terminal operation and while transiting between the terminal and the en route environment.

transponder The airborne radar beacon receiver/transmitter portion of the **Air Traffic Control Radar Beacon System (ATCRBS)** that automatically receives radio signals from the ground and selectively replies with a specific reply pulse or pulse group only to those interrogations being received on the mode to which it is set to respond. *Mode A* provides 4096 codes normally used by ATC in the United States. *Mode C* adds the capability of automatic altitude reporting.

transverse Gs Accelerations experienced in a fore-and-aft direction.

trim tabs Secondary flight controls normally located on the primary flight controls that, when displaced, reposition the primary control surface, relieving control system forces. An airplane must be in trim to exhibit its design stability characteristics.

tropopause The boundary zone that separates the **troposphere** and the **stratosphere**.

troposphere The layer of the earth's **atmosphere** lying closest to the surface; the most active area for weather of all types. The troposphere extends to an altitude of 29,000 feet at the poles and to 54,000 feet at the **equator**.

trough An elongated low-pressure area.

TRSA See **terminal radar service area**.

true airspeed (TAS) Equivalent airspeed corrected for air density; the measure of the aircraft's actual speed through a mass of air. For airspeeds below 200 knots, **calibrated** and equivalent **airspeeds** can be considered the same. See also **airspeed**.

true altitude   An object's actual height above mean sea level; calibrated altitude corrected for nonstandard atmospheric conditions.

true course (TC)   An aircraft's course with respect to true north; a straight line *(true course line)* plotted on a chart based on a Lambert conformal conic projection, such as a **sectional** aeronautical **chart**.

true heading (TH)   The **true course**, measured in degrees, plus or minus a **wind correction angle**.

TUC   See **time of useful consciousness**.

tule fog   See **radiation fog**.

turbocharged, turbocharger   See **supercharger**.

turbulence   Irregular motion of the **atmosphere** resulting from unstable air; land flow or mountain flow, **wind shear**, and other phenomena. See also **clear air turbulence, land flow turbulence, mountain wave, wing tip vortices**.

turn and slip indicator   See **turn coordinator**.

turn coordinator   A **gyroscopic instrument** that displays the aircraft's rate of turn and the quality of the turn (degree of **rudder** and **aileron** coordination). The **gyroscope** is canted (angled) in a restricted mounting and reflects the rate of turn by banking a miniature airplane on the instrument face in the direction of turn appropriate to the turn rate being experienced. The lower portion of the instrument contains an **inclinometer**, which displays turn coordination. The *turn and slip indicator* is an older style instrument that performs a similar function, but with a needle and reference indices (calibrated for a standard rate turn) above an inclinometer. See also **standard rate of turn**.

TWEB   See **Transcribed Weather Broadcast**.

type of aircraft   A subdivision of aircraft **class**; the specific make and model of the aircraft, such as Beechcraft Skipper model 177 or Boeing 747B.

ultrahigh frequencies (UHF)   The frequency band between 300 and 3000 MHz; the bank of radio frequencies used for military air/ground voice communications, **TACAN, DME,** and **ILS glide slope navaids**.

uncontrolled airport   An airport without a functioning control tower.

uncontrolled airspace   That portion of the airspace that has not been designated as a **continental control area, control area, control zone, terminal control area,** or **transition area**.

undercarriage   An aircraft's landing gear.

UNICOM   A nongovernment air/ground radio communication facility that may provide airport advisory service at certain airports. Locations and frequencies of UNICOMs are shown on aeronautical charts and publications.

universal mounting   The suspension of a **gyroscope** by means of three or more gimbals, which allows the spin axis to turn and tilt. See also **precession**.

unstable air   See **stability (atmospheric)**.

upslope fog   Fog that occurs when a mass of moist air is lifted into a cooler region, such as when winds move against a mountainside.

upwind leg   See **takeoff leg**.

usable fuel   The fuel capacity of the aircraft less *unusable fuel*, or the weight of fuel remaining in the tanks and lines that,

because of the design, is not available to the engine.

useful load   Everything that can be added to the **basic empty weight** of the aircraft until the maximum ramp weight is attained. Useful load includes **usable fuel** and **payload**.

vacuum system   A system using an air-pressure or a vacuum pump to energize the **gyroscopic instruments**. An engine-driven pump provides a suction force through a series of tubes that draws air over the gyro rotors and keeps them spinning. A cockpit vacuum pressure gauge shows if the pressure generated by the pump is adequate to power the system.

Valsalva technique   A method of clearing an ear block on ascent or descent by pinching the nostrils closed and blowing *gently*.

vapor lock   Bubbles of air or gasoline vapor that form a block in a fuel line. Vapor lock is precipitated by fuel that vaporizes too easily and fuel lines that feature many sharp bends.

variation   The angular difference between true north and magnetic north for any given location. Variation values are depicted on aeronautical charts used for VFR navigation. See also **compass variation**.

VASI   See **visual approach slope indicator**.

vector   A physical quantity having magnitude and direction; a **magnetic heading** issued by a controller to an aircraft to provide navigational guidance by radar.

velocity   An object's speed and direction of movement.

venturi tube   A tube with a local constriction, used to demonstrate **Bernoulli's Principle**.

vertical axis   An imaginary reference line that runs through the top and bottom of an aircraft and the **center of gravity**. Movement about the vertical axis is called **yaw**.

vertical speed indicator (VSI)   The cockpit flight instrument that measures and displays the rate of change in altitude; also called the *rate of climb indicator*.

vertical stabilizer   The **airfoil** and structural member in the empennage group used to stabilize the aircraft about its **vertical axis**. The **rudder** is usually attached to the trailing edge of the vertical stabilizer, and by its movements, it changes the airfoil characteristics of the stabilizer so that desired **yaw** changes occur.

vertigo   See **spatial disorientation**.

very high frequencies (VHF)   The frequency band between 30 and 300 MHz. Portions of this band, 108 to 118 MHz, are used for certain **navaids**; 118 to 136 MHz are used for civil air/ground voice communications. Other frequencies in this band are used for purposes not related to air traffic control.

VFR   See **Visual Flight Rules**.

VFR planning chart   A medium-scale chart used for preliminary flight planning by VFR pilots. It shows much of the same information depicted on **sectional charts** but with somewhat fewer details. The VFR planning chart is frequently wall mounted by **FBOs** and flying schools.

VFR terminal control area chart   A large-scale chart (4 miles to the inch) depicting the **TCA** of a particular airport. In addition to data such as that on **sectional charts**, information includes TCA operational data relevant to VFR flights, such as ATC frequencies, call-up points, lateral boundaries, ceilings, and floors.

VHF omnidirectional range (VOR)   A ground-based **navaid** transmitting VHF navigational signals (called **radials**) 360 degrees in azimuth, oriented from magnetic north. Used as the basis for navigation in the national airspace system. The VOR periodically identifies itself by Morse code and may have an additional voice identification feature. Voice features may be used by ATC or FSS for transmitting instructions and information to pilots.

victor airways Low-altitude federal airways connecting **VOR** stations.

virga Precipitation that evaporates before reaching the ground.

visibility (prevailing) See **prevailing visibility**.

visual approach slope indicator (VASI) An airport lighting facility providing vertical visual approach slope guidance to aircraft during approach to landing by radiating a directional pattern of high-intensity red and white focused light beams. The aircraft is on path if red appears over white, above path if white appears over white, and below path if red appears over red. Some airports serving large aircrafts have three-bar VASIs that provide two visual glide paths to the same runway, based on the aircraft's approach speed and required angle of descent.

Visual Flight Rules (VFR) Rules that govern the procedures for conducting flight under visual conditions. The term *VFR* is also used in the United States to indicate weather conditions that are equal to or greater than minimum VFR requirements. In addition, the term is used by pilots and controllers to indicate type of **flight plan**.

visual meteorological conditions (VMC) Meteorological conditions expressed in terms of visibility, distance from clouds, and ceiling equal to or better than specified minimums; conditions in which flight can be maintained by outside visual references continuously available to the pilot. VMC is not necessarily the same as VFR, which is a specific set of conditions under which visual flight is to be conducted.

visual routes (VR) High-speed, low-altitude military training routes where operations are conducted only under VFR conditions.

VMC See **visual meteorological conditions**.

voltage The amount of electromotive (or "electron-pushing") force in a material or system; the electrical potential difference between materials, measured in *volts*.

voltage regulator A device used to control or regulate the output voltage of a **generator** or **alternator**.

volt (V) See **voltage**.

VOR See **VHF omnidirectional range**.

VOR head The display unit on a VOR radio receiver.

VOR receiver checkpoint A geographic point at which or special signal whereby a VOR receiver may be checked for accuracy, including (1) an FAA **VOR test facility (VOT)** or a radiated test signal from an appropriately rated radio repair station; (2) a certified airborne checkpoint; and (3) a certified ground checkpoint located on an airport's surface.

VORTAC Combination **VOR** and **TACAN** ground facility; a VOR station with **DME** capability for appropriately equipped aircraft.

VOR test (VOT) facility A ground facility that emits a test signal to check VOR receiver accuracy. A VOT signal may be used while airborne only at specific altitudes and areas authorized in the *Airport/Facility Directory*.

VR See **visual routes**.

V speeds Reference speeds used by the FAA and in most airplane flight manuals, many of which correspond to markings on the **airspeed indicator**. The letter V stands for *veloc-*

ity and is usually accompanied by a subscript denoting the referenced speed, such as V_{NE} (the never-exceed speed of the aircraft) and V_x (the **best angle of climb** speed). A complete list of V speeds can be found in FAR Part 1: Definitions and Abbreviations.

V_a See **maneuvering speed**.

V_{FE} Maximum flap extension speed. On airspeed indicators with color-coded markings, this is the high-speed end of the white arc.

V_{NE} Never-exceed speed. On airspeed indicators with color-coded markings, this is the red-line speed.

V_{NO} Maximum speed for normal operation. On airspeed indicators with color-coded markings, this is the high-speed end of the green arc.

V_{SO} Stall speed in the landing configuration. On airspeed indicators with color-coded markings, this is the low-speed end of the white arc.

V_{S1} Stall speed in a specified configuration (normally, curise configuration). On airspeed indicators with color-coded markings, this is the low-speed end of the green arc.

V_x See **best angle of climb** speed.

V_y See **best rate of climb** speed.

WAC See **world aeronautical chart**.

wake turbulence See **wing tip vortices**.

warm front The boundary between two masses of air indicating the place where warm air is replacing colder air.

warning area Airspace that may contain hazards to nonparticipating aircraft in international airspace.

waypoint As used in **area navigation (RNAV)**, a predetermined geographical position used for route and instrument approach definition or progress reporting purposes that is defined relative to a **VORTAC** station position. Waypoints allow pilots using RNAV to avoid overflying the VORTAC station, reducing airspace congestion and allowing more efficient routing to many airports.

WCA See **wind correction angle**.

weather depiction chart Prepared from the **surface analysis chart**, a chart that displays all areas where IFR is in effect—that is, where visibility is below 3 miles and/or the ceiling is less than 1000 feet—and where **marginal VFR (MVFR)** conditions—visibility 3 to 5 miles and ceiling of 1000 to 3000 feet, inclusive—are present. An abbreviated **station model** gives visibility values, obstructions to vision, and sky condition for each reporting station.

weight and balance record Logbooks and data sheets recording the *changes* to an airplane's configuration that affect weight and balance. All items added to or deleted from an aircraft's **basic empty weight** should be recorded in these documents, along with their weight and **fuselage station number**.

weight-moment envelope Chart that shows the minimum and maximum moments for any given weight.

WH See **hurricane advisory**.

wind cone See **wind sock**.

wind correction angle (WCA) The angular difference between an aircraft's **true course** and **true heading**; the amount of upwind heading correction needed to counteract **drift** due to **crosswinds**.

wind level The altitude at which and above which the winds tend to follow the isobaric lines; the flow of winds above the **friction level**.

windmilling propeller A **propeller** turning without power in the free airstream, similar to the motion of a windmill. A windmilling propeller can add considerably to total airplane **drag**, increasing minimum controllable speeds for multiengine airplanes and decreasing gliding distances for single-engine craft. Multiengine airplanes nearly always have a propeller *feathering system* that rotates a controllable pitch propeller on an inoperative engine so that its leading and trailing edges are parallel to the flight path, halting rotation.

winds and temperatures aloft forecast (FD) Teletyped forecast issued every 6 hours for winds and temperatures at selected altitudes. Because of terrain effects, no forecasts are made for levels less than 1500 feet above station elevation.

wind shear A change in wind speed and/or direction in a short distance, resulting in a tearing or shearing effect. It can exist in a horizontal or vertical direction and occasionally in both.

wind sock A hollow cone made of weatherproof, flexible material that inflates with pressure from the wind and points its smaller (trailing) end downwind. Wind speed can be estimated by the degree of wind sock inflation, and the amount of crosswind can be estimated by observing its orientation with respect to the runway.

wind T A weather vane device resembling an airplane, designed to pivot freely into the wind.

wind up method A technique in solving triangle of velocity problems on the wind face of a **navigational computer** in which the wind arrow is placed "up" toward the top of the computer.

wing flaps See **flaps.**

wings The major lift-producing structure of an airplane.

wing tank drains Small valves placed at the lowest point in each wing fuel tank used to draw off any water (which is heavier than **avgas**) that may have condensed in the tank. Drained water and other contaminants can usually be detected within a transparent container below an upper layer of colored gasoline. If more than 2 or 3 tablespoons of water are present in any given sample, an **A&P mechanic** should be consulted.

wing tip vortices Rotating currents of air thrown off a lift-producing wing; generally called *wake turbulence*. The heavier the airplane and the more lift being produced, the more powerful the vortex.

world aeronautical chart (WAC) Similar in markings and format to **sectional charts** but with fewer details and smaller scale (16 miles to the inch). WACs are favored by pilots flying at intermediate or high altitudes and covering long distances.

yaw Movement of aircraft about its **vertical axis**. Yaw is controlled by the **rudder**. See also **adverse yaw**.

yaw stability The tendency of an airplane to assume a straight flight path after yaw displacement.

Z time See **Coordinated universal time (UTC)**.

zulu time See **Coordinated universal time (UTC)**.

Index

Index to Federal Aviation Regulations